Marine Science

for Cambridge International AS & A Level

COURSEBOOK

Matthew Parkin, Melissa Lorenz, Claire Brown & Jules Robson

CAMBRIDGE
UNIVERSITY PRESS

University Printing House, Cambridge CB2 8BS, United Kingdom

One Liberty Plaza, 20th Floor, New York, NY 10006, USA

477 Williamstown Road, Port Melbourne, VIC 3207, Australia

314–321, 3rd Floor, Plot 3, Splendor Forum, Jasola District Centre, New Delhi – 110025, India

79 Anson Road, #06–04/06, Singapore 079906

Cambridge University Press is part of the University of Cambridge.

It furthers the University's mission by disseminating knowledge in the pursuit of education, learning and research at the highest international levels of excellence.

www.cambridge.org
Information on this title: www.cambridge.org/9781108795944

© Cambridge University Press 2020

This publication is in copyright. Subject to statutory exception and to the provisions of relevant collective licensing agreements, no reproduction of any part may take place without the written permission of Cambridge University Press.

First published 2017
Second edition 2020

20 19 18 17 16 15 14 13 12 11 10 9 8 7 6 5 4 3 2 1

Printed in Mexico by Editorial Impresora Apolo, S.A. de C.V.

A catalogue record for this publication is available from the British Library

ISBN 978-1-108-86606-4 Coursebook with Digital Access
ISBN 978-1-108-79142-7 Digital Coursebook (2 Years)
ISBN 978-1-108-79144-1 Coursebook - eBook

Cambridge University Press has no responsibility for the persistence or accuracy of URLs for external or third-party internet websites referred to in this publication, and does not guarantee that any content on such websites is, or will remain, accurate or appropriate. Information regarding prices, travel timetables, and other factual information given in this work is correct at the time of first printing but Cambridge University Press does not guarantee the accuracy of such information thereafter.

....

NOTICE TO TEACHERS IN THE UK
It is illegal to reproduce any part of this work in material form (including photocopying and electronic storage) except under the following circumstances:
(i) where you are abiding by a licence granted to your school or institution by the Copyright Licensing Agency;
(ii) where no such licence exists, or where you wish to exceed the terms of a licence, and you have gained the written permission of Cambridge University Press;
(iii) where you are allowed to reproduce without permission under the provisions of Chapter 3 of the Copyright, Designs and Patents Act 1988, which covers, for example, the reproduction of short passages within certain types of educational anthology and reproduction for the purposes of setting examination questions.

....

Exam-style questions have been written by the authors. In examinations, the way marks are awarded may be different. References to assessment and/or assessment preparation are the publisher's interpretation of the syllabus requirements and may not fully reflect the approach of Cambridge Assessment International Education.

Cambridge International recommends that teachers consider using a range of teaching and learning resources in preparing learners for assessment, based on their own professional judgement of their students' needs.

Cambridge International copyright material in this publication is reproduced under licence and remains the intellectual property of Cambridge Assessment International Education.

DEDICATED TEACHER AWARDS

Teachers play an important part in shaping futures. Our Dedicated Teacher Awards recognise the hard work that teachers put in every day.

Thank you to everyone who nominated this year, we have been inspired and moved by all of your stories. Well done to all of our nominees for your dedication to learning and for inspiring the next generation of thinkers, leaders and innovators.

Congratulations to our incredible winner and finalists

WINNER

Ahmed Saya
Cordoba School for A-Level, Pakistan

Sharon Kong Foong
Sunway College, Malaysia

Abhinandan Bhattacharya
JBCN International School Oshiwara, India

Anthony Chelliah
Gateway College, Sri Lanka

Candice Green
St Augustine's College, Australia

Jimrey Buntas Dapin
University of San Jose-Recoletos, Philippines

For more information about our dedicated teachers and their stories, go to
dedicatedteacher.cambridge.org

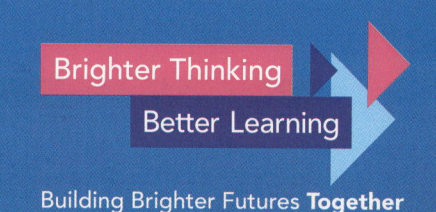

CAMBRIDGE UNIVERSITY PRESS

Brighter Thinking
Better Learning

Building Brighter Futures Together

Contents

Introduction		v
How to use this series		vi
How to use this book		vii
Introduction to command words		ix

1 Water
- 1.1 Particle theory and bonding — 3
- 1.2 Solubility in water — 8
- 1.3 Density and pressure — 17

2 Earth processes
- 2.1 Tectonic processes — 33
- 2.2 Weathering, erosion and sedimentation — 41
- 2.3 Tides and ocean currents — 44

3 Interactions in marine ecosystems
- 3.1 Interactions — 64
- 3.2 Feeding relationships — 66
- 3.3 Nutrient cycles — 82

4 Classification and biodiversity
- 4.1 The classification of marine organisms — 103
- 4.2 Key groups of marine organisms — 106
- 4.3 Biodiversity — 125
- 4.4 Populations and sampling techniques — 127

5 Examples of marine ecosystems
- 5.1 The open ocean — 154
- 5.2 The tropical coral reef — 157
- 5.3 The rocky shore — 169
- 5.4 The sandy shore — 171
- 5.5 The mangrove forest — 174

Practical skills
- Introduction to practical skills — 186
- Experimental planning including making estimates, predictions and hypotheses — 187
- Presentation of data and observations — 198
- Evaluation of procedures and data — 200
- Analysis of data and conclusions — 201

6 Physiology of marine organisms
- 6.1 General cell structure — 211
- 6.2 Movement of substances — 230
- 6.3 Gas exchange — 239
- 6.4 Osmoregulation — 250

7 Energy
- 7.1 Photosynthesis — 267
- 7.2 Chemosynthesis — 285
- 7.3 Respiration — 288

8 Fisheries for the future
- 8.1 Life cycles — 305
- 8.2 Sustainable fisheries — 312
- 8.3 Marine aquaculture — 339

9 Human impacts on marine ecosystems
- 9.1 Ecological impacts of human activities — 371
- 9.2 Global warming and its impact — 393
- 9.3 Ocean acidification — 399
- 9.4 Conservation of marine ecosystems — 404

Glossary	440
Acknowledgements	455
Index	456

> Introduction

This second edition of the *Cambridge International AS & A Level Marine Science Coursebook* has been written to help you acquire the knowledge and skills required by the Cambridge International AS & A level Marine Science syllabus (9693). The book provides full coverage of the revised syllabus and reflects the slightly different demands of the new content.

The chapters are arranged in the same sequence as the syllabus. Chapters 1 to 5 cover the AS syllabus and Chapters 6 to 9 cover the full A Level syllabus. Each chapter has similar features to help you, including: key words and command words, maths skills, test yourself questions, practical activities, case studies that look at real-life scenarios, and exam-style questions. Look at the 'How to use this book' section for more information about each feature.

In order to succeed in your course, you will need to develop a number of skills. These include applying your knowledge to unfamiliar situations, using mathematical and statistical skills to determine population sizes, species diversity etc., as well as recalling key facts. Working through the questions and activities in this coursebook will help you to hone these skills.

Although the book is arranged as a series of discrete chapters, it is important to remember that the topics and skills in these chapters link to each other. Practical skills are an important part of the AS & A Level Marine Science course. You should become familiar with certain 'core' practicals, and understand how to plan practical investigations and analyse the data. Most chapters contains practical activities for you to carry out and develop your skills. The exam-style questions at the end of each chapter also include practical of each chapter include practical questions the practical skills chapter explains the nature of scientific investigation.

Further exercises, exam-style questions and practical activities can be found in the *Cambridge International AS & A Level Workbook* published by Cambridge University Press.

Marine science is a unique and engaging subject that requires you to have an understanding of subjects such as biology, geography, geology, physics, chemistry and even sociology. This coursebook will cover material from all of these areas and look at both established knowledge and some of the recent exciting developments in our understanding of the marine world. It will help you to appreciate topical issues, such as the effects of human activity, by looking at real case studies. Our oceans are the lifeblood of the planet and they have never been as threatened by human activity as they are now. Never a day goes by without some mention of new threats to the marine environment, be it plastic, climate change or overfishing. A thorough knowledge of marine science is essential if we are to prevent further damage and educate the world about them. People study marine science for a variety of reasons: a route into further study through marine science courses at universities; to help develop careers that are linked to the seas such as fishing, aquaculture or tourism; or simply for pure interest in our marine world. Whatever reasons you have for studying marine science, we hope you enjoy learning about this fascinating subject.

The information in this section is taken from the Cambridge International syllabus based on the 9693 syllabus for examination from 2022. You should always refer to the appropriate syllabus document for the year of your examination to confirm the details and for more information. The syllabus document is available on the Cambridge International website at www.cambridgeinternational.org.

CAMBRIDGE INTERNATIONAL AS & A LEVEL MARINE SCIENCE: COURSEBOOK

> How to use this series

This suite of resources supports students and teachers following the Cambridge International AS & A Level Marine Science syllabus (9693). All of the books in the series work together to help students develop the necessary knowledge and scientific skills required for this subject.

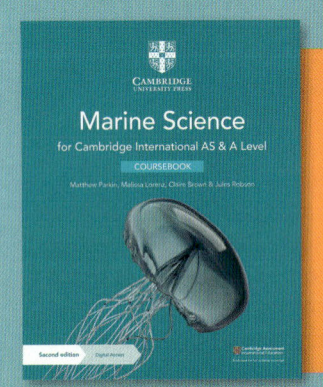

The coursebook covers the full Cambridge International AS & A Level Marine Science syllabus, with the chapter structure following the syllabus order. Each chapter includes exercises to develop problem-solving skills; practical activities to help students develop investigative skills; and international case studies and projects to illustrate phenomena in real-world situations. There is a new practical skills chapter that introduces students to experimental planning, presenting data and evaluating experimental methods, with examples and questions.

The teacher's resource supports and unlocks the projects, questions and practical activities in the coursebook, as well as providing detailed lesson ideas and plans. It includes support notes and sample data for the practical activities in the workbook and coursebook. It also contains answers to all questions in the coursebook and workbook.

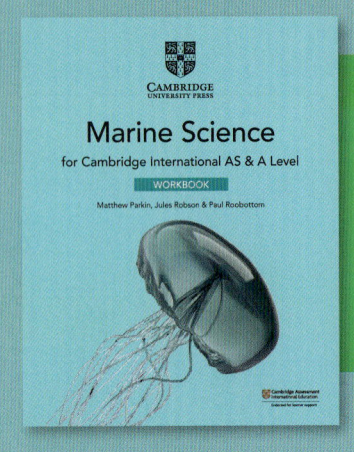

The workbook contains engaging exercises and exam-style questions to develop scientific skills such as problem-solving, handling and applying information, and mathematical skills for science. It also contains practical activities for each syllabus topic area, to support students' investigative skills, including planning experiments and data exercises.

> How to use this book

Chapters 1–5 of the coursebook cover the topics that you will study for Cambridge International AS Level Marine Science. Chapters 6–9 cover the topics that you will study at A Level. Throughout this book, you will notice lots of different features that will help your learning. These are explained below.

LEARNING INTENTIONS

These set the scene for each chapter, help with navigation through the coursebook and indicate the important concepts in each topic.

BEFORE YOU START

This contains questions and activities on the topic knowledge that you will need before starting a chapter.

PRACTICAL ACTIVITY

Practical activities give you the opportunity to test out the theory that you have learnt in a chapter and investigate a topic for yourself. You will find it particularly helpful to cover the Core practical activities, as these are taken directly from the AS & A Level Marine Science syllabus.

COMMAND WORDS

Words that might be used in exams are highlighted in the exam-style questions when they are first introduced. In the margin, you will find the definition of these words. You will also find a helpful 'Introduction to Command Words' page at the front of this book.

Test yourself

Test yourself questions appear at the end of each section in a chapter. These give you the chance to check that you have understood the topic that you have just read about.

REFLECTION

Reflection questions follow on after each practical activity. These ask you to look back on the practical and encourage you to think about your learning.

SCIENCE IN CONTEXT

This feature presents real-world examples and applications of the content in a chapter, encouraging you to look further into topics. There are discussion questions at the end which look at some of the benefits or problems of these applications.

KEY WORDS

Key vocabulary is highlighted in the text when it is first introduced. Definitions are then given in the margin, which explain the meanings of these words and phrases. You will also find definitions of these words in the Glossary at the back of this book.

PROJECT

Projects give you the opportunity to work collaboratively with other students. Your group will explore a particular question or topic, and will then present the outcome via various creative methods. Afterwards, you can reflect on or assess the project with the 'Thinking about your project' questions.

CASE STUDY

Case studies take an in-depth look at a topic in the chapter and present it in a real-world setting. This will help you to discuss issues relating to this topic.

Note: This type of box shows extension content that is not part of the syllabus.

MATHS SKILLS

Maths skills contain background information, worked examples and practice questions that will help you to develop the mathematical awareness that is needed for your Marine Science course.

EXAM-STYLE QUESTIONS

Questions at the end of each chapter provide more demanding exam-style questions, some of which may require you to use your knowledge from previous chapters.

SELF-EVALUATION CHECKLIST

At the end of each chapter, you will find 'I can' statements which match the learning intentions at the beginning of the chapter. You might find it helpful to rate how confident you are for each of these statements when you are revising. You should revisit any topics that you rated 'Needs more work' or 'Almost there'.

I can:	See section…	Needs more work	Almost there	Ready to move on

EXTENDED CASE STUDY

Each chapter is followed by a longer case study, which illustrates a more complex topic in a real-world setting. This will help you to think about this topic and discuss issues relating to it in more depth.

Practical Skills chapter

This chapter contains some additional features to support your learning.

A Level content

If you are studying A Level Marine Science, you will find that any relevant content beyond AS Level in this chapter is highlighted in blue font.

EXAMPLES

You will find examples throughout this chapter that present practical activities that you may encounter as part of your Marine Science course. These conclude with 'Now you try' questions that encourage you to think about various aspects of the practical for yourself.

SUMMARY

At the end of each section in this chapter, you will find a summary. This list summarises the steps that you should take to complete some of the key skills relating to practical activities.

Introduction to command words

Command words are verbs used within the questions of examination papers that can give you insight in how to go about answering the question. These words can help you determine much about the expected answer for the question that is being presented. Used as clues, these words can help determine the length and depth of knowledge an answer requires, the appropriate style of response, and differentiate between similar questions that need different responses. Being comfortable with the general definitions and standard expectations for each of the command words listed below can really help you navigate your way through your papers.

Analyse: examine in detail to show meaning, identify elements and the relationship between them
Guidance: This is a higher level, and typically higher mark, question requiring multiple details. Your response to 'analyse' questions is likely to be longer than to other types of questions.

Assess: make an informed judgement
Guidance: This command word will typically be used in a scenario that was not expressly taught through the syllabus. You will need to pull related information and apply it to the situation to create your judgement.

Calculate: work out from given facts, figures or information
Guidance: In these questions, you will need to do maths to arrive at the answer. Make sure to include any units and show your working.

Comment: give an informed opinion
Guidance: These are shorter response questions where you will apply general knowledge to a new scenario. Make sure you justify your opinion with supporting details.

Compare: identify / comment on similarities and/or differences
Guidance: These questions vary in length so use the provided marks to determine how many points of comparison you need to provide. Make sure you do not repeat the same points within your answer – each mark will only be given once no matter how many times you have reworded it.

Consider: review and respond to given information
Guidance: These questions are higher level and generally require data analysis in the context of a case study.

Contrast: identify / comment on differences
Guidance: These questions vary in length so use the provided marks to determine how many points of contrast you need to provide. Focus entirely on the differences between the provided situations.

Define: give precise meaning
Guidance: Try to word your definitions as precisely as possible with all major identifying features. This is a concise response that should not be longer than a sentence.

Demonstrate: show how or give an example
Guidance: Make sure to provide a step-by-step method for how the process being asked about works or use an example to illustrate the process.

Describe: state the points of a topic / give characteristics and main features
Guidance: Most commonly confused with 'explain', 'describe' means to answer *what* is happening. This could be in reference to describing the data (for example, it increases or decreases), the process, or the meaning of a term. At no point should you try to write about how or why something is happening, as that is the meaning of the 'explain' command word.

Develop: take forward to a more advanced stage or build upon given information
Guidance: This term is asking you to use background knowledge in a novel situation to predict the step or process in the situation. This question requires a higher-level response.

Discuss: write about issue(s) or topic(s) in depth in a structured way
Guidance: Questions using this command word are generally longer response and required the use of details

to support the your knowledge about a topic. In general, responses to 'discuss' questions require the use of multiple well-written paragraphs.

Evaluate: judge or calculate the quality, importance, amount or value of something
Guidance: For 'evaluate' questions, you will need to create an opinion or choose a side about the topic in question. You will then need to support your thesis using details from either your background knowledge or information provided within the question.

Examine: investigate closely, in detail
Guidance: These questions typically will have you look over a data set to pull information out of. Depending on the style of this type of question, 1-2 sentences is probably sufficient, but use the marks provided to determine how much detail is needed.

Explain: set out purposes or reasons / make the relationships between things evident / provide why and/or how and support with relevant evidence
Guidance: Often confused with 'describe', 'explain' questions require you to write about why or how something happens. In order to succeed with these questions, it is important to provide reasons and clear connections within your answer. Unless expressly stated, it is not necessary to outline *what* is happening, just *why* or *how*.

Give: produce an answer from a given source or recall / memory
Guidance: Questions using 'give' are generally short response and may not even need a complete sentence. They may require you to recall something from memory or locate in on a graph or data set.

Identify: name / select / recognise
Guidance: This command word requires a brief, direct response.

Justify: support a case with evidence / argument
Guidance: Used to encourage you to include many details, this command term will be seen with high-mark questions. You should prepare a well-organised response of at least one paragraph. You may also need to create an opinion statement based on the question asked, indicating which part of the argument you are supporting.

Outline: set out main points
Guidance: While you can use a paragraph to answer an 'outline' question, a detailed, bulleted list is also appropriate. Make sure to include enough detail to clarify each point. This command word is often used to gain an understanding of a process or theory.

Predict: suggest what may happen based on available information
Guidance: Questions using this command term do not expect you to get the information through recall. Rather, the expectation is that you can use background information in conjunction with the information or data provided in the question to make a best guess about what may happen next. For example, you may see 'predict' when discussing data or behavior of organisms or the physical ocean.

Sketch: make a simple freehand drawing showing the key features, taking care over proportions
Guidance: Use a pencil to draw the process or graph being requested. Make sure to label major features as necessary. If data is provided, make sure your proportions are appropriate to represent the numbers given (for example trophic pyramids).

State: express in clear terms
Guidance: This command term indicates that the response needed will be short. This can be used to have you identify important data points on a graph, provide the term that matches a definition, or in other situations where only a one- or two-word response would be appropriate.

Suggest: apply knowledge and understanding to situations where there are a range of valid responses in order to make proposals
Guidance: Similar to 'predict', 'suggest' asks you to combine information from the question with other information learned during the course. Generally, 'suggest' questions have a wide variety of appropriate responses that could be used to produce a successful answer. Make sure to provide a clear line of reasoning for the suggestion being made.

Summarise: select and present the main points, without detail
Guidance: Similar to 'outline', a bulleted list can be appropriate for a question using the 'summarise' command term. Make sure to list out all of the important aspects of the process or theory being asked about, but refrain from adding unnecessary details or evidence unless specifically asked for it in the question (that is, if they ask you to *summarise* and *explain*).

Chapter 1
Water

LEARNING INTENTIONS

In this chapter you will learn how to:

- use the kinetic particle theory to explain the changes of state in water, between solid, liquid and gas
- describe how the structure of atoms leads to the formation of different bonds such as covalent, ionic, and hydrogen bonds
- explain how hydrogen bonding provides special properties to water
- explain the terms solute, solvent, solution and solubility in order to apply these terms to the dissolution of substances in the ocean
- explain the impacts of physical factors, such as temperature and salinity and pressure, on the solubility of salts and gases in seawater
- explain how run-off, precipitation and evaporation impact the salinity of seawater
- describe the pH scale and techniques used to measure pH in water
- explain the effects on the density of seawater caused by water temperature, pressure and salinity
- state why ice floats and explain why this is important as a thermal insulator and habitat to marine organisms
- describe how temperature and salinity gradients form in water columns to produce ocean layers and how subsequent mixing of these layers may occur.

CAMBRIDGE INTERNATIONAL AS & A LEVEL MARINE SCIENCE: COURSEBOOK

BEFORE YOU START

- With a partner discuss your understanding of the term 'atom'. Sketch a labelled diagram to show what you understand atoms to be made from. Compare your drawing to others in class and review with your teacher.
- We use water to clean clothes, dishes and our own bodies. Discuss with a partner why water is so good for cleaning.
- Write one or two questions about what affects the density of seawater on a sticky note and post them on the board. With your class, compare and organise your questions into topics for discussion.

THE STUDY OF SEAWATER

When beginning your studies in marine science it helps to gain a scientific understanding of the properties of seawater. After all, 71% of our planet is covered in water and the vast majority of that water (about 97%) is held in the oceans. Some people may think that seawater is simply saltwater – they may think that, if you add some table salt to a glass of water, you can recreate seawater that is suitable for fish and other organisms to live in. But this is not true.

Seawater is a complex mix of chemicals. In fact, nearly every **element** in the Periodic Table has been located, usually combined with other elements as many different **compounds**, within the ocean's vast waters. Water itself is made from hydrogen and oxygen; it interacts with all the other substances dissolved or immersed in it. These substances interact with the water **molecules** to support life in our oceans. The concentrations of these elements and their compounds determine what organisms are capable of living within different marine ecosystems, and how they will survive.

It is imperative, then, to know how these substances interact together and how water molecules function to support life. To begin that study, we must look to the **atom** and build our way up from there.

Questions

1. Do you agree that starting with the simplest form and working up is the best way to begin? Why or why not?
2. Which of our senses can we use to try to determine what is in a sample of seawater? How reliable are these senses and can you suggest other methods or equipment to determine what is in the sample of seawater?

KEY WORDS

element: a substance that cannot be chemically broken down into a simpler substance

compound: a substance containing two or more elements chemically bonded together

molecule: a group of atoms covalently bonded together

atom: the smallest particle an element can be divided into and still be the same substance

1.1 Particle theory and bonding

An atom is the smallest particle an element can be separated into and still be the same substance. Atoms are the particles found in everything around and within us.

Atomic movement

The **kinetic particle theory (particle theory)** describes all matter as a collection of particles that are in constant, random motion, even if those movements are only small vibrations. The amount of movement a particle has is determined by the amount of energy it has. The chair you are sitting on, the water you are drinking, and the air you are breathing are all examples of many particles that have joined together to create materials. Matter generally exists in three states: solid, liquid, or gas (Figure 1.1). As energy is transferred away from, or transferred to, these molecules, the state of matter may change as the movement of the *molecules* within the matter changes.

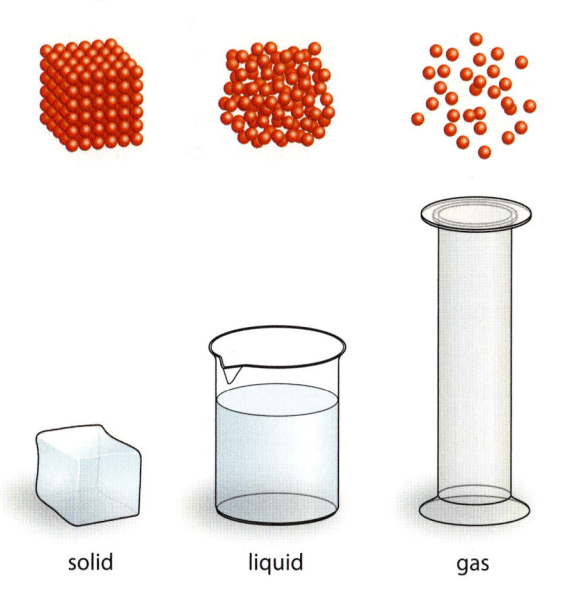

Figure 1.1: The states of matter and the arrangement of their particles.

Water molecules can be used to demonstrate particle theory. When liquid water cools down, the movement of the water molecules slows until they arrange in a regular structure called a lattice. The molecules become fixed in position in this lattice resulting in a solid (ice) forming. As more molecules join the lattice the ice crystals grow larger.

When ice is heated the water molecules are given more energy, resulting in them vibrating faster until the forces holding the molecules together start to break. The water molecules nearest the outer surfaces of the ice crystals break free and are able to flow away from the crystals, taking the shape of the container they are in. The water molecules are closely packed to each other in a liquid but able to move freely past each other; this explains why liquids can take the shape of their container but cannot be compressed – they are already very close to each other.

When liquid water is heated the particles gain more energy, making them move faster and slightly further from each other. Some of the collisions between water molecules transfer enough energy for molecules at the upper surface to escape the forces attracting them to other molecules, and they can evaporate into the air above. This process is essential to the water cycle and occurs faster as the surface water becomes warmer. When water approaches its boiling temperature (100 °C at 1 atmosphere pressure), all the water molecules have enough energy to break the forces holding them together and water rapidly evaporates (boils). **Water vapour** is the term given to gaseous water (both from evaporation and boiling).

A brief understanding of atoms

Atoms are made of three smaller subatomic particles that, depending on their numbers, give the atom its characteristics (or properties). These subatomic particles are **protons**, **neutrons** and **electrons**. Protons are positively charged, neutrons are neutral (they have no

> **KEY WORDS**
>
> **kinetic particle theory (particle theory):** the theory of how particles (such as atoms and molecules) move in relation to each other and the amount of energy within the system
>
> **water vapour:** gaseous phase / state of water; produced when liquid water evaporates or boils
>
> **proton:** a positively charged subatomic particle contained within the nucleus of an atom
>
> **neutrons:** a neutral subatomic particle contained within the nucleus of an atom
>
> **electron:** a negatively charged subatomic particle that orbits the nucleus of an atom

electrical charge), and electrons are negatively charged. An atom has an equal number of electrons and protons, so they are neutral.

Protons, neutrons, and electrons are arranged within the atom to provide stability and structure (see Figure 1.2). At the centre of the atom is the **nucleus**. The nucleus is made of the neutrons and protons. Electrons move around the nucleus in orbits called **shells**. These shells vary in size and distance from the nucleus depending on how many electrons are present. The first shell nearest the nucleus can hold two electrons. This is the only shell present in both hydrogen and helium. The next two shells hold up to eight electrons. Atoms are at their most stable when their outermost shell containing electrons is full.

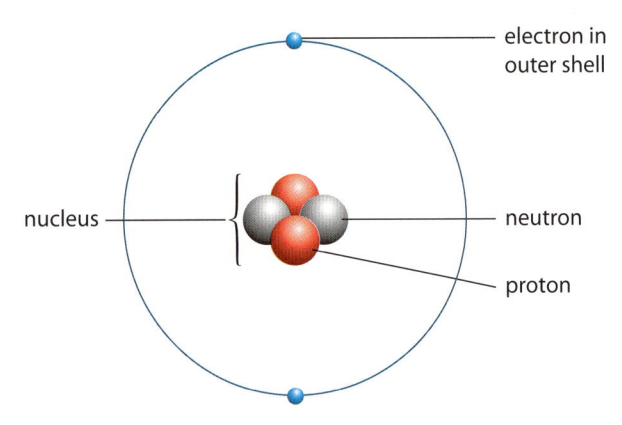

Figure 1.2: The atomic structure of helium showing the relative positions of the protons, neutrons and electrons.

The Periodic Table you might see hanging on the wall in many science classes lists all the known types of atoms. These different types of atoms are called elements. An element is made of atoms that have a specific number of protons. This **atomic number** never varies and helps us to identify the characteristics of elements. Seawater is a mixture of different elements and compounds. Examples of elements we find in the ocean include carbon, hydrogen and oxygen.

Bonding properties of atoms

When individual atoms come together to form different substances, they form **bonds**. A substance with a specific ratio of different elements bonded together, such as water, is called a compound. A water molecule is two atoms of hydrogen bonded to one atom of oxygen. Water molecules always have a 2[H]:1[O] ratio. A compound's properties can be very different from those of the elements that it is made of. For instance, at room temperature, both hydrogen and oxygen are gases which require very low temperatures and high pressures to become liquid. When combined in a 2H:1O ratio, however, water can be formed, which is liquid at room temperature. The new characteristics a compound develops through bonding are called **emergent properties**.

The type of bond formed between the atoms of a compound will also play a part in the emergent properties of the compound. There are three major categories of bonds that we will discuss: **covalent bonds**, **ionic bonds** and **hydrogen bonds**. All three bond types play a major role in how the ocean works and how organisms can make the ocean their home.

Covalent bonds

A covalent bond forms when two atoms share a pair of electrons. Covalent bonding occurs in most non-metal elements, and in compounds formed between non-metals.

Because the atoms are sharing the electrons, both atoms have complete outer shells. This sharing of electrons also makes this type of bond between atoms one of the strongest, requiring a large amount of energy to break.

KEY WORDS

nucleus: the positively charged central core of an atom that is made of protons and neutrons

shells: each of a set of orbitals around the nucleus of an atom that can be occupied by electrons

atomic number: the number of protons contained in the nucleus of an atom

bond: a strong force of attraction holding atoms together in a substance

emergent properties: characteristics that are present within a compound or molecule of two or more different elements that those elements do not possess on their own

covalent bond: chemical bond that involves the sharing of electron pairs between atoms

ionic bond: chemical bond that involves the attraction between two oppositely charged ions

hydrogen bond: a weak bond between two molecules due to the electrostatic attraction between a hydrogen atom in one molecule and an atom of oxygen, nitrogen or fluorine in the other molecule

Compounds with covalent bonds are able to exist as a solid, liquid or gas at room temperature and normal atmospheric pressure. Therefore, it should come as no surprise that water is one of the most prevalent covalent compounds on our planet. Each water molecule contains two covalent bonds connecting the oxygen atom to each of the hydrogen atoms (Figure 1.3). These bonds form when an oxygen atom, which only has six electrons in its outermost shell, reacts with two hydrogen atoms, with only one electron each. The hydrogen atoms share their individual electrons with the oxygen atom. The shared electrons orbit around the atoms connected in the bond, filling the outer shells of the oxygen and the hydrogen. Many compounds in seawater have covalent bonds (Figure 1.4). As seen in Figure 1.4 (b) carbon dioxide has four covalent bonds as the single carbon molecule forms a double bond with each oxygen molecule. A double bond occurs when molecules share two pairs of electrons instead of just one.

Carbon dioxide, needed by plants for photosynthesis, and oxygen, needed by organisms for respiration, also use covalent bonds to hold their atoms together. In photosynthesis, the glucose produced through photosynthesis is also a covalently bonded carbohydrate. This is important because a lot of energy is stored in the covalent bonds that join molecules, making glucose a useful molecule for holding chemical energy. In ecosystems where photosynthesis is not possible, some bacteria use the process of chemosynthesis to break apart the covalent bonds within the molecule sulfur dioxide in order to obtain the energy needed for survival (see Chapter 7). In each instance, these atoms are sharing one or more pairs of electrons creating strong chemical bonds.

Ionic bonds

An **ion** is an atom that has gained or lost an electron from its outer shell. This change in the number of electrons gives the atom an electrical charge. An electron will move from one atom, which results in either filled or empty outer electron shells. If an atom loses an electron, the ion created will have a positive charge because the protons in the nucleus (positive charge) now outnumber the electrons in the outer shell (negative charge). If an atom gains an electron, the ion created will be negatively charged due to an excess of electrons compared to protons.

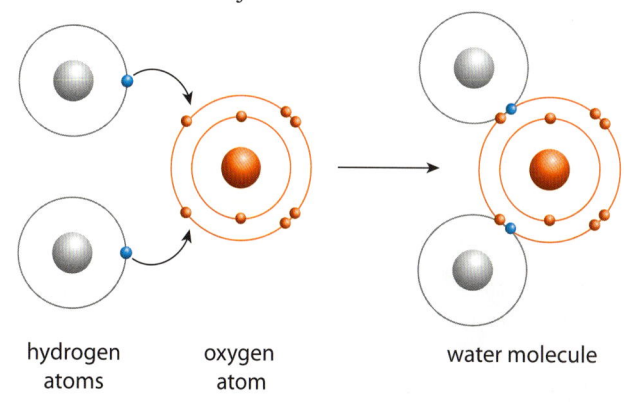

Figure 1.3: The formation of the covalent bonds in water molecules. The red circles represent electrons from the oxygen atom and the blue circles represent electrons from the hydrogen atoms.

> **KEY WORD**
>
> **ion:** an atom or molecule that has lost or gained one or more electrons creating an electrical charge

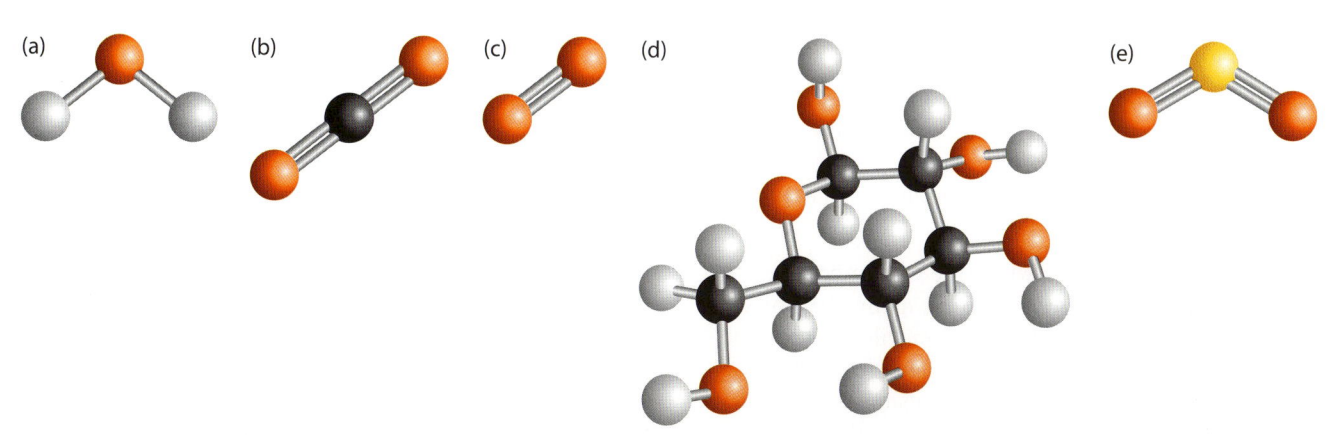

Figure 1.4: Common covalently bonded molecules in seawater: (a) water (H_2O); (b) carbon dioxide (CO_2); (c) oxygen (O_2); (d) glucose ($C_6H_{12}O_6$); and (e) sulfur dioxide (SO_2).

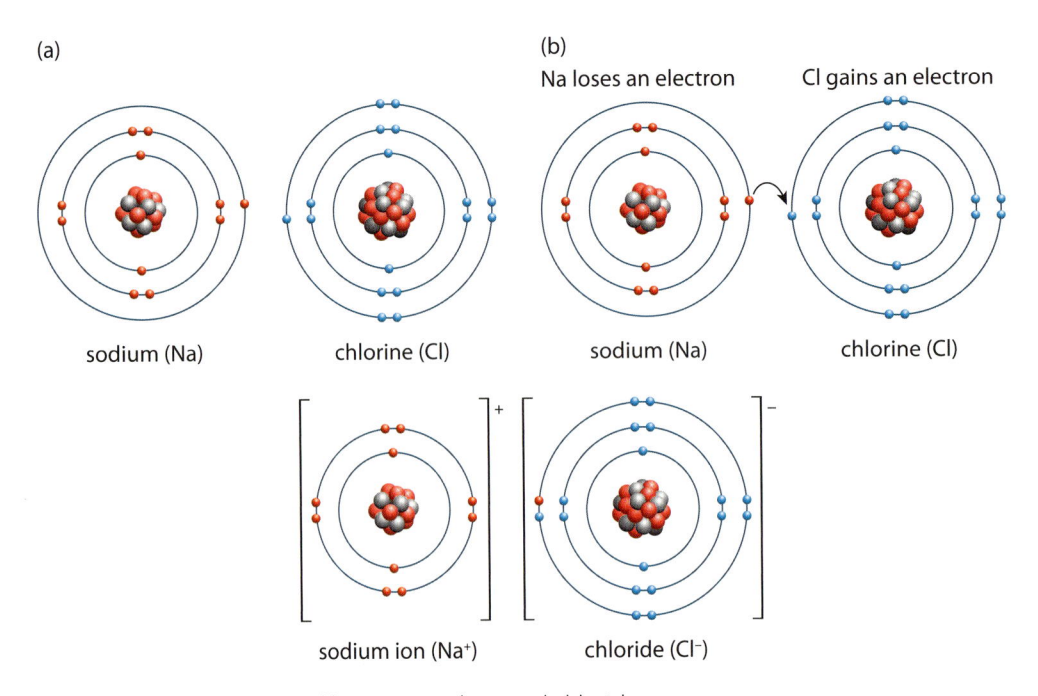

Figure 1.5: The formation of an ionic bond between sodium and chloride atoms.

So, how do ionic bonds form? When an ion loses an electron, its positive charge is attracted to the newly formed negative ion that gained its electron. This electrostatic attraction causes an ionic bond to form.

The process of forming an ionic bond is seen in Figure 1.5. In step (a) sodium and chloride both have incomplete outer shells, with sodium having a single electron and chloride having seven. In step (b) sodium's single electron breaks away and moves to complete chloride's outer shell, making both ions more stable in the process. In step (c) sodium has a positive charge, chloride has a negative charge. The electrostatic attraction between the positive sodium ions and negative chloride ions creates an ionic bond.

It is important to remember that many atoms of sodium and chlorine react together in this way, and the resulting positive and negative ions can create solids that have a three-dimensional ionic lattice structure, a small part of which is shown in Figure 1.6.

Salts are made from ions, which are very important compounds in our oceans, There are many types of salts found in the ocean, including sodium chloride (NaCl), calcium carbonate ($CaCO_3$), and magnesium sulfate ($MgSO_4$). These salts are all formed using ionic bonds. Chemical diagrams of the ions in these salts can be found in Figure 1.7.

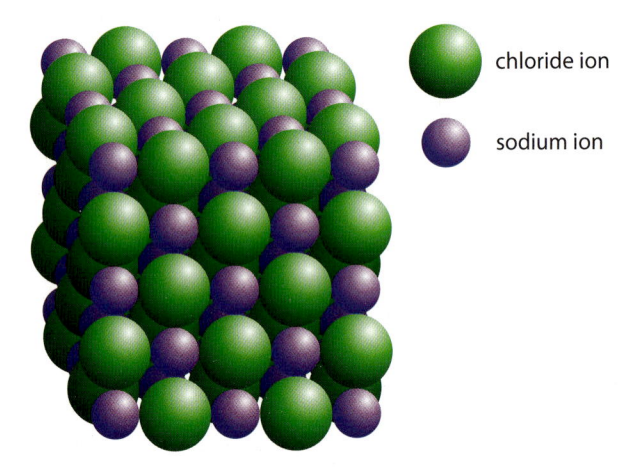

Figure 1.6: Ionic lattice structure of sodium and chloride ions.

Figure 1.7: Chemical diagrams of sodium chloride (a), calcium carbonate (b), and magnesium sulfate (c).

Hydrogen bonding

A hydrogen bond is a weaker bond that can occur between molecules containing a hydrogen atom bonded to an atom of oxygen, nitrogen or fluorine. Water is an example of such a molecule, as it has two hydrogen atoms bonded to an atom of oxygen. When creating this covalent bond, the oxygen and hydrogen atoms share electrons unequally. The oxygen atom has a much stronger attraction to the bonding pair of electrons between oxygen and hydrogen, resulting in these being pulled closer to the oxygen atom than the hydrogen atom. This unequal sharing causes a partial charge on the atoms involved in the bond: the hydrogen atoms are partially positive ($\delta+$), and the oxygen atom is partially negative ($\delta-$). When molecules have a partial charge on each end as water does, they are referred to as **polar**. Due to this polarity, the more positive hydrogen atoms of one water molecule will be attracted to the more negative oxygen atoms of a nearby water molecule (Figure 1.8) creating a dipole – a molecule with a separation of partial positive and negative charges.

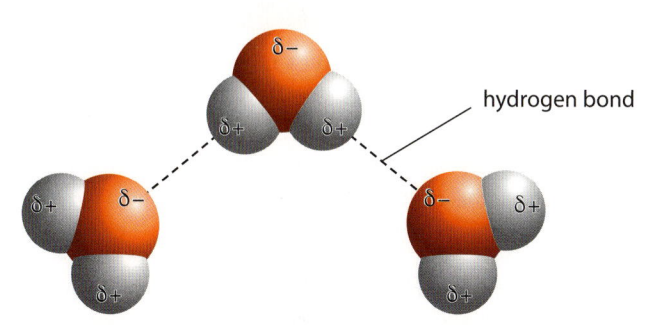

Figure 1.8: Hydrogen bonding in water.

While hydrogen bonds are easily broken, they have an incredible impact on the properties of water due to the sheer number of water molecules found within a single droplet of water. Therefore, many hydrogen bonds are continually forming between water molecules.

One of the reasons seawater is unique is because of the many different elements and compounds that can be found within it. This exceptional variety is due to water's properties as a **solvent**. A solvent is a material capable of dissolving other substances. The partial charges on the water molecule allow water to interact with charged ions from many ionic compounds as well as many covalent substances, including glucose and gases from the atmosphere. The partial charges on the water molecule allow it to form bonds with an unusual number of substances, making water one of the best solvents on the planet. In fact, water is often referred to as the universal solvent. More information regarding water's solvent capabilities can be found in Section 1.2.

The **density** of water is also impacted by hydrogen bonds. As previously mentioned, as the energy within matter lowers, so too does the movement of the individual particles making up that matter. So, as water nears its freezing point (0°C), the water molecules slow their movement and gather closely together, allowing the hydrogen bonds to become stronger. The hydrogen bonds then help keep the water molecules at perfectly symmetrical distances from each other, forming a crystal lattice-like shape. The shape formed upon freezing actually spreads the molecules out further than they were just prior to freezing. Because fewer water molecules can fit into the same space, the density of solid ice is actually less than that of liquid water. Water is one of the few substances on earth that can claim a solid state that is less dense than the liquid. More information on water density and the impacts of temperature can be found in Section 1.3.

Specific heat capacity, the amount of heat required to change one kilogram of mass by one degree Celsius, is yet another property of water that relates to its hydrogen bonding properties. Water has one of the highest specific heat capacities due to the number of hydrogen bonds holding the molecules together. This property allows water to act as a great temperature buffer and helps moderate our planet's climate. The size of our oceans allows them to hold a great deal of heat before they actually change temperature creating mild climates along coastlines worldwide.

> **KEY WORDS**
>
> **polar:** when opposite sides of a molecule have contrasting (partial) electrical charges
>
> **solvent:** a substance which is able to dissolve other substances
>
> **density:** a measure of the mass of a defined volume of water
>
> **specific heat capacity:** the heat required to raise the temperature of the unit mass of a given substance by one degree Celsius

Test yourself

1. Sketch a carbon atom. Label the nucleus, electrons, protons and neutrons.
2. How do compounds differ from elements?
3. What determines the number of covalent bonds that an atom can form?
4. How will you remember the differences between the different types of bonds?

1.2 Solubility in water

As we saw in Section 1.1, a solvent is a material capable of dissolving other substances and water is one of the greatest solvents on earth. The substance that is dissolved by a solvent is called a **solute**. There are many solutes in seawater, such as sodium chloride, carbon dioxide, oxygen and calcium carbonate. The mixture of solutes and solvent is referred to as a **solution**.

Understanding solubility

Solubility refers to the extent to which a particular solute, such as sodium chloride, can be dissolved in a solvent, such as water. This combination then creates a solution, such as seawater. In general, sodium chloride and other soluble salts dissolve easily into water through **dissolution** of ions. This is a result of the polarity of the water molecule and its ability to interact with ions from ionic substances. As we saw in Section 1.1, sodium chloride is an ionic compound formed through the attraction of sodium ions to chloride ions after the transfer of an electron from sodium to chlorine. The change in distribution of electrons gives both atoms an electrostatic charge that water molecules are attracted to. When placed in water, the sodium and chloride ions are easily dissolved when their ionic bonds are broken by the water molecules. At this point, the partially positive hydrogen ends of the water molecules will surround the negatively charged chloride ions and the partially negative oxygen ends of the water molecules will surround the positively charged sodium ions (Figure 1.9).

Solubility can be impacted by physical factors within the seawater, particularly temperature. Repeated studies have found that as the temperature of seawater rises, the rate of dissolution of salts increases as well. This is because as water heats up, the individual water molecules move faster. This movement helps mix the ions into the water making it easier for water molecules

> **KEY WORDS**
>
> **solute:** a solid that dissolves in a solvent
>
> **solution:** a mixture of a solute dissolved in a solvent
>
> **solubility:** the ability of a solute to dissolve within a solvent (such as water)
>
> **dissolution:** the process of being dissolved

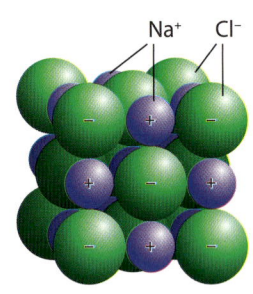

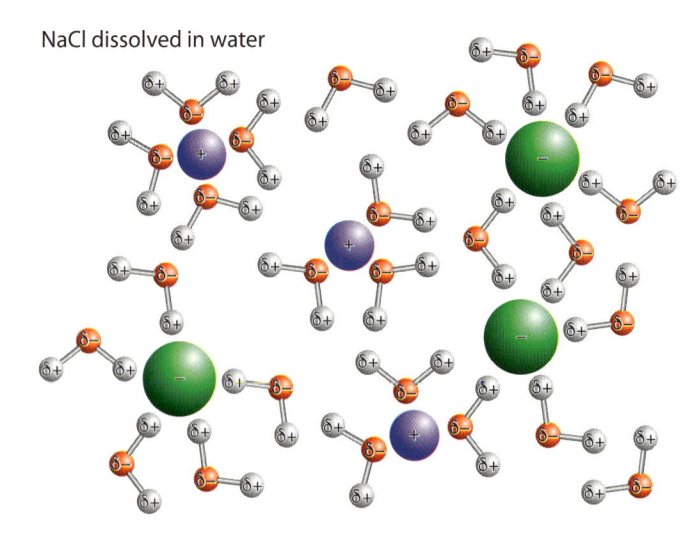

Figure 1.9: A comparison of sodium chloride solid molecular structure and its dissolved structure in water.

to break the ionic bonds and surround the positive and negative ions that are left. So, the warmer the water, the saltier it can be.

Salinity

When studying the chemistry of the ocean, traditionally you start by looking at the salinity of seawater. Salinity is a measure of the concentration of dissolved salts in seawater. The unit used for salinity is parts per thousand (ppt or ‰). This unit was originally derived using the traditional method for discovering the salinity of a solution called total dissolved solids (TDS). Using this method, scientists would boil 1000 g of seawater until all of the water present had evaporated. The solutes left behind, usually ions called salts, were then weighed, making them the 'parts' that make up 1000 g of water. After hundreds of years of water samples, scientists now know that the average salinity of the open ocean is 35 ppt.

While 35 ppt is the average salinity of ocean water, the actual salinity at any given location does vary locally thanks to the water cycle. Precipitation (for example, rain or snow) lowers the salinity of a body of water by diluting the salt in the seawater with incoming fresh water. After it rains, the water will flow over or into the Earth's surface. Eventually, most of this water, as part of the hydrological cycle, finds its way to the oceans as run-off, either directly by first flowing into a river, or through flows of groundwater (water moving through soil and porous rocks). In areas of ocean with fresh-water run-off, the salinity may be much lower than the open ocean. This lower salinity is caused by the addition of fresh water, rather than the removal of salts. It is important to note that as run-off flows over city streets or through farmers' fields, it dissolves many substances and carries them along. These substances could include vital nutrients, pesticides, fertilisers, oils and other pollutants capable of changing the salinity or quality of the water it is entering as well.

Evaporation will cause salinity levels to rise due to the removal of water from the solution rather than the addition of salts. It is important to note that only water is removed through evaporation; all solutes are left behind. Salinity higher than 35 ppt is often found in regions with above-average evaporation rates and a limited fresh-water inflow. When the salts are even more concentrated, the water is described as hypersaline. The most hypersaline environment in the world is Don Juan Pond in Antarctica. Scientists refer to this region as the McMurdo Dry Valleys due to the lack of precipitation

Figure 1.10: An aerial view Don Juan Pond located in the McMurdo Dry Valleys of Antarctica.

in the area. That lack of rain and snow causes this pond to have a salinity of 440 ppt, which is twelve times saltier than the ocean. The salinity is so high that even in −50 °C weather, the pond does not freeze (Figure 1.10). For more information about the freezing point of water and salinity, see Core Practical 1.1.

KEY WORDS

salinity: a measure of the quantity of dissolved solids in ocean water, represented by parts per thousand (ppt) or ‰

precipitation: water that falls from the atmosphere to the Earth's surface as rain, sleet, snow or hail

run-off: the flow of water from land caused by precipitation

evaporation: a change in state from liquid to gas below the boiling point of a substance

hypersaline: when a body of water has a salinity level greater than 40‰

CORE PRACTICAL ACTIVITY 1.1: INVESTIGATING THE EFFECT OF SALINITY ON THE FREEZING POINT OF WATER

Introduction

As the molecules of water are cooled, their movement slows and they form a lattice pattern that creates the solid ice. The temperature at which liquid water turns to solid ice is called the freezing point. This property of water has major implications for marine organisms. Organisms cannot swim through ice; however, much of our Arctic and Southern Oceans have thriving ecosystems despite the large volume of water that freezes each year. This is at least partially due to the presence of salts in seawater. Throughout this investigation, you will study how increased salinity impacts the point at which water freezes.

Equipment

You will need:

- temperature probe *or* digital thermometers
- 4 × medium test tubes marked $0.5\,mol\,dm^{-3}$, $1.0\,mol\,dm^{-3}$, $1.5\,mol\,dm^{-3}$ and $2\,mol\,dm^{-3}$
- 4 × 100 ml beakers marked $0.5\,mol\,dm^{-3}$, $1.0\,mol\,dm^{-3}$, $1.5\,mol\,dm^{-3}$ and $2\,mol\,dm^{-3}$
- 1 litre beaker *or* flask *or* graduated cylinder
- $400\,cm^3$ beaker
- freezer
- ice cube trays
- plastic bag
- rubber hammer
- digital balance
- black marker
- 230 g sodium chloride
- access to tap water (to create ice)
- $500\,cm^3$ of distilled water (to create solutions)

Safety considerations

- Follow all usual laboratory safety rules.
- Wear safety goggles, lab coats and gloves while in the laboratory.
- Handle glassware carefully.

Before you start

1. Why are you using distilled water to create the solutions instead of tap water?
2. In this investigation, the independent variable is the amount of sodium chloride added to the water, and the dependent variable is the freezing point of the solution. What are *two* other variables that will need to be controlled in order to receive accurate results?
3. What do you predict will happen to the freezing point of water as sodium chloride is added to it?

Method

1. Create a results table in your notebook similar to Table 1.1.
2. Create your ice.
   a. Using the beaker or graduated cylinder, mix 200 g of Sodium chloride into $1\,dm^3$ of tap water.
   b. Pour the solution into ice trays.
   c. Place the trays in the freezer and leave them overnight.
3. The next day, label the four beakers and test tubes as Sodium chloride $0.5\,mol\,dm^{-3}$, Sodium chloride $1.0\,mol\,dm^{-3}$, Sodium chloride $1.5\,mol\,dm^{-3}$, Sodium chloride $2.0\,mol\,dm^{-3}$.
4. Prepare each of the solutions below in the appropriately labelled beaker:
   a. Sodium chloride $0.5\,mol\,dm^{-3}$ – mix $100\,cm^3$ of distilled water with 2.9 g of sodium chloride
   b. Sodium chloride $1.0\,mol\,dm^{-3}$ – mix $100\,cm^3$ of distilled water with 5.8 g of sodium chloride
   c. Sodium chloride $1.5\,mol\,dm^{-3}$ – mix $100\,cm^3$ of distilled water with 8.7 g of sodium chloride
   d. Sodium chloride $2.0\,mol\,dm^{-3}$ – mix $100\,cm^3$ of distilled water with 11.6 g of sodium chloride
5. Using the ice cubes prepared the previous day, create an ice bath.
   a. Place the prepared ice cubes in a large plastic bag.
   b. Using the rubber hammer (or appropriate substitute) carefully crush the ice.
   c. Fill the $400\,cm^3$ beaker with the crushed ice.
6. Pour the solution in each beaker into its marked test tube to the halfway mark.
7. Put a digital thermometer into each tube.
8. Add the test tubes to the ice bath.

> **CONTINUED**
>
> ### Results
>
> 1 Observe the test tubes and record the temperature when the first ice crystals begin to form along the surface into a copy of Table 1.1.
>
> | Concentration of sodium chloride in solution / mol dm^{-3} | Freezing point of solution / °C |
> |---|---|
> | 0.5 | |
> | 1.0 | |
> | 1.5 | |
> | 2.0 | |
>
> **Table 1.1:** Data table for measuring freezing point.
>
> 2 Create a line graph of *Concentration of sodium chloride in solution* (x-axis) against *Freezing point of solution* (y-axis).
>   a Create a scale for each axis based on your data. Your scale should be large enough that your data takes up more than half of the available space both vertically and horizontally.
>   b As your temperatures will be below 0 °C, your x-axis should be at the top rather than along the bottom, so the y-axis can better represent the negative numbers.
>   c Remember to use a ruler to create straight lines that will connect your carefully plotted data points.
>
> ### Evaluation and conclusions
>
> 1 Identify the solvent and the solute in our solutions.
> 2 Compare the solubility of the sodium chloride when you are adding 2.9 g to the solubility of the sodium chloride when you are adding 11.6 g.
> 3 Describe the change in temperature as the concentration of sodium chloride increased.
> 4 Predict the freezing point of a solution with 40 g cm^{-3}.
> 5 How could you extend this experiment to test for other factors which may impact freezing point?

> **REFLECTION**
>
> After completing Core Practical Activity 1.1, think about these questions:
>
> 1 How could you improve your results for this practical?
> 2 Do you think this practical helped your understanding of this concept? Why or why not?

Mixing of the layers

The surface layer of the ocean, from zero to around 200 m deep, is the best-mixed area of the ocean. As the wind blows across the surface of the ocean, currents and turbulence are created. This water movement mixes the upper 200 m or so of the ocean, making it fairly uniform in both temperature and salinity.

Mixing of the layers within the ocean is typically density driven. For example, if the surface of the ocean cools, the density of the water will increase due to the temperature change. As the density increases, the water sinks, carrying with it all the nutrients and dissolved gases that it contained at the surface, mixing with the higher density water that is rising. This can happen in cold ocean as well when the density changes due to changes in salinity levels. Both the **halocline** and **thermocline** are considered areas of mixing where significant changes in the abiotic factors of the ocean happen.

> **KEY WORDS**
>
> **halocline:** a layer of water below the mixed surface layer where a rapid change in salinity can be measured as depth increases
>
> **thermocline:** a layer between two layers of water with different temperatures

The deep ocean, or bottom layer of the ocean, is uniform, like the surface. The deep ocean tends to be very cold, salty and dense. There is oxygen and other gases present in this layer, but they are limited.

The pH scale

Potential of hydrogen, more commonly referred to as **pH**, is an important abiotic factor for the survival of aquatic organisms in a marine environment. This is used to measure the concentration of hydrogen ions in water. Hydrogen ions are spontaneously created in pure water when the water molecules will split into hydrogen ions (H^+) and hydroxide ions (OH^-). Solutions with high concentrations of hydrogen ions compared to pure water are **acidic** (called acids), while solutions with low concentrations of hydrogen ions are called **alkaline** (you may have also seen this referred to as 'basic'). Because pure water is the point of comparison, it is considered **neutral**. For scientists to easily determine the pH of a solution, they created the logarithmic **pH scale** (Figure 1.11). Using this scale, solutions with a pH:

- below 7.0 are acidic
- at 7.0 are neutral
- above 7.0 are alkaline.

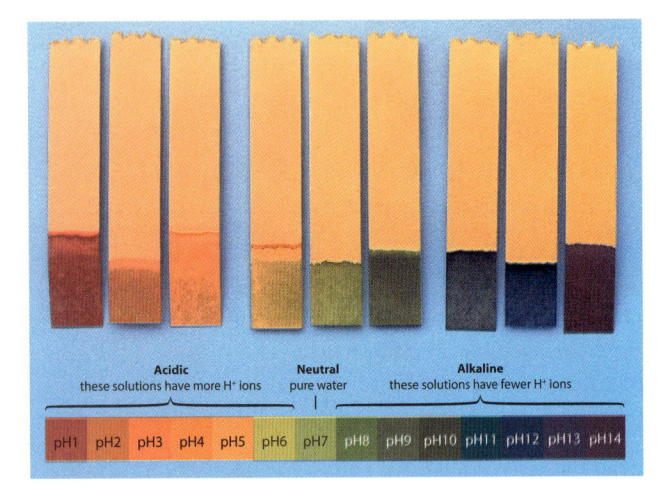

Figure 1.11: The colour pH scale used with universal indicator paper to determine hydrogen ion concentrations within a solution.

The pH of the world's oceans has been slightly alkaline since before we ever began collecting data. Historically, the pH of the open ocean has been an average of 8.2; however, there has been a recent drop in the worldwide average to an 8.1 pH due to increasing levels of carbon dioxide (CO_2) in our atmosphere. This seems like a small drop; but it is easy to misjudge the readings on the pH scale because it is not linear. In a linear scale, a 0.1 decrease in pH would indicate a 1% increase in acidity. Instead, because this scale is logarithmic, a 0.1 decrease in pH is actually a 25% rise in acidity. Small changes in pH, therefore, can bring drastic issues to the environment.

Scientists typically use one of three methods to measure the pH of water samples: litmus indicator, universal indicator and pH probes. Litmus indicator and universal indicator are both solutions, but they are also commonly used as papers where an absorbent paper has been soaked in the solution and allowed to dry, providing a simple and easier method to test with these indicators that can be dipped into a solution. Once in contact with the solution being tested, the indicator begins to change colour. Litmus indicator only determines if a substance in an acid or an alkali, it cannot show how strong an acid or alkali is. Universal indicator shows a range of strengths for acids and alkalis: scientists then compare the colour of the paper to the colour pH scale provided to give a whole number pH. These methods are quick, but also subjective, leading the scientist to try to determine the pH as closely as possible. Electronic pH probes can also be used to determine pH. These probes measure the hydrogen-ion concentration within a solution to provide a numerical read-out that is more precise and less subjective than the other methods.

> **KEY WORDS**
>
> **pH:** a numeric value expressing the acidity or alkalinity of a solution on a logarithmic scale
>
> **acidic:** having a pH below 7
>
> **alkaline:** having a pH above 7
>
> **neutral:** having a pH that equals 7
>
> **pH scale:** a logarithmic scale that measures the ratio of hydrogen ions to hydroxide ions

CORE PRACTICAL ACTIVITY 1.2: DETERMINING THE PH OF WATER

Introduction

When studying aquatic environments, like the ocean, it is important to understand how changes in pH can alter the ability of some organisms to survive or reproduce within an environment. Therefore, when checking water quality, scientists often test the pH of the water using one of three methods: universal indicator, litmus indicator or pH probes. Each method measures the concentration of hydrogen ions, H^+, within the solution being studied. After testing, each method provides a number value between 0 and 14 along the pH scale. Those numbers between 0 and 6.9 are considered acidic, a 7.0 is considered neutral, and 7.1 to 14.0 are considered alkaline. As the pH scale is logarithmic, a decrease of 1 indicates that 10 times more hydrogen ions are present within the solution. This change can greatly alter the environment for organisms sensitive to pH.

Equipment

You will need:
- distilled water (up to 60 cm^3 per group plus extra for rinsing test tubes and pH probe)
- white vinegar (10 cm^3 per group)
- seawater or a solution of 35 g NaCl per litre of tap water (20 cm^3 per group)
- pond water (20 cm^3 per group)
- universal indicator solution or paper with corresponding colour chart
- litmus indicator solution (or red and blue litmus papers)
- baking soda (0.5 mg per group)
- pH probe
- 5 × test tubes (wide enough to fit the pH probe)
- test tube rack
- 2 × small beakers
- dropping pipettes

Safety considerations

- Wear safety goggles, lab coats and gloves while in the laboratory.
- Handle glassware carefully.
- Check the Material Safety Data Sheets (MSDS) for the universal indicator solution used, and follow necessary safety precautions.

Before you start

1. Which properties of distilled water make it appropriate to use for cleaning and calibrating equipment?
2. What purpose might the vinegar and baking soda serve in a pH experiment?
3. Ocean acidification is a major concern for scientists due to potential impacts on marine organisms. What organisms do you think are at the greatest risk and why?

Method

1. For each solution listed in the results table, predict whether it will be acidic, neutral, or alkaline, and record your prediction in a copy of Table 1.2.
2. Create a solution of vinegar and distilled water in one of the small beakers by combining 10 cm^3 acetic acid with 10 cm^3 distilled water. Set aside.
3. Create a solution of baking soda and distilled water in the second small beaker by combining 5 mg of baking soda and 20 cm^3 distilled water. Set aside.
4. Pour approximately 1 cm depth of distilled water into a test tube.
5. Using universal indicator to measure pH:
   a. With solution:
      i. Add a few drops of universal indicator to each solution.
      ii. Wait for colour change.
      iii. Compare colour to associated pH colour chart and note results in table.
   b. With universal indicator paper:
      i. Dip the indicator paper into the solution for about 1 second.
      ii. Allow the paper to dry completely.
      iii. Compare colour to associated pH colour chart and note results in table.

CONTINUED

6. For each of the remaining test tubes, pour approximately 1 cm depth of the remaining solutions (vinegar solution, baking soda solution, seawater, and pond water) so that each test tube only contains one solution.
7. Repeat step 5 for each test tube.
8. Rinse all test tubes with distilled water.
9. Create new samples of each solution as before.
10. Use litmus indicator solution or papers to see if each solution is acidic, alkaline or neutral.
11. Record the results of the litmus indicator in the table (acidic, alkaline or neutral).
12. Rinse all test tubes with distilled water.
13. Create new samples of each solution as before.
14. Using pH probe, determine the pH of each solution.
15. Note all pH readings in the results table.

Results

	Prediction: acidic, neutral, alkaline	Colour and pH of universal indicator	Results of litmus indicator	pH probe reading
distilled water				
vinegar solution				
baking soda solution				
seawater				
pond water				

Table 1.2: Data table for measuring pH.

Evaluation and conclusions

1. Did each method provide uniform results for each solution? Why do you think different methods may have produced slightly different results?
2. Pond water may be slightly acidic to slightly alkaline. Where did your solution fall on the pH scale? Suggest a reason for that reading.
3. Predict what the pH would be if the vinegar solution were added to the baking soda solution. Suggest an explanation for your prediction.

> **REFLECTION**
>
> After completing Core Practical Activity 1.2, think about these questions:
>
> 1 Your results may be different from those of other groups. Why might that be?
> 2 What problems did you encounter when working through this practical? How do you think they could have impacted your results?

The solubility of gases in seawater

Gases in the atmosphere (nitrogen, carbon dioxide and oxygen) are in a state of equilibrium with the gases dissolved in ocean water. As the concentration of a particular gas in the atmosphere increases (carbon dioxide, for instance), the concentration of that gas in seawater also rises. Mixing, as a result of **turbulence** and wave action, works to maintain this equilibrium. The more turbulence there is, the easier it is for gases in the atmosphere to dissolve into the ocean. This can lead to higher concentrations of carbon dioxide and oxygen within the upper 200 m depth of the ocean than are found in the water below this. Factors contributing to the concentration of gases in seawater include the following.

> **KEY WORD**
>
> **turbulence:** irregular changes in the speed and direction of fluid movement

Gas solubility

Carbon dioxide is very soluble in seawater because of its ability to form carbonic acid, a weak acid, when introduced to water. Oxygen, however, has a low solubility because it does not chemically combine with the water molecules. This means that the level of carbon dioxide held by seawater is higher than that of oxygen.

Water temperature

Cold water can dissolve more gas than water at warmer temperatures. When water increases in temperature its molecules move faster. This results in dissolved gas molecules evaporating from the surface of water more quickly. All gases are less soluble in warmer water for the same reason. This means that water found near the poles will dissolve more oxygen than water found in the tropics (Table 1.3). The concentration of dissolved oxygen is particularly important to aquatic organisms, so increases in temperature can have a significant impact on the range of organisms that the water can sustain.

Temperature of water / °C	Concentration of dissolved oxygen / mg dm^{-3}
0	14.6
5	12.8
10	11.3
15	10.2
20	9.2
25	8.4

Table 1.3: Relationship between temperature and the maximum concentration of dissolved oxygen in fresh water.

Atmospheric pressure

The solubility of gases increases with increasing pressure. Atmospheric pressure plays a role in how soluble gases are at the ocean's surface. When atmospheric pressure increases, the equilibrium of gases in the atmosphere and those dissolved in the ocean changes – there is a greater concentration of the gas in the atmosphere, this pushes more of those gas molecules to dissolve in the seawater and increase the concentration of dissolved gases in the surface waters of the ocean. When atmospheric pressure decreases, during a tropical cyclone for instance, this equilibrium shifts the other way and more of the dissolved gas molecules escape from the surface and enter the atmosphere.

Water pressure due to depth

As you travel deeper into the ocean, the pressure of the water above you continues to increase due to the sheer mass of the water. With that increasing pressure, gases are better able to dissolve into the water and stay dissolved in the water. Note that, when describing depth of water be very careful with your wording – try to use words such as 'deeper' or 'shallower' instead of 'higher' or 'lower'. A statement such as 'higher depths' is ambiguous because a high value is deeper, but a low value could mean something is higher up in the ocean.

The salinity of the seawater

Gases are better able to dissolve in water with lower levels of salinity because there are less solutes taking up space between the water molecules and so more water molecules are able to interact with gas molecules and dissolve them. This can be seen very clearly if you add a teaspoon of salt to a carbonated drink such as sparkling water or cola – when the salt is added the gas molecules are released very quickly as the liquid fizzes up. Gases, like oxygen and carbon dioxide, are most soluble in fresh water entering the ocean from rivers, such as in estuaries; as the fresh water mixes with salt water in the sea, the solubility of these gases decreases. Therefore, you would expect to find higher levels of oxygen in an estuary than in the open ocean.

Impact of solubility on marine life

Organisms and dissolved gases are intricately linked. Carbon dioxide and oxygen are both necessary for the survival of marine organisms. At the surface, producers take in dissolved carbon dioxide for use in photosynthesis and then release oxygen as a result. All living organisms use dissolved oxygen for respiration. Nitrogen gas is transformed into ammonia by nitrogen-fixing bacteria, making the nitrogen easier for other organisms to use for protein creation.

As a key requirement for respiration, the concentration of **dissolved oxygen (DO)** is incredibly important in the marine environment. In general, oxygen has a low solubility in water, and this characteristic is impacted further by temperature, salinity and pressure causing the concentration of DO to vary greatly throughout the ocean. As temperature and salinity increase, the concentration of DO decreases. The solubility of oxygen generally increases with depth due to both the decrease in temperature and the increasing pressure of the water above.

The area of the ocean with the greatest concentration of dissolved oxygen is the top 100 m of the ocean, known as the surface layer. Within this layer, the dissolved oxygen concentration can reach 'supersaturation'. This means there is more oxygen dissolved in the seawater than it would normally be able to carry. Two major factors work together to increase the amount of dissolved oxygen to supersaturation level: the motion of the water and photosynthesis by producers. The more turbulent the water, the more oxygen is mixed into it by the movement of the waves. Meanwhile, producers, like **phytoplankton** and algae, carry out photosynthesis using light from the Sun to create glucose (for the producer) and generate oxygen as a by-product that is released into the ocean's waters. Photosynthesis can only take place in the upper layer of the ocean, called the photic zone, where light is able to penetrate and be used by producers. This release of oxygen increases the concentration of dissolved oxygen in the surface layer. Dissolved oxygen is removed from the surface layer by the respiration by all organisms. The concentration of DO can also vary tremendously with latitude, as tropical waters have much higher temperatures, reducing the concentration of DO that the water can dissolve. Polar waters are much colder and therefore able to dissolve a much higher concentration of DO.

Below the surface layer of the ocean, the concentration of dissolved oxygen changes dramatically. As the depth of the ocean increases, the level of dissolved oxygen decreases until it reaches the **oxygen minimum layer**. The oxygen minimum layer typically occurs at a depth of around 500 m but has been found anywhere between 100 m and 1000 m deep depending on location. At this point, the level of DO can sometimes nearly reach zero due to a lack of oxygen being introduced into the water and consumers still performing respiration to survive.

Some organisms, such as the vampire squid, are capable of living within the oxygen minimum zone, despite the lack of dissolved oxygen, but they do need special adaptations for survival. Most of the organisms found here are fairly inactive, which reduces their need for oxygen. The gills of the fish in this area are incredibly efficient at extracting oxygen from water, even at the low levels present in this layer. Additionally, many of the organisms here have a specially adapted form of haemoglobin, a blood protein responsible for carrying oxygen throughout the body.

> **KEY WORDS**
>
> **dissolved oxygen (DO):** concentration of oxygen dissolved in a solution
>
> **phytoplankton:** microscopic photosynthetic organisms that live in the upper, sunlit layers of water
>
> **oxygen minimum layer:** the layer within the ocean where the concentration of dissolved oxygen is at its lowest, typically found below the photic zone between 100 m and 1000 m deep

After passing through the oxygen minimum layer, the DO concentration begins to increase with depth as expected. Several reasons exist for this increase in oxygen as you move deeper (Figure 1.12).

- Falling detritus is colonised by bacteria that decompose the organic matter carrying out aerobic respiration which uses up oxygen. As this detritus falls below the photic zone the oxygen cannot be replaced by photosynthesis. Below the oxygen minimum layer this decomposition has been completed and there is less respiration carried out by these bacteria.
- The organisms found below the oxygen minimum layer are in an area with very few food resources. This lack of food reduces the need for the organisms to respire, so they survive with less oxygen.
- The solubility of oxygen increases as the temperature decreases. As you go deeper into the ocean, the temperature decreases to near-freezing. The lower temperature means more oxygen can stay dissolved in the water.
- As pressure increases, the solubility of oxygen increases. For every 10 m you sink into the ocean, the pressure increases by one atmosphere.

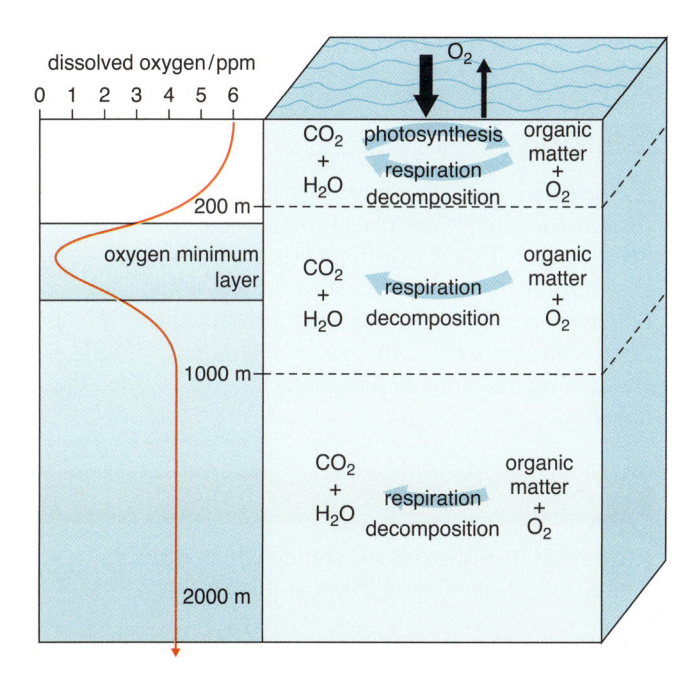

Figure 1.12: Oxygen minimum layer in the eastern tropical Pacific Ocean and the biological processes responsible.

Test yourself

5 What makes seawater a solution? How could you test this to verify your answer?

6 How does the salinity of seawater differ in areas where precipitation is greater than evaporation, compared to areas where evaporation is greater than precipitation?

7 How does the solubility of a gas impact its availability to marine life?

1.3 Density and pressure

Density is the mass of a defined volume of water divided by its volume. The formula for density is:

$$\text{density (kg m}^{-3}) = \frac{\text{mass (kg)}}{\text{volume (m}^3)}$$

When discussing density in seawater, the denser the water is, the lower it will sit in the **water column**. The least dense water will rise to the surface of the water column and the densest water will sink to the bottom. Temperature, salinity and water pressure all play a role in determining the density of seawater.

Temperature

Temperature is the factor most responsible for changes in density. As the temperature of seawater increases, density decreases. Warmer water tends to float near the surface of a body of water, and this is exposed to heating by the Sun, causing this layer to get even warmer and less dense. This warm layer is often fairly shallow and sits on top of colder, denser water. Between the two layers is an area where the temperature abruptly changes, known as the thermocline (Figure 1.13). Water at the surface may reach 25 °C or higher in tropical seas but is more likely to be 1 °C at depths of 2000 m or more. In polar seas, the temperature **gradient** in a

> ### KEY WORDS
>
> **water column:** a vertical section of water from the surface to the bottom; useful concept when discussing changes in the abiotic factors within the body of water
>
> **gradient:** the rate of change in the y-axis value as the x-axis value increases

thermocline is less drastic. In these areas, the surface water is likely to be close to freezing and remain at a fairly constant temperature with increasing depth.

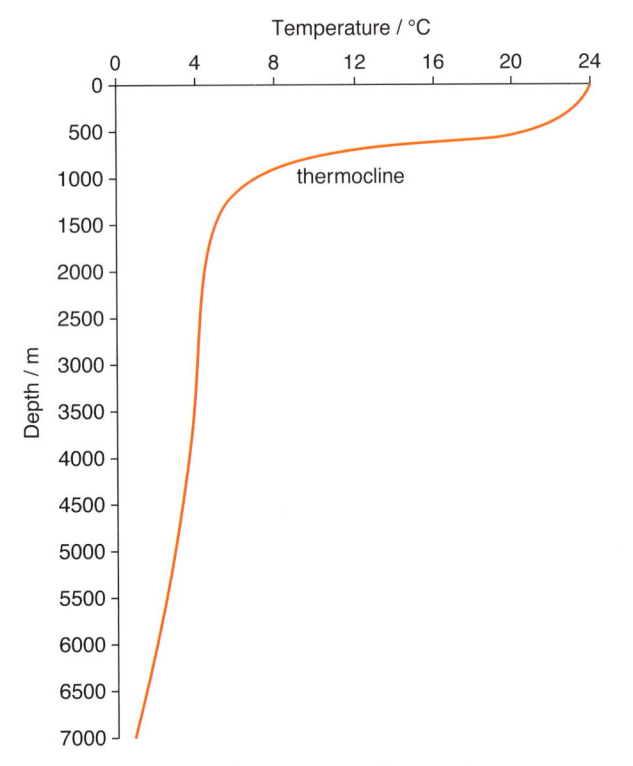

Figure 1.13: Thermocline in a typical tropical sea.

Why is it that the water at the bottom of the ocean does not freeze? The answer has two parts: salinity and density. As salinity increases, the freezing point of water decreases, making it more difficult to create ice. For more information, see Core Practical 1.1. When water begins to freeze, the individual water molecules begin to arrange into a lattice pattern (as you saw in Section 1.1) due to the hydrogen bonds holding them together. These bonds hold the water molecules at a slightly greater distance from one another, which is different from the arrangement in liquid water where the molecules of water are constantly making and breaking hydrogen bonds with each other as they move past each other. This reduces the density of ice compared to liquid water, which causes ice to float at the surface of liquid water. Therefore, even if the water freezes on the bottom of the ocean, unlikely due to the salinity, it would float to the surface rather than remain at the bottom of the ocean.

The property of water that allows ice to float is of vital importance for marine organisms. If ice stayed at the bottom of the ocean, the ocean would freeze entirely from the bottom to the surface, which would leave marine organisms nowhere to go in the dead of winter. When ice forms on a body of water it begins to act as a **thermal insulator**, reducing the rate of further heat loss from the water beneath it. This means the water under the ice is warmer than the water exposed to the freezing air above the ice, allowing marine organisms to stay at a temperature that is better suited for their adaptations. The floating ice sheets provide a habitat for animals such as penguins or polar bears to hunt from. Additionally, the underside of icebergs and ice sheets functions as a habitat for species of phytoplankton and algae that can grow there. The growth of these producers helps support the Arctic and Antarctic ecosystems throughout the winter months when the food supply should be too low to maintain the food web.

Pressure

As pressure increases with increasing depth, so too does the density of seawater. There is approximately a 2% change in is density due to the pressure differences between the abyssal floor and the surface. This is due to the water pressure due to increasing depth acting on the individual molecules in the seawater. With increased pressure, the molecules are pushed closer together, forcing more molecules into smaller volumes. Therefore, there is more mass contained within the same volume of water. An area of water where the density changes quickly with depth is referred to as a **pycnocline**.

Salinity

As the salinity of water increases, the density increases; therefore fresher, lower density water floats on saltier, denser water. This is why in an estuary fresh water sits above the saltwater. Between the less saline, and therefore less dense, surface waters and the more saline, denser, bottom waters, there is an area where salinity changes significantly with depth. This area is called the halocline.

> **KEY WORDS**
>
> **thermal insulator:** a substance which reduces the rate of transfer of thermal energy
>
> **pycnocline:** a layer of water between two layers of water with different densities

1 Water

This would indicate that the saltiest water in the ocean is at the seabed. For the most part this is true, but there is one exception: tropical seas. In tropical seas between 30°N and 30°S, the surface temperatures create high evaporation rates at the surface. This results in a very warm, but also very salty, layer across the surface of the ocean. This layer floats on the surface, in spite of its increased salinity, because the temperature is so high. Just below that layer, the salinity profile shows a steep decrease in salinity, the halocline, until 750 m, followed by a slow increase, as expected (Figure 1.14).

In non-tropical oceans the halocline can be in the reverse direction, since a greater rate of precipitation than evaporation can result in lower salinities at the surface, as we find in estuaries, and the salinity therefore increases as you move deeper.

Mixing of layers in the ocean

Calm, still waters in the ocean lead to the formation of distinct layers due to temperature and salinity differences as you move deeper. These layers can be mixed by several factors, including strong winds and wave action (especially in stormy weather), and by currents and upwellings pushing water of different densities together. This mixing can cause thermoclines and haloclines to weaken or break down completely. For example, temperate waters generally only experience a thermocline in the summer months when the surface waters are heated by more intense sunlight and the weather is generally calmer. Stormier weather in the autumn months causes the thermocline to weaken until it

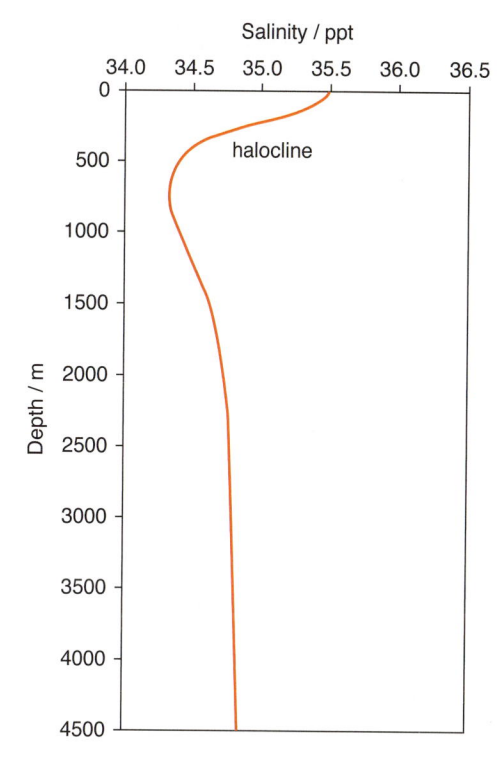

Figure 1.14: Typical halocline in a tropical sea.

eventually disappears completely. It will not reappear until warmer weather returns in the late spring. This mixing is due to great forces from strong winds or currents churning the water to considerable depths; the passing of ships or large animals such as whales has virtually no impact on mixing these layers of water.

CASE STUDY 1.1: DISCOVERING THE COMPOSITION OF SEAWATER

The Challenger expedition was the first true scientific study of the open ocean. Led by Charles Wyville Thomson, the expedition took place between December 1872 and May 1876 aboard a modified British warship named the *HMS Challenger*. After petitioning for years, the Royal Society of London, of which Thomson was a member, was able to purchase an outdated warship from the Royal Navy. To prepare for the journey, 15 of the *HMS Challenger*'s 17 cannons were removed and the space created by their removal was fitted with scientific laboratories (Figure 1.15). When the *HMS Challenger* set sail, among the nearly 250-person crew were seven scientists and an official expedition artist to document the scientists' findings.

Figure 1.15: An illustration of the natural history workroom aboard the *HMS Challenger*.

CONTINUED

The laboratories on board enabled the scientists to collect an incredible amount of data in the fields of natural history and chemistry over the course of the 68 890 nautical-mile scientific voyage. In fact, they collected so much data that once they returned to land it took nearly 20 years for all of their findings to be analysed and published in a 50-volume report containing nearly 30 000 pages. Within those findings, more than 4000 new species of marine life were discovered as well as some necessary pieces of chemical oceanography.

When the *Challenger* returned to England in 1876, the water samples taken during the voyage were sent to a well-known chemist, William Dittmar. After years of analysing the samples, Dittmar discovered a multitude of evidence that the same six ions made up the majority of the solutes in seawater: chloride, sodium, sulfate, magnesium, calcium, and potassium. Additionally, he found that, regardless of the concentration of salts in the water, the ions were always present in the same percentages within the seawater. This phenomenon, first proposed by Johan Georg in 1865, is now called the **principle of constant proportions**. Even with the modern technology of today, scientists continue to revisit this research and come to the same conclusions. Dittmar's theory of constant proportions holds true for the open ocean and, generally, for coastal regions.

Thanks to William Dittmar and his evidence solidifying the theory of constant proportions, we now know chloride (Cl^-) ions in the open ocean account for 55% of the ions present and sodium ions (Na^+) follow at 30%. It really should be no surprise, then that seawater tastes like table salt – the common name for the compound sodium chloride (NaCl). Four other ions can also be found in regular proportions within our oceans: sulfate (SO_4^{2-}), magnesium (Mg^{2+}), calcium (Ca^{2+}), and potassium (K^+). Their proportions can be seen in Table 1.4.

In 2018, scientists met from all over the globe to share new data on ocean salinity investigations at the Ocean Salinity Conference in Paris, France. These scientists worked to share new data gathered from modern technology such as satellite observations and computer models. While the theory of constant proportions has not changed, scientists are able to monitor changing salinity to look at variations in the way currents flow and the impacts of these changes on our freshwater cycle.

Ion	Mean concentration in seawater / parts per thousand	Ratio of ion : total salts / percentage (%)
chloride (Cl^-)	19.35	55.04
sodium (Na^+)	10.75	30.61
sulfate (SO_4^{2-})	2.70	7.68
magnesium (Mg^{2+})	1.30	3.69
calcium (Ca^{2+})	0.42	1.16
potassium (K^+)	0.38	1.10
minor ions	0.10	0.72

Table 1.4: Concentrations of the six most common ions in seawater.

Questions

1. Charles Wyville and the Royal Society of London spent years trying to convince the British government to send a scientific ship to learn about the world's oceans. The British government did not see the potential benefits of such an endeavour. Suggest how the benefits justified the cost of the expedition.

2. Scientists still struggle to receive funding even though less is known about the contents of our oceans than the surface of Mars. Why do you think scientific exploration of our oceans is still in the position of having to justify support?

3. Using the data presented in Table 1.4, create a pie chart to represent the percentages of ions in ocean water.

4. According to studies conducted by Dittmar and many chemists since, chloride ions make up 55% of the ions present in seawater. Besides sodium chloride, what ionic compounds could be formed with chloride from the ions listed?

1 Water

> **KEY WORD**
>
> **principle of constant proportions:** the ratio of any two major ions dissolved in seawater is constant

MATHS SKILLS 1.1

GRAPHING DENSITY AND TEMPERATURE

Density is a major component of survival for marine organisms. The formula for density is:

$$\text{density (kg m}^{-3}) = \frac{\text{mass (kg)}}{\text{volume (m}^3)}$$

You need to remember this formula so you can calculate density if you are given the mass and volume of an object or body of water. Conversely, you should be able to use this formula to determine either mass or volume, as well. A good starting point is to know that the density of freshwater at sea level is 1000 kg m^{-3}; however, the density of seawater, with a salinity of 35 ppt, is slightly higher due to the mass of the ions dissolved within the solution. This density will vary with depth and temperature.

Worked example

In Table 1.5, data has been collected for you about the density of seawater at different temperatures. This data assumes pressure remains the same at 101 kPa, which is the average atmospheric pressure at the sea surface.

Temperature of seawater / °C	Density of seawater / kg m^{-3}
30	1021.76
25	1023.37
20	1024.79
15	1026.00
10	1026.98
5	1027.70
0	1028.13
−5	1028.22
−10	1027.90

Table 1.5: The density of seawater at various temperatures.

You will need to be able to graph data sets for different experiments throughout this course. Make sure to plan your graph appropriately. When plotting data, it is important to begin by identifying which variable belongs on the *x*-axis and which belongs on the *y*-axis. The simplest way to do this is to determine which variable is the independent variable or the variable that is being controlled by the scientist. Usually, the independent variable is the variable with a regular, easily predicted pattern; in this case, the temperature of the seawater was controlled by the researcher, and is normally the first column of data in a results table. Generally, your independent variable will lie on the *x*-axis. (This may not always be the case, but it is the normal rule – a notable exception is graphs plotted against depth; the depth is usually the independent variable but we plot depth on the *y*-axis to match the actual changes in depth in the ocean. This has an impact on how the gradient is measured.)

Next, you will need to figure out the scale of your axes. Your scale should represent the data so it is easy to see trends. To do this, you must find the range of your data. In this case our range is $1028.22 - 1021.76 = 6.46$. Many people would start numbering their *y*-axis from zero out of habit, but that will not showcase the data and the changes that need to be analysed. It is important to note that axes do not need to start at zero. In fact the most important consideration is the spread of your data – the points (when plotted) must occupy over half the scale on each axis. They must also have consistent intervals between numbers of the axis. In Figure 1.16, a graph has been started for you with appropriate intervals and scale on the *y*-axis.

> CAMBRIDGE INTERNATIONAL AS & A LEVEL MARINE SCIENCE: COURSEBOOK

CONTINUED

Questions

1 Using the rest of the data, complete the graph.
2 Using the data presented in your graph, describe the shape of your graph.
3 At 1.9 °C the density of seawater is 1028.21 kg m^{-3}. If you were to add that data point to your graph, would the pattern change? Why or why not?
4 What do you predict would happen to the density of the seawater if the pressure was increased from 101 kPa to 101 000 kPa? Justify your response.
5 What would happen to the line on your graph if the y-axis had started at zero instead of 1020?

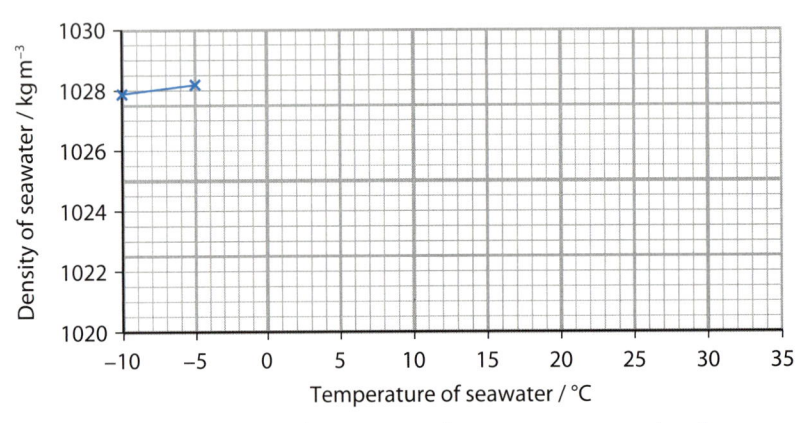

Figure 1.16: Line graph comparing the density of seawater and temperature at sea level.

Test yourself

8 What impact do temperature and salinity have on density?
9 Sketch what you would expect the temperature profile with depth to look like in an Arctic environment. What clues did you use to create your profile?

PROJECT: ATOMIC BONDING PLAY

Work with fellow students to create a play showing how different types of bonds form between atoms in the ocean. These plays can be serious or silly as long as they detail the processes the atoms go through (for example, the sharing or exchange of electrons). Your performance should be no longer than three minutes and focus on one type of bond with examples that are commonly found in marine ecosystems. The use of props is encouraged (for example, a beach ball could represent an electron).

Thinking about your project

- Now that you have performed your play and watched others, do you feel more comfortable with the bonding processes in atoms?
- How would you rate your group's performance in comparison to the other groups?
- What changes would you make to your play if you could do it over again?

1 Water

EXAM-STYLE QUESTIONS

1   a   Through the use of an annotated diagram, **describe** covalent bonding in a water molecule. [3]
    b   **Explain** how water changes state from a liquid to a gas with reference to hydrogen bonds. [3]
    c   When creating the solid form of water, ice, individual water molecules link together through the attractive forces of hydrogen bonds, forming a lattice structure. **State** how this change in structure affects the density of ice compared to liquid water. [1]
    d   Explain how the change you identified in **1c** impacts the organisms in Arctic ecosystems. [3]
    e   Using knowledge gained in your practical, **predict** the temperature of the water below the ice in the arctic ecosystems mentioned in **1d** and **suggest** a reason why. [2]

    [Total: 12]

2   a   **Define** the term *salinity*. [1]
    b   **Outline** the effect evaporation and freezing have on salinity. [2]
    c   Explain why the salinity of water in the open ocean tends to be higher than that near the coastlines. [2]
    d   Explain how salinity and temperature affect the density of seawater creating layers within the ocean, and how mixing of these layers occurs. [6]

    [Total: 11]

3   Scientists studying dissolved oxygen rates in aquatic ecosystems collected data from the surface of a river, the open ocean, and a tropical lagoon. The salinity at each collection site is 3 ppt, 35 ppt, and 40 ppt, respectively. The data is shown in Table 1.6.

	Dissolved oxygen (DO) / mg L^{-1}			Mean DO concentration / mg L^{-1}
	Collection 1	Collection 2	Collection 3	
River mouth	10.0	11.1	10.3	
Open ocean	7.5	5.2	8.1	
Tropical lagoon	3.2	3.7	2.9	

Table 1.6: Data collected regarding dissolved oxygen concentrations.

   a   Complete a copy of Table 1.6 by **calculating** the mean dissolved oxygen concentration for each environment. [3]
   b   Describe how means were calculated for each environment. [2]
   c   **Compare** the data for the three environments. [2]
   d   Suggest explanations for the differences in DO concentration in these habitats. [8]

   [Total: 15]

COMMAND WORDS

describe: state the points of a topic / give characteristics and main features

explain: set out purposes or reasons / make the relationships between things evident / provide why and/or how and support with relevant evidence

state: express in clear terms

predict: suggest what may happen based on available information

suggest: apply knowledge and understanding to situations where there are a range of valid responses in order to make proposals

define: give precise meaning

outline: set out main points

calculate: work out from given facts, figures or information

compare: identify / comment on similarities and/or differences

CONTINUED

4 Scientists are attempting to find a correlation between sea surface temperatures and ocean acidity to indicate that global warming is impacting ocean acidification. These scientists have already collected temperature data for ten sites along the Great Barrier Reef (Figure 1.17).

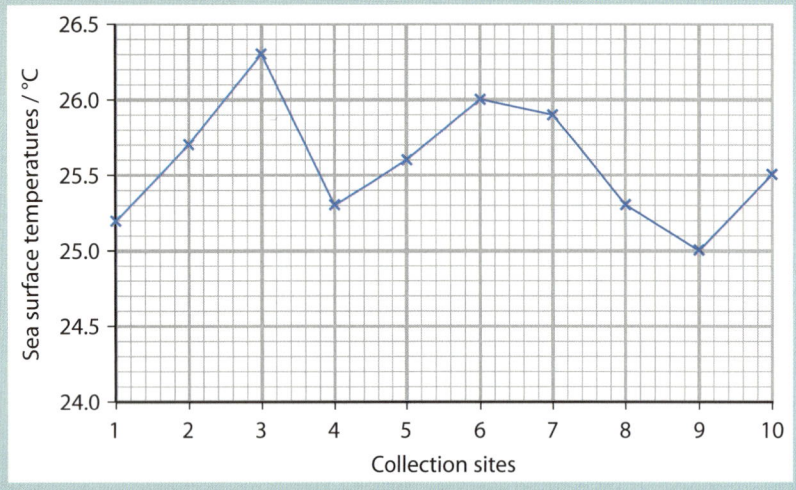

Figure 1.17: A student's graph of the seas surface temperatures at ten collection sites on the Great Barrier Reef, Australia.

- **a** Identify the 'best' technique for the scientists to collect pH data from the same ten sites where temperature data was collected, and how they would ensure the results are reliable. [2]
- **b** Suggest reasons why the technique you chose in part (**a**) would be the best choice in this instance. [3]
- **c** In a healthy ocean, state the pH levels you would expect to find. [1]
- **d** A student plotted the data collected by the scientists on the graph seen in Figure 1.17. Identify the error made by the student when graphing his data and explain why it is incorrect. [2]
- **e** Using the data in Table 1.7, plot a graph of the pH values on a copy of Figure 1.17. [4]

Collection site	pH
1	8.15
2	8.21
3	8.34
4	8.20
5	8.22
6	8.24
7	8.20
8	8.19
9	8.24
10	8.30

Table 1.7: pH values collected at ten collections sites on the Great Barrier Reef, Australia.

> **COMMAND WORD**
>
> **identify:** name / select / recognise

CONTINUED

f To what extent does the graph support a correlation between sea surface temperatures and ocean pH? [1]

[Total: 13]

5 a *Sketch* an annotated diagram depicting the creation of an ionic bond formed from a sodium atom and a chloride atom. [4]

b Complete a copy of Table 1.8 with each compound's bond type, chemical formula and chemical name. [6]

> **COMMAND WORD**
>
> **sketch:** make a simple freehand drawing showing the key features, taking care over proportions

Diagram	Bond types	Chemical name	Chemical formula
$Ca^{2+}[CO_3]^{2-}$ structure			
glucose ring structure			
H_2O structure			

Table 1.8: The bond types of common compounds found in seawater.

[Total: 10]

6 Seawater is a solution made of many solutes including ions and covalent molecules.

    a Define the following terms:

        i solute [1]

        ii solvent [1]

    b Suggest a reason why scientists think a warming ocean may have a higher salinity. [2]

    c State the most abundant ionic compound found in seawater. [1]

[Total: 5]

CONTINUED

7 Scientists were conducting research in the waters off the Southern California coastline. They took measurements of temperature and dissolved oxygen concentration from the sea surface to approximately 300 m down. See the results in Figure 1.18.

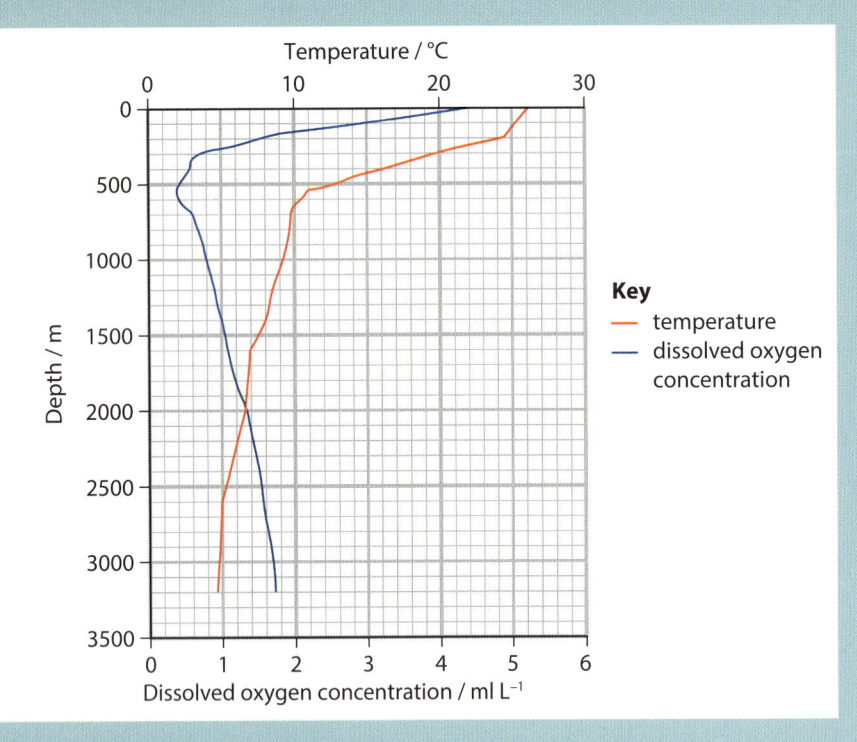

Figure 1.18: A comparison of DO levels and temperature off the coast of Southern California.

- **a** State the term used to describe the region of a water column where there is a drastic change in water temperature. [1]
- **b** State the approximate range of depths during which this drastic temperature change occurs. [1]
- **c** Use Figure 1.18 to find the following information:
  - **i** the depth at which the dissolved oxygen concentration is 0.4 ml L^{-1} [1]
  - **ii** the temperature at 1000 m. [1]
- **d** Figure 1.18 shows an area of extremely low oxygen concentration at 500 m deep.
  - **i** State the name for that region of the ocean. [1]
  - **ii** Explain why the oxygen at this level is so low. [4]
- **e** Oxygen concentrations begin to rise after 500 m deep. Explain how that is possible. [3]

[Total: 12]

1 Water

SELF-EVALUATION CHECKLIST

I can:	See section...	Needs more work	Almost there	Ready to move on
use the kinetic particle theory to explain the changes of state in water, between solid, liquid and gas	1.1			
describe how the structure of atoms leads to the formation of different bonds such as covalent, ionic and hydrogen bonds	1.1			
explain how hydrogen bonding provides special properties to water	1.1			
explain and compare the terms solute, solvent, solution and solubility in order to apply these terms to the dissolution of salt in the ocean	1.2			
explain the impacts of temperature and salinity on the solubility of salts and gases in seawater.	1.2			
explain how run-off, precipitation and evaporation impact the salinity of seawater	1.2			
describe the pH scale and know three techniques used to measure pH in water	1.2			
explain the effects on the density of seawater caused by water temperature, pressure and salinity	1.3			
state that the reason ice can float is because the density of ice is lower than seawater and discuss the importance of that to marine organisms.	1.3			
describe how temperature and salinity gradients form in water columns to produce ocean layers and how subsequent mixing of these layers may occur	1.3			

EXTENDED CASE STUDY: THE DEAD SEA

The Dead Sea is a hypersaline lake located in the Middle East in the Jordan Rift Valley. At 377 m deep, the Dead Sea is considered to be the deepest hypersaline lake in the world. This depth also helps make the Dead Sea the lowest elevation on land, at 423 m below sea-level.

The waters of the Dead Sea are replenished by the Jordan River which flows into the northern end of the lake. This 50 km long and 15 km wide body of water is considered to be one of the saltiest places on Earth.

The salinity of the water in the Dead Sea ranges from 280 ppt to 350 ppt. As typical ocean water contains salinity levels of only 35 ppt, the waters of the Dead Sea are, on average, 8.5 times as salty. However, the salinity levels vary depending on the time of year and where in the water column the measurement was taken. Salinity typically decreases in the winter and spring as there is more inflow from the Jordan River during these times, although that water has been dwindling for years as neighbouring countries divert more and more of the river for their country's needs. Measurements taken nearest the immediate surface tend to be higher than the waters directly below because of the high evaporation rates in the desert-like conditions of the Jordan Rift Valley. Evaporation rates are so high that salt crystals actually from along the surface and shore of the water (Figure 1.19). As you dive deeper into the water column you see a general trend of increasing salinity as you reach the bottom.

Due to the high salinity levels in the bottom water, the lake has historically had two different water masses existing simultaneously within its confines. The last time this happened lasted for nearly

Figure 1.19: Salt crystals on the surface of the Dead Sea.

CONTINUED

three hundred years and ended in the late 1970s. In this case, the first 40 metres of the Dead Sea maintained an average salinity that was just under 300 ppt. The most common salts found in this layer were bicarbonates and sulfates – very different from the open ocean where these salts occur at much lower percentages. Below the surface layer was a transition zone where the water's temperature decreased while the salinity gradually increased, creating both a thermocline and halocline. Below this transition zone, at approximately 100 metres, the water became more uniform with a constant temperature and salinity. The salts present in the water saw a drastic shift to hydrogen sulfide, magnesium, potassium, chlorine, and bromine. The high concentrations of salt made this water incredibly dense, preventing it from ever rising to the surface and, in essence, creating a permanent bottom layer with distinctly different characteristics from the surface layer.

Cultural history

For thousands of years, the Dead Sea has been a vacation destination. The salty waters are rumoured to have healing powers because of its mineral content. It is believed that soaking in these ion-laden waters can help reduce skin disorders, such as psoriasis and acne, and alleviate joint pain from arthritis. Many tourists will cover their bodies in the mineral-enriched muds hoping for health benefits. Science has yet to conclusively say any of these rumours are true and yet they have persisted throughout history. According to historical legend, the first health spa was located at the Dead Sea for Herod I (37–34 BCE).

However, if you are trying to get a work-out in these waters, you might want to visit somewhere else. Swimming here is really just floating as bathers are buoyant on the incredibly dense waters (Figure 1.20). Tourists have been seen reading the newspaper while floating on their backs with no problem.

It is ironic that the Dead Sea has always been considered a place of health and healing considering salinity levels make it impossible for most organisms to live there. Humans have even been killed by accidentally swallowing the water.

Figure 1.20: A man floats on his back in the Dead Sea.

The salt content is so high that even a mouthful of water can shut down your kidneys and damage your heart, which is why lifeguards are always on duty on a beach where no one drowns. Only a few species of archaea, bacteria and fungi are capable of making their homes in the Dead Sea on a continuous basis. In recent history, there has only been one occasion where new life has made its way into the sea. A particularly rainy winter in 1980 reduced the salinity so much that a new type of algae became established and turned the waters red, an unusual occurrence.

Profiting from salinity

People have always taken salt in small amounts from the Dead Sea. After all, it washes up on the shores. That changed when the Dead Sea Works was established to produce a major component of fertilisers: potash. Potash is the common name for potassium chloride and it has been mined from the Dead Sea in great quantities since 1929. Potash is such an important and expensive part of fertilisers that it is often referred to as 'white gold'. In order to remove potash from the waters of the Dead Sea, shallow evaporation pools have been created in the southernmost portion of the lake (Figure 1.21). This allows sunlight to evaporate water from the brine and leave the salts behind. However, in order to make these pools successful, the southern end of the Dead Sea has had several barricades, or dykes, built to prevent water from the Jordan River from

CONTINUED

flowing in naturally. This allows the corporations mining the potash, such as Dead Sea Works, to control rainwater flow.

Unfortunately, this evaporation process, which has been happening for nearly 100 years, has caused a severe drop in water levels. Between 1970 and 2018, the water levels in the Dead Sea dropped an average 1 metre year^{-1}. This reduction in surface water has allowed groundwater to move below the surface, dissolving subterranean caverns in the salt layer below the lake leading to sinkholes when the underground salt structures collapse. Several hundred sinkholes have formed around the Dead Sea, many in areas that are popular with tourists. It will not surprise you that resorts in this area are now turning even the sinkholes into tourist attractions. Concerned over this water loss the governments of countries neighbouring the Dead Sea have been in talks about how to restore water levels and conserve the water of the Jordan River.

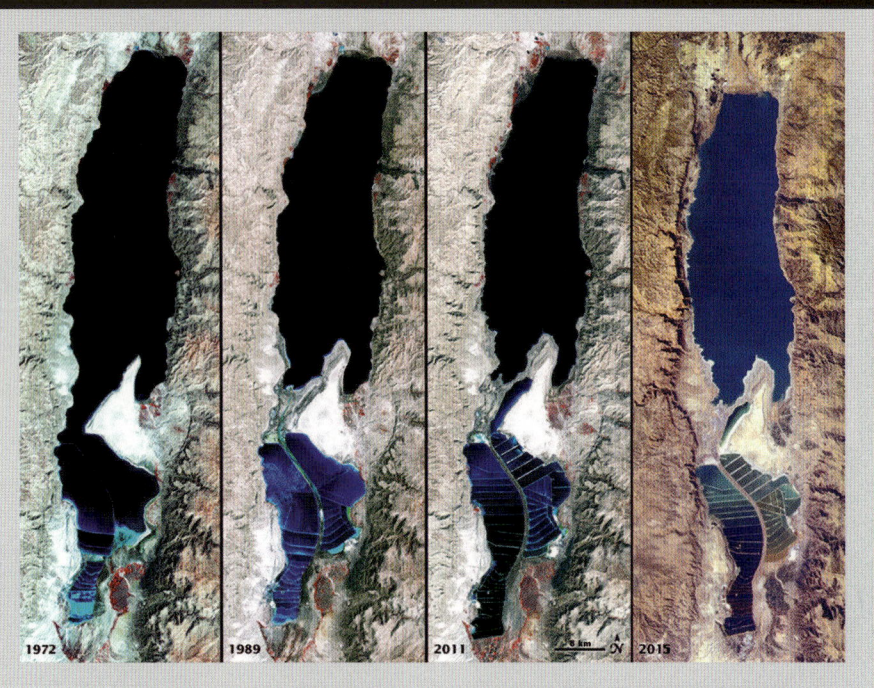

Figure 1.21: Aerial views of the Dead Sea taken in 1972, 1989, 2011 and 2015.

Questions

1. Unlike the Dead Sea, in the open ocean potassium is a minor component in seawater. When seawater is evaporated, which minerals would you expect to find the most of?

2. Based on your knowledge of run-off, why do you think the levels of potassium are so high in the Dead Sea?

3. Evaporation is a major factor in the salinity of the Dead Sea. What role does it play in the ocean?

4. How does the increased salinity of the Dead Sea due to the fertiliser industry impact upon the microscopic organisms that live there?

5. Do you believe the history and culture of the Dead Sea should play a role in trying to save it? How?

Chapter 2
Earth processes

LEARNING INTENTIONS

In this chapter you will learn how to:

- describe the structure of Earth's geology with regard to the continental crust, oceanic crust, mantle and core
- describe and apply the theory of plate tectonics
- describe the formation of hydrothermal vents and other features that make up the ocean floor
- compare weathering and erosion
- describe sedimentation and explain how the speed of water and size of particles affect transport of particles to and from shorelines.
- Identify examples of varying types of littoral zone and describe how the processes of weathering, erosion and sedimentation create these ecosystems.
- explain how different tides with varying tidal ranges are impacted by many physical factors allowing for interpretation of tide tables and graphs
- discuss how ocean currents and upwelling are created and influenced by abiotic factors in the environment which lead to the formation of the global ocean conveyor belt and the El Niño Southern Oscillation cycle in the Pacific Ocean.

BEFORE YOU START

- Working with a partner, create a word map to represent the three plate boundaries types in the theory of plate tectonics. Write down everything you remember about each, including how they are formed, how they move, and what they can create. Use lines to connect the concepts that are related.

- As a class, list as many different types of ocean shores as you can think of. For each one, describe how weathering, erosion and sedimentation played a part in its creation.

- Think out loud with a partner about all the ways tides differ from ocean currents. Create a list to share with the class.

STUDYING THE OCEAN WITH WAR-TIME TECHNOLOGY

Coastal environments, such as **estuaries** and rocky shores, are some of the most studied marine environments worldwide. These environments are readily accessible for scientists, so it is easier to conduct studies and experiments on the coast since no special equipment is needed to get there.

This love of the coast is not restricted to scientists, though. Every time you spend a day relaxing or walking on the beach, you are enjoying a small piece of the **littoral zone**.

People started studying the sea from dry land, but they soon wanted to know more about the creatures that live within these vast bodies of water.

For thousands of years, tales of sea monsters such as the Kraken have tormented sailors voyaging across vast oceans for months at a time, wondering what really lay in the depths below their ships. They were even unaware how deep the oceans were or the shape of the seafloor until the twentieth century when technology used to explore the seabed was designed.

During the First World War, many countries needed to be able to detect enemy submarines in the ocean. Scientists adapted a tool that used blasts of sounds and their echoes to locate icebergs into a new technology that could be used to find submarines. This new invention was called sound navigation and ranging (SONAR). SONAR works in much the same way whales and dolphins use echolocation to find prey. Since then, SONAR has enabled scientists to map the ocean floor, and some amazing discoveries have been made using SONAR equipment. Instead of flat, barren plains stretching from shore to shore, scientists found mountain ranges dividing ocean floors and sea trenches sinking deeper than the height of the tallest mountains. This technology has been used for studies throughout the oceans, changing preconceived notions and providing evidence for new theories about the geology of our planet.

Questions

1. SONAR technology was created for war but ended up supporting marine scientists all over the globe. Can you think of any other technologies or inventions that were created for one purpose but helped make new discoveries in a completely unrelated field?

2. Is it ethical for scientists to use data collected during war time to make new discoveries in unrelated fields?

KEY WORDS

estuary: a partially enclosed, tidal, coastal body of water where fresh water from a river meets the saltwater of the ocean

littoral zone: the benthic, or bottom, zone between the highest and lowest spring tide water marks on a shoreline; also referred to as the intertidal zone

2 Earth processes

2.1 Tectonic processes

The Greek word *tektōn* is a noun meaning 'builder' or 'carpenter'. For this reason, those forces on and within Earth that help build the geological features that give character to our planet – mountains, trenches, volcanoes – are called tectonic processes. Studying these processes and the formations that result on our ocean floor can give scientists great insight into what our planet once was, and what it may become.

The structure of Earth's interior

Until the early part of the twentieth century, most people thought Earth was a large rock of singular density and structure. Due to advancements in technology and detailed studies of the vibrations created by **earthquakes**, scientists now know that is not true. In fact, the inside of planet Earth is made of a series of rock layers of varying densities, mineral make-ups, and form. Scientists have divided the Earth's interior into three distinct layers: the **crust**, the **mantle** and the **core** (Figure 2.1).

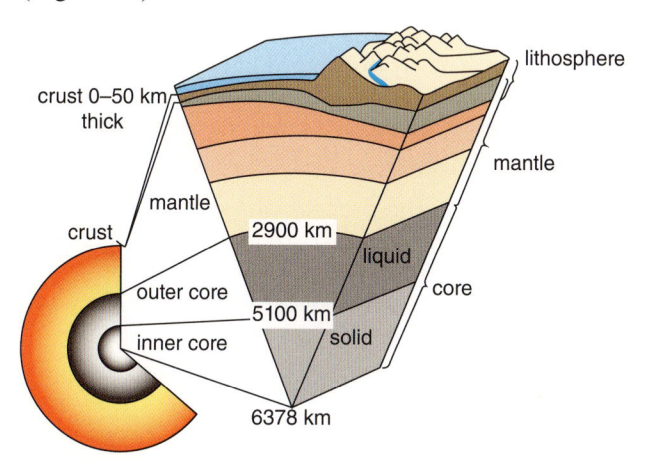

Figure 2.1: A diagram of the Earth's interior.

The core is a hot sphere of dense elements, mostly iron and nickel, found at the centre of the Earth. The core is made of a solid inner sphere (the inner core) covered by a liquid outer layer (the outer core) with a combined radius of approximately 3485 km. The density of the core varies between 9900 kg m^{-3} and 13 000 kg m^{-3}, with the highest densities toward the centre of the Earth.

The mantle is a layer of hot, semisolid rock capable of very slow movement over geological timescales, that surrounds the core. This is the thickest layer of our planet and extends to a depth of 1,802 miles. The uppermost portion of this layer of the mantle is highly viscous and capable of deforming due to high temperatures.

The crust is the outermost layer of Earth's structure and, therefore, the layer humans are most familiar with. This layer is made of solid rocks. It ranges in size from 5 km thick beneath ocean basins to 70 km thick beneath the continents. The thinnest crust is **oceanic crust**. This crust is composed of primarily basaltic rocks filled with iron and magnesium. It is much denser than the thicker **continental crust**, which tends to be made of granite and similar rocks. The varying densities of crust types is important when discussing the theory of plate tectonics.

The theory of plate tectonics

In 1912, a German scientist named Alfred Wegener proposed the theory of **continental drift**. Wegener's theory was that, more than 300 million years ago, all the continents on Earth were joined as a single landmass, known as Pangea. Wegner theorised that, over the course of millions of years, Pangea began to split, and its pieces have been slowly moving further away from each other ever since.

> **KEY WORDS**
>
> **earthquake:** a sudden release of energy inside the Earth that creates seismic waves; usually caused by movement of tectonic plates or volcanic activity
>
> **crust:** the outermost layer of rock on Earth
>
> **mantle:** a region of molten rock within the interior of the Earth, between the core and the crust
>
> **core:** the dense, central region within Earth
>
> **seismic:** having to do with vibrations of the earth's crust; earthquakes
>
> **oceanic crust:** the dense, basaltic layer of crust that makes up the bottom of the ocean basins
>
> **continental crust:** the thicker, less dense crust that makes up the foundation of the continents
>
> **continental drift:** a theory supporting the possibility that continents are able to move over Earth's surface

Wegener first began to develop his theory after looking at the shape of modern continents and noticing they could fit together like a jigsaw puzzle. Wegener then began looking at studies by other scientists. When Wegener began to compare geological structures (mountains) between continents, he found evidence that the rock layers in South Africa match those in Brazil. He discovered that the structure of the Appalachian Mountains in the United States closely matches that of the mountains in the West Highlands of Scotland. Wegener then argued that the shape of the coastlines with matching geological features – South America and Africa, North America and Europe – fit together nearly seamlessly. Looking further, he noticed identical fossilised (and occasionally living) plants and animals had been found on the coasts of different continents separated by oceans. Believing he had a strong argument with three lines of evidence, Wegener presented his theory, as seen in Figure 2.2.

Wegener's theory was not initially well received. Despite the evidence he presented, his peers were not convinced that continental drift had ever happened. This was partly because Wegener did not suggest a logical mechanism by which the continents moved. Originally, Wegener stated continents were able to plough through the oceanic crust in the same way as an iceberg moves through water. Other scientists pointed out that this would change the shape of the continents, refuting the evidence Wegener was relying on to support his theory. Instead, scientists at the time insisted on the idea of non-moving continents with long-gone land bridges for animals and plants to cross in order to explain the patterns of fossils.

For the next 50 years, scientists were split: there were the 'drifters' who supported Wegener's theory, and the 'fixists' that opposed Wegener's theory.

Scientists used new technologies to find overwhelming evidence and multiple new discoveries in the fields of geology, morphology and ecology of the oceans. This new evidence led to a revision of Wegener's theory of continental drift in the 1960s.

The revised theory, the theory of **plate tectonics**, included a mechanism for how the continents were able to move across Earth's surface, a factor missing from Wegener's original theory. The theory of plate tectonics suggests that the **lithosphere** is broken into sections called tectonic plates. Each of these plates floats independently on the highly viscous mantle below, allowing for incremental movement of continents over time. To support this revised theory, scientists combined the evidence previously presented by Wegener (distribution of fossils, geological matching of rock formations, and the jigsaw-like fit of the continents) with newly discovered lines of evidence:

> **KEY WORDS**
>
> **plate tectonics:** the process where large sections (plates) of the Earth's crust are in constant movement over the fluid mantle, causing earthquakes and volcanoes at the borders between the plates
>
> **lithosphere:** the outermost layer of the Earth's crust

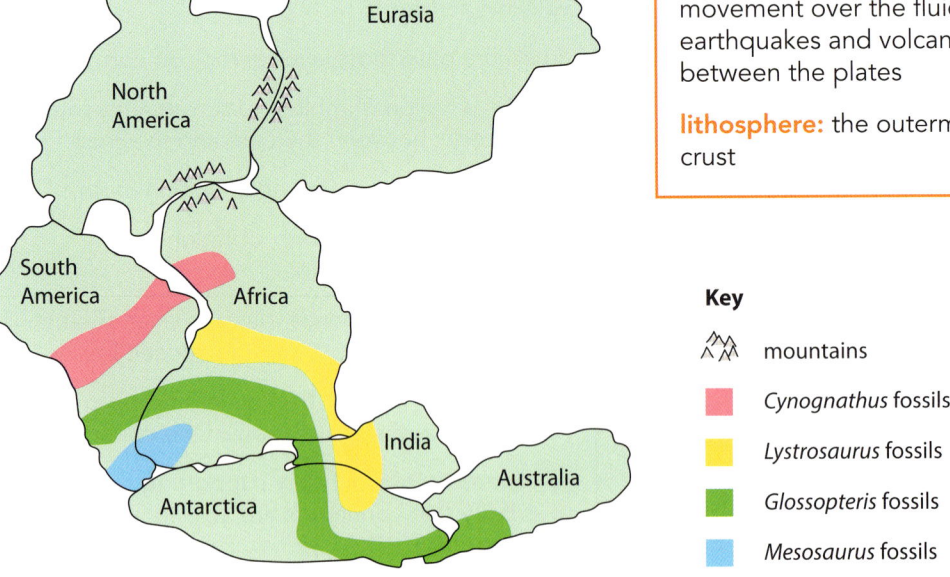

Figure 2.2: The proposed theory of Pangaea with fossil and geological evidence.

seafloor spreading and **paleomagnetic stripes** on the ocean floor.

Seafloor spreading

With the invention of SONAR in the 1940s, new evidence of plate boundaries came to light on the bottom of the ocean. The data collected while looking for submarines showed mountains and trenches lining the edges of plate boundaries. These geological features created a clear, predictable map of where the tectonic plates were separated. Marie Tharp, a geologist and oceanic map-maker, and her partner Bruce Heezen, a geologist, collaborated for 20 years to collect ocean floor mapping data in order to create an accurate, scientific map of the seabed. This map (Figure 2.3), called the World Ocean Floor, revolutionised Earth science after its publication in 1977, because of the prominent presence of the **mid-ocean ridge**. This map is responsible for convincing many scientists to accept the theory of plate tectonics and seafloor spreading.

Figure 2.3: The World Ocean Floor by Marie Tharp and Bruce C. Heezen.

Magnetic polarity reversal

For those scientists needing further evidence of seafloor spreading and the movement of the continents, more evidence was discovered due to anti-submarine technology during the Second World War. In search of submarines, magnetometers were attached to naval vessels in addition to SONAR technology. Scientists were then able to study magnetism on the ocean floor using those magnetometers. The evidence they found surprised them. The magnetic field of the ocean floor was laid out in alternating stripes of normal **polarity** and reversed polarity. Scientists refer to this phenomenon as paleomagnetic stripes.

The fact that the ocean floor was magnetic was not the surprise. Sailors had known for more than 100 years that the basaltic rocks lining the ocean floor were magnetic. It was the striped pattern that was unexpected. Further research showed that the striped pattern had an origin around the mid-ocean ridges, where the crust is weakest and magma often pushes through (Figure 2.4). This magma held the explanation.

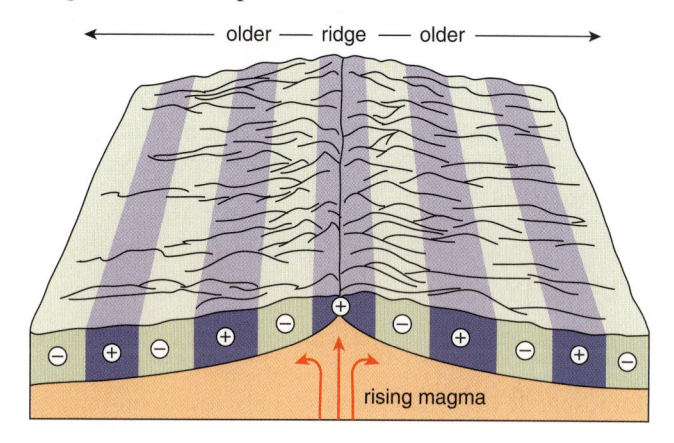

Figure 2.4: Diagram of seafloor spreading and magnetic reversal.

Basaltic rocks, the type commonly found on the seabed, are an example of an igneous rock. Igneous rocks are created when molten magma from a volcanic eruption cools and hardens. Within igneous rocks is a naturally magnetic iron material called magnetite, which is why basalt is magnetic. When molten magma first reaches the Earth's surface, the particles of magnetite within it align with the Earth's magnetic field. Once the magma begins to harden, the magnetite is locked in place, holding information about the Earth's magnetic field at the time the rock was formed. Scientists have found that the Earth's magnetic field reverses on average every 250 000 years, changing magnetic north to magnetic south.

KEY WORDS

mid-ocean ridge: a mountain range with a central valley on an ocean floor at the boundary between two diverging tectonic plates, where new crust forms from upwelling magma

paleomagnetic stripes: the pattern of magnetic stripes on the ocean floor due to reversals in the Earth's magnetic field and seafloor spreading.

polarity: having two opposite states of being on either end (such as the North and South pole, or the positive and negative end of a magnet)

This information, when applied to the ocean floor, provides unique evidence in support of the theory of plate tectonics.

At **divergent boundaries**, where mid-ocean ridges form, scientists now know the seabed is spreading because of magma rising from the mantle and hardening into igneous rocks. When the magnetic properties of the rocks at these boundaries were measured, scientists confirmed that the rocks lay in alternating stripes of magnetic polarity radiating away from the boundary in parallel lines. These stripes differed in width based on the length of time between each reversal, providing the strongest evidence in support of seabed spreading and plate tectonics.

Plate boundaries and the ocean features they form

Lithospheric (tectonic) plates are only able to move if the mantle is moving as well. The movement of the mantle is caused by **convection currents** within the mantle. Convection currents happen when the molten rock of the mantle moves because of density changes in the rock caused by temperature differences. In other words, as the molten rock is heated, it becomes less dense as the molecules spread out. The less dense rock moves upwards in the mantle towards the crust in order to float on top of the denser rock. Then, as the rock begins to cool, it begins to sink towards the warmer core. This forms a circular cell of flowing molten rock capable of moving the lithospheric plate lying on top of it. Because the plates are heavy and the convection currents in the mantle move so slowly, the plates move only 2–5 cm per year. However, even this small movement causes the plates to meet and form three types of boundary: convergent, divergent and transform. Each boundary type has identifiable characteristics and geological features (Figure 2.5).

> **KEY WORDS**
>
> **divergent boundary:** where two tectonic plates are moving away from each other
>
> **convection current:** the movement of fluids or air based on density differences caused by differing temperature

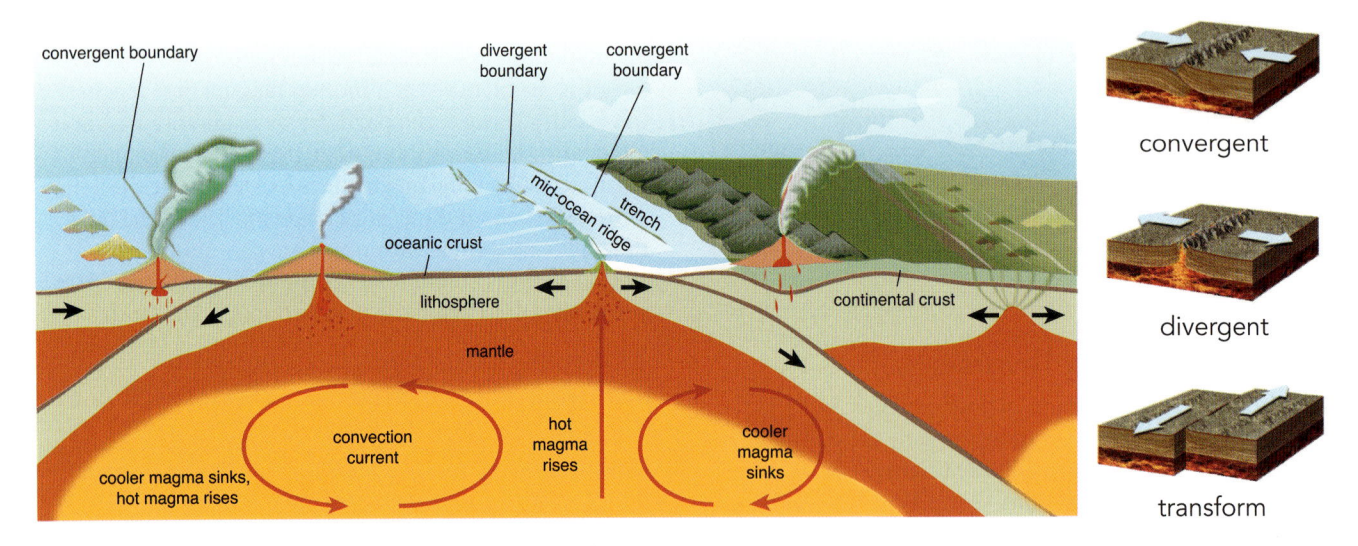

Figure 2.5: Visual representation of plate boundaries and their features.

Convergent boundaries

Convergent boundaries form when two tectonic plates are moving towards each other. When the two plates are of varying densities, a **subduction** zone will form. This happens when the denser oceanic plate is forced underneath the other, less dense, continental plate. These areas are known as destructive zones because, after being forced below the continental crust, the oceanic crust is destroyed by the heat reshaping it into molten magma within the mantle.

Trenches

Trenches are long, narrow, deep canyons in the seabed that only form at subduction zones within convergent boundaries due to these processes. The deepest part of the ocean, known as Challenger Deep, exists within the Marianas Trench in the western Pacific Ocean. Challenger Deep is 11 034 m deep, which is deeper than Mount Everest is tall (8 848 m). Other common features along subduction zones and convergent boundaries are **volcanoes**, earthquakes and **tsunamis**.

Divergent boundaries

Divergent boundaries are areas where two tectonic plates are moving away from each other, which may allow molten magma from the mantle to push through to the crust. These areas are constructive zones. As the magma, driven by convection currents, pushes through the opening in the crust, spreads out and solidifies in the cold ocean waters at the bottom of the sea, creating new seafloor. The new rocks created through this process eventually build up and form underwater mountain ranges called mid-ocean ridges. As mid-ocean ridges continue to build new crust, there is an eventual movement away from the divergent boundary, causing seafloor spreading. This spreading action helps move tectonic plates towards convergent boundaries on the opposite side of the planet. This process, over the course of millions of years, is responsible for a shrinking Pacific Ocean and growing Atlantic Ocean. Located within these mid-ocean ridges are volcanoes and **hydrothermal vents**.

Transform boundaries

Transform boundaries are areas where two plates slide laterally next to each other. No crust is created or destroyed at transform boundaries, leading scientists to refer to them as conservative regions. However, transform boundaries are areas of great seismic activity. The increased friction between plates at these boundaries causes small cracks called faults to form. The pressure that builds up in these fault lines can lead to earthquakes and tsunamis. The most common ocean feature found along transform boundaries are **abyssal plains**, which are flat deep areas of the seafloor where sediment accumulates. Abyssal plains may also form near divergent boundaries on either side of the mid-ocean ridge.

Volcanoes

A volcano can be formed at a convergent boundary when pressure begins to build up between the oceanic and continental plates. At this pressure point, the Earth's crust begins to thin, allowing hot gases and magma to rise through the opening creating an eruption. This lava quickly cools and solidifies into new rock. Over time, the new rock builds up creating a volcano. Volcanoes that rise above sea-level form new islands like those in the Hawaiian and Philippines archipelagos.

KEY WORDS

convergent boundary: when two or more tectonic plates come together

subduction: the process where one lithospheric plate slides below another at a convergent plate boundary

trench: a long, narrow and deep depression on the ocean floor with relatively steep sides; caused by convergent plate boundaries

volcano: a mountain or hill with a crater or vent through which lava, rock fragments, hot vapour and gas are being forced from the Earth's crust

tsunami: a seismic sea wave created by an underwater earthquake or volcanic event; not noticeable in the open ocean but building to great heights in shallow water

hydrothermal vent: an area where cold ocean water that has seeped into the Earth's crust is superheated by underlying magma and forced through vents in the ocean floor

transform boundary: when two plates are moving in an antiparallel direction, creating friction between them

abyssal plain: a flat, sandy region of the ocean floor found between trenches and the continental rise

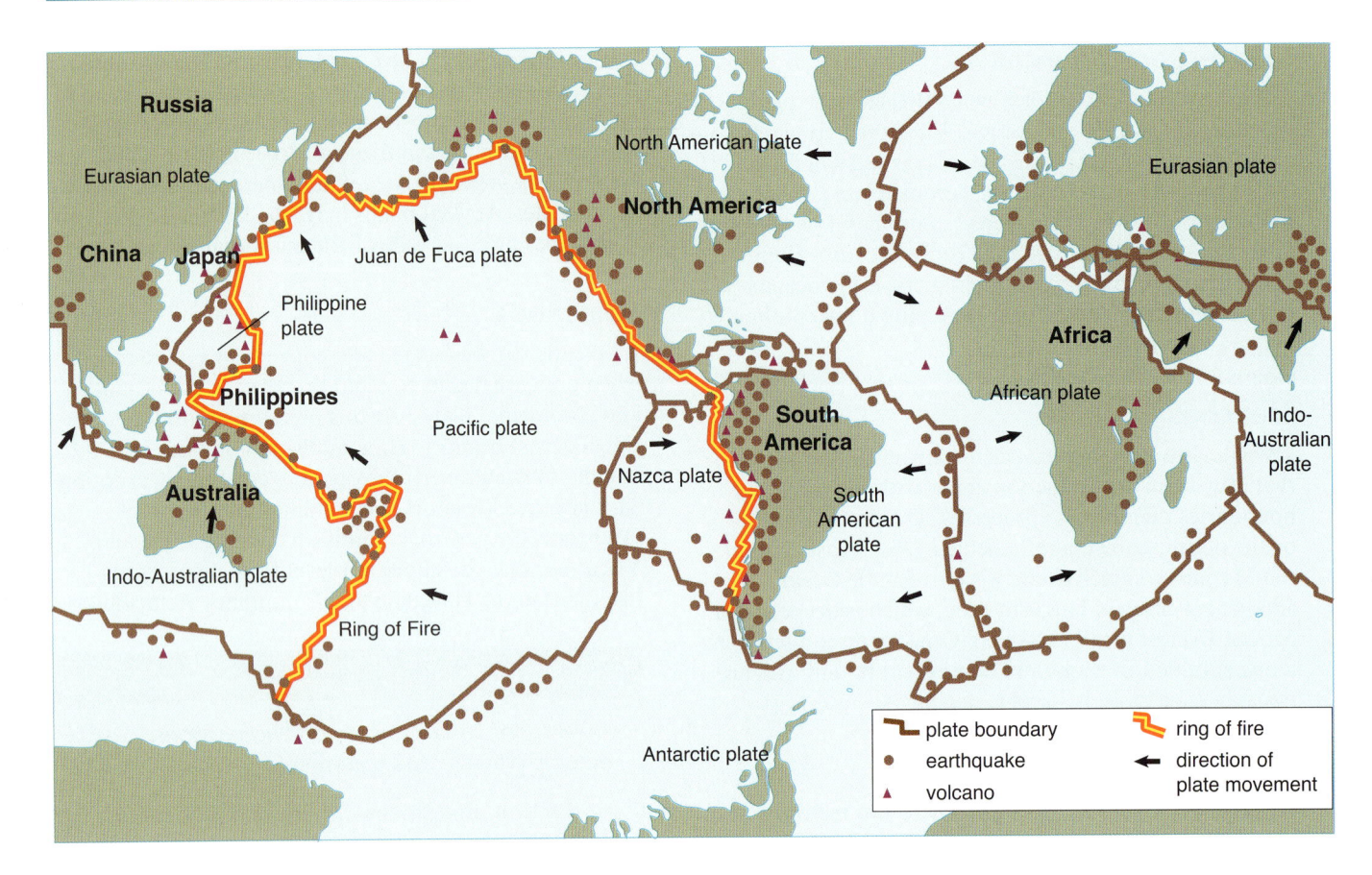

Figure 2.6: The Pacific Ring of Fire with tectonic plate movement.

However, many volcanoes are located under the ocean's surface, creating new seabed when the magma cools after erupting. Of these underwater volcanoes, most lie along the convergent plate boundaries surrounding the Pacific Ocean. Together, they create what is known as the Ring of Fire (Figure 2.6). The areas that border the Ring of Fire are hotspots for volcanic and seismic activity.

Volcanoes can also be found at divergent boundaries and areas where the crust is very thin. In this case, there is little pressure added; however, magma still rises from the mantle to the seafloor. Once again, the nearly freezing water on the seafloor cools the molten rock, solidifying it. This new rock continues to build upon itself, eventually forming a volcano.

Earthquakes

Earthquakes occur after there has been a sudden release of energy from the movement of the Earth's crust. When two plates are moving past each other, at either a convergent or transform boundary, they may get stuck. When this happens, the pressure for them to move builds and builds until there is a sudden slippage of one of the plates that releases stored potential energy in a sudden burst. This burst of energy releases seismic waves that move through the lithosphere, making everything on top of the crust shake, creating an earthquake. Volcanoes are also capable of causing an earthquake when they release enormous amounts of energy during an eruption.

Tsunamis

Sudden releases of energy on the seabed, either through an earthquake or a volcanic eruption, can lead to tsunamis. Tsunamis are long-wavelength, high-energy waves created by seismic activity. Figure 2.7 shows how a tsunami can form. When an earthquake occurs on the seafloor (A), stored energy is released to the seabed (B). This energy displaces the large volume of water lying above the seafloor. The water holds on to this energy and begins to move very quickly but unnoticeably through deep ocean water (C). However, as the tsunami reaches shallow, coastal waters, the wave slows down and grows exponentially in height (D). These large, high-energy waves can be incredibly destructive. Tsunamis are sometimes called 'tidal waves', but this is inaccurate because the tides have nothing to do with the creation of tsunamis.

2 Earth processes

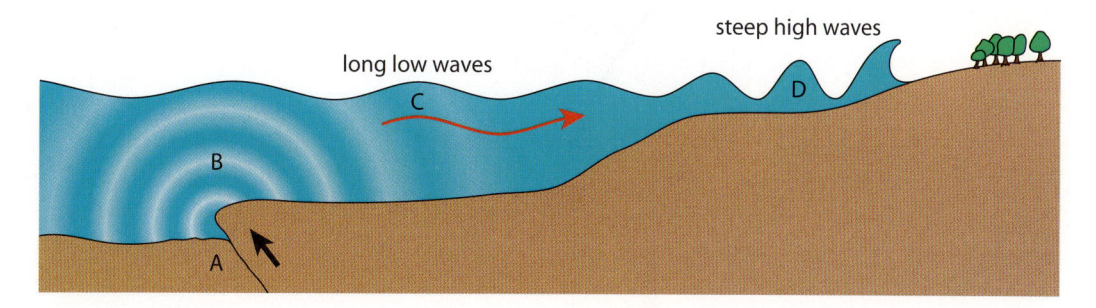

Figure 2.7: Illustration depicting formation of a tsunami at convergent boundary.

Mid-ocean ridges

At the constructive zone created by divergent boundaries, another landform is created – the mid-ocean ridge. These underwater mountain ranges build over time as magma pushes through the weakened crust at these boundaries and solidifies, creating new rocks on the seafloor. The new rocks grow in size until they become mountains. As mid-ocean ridges continue to build new crust, there is an eventual movement away from the divergent boundary, leading to further seafloor spreading. Located within these mid-ocean ridges are volcanoes and hydrothermal vents.

Hydrothermal vents

Hydrothermal vent systems were discovered in 1977 along the Galápagos Rift in the Pacific Ocean by scientists from Woods Hole Oceanographic Institute (WHOI) using the deep sea submersible ALVIN (Figure 2.8). Hydrothermal vents (Figure 2.9) occur in deep ocean water, usually 2000 m or more below sea-level, within mid-ocean ridge systems. At this depth, the pressure is over 20 265 kPa and there is no light. In Figure 2.9 you can see the structure of the vent formation with the superheated water being forced from the vent taking a familiar shape. The depth, lack of sunlight and intense pressure are unique circumstances for the development of an ecosystem (for more information, see Chapter 7).

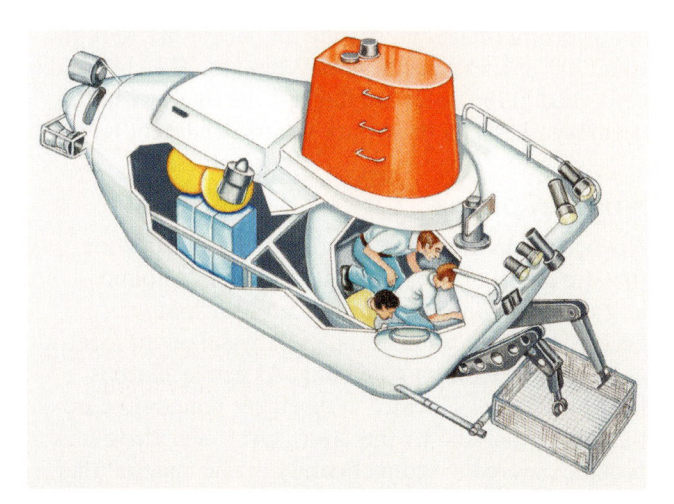

Figure 2.8: A cross-section illustration of the submersible ALVIN used by the Woods Hole Oceanographic Institute.

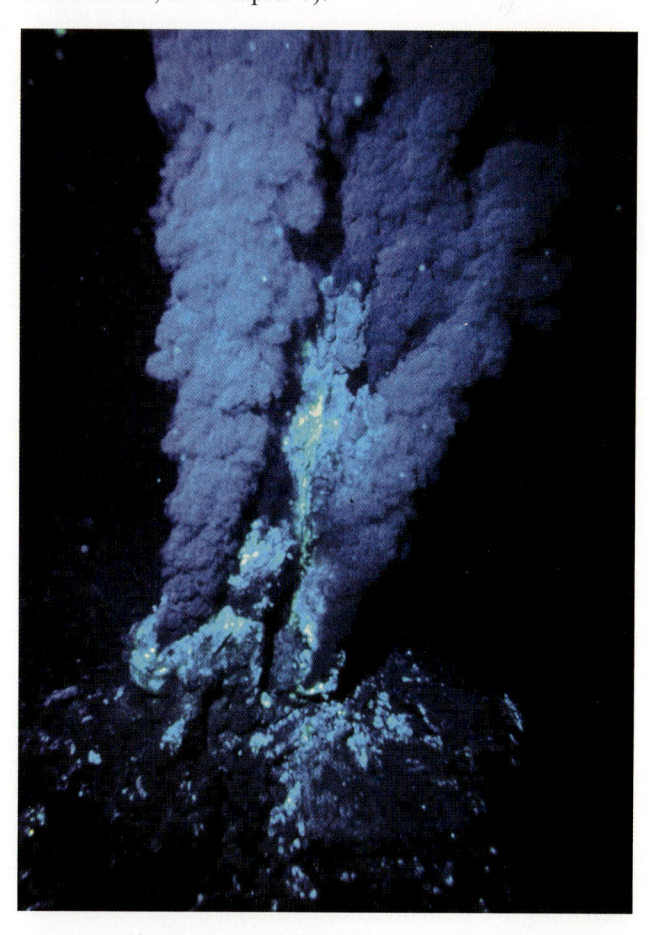

Figure 2.9: The Spire hydrothermal vent on the Mid-Atlantic Ridge.

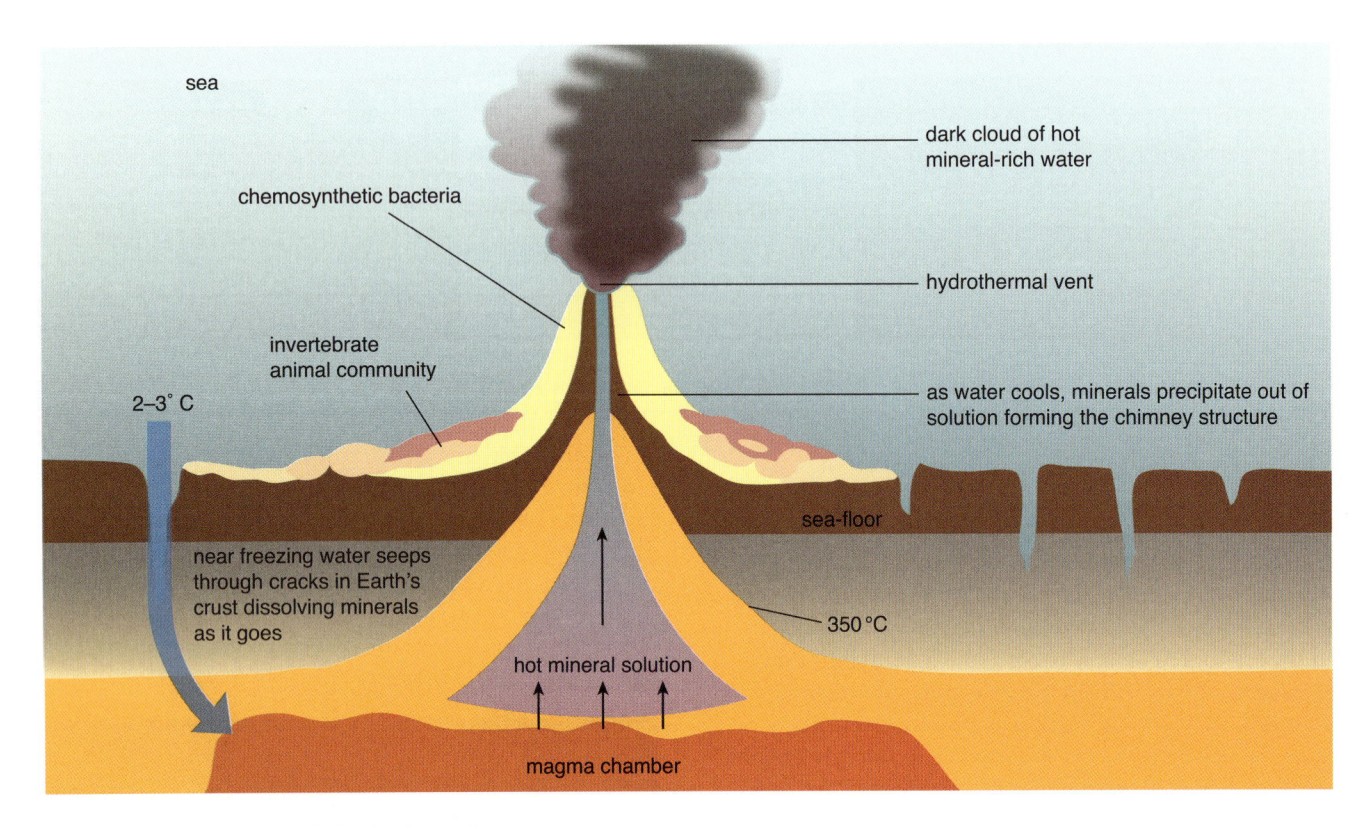

Figure 2.10: Formation of a hydrothermal vent.

Hydrothermal vents are formed when cold ocean water seeps through cracks in the thin crust surrounding divergent boundaries (Figure 2.10). As the water moves through the crust to an area directly over a magma chamber, it dissolves minerals (for example iron, copper and zinc sulfides) from the rocks, turning it black. Once heated by the magma, the water reaches temperatures well over 100 °C but never boils because of the extreme pressure in the region. This superheated water then escapes the crust through a fissure above.

As the superheated water meets the near-freezing water on the ocean floor it begins to cool. As the water cools, minerals, including ions of copper, sulfides, zinc, and iron, precipitate out of solution. These minerals form solids, which settle near the fissure, piling on top of each other due to their lack of solubility in cold water. This forms a chimney, or vent, for the superheated water that can be up to 60 m high. The mineral-rich, pressurised water released by hydrothermal vents is often at temperatures over 350 °C and is referred to as a 'plume'. Due to the abnormally high temperatures and strong, seemingly toxic, chemical composition of the water released from the vents, a hydrothermal vent plume can often be detected from quite a distance away using modern technology. Organisms, particularly tube worm larvae, rely on locating the unique chemical signatures of a vent plume when attempting to settle in a new colony.

Hydrothermal vents can be classified as either 'black smokers' or 'white smokers' based on the mineral composition and, to a lesser degree, the temperature of the water they release. The title of 'smoker' is misleading however, as there is no smoke to be found at a hydrothermal vent, despite the smoke-like look the water has as it escapes from the chimney. The chemicals contained in the water are the basis for energy capture, chemosynthesis, in these dark waters (Chapter 7).

Abyssal plains

Abyssal plains are flat deep areas of the ocean floor that are essentially feature-less. They can be found at transform boundaries or in the wide expanse of ocean floor between boundaries. Abyssal plains form as a result of seafloor spreading. As new seafloor is formed, the rocks formed at divergent boundaries are pushed further and further away. Over time, these rocks become covered in sediment and organic material that falls to the seafloor. As sedimentation continues to occur, it covers the rocks and leads to the smooth, flat appearance of the abyssal plain.

Test yourself

1. Compare the theory of continental drift with the theory of plate tectonics.
2. Describe how tsunamis are formed.
3. How are divergent and convergent boundaries related to the rock cycle?
4. Would you describe the hydrothermal vent environment as extreme? Why or why not?

2.2 Weathering, erosion and sedimentation

Weathering is the breaking down of rocks into smaller pieces over time. This can occur due to exposure to the atmosphere, moving water and biological organisms. Weathering tends to occur in the same place with little movement of the particles involved, making it a different process than **erosion** which involves the movement and transportation of rocks and minerals by natural agents to new locations. **Sedimentation** happens when those new materials reach their new location and are left there to accumulate.

> **KEY WORDS**
>
> **weathering:** The wearing down or breaking of rocks through physical, chemical or organic means
>
> **erosion:** a natural process where material is worn away from the Earth's surface and transported elsewhere
>
> **sedimentation:** the deposition of suspended particles from water

Weathering

There are three categories of weathering: chemical, physical and organic (biological).

Chemical weathering

Chemical weathering occurs when the chemical composition of rocks changes through exposure to water or oxygen. We see this in nature when new rocks are exposed to precipitation through uplift. When it rains, water moves over the rocks dissolving ions as it moves, particularly Calcium (Ca^{2+}), and transporting them into the ocean as run-off.

Physical weathering

Physical weathering (also known as mechanical weathering) is caused when rocks are broken into smaller pieces without changing their chemical composition. Temperature change is one method of physical weathering. The constant heating and cooling of rocks or sudden temperature change can weaken a rock's structure and make it more likely to break apart. It can also create cracks in the exterior surface. Physical weathering also happens when water gets into the cracks of those rocks and freezes. The expanding ice forces the sides of the rock to expand as well, increasing the size of the initial crack.

Ocean waves are capable of great changes in a coastline by weathering rock through the constant motion of the water. This example of physical weathering also works in conjunction with chemical weathering as the salts in the seawater often change the chemical composition of the rocks. The combined work of physical and chemical weathering increases the ability of the waves to change the shape of the shoreline.

Organic (biological) weathering

Organic (biological) weathering relies on living organisms to complete the weathering process. This could be a form of chemical weathering (for example, when lichen attaches to the basaltic rock of a newly created volcanic island). The lichen release special compounds that break down the rock into smaller particles, aiding the production of soil for the ecosystem. Organic weathering is also closely linked to physical weathering. We see this combined weathering when the roots of a tree grow into the cracks in a rock. As the roots grow in length and width, they slowly force the root to move further apart, causing the rock to eventually break apart.

Erosion

There are four types of erosion that work to move sediments and rocks to new locations: ice, gravity, wind and water.

Ice erosion

Ice erosion is a type of erosion most closely associated with glaciers. As a glacier moves over land, its weight crushes and breaks the rocks below, weathering them. However, the sediments that are formed are carried within the bottom of the glacier as it moves. As the glacier reaches new locations, it releases these sediments depositing them far from where they were picked up.

Gravity erosion

Gravity works as a form of erosion in conjunction with weathering. This type of erosion tends to feature in movies when someone is standing on a cliff edge that begins to crack (an example of weathering) and then a large chunk of the cliff drops down to the ravine or ocean below due to gravitational forces. The gravity helps move that rock from location A, the cliff edge, to location B, the ocean below, thus making gravity a source of erosion.

Wind erosion

Wind erosion occurs when the wind blows, picking up small pieces of sand or sediment. These particles are then carried to new locations. For example, the sand being blown in your face if you go to the beach on a windy day, or when sand from the Sahara Desert arrives in North America because it was carried by the winds of a hurricane.

Water erosion

Water is a source of erosion due to its ability to pick up sediments and carry them through runoff or down rivers on the way to the ocean. Whether water is working as an erosive agent or weathering agent can often be confusing because water can be both at the same time. An example of this is a canyon. These are often formed when a river moves over the same rocks for thousands or millions of years. Slowly, the water weathers the rocks breaking them into smaller and smaller pieces. At the same time, the water is eroding the material that has broken by carrying it away on the river to a new location. It is important to differentiate between the two steps of weathering (breaking apart) and erosion (carrying away) even though they may be happening simultaneously.

Sedimentation

Sedimentation is the third part of the journey that sediments take through water erosion. After they are broken down (weathering) and transported (erosion), the particles suspended in the water must be delivered somewhere. The delivery, or **deposition**, of these particles in a new location is called sedimentation. For example, when water in the Nile River carries sediments as suspended particles and then leaves them at the river mouth into the Mediterranean Sea forming a **delta**, that deposition process is called sedimentation.

Particle size and water speed have the greatest impacts on the rates of sedimentation. Table 2.1 shows some different categories and diameters of sediments commonly found on sea shores. In general, the faster the water is moving the larger the size of the particles it can carry. As water begins to slow, larger particles begin to fall out of suspension and deposit themselves. Larger pieces of rock or gravel may not be able to be carried very far or at all, even in swiftly moving water. The smallest particles, like those of silt, can stay suspended in the water for a very long time, allowing them to travel great distances. In fact, water must be very still for long periods of time before silt particles will deposit themselves. Water's ability to carry sediments and how it deposits them is what gives it the ability to help shape coastlines.

Particle type	Diameter / mm	Comparative sedimentation rates
silt	0.002–0.02	slowest
fine sand	0.02–0.2	medium
coarse sand	0.2–2.0	fastest
gravel (small stones)	>2.0	

Table 2.1: Diameters of common sediment types.

The littoral zone

The area of the ocean most commonly studied is the littoral zone. This is the area of the shore where land meets sea. It is also known as the intertidal region. The littoral zone is the area of a shoreline that falls between the highest high-water mark and lowest low-water mark during a spring tide. This area of the ocean is varied and is categorised according to:

- the shape of the shore
- wave action and erosion
- the substrate that makes up the shore
- the organisms that live there.

Morphology of the littoral zone

The shape of the sea shore depends primarily on the geology of the land lying closest to the shore and the level of exposure that shore has to the processes of weathering, erosion and sedimentation. This means sea shores may be nearly flat areas covered in fine particles of silt, or nearly vertical areas with large rocks. Scientists that study the different shape and make-up of sea shores are studying the **morphology** of that shore. The two factors that scientists

> **KEY WORDS**
>
> **deposition:** a geological process where sediments, soil and rocks are added to a landform or land mass
>
> **delta:** a low-lying triangular area at the mouth of a river formed by the deposition of sediments
>
> **morphology:** the study of the forms of things

focus on when studying morphology are the *slope* of the shore and the *size of the sediment* found on the shore.

Rocky shores

Rocky shores are areas of shoreline characterised by the presence of a rocky substrate (Figure 2.11). Rocky shores vary widely in slope from nearly vertical cliff faces to wide flat expanses of rocks. The size of the rocks making up the shore also varies from very large boulders to much smaller pieces of gravel and pebbles.

Figure 2.11: A rocky shore in Mallorca, Spain.

Rocky shores tend to be made of granite or igneous rocks, which are incredibly resistant to weathering and take a much longer time to break down than softer rocks such as sandstone. Rocks along these shores often exist in a gradient, with the largest rocks occurring farthest from the water at the high-water mark and the smallest rocks occurring nearer the low-water mark. Scientists believe this gradient is caused by the pounding of waves wearing away those rocks closest to the water line first and not being able to reach those farther up the shore. These shores are the most resistant to erosion even though they tend to be the most open and exposed. Very little sedimentation is able to happen along rocky shores due to the speed of the water coming in.

Sandy shores

A normal sandy shore is made of loose deposits of sand (silica), small pieces of gravel, and shells. Sandy shores are formed by the erosion of sandstone and sedimentation of sand particles by waves. Sandy shores are constantly in motion as the wind and ocean moves the sand up and down the beach. These shores tend to have a gradual slope towards the ocean.

Muddy shores

Muddy shores are found in protected regions and are least exposed to weathering and erosion. There is usually a very shallow slope or no slope at all on muddy shores, which is why they're often called 'mud flats'. A lack of erosion and little to no water movement allows the deposition of a layer of very fine silt particles and organic materials. For this reason, sedimentation is the primary factor in the formation of muddy shores.

Estuaries

Estuaries form in sheltered or partially enclosed areas where fresh water and salt water meet; this mix of water is called brackish. Because these areas are sheltered from the weathering and erosive action of waves, the bottom is often made of fine sand and silt that falls out of suspension when the water is still. The water in estuaries is very murky, with high **turbidity** as a result of the fine sediments. Other names for estuaries include bays, lagoons, sounds and sloughs.

> **KEY WORD**
>
> **turbidity:** the level of transparency loss water has due to the presence of suspended particles in the water; the higher the turbidity, the harder it is to see through the water

Deltas

Deltas form at the mouth of a river where it meets the sea. These shores are named after the Greek letter delta (Δ) because they usually have a triangular shape (Figure 2.12). As a river flows towards its mouth, it picks up sediment along the way through erosion. The river begins to widen as it approaches the sea, slowing down the speed of the water. When the water slows enough, the sediments begin to settle on the bottom of the river. Over time, these sediments deposit and accumulate into sandbars and other small landmasses, forming a wide fan-shaped structure resembling a branching tree. If the landmasses build up enough, it is possible for the delta to form new tributary channels of the river. Two of the most well-known river deltas are the:

- Mississippi River Delta, leading to the Gulf of Mexico in the United States
- Nile River Delta, draining into the Mediterranean Sea in Egypt.

Figure 2.12: Nile River Delta.

Test yourself

5 Describe the differences between weathering and erosion.

6 Which of the major littoral zone habitats discussed are primarily created through sedimentation and deposition?

7 Outline the role that erosion plays in creating a rocky shore.

2.3 Tides and ocean currents

Two concepts that are often confused in marine science are tides and currents. Although they are both responsible for the movement of large amounts of water, tides and currents are very different in the way they are formed. Both play a significant role in the daily lives of humans around the world.

Tides

A **tide** is the regular rise and fall of bodies of water as dictated by the gravitational interactions of the Moon, Earth and Sun. Tides can be found in all coastal areas as well as large lakes. Most coastal areas have tides with an interval of 12.5 hours, creating two high tides and two low tides each day. Tidal patterns like this are called **semi-diurnal** and the tides are easy to predict. Areas with only one high tide and one low tide each day have a **diurnal** tidal pattern.

Tidal range

Tidal range, or tidal amplitude, is the difference in height between the low-water mark and the high-water mark on a coastline (Figure 2.13). Tidal range varies all over the world and from day to day. In some places, the average tidal range daily is nearly 12 m while in others, the tidal range is close to zero. This variance is due to:

- the gravitational effects of the Moon, Earth and Sun
- physical features of the coastline where the tide is occurring
- environmental factors such as wind, air pressure and size of the body of water.

In the open ocean, tidal ranges are small (approximately 0.6 m). The difference between high and low tide is mostly unnoticeable, unless you enter the continental margin, where the water begins to shallow. Small bodies of water, such as the Mediterranean or Red Sea, also have tidal ranges, but they are minimal. Small tidal ranges even occur in large lakes, such as Lake Superior in the northern United States, but the effect is usually masked by the winds blowing across the lake.

The shape of the coastline plays a significant role in the size of the tidal range. If the tide is entering a particularly narrow channel (for example, a river mouth or entrance to an estuary) the tidal height is increased because the water is being forced into a smaller area. If, however, the tide is happening along an open beach, the tidal height is much shorter because the same volume of water is more spread out.

An extreme example of the coastline changing the tidal amplitude is the Bay of Fundy in Canada, home to the highest tidal range in the world. The average spring tide range here is 14.5 m. The highest water level recorded in the Bay of Fundy, 21.6 m, occurred during the tropical cyclone Saxby Gale in 1869, providing evidence of another physical factor affecting tides: the weather.

> **KEY WORDS**
>
> **tide:** the periodic rise and fall of the surface of the ocean resulting from the gravitational pull of the Moon and Sun
>
> **semi-diurnal:** occurring twice daily
>
> **diurnal:** occurring daily
>
> **tidal range:** the difference in height between the high-tide mark and the low-tide mark over the course of a day; also called the tidal amplitude

2 Earth processes

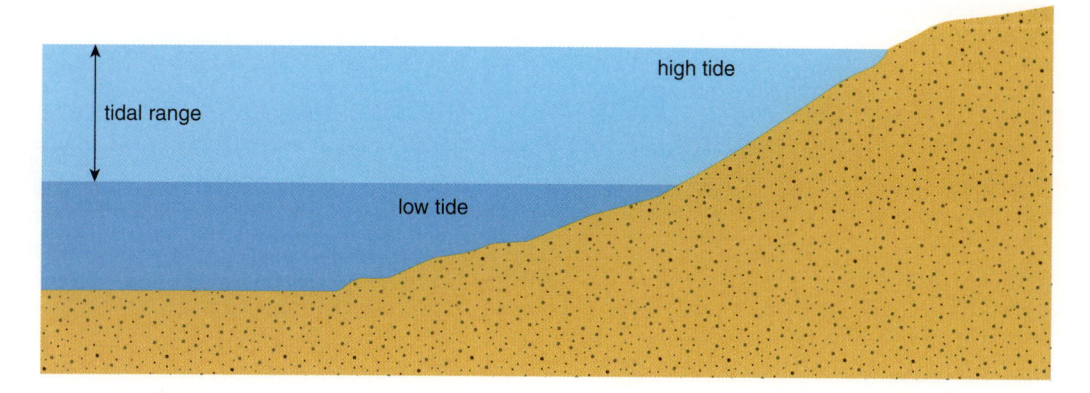

Figure 2.13: How to determine tidal range.

Weather is a major factor in tide heights. Changes in wind and air pressure can have incredible effects on tidal range. During a tropical cyclone, air pressure is much lower than usual, allowing water to swell. There are also high winds capable of pushing water onto the shore. Combined, these two factors can create a **tidal surge**, which is a dangerous rising of water higher than the predicted levels of the tide.

Spring and neap tides

Spring tides create the greatest tidal range for coasts. These tides are not reliant on seasons, but rather on phases of the Moon. Spring tides occur during the phases of new moon (when the Moon is dark) and full moon. Therefore, a spring tide can be predicted to happen twice a month in most cases.

During spring tides, the Earth, Moon and Sun are in a straight line, with either the Earth between the Sun and Moon or the Sun and Moon on one side of Earth (Figure 2.14). This alignment amplifies the gravitational effects the Moon and Sun have on Earth, creating a larger than average ocean bulge. This results in the highest of the high tides and the lowest of the low tides for a given shoreline, creating a larger than average tidal range.

Neap tides have the smallest tidal range, with the highest low-tide marks and the lowest high-tide marks. During these tides, the Sun and Moon are at a right angle to each other, with the Earth as the pivot point (Figure 2.14). Neap tides occur during the first- and third-quarter moon phases. During this time, the Sun and Moon are pulling the ocean in opposite directions, creating a smaller than average ocean bulge.

Currents

Within any large body of water, you will find **currents**. In the ocean, currents are the continuous, directional movement of seawater. Currents carry nutrients, dissolved gases, heat and even organisms with them. Currents have significant impact on ecosystems and global climate. Currents are created by different physical forces acting on the water, such as wind, temperature, salinity, density, the **Coriolis effect** and the shape of the seabed. There are two major types of currents in our oceans: surface currents and deep-water currents.

KEY WORDS

tidal surge: the coastal flooding of of an abnormally high seawater level associated with low pressure weather systems; also called a storm surge

spring tide: a tide that occurs when the Sun and Moon are aligned, causing the largest tidal range

neap tide: a tide that occurs when the Moon and Sun are at right angles from each other, causing the smallest tidal range

current: a continuous physical movement of water caused by wind or density

Coriolis effect: a force that results from the Earth's rotation that causes objects or particles in motion to deflect to the right in the Northern Hemisphere and to the left in the Southern Hemisphere

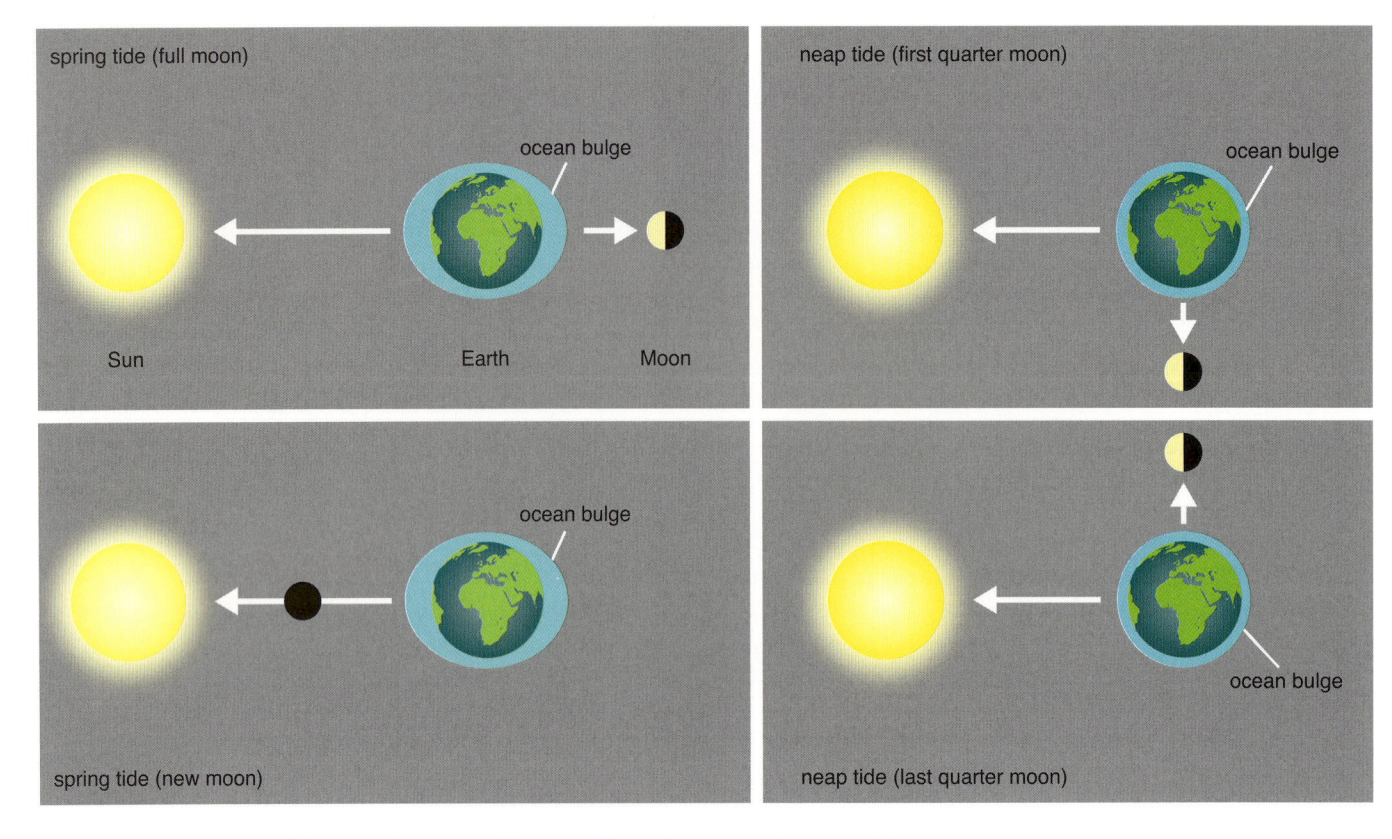

Figure 2.14: Positions of the Sun, Moon and Earth and how that determines the tide.

MATHS SKILLS 2.1

GRAPHING AND INTERPRETING TIDAL DATA

Graphing data sets is an important skill in science. Equally important is being able to determine what the data means. The following data set shows the height of the tides above and below mean sea-level for Barcelona, Spain (Table 2.2).

Date	High-tide level / m	Low-tide level / m	Tidal range / m
01 June	0.55	0.50	0.05
02 June	0.59	0.46	0.13
03 June	0.66	0.31	
04 June	0.76	0.13	
05 June	0.90	−0.06	
06 June	0.98	−0.23	
07 June	1.05	−0.37	
08 June	1.13	−0.46	
09 June	1.18	−0.50	
10 June	1.19	−0.48	
11 June	1.15	−0.42	

Table 2.2: Height of tides above and below mean sea-level in Barcelona, Spain.

2 Earth processes

CONTINUED

Date	High-tide level/m	Low-tide level/m	Tidal range/m
12 June	1.05	−0.31	
13 June	0.90	−0.17	
14 June	0.72	−0.02	
15 June	0.53	0.12	
16 June	0.34	0.2	

Table 2.2: Height of tides above and below mean sea-level in Barcelona, Spain. (continued)

Worked example

Tidal range is determined by subtracting the low-tide value from the high-tide value.

high tide − low tide = tidal range

As an example, 01 June and 02 June have been completed for you:

01 June: 0.55 − 0.50 = 0.05

02 June: 0.59 − 0.46 = 0.13

You will need to plot this data to see the trends in tidal range more clearly. Figure 2.15 has begun the graphing process for you. Use this as a guide when creating your own graph.

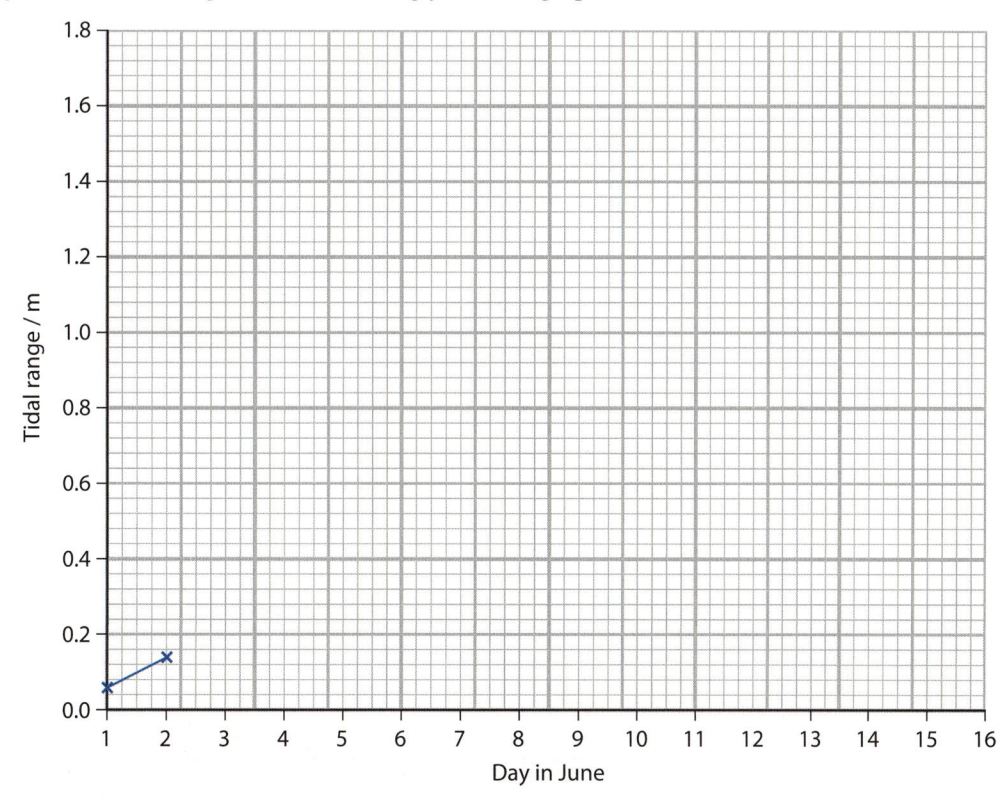

Figure 2.15: Worked example for the tidal range in Barcelona, Spain between 01 June and 16 June.

> **CONTINUED**
>
> **Questions**
>
> 1. Calculate the tidal range for each of the remaining dates and complete Table 2.2.
> 2. a Using standard graphing paper, create a graph representing the change in tidal range over time. Make sure your independent variable (date) is on the *x*-axis and your dependent variable (tidal range) is on the *y*-axis. Do not forget to include the units for your variables.
>   b Using your knowledge of tides, circle the date(s) of the spring tide(s) on your graph, and explain your choice.
>   c Using your knowledge of tides, draw a square around the date(s) of the neap tide(s) on your graph, and explain your choice.

Surface currents

Surface currents are typically driven by the wind. These currents are steady and dependable as a result of global wind patterns caused by an uneven heating of the Earth's surface by the Sun. Areas with large amounts of solar radiation (the equator) have excess heat energy in the air, causing the air to rise in the atmosphere. As the air rises, it begins to transfer away some of its heat energy until it begins to sink in areas with less radiation and cooler temperatures. This movement of air in convection currents forms predictable winds, leading to constant surface sea currents at different latitudes (Figure 2.16).

In the Northern Hemisphere, these currents tend to have a clockwise spiral, while in the Southern Hemisphere they have a counter-clockwise spiral. These spiral patterns are caused by the Coriolis effect. The Coriolis effect is a result of the Earth's rotation. As an object moves across the rotating Earth, the object swerves slightly to the left or right rather than travelling in a

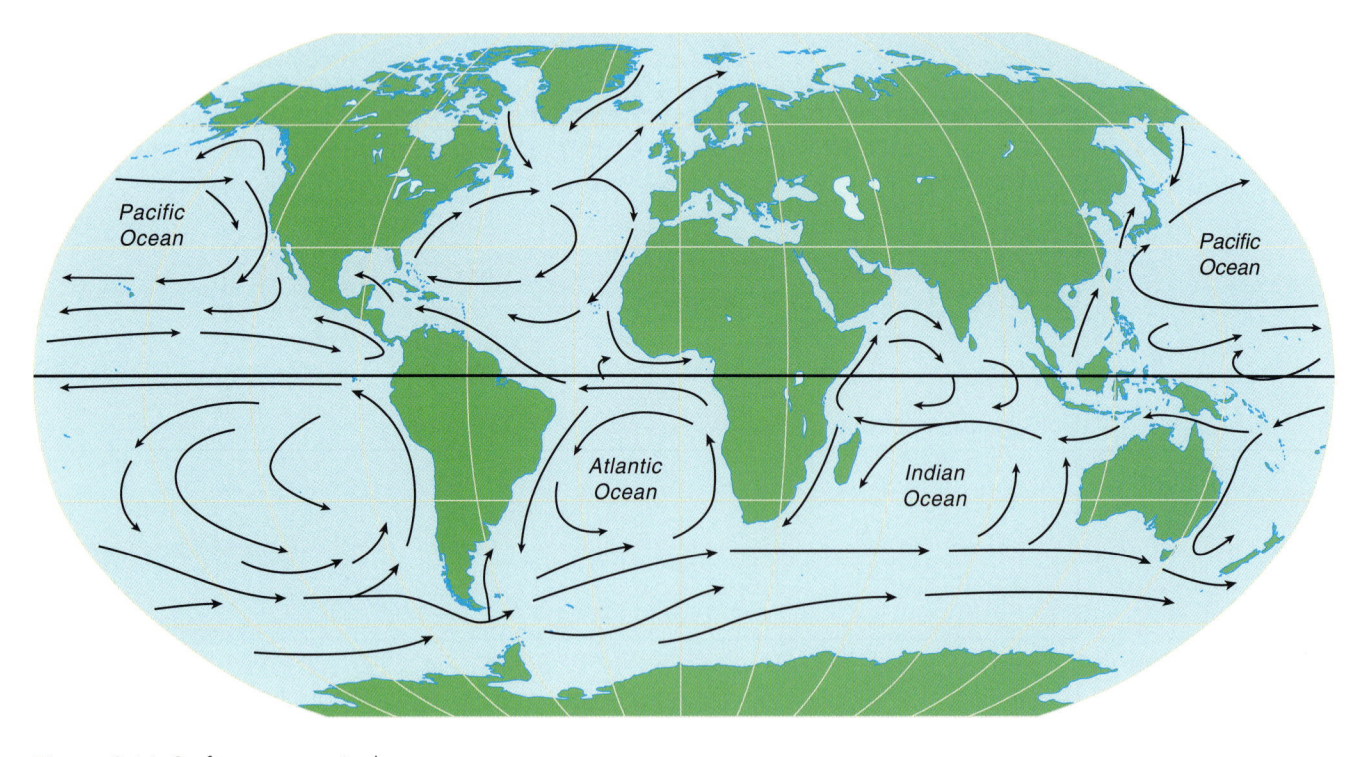

Figure 2.16: Surface currents in the ocean.

straight line. So, as wind blows the seawater across the ocean surface, the rotation of the Earth actually deflects the water at a 45° angle. That is why wind and currents have spiral patterns away from the equator in both hemispheres (Figure 2.17).

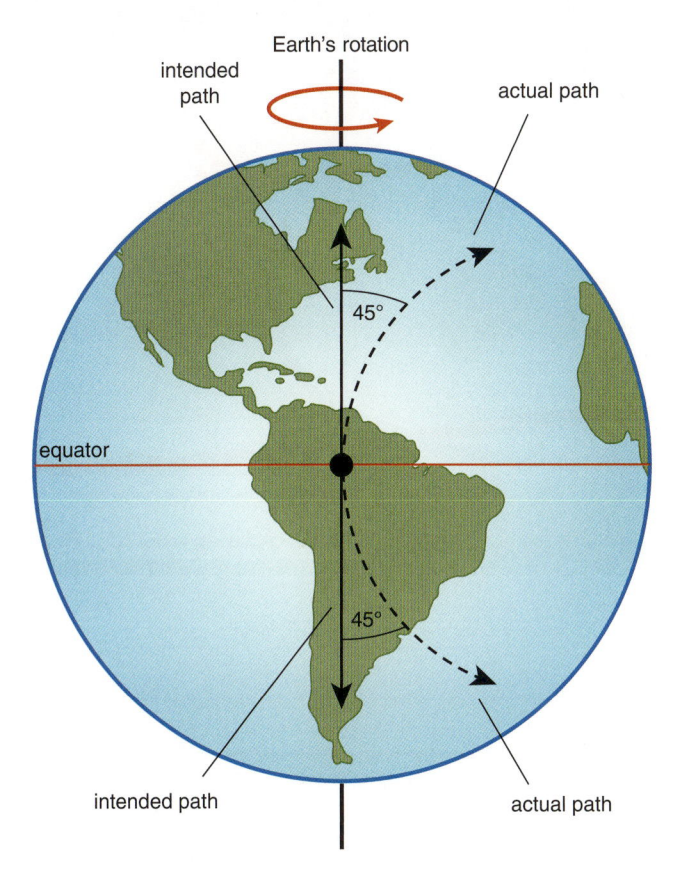

Figure 2.17: Diagram of the Coriolis effect on objects moving over the Earth's surface.

Deep currents

Deep-water currents are driven by differences in density caused by salinity and temperature, hence the term **thermohaline circulation**. These currents happen along the ocean floor and cannot be detected by satellite imagery the way surface currents can. The movement of these currents over the planet is called the **global ocean conveyor belt** (Figure 2.18). These slow-moving currents carry a huge volume of water: more than one-hundred times the flow of the Amazon River in Brazil.

The global conveyor belt starts in the Arctic when cold water freezes into sea ice, leaving behind the salts, which do not freeze. This denser, high salinity water begins a process known as **downwelling**, causing a mixing of the water column, until it reaches the bottom of the ocean. The water then begins moving south through the Atlantic Ocean towards Antarctica.

In Antarctica, the global conveyor belt picks up more cold water before the current divides. One part of the belt goes towards the Indian Ocean and the other towards the Pacific Ocean. In the Indian Ocean, this cold water moves northwards towards the equator, bringing nutrients to the eastern African coasts. The water increases in temperature as it moves towards the equator, so it begins to rise to the surface. When the water cannot rise any higher, it loops back through the south Indian Ocean as a warm surface current.

The cold bottom water of the global conveyor belt in the Pacific Ocean moves through the equator toward the northern Pacific. As this water increases in temperature it also rises, becoming a warm surface current along the western coast of North America. This warm current then wraps around the northern coast of Australia and reconnects with the Indian Ocean portion of the global conveyor belt. Together, these warm currents flow through the Atlantic Ocean back towards the North Pole, where the entire process will begin again.

The global conveyor belt is vital to our global climate patterns. When the cooler currents flow past continental coastlines, they bring cooler, drier weather than might otherwise be expected based on the latitude of the area. Conversely, warm water currents bring warm, wet air to areas that would normally be much colder. This is a reason why the weather in coastal cities tends to be milder than that of cities farther inland or in landlocked regions of the world.

KEY WORDS

thermohaline circulation: large-scale ocean circulation caused by density differences due to temperature and salinity changes in the world's ocean

global ocean conveyor belt: constantly moving systems of deep-ocean water driven by thermohaline circulation

downwelling: the downward movement of water in the sea due to density differences

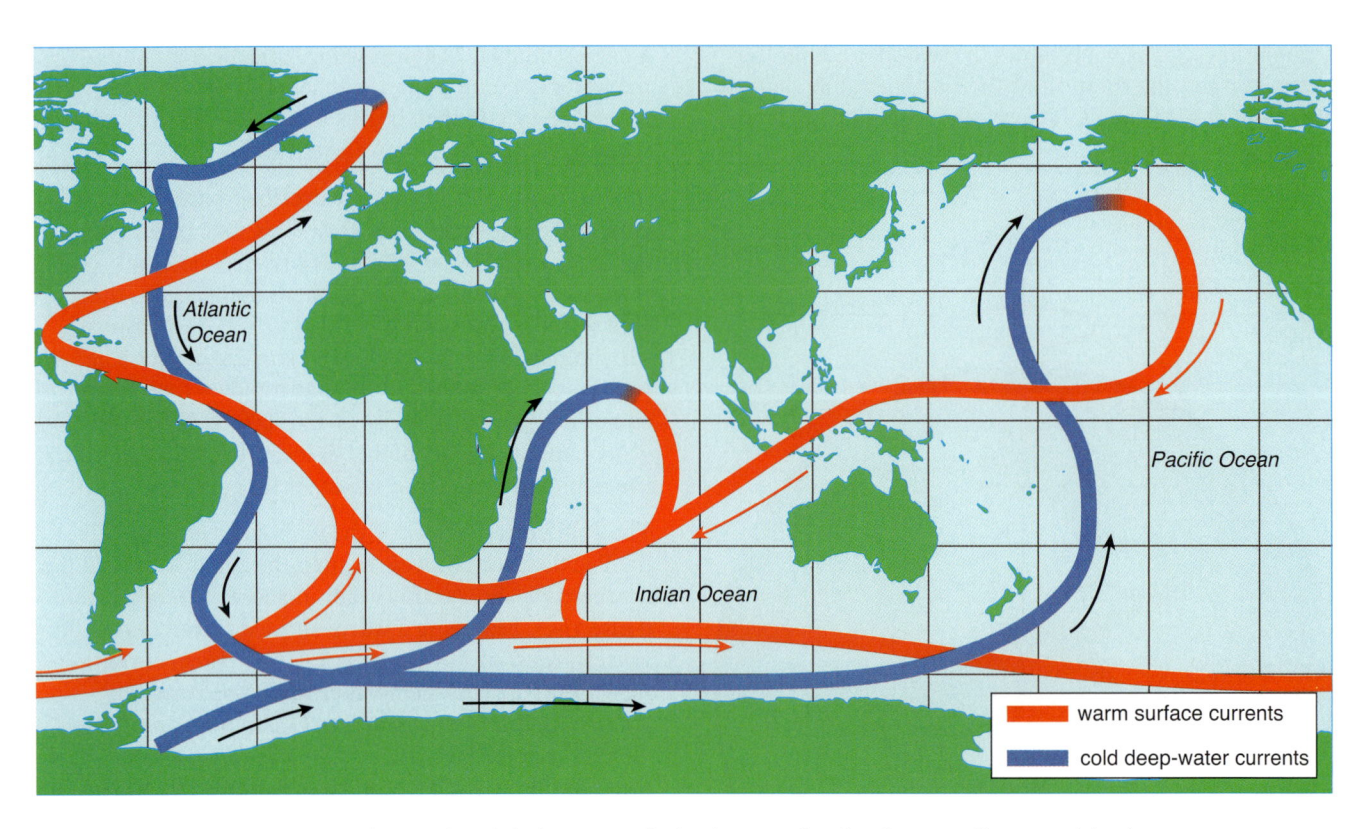

Figure 2.18: Thermohaline circulation (the global conveyor belt) showing the distribution of heat worldwide.

Upwelling

Upwelling is the movement of cold, nutrient-rich water from the seabed vertically to the ocean's surface. Upwelling can be caused by winds forcing the warmer surface water away from the coastline and creating a low pressure zone that brings colder water to the surface (Figure 2.19). Upwelling can also be caused by the topography of the seabed. A mid-ocean ridge, or sea mount, can deflect a cold water current upwards, causing upwelling. This movement of nutrient-rich water upwards acts as fertiliser for surface waters, increasing the productivity of producers in the area. An excess of producers and biomass then increases the biomass of consumers, making areas with upwelling very healthy ecosystems with a lot of biological productivity.

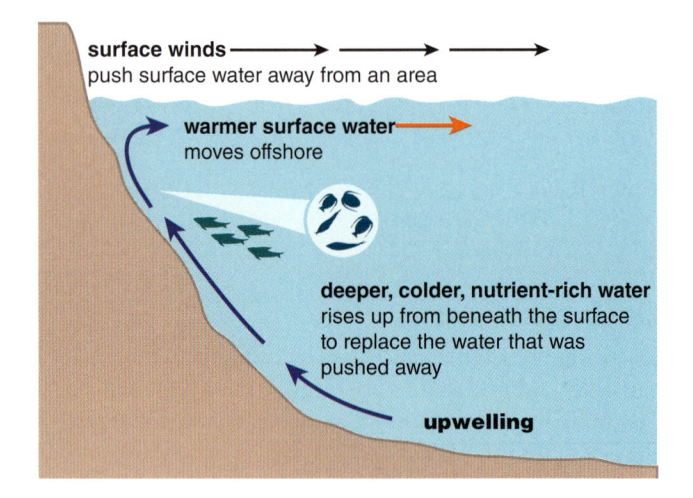

Figure 2.19: The process of upwelling as a result of surface winds.

> **KEY WORD**
>
> **upwelling:** the movement of cold, nutrient-rich water from deep in the ocean to the surface

El Niño Southern Oscillation

Every three to five years (sometimes as long as seven years), the weather pattern in the equatorial region of the Pacific Ocean changes. The change is referred to the El Niño Southern Oscillation (ENSO). ENSO includes changes in ocean currents, wind currents, rainfall and the development of tropical cyclones.

Normal conditions

Under normal conditions (Figure 2.20), currents flowing north along the west coast of South America bring cold, nutrient-rich water towards the equator. This flow of water is part of the global conveyor belt. As strong south-westerly winds blow water away from the coast of South America, the cold, nutrient-rich water moves toward the surface, causing upwelling and high levels of productivity off equatorial South America. This leads to large numbers of small fish (for example anchovies and sardines), which support a substantial fishery industry, along with many species of sea birds and large marine consumers.

However, on the other side of the Pacific, these westerly winds push large amounts of warm water towards Australia and Asia. The water levels in the western Pacific Ocean are about 0.5 m higher than those found in the eastern Pacific Ocean. The warm water that has been pushed west evaporates, creating massive storm clouds and bringing large amounts of much-needed rain to Australia and Asia, while keeping the eastern Pacific fairly dry.

El Niño and La Niña conditions

There are two opposing phases in ENSO: **El Niño** and **La Niña**. During El Niño, the prevailing trade winds that normally blow from east to west along the equator stop blowing in their normal pattern. Instead, these winds reduce, preventing warm water and moist air from moving to the west (Figure 2.21). The warm water builds up along the coast of South America, stopping the upwelling that usually occurs when the **Humboldt Current** brings cold water to the surface. Indonesia and Australia experience drought conditions, because of a reduction in rainfall, while Peru and the eastern Pacific experience increased rainfall.

> **KEY WORDS**
>
> **El Niño:** a warm current that develops off the coast of Ecuador around December, which can cause widespread death within local food chains
>
> **La Niña:** a cold current that develops off the coast of Ecuador and spreads across the Pacific, reducing sea surface temperatures for extended periods of time
>
> **Humboldt Current:** a coldwater current with low salinity levels that flows north along the western coast of South America; also called the Peru current

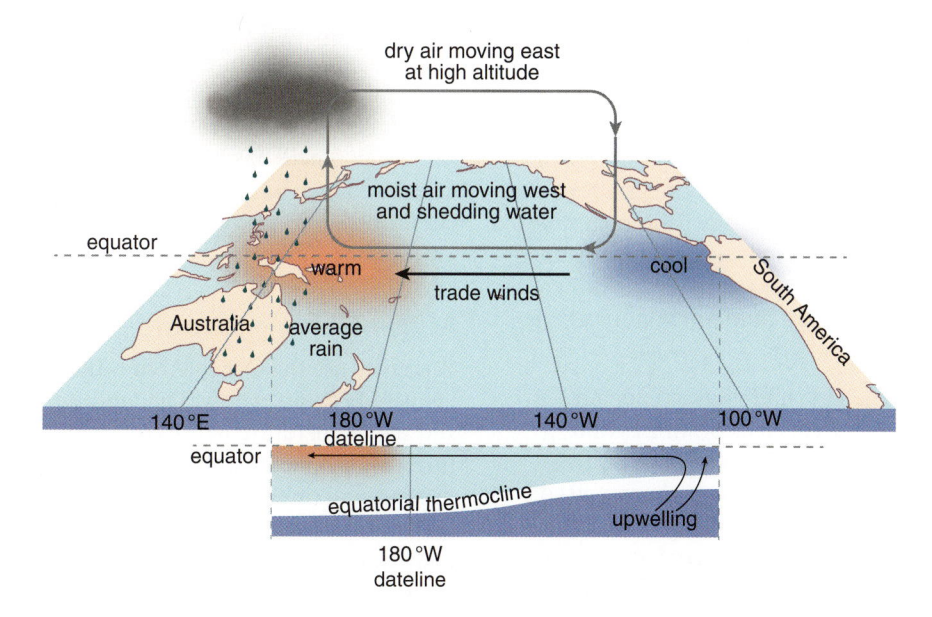

Figure 2.20: Normal weather conditions in the equatorial Pacific Ocean.

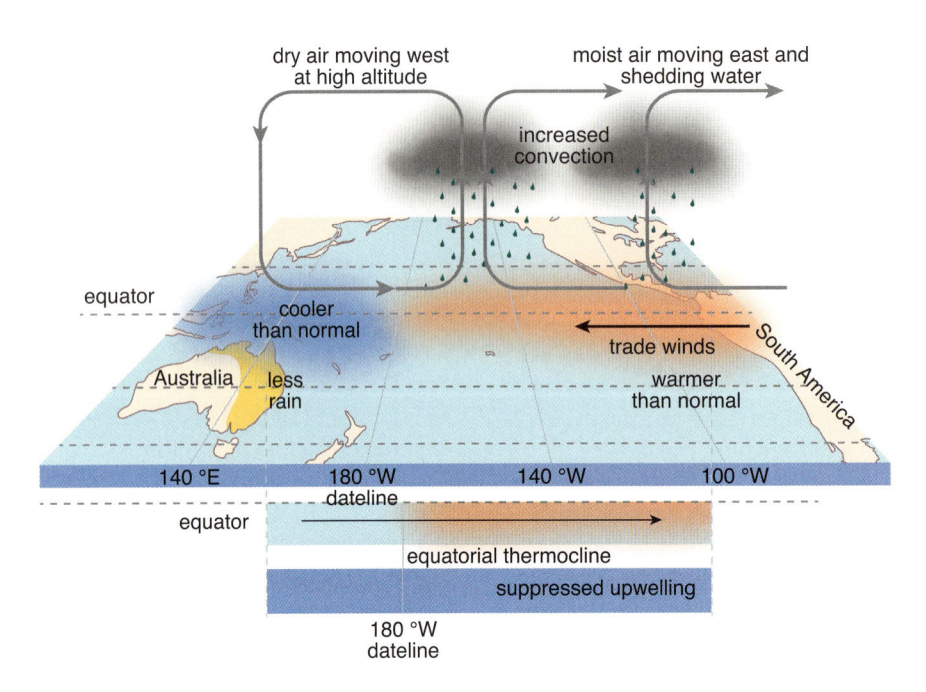

Figure 2.21: El Niño conditions in the equatorial Pacific Ocean.

Without the upwelling off the South American coast, there is no fresh supply of nutrients or colder water to reduce surface temperatures. As a result, many cold-water species die and primary productivity goes into a steep decline due to lack of nutrients. The lack of producers impacts upon every other level of the local food webs. This causes both the ecosystems and the fishing industries to fail during these times.

The destruction of the fisheries industry is actually how El Niño came to be named. The Peruvian fishermen were the first to notice the change in sea surface temperatures and how that impacted the fishing. When the waters became usually warm for December, they could not catch any fish. This meant the fishermen were able to stay at home with their families for the Christmas holiday. Eventually, the phenomena came to be known as El Niño, Spanish for 'the boy child', in honour of the baby Jesus in their Christian faith.

La Niña, Spanish for 'the girl child', has a tendency to immediately follow the occurrence of an El Niño event and generally follows the opposite pattern. This is a cooling phase rather than a warming phase caused by stronger than average trade winds off the coast of Peru. These stronger winds allow more cold, water from the Humboldt Current to rise to the surface bringing with it extra nutrients leading to more phytoplankton and greater productivity in the region. While the standards for determining a La Niña event vary, they all require at least three months during which the sea surface temperature is 3–5 °C below the usual average. The impacts of La Niña are prominently felt in North America, leading to an increase in hurricane activity in the Atlantic basin.

Both El Niño and La Niña are naturally occurring phenomena, but their exact cause is not known. A problem with determining the cause is that not all El Niño or La Niña years begin or progress in the same way. There has been some speculation that climate change increases occurrence of these alternate conditions, but it is unlikely that this is the only factor involved.

Major El Niño events

Scientists use the Oceanic Niño Index (ONI) to identify El Niño events. The ONI tracks average sea-surface temperature in the equatorial Pacific region in three-month increments. If there are five consecutive overlapping three-month periods with sea-surface temperatures at or more than +0.5 °C above average temperatures, they consider it to be an El Niño event. There have been a few 'very strong' El Niño events in the past few decades according to the ONI.

- 1982–83: sea-surface temperatures rose to 2.1 °C above average and caused massive flooding along the eastern Pacific basin.
- 1997–98: the strongest El Niño event recorded so far, sea-surface temperatures rose 2.3 °C above the average temperature.
- 2015–16: scientists have rated this event as equal in power to the 1997–98 event as sea-surface temperatures rose 2.3 °C above the average sea-surface temperature again before beginning to dissipate in May 2016. This event caused a record-breaking sixteen tropical cyclones in the Pacific Ocean.

Test yourself

8 Imagine you owned a seaside home. A bad storm brought heavy winds and high surf to your coastline. Would you prefer it to be during a new moon or a quarter moon? Why?

9 Compare and contrast a current and a tide.

10 What are the effects of El Niño and La Niña on local ecosystems?

CASE STUDY 2.1: EL NIÑO, LA NIÑA, HURRICANES AND CLIMATE CHANGE

The El Niño Southern Oscillation (ENSO) has a significant impact on the climate conditions over the Pacific Ocean, as would be expected due to its immediate location. However, the global conveyor belt uses ocean currents to carry heat energy over our planet. This movement of heat energy magnifies the impacts of ENSO so its effects can be felt globally. In fact, both phases of ENSO, El Niño and La Niña, are capable of impacting the formation and strength of hurricanes in the Atlantic Ocean (Figure 2.22).

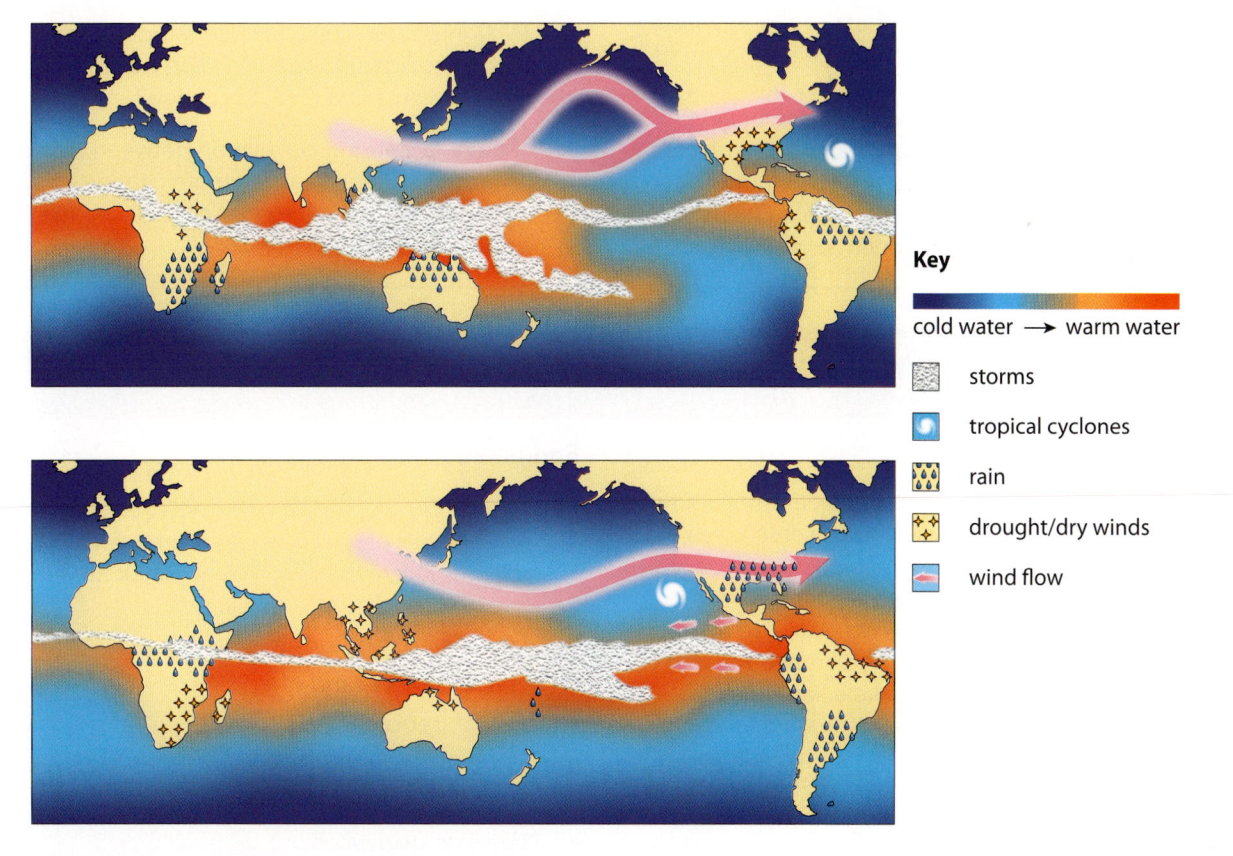

Figure 2.22: A comparison of El Niño and La Niña.

CONTINUED

During El Niño, fewer hurricanes are seen in the Atlantic due to changes in air pressure and wind velocity. However, in La Niña years, conditions in the Caribbean and Central Atlantic are highly favourable for the formation of hurricanes.

The consequences of ENSO on ecosystems and hurricane formation are why scientists have spent so much time studying the oscillation. In fact, scientists have been studying El Niño since the early twentieth century when Peruvian fishermen made the connection between water temperature and the quality of the fish catch that year. Recently ENSO has become a concern alongside climate change. The way these two phenomena react in conjunction with each other is still open to much speculation.

One method scientists use to track climate change is monitoring sea surface temperatures, which have been rising uncharacteristically in recent years. Since sea surface temperatures in the equatorial Pacific also rise as part of the El Niño phase, many scientists worry that increased global sea surface temperatures will increase the intensity and frequency of El Niño. This brings with it concerns about the damages El Niño causes to the marine ecosystems off the coast of Peru as well as the country's economy. Other scientists worry that more frequent El Niño events will also bring more frequent or stronger La Niña. While this may help offset the unfavourable ecological conditions brought by El Niño to Peru, it may also create even better conditions for hurricane production in the Atlantic. Specifically, scientists are concerned about a lengthening of the hurricane season in the North Atlantic.

Regardless of which phase will bring the worst conditions, recent data is indicating that we can expect to see these events happening at a more frequent pace. While scientists cannot guarantee that climate change is the cause between more frequent ENSO events, it is interesting to see such a strong correlation between the two.

Questions

1 Using the information above, and Figure 2.22, state which image in Figure 2.22 (top or bottom) represents each phase of the ENSO. Justify your response with details from the image.

2 Why might using sea surface temperatures alone provide a false correlation between ENSO events and climate change?

3 If there is a strong correlation between increase in ENSO frequency and climate change, why cannot scientists agree that climate change causes ENSO?

PRACTICAL ACTIVITY 2.1: INVESTIGATING SETTLEMENT SPEEDS IN SEDIMENTS OF VARYING SIZES

Introduction

Sediment-settling tubes are used to determine how quickly different diameter sediments settle when water stops moving. This can help us determine how much erosion and sedimentation is happening on different shorelines by allowing us to see how long it takes before sediments settle once water is still. In this practical you will make a sediment tube to investigate the settling times of three different sediment types: sand, pebbles and diatomaceous earth.

Equipment:

You will need:

- 45 cm clear plastic watertight tube with PVC caps on both ends, or a clear plastic tennis ball can with a lid
- cup of fine sand or silt
- cup of coarse sand
- cup of pebbles
- enough water to fill the tube
- electrical or duct tape
- timer or stopwatch

CONTINUED

Safety considerations

Follow all laboratory safety rules.

Wear safety goggles, lab coats and gloves while in the laboratory.

Do not eat or drink any of these materials.

Before you start

1. Which of the sediments mentioned in the introduction would you expect to settle the fastest in water? Why?
2. How long do you predict it will take before all of the sediment has settled?
3. In this investigation, you will be measuring sediment-settling time. Does this make time a dependent or independent variable? Why?

Method

1. Make sure the tube is capped at one end.
2. Pour approximately one-third of the fine sand or silt into the tube.
3. Add water to fill the tube within 3–5 cm of the top.
4. Place the remaining cap on the open end and secure with tape.
5. Gently shake the tube so that all the sediment is mixed in the water.
6. Set the tube down on a flat surface and allow the material to settle. Be careful not to jostle the table.
7. Start timing as soon as the tube is set down.
8. Time how long it takes for the sediment to settle to the bottom.
9. Record settling times in a copy of Table 2.3.
10. Repeat the method two more times.
11. Repeat steps 1–10 with the coarse sand, and then with the pebbles.
12. After all results are collected, calculate the mean settling time for each sediment type.

Results

	Time to settle		
	Fine sand or silt	Coarse sand	Pebbles
Trial 1			
Trial 2			
Trial 3			
Mean			

Table 2.3: Settling times for different sediment types.

Evaluation and conclusions

1. Which unit for time, seconds or minutes, do you think would be best to record the time for the sediment to settle? Why?
2. Using the data you collected, describe the settling rates of these sediments.
3. How does this tube represent the sedimentation seen on different types of shores?
4. Based on this tube and your knowledge of substrate types, rank the wave action found on these shores (sandy, rocky and muddy) from greatest to least.
5. Explain why you ranked each shore the way you did.

REFLECTION

After completing Practical Activity 2.1, think about these questions:

1. How accurate do you think your measurements were? Why?
2. How can scientists use models like this one to build an understanding of how our oceans function?

PROJECT: REPORTING ON EARTH PROCESSES

Work in a group of three or four. Together, you will create a short video segment as news reporters. Each group will choose a different topic from the chapter (plate boundaries, volcanoes, tides, currents, El Niño and so on) and find real data and examples to present in your video. The video you create should provide an explanation of how these processes work in the real world using props to support your given topic. You can create diagrams, charts, graphs or models. If technology is available, you may be able to work on this in class. If you do not have technology, you could act out your segments in person. The final product should be approximately one-minute long, but no longer than two minutes, and you should be able to be show the video in class.

Thinking about your project

What resources did you use while working on your video? Which ones were especially helpful? Which ones would you use again?

What did you think other students did well when you watched their videos? Are there any areas in your video you would like to improve on?

EXAM-STYLE QUESTIONS

1. **a** Define what is meant by the term *littoral zone*. [1]
   b Compare the formation of a rocky shore to the formation of a sandy shore. [4]
   c State a defining feature that distinguishes a delta from an estuary. [1]
   [Total: 6]

2. **a** State **three** major lines of evidence supporting the theory of plate tectonics. [3]
   b Describe the movement at each of the following plate boundaries and state one feature located there:
      i transform boundary [2]
      ii convergent boundary [2]
      iii divergent boundary. [2]
   [Total: 9]

3. **a** State where you would expect to locate hydrothermal vents. [1]
   b Outline how hydrothermal vents form. [4]
   c Hydrothermal vents are considered to be extreme environments. Describe how that may impact the organisms that live there. [3]
   [Total: 8]

4. *Tevnia* are a species of tube worms typically found at hydrothermal vent ecosystems. These marine invertebrates have free-swimming planktonic larvae and eventually grow into adults that form a symbiotic relationship with chemosynthetic bacteria.

CONTINUED

Researchers wanted to determine if high pressure attracted the tube worm larvae to settle in that ecosystem. Three containers of seawater were set up. Each container was kept at a different pressure:

- 0 kPa (to represent sea-level)
- 10 100 kPa (to represent a mid-level depth in the ocean)
- 250 000 kPa (to represent the pressure at a hydrothermal vent)

Approximately 250 larvae were released into each container. Temperature, pH and salinity were carefully controlled. After three days, the numbers of larvae that had settled within each container were counted. The results are shown in Table 2.4.

Container pressure / kPa	Number of tube worm larvae settled
0	15
10 100	87
25 000	95

Table 2.4: Number of tube worm larvae settled in each container.

    a Using the data in Table 2.4, describe the effect of pressure on the attachment of *Tevnia* larvae. [2]

    b The attachment of *Tevnia* is also affected by other factors, including pH.

       Outline a laboratory-based experiment to determine whether pH plays a role in settlement of *Tevnia*. [5]

[Total: 7]

5 a Outline the principles behind the Coriolis effect. [4]

    b Describe the impact the Coriolis effect has on the formation of surface currents. [2]

    c Not including the Coriolis effect, state **two** physical factors that could impact the flow of ocean currents. [2]

[Total: 8]

6 a **Discuss** the impact of the alignment of the Sun, Moon and Earth on tidal range. [5]

    b Horseshoe crabs, like many marine species, come to shore when it is time to mate. While on shore, the female horseshoe crab will dig a hole and lay her eggs while the males fertilise them. The eggs take about two weeks to hatch, during which time they need to stay buried. Once hatched the tiny larvae need to get into the water as quickly as possible to avoid predators.

> **COMMAND WORD**
>
> **discuss:** write about issue(s) or topic(s) in depth in a structured way

> **CONTINUED**
>
>   **i** Given what you know about tides, predict when horseshoe crabs probably come to shore to mate. [1]
>
>   **ii** Discuss your response with reference to tidal range. [3]
>
>   [Total: 9]
>
> **7** The Benguela current flows along the western portion of southern Africa from Cape Point in the south northward. Each year it brings cold, nutrient-rich waters to the coastlines in this region.
>
>   **a** State the name of the process described above. [1]
>
>   **b** Explain how the process named above is able to support large numbers of fish and marine predators. [4]
>
>   **c** Unlike South America, the southern portion of Africa does not have an El Niño event disrupting the constant flow of cold water. Describe the difference in the levels of phytoplankton in the waters off Southern Africa and the waters in Peru during an El Niño event. [2]
>
>   [Total: 7]
>
> **8** Figure 2.6 shows the Earth's major tectonic plates and their boundaries. The arrows show the movement of the plate.
>
>   **a** Complete a copy of Table 2.5 by naming the type of plate found at the listed boundary. [4]
>
> | Plate boundary | Boundary type |
> |---|---|
> | Australian Plate – Pacific Plate | |
> | South American Plate – African Plate | |
> | Pacific Plate – North American Plate | |
> | North American Plate – Eurasian Plate | |
>
> **Table 2.5:** Plate boundary types.
>
>   **b** Describe how a tsunami is formed at a tectonic plate boundary. [5]
>
>   **c** With reference to Figure 2.6, state **two** plates where a tsunami may form. [1]
>
>   [Total: 10]

2 Earth processes

SELF-EVALUATION CHECKLIST

I can:	See section...	Needs more work	Almost there	Ready to move on
describe the structure of Earth's geology with regard to the continental crust, oceanic crust, mantle and core	2.1			
describe and apply the theory of plate tectonics	2.1			
describe the formation of hydrothermal vents and other features that make up the ocean floor	2.1			
compare weathering and erosion	2.2			
describe sedimentation and explain how the speed of water and size of particles affect transport of particles to and from shorelines	2.2			
identify examples of varying types of littoral zone and describe how the processes of weathering, erosion and sedimentation create these ecosystems	2.2			
explain how different tides with varying tidal ranges are impacted by many physical factors allowing for interpretation of tide tables and graphs	2.3			
discuss how ocean currents and upwelling are created and influenced by abiotic factors in the environment which lead to the formation of the global ocean conveyor belt and the El Niño Southern Oscillation (ENSO) cycle in the Pacific Ocean	2.3			

EXTENDED CASE STUDY: TSUNAMIS AND THEIR GEOLOGICAL MARK

Tsunamis are a phenomenon that has fascinated the world for some time. A truly destructive force, they are often featured in the most dramatic entries of the 'disaster movie' genre. On screen, tsunamis are generally portrayed as a giant wave towering above the shoreline. Except for the largest of tsunamis, this picture is not accurate. In most cases, tsunamis appear as if they are an exceptionally large high tide coming in more quickly than usual. This appearance of a 'tide' is what gave rise to the common name 'tidal wave' despite the inaccuracy. Tides do not cause tsunamis. Tsunamis can be caused by earthquakes at convergent or transform boundaries that shake violently enough to displace the large volume of water above them or by volcanic eruptions, large landslides, or glaciers splitting and falling into the sea.

Tsunamis are capable of causing incredible damage to areas of the world located near the sea. While most common in the Pacific Ocean along the Ring of Fire, tsunamis have also happened in the Indian Ocean, Mediterranean and Norwegian Seas and are, therefore, a danger to many parts of the world.

CONTINUED

The case for an early warning system

One of the deadliest tsunamis in modern times became international news in 2004. It all started when the Indian Ocean Earthquake began in the early hours of 26 December off the coast of northern Sumatra. This earthquake would rank a 9.0 magnitude, making it the third largest earthquake ever recorded. The earthquake and its aftershocks were able to trigger a series of tsunamis reaching up to 30 m in height along multiple areas on the coast of the Indian Ocean. Following the tsunamis, massive damage and casualties were reported from 14 countries. Estimates have put the total death toll of these tsunamis at more than 225 000 people, with the largest losses in Indonesia, Sri Lanka, India and Thailand. The Indonesian city of Banda Aceh was arguably the most impacted by the tsunami with more than 167 000 people reported dead in that region alone. Damage from the tsunami was still visible months and years after the event (see Figure 2.23).

Figure 2.23: Aerial views of the coastline of Banda Aceh city, Indonesia, eight months after the 2004 Indian Ocean Earthquake and tsunami.

There was a delay of several hours between when the earthquake began and when the tsunamis struck land. It has been argued that many of these lives could have been saved if an early warning system for tsunamis had been put in place prior to 2004. However, early warning systems are expensive and require a complicated network of sensors to detect tsunamis in deep water where they change the ocean height by a tiny amount. In order to be truly effective, the system would also need an information infrastructure that could send out a warning to the coastal populations in the many nations that surround the Indian Ocean. Justifying the need for such an detailed and pricey system would be hard to do in area overwhelmed by so much poverty – there had not been a major tsunami in that region since the 1883 eruption of Krakatau. After the 2004 tsunami, Indonesia, with the help of the UN, installed a complicated tsunami warning system anyway.

Unfortunately, for the Indonesian region, there was a repeat of the Krakatau eruption and tsunami in December of 2018. The powerful volcano Anak Krakatau, literally '*the child of Krakatau*', began to erupt on 22 December and, due to the violent shaking caused by the eruption, a part of the volcanic island collapsed into the Sunda Strait. The sheer weight of the rock caused an underwater landslide that displaced an enormous amount of seawater. This displacement, much like that of an earthquake, triggered a tsunami that rose the high-tide level by an additional 90 cm in Lampung. More than 430 people died and 14 000 more were injured during the tsunami in spite of the early warning system. This is because maintaining the system is expensive and difficult to do, so by 2012 the sea level detection buoys that detect changes in sea height were non-operational. This means the system in place relies entirely on detecting seismic activity from earthquakes; there is no way for it to detect tsunamis caused by volcanic eruptions.

Searching for fossilised tsunamis

Justifying better warning systems and their maintenance is leading some scientists to look backward to find evidence of previous tsunamis through both the oral history of aboriginal tribes and the geology of areas that may have been affected by a tsunami. Anthropologists were concerned after the tsunamis hit that the aboriginal tribes on nearby islands may have been wiped out by the tsunamis. Once they were able to reach out to these people, however, they found that they suffered very few casualties. The oral traditions of

CONTINUED

the tribes that had been passed down warned of a 'wall of water' that followed a shaking ground, so when they felt the earthquake, they evacuated to higher ground.

In terms of geology, scientists are now trying to find evidence of tsunami deposits, called *tsunamiite* (see Figure 2.24). Tsunamiite is a term that was introduced in the 1980s to describe a particular formation of sediments that is left behind by tsunamis as the water slowly returns to the sea. These deposits tend to be found in low-lying lagoons on the coasts of areas impacted by tsunamis. As the waves move through the ocean, the speed of the water allows them to pick of sediments of all sizes, stones, shells, bits of coral and more. Once the wave makes landfall and begins to recede, it slows. The slowing of the water allows the large rocks and sediments to fall out of the solution and deposit themselves and, through sedimentation, create large geological formations that can be examined by geologists. These new rocks often have a number of subdivisions dependent on the number of successive tsunami waves within an incident. The location of tsunamiite deposits can also tell scientists how high the waves were and how far inland the flooding extended. The movement of large boulders can also be an indicator of a tsunami, but is inconclusive as it can also be a result of a tropical cyclone.

Figure 2.24: Tsunami waves from the 2004 Indian Ocean earthquake deposited this tsunamiite, a thick pile of sorted gravel and sands, onto a low-lying coastal plain. Photo taken five years after impact.

Identifying tsunamiite and linking it to historically-known tsunami and earthquake events can allow scientists to model future tsunamis based on a set of conditions. This is helpful in designing warning systems and creating action plans to prevent future damage. An example of this happened in Japan. Using geological data, scientists in 2007 were able to provide information to the company that ran the Fukushima Daiichi Nuclear Power Plant that predicted there would be another large, tsunami-causing earthquake within the next three decades. The company revised their estimates of predicted tsunami heights, nearly doubling the predicted height of a tsunami at the nuclear power site, but unfortunately, they took no action to increase the size of the wall around the plant for protection. When the tsunami hit in 2011, the flooding was almost identical to that predicted by the scientists and the damage was catastrophic.

Questions

1. Explain how a tsunami would be able to create a rock formation that is different from those created by the usual wind-driven waves.

2. Using the knowledge gained in Practical activity 2.1, explain which shore type you would be most likely to find a deposit of tsunamiite.

3. Using the same practical activity, describe where you would expect to find the largest pieces of sediment within the actual tsunamiite rock.

4. How can the theory of plate tectonics be applied to explain why there are more tsunamis in regions within and surrounding the Pacific Ocean than those bordering the Atlantic Ocean?

5. Oral traditions were able to help aboriginal tribes in Indonesia survive the tsunami. If impoverished regions such as those surrounding the Indian Ocean cannot afford an early alert system for tsunamis, would educating the public on the possible warning signs of a tsunami be a good alternative? Justify your response.

Chapter 3
Interactions in marine ecosystems

LEARNING INTENTIONS

In this chapter you will learn how to:

- describe the three main types of symbiotic relationship and describe examples of each one
- represent feeding relationships as food chains or food webs and be able to describe the organisms in these relationships in terms of their trophic level
- explain how photosynthesis provides energy to the food chain and summarise the process as a word equation
- give the word equation for respiration
- define productivity and explain how high productivity can affect food chains
- explain why energy is lost at each stage of the food chain

3 Interactions in marine ecosystems

CONTINUED

- draw pyramids of number, energy and biomass and be able to explain and interpret their shapes
- explain what a nutrient is and be able to give the biological roles of nitrogen, carbon, magnesium, calcium and phosphorus
- draw simple diagrams to show how carbohydrates, proteins and lipids are made up from smaller molecules
- explain how nutrients in the ocean are depleted and replenished
- describe the different stages in the carbon cycle including combustion, photosynthesis, decomposition, fossil fuels and the formation and weathering of rocks.

BEFORE YOU START

- In small groups, think of as many ways as you can in which organisms of different species can interact. Divide your list into positive and negative interactions.
- In pairs, discuss what you already know about food chains. If you can, draw and label a simple food chain.
- Write down any examples of nutrients you have heard of and the reasons you think they are needed by living organisms.

THE IMPORTANCE OF PHYTOPLANKTON

Around three billion people rely on marine ecosystems for their food. These people obtain the majority of the protein in their diet from farmed or wild caught fish and other seafood. What they may not realise is that, ultimately, much of the energy in their food has come from tiny organisms called phytoplankton. This word comes from the Greek meaning 'drifting plants'. Phytoplankton are tiny, microscopic organisms which float in the upper sunlit layers of the water. Like land plants, they contain **chlorophyll** which enables them to **photosynthesise**. They carry out more than half of all the photosynthesis on Earth, producing up to 160 billion tonnes of **carbohydrates** every year.

The ability of the phytoplankton to capture the energy in sunlight and to fix it into carbohydrates is essential to life in the oceans. Many of the **consumers** must gain their energy from either eating the phytoplankton directly, or from eating other animals who have eaten the phytoplankton. Even if you do not eat seafood you are benefitting from these tiny organisms, as more than half of the oxygen you breathe will have come from their photosynthesis.

KEY WORDS

chlorophyll: a pigment found in plants and algae that is used to absorb sunlight for photosynthesis

photosynthesis (photosynthetic, photosynthesise): the process of using light energy to synthesise glucose from carbon dioxide and water to produce chemical energy

carbohydrate: organic compounds occurring in living tissues that contain carbon, hydrogen and oxygen (for example, starch, cellulose and sugars); carbohydrates can be broken down in the process of respiration to release energy

consumer: an animal which feeds on other organisms to gain energy from food

> **CONTINUED**
>
> NASA, the United States' civilian space programme, monitors the levels of phytoplankton in the oceans using satellite imagery, comparing the colour of the water to the colour of chlorophyll and other pigments. NASA has found that, overall, phytoplankton populations have declined over the last decade. This may be because the surface of the ocean is increasing in temperature. This in turn decreases the mixing between the nutrient-rich lower layers of water and the upper sunlit layers. Fewer nutrients means less growth and reproduction of phytoplankton. In contrast, marine dead zones are formed where excess fertilisers enter the water. In these areas productivity reaches such a peak that the ecosystem becomes unbalanced. The phytoplankton population initially increases very rapidly in a phenomenon known as an **algal bloom**. As the cells die and are decomposed by bacteria the levels of oxygen fall. Eventually the oxygen levels become so low that little life can remain.
>
> **Questions**
>
> 1 Marine dead zones are often formed when agricultural fertilisers enter the water. This reduces the population of fish available to catch and use as food. However, if we do not use the fertilisers there will be a reduction in the yield of food crops. Discuss, in pairs, what should be done about this problem and the impacts on land and ocean ecosystems.
>
> 2 Think about why an organisation such as NASA might need to monitor the phytoplankton in the ocean. Discuss, in groups, the reasons that this might be important and whether you think it is a good use of resources.

3.1 Interactions

Ecological interactions describe how a pair of organisms living together in a **community** can affect one another. Some of these interactions are **mutualistic** and have a positive effect on both organisms. Others such as **predation** and **parasitism** are harmful to one of the species involved. **Competition** is harmful to both organisms as they are both trying to use the same resources. However, all of these relationships are vital to the ecosystem as they allow the transfer of energy from one organism to the next.

Symbiosis is a relationship between two or more organisms of different species which live physically close to each other. The word comes from a Greek term which means 'living together'. The smaller organism is the symbiont and the larger organism is the host. There are several different types of symbiosis including:

- parasitism – where the symbiont benefits but the host is damaged (for example, copepods and marine fish)
- **commensalism** – where the symbiont benefits but the host remains unaffected (for example, manta rays and remora fish)
- mutualism – where both organisms benefit from the relationship (for example, boxer crabs and anemones).

> **KEY WORDS**
>
> **algal bloom:** a rapid increase in a population of algae
>
> **community:** all the different populations interacting in one habitat at the same time
>
> **mutualism (mutualistic):** a relationship between two different organisms where both organisms benefit
>
> **predation:** a relationship between two organisms where a predator hunts, kills and eats a prey animal
>
> **parasitism:** a relationship between two organisms where the parasite obtains benefit at the expense of the host
>
> **competition:** a relationship between two organisms where both species are negatively affected as they are trying to use the same resources
>
> **symbiosis:** a relationship between two or more organisms of different species which live physically close to each other
>
> **commensalism:** a relationship between two organisms where one organism benefits and the other is neither harmed nor benefitted

3 Interactions in marine ecosystems

Types of relationships

The parasitic relationship between copepods and marine fish

Copepods are tiny shrimp-like crustaceans found both in freshwater and saltwater. They are one of the most abundant life forms on Earth and there are thousands of different species. About half of the species are parasitic and these cause major problems for the aquaculture of marine fish as infection can lead to substantial economic losses. An example of copepod parasites are the sea lice which include more than 500 species. Two of the most common are *Lepeophtheirus salmonis* and *Caligus elongatus*.

Sea lice are **ectoparasites** which means they live on the *outside* of their host as shown in Figure 3.1. (**Endoparasites**, such as tapeworm, are found *inside* the host's body.) Sea lice feed on mucus, tissues and blood. This can lead directly to the death of the host fish if enough lice are attached, particularly if they are attached to the gills or to the more vulnerable juvenile fish. Even a lesser infestation will reduce the growth rate of the fish and may leave them open to infection through the damaged tissues. The lice not only cause problems for farmed species but can spread to wild populations. In doing so, they can act as vectors for other diseases, including infectious salmon anaemia, a virus which causes severe losses to fish farming. In this relationship, the fish (host) is negatively affected, and the sea louse (parasite) gains food and is positively affected.

The commensal relationship between manta rays and remora fish

Remora fish (also known as suckerfish) have a modified dorsal fin which can create suction and attach the fish to smooth surfaces. The skin of a manta ray is one such surface (Figure 3.2). The remora fish is able to cling with a force of three times its own weight and it has even been studied as way to create new adhesive technology.

This is an example of **phoresis**, a type of commensal relationship where the host remains unaffected and the symbiont uses the host for transport. In this case, the manta ray is unaffected but the remora benefits as it does not have to use its own energy to travel. It is also possible for this relationship to become mutualistic as there are cases where the remora have been recorded eating the parasites which affect the rays.

> **KEY WORDS**
>
> **ectoparasite:** a parasite, such as a flea or a louse, which lives on the outside of its host
>
> **endoparasite:** a parasite, such as a tapeworm, which lives inside the body of its host
>
> **phoresis:** a commensal relationship where one organism attaches itself to another in order to travel

Figure 3.1: Sea lice attached to a juvenile salmon.

Figure 3.2: A manta ray with two attached remora fish.

The mutualistic relationship between boxer crabs and anemones

Boxer crabs (sometimes known as pom-pom crabs) are small crabs (less than 2 cm across) from the genus *Lybia*. Its name comes from the anemones which the crabs hold in their claws which look like boxing gloves or pom-poms (Figure 3.3).

Figure 3.3: Boxer crab holding anemones.

As this is a mutualistic relationship, both organisms benefit. Anemones have stinging cells called cnidocytes on their tentacles. The crab makes use of these by holding the anemones in its claws and using them for defence. The anemone gains easy access to food and will also use its tentacles like mops to pick up debris and food from the crab's hiding place. A crab without an anemone may try to steal one from another crab. Recently it has been found that most crabs carry two anemones which are clones of each other. This suggests that, once a crab has one anemone, it splits it into two, one for each claw. Crabs have also been observed directly feeding their anemones. The evidence, therefore, seems to be that the crabs actively feed and cultivate their anemones, rather like looking after a pet.

Test yourself

1. Complete a copy of Table 3.1 using the symbols below to show the effects of different interspecies relationships on both the host and the symbiont:
   - 0 species is unaffected
   - – species is harmed
   - + species benefits.

Relationship	Host	Symbiont
mutualism		
parasitism		
commensalism		

Table 3.1: Different interspecies relationships.

2. Compare parasitism and commensalism.
3. Give an example of a symbiotic relationship. Name **two** organisms which are involved in this type of relationship and list the cost or benefit to each organism.

3.2 Feeding relationships

Ultimately, all life on Earth is dependent on the energy that can be fixed into carbohydrates by **autotrophic** organisms. An autotroph is able to make its own food by forming organic compounds from simple inorganic molecules. Marine ecosystems contain both photosynthetic and **chemosynthetic** organisms. Photosynthetic organisms capture the energy in the sunlight, whereas chemosynthetic organisms are able to use the energy in chemicals that are dissolved in the water.

Photosynthesis can only take place in the sunlit upper layer of the ocean. Therefore, about 90% of all marine life is found in this area. The ability of the chemosynthetic organisms to produce carbohydrates is an important adaptation to living in extreme conditions. They are found near hydrothermal vents, which are fissures or gaps in the ocean floor. There is no light, so photosynthesis is not possible. It was originally thought that the only way in which energy could reach these lower parts of the ocean was when organisms died and

> **KEY WORDS**
>
> **autotroph (autotrophic):** an organism that can capture the energy in light or chemicals and use it to produce carbohydrates from simple molecules such as carbon dioxide
>
> **chemosynthesis (chemosynthetic):** the production of organic compounds by bacteria or other living organisms using the energy derived from reactions with inorganic chemicals

3 Interactions in marine ecosystems

their remains fell to the bottom. This view was not challenged until the vent communities were discovered in the 1970s.

Other organisms known as consumers have to obtain their energy by feeding on the autotrophs. These are also known as **heterotrophic** organisms. The **primary productivity** of an ecosystem relates to how much energy is fixed into carbohydrates (new organic matter). Estuaries, swamps and marshes are the most productive ecosystems per unit area. However, the most productive ecosystems overall are the oceans, because they cover such a high proportion of the Earth's surface.

Consumers can be put into different categories depending on how close they are to the producer in the **food chain**. Primary consumers feed directly on the producer, secondary consumers feed on the primary consumer, tertiary consumers feed on the secondary consumers, and quarternary consumers feed on the tertiary consumers. It is very rare to find more consumers than this due to the decrease in the available energy at each stage of the process.

There are different types of consumer depending on the food they eat. **Herbivores** are animals which feed only on plants and algae (producers). For example, parrotfish and angelfish graze on the algae on coral reefs. **Carnivores** are animals which feed only on other animals. Many of these animals are also **predators** which means that they catch and kill their **prey**. Seals are predators which feed on a range of organisms including squid, shrimp and fish. **Omnivores**, by contrast, eat both plants and animals. Many species of crab are omnivorous, feeding on algae, juvenile fish and small invertebrates. In marine ecosystems, zooplankton are important consumers and include copepods, foraminifera and krill. Non-parasitic copepods are small herbivores that feed on diatoms. Foraminifera are single-celled animals with calcium carbonate shells which are often omnivorous and feed on algae and copepods. Krill are shrimp-like omnivores that feed on other zooplankton species and phytoplankton. Krill are an important food source for birds, fish, seals and baleen whales.

All organisms will eventually die and the nutrients in their bodies will be broken down by **decomposers**. These are bacteria and fungi which are able to break down dead organic matter. The decomposers are, therefore, the last stage in any feeding relationship, returning nutrients to the environment where they can be absorbed by the producers.

> **KEY WORDS**
>
> **heterotroph (heterotrophic):** an organism that cannot make its own food and instead relies on consuming other organisms; all animals, fungi and protozoans are heterotrophic, as well as most bacteria
>
> **primary productivity:** the rate of production of new biomass through photosynthesis or chemosynthesis
>
> **food chain:** a way to describe the feeding relationships between organisms
>
> **herbivore:** an animal which feeds only on producers (plants or phytoplankton)
>
> **carnivore:** an animal which feeds on other animals
>
> **predator:** an animal which hunts, kills and eats other animals
>
> **prey:** an animal which is eaten by predators
>
> **omnivore:** an animals which feeds on other animals and on producers
>
> **decomposers:** bacteria and fungi which break down dead organic matter and release the nutrients back into the environment

Predation

One of the most important feeding relationships is that between a predator and its prey. A predator is an animal that catches, kills and eats another animal. Predators can be secondary, tertiary or quaternary consumers. Marine predators include sharks and carnivorous fish that eat zooplankton (planktivores) or fish (piscivores). Predators are often well adapted by being fast and agile. They may also have camouflage, large teeth, poison or the ability to hunt in packs.

Prey are the animals that are eaten by the predators. A well-adapted prey animal will often have camouflage, defensive spines, the ability to hide in safe places, or the ability to flee.

Predator–prey relationships may be an example of coevolution. Here, the predator and prey species have evolved together in response to changes in each other's morphology and physiology.

Predator–prey relationships are crucial for keeping a healthy balance of populations within the ecosystem.

For example, without starfish (Figure 3.4) there would be no natural predators to control the numbers of mussels, sea urchins and shellfish. If the populations of these organisms became too large, they would potentially be able to destroy a kelp forest. This would negatively affect the other species feeding on or living within the kelp.

Figure 3.4: Starfish eating mussels.

Food chains and food webs

These feeding relationships between organisms can be represented by food chains and **food webs**. A food chain is a linear relationship beginning with the producer and then moving through the primary consumers and predators. A food web shows all the different interrelated feeding relationships within one ecosystem. In both food chains and food webs, arrows represent the direction in which energy, **biomass** and nutrients are transferred. An example of a food web is shown in Figure 3.5.

> **KEY WORDS**
>
> **food web:** a way to show all the different feeding relationships in an ecosystem
>
> **biomass:** the mass of living material in an area; it can be measured as dry mass (without the water) or wet mass (with the water)

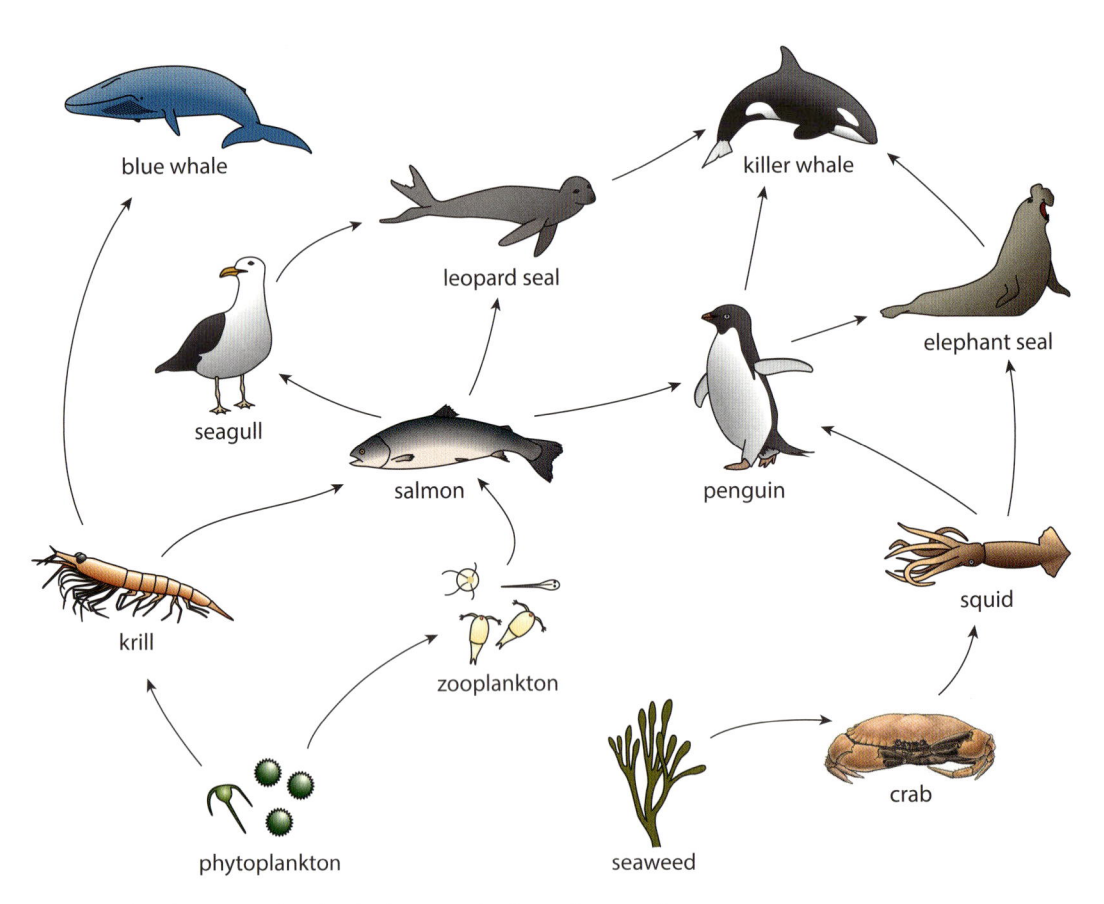

Figure 3.5: An example of a marine food web showing the flow of energy between organisms.

The 'feeding level' in a food chain is called the **trophic level**. The first trophic level is made up of the producers, the second trophic level is the primary consumers, the third trophic level is the secondary consumers and so on. Within a food chain each organism can only occupy one trophic level. However, in a food web, organisms may occupy more than one trophic level. This is particularly true of omnivores who may be feeding on producers (making them part of the second trophic level) and other consumers (third or fourth trophic level). Organisms which are feeding on more than one species are not dependent on only one food source. This means that, if the population of one prey species or producer declines, there will be an alternative source of food. This also means that the numbers of organisms of each species in a food web are interrelated.

In general, food chains can be summarised as:

producer → primary consumer → secondary consumer → tertiary consumer → quaternary consumer

or:

first trophic level → second trophic level → third trophic level → fourth trophic level → fifth trophic level

An example of a marine food chain is:

dinoflagellates → shrimp → tuna → marlin → shark

The organism at the end of the food chain (the shark in the above example) is known as a top carnivore or an **apex predator**. These organisms have no natural predators of their own.

Productivity

Primary productivity is the rate of production of new biomass (living material) per unit area by autotrophic organisms. This takes place through either photosynthesis or chemosynthesis. These processes allow light or chemical energy to be fixed into useable organic molecules, and as such are the basis of all food chains and food webs. The main way in which energy is fixed is through photosynthesis. On land, the majority of photosynthesis is carried out by green plants, but in the oceans it is mainly carried out by phytoplankton. Most of these tiny algae are single-celled and simply float with the current in water. As well as the phytoplankton, there are much larger algae (macroalgae), such as kelp and rooted plants called seagrass (Figure 3.6). These organisms are all **photoautotrophs**, meaning they are able to make their own food using light from the sun.

Photosynthesis

Photosynthesis is a process in which two inorganic compounds, carbon dioxide and water, are combined to produce glucose. Glucose is a useable organic compound. Oxygen is produced as a by-product.

$$\text{carbon dioxide} + \text{water} \xrightarrow[\text{chlorophyll}]{\text{light}} \text{glucose} + \text{oxygen}$$

KEY WORDS

trophic level: the position an organism occupies in the food chain or food web

apex predator: an organism at the end of the food chain which has no natural predators

photoautotroph: an organism which is able to use light energy to synthesise organic compounds

Figure 3.6: Important marine photoautotrophs: **(a)** phytoplankton; **(b)** kelp; **(c)** seagrass.

The energy to do this comes from sunlight and must be absorbed by pigments in the plants or algae. The most common pigment is chlorophyll, which is found in organelles called chloroplasts (Figure 3.7). To show that light and chlorophyll are both necessary, they can be written above and below the arrow in the equation. You can read more about the different pigments needed for photosynthesis in Chapter 7.

Factors affecting photosynthesis

The rate of photosynthesis can be affected by several different factors. These include:

- temperature
- concentration of carbon dioxide
- nutrients
- amount of light.

In a marine environment, the most important factors are likely to be the availability of nutrients and light.

- **Temperature and carbon dioxide**

In marine environments there is always an abundance of water, and the water contains dissolved carbon dioxide. Although the reactions of photosynthesis are affected by the temperature, the temperature of each area in the ocean is very stable and so has little effect on the rate of photosynthesis.

- **Nutrients**

Algae and plants both need nutrients in the form of mineral ions in order to grow. A lack of a particular nutrient, therefore, affects the rate of productivity of new biomass because it affects the rate of growth. Later in this chapter you can read about the roles of the major nutrients.

- **Light**

Photosynthesis can only take place within a relatively thin layer of the ocean which has enough light. This sunlit zone is called the **photic zone** and is the only layer where enough light penetrates for photosynthesis to take place (Figure 3.8). This means that the vast majority of the biomass in the open ocean is contained within the upper 200 m of water.

> **KEY WORD**
>
> **photic zone:** the surface layer of the ocean which receives sunlight

The sunlight is scattered and absorbed by the water. The amount of light reflected will depend on the state of the water. When there are waves, more light is reflected because the waves act like lenses and focus the light. When the light penetrates the surface of the water it is refracted because light travels more slowly in water than in the air. Finally, solid particles within the water also scatter and absorb the light.

The sunlight which is absorbed by the water also increases the temperature. When the temperature increases, the molecules of water have more kinetic energy and move more quickly, so the warm water is less dense and, therefore, more buoyant than cold

Figure 3.7: Single-celled alga with green chloroplasts visible.

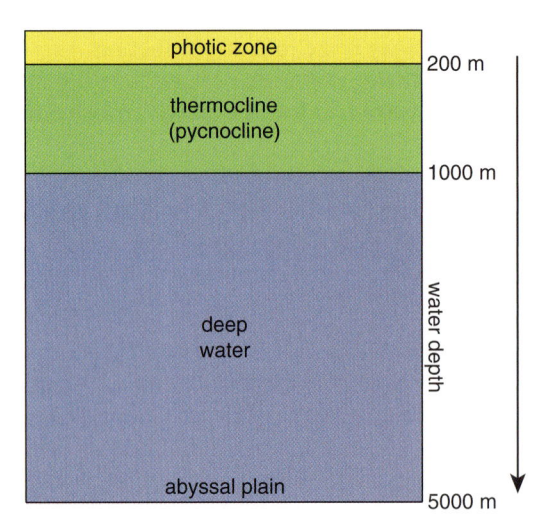

Figure 3.8: Layers of water in the ocean.

water. The thin layer of warm water floats on top of the colder deep water; the transition between the two is called the thermocline. It can also be referred to as a pycnocline, which is simply related to the different densities of the layers rather than the temperature. There is little mixing between the two layers because a source of energy (such as wind) is needed to push the warm water down. This is very important to the phytoplankton as it keeps them floating near the surface where they have access to light.

Without the thermocline, there would be much more mixing of the water and currents would carry the phytoplankton down and away from the light. This would reduce the rate of photosynthesis and, therefore, the productivity. However, the thermocline also prevents nutrient-rich water from mixing with the upper layers and, therefore, limits the productivity. Generally, the deeper the water, the higher the nutrient levels but the lower the light. There is normally a point near the thermocline where the productivity is highest as there is enough light for photosynthesis and enough nutrients for growth.

The light varies with the seasons, particularly at high latitudes. In spring, the average length of the day and the intensity of light both increase. This is clearly an advantage in terms of photosynthesis, and productivity is, therefore, higher in spring and summer than it is in winter. Often it is nutrient availability that limits the rate of photosynthesis in spring and summer, and light which limits it during autumn and winter.

Chemosynthesis

There are some ecosystems, such as those found around hydrothermal vents, where light is not available for productivity. Chemosynthesis is a process where carbon dioxide is turned into useable organic molecules using the energy stored in dissolved chemicals such as hydrogen sulfide. The chemicals dissolve in heated water in the undersea crust as it makes its way back to the surface to emerge from the vents. **Chemoautotrophs** are species of bacteria that are able to make their own food using chemical energy. Each species uses different chemicals as their energy source and produces different sugars.

Chemosynthetic bacteria were first discovered in hydrothermal vents in the ocean floor in 1977. The vents are found at depths varying from around 2000 m in the Galápagos Ridge to 7700 m in the Mid-Atlantic Ridge. At these depths there is no light, there are no phytoplankton and, therefore, there can be no photosynthesis. Chemosynthesis is the only way in which life is possible in such an inhospitable environment. The species able to survive here are all examples of **extremophiles**, which means that they are able to survive very harsh conditions. At these vents there is extremely high pressure, as well as water temperatures that can vary from 2 °C to 400 °C.

Up to 75% of animal species at hydrothermal vents depend on mutualistic relationships with chemosynthetic bacteria for at least some of their food. For example, mussels at these vents have mutualistic bacteria living in their gills but are also able to filter feed.

Similarities and differences between photosynthesis and chemosynthesis

Both photosynthesis and chemosynthesis use carbon dioxide and require an energy source to produce sugars. In photosynthesis, oxygen is produced as a by-product. In chemosynthesis, the by-products vary depending on the chemicals that are used, although sulfur is often produced. There is, therefore, only one possible equation for photosynthesis compared with several different equations for chemosynthesis. In both processes, the sugars produced are used to provide metabolic energy through **respiration**, or built up into the other chemicals needed by the organism which adds to the biomass.

Respiration

Respiration is the process by which all living things release the chemical energy stored in organic molecules such as carbohydrates. This energy is then used to carry out all the different metabolic reactions within

> **KEY WORDS**
>
> **chemoautotroph:** an organism which is able to use chemical energy to synthesise organic materials
>
> **extremophile:** an organism that is adapted to survive extreme temperature, pressure, salinity or pH
>
> **respiration:** the process by which all living things release energy from their food by oxidising glucose

the organism. Aerobic respiration requires a supply of oxygen and glucose and produces carbon dioxide and water.

$$\text{glucose} + \text{oxygen} \rightarrow \text{carbon dioxide} + \text{water}$$

As well as the useable energy the organism needs, respiration produces heat energy, which is transferred to the environment.

The link between photosynthesis and respiration

Primary productivity is the amount of new biomass made by the producers. But not all of this biomass is available for the consumers to eat. Some of the carbohydrate produced is not stored but is oxidised during respiration to provide energy. It is this net primary production which remains after respiration that is available to pass on to the consumers.

Secondary production (the rate of production of new biomass by consumers, using the energy gained by eating producers) is the amount of biomass produced by heterotrophs after eating the producers. Hence the more productive an ecosystem, the more energy is available to pass along the food chain. In the marine environment, there is no large-scale accumulation of biomass as there is in savannahs and forests on land. However, the reproductive rate of the phytoplankton is very high so there is a constant source of new organisms which photosynthesise. Carbon dioxide from the atmosphere dissolves in the water and is then available for photosynthesis. When it is fixed into glucose it is stored as phytoplankton biomass. Much of this 'locked up' carbon dioxide sinks to the floor of the ocean when organisms die. This process is discussed later in this chapter in Section 3.3.

Measuring productivity

Primary productivity can be estimated in several different ways including:

- using the rate of photosynthesis of producers
- using the rate of increase in the biomass of producers
- using satellite imagery to measure the amount of chlorophyll.

For example, the higher the rate of growth of producers, the higher the amount of chlorophyll present. Net primary production (NPP; the amount of energy that is left over after respiration to be made into new plant biomass) and gross primary production (GPP; the amount of light or chemical energy fixed by producers in a given length of time in a given area) are usually given as units of energy per unit area per unit of time (for example, $kJ\,m^{-2}\,year^{-1}$). However, the units used vary depending on the method of measurement chosen.

> **Note:** gross primary production and net primary production are extension content, and are not part of your syllabus.

Rate of photosynthesis

The rate of photosynthesis can be found by looking at the change in either the oxygen or carbon dioxide concentrations. If photosynthesis is taking place, there will be a decrease in the concentration of carbon dioxide and an increase in the concentration of oxygen.

Because the majority of marine producers are single-celled phytoplankton, they can be easily kept in a closed system such as a bottle. When the bottle is in the light, both photosynthesis and respiration will take place. When the bottle is in the dark, there will be no photosynthesis but respiration will continue. If we assume that the rate of respiration remains relatively constant, we can compare the readings of bottles kept in the dark and light to work out the rate of photosynthesis (Figure 3.9). The oxygen level needs to be taken using a dissolved oxygen sensor. There are three readings to take:

- an initial reading before the experiment begins
- the reading in the light bottle at the end of the experiment
- the reading in the dark bottle at the end of the experiment.

3 Interactions in marine ecosystems

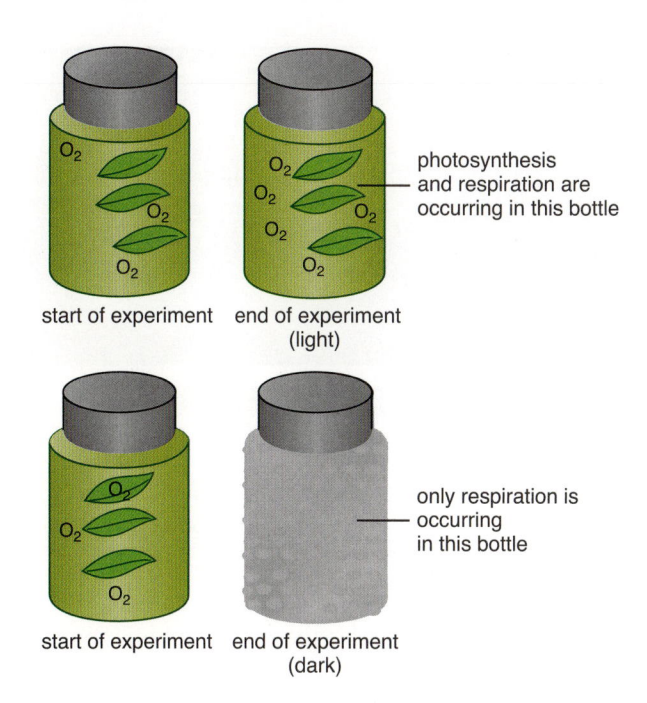

Figure 3.9: The light- and dark-bottle method for measuring productivity. The bottles on the left represent start of experiment and the bottles on the right represent end of experiment.

	Mass of oxygen / mg dm^{-3} h^{-1}	
	Start of experiment	End of experiment
Light bottle	8	19
Dark bottle	8	2

Table 3.2: A sample set of results from the light- and dark-bottle method.

The results would be tabulated as shown in Table 3.2.

In the dark bottle, the only process taking place is respiration, so the mass of oxygen in this bottle decreases. In the light bottle, the rate of photosynthesis is higher than the rate of respiration, so the mass of oxygen increases.

The difference in the mass of oxygen at the start and the mass in the light bottle at the end is net primary productivity. The difference between the oxygen at the start and the oxygen in the dark at the end is respiration. The gross primary production is the difference between the light and the dark bottles at the end of the experiment.

In this example:

NPP = $19 - 8 = 11$ mg O_2 dm^{-3} h^{-1}

Respiration = $8 - 2 = 6$ mg O_2 dm^{-3} h^{-1}

GPP = $19 - 2 = 17$ mg O_2 dm^{-3} h^{-1}

This technique can be extended to investigate the effect of light on productivity. Samples are removed from different depths in the water and placed into pairs of light and dark bottles. The bottles are then suspended at the same depth the samples were removed from. The calculations are carried out as described to work out the net primary production, gross primary production and respiration at each depth.

Generally, the productivity increases moving towards the region below the surface of water with the maximum concentration of chlorophyll, and then decreases as the amount of light begins to limit the rate of photosynthesis (Figure 3.10). At the point where the rates of respiration and photosynthesis are equal, there is no change in the amounts of carbon dioxide or oxygen, and the net productivity is zero. The light intensity at this depth is known as the **compensation point**. Immediately below this depth, there is still light available but producers are unable to survive because the rate of respiration would be greater than the rate of photosynthesis. This part of the photic zone is

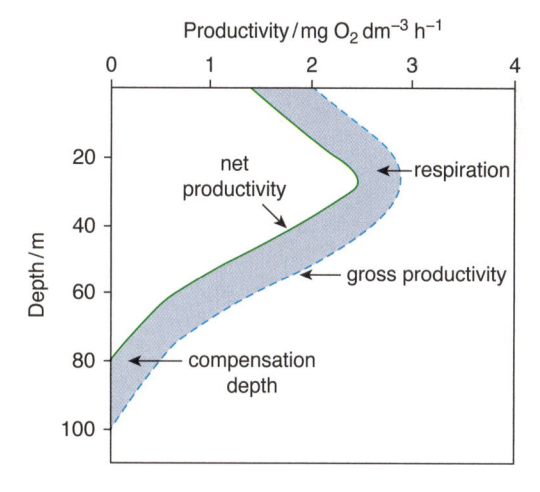

Figure 3.10: Productivity at different depths as measured by the light- and dark-bottle method.

KEY WORD

compensation point: the light intensity at which the rate of photosynthesis and the rate of respiration are equal

sometimes called the disphotic zone (the layer of water in the ocean where there is a low level of light which is not sufficient for photosynthesis; it is sometimes also referred to as the twilight zone) Around 90% of marine life is, therefore, found above the depth of the compensation point. This upper area, with sufficient light for photosynthesis is called the euphotic zone (the upper 80 m of the water where there is enough light for photosynthesis to take place).

> **Note:** disphotic zones and euphotic zones are extension content, and are not part of your syllabus.

Changes in biomass

Scientists can measure the rate of accumulation of biomass by harvesting producers after a set amount of time, drying them to remove variations in the water content, and then finding the mass. If they know the size of the area the producers came from, they can work out the biomass per unit area per year to give an estimate of the net primary production. As the producers would have been respiring while growing, scientists are unable to measure the gross primary production. There are difficulties with this method, however, as you cannot measure the biomass that has already been consumed by heterotrophic organisms. This may also be true for the light- and dark-bottle method if small heterotrophic organisms are not sieved out before the experiment begins.

Satellite imagery

Scientists can monitor the productivity of the oceans by using satellite imagery to measure the colour of the surface layers of water. This can be used to follow the changes in chlorophyll concentration and, therefore, the amount of producers present (Figure 3.11).

In Figure 3.11, the most productive areas are found in the tropics and at the higher latitudes, which are shown in green and orange. The least productive areas, shown in purple and blue, tend to be where there is a smaller supply of nutrients from the deeper waters, perhaps because of wind patterns. There are problems with this method of measurement, though, because the relationship between chlorophyll concentration and biomass is not fixed. It depends on the individual species present and their adaptations.

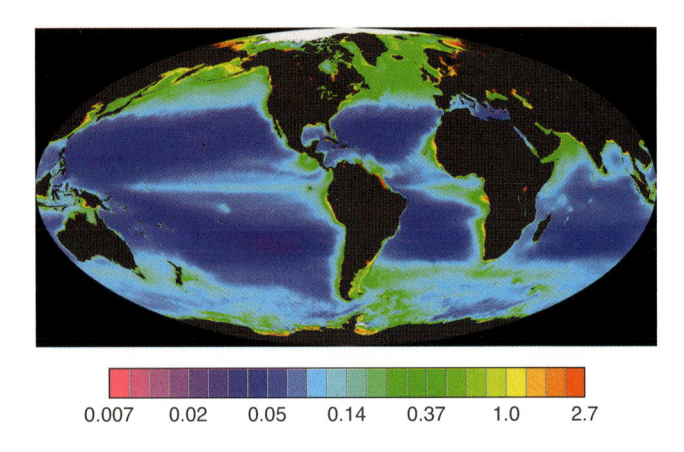

0.007   0.02   0.05   0.14   0.37   1.0   2.7

Figure 3.11: False-colour picture showing annual mean amount of chlorophyll *a* in the oceans (NASA *aqua modis*).

The satellites can only indicate relatively shallow depths and cannot penetrate the entire euphotic zone where production is taking place. However, the satellite images give a very useful summary of differences in productivity and enable scientists to monitor any changes. In 2016, researchers at Sheffield University discovered that water from melting giant icebergs in the Southern Ocean contains nutrients that increase the growth of the local phytoplankton (Figure 3.12). These giant icebergs can be more than 18 km in length. Scientists studied the satellite images and found that the increased productivity caused by these icebergs lasts for at least a month after they pass through an area and can extend for up to 600 miles.

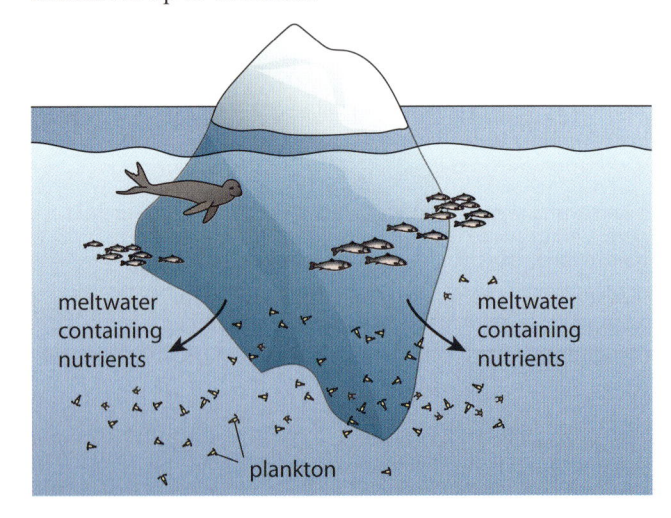

Figure 3.12: The meltwater from icebergs increases productivity.

The influence of changes in productivity on the food chain

The higher the productivity, the more biomass accumulated by the producers and, therefore, the more biomass available for the consumers to eat. This means that, in general, higher productivities lead to more abundant populations of consumers, and longer food chains. The most productive areas of the oceans tend to be those areas with high levels of nutrients from upwelling. In tropical areas, there are high levels of light but it is also warm, which leads to a strong thermocline and little mixing of nutrients from deeper waters. In contrast, polar waters are nutrient rich because it is very cold and there is only a weak thermocline. Polar waters can have long food chains as the productivity is high enough to maintain populations at several different trophic levels. It is not unusual to have five or even six trophic levels in these food chains. However, productivity is only high in the summer when the light levels are higher.

There does come a point when productivity can be too high. This leads to effects that are similar to the process of **eutrophication** seen in fresh-water ecosystems. If the levels of nutrients increase too much or too rapidly, phytoplankton may rapidly increase in a phenomenon known as an algal bloom.

> **KEY WORD**
>
> **eutrophication:** the process by which a body of water becomes enriched in dissolved nutrients (such as nitrates and phosphates) that stimulate the growth of producers, usually resulting in the depletion of dissolved oxygen

In these circumstances, up to five million cells per litre can be produced, which is damaging to the ecosystem. This density of algae is so high that it can clog the gills of fish so that they are unable to obtain enough oxygen. Once the algal cells die, they are broken down by bacterial decomposers so there is also an increase in bacterial populations. The bacteria respire and grow and use up the oxygen in the water, which can lead to hypoxic conditions (lacking oxygen). This also kills heterotrophic organisms because without oxygen they cannot respire.

If the algal species involved also produce toxins, the effects can be even worse because the organisms that ingest them will be poisoned. This can cause mass mortality in aquatic organisms such as dolphins, manatees and whales, as well as food poisoning in people who eat contaminated shellfish.

Energy transfer through the food chain

Only a small amount of the radiation from the Sun is fixed by the Earth's producers. Some of the radiation never reaches the producers because it is reflected back into space. Of the light that does reach the ocean, some is absorbed, reflected or scattered by the water. The remainder is available to the producers – but even then it cannot all be used. Some light is the wrong wavelength for the pigments of producers to absorb. Chlorophyll, for example, absorbs red and blue light but reflects green light (which is why it appears to be green). Of the light that is the correct wavelength, some will miss the chloroplasts and still not be absorbed (Figure 3.13).

Photosynthesis itself is not completely energy efficient. Energy is lost as heat during the various chemical reactions which take place during the process. It has been estimated that producers worldwide only fix about 0.06% of the total solar energy available. In aquatic ecosystems this figure can be as high as 1%.

Some of the glucose produced in photosynthesis is used in respiration. This means that only the net production of biomass is available to the next trophic level. The energy stored in biomass is passed to heterotrophic organisms when they ingest, digest and absorb the nutrients from the producers. These nutrients can then be assimilated into new biomass. If the producers are phytoplankton, then the entire cell is usually ingested by the primary consumers, passing on all the available energy. However, in the case of macroalgae and rooted plants such as seagrass, there are parts of the producer that are not eaten (the roots, for example). The energy stored in these parts is not available to the next trophic level, although it may later re-enter the ecosystem through decomposition when the plant dies.

Secondary production is the production of new biomass by the consumers. It can involve animals eating the phytoplankton, macroalgae and seagrass, or animals eating other animals. Decomposers such as bacteria and fungi break down dead organic matter to obtain the nutrients they need. This also releases nutrients back into the ecosystem.

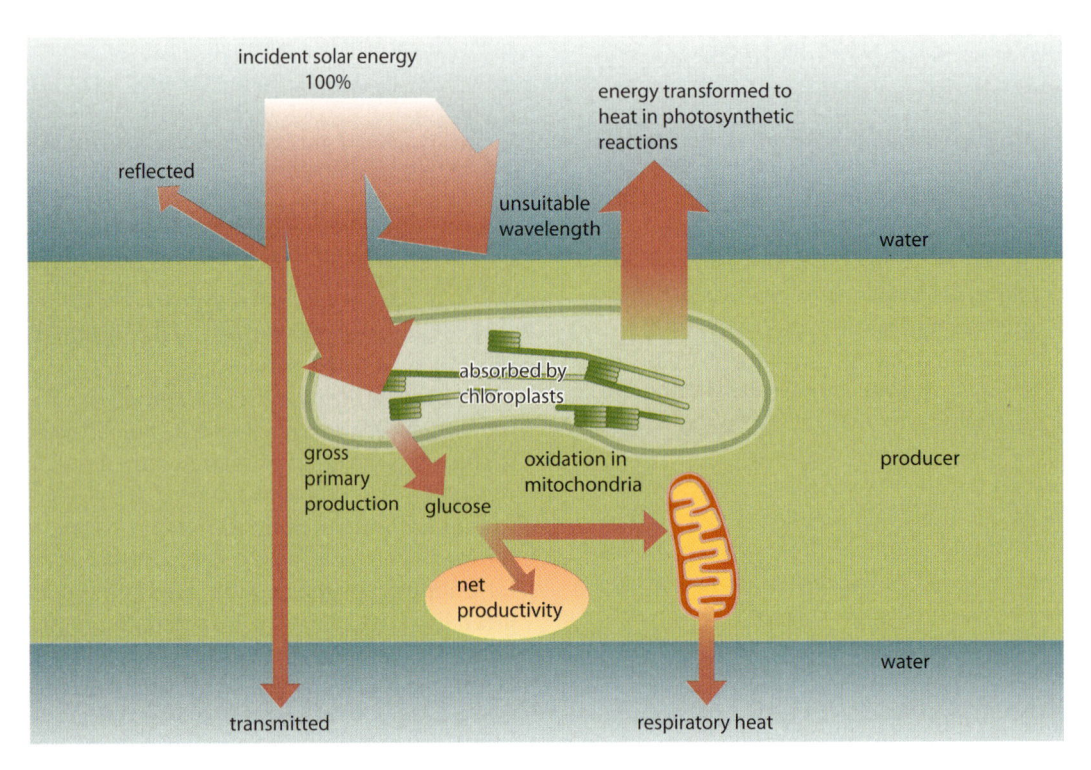

Figure 3.13: The fate of light energy falling on producers in the ocean.

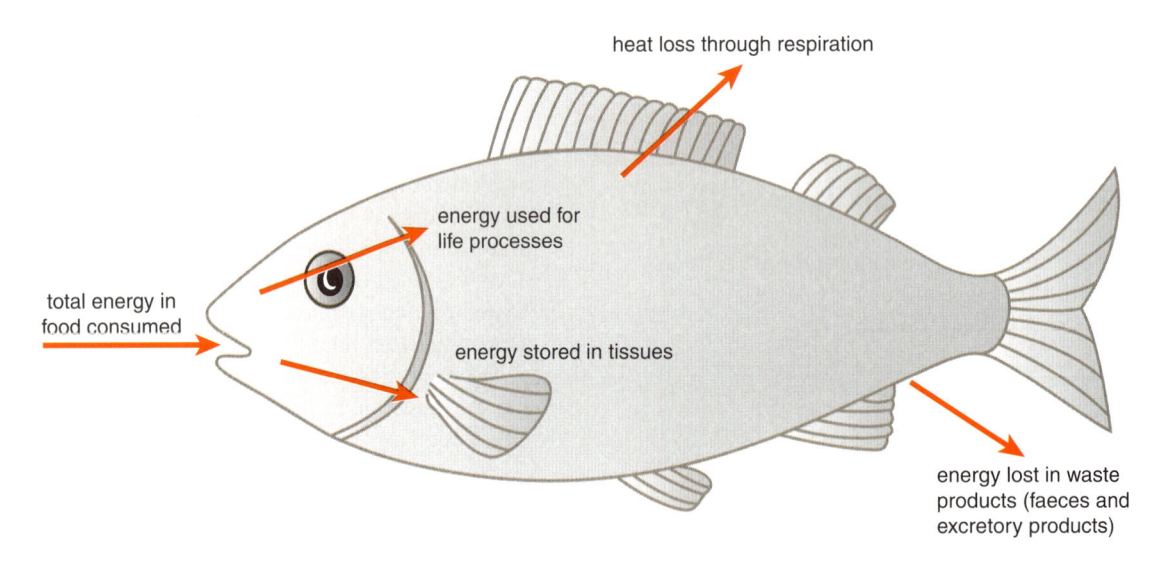

Figure 3.14: Energy transfer into and out of a consumer.

Secondary production depends on:

- the biomass available in the producers
- the amount of energy lost through respiration by the consumers
- the amount of energy lost in waste products such as urine (Figure 3.14).

Most saltwater fish only lose small amounts of urine and excrete most of their nitrogenous waste through their gills in the form of ammonia. Undigested food is egested as faeces.

These energy transfers can also be expressed as a formula:

$$C = P + R + F + U$$

Where C is the energy consumed, R is the energy used in respiration, F is the energy in faeces, U is the energy in urine and other excreted waste products of metabolism, and P is the energy left over for the production of new biomass by the animal.

The energy of production (P) is then available to pass on to the next trophic level.

Typically, the efficiency of transfer between trophic levels is around 10%, but it varies depending on:

- how much of the food is eaten
- how easy it is for the consumer to digest and assimilate the nutrients
- how much energy is used for movement
- how much is lost in the waste products of metabolism.

Some organisms are easier to digest and assimilate than others: generally, consumers find it easier to assimilate the energy in other animals than the energy in producers. If it is easier to assimilate the energy, then more of it will be passed to the next consumer. In addition, some organisms at each trophic level escape being eaten and the energy stored in their biomass will never pass to the next level.

Most fish are ectothermic (an organism that maintains its body temperature by exchanging heat with its surroundings, which means that their body temperature varies with the environmental temperature. The ocean sunfish, for example, is a secondary consumer that eats zooplankton, tiny animals present in the water that feed on the phytoplankton. The ocean sunfish is ectothermic and does not use energy in respiration to keep its body temperature higher than that of the surrounding water.

Tuna are endothermic (an organism that maintains its body temperature by generating heat in metabolic processes), which means that they must expend energy maintaining their body temperature. Tuna occupy two trophic levels in the same food web, Processes that add nutrients to surface layer as secondary consumers eating zooplankton, and as tertiary consumers eating small crustaceans that have already fed on the zooplankton.

> **Note:** ectothermic and endothermic are extension content, and are not part of your syllabus.

Small sharks feed on both the sunfish and the tuna but the efficiency of energy transfer is higher from the sunfish. Assuming that the sunfish and tuna take in similar amounts of energy, the tuna use more of this in respiration to keep warm so there is less to pass to the sharks. In general, the efficiency of transfer from ectothermic organisms ranges from 5% to 15%, and the efficiency of transfer from endothermic organisms ranges from 1% to 5%. The efficiency of transfer between the different trophic levels determines how many levels there are in the ecosystem. The higher the efficiency of transfer, the more trophic levels the ecosystem can support.

Illustrating feeding relationships

We can show the relationships between the different trophic levels using pyramids of number, biomass and energy. These are made up of horizontal bars arranged in a pyramid shape to show a particular food chain. They can be drawn to scale or simply sketched to give an idea of the changes as energy is transferred along the food chain. Producers are always at the bottom, followed by primary consumers, secondary consumers and tertiary consumers. Although energy is transferred to decomposers once the producers and consumers die, it is not often shown on the pyramid.

Pyramids of number

A **pyramid of numbers** simply shows the number of organisms present in each trophic level at a particular moment in time. The size of each horizontal bar is proportional to the number of organisms. In theory, this should be quite simple but, in practice, it is actually rather difficult. It is often hard to estimate accurately the number of organisms present, and even once this has been achieved it can be difficult to show them to scale. For example, a typical oceanic food chain is:

Phytoplankton → zooplankton → Ocean sunfish → shark

> **KEY WORD**
>
> **pyramid of numbers:** a diagram that shows the number of organisms in each trophic level of a food chain

There could be millions of cells of phytoplankton and only one or two sharks. Finding a scale to show this is impossible. For this reason, many pyramids of numbers are sketched rather than drawn to scale (Figure 3.15). In addition, much of the phytoplankton is consumed very quickly after it is produced. Thus, if the numbers present in an ecosystem are counted after most have been eaten, the pyramid will be inverted (upside down) and it will look as though there are fewer phytoplankton than zooplankton. The number of organisms in an ecosystem will also vary depending on factors such as the time of year or the amount of fishing. This means that the pyramid can only show the numbers in each trophic level at a particular moment in time. Pyramids of number also do not take into account the size of organisms, which can lead to odd-looking pyramids. For example, if several small parasites feed on one large fish you will see an inverted pyramid.

Pyramids of biomass

Instead of finding the number of each organism, we could measure their total biomass. This overcomes the difficulties of having organisms of different sizes, such as the parasites in the last example. It does not, however, solve the issues caused by phytoplankton being eaten before they can be measured. It is possible that the biomass of organisms within an ecosystem could increase or decrease after measurements are taken which will make the pyramid inaccurate.

It is difficult to find the biomass of each trophic level accurately. Organisms vary in the amount of water they contain, and this water does not contribute to their biomass. For this reason, dry mass should be used, with the water removed by evaporation. To do this, the organisms must be killed, which is not feasible or desirable when measuring the biomass of the entire food chain. Instead, there are conversions available to change the mass of living material into dry mass. This still means that every individual must be found and weighed. Alternatively, the dry mass of a sample can be taken and then multiplied by the total number of organisms to give the total average dry mass. Both of these methods will give an estimate of the total biomass but neither of them will be completely accurate.

A **pyramid of biomass** may still be inverted as the total amount of biomass in phytoplankton at any one time is small because they are eaten very quickly. However, their reproductive rate is very high so they reproduce quickly enough to provide enough biomass to maintain the population of consumers. In other words, the amount of biomass is low but the rate of production of biomass is high. This snapshot view of the biomass at a particular moment in time is known as the standing crop (Figure 3.16).

> **KEY WORD**
>
> **pyramid of biomass:** a diagram that shows the biomass present in each trophic level of a food chain

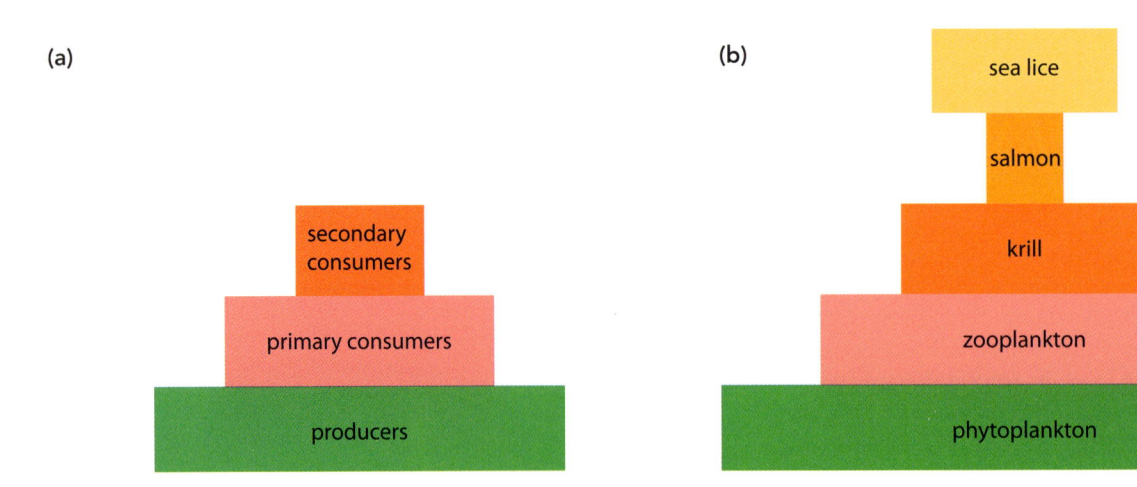

Figure 3.15: (a) A generalised pyramid of numbers; (b) A pyramid of numbers for a marine ecosystem showing small parasites feeding off a large fish.

3 Interactions in marine ecosystems

Figure 3.16: **(a)** Pyramid of biomass showing the decrease in biomass through the food chain; **(b)** Inverted pyramid of biomass showing the problems caused by the standing crop of rapidly reproducing phytoplankton.

Pyramids of energy

A **pyramid of energy** shows the rate of production of biomass rather than the standing crop, so is always pyramid shaped (Figure 3.17). It involves finding the energy in each trophic level of the food chain, which is a complex procedure. Data is collected over a long period of time, normally a year. Often conversion tables are used that will convert dry biomass into energy production. The units for pyramids of energy are $kJ\,m^{-2}\,year^{-1}$ so it will not be a standing crop but a measurement of the energy available over the entire year. Although pyramids of energy are the most difficult to produce, they are probably the most useful in terms of understanding the ecosystem.

> **KEY WORD**
>
> **pyramid of energy:** a diagram that shows the amount of energy in each trophic level of a food chain

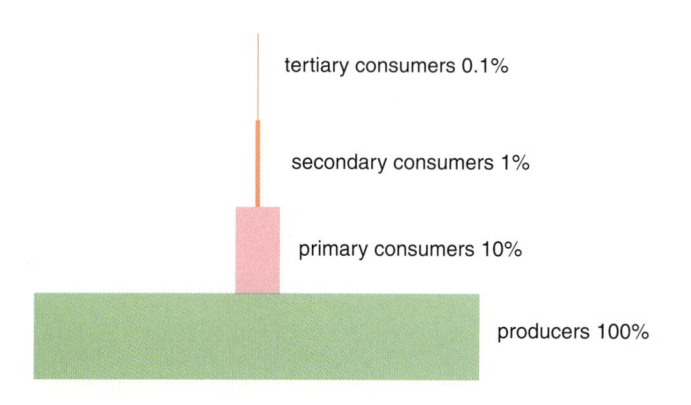

Figure 3.17: A generalised pyramid of energy showing the approximate transfer between tropic levels.

Pyramids of number, biomass and energy during an algal bloom

During an algal bloom we would expect the numbers, biomass and energy of phytoplankton to increase, followed by the numbers, biomass and energy of zooplankton and other consumers, as there is more energy to pass along the food chain. Once animals start to die due to the hypoxic conditions, the numbers and biomass will decrease again. As this takes place, there will be less energy to pass down the food chain so the energy in each trophic level will also decrease. However, often the phytoplankton which grow most during a bloom are inedible species of cyanobacteria. The proportion of edible cells in the phytoplankton decreases. This means that the figures for zooplankton do not increase as much as expected. In this situation, the bar for phytoplankton would be bigger than normal in all three types of pyramid. The bar for zooplankton would be smaller than expected, as with less energy and biomass passing along the food chain there will also be fewer zooplankton.

Test yourself

4 State the **two** ways in which new biomass is produced in the ocean.

5 Explain why ocean productivity is limited to the first 200 m in depth.

6 Explain why organisms need to respire.

7 Explain why is it best to use dry mass to produce pyramids of biomass

8 Describe what an inverted pyramid is and explain what might cause it.

CORE PRACTICAL ACTIVITY 3.1: INVESTIGATE THE EFFECT OF LIGHT INTENSITY ON THE RATE OF PHOTOSYNTHESIS

In this practical you will investigate the effect of light intensity on the rate of photosynthesis by using an aquatic plant such as *Elodea* or *Cabomba*. Aquatic plants like this have a special kind of spongy tissue in their stems called aerenchyma which enables them to transport the oxygen produced during photosynthesis around the plant. This means even those parts of the plant which cannot photosynthesise (such as the roots) will be supplied with oxygen for respiration. This is important as there is less oxygen dissolved in the water than there is in the air and so the roots would be at risk from the lack of oxygen available for respiration.

Light is an important limiting factor for photosynthesis and is only available in the photic layer of the ocean. This investigation will enable you to investigate how the rate of photosynthesis is affected by the light intensity by counting the bubbles of oxygen which are released from the aerenchyma. The faster the rate of photosynthesis, the more oxygen will be produced and the more bubbles you will be able to count.

Equipment:

You will need:
- a cut stem of an aquatic pondweed, about 5 cm long
- test tube
- large beaker
- lamp
- meter ruler
- timer
- thermometer
- enough sodium hydrogencarbonate solution to fill the test tube.

Safety considerations

Sodium hydrogencarbonate is not hazardous.

It is possible, but unlikely, that an infection could be picked up when handling pondweed and pondwater so follow normal hygiene procedures, cover cuts and wash hands afterwards.

Before you start

1. Name the independent and dependent variables in this practical.
2. Explain why the sodium hydrogencarbonate is added to the pondweed.
3. Why do you think we have the pondweed tube in a beaker of water with a thermometer?
4. Predict the pattern of results as the lamp is moved further away from the pondweed.

Method

1. Switch all the lights off in the room.
2. Place the pondweed in the test tube with the cut end at the top.
3. Fill the test tube with sodium hydrogencarbonate solution, making sure it completely covers the pondweed.
4. Fill the beaker with warm water. Measure and record the water's temperature.
5. Place the test tube of pondweed into the beaker.
6. Position the lamp close to the beaker and measure the distance from the beaker to the lamp.
7. Allow two minutes for the pondweed to adjust to the light intensity.
8. Count the number of bubbles released over a one-minute period.
9. Wait another minute.
10. Count the bubbles for a second one-minute period.
11. If your two values are very different, repeat for a third time and then ignore the anomaly when calculating the mean.
12. Move the lamp 20 cm further away and repeat all the steps.
13. Continue at further intervals of 20 cm up to 100 cm.
14. At each stage, measure the temperature of the water in the beaker and add hot or cold water to try to keep it constant.

CONTINUED

Results

Record your results in a results table as shown below (Table 3.3).

Calculate the mean average number of bubbles released at each distance.

distance from lamp / cm	temperature / °C	number of bubbles released in one minute			
		1	2	3 (if required)	mean

Table 3.3: The effect of light intensity on photosynthesis.

You may wish to convert the distances to approximate light intensities. This can be done using the formula:

$$\text{light intensity} = \frac{1}{\text{distance}^2}$$

You should now plot a graph with the independent variable (light intensity or distance) on the x-axis, and the dependent variable (average number of bubbles per minute) on the y-axis. Join the points with straight lines.

Evaluation and conclusions

1. Describe the shape and pattern of your graph.
2. If there are any anomalous results, circle them on the graph.
3. State the gas we assume is inside the bubbles.
4. Suggest how you could test your answer to question 3.
5. Explain the pattern of your graph.
6. The bubbles may not have all been the same size. Explain what effect this could have on the reliability of the results.
7. Suggest how you could improve the experiment so that different sized bubbles do not affect the results.

REFLECTION

After completing Core Practical Activity 3.1, think about these questions:

1. Discuss any difficulties you had with this experiment and how you could avoid them in the future. If there were no difficulties then discuss what else you could investigate using the same apparatus.
2. Describe how this practical has increased your understanding of photosynthesis in the ocean. If it has not altered your understanding then describe what else you still need to find out to help with this.

3.3 Nutrient cycles

Nutrient cycles show the essential movement and recycling of the elements that are necessary for organisms to live and grow. The carbon and nitrogen cycles are probably the best known and most clearly understood, but there are many other elements that are important. These include phosphorus, calcium and magnesium. Each of these elements is required for a different biological role within living organisms. Nitrogen is used to make amino acids, proteins and DNA. Carbon is found in all organic compounds. Magnesium is used to make chlorophyll and is essential for photosynthesis. Calcium is used to make bones, shells and coral skeletons. Phosphorus is used to make bones and DNA.

All nutrient cycles have a biotic and an abiotic phase (Figure 3.18). A **nutrient** moves from the abiotic to the biotic phase when it is absorbed and **assimilated** by producers. A nutrient is a substance which is needed for growth, repair, energy or the normal metabolism of an organism.

The biotic phase

In the carbon cycle, carbon dioxide (an inorganic molecule that is part of the abiotic cycle) is fixed during photosynthesis into glucose. This can later be converted into the other molecules needed by the producer (for example, starch). It has been assimilated and is now part of the biotic cycle. During the biotic phase, nutrients are moved from one organism to the next by feeding. So nutrients move along the food chain from the producers to the consumers. Some will be lost from each organism by egestion and excretion and the rest will remain within organic compounds until the organism dies. In this biotic part of the cycle, nutrients will be found as organic compounds such as carbohydrates, lipids and proteins.

> **KEY WORDS**
>
> **nutrient cycles:** the movement and exchange of elements that are essential to life, from inorganic molecules, through fixation and then into living organisms, before being decomposed back into inorganic molecules
>
> **nutrient:** a chemical that provides what is needed for organisms to grow, repair damaged cells or tissues, release energy or for their metabolism
>
> **assimilation:** the conversion of a nutrient into a useable form that can be incorporated into the tissues of an organism
>
> **primary producers:** organisms that produce biomass from inorganic compound; in almost all cases these are photosynthetically active organisms

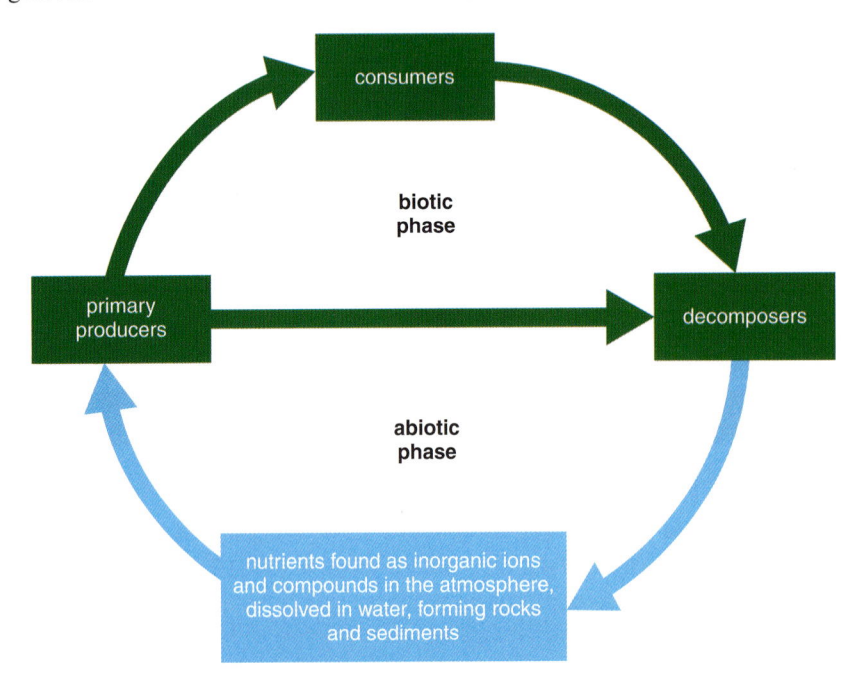

Figure 3.18: A generalised nutrient cycle showing the movement from the biotic to the abiotic phases.

3 Interactions in marine ecosystems

Carbohydrates, lipids and proteins

Carbohydrates, lipids and proteins are three very important **polymers** in living organisms. A polymer is a large molecule made from many repeating smaller sub-units called **monomers**. The monomers are joined together during condensation (a reaction where two molecules bond to form a larger molecule with water being released as a by-product) reactions where a molecule of water is removed in order to form the chemical bonds between them. They can be broken down again by hydrolysis reactions where a molecule of water is added to break each chemical bond.

> **Note:** hydrolysis and condensation are extension content, and are not part of your syllabus.

Carbohydrates

Carbohydrates are molecules made from carbon, hydrogen and oxygen. They are the most abundant biological molecules on Earth and are used for energy and to provide structure.

An example of a carbohydrate used for energy is **starch**, which is the energy storage molecule in plant and algal cells. Starch is made from many glucose molecules joined together into long chains by glucosidic bonds. Starch is a mixture of two types of chains formed from these glucose molecules.

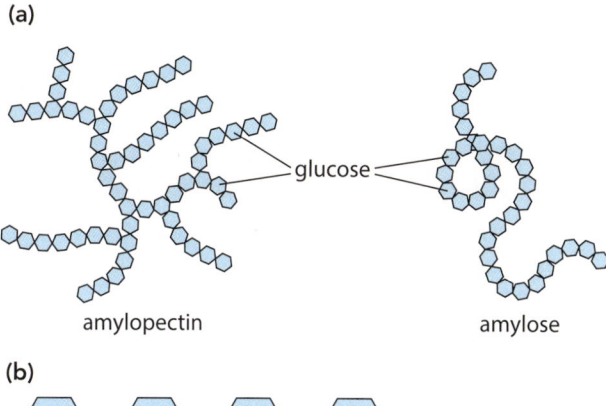

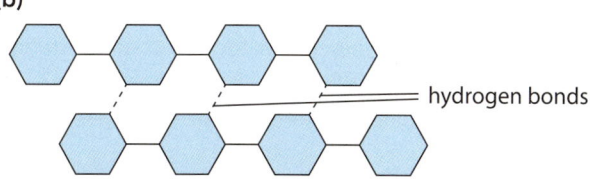

> **Note:** amylose and amylopetin are extension content, and are not part of your syllabus.

Amylose (one of the components of starch which is made from chains of glucose molecules with no branches chains are unbranched and can coil up easily, which makes them compact for storage. Amylopectin (one of the components of starch which is made from chains of glucose molecules with branches) chains do have branches which means that they have more 'end' molecules which can be easily broken off in hydrolysis to provide glucose for respiration (Figure 3.19a). Starch is a suitable molecule for storage because it is insoluble. It will not affect the water potential of the cell so will not cause water to move in or out of cells by osmosis.

An example of a carbohydrate used for structure is **cellulose** which forms the basis of cell walls in plant and green algal cells. Like starch, cellulose is made from chains of glucose molecules. However, the chains in cellulose are very long and have no branches. Many chains lie alongside each other to form microfibrils, rather like the way a rope is formed from many thinner strands of thread. The individual cellulose molecules are joined together by hydrogen bonds. Many microfibrils join together to form fibrils and the fibrils in turn join together to form cellulose fibres. This makes the cellulose molecule extremely strong and enables plants to remain upright despite their lack of a skeletal structure (Figure 3.19b).

> **KEY WORDS**
>
> **polymer:** a large molecule made from many repeating sub-units
>
> **monomer:** the smallest unit of a polymer; monomers are able to join chemically to form longer molecules
>
> **starch:** a carbohydrate made from chains of glucose molecules joined together
>
> **cellulose:** an important component of plant cell walls which is made from many straight chains of glucose molecules held together by hydrogen bonds

Figure 3.19: **(a)** Starch is formed from chains of glucose molecules, amylopectin has branched chains and amylose chains are unbranched; **(b)** Cellulose is formed from many long branches of glucose with hydrogen bonds between them.

Lipids

Lipids are made from carbon, hydrogen and oxygen. Some types of lipid also contain phosphorus and nitrogen. One of the most common classes of lipid is fats or triglycerides which are used for energy storage, insulation and protection. Other lipids include phospholipids which are the main component of membranes in living cells and steroids which form the basis of many hormones.

Triglycerides are formed entirely from carbon, hydrogen and oxygen. They are made from three long **fatty acid** molecules joined to a glycerol molecule by ester bonds (Figure 3.20). The ester bonds are formed by a condensation reaction and can be broken down by a hydrolysis reaction. The long fatty acid chains are **hydrophobic** which makes lipids insoluble in water.

> Note: phospholipids is extension content, and is not part of your syllabus.

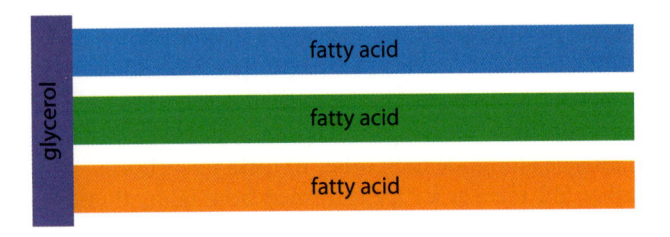

Figure 3.20: Triglyceride formed from three fatty acid chains and glycerol.

Proteins

Proteins are polymers formed from amino acids. Proteins contain carbon, hydrogen, oxygen, nitrogen and sulfur. There are 20 amino acids which form proteins. The amino acids can be joined together in different orders to form all the different proteins needed in living organisms. The order of amino acids in a protein is determined by the DNA which is found in the nucleus of the cell. Thus our genetic code is really a code to build proteins. Proteins are important in all living cells, forming, among other things:

- enzymes, which speed up chemical reactions
- hormones, which are chemical messengers
- part of bones, muscles, skin, cartilage and blood in animals
- part of the cell wall in plants.

The amino acids in proteins are joined together by peptide bonds which are once again formed in a condensation reaction (Figure 3.21). Each chain of amino acids can be folded in a specific way to achieve all the different types and shapes of protein needed by living organisms.

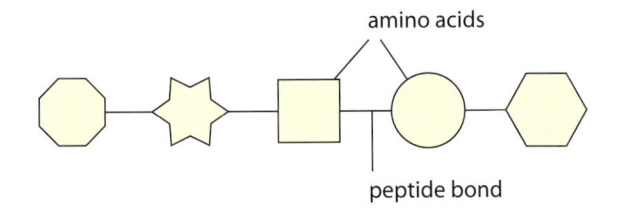

Figure 3.21: A short length of a protein formed from amino acids.

The abiotic phase

After death, organisms must be broken down by decomposers, which results in nutrients returning to their inorganic form and the abiotic part of the cycle. During this part of the cycle, nutrients can be found in several different forms:

- as ions dissolved in water (for example, Mg^{2+}, CO_3^{2-}, PO_4^{3-} and NO_3^-)
- as gases in the atmosphere (for example, CO_2)
- forming sediment that can later become rocks.

KEY WORDS

triglyceride: a type of lipid which is made from a glycerol molecule joined to three fatty acid chains

fatty acid: lipid molecules that are a major constituent of triglycerides and phospholipids

hydrophobic: a molecule without a charge which repels water molecules

3 Interactions in marine ecosystems

Reservoirs in nutrient cycles

A reservoir is part of the abiotic phase of the nutrient cycle where soluble nutrients can remain for long periods of time. The ocean is an important reservoir for many elements. The **residence time** is the average time a particle spends in a system. Average residence times for nutrient ions in the ocean tend to be very long because some of them fall to the bottom in faeces or dead organisms. They can remain in sediment on the ocean floor for thousands or even millions of years (Table 3.4).

Nutrient	Average residence time / years
phosphate (phosphorus)*	20 000–100 000
magnesium	17 000 000
hydrogencarbonate** (carbon)*	100 000
nitrogen	2000
calcium	1 000 000

*Where the nutrient is found as an ion, the element is given in parentheses

**Sometimes called bicarbonate

Table 3.4: Approximate residence times for different nutrients in the ocean.

The time the same nutrients spend in just the surface layer of the ocean is much shorter because they are constantly being used and recycled by the organisms living there. This surface reservoir is of particular importance because it enables the high productivity of phytoplankton. After light intensity, nutrient availability is often the main limiting factor for growth of producers.

Phytoplankton are found in the surface layer of the ocean where there is plenty of light. It is the concentration of nutrients that determines the rate of growth. The higher the rate of growth of phytoplankton, the higher the rate of photosynthesis and the higher the productivity. As discussed earlier, the productivity of the phytoplankton determines how much energy can be transferred to the next trophic level. In general, the amounts of nitrogen and phosphorus limit the rate of growth because they are found in the lowest concentrations in the water. This means that there is usually slightly less than is needed by the producers. If the concentrations increase, the productivity increases. The average concentrations of ions dissolved in the water at the ocean surface are shown in Table 3.5.

Ion	Average concentration in seawater / ppm
chloride	19 345.00
sodium	10 752.00
sulfate	2701.00
magnesium	1295.00
calcium	416.00
hydrogencarbonate	145.00
nitrate	0.50
phosphate	0.07

Table 3.5: Average concentrations of some of the ions found dissolved in seawater.

Processes that replenish nutrient reservoirs

There are five main processes that add nutrients to replenish the reservoir within the surface layer. These are:

- dissolving in the water from the atmosphere
- **excretion** and decomposition
- upwelling
- run-off
- tectonic activity.

The relative importance of these processes depends on each nutrient. For nutrients present in high concentrations in the atmosphere, dissolving will add more to the reservoir than run-off, for example.

Dissolving of atmospheric gases

Nitrogen and carbon are both present in the Earth's atmosphere and are therefore both able to dissolve directly into the water. Nitrogen is present in the form of nitrogen gas, N_2, and carbon as carbon dioxide gas, CO_2. The amount of gas that can dissolve in the water depends on several factors.

> **KEY WORD**
>
> **residence time:** the average time that a particle spends in a particular system
>
> **excretion:** the process of eliminating the waste formed from the chemical reactions within living cells

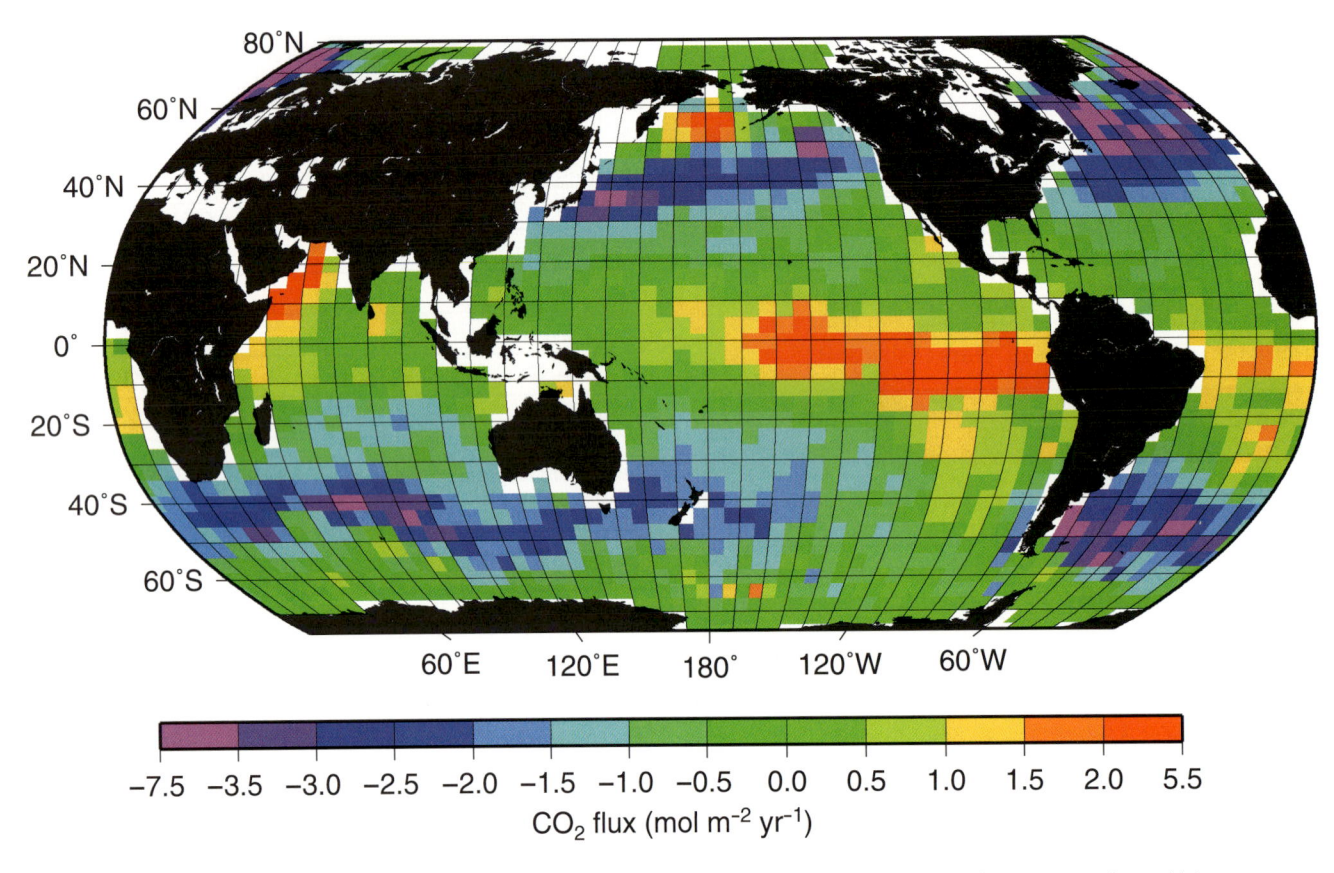

Figure 3.22: Movement (flux) of carbon dioxide into and out of the ocean over the course of a year. Purple and blue areas are carbon sinks; yellow and red areas are carbon sources; green areas are at an equilibrium, with the same amount of carbon dioxide dissolving as being released.

These include:
- the temperature of the water
- the atmospheric concentration of each gas
- the amount of mixing of water at the surface.

In some areas, there will be more gas dissolving in the water than there is diffusing back into the atmosphere. These areas are known as **sinks**.

In other areas, more gas will diffuse into the atmosphere than is dissolving into the water. These areas are called **sources**.

> **KEY WORDS**
>
> **sink:** an area where there is a net loss of material (for example, where more gas dissolves into the ocean than diffuses into the atmosphere)
>
> **source:** an area where there is a net gain of material (for example, where more gas diffuses into the atmosphere than dissolves in the ocean)

Generally, the overall concentration remains at an equilibrium, with the same amount dissolving into the ocean as is removed by diffusion back into the atmosphere (Figure 3.22).

Excretion and decomposition

Excretion is the removal of the waste produced by the chemical reactions which take place within living things. For example, the carbon dioxide produced during respiration is excreted from the lungs of mammals and the gills of fish. Nitrogenous waste is excreted by most marine organisms either in the form of urea dissolved in urine (mammals) or ammonia (fish). In this way some of the nutrient ions contained within living organisms are returned to the water.

Dead organic matter and some excretory products need to be broken down by decomposers. These are fungi and bacteria which secrete enzymes to digest large organic molecules. The decomposers then absorb the products. For example, proteins are broken down into amino acids and complex carbohydrates are broken down into glucose. The glucose can then be used by the decomposers for respiration which will return carbon dioxide to the surface layer. Amino acids are converted to ammonia and nitrates by other species of bacteria and can then be used by phytoplankton for growth. Decomposition is also an important process in the deeper parts of the ocean and the nutrients formed here will be returned during the process of upwelling.

Upwelling

Upwelling is where cold water from the deep ocean is brought to the surface. These deep waters have higher concentrations of nutrients than those at the surface because of the tendency for the remains of living things to sink. So faecal matter and dead organisms sink from the surface layers to the deeper parts of the ocean. Here they may be broken down by decomposers and the nutrient ions returned to the water. During upwelling this nutrient-rich water rises to the surface where it effectively fertilises the surface layers and increases productivity. Areas with high levels of coastal upwelling tend to be the most productive and have high catches of commercially important fish. It has been estimated that 25% of fish are caught from just 5% of the ocean where there are high levels of upwelling.

Coastal upwelling is caused when winds blow parallel to the shore (Figure 3.23). This displaces the warm surface layer, which moves further offshore and has to be replaced by water from deeper in the ocean. If the wind is moving in the opposite direction and drives the water towards the coastline, it is also possible for downwelling to occur. This removes nutrients from the surface layers of the ocean.

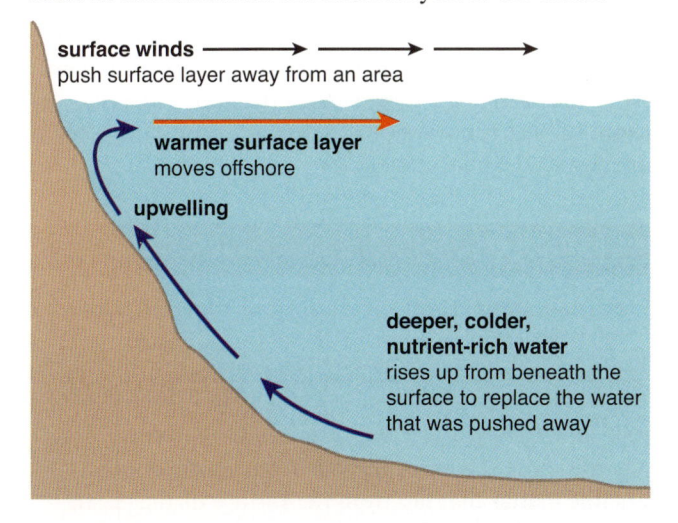

Figure 3.23: Coastal upwelling caused by surface winds.

Run-off

Run-off is part of the water cycle; water flows into streams and rivers and from there to the ocean. During the water cycle, water evaporates from rivers, lakes, oceans and streams. It condenses into clouds in the atmosphere and from there falls on the land as precipitation (Figure 3.24). Some of the precipitation enters the soil in a process called infiltration (part of the water cycle where water soaks into the soil from ground level and moves underground). The rate of infiltration is affected by the characteristics of the soil. Sandy soil, which is formed from large particles with relatively large gaps between them, has a high infiltration rate, compared with clay soil, which has a low infiltration rate. The higher the infiltration rate, the lower the rate of surface run-off. In other words, the more impermeable the ground, the more surface run-off there is.

As the water flows towards the sea it leaches (a process during which water-soluble nutrients are removed from the soil and dissolve in water that is flowing to the sea (run-off)) nutrients from the soil. This means that water-soluble nutrient ions dissolve in the water. Run-off can also collect other substances as it flows, such as oil, heavy metals, pesticides and sewage. These all end up in the ocean. Excess nutrients in run-off can lead to marine dead zones and harmful algal blooms. Marine dead zones are discussed in the extended case study.

> **Note:** infiltration and leaching are extension content, and are not part of your syllabus.

Tectonic processes

Tectonic processes add nutrients to the water in two main ways. At hydrothermal vents nutrients dissolve in the water as it passes over a magma chamber. When the superheated water is released from the vent and meets the cold seawater, some of the mineral ions precipitate out and form the solid chimney. However, many minerals which are essential for life remain dissolved in the water where they are available to the organisms living near the vents. These are particularly important for the process of chemosynthesis which uses sulfides. Without this, there would be no life at this depth as there is no light. Some of the nutrients added in this way will eventually reach the surface layer through the process of upwelling.

Erosion and weathering are also important in adding nutrients to the reservoir in the ocean. Tectonic activity

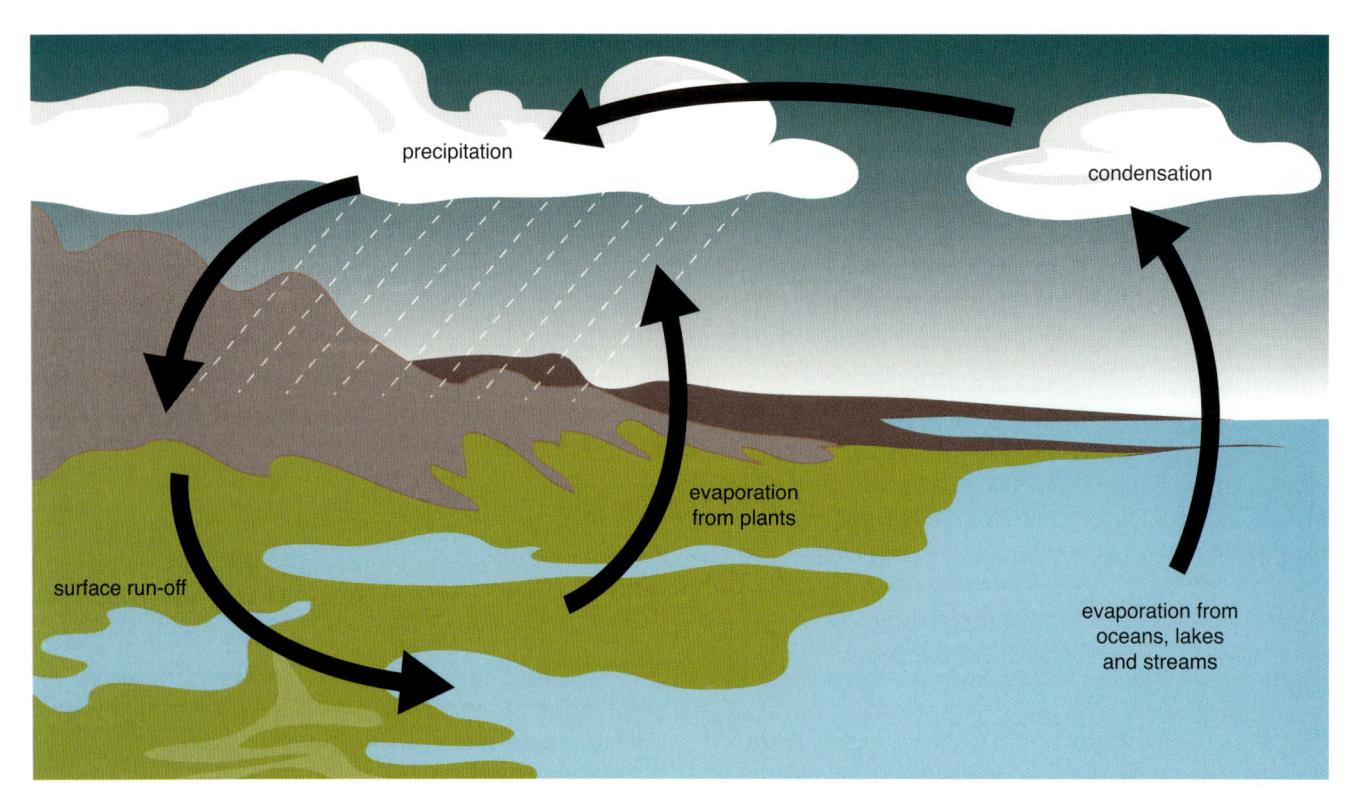

Figure 3.24: Summary of the water cycle.

such as the release of magma from volcanoes as well as the formation of mountains adds fresh rock to Earth's surface. At a convergent plate boundary between a continental and an oceanic plate, the more dense oceanic plate is subducted and pulled beneath the continental plate (see Chapter 2). In contrast, at convergent plate boundaries between two dense continental plates, a mountain can form. The Himalayas are a mountain range which formed in this way. The fresh rock added in these processes can then be eroded and weathered. Soluble nutrients will dissolve in rainwater and run-off into rivers and streams and from there into the ocean.

Ash from volcanic eruptions has also been shown to fertilise the ocean and lead to an increase in primary productivity. When the ash lands in the water, mineral ions such as phosphate, iron and magnesium dissolve and add to the reservoir.

Processes that remove nutrients from the surface layer

The main way in which nutrients are removed from the surface layer is through uptake and assimilation by producers. They fix the inorganic ions into useable organic compounds that consumers feed on. In this way, the nutrients are able to move through the food chain. For example, phytoplankton take up nitrate ions and use them to produce amino acids. These are then built up into proteins that form part of the phytoplankton structure. Zooplankton eat the phytoplankton and digest these proteins, using the amino acids released in digestion to produce their own proteins. Small fish then eat the zooplankton and the process continues. Once the nutrients have entered the food chain there are different paths they can take. Some sink to the floor as **marine snow**, some are incorporated into coral reefs, and some are removed by harvesting.

> ### KEY WORD
>
> **marine snow:** particles of organic material that fall from surface layers to the deeper ocean

Marine snow

Marine snow is the name given to the particles of organic matter that fall from the surface of the ocean to the deeper water. It is made up of faeces from the organisms living in the surface layers, as well as dead animals, phytoplankton and zooplankton. It is called marine snow because it looks like snow – small, white particles floating in the water (Figure 3.25).

Figure 3.25: Marine snow in the water.

This continuous fall of organic matter provides food for many organisms that live deeper in the ocean. Some of it is fed on by zooplankton and fish as it falls, some is eaten by filter feeders much deeper down. Much of it is not eaten at all and forms part of the sediment at the bottom of the ocean. Some of the nutrients in the sediment are released into the water by processes such as erosion and dissolving, others remain in the sediment for many years.

Harvesting

Harvesting refers to the removal of marine species by humans. According to the United Nation's most recent figures, the total capture of fish in 2016 was 90.9 million tonnes. Other animal species are also included in this figure despite not being fish. These include crustaceans, such as crabs and lobsters, and molluscs, such as mussels and squid. Macro-algae such as seaweeds can also be harvested both for use as foods and in industrial processes such as the manufacture of gels and fertilisers. All the nutrients present in these species are removed when they are harvested from the ocean. However, many of the nutrients eventually find their way back to the ocean through the normal cycling of nutrients. For example, fish may be eaten and digested by humans and some of the nitrogen-containing compounds are then lost in urine, which ends up in sewage. In many areas, sewage is released into rivers and oceans after only being partially treated. In some areas, raw sewage is released. In this way, the nitrogen-containing compounds present in the original fish return to the ocean.

The carbon cycle

Carbon is needed by living things because it is the basis of all organic materials. Carbohydrates such as glucose and starch, lipids, proteins, and nucleic acids such as DNA are all based on chains of carbon molecules. Carbon enters the biotic phase of the cycle through the fixation of carbon dioxide in photosynthesis. Carbon dioxide is then released through respiration by all living things.

The main way carbon enters the ocean is by dissolving of carbon dioxide gas from the atmosphere. Carbon dioxide dissolves in water to form **carbonic acid** (H_2CO_3). This then dissociates (a reversible chemical change where the molecules of a single compound separate into two or more other substances) into hydrogencarbonate ions (HCO_3^-) and hydrogen ions (H^+) in a reversible reaction. Hydrogencarbonate dissociates further into carbonate ions (CO_3^{2-}) and hydrogen ions (H^+). So, in solution, there is a dynamic equilibrium between carbon dioxide, hydrogencarbonate and carbonic acid. In seawater, 89% of the dissolved inorganic carbon is found as hydrogencarbonate, 10% is carbonate and 1% is dissolved carbon dioxide.

> **Note:** dissociation and Carbonic acid formation are extension content, and are not part of your syllabus.

KEY WORD

carbonic acid formation: a weak acid made of carbon dioxide dissolved in water

The reactions in this equilibrium are:

carbon dioxide + water ⇌ carbonic acid

$$CO_2 + H_2O \rightleftharpoons H_2CO_3$$

carbonic acid ⇌ hydrogencarbonate ion + hydrogen ion

$$H_2CO_3 \rightleftharpoons HCO_3^- + H^+$$

hydrogencarbonate ion ⇌ carbonate ion + hydrogen ion

$$HCO_3^- \rightleftharpoons CO_3^{2-} + H^+$$

The algae and photosynthetic bacteria that make up the phytoplankton are able to take in dissolved forms of carbon dioxide and use it in photosynthesis. It is fixed into glucose, which can then be used to form other compounds needed by the phytoplankton. When the phytoplankton are eaten by zooplankton, the carbon-containing compounds are broken down during digestion. The zooplankton then assimilate them into their own biomass. This process is repeated when the zooplankton are eaten by other consumers.

At each stage, the organisms are respiring so they release carbon dioxide back into the water. From here it can diffuse back into the atmosphere. When the organisms die, some of the organic matter is broken down by decomposers and returns to the water as dissolved inorganic carbon. Some of the organic matter falls to the ocean floor as marine snow, where it may remain for long periods of time.

The flux of carbon between the ocean and the atmosphere is around 90 gigatonnes per year. This mean that the same amount of carbon dioxide dissolves into the ocean as diffuses back into the atmosphere. However, there are also approximately 2 gigatonnes of carbon each year added to the ocean through human activities such as the combustion of fossil fuels. This makes the oceans a very important carbon sink in terms of reducing atmospheric carbon dioxide. But the risk is that the ocean will become more acidic because of the extra carbonic acid formed. It has been estimated that since the 18th century, the pH of the ocean has decreased by 30%. This can have negative effects on the ecosystem. For example, a low pH triggers chemical reactions that decrease the concentration of carbonate ions; this makes it more difficult for corals to produce their calcium carbonate skeleton. This can also affect other species with calcified shells, including oysters and clams. If the water becomes even more acidic, it can dissolve the coral skeletons and the shells of other organisms, making them weaker and more vulnerable to damage.

Some scientists have suggested that artificially fertilising the ocean with iron would increase the productivity of the phytoplankton and mean that more carbon dioxide could be absorbed. This has been put forward as a possible way to reduce the amount of carbon dioxide in the atmosphere. The theory is that, since iron is often a limiting factor for phytoplankton growth, adding more will cause increased growth rates and thus increased use of carbon dioxide. This process is known as ocean seeding or iron fertilisation. Trials have shown that ocean seeding does increase the growth of phytoplankton but there are risks to this procedure. If the productivity increases too much, a harmful algal bloom could take place. The long-term effects of altering the ecosystem in this way are not clearly understood. If more carbon dioxide is absorbed, the pH of the water could decrease further, causing harm to many different species.

Respiration and photosynthesis are part of the short-term carbon cycle. This cycle can take as little as a few days in the case of an algal bloom, or hundreds of years in the case of an oak forest.

However, there are also much longer term processes which affect the carbon cycle. The organic matter which falls to the bottom of the ocean as marine snow contains carbonate ions, for example, in corals and the shells of sea animals. As the sediment builds up, the layers at the bottom are compacted by the pressure of the layers above. Over long periods of time this can them form **sedimentary rocks**, such as limestone on the ocean floor. This process removes carbon from the carbon cycle. Eventually sedimentary rock from the ocean may end up being part of a landmass through a process called **marine uplift**. This can be a slow process through the gradual movement of tectonic plates or a much quicker process during an earthquake. Once the rock is exposed to the rain and waves it will be subjected to erosion and weathering. The carbon stored in the rocks will be released as carbon dioxide as part of the chemical weathering process. For example, when sulfur dioxide in the atmosphere dissolves in the rain it forms weak sulfuric acid. This reacts with the calcium carbonate in limestone rocks to form calcium sulfate, water and carbon dioxide which returns to the carbon cycle. The sediments in the oceanic crust can also be subjected to subduction at convergent plate boundaries as described in Chapter 2. In this case the carbon stored in the rocks can later be returned to the cycle through volcanic eruptions.

Another part of the long-term carbon cycle is the formation of **fossil fuels**. Coal is formed from dead plants whereas oil and gas are formed from the organic matter which falls to the bottom of the ocean and form a sediment. Sometimes the sediment is buried in mud, as the layer of mud gets thicker it is subjected to heat and pressure from the Earth's core. This changes the chemical structure and forms the fossil fuels. The process takes up to 650 million years and removes carbon from the cycle. The carbon is returned when the fossil fuels are burned. Combustion of course is much quicker than the formation of fossil fuels and so can lead to an imbalance in the carbon dioxide in the atmosphere. This is discussed in detail in Chapter 9. A summary of the carbon cycle is shown in Figure 3.26.

> **KEY WORDS**
>
> **sedimentary rock:** rock formed by the deposition of particles on the ocean floor
>
> **marine uplift:** a process by which the floor of the ocean rises, possibly to the extent that it is no longer beneath the water
>
> **fossil fuels:** buried organic materials from dead plants and animals which have been converted into oil, coal or natural gas by exposure to heat and pressure in the Earth's crust

3 Interactions in marine ecosystems

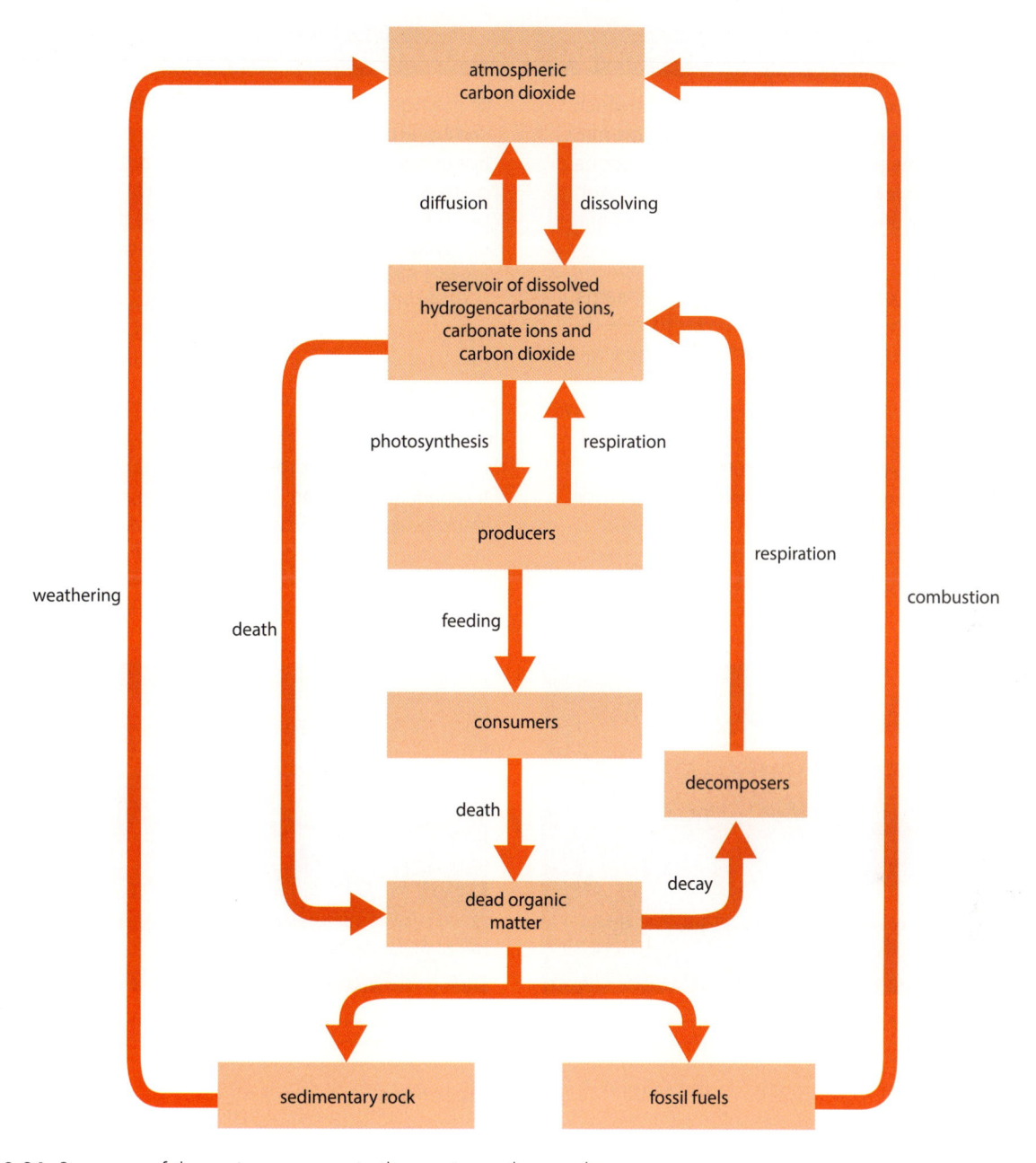

Figure 3.26: Summary of the main processes in the marine carbon cycle.

Test yourself

9 a Describe what is meant by the words *biotic* and *abiotic* with reference to nutrient cycles.

  b Explain how nutrients move from the abiotic to the biotic part of a nutrient cycle.

10 a Describe how nutrients move within the biotic part of the cycle.

  b Name **two** places where you would find nutrient ions within the abiotic part of a nutrient cycle.

11 Explain why harvesting is important in marine nutrient cycles and explain whether you think it is beneficial or harmful.

12 Draw simple diagrams to show the structure of a lipid, a named carbohydrate and a protein.

CASE STUDY 3.1: THE IMPORTANCE OF SALMON TO THE GROWTH OF TREES

Harvesting by humans is an important way in which nutrients are removed from the marine environment. However, nutrients are also removed by migrations of marine organisms such as salmon to fresh-water areas where they are eaten by predators like bears and eagles.

Each year salmon return to the fresh-water streams and lakes where they were born in order to breed (Figure 3.27). For successful reproduction, the streams need to be shaded by trees so that the water is not too warm. Warm water contains less oxygen, so fewer eggs are able to survive. The trees help to prevent soil erosion, stopping sediment from entering the streams and keeping the water clear for the salmon. Large populations of insects live in the trees and provide food for the young salmon once they hatch. The trees are, therefore, important for the survival of the salmon.

of the normal cycling of nutrients. From here they can be absorbed through the roots of the trees. For example, nitrates are often a limiting factor for plant growth. The fish provide up to 120 kg nitrogen per hectare of forest, which enables the trees to grow up to three times faster than they would without the added nitrates. In this way, a positive feedback loop is formed. The more salmon that are deposited, the better the trees grow, and the better the trees grow, the better the conditions in the stream for the spawning of salmon.

This has important implications for conservation of both salmon and forests, as each helps the other to survive. Since the 1990s there have been sharp declines in the numbers of Pacific salmon. In order to conserve the salmon populations, the forests must be protected. And in order to conserve the forests, there need to be enough salmon spawning each year.

Figure 3.27: Spawning Pacific salmon moving upstream.

Figure 3.28: An eagle catching a salmon.

It has become clear that not only do the salmon need the trees, but the trees need the salmon. As millions of salmon move through the waters of the Pacific Northwest coast of the USA, they provide huge amounts of food for bears and eagles (Figure 3.28). It has been estimated that each bear fishing in British Columbia, for example, can catch 700 salmon during the spawning period. Although the bears kill the salmon in the water, they move away from the water to eat. Roughly half of each salmon carcass is consumed by the bear, with the rest feeding scavenger species and insects.

The compounds from the decomposing salmon eventually find their way back into the soil as part

Questions

1. a Explain why the growth of trees is important for the survival of salmon.

   b Explain how the salmon increase the growth of the trees.

2. Suggest a type of organism, other than the trees, that would benefit from the nutrients within the salmon.

3. Imagine that you are working in conservation. Explain whether you would start by conserving the forests or the salmon and justify your answer.

3 Interactions in marine ecosystems

MATHS SKILLS 3.1

INTERPRETING ENERGY DIAGRAMS AND DRAWING PYRAMIDS OF ENERGY

Energy diagrams are another way of showing the flow of energy through an ecosystem (Figure 3.29). They show the energy entering the ecosystem from the Sun, moving through producers and being lost as a result of respiration and excretion. The main point to remember is that all the energy has to go somewhere, so the values on the arrows going into a box must always equal the sum of the values on those coming out. The units can be given as $kJ\,m^{-2}\,year^{-1}$ or simply arbitrary units. Arbitrary units are relative units of measurement to allow comparison. For example, if there is twice as much energy in producers as in primary consumers the arbitrary units could be 5 and 10 or 50 and 100, it does not matter.

Worked example

```
                    energy from
                      sunlight
                    1.6 × 10^6
                         │
                         ▼
      43137      ┌─────────────────┐     23009
    ◀───────────│  energy in       │───────────▶
                │  producers 72567 │
                └─────────────────┘
                         │ 6421
                         ▼
       Y        ┌─────────────────┐      2389
    ◀───────────│  energy in primary │───────────▶
                │    consumers    │
                └─────────────────┘
                         │ 598
                         ▼
       X        ┌─────────────────┐       67
    ◀───────────│  energy in secondary │───────────▶
                │    consumers    │
                └─────────────────┘
         ┌──────────┐                ┌──────────┐
         │respiration│                │decomposers│
         └──────────┘                └──────────┘
```

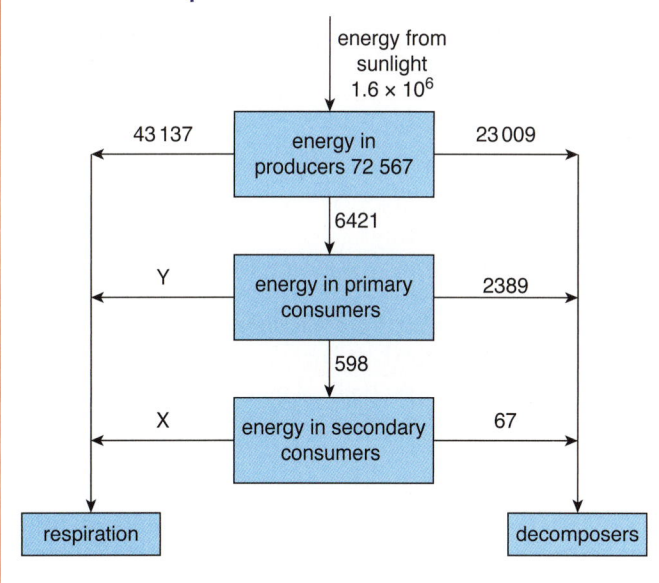

Figure 3.29: Worked example of an energy flow diagram (units are $kJ\,m^{-2}\,year^{-1}$).

1. How much energy is being lost in respiration by the secondary consumers shown in Figure 3.29?

   Remember that the energy entering the secondary consumers must equal the energy leaving.

   From the diagram, you can see that $598\,kJ\,m^{-2}\,year^{-1}$ enters the secondary consumers (the 'in arrow') and $67\,kJ\,m^{-2}\,year^{-1}$ ends up being passed to the decomposers.

   The only other arrow is the respiration arrow (labelled X).

   So, the energy lost in respiration, X, must be equal to $598 - 67 = 531\,kJ\,m^{-2}\,year^{-1}$.

   You can check your answer by making sure the arrows add up:

   The 'in arrow' is 598 and the 'out arrows' are 531 and 67.

   $531 + 67 = 598$, so the answer is correct.

2. What percentage of the energy from the sun is transferred to the producers?

   It is useful to calculate a percentage as it allows you to compare different ecosystems where the initial energy inputs might be different. The percentage is the energy which is transferred divided by the energy that was in the previous trophic level and then multiplied by 100.

   The energy transferred to the producers was $72\,567\,kJ\,m^{-2}\,year^{-1}$ and the energy in the previous trophic level (the Sun) was $1.6 \times 10^6\,kJ\,m^{-2}\,year^{-1}$.

   So, the percentage transferred is:

   $$\frac{72567}{1.6 \times 10^6} \times 100 = 4.54\%$$

   You may also be given similar information in the form of a pyramid of energy. In this case, just use the figures in the pyramid in your percentage calculation. Always divide the figure in any particular trophic level by the figure for the previous level and then multiply by 100.

   For example:

   $$\frac{\text{energy in primary consumers}}{\text{energy in producers}} \times 100$$

3. Draw a pyramid of energy which shows the energy in producers, primary and secondary consumers.

   You will not have to draw an energy flow diagram but you may have to draw a pyramid of energy. If you are asked to draw it to scale, consider each bar of the pyramid to be like the bar on a bar chart. In this case, the data will often be given in arbitrary units to make it easier to fit into one scale.

CONTINUED

If you are asked to sketch a pyramid of energy (or numbers or biomass) it does not have to be drawn to scale, the bars must simply be larger or smaller depending on the numbers you are given. The producers are always drawn as the lowest bar, followed by the primary consumers and then secondary consumers until you reach the top of the food chain. Label each bar with the name of the organism from the food chain you are drawing.

Questions

1. **a** Calculate the amount of energy used in respiration (Y) by the primary consumers in Figure 3.29.
   b Calculate the percentage of energy transferred between producers and primary consumers.

2. **a** Sketch a pyramid of energy for the following data: fish 86 arbitrary units, zooplankton 912 arbitrary units, phytoplankton 8000 arbitrary units.
   b Use the data from your pyramid to calculate the percentage of energy which is transferred from the zooplankton to the fish.
   c The average percentage of energy transferred between producers and primary consumers is 10%. Suggest why the transfer in this food chain between phytoplankton and zooplankton is higher than this.

PROJECT: MARINE RELATIONSHIPS CARTOON

Work in small groups to produce a cartoon which illustrates the relationship between two marine organisms. The type of relationship should be one studied in this chapter (for example, mutualism) but you must do research to find your own example. Your cartoon should show the type of relationship and how it affects both organisms, preferably in an interesting or creative way.

Thinking about your project

Each group should look at one other cartoon and think about the following questions:

- Does it explain what the relationship is?
- Would someone who has not studied this chapter understand what was happening?
- Is it obvious which organism benefits or is harmed and why?
- Is it interesting to look at?

Give the other group a mark out of five for each category and total their final mark out of 20. Write down one thing you really liked about it and one piece of advice for making it even better.

EXAM-STYLE QUESTIONS

1. **a** **i** Describe what is meant by the term *productivity*. [3]
      ii **Give** three factors that can affect productivity. [3]
   b **i** Explain the difference between *gross primary production* and *net primary production*. [3]
      ii The gross primary production in an ecosystem is $78\,935\,kJ\,m^{-2}\,year^{-1}$ and the energy lost in respiration is $23\,674\,kJ\,m^{-2}\,year^{-1}$. Calculate the net primary production. [2]

   [Total: 11]

COMMAND WORD

give: produce an answer from a given source or recall / memory.

Note: Gross and net primary production (GPP, NPP) is extension content, and is not part of your syllabus.

CONTINUED

2 a Describe the process of photosynthesis [4]

   b Explain why photosynthesis does not occur at hydrothermal vents on the ocean floor. [2]

   c The solar energy falling on the ocean is $1.7 \times 10^6 \, kJ \, m^{-2} \, year^{-1}$ and the phytoplankton are able to use $18\,754 \, kJ \, m^{-2} \, year^{-1}$ of this.

   i Calculate the percentage of the Sun's energy that is used by phytoplankton. Show your working. [2]

   ii Explain why 100% of the energy is not used. [3]

   [Total: 11]

3 Study the graph in Figure 3.30, which shows the approximate chlorophyll concentrations off the coast of California over the course of one year.

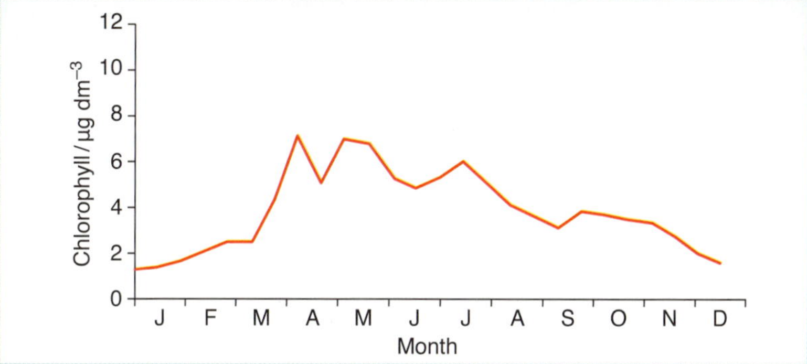

Figure 3.30 Approximate chlorophyll concentrations on the California coast in one year.

   a Describe the trend or patterns shown. [3]

   b Explain why the amount of chlorophyll increases in March. [5]

   c Suggest and explain what will happen to the population of zooplankton in March and April. [2]

   d Within this ecosystem, herring feed on the zooplankton and mackerel feed on the herring. There are 809 phytoplankton, 37 zooplankton, 11 herring and one mackerel. Draw the pyramid of numbers for this food chain. [3]

   [Total: 13]

4 a i Describe how nutrient-rich water from deep in the ocean enters the reservoir of nutrients at the surface. [2]

   ii Describe **two** other ways in which nutrients enter surface layers. [2]

   b i Explain the benefit of increased nutrients in surface layers. [2]

   ii Suggest how increased nutrients in surface layers could be harmful. [2]

   c Give an example of an essential element needed by living organisms and state what it is used for. [2]

   [Total: 10]

CONTINUED

5 a With reference to named examples, explain the meaning of each of the following terms:
  i Parasitism [3]
  ii Commensalism [3]
b <u>Contrast</u> producers and consumers. [3]
[Total: 9]

> **COMMAND WORD**
>
> **contrast:** identify / comment on differences

6 A student wanted to investigate the effect of light intensity on the rate of photosynthesis in pondweed by counting the bubbles coming from the stem.
  a Describe how this experiment should be set up to obtain accurate results. [5]
  b Give **two** variables which must be controlled. [2]
[Total: 7]

7 Study the graph in Figure 3.31 which shows the biomass of phytoplankton and zooplankton round the Norwegian coast over the course of a year.

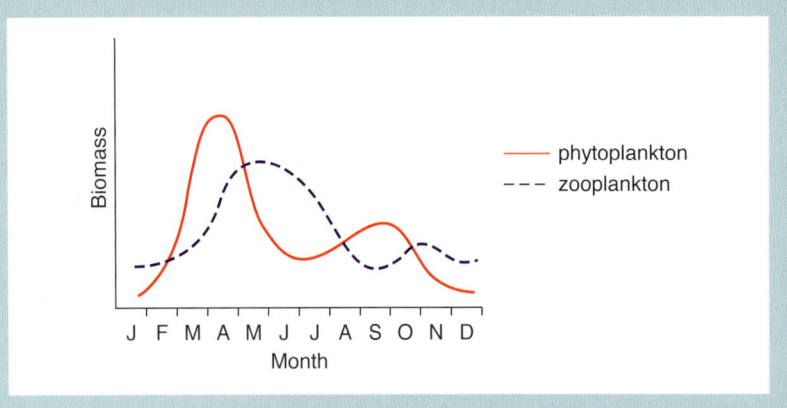

Figure 3.31: The biomass of phytoplankton and zooplankton round the Norwegian coast over the course of a year.

  a Sketch a pyramid of biomass to show the phytoplankton and zooplankton in March. [2]
  b Explain why there is normally more biomass in the producers than in the consumers. [3]
  c Describe how the pyramid of biomass would be different in July. [2]
  d Explain why the pyramid of biomass would be different in July. [1]
[Total: 8]

8 Figure 3.32 shows a food chain from a marine ecosystem. The figures show the energy in each trophic level in winter in arbitrary units.

phytoplankton 5000 → zooplankton 589 → sardine 61 → tuna 4

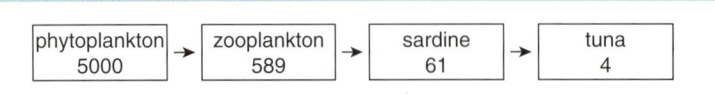

Figure 3.32: A food chain from a marine ecosystem showing the energy in each trophic level in arbitrary units.

CONTINUED

    a Calculate the percentage of the energy transferred between the phytoplankton and the zooplankton. Show your working. [2]

    b Explain why there is less energy in the consumers than in the producers.. [3]

    c i Suggest what would happen to the energy in each level during summer. [3]

        ii Suggest what might happen to the food chain if fertilisers from coastal farmland drain as run-off into the water. [3]

            [Total: 11]

9 a Complete a copy of Table 3.6 to show the uses of different nutrients. [3]

Nutrient	Biological use
nitrogen	
calcium	
phosphorus	

Table 3.6: Uses of different nutrients

    b i Describe the process of run-off. [3]

        ii Describe the effect of run-off of nitrogen fertilisers on producers. [3]

        iii Explain how this will affect the consumers in the food chain. [2]

            [Total: 11]

10 Salmon were sampled at a site in the Atlantic Ocean once per year and checked for sea lice. Table 3.7 shows the results.

Year	Number of salmon caught at sampling site	Proportion of salmon infested with sea lice/%
2007	356	1.7
2008	302	4.3
2009	340	4.4
2010	253	4.6
2011	307	6
2012	105	7.4
2013	68	5.3
2014	35	8.2
2015	32	8.9
2016	15	11.4

Table 3.7: The proportion of salmon infested with sea lice in the Atlantic between 2007 and 2016

> CAMBRIDGE INTERNATIONAL AS & A LEVEL MARINE SCIENCE: COURSEBOOK

CONTINUED

a   Plot a graph to show the changes in the number of salmon each year. [4]
b   Describe the pattern of the graph. [2]
c   **Evaluate** the evidence that sea lice affect the health of the salmon. [4]

[Total: 10]

COMMAND WORD

evaluate: judge or calculate the quality, importance, amount or value of something

SELF-EVALUATION CHECKLIST

I can:	See section...	Needs more work	Almost there	Ready to move on
describe the three main types of symbiotic relationship and describe examples of each one	3.1			
represent feeding relationships as food chains or food webs and be able to describe the organisms in these relationships in terms of their trophic level	3.2			
explain how photosynthesis provides energy to the food chain and summarise the process as a word equation	3.2			
give the word equation for respiration	3.2			
define productivity and explain how high productivity can affect food chains	3.2			
explain why energy is lost at each stage of the food chain	3.2			
draw pyramids of number, energy and biomass and be able to explain and interpret their shapes	3.2			
explain what a nutrient is and be able to give the biological roles of nitrogen, carbon, magnesium, calcium and phosphorus	3.3			
draw simple diagrams to show how carbohydrates, proteins and lipids are made up from smaller molecules	3.3			
explain how nutrients in the ocean are depleted and replenished	3.3			
describe the different stages in the carbon cycle including combustion, photosynthesis, decomposition, fossil fuels and the formation and weathering of rocks	3.3			

3 Interactions in marine ecosystems

EXTENDED CASE STUDY: THE GULF OF MEXICO DEAD ZONE

Figure 3.33: The Gulf of Mexico and surrounding countries.

The Gulf of Mexico is an ocean basin surrounded by the United States, Mexico and Cuba (Figure 3.33). It is approximately 1500 km wide and is connected to both the Atlantic Ocean and the Caribbean Sea.

A dead zone is an area of water where oxygen levels have become very low (hypoxic). This means that there is insufficient oxygen for respiration, and organisms either die or move to a different area where the dissolved oxygen levels are higher. Dead zones occur near coastlines where there are high levels of nutrients washing off agricultural land. The first dead zone was reported in the early twentieth century and since then the numbers have increased every year. (Figure 3.34). It has been estimated that between 1950 and 2018 the overall level of oxygen in the oceans dropped by 77 billion tonnes.

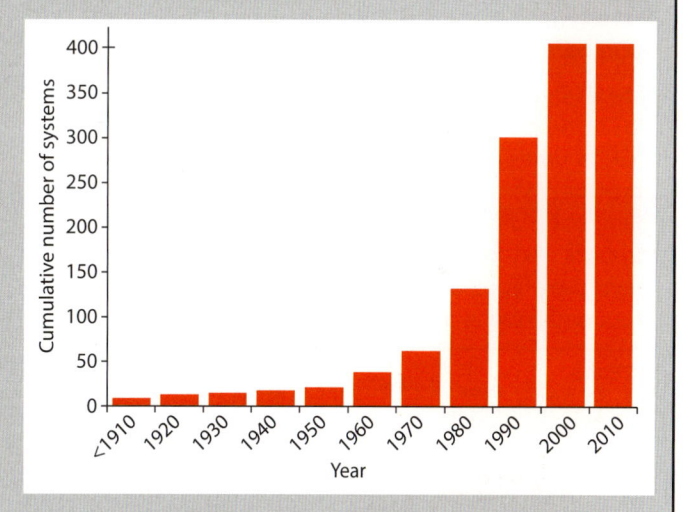

Figure 3.34: Number of dead zones by decade.

Formation of dead zones

Dead zones form when excess nutrients such as phosphates and nitrates enter the water. These primarily come from chemical fertilisers and waste such as sewage. Dead zones can also form naturally if changes in wind and currents alter the upwelling of nutrients from deep water.

When the excess nutrients enter the water, they massively increase the growth of algae, leading to an algal bloom. Phosphates and nitrates tend to increase the growth of blue-green cyanobacteria, which are not eaten by many zooplankton. This means that their numbers can build up unchecked. When the organisms die they sink to the bottom, where they provide a food source for the bacteria, which break them down in the process of decomposition. The numbers of bacteria rapidly increase and their respiration uses up the majority of the oxygen dissolved in the water. The water, therefore, becomes hypoxic and other aquatic organisms die.

CONTINUED

The Gulf of Mexico

The Gulf of Mexico dead zone is interesting for two reasons. First, it is the second largest dead zone in the world. Second, it is seasonal and its size fluctuates depending on the weather conditions each year. The Mississippi River drains into the Gulf and has the largest drainage basin of any river in North America. The levels of nutrients it washes into the Gulf are correspondingly large. Twelve million people live in areas that border the Mississippi and that discharge treated sewage into the water. The majority of the land near the Mississippi is farmland so rainwater constantly washes fertilisers into the water. About 1.7 million tonnes of nutrients are released into the Gulf of Mexico from the Mississippi every year. In the spring and summer this causes algal blooms and the development of the dead zone. The size of the dead zone varies; on average it is around $13\,000\,km^2$. The largest recorded dead zone here was in 2017 when it reached $22\,730\,km^2$.

Interestingly, a year later, during the summer of 2018, the dead zone returned to an average size. During times of heavy flooding the dead zone tends to be very large. In the late summer of 1998 the dead zone disappeared because there was a severe drought and the amount of water entering the Gulf decreased significantly. Figure 3.35 shows the size of the dead zone in an average year.

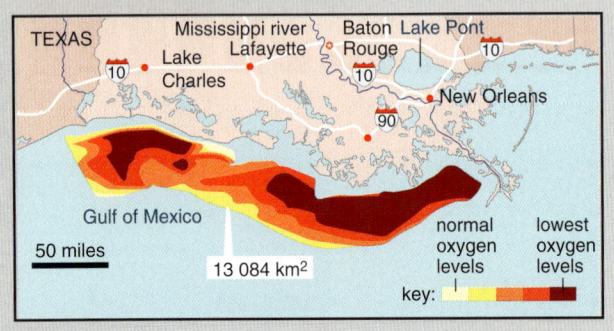

Figure 3.35: An average sized dead zone in 2018.

The fresh water flowing into the Gulf from the Mississippi is less dense than the seawater and so forms a layer on the top. This means that the deeper water, where the hypoxia occurs, is cut off from a resupply of oxygen from the atmosphere. The dead zone, therefore, persists until the water mixes again, either because of a hurricane or when cold fronts form in the autumn and winter.

The effects of the dead zone

The seafood industry in the Gulf of Mexico is very important. The Gulf provides the United States with the majority of its farmed oysters and shrimp, as well as being a source for several types of fish. The National Oceanic and Atmospheric Administration (NOAA) has estimated that the dead zone costs the tourism and fishing industries US$82 million per year. When fish move out of the dead zone because of the lack of oxygen, fishers have to travel further to catch them. This costs both time and money. Shrimp are often unable to escape the dead zone and instead are simply killed, reducing the population and making them harder to catch in the future.

Reducing the size of the dead zone

The main way to reduce the size of any dead zone is to reduce the level of nutrients entering the water. In 1997 the Gulf of Mexico Watershed Nutrient Task Force was formed with the aim of reducing the average size of the dead zone to $5000\,km^2$. Strategies that can be used include reducing the use of inorganic fertilisers on farms, as well as altering the timing of their use to avoid leaching by rainwater. Management of flood plains is important because an increased area of flood plains means that less floodwater makes its way into the Gulf and nutrient-rich sediment is captured. Farmers are being encouraged not to drain wetlands but to leave them in their natural state to improve soil quality and reduce erosion. Waste treatment processes are being improved to reduce the discharge of nutrients into the water and to avoid animal waste entering waterways at all.

Questions

1. Describe how a dead zone forms.
2. Suggest why the number of dead zones has increased since they were first discovered.
3. Explain why the Gulf of Mexico dead zone varies in size each year.
4. Explain why the Gulf of Mexico dead zone is seasonal.
5. Summarise the control measures being taken to reduce the size of the Gulf of Mexico dead zone and explain how each measure works.

Chapter 4
Classification and biodiversity

LEARNING INTENTIONS

In this chapter you will learn how to:

- understand the classification of species and binomial nomenclature system
- construct and use simple dichotomous keys and make biological observations and drawings
- understand the role of phytoplankton as producers and zooplankton as consumers
- state the main features of typical adult echinoderms, crustaceans, bony fish, cartilaginous fish, macroalgae and marine plants
- understand the ecological and economic importance of these marine organisms, including named examples
- explain the genetic, species and ecological biodiversity of marine environments
- understand the importance of maintaining marine biodiversity
- explain the terms ecosystem, habitat, niche, species, population and community
- explain and identify biotic and abiotic factors in marine ecosystems
- describe sampling and field work methods used in the littoral zone and interpret different types of correlations.

> **BEFORE YOU START**
>
> - Working in small groups, spend one minute brainstorming as many different marine habitats that you can think of. Compare your results with another group and add any suggestions that you missed. Repeat the exercise by spending one minute brainstorming as many different marine species that you can think of. Then, on a large sheet of paper, divide them into groups depending on their similarities and differences. When you have done this, share your results with another group and see if they can add an example to each of your groups.
>
> - Biodiversity is a measure of the range of organisms in a habitat. Sketch out a potential plan of ideas regarding how you might measure this on (a) a coastal shore and (b) a coral reef.

OUR AQUATIC HERITAGE

Earth looks blue from space. That is because water covers more than 70% of its surface. The **oceans** and their submarine havens are crucial for all life on Earth. Oceans are where life evolved more than 3.5 billion years ago and they remain home to an enormous biodiversity of organisms. The world ocean contains 99% of Earth's habitable space. An estimated 50–80% of all life on Earth is found in the sea. Given that approximately 95% of the oceans remains unexplored, it is impossible to know the exact number of species that live there, but the final number could be as high as one million. A recent census of marine life discovered more than 600 potential new species on average per year, scientists estimate that 91% of marine organisms have yet to be discovered.

Life evolved in the ocean and spread from there onto land. Competition within marine organisms, as well as changes in the ocean's temperatures and salinity, meant that some aquatic plants and animals began to evolve to live on the land more than 425 million years ago. The interface where oceans and land meet has a rich variety of coastline communities. **Seas** and estuaries host a range of productive and ecologically critical habitats such as mangroves, seagrass beds, kelp forests, and sandy, rocky and muddy shores.

The term ecology is derived from the Greek word 'oikos' meaning 'house'. Marine ecologists study oceanic organisms in their natural habitats to find the connections between both the organisms' homes and their habitats, and the connections between the organisms, as they are all interconnections that underlie our ecological understanding of marine ecosystems. By doing so, they aim to understand the factors that control the distribution and abundance of marine life. To do this, it is important to be able to classify, measure and sample the maritime conditions. We must strive to understand how humans are responsible for the short and long term altering of the marine environment. By doing so, we can highlight its importance and pass on the responsibility of conserving aquatic biodiversity for future generations.

Questions

1. Humans have been to the Moon more times that they have been to the deepest parts of the Earth's oceans. Discuss why you think this may be.

2. Discuss why we should conserve aquatic biodiversity for future generations. Suggest different ways that this could be achieved.

KEY WORDS

ocean: a continuous mass of seawater on the Earth's surface, its boundaries formed by continental land masses, ridges on the ocean floor or the equator

seas: smaller and less deep bodies of seawater that are partially enclosed by land; they are found where the ocean and land meet

4.1 The classification of marine organisms

One way to make sense of the enormous biotic variety found in our oceans is using a **taxonomic hierarchy**. A taxonomic hierarchy classifies aquatic life into taxonomic groups based on the features, relationships and evolutionary pathways that they share.

Taxonomic hierarchy sorts each species into a series of similar groups of organisms or taxa. Similar species are grouped into a genus (plural: genera) which are in turn linked into a family, an order, a class, a phylum (plural: phyla), a kingdom, and then a domain. Figure 4.1 shows the taxonomic hierarchy for the blue shark, *Prionace glauca*.

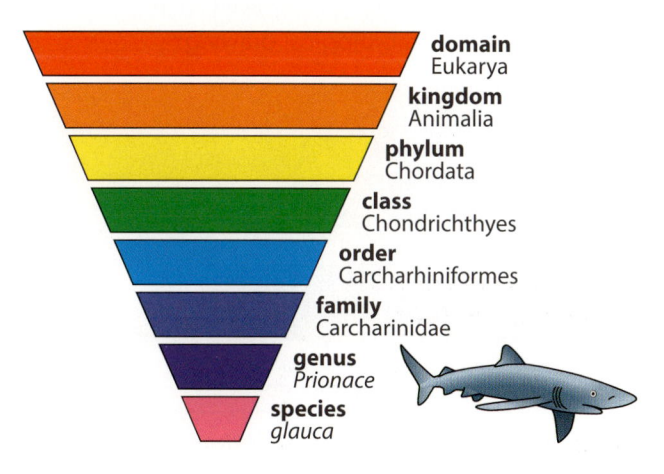

Figure 4.1: Taxonomic hierarchy for the blue shark, *Prionace glauca*.

We give each marine organism a name in Latin composed of two parts, the genus followed by the species. This naming system is called **binomial nomenclature**. It was first formulated in 1736 by Carolus Linnaeus, a Swedish botanist. The genus is given a capital letter, whereas the species is always lower case. In print, a binomial name always appears in italic. For example, the Latin binomial name for the Galápagos penguin is *Spheniscus mendiculus*. When you write a binomial name by hand, you should underline it (for example <u>Spheniscus mendiculus</u>).

When marine scientists try to determine which species a specimen belongs to, they often use a dichotomous key. A **dichotomous key**, such as Table 4.1, is a series of choices between alternative characteristics, with a direction to another stage in the key. Choices are made until the species is identified. You can use Table 4.1, together with Figure 4.2 which shows the characteristic features of a blue shark, to identify the blue shark as shark species F.

Step	Characteristic	Common name
1a	Kite like shape to body … Go to 2	
1b	Non kite like shape to body… Go to 3	
2a	Hornlike appendages on snout	Shark spp A
2b	No hornlike appendages on snout	Shark spp B
3a	Six gill slits	Shark spp C
3b	Five gill slits … Go to 4	
4a	Spines on dorsal fin	Shark spp D
4b	No spines on dorsal fin … Go to 5	
5a	Long point on end of snout	Shark spp E
5b	No long point on end of snout … Go to 6	
6a	Big eyes surrounded by a small ring	Shark spp F
6b	Eyes on end of hammer-like projection	

Table 4.1: Dichotomous key for shark identification.

KEY WORDS

taxonomic hierarchy: the classification of the species within living organisms by describing the domain, kingdom, phylum, class, order, family, genus and species

binomial nomenclature: the two-part Latin name given to each species comprising the genus followed by the species

dichotomous key: an identification tool utilising a series of choices between alternative characters, with a direction to another stage in the key, until the species is identified

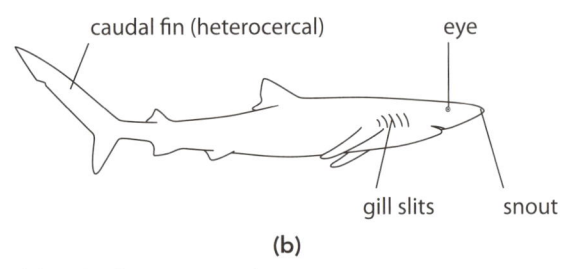

Figure 4.2: (a) Photograph of a blue shark; (b) Biological drawing of a blue shark, *Prionace glauca*.

CORE PRACTICAL ACTIVITY 4.1: MARINE BIOLOGY OBSERVATIONS AND DRAWINGS

Introduction

When investigating life in the ocean, it is important that marine scientists can make biological drawings of either live specimens or from photographs of a specimen. To do this you do not have to be a great artist as the aim is simply to produce a clear outline of the main biological features.

Before you start

1. Discuss in pairs why marine scientists make **biological drawings**.
2. Make a list of the external features that you may be able to label from each of the following marine groups:
   a. Echinoderm
   b. Bony fish
   c. Cartilaginous fish
   d. Macroalgae
   e. Marine plant.

Equipment

Before you start, ensure you have all the equipment you will need:

- a sharp hard (minimum HB) pencil
- eraser, pencil sharpener and ruler
- plain paper.

> **KEY WORD**
>
> **biological drawings:** a scientific drawing that records an image and important features of the specimen

Method

Use the photograph of a stickleback fish in Figure 4.3 to make a biological drawing:

Figure 4.3: Photograph of a stickleback fish.

1. Write the title of the specimen at the top of a piece of plain paper.
2. Begin drawing by using a sharp HB pencil to make an outline of the specimen. The drawing should be at least half the size of the space provided, with room on each side for labels if required.
3. No shading is permitted so only use smooth continuous bold lines to show the features. If a drawing error is made then an eraser can be used to make corrections.
4. Try to ensure that the scale of the image is appropriate (for example, the length of the tail is in the correct ratio to the length of the whole fish).
5. You need to look very carefully at the specimen if you are to be scientifically accurate with your drawing. An example could be whether the stickleback has two or three spines.

4 Classification and biodiversity

CONTINUED

6 Try to also ensure that the position and size of an observable feature is biologically correct (for example, where do the dorsal fins start compared to the anal fin?)

7 Labels are a good way to name and describe characteristics visible in the specimen. Labels should be printed clearly and in ink. The labels should be to the sides of the image and the label lines should be horizontal. Label lines should be drawn in pencil with a ruler and you need to ensure they touch the site being identified.

8 Add the following labels to your diagram: Operculum, Lateral line, Pectoral fin, Caudal fin, Anal fin, Pelvis fin, Dorsal fin, Dorsal spines, Eye, Mouth.

9 If you are simply asked to 'add labels' then the name of an observed feature is all that is required. In annotated diagrams, the label should however also include an explanation for how that feature is an adaptation for living in a marine ecosystem, such as: *'The operculum is essential for ventilation as it is a bony flap that covers and protects the gills.'*

Results

The results for this experiment should be a labelled diagram. It should be large, drawn in pencil and labelled with ruled label lines. There should be no sketching or shading.

Evaluation and conclusions

1 Explain what makes a good biological drawing.
2 Suggest why biological drawings are different from an artistic representation of the organism.

REFLECTION

After completing Core Practical Activity 4.1, swap your biological drawing with another member of the class. How do they compare? How could they be improved?

Test yourself

1 Complete the spaces in a copy of Table 4.2 to describe the taxonomic hierarchy for the Galápagos penguin, *Spheniscus mendiculus*.

Taxonomic hierarchy	Galápagos penguin
	Eukarya
	Animalia
	Chordata
	Aves
	Sphenisciformes
	Spheniscidae

Table 4.2:

2 a Figure 4.4 is a biological drawing of a crayfish. List **three** features of the drawing that are good and three features that could be improved.

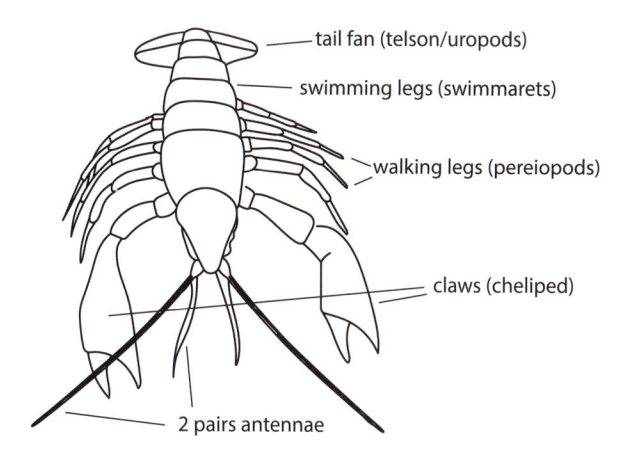

Figure 4.4: Biological drawing of a crayfish.

Labels: tail fan (telson/uropods); swimming legs (swimmarets); walking legs (pereiopods); claws (cheliped); 2 pairs antennae

b Draw a diagram of a coral polyp from Figure 4.5. Add labels to indicate the location of the following structures: mouth, tentacle, nematocyst.

Figure 4.5: Coral polyp.

4.2 Key groups of marine organisms

There is an enormous variety of marine organisms ranging in size from microscopic viruses, bacteria and plankton, through to the largest animal on Earth, the blue whale, that can weigh up to 180 000 kg and is more than 30 m in length. Marine producers include phytoplankton, macroalgae and marine plants. They are crucial to the marine food web as they photosynthesise to transform light energy from the Sun into chemical energy (food energy) used by marine consumers. Each trophic group plays a crucial ecological role within the marine web of life.

In this section we will explore a sample of aquatic life by comparing the characteristics of eight groups of marine organisms:

- phytoplankton
- zooplankton
- echinoderms
- crustaceans
- bony fish
- cartilaginous fish
- macroalgae
- marine grasses.

We will also explore the ecological and economic importance of each group. We will use a range of specific examples of organisms that play pivotal roles in the ecology of their aquatic habitats: crown of thorns starfish (COTS), Antarctic krill, Peruvian anchoveta, blue shark, kelp and seagrass. The abundance and distribution of these keystone species is indicative of not only the health of the ecosystem but also mankind's impact on the marine environment.

Keystone species are consumers that affect biodiversity to a greater extent than would be expected from their population numbers. Keystone species control other species by means of grazing, predation and competition. They may also be capable of ecosystem engineering by physically modifying the habitat. Without keystone species, the ecosystem would be dramatically different or cease to exist altogether. Keystone species are important in conservation programmes that focus resources on maintaining such species, rather than attempting to protect and manage all endangered species in a habitat that is at risk.

> **KEY WORDS**
>
> **plankton:** microscopic free floating marine organisms
>
> **zooplankton:** planktonic consumers that are either floating or weakly swimming animals
>
> **echinoderms:** a marine invertebrate group with pentaradial symmetry and tube feet
>
> **cructaceans:** a marine invertebrate group with a hard exoskeleton, ten jointed legs and a nauplius larval stage
>
> **bony fish:** fish that have a bony skeleton and belong to the class Osteichthyes
>
> **cartilaginous fish:** fish that have jaws and skeletons made only of cartilage and belong to the class Chondrichthyes
>
> **macroalgae:** marine producers such as kelp and seaweeds
>
> **marine grasses:** aquatic flowering plants that are often found in estuarine and coastal environment
>
> **keystone species:** an organism that plays a unique and crucial role in the way an ecosystem functions; without keystone species, the ecosystem would be dramatically different or cease to exist altogether

4 Classification and biodiversity

Keystone species

Plankton

Plankton are microscopic organisms that have limited mobility. They simply float with the current in water. (The word plankton is derived from Greek, and means 'wandering'.) Plankton are divided into two groups: phytoplankton and zooplankton. Phytoplankton are producers that obtain their nutrition by using the energy in light through photosynthesis. Zooplankton are consumers that gain their nutrition from the food energy in producers or consumers.

Phytoplankton

There are many different species of phytoplankton. In the open ocean, most are free floating and are found in surface water where light intensity is highest. They have no need to settle on a substrate and are carried wherever the ocean currents take them. Phytoplankton can be divided into three groups depending on their size: picoplankton (0.2–2 µm); nanoplankton (2–20 µm); and microplankton (20–200 µm). Each group of phytoplankton exist with slightly different adaptations and niches.

Diatoms (Figure 4.6a) are unicellular phytoplankton found in the oceanic surface water. There are more than a hundred different genera but all have intricate cell walls of silica, which often have extraordinarily beautiful designs. They are able to reproduce very rapidly when conditions are optimal and blooms are often seen in spring. This is when light intensity and temperature are rising and upwelling of mineral ions into the surface waters occurs. The blooms tend to appear and then rapidly disappear because of consumption by primary consumers such as planktonic crustaceans and krill, and depletion of mineral ions. Phytoplankton are important in removing carbon dioxide from the atmosphere and form the base of many marine food webs.

Dinoflagellates (Figure 4.6b) are also unicellular protoctists but do not have the silica cell wall that diatoms have. Like diatoms, they live in the upper surface waters of oceans and can undergo rapid reproduction to produce algal blooms when conditions are optimal. The blooms of some species of dinoflagellate produce toxins that can poison fish and accumulate in shellfish. Contaminated shellfish that are eaten by other organisms, including humans, can cause poisoning. Blooms of dinoflagellates that produce toxins are called harmful algal blooms (HABs) and include red tides, which cause areas of the ocean to turn red. Pollution caused by the run-off of fertiliser from fields

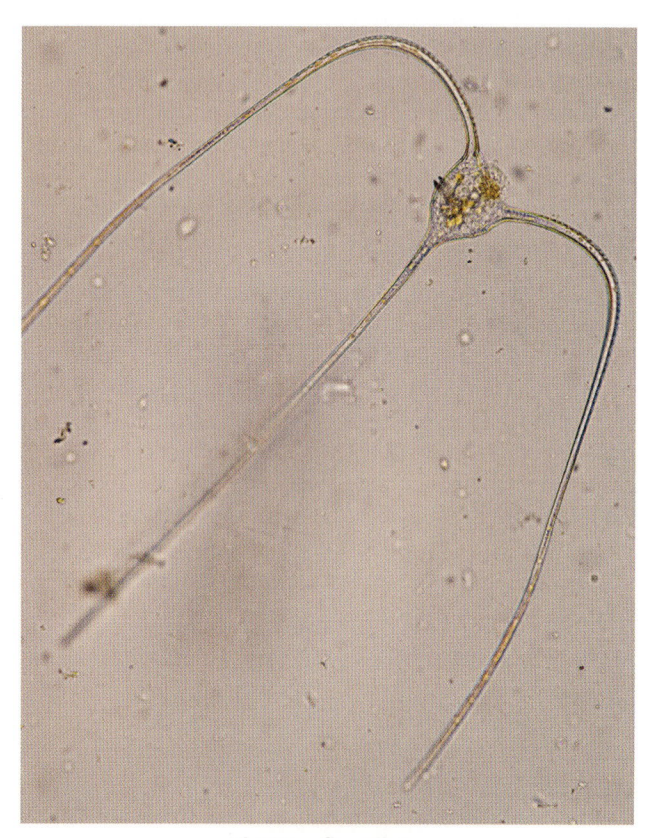

(a) Diatoms

(b) Dinoflagellate

Figure 4.6: Phytoplankton: (a) Diatoms; (b) Dinoflagellate.

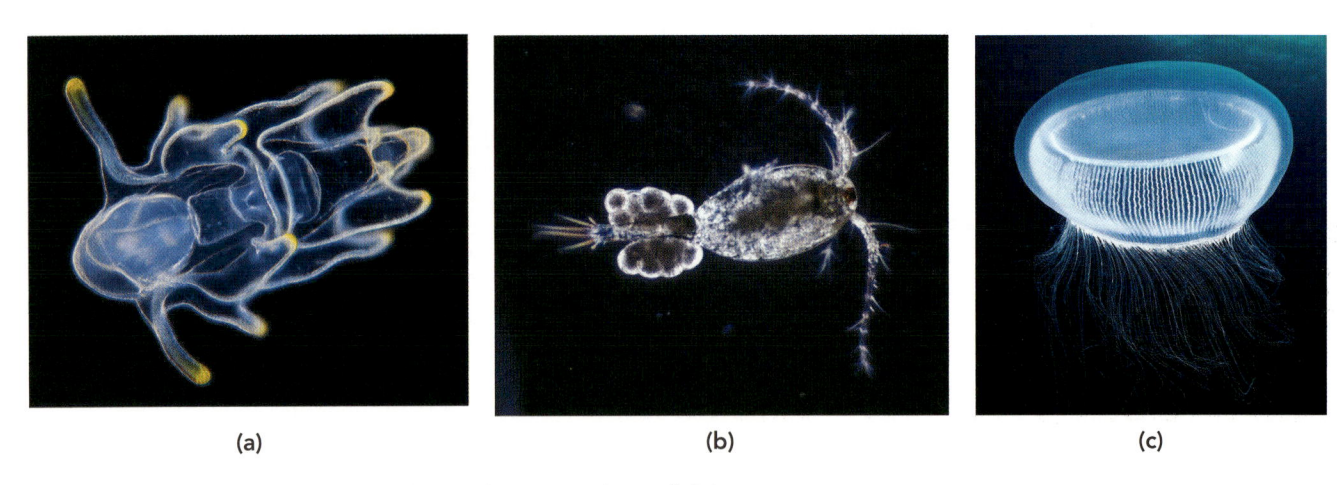

Figure 4.7: Zooplankton: (a) seastar larvae; (b) copepod; (c) jellyfish.

is the source of many blooms of dinoflagellates and, as farming has become more intense, the number of harmful algal blooms has increased. (Human impact on marine waters will be discussed further in Chapter 9.) Some dinoflagellates bioluminesce, and this can often be seen at night on the ocean or at the coast, when impressive displays can occur in the evening. They bioluminesce as a defence mechanism since it tends to attract large predators into the area which then consume predators of the dinoflagellates.

Zooplankton

Zooplankton are important consumers and include larvae, copepods and larger animals such as jellyfish. Zooplankton migrate vertically in the water column each day, to feed on phytoplankton in the photic surface layer. Zooplankton provide a critical link in the food chain between the primary producers and larger consumers including shellfish, fish and whales. Zooplankton are sensitive to environmental change and can be killed by pollution, microplastics, ocean acidification or increases in water temperature due to global warming.

Many marine organisms have a complex life cycle where the eggs develop into **larvae** before turning into juveniles and then adults. Larvae include the planktonic stage of nearly all species of fish and invertebrates, such as seastar (Figure 4.7a). The larvae are adapted to life floating in the ocean (for example, some species of fish larvae have oil globules that give them added buoyancy).

Copepods (Figure 4.7b) are crustaceans and comprise the most abundant and diverse group of zooplankton. They are small herbivores that feed on diatoms. Copepods bodies are divided into three sections: the head, thorax and abdomen. Two antennae protrude from the head and aid in swimming, while two to four pairs of appendages extend from the thorax. Their tough exoskeleton is made of calcium carbonate and can include spikes that provide protection as well as an increased surface area : volume ratio for better flotation.

Jellyfish species (Figure 4.7c) live in every part of the ocean and belong to the same group (cnidarian) as corals and sea anemones. Many of these soft-bodied, fragile organisms are made of two parts: a transparent bell, called a medusa, with tentacles dangling from it. The medusa can be as large as 1 m with the tentacles extending to 65 m. In contrast to larvae, jellyfish remain planktonic throughout their entire life and the pulsing of the medusa provides a limited mobilty. Jellyfish are predators that survive by using stinging cells called nematocysts on their tentacles to kill other plankton and larval fish.

Other examples of zooplankton include krill. Krill are shrimp-like carnivores that feed on other zooplankton species and phytoplankton. Krill are important food sources for birds, fish, seals and baleen whales.

> ### KEY WORD
>
> **larvae:** a planktonic stage of development which occur between the egg and juveniles; found in nearly all species of fish and invertebrates

4 Classification and biodiversity

| seastars (starfish) | brittle stars | sea lilies | sea cucumbers | sea urchins |

Figure 4.8: The five main classes of echinoderms.

Echinoderms

Echinoderms are a phylum of marine invertebrate and include creatures such as seastars (also known as starfish), sea urchins, sea cucumbers, sea lilies and brittle stars (see Figure 4.8). There are more than 7000 species of echinoderms, which can be found in a range of sea floor habitats from the intertidal zone to the benthic depths.

Their name comes from the Greek for their characteristic 'spiny skin' which is composed of a thin layer of skin over a hard calcium carbonate skeleton (see Figure 4.9). Echinoderms have planktonic larvae that develop into adults with **pentaradial symmetry**: five arms (or fans) radiating from a central body cavity which contains a mouth and anus. Echinoderms move via a system of water-filled tubes that increase and decrease the hydraulic pressure in the **tube feet** arranged in grooves on the underside of each arm. The tube feet (Figure 4.9b) are used by seastar to open the shells of bivalve molluscs such as oysters and clams. The seastar's stomach is then everted (turned inside out) and enters the opened shell. The stomach releases enzymes that digest the prey before the nutrients are absorbed. The sticky tube feet act as tiny suction cups that help it adhere to the seafloor. The tube feet also help in gaseous exchange for respiration by taking in oxygen and releasing carbon dioxide.

> **KEY WORDS**
>
> **pentaradial symmetry:** five arms (or fans) radiating from a central body cavity
>
> **tube feet:** tubular projections that that assist in locomotion, feeding and respiration

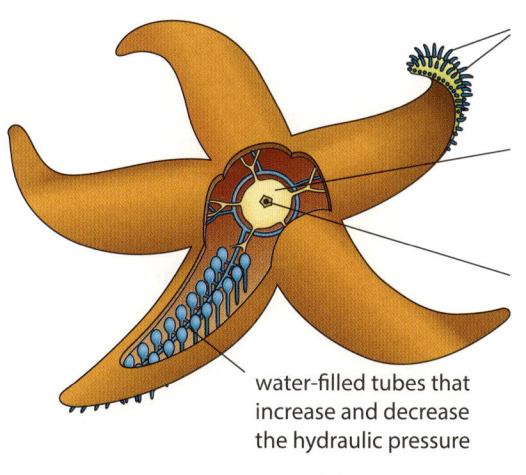

- tube feet help with locomotion, feeding, respiration and sticking to the seafloor
- the stomach is inverted through the mouth on the seafloor surface for digestion of molluscs
- egestion is via the anus on the top surface
- water-filled tubes that increase and decrease the hydraulic pressure

(a) (b)

Figure 4.9: (a) Main features of an adult echinoderm;) **(b)** tubed feet.

Ecological importance of echinoderms

Some echinoderms are keystone species forming unique and crucial ecological components within marine ecosystems. Examples of echinoderm species can be found in a variety of habitats including coral reefs, kelp forests and sandy shores.

Coral reefs

The crown-of-thorns starfish (COTS) (*Acanthaster planci*) is an example of an echinoderm that is a keystone species in coral reef communities. The COTS feeds on the fastest growing coral species. By doing so, it supports the colonisation of slower growing coral species. This increases the coral biodiversity on the reef, which in turn provides more niches for other marine organisms to occupy, increasing the overall biodiversity of a reef. The removal of the COTS predators can, however, lead to an explosion in their population. These COTS outbreaks can lead to destruction of large areas of coral which in turn severely damages the coral reef biodiversity. COTS are key to the delicate relationship between other organisms within the coral reef community and can promote and damage the reef's biodiversity. (You will explore this topic further in the COTS case study in Chapter 5.)

Kelp forests

In kelp forests, echinoderms such as sea urchins feed on the kelp holdfast and are predated by sea otters. When the predator–prey balance is not in equilibrium (for example, if sea urchins are over-harvested) then ecosystems can become overrun by kelp. Similarly, if local sea otter populations are hunted to extinction for their fur, then sea urchins proliferate, leading to the destruction of kelp forests (kelp barrens).

Sandy shores

On sandy shores, echinoderms such as sea cucumbers filter seawater, and burrow into the substrate, providing increased oxygen to organisms that live hidden in the sand. Sea cucumbers' planktonic larvae form an important part of the food chain for plankton-eating (planktivorous) fish. They also ingest sand along with their food and the nitrogenous waste produced by sea cucumbers is an important nutrient for marine habitats.

Economic importance of echinoderms

Echinoderms can have both positive and negative effects on coastal economies. Sea cucumbers and sea urchins can be a source of income when they are used in agriculture, fishing, food and scientific industries. COTS can, however, damage the ecotourism industry when they destroy the kelp beds or coral reefs frequented by dive companies.

Sea cucumbers (Figure 4.10) are considered a delicacy in Chinese cuisines and their commercial harvesting can play a pivotal role in local economies. In the Galápagos Islands, fishermen began large-scale harvesting of sea cucumbers in 1992. Initially, there was no control and up to 150 000 per day were collected. This led to an 80% decrease in the sea cucumber population. In 1999, a fishing season and minimum catch size were introduced but failed to prevent continued over-harvesting. In 2005, the resultant collapse of the sea cucumber population led to a political crisis on the islands as the local fishermen reliant on the industry lost their means of income. Sea cucumbers are also the source of pharmaceutical drugs that inhibit the growth rate of some cancers.

Figure 4.10: Sea cucumber.

Sea urchins are eaten in Japan, New Zealand, Peru, Spain and France. Farmers also add sea urchin's calcium carbonate rich endoskeleton to acidic soil to raise the soil's pH. Research scientists also use sea urchins as model organisms to help study developmental biology.

Crustaceans

Aquatic crustaceans have adapted to live in salt, brackish or fresh water and can be found in almost all aquatic habitats. They include crabs, crayfish, lobster, krill, shrimp (Figure 4.11), prawns, barnacles, copepods, amphipods and fish lice. Crustaceans have a distinctive planktonic larval form called a **nauplius**.

> ### KEY WORD
> **nauplius:** distinctive larval stage of crustaceans

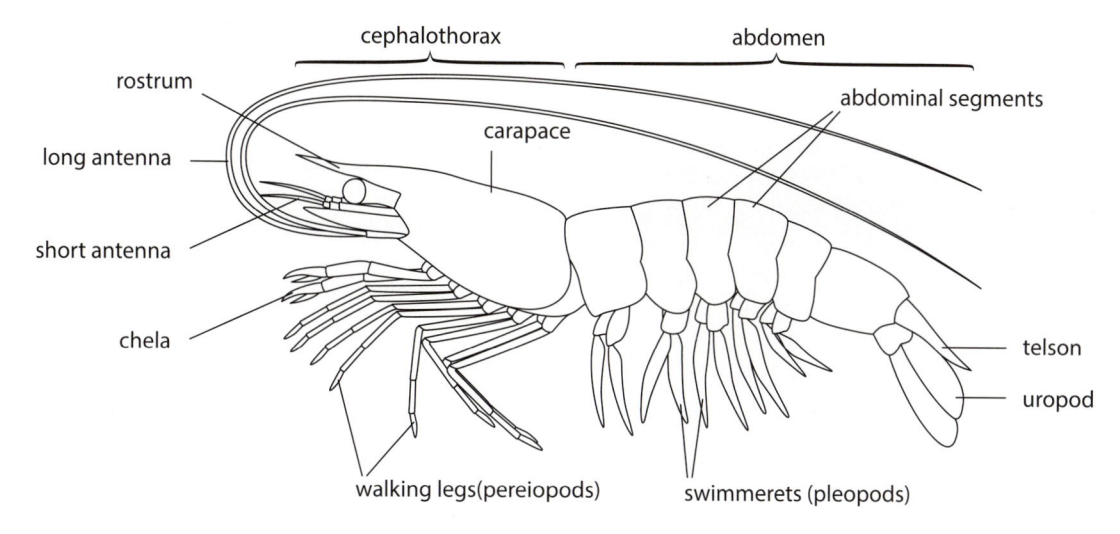

Figure 4.11: Biological drawing of a shrimp.

The name crustacean comes from the Latin for 'hard shell'. They are characterised by a hard exoskeleton made of calcium and a polysaccharide called chitin. The outside of the exoskeleton provides protection from predators and water loss, while the inner part provides support for the attachment of the muscles. It is divided into a cephalothorax and a segmented abdomen.

The cephalothorax is a combined head and thorax (as crustaceans have no neck) which contains the heart, gills, and stomach. The dorsal side is protected by a **carapace**. Crustaceans have two pairs of antennae: one pair is shorter, called antennules. The head has two compound eyes and three pairs of mouthparts (one pair of mandibles and two pairs of maxillae) which can be used for defence and feeding.

> **KEY WORD**
>
> **carapace:** the part of the exoskeleton that protects the dorsal side of the cephalothorax

Crustaceans, like all arthropods, have jointed legs. Unlike insects (three pairs) and arachnids (four pairs), crustaceans have at least five pairs of legs so can be described as decapods or ten-legged. Another distinguishing feature that separates them from other groups of arthropods, is that the legs have two-parts limbs. The cephalothorax has claws (chela) as well as walking legs (pereiopods) that can also be used to gather food. The abdomen is split into separate sections (segmented) and contains swimmerets (pleopods) which are swimming legs that can also assist in reproduction (for example, the first pair may be enlarged in males and used to pass sperm to the eggs on the female's swimmerets). The abdomen ends in ends in a fan-shaped tail (uropod and telson).

Ecological importance of crustaceans

Crustaceans play an important role in many marine ecosystems, as they can be found ranging from deep sea benthic habitats (for example amphipods), through to surface pelagic waters, where the nauplius larvae drift in the zooplankton soup. Scavenging crustaceans are crucial to the recycling of mineral nutrients as they often occupy the niche of detritivores consuming dead and decaying matter. By helping in the breakdown of detritus, they accelerate the conversion of complex organic matter into inorganic ions by decomposers such as bacteria.

Crustaceans also assist in maintaining the health of seagrass meadows where shrimps graze on the algae that grow on the blades of these marine plants. Without these crustacean primary consumers, the algae would block sunlight preventing photosynthesis and so reducing the growth rate of seagrass beds. Crustaceans are also the food source for many marine organisms. Marine birds feed on mud crabs commonly found in intertidal mangroves forests. Similarly, smaller crustaceans, such as copepods and krill, are crucial trophic component on marine food chains.

Krill form a biomass of 110 billion kg in the Southern Ocean and are a vital part of the Antarctic food chains, being consumed by a variety of organisms, including fish, birds, squid, whales, seals and penguins. Krill are a group of about 80 different species of crustaceans. Antarctic krill (*Euphausia superba*) are one of the most important krill species in these polar waters of the Southern Ocean (Figure 4.12).

Figure 4.12: Antarctic krill.

Antarctic krill have a high reproductive capacity: the females can lay up to 10 000 eggs that can result in swarms that contain 30 000 individuals per cubic metre. Melting ice in spring and summer produces a layer of less-saline water on the Southern Ocean's surface, together with increased nutrients and sunlight. These changes in abiotic conditions lead to a massive increase in phytoplankton, known as a bloom. The phytoplankton blooms feed krill, which subsequently become very abundant.

Global warming can result in a decrease in krill population due to the rise in ocean temperatures leading to a change in ocean currents and a retreat in the Antarctic sea ice.

Krill are also a target species for commercial fisheries and the annual global krill harvest is up to 20 million kg. Over-harvesting of krill can lead to a decrease in the krill population. The lower krill abundance reduces their grazing on phytoplankton. This can result in even larger phytoplankton blooms which can produce toxins harmful to other organisms in the ecosystem. Krill are also highly susceptible to overfishing of other Antarctic fauna, such as Antarctic squid. Despite krill being only one component of the diet of squid, the dramatic fluctuations in squid numbers due to their overfishing can directly affect the krill abundance.

Economic importance of crustaceans

Crustaceans are of great economic importance to humans. The larger crustaceans, such as prawns, shrimps, krill, crabs, crayfish and lobsters, are consumed by humans. The small zooplanktonic crustaceans, such as copepods and krill, form the largest animal biomass on Earth and are a crucial trophic link in maritime food webs that support the seafood we eat. Crabs, lobster and krill fishing are major industries, as they are considered a delicacy all over the world. Krill is eaten in certain countries (for example in Japan where it is known as okiami). Krill is also caught for use as an aquaculture and aquarium feed or as bait in sport fishing or in the pharmaceutical industry. Krill oil contains omega-3 fatty acids and antioxidants and is sold as a dietary supplement to lower blood lipid and help alleviate arthritis pain.

Crustaceans can also be harmful to aquaculture industry as they can slow the growth rate of the fish or molluscs being farmed. Water fleas are considered a pest as they eat smaller zooplankton that are an important food for juvenile fish in fish farms. Fish lice are copepods that are parasites on fish. Some species of fish lice suck blood while clinging to scales on the outside of the fish, while other species enter the fish via its gills and are internal parasites. Pea-crabs enter their oyster hosts as larvae and remain there as they feed and grow.

Bony fish

96% of fish have a bony skeleton and belong to the Class: *Osteichthyes*. They can be recognised by their external features (Figure 4.13a).

- **Gills** Delicate pink membranous structures that provide a large surface area for exchange of oxygen and carbon dioxide between seawater and the blood in fish. They are supported by bony structures called gill arches.

- **Operculum** A thin bony flap of skin covering and protecting the gills. As it opens and closes, it allows sea water containing dissolved gases to flow over the gills and thus enables ventilation and gaseous exchange.

- **Lateral line** A canal that can be seen on the head and the side of the body in bony fish. It contains

> **KEY WORDS**
>
> **gills:** the gaseous exchange surfaces of fish
>
> **operculum:** a thin bony flap of skin covering and protecting the gills
>
> **lateral line:** a canal on the head and the side of the fish that contains sense organs; it is externally visible in bony fish but in cartilaginous fish it is under the skin

4 Classification and biodiversity

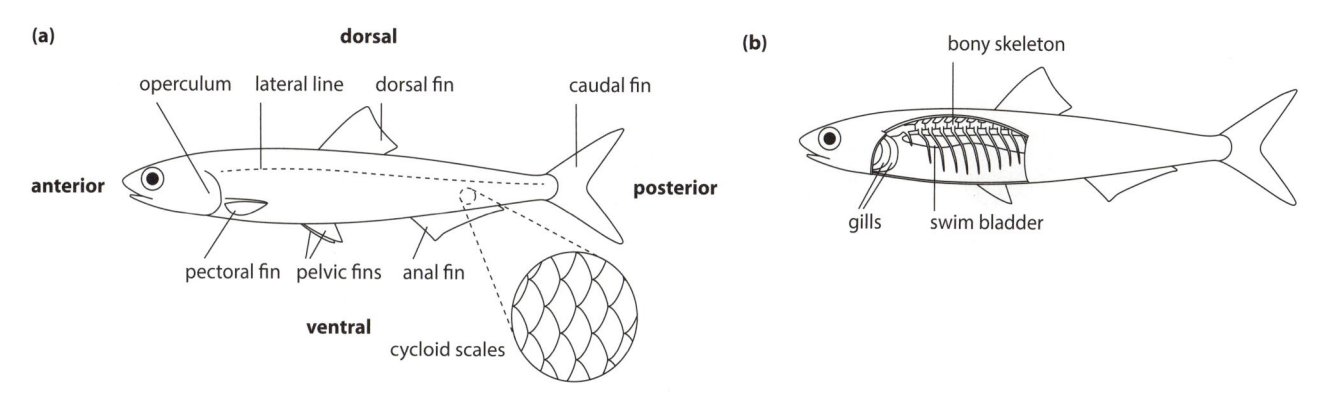

Figure 4.13: **(a)** the external features of bony fish; **(b)** the internal features of bony fish.

sense organs that can detect changes in the electric field (electroreceptors), as well as vibrations in the water (mechanoreceptors). This assists in shoaling behaviour, navigation and detecting prey.

- **Scales** Made of bone. Covered by skin and mucus. Scales help protect the fish as well as reducing drag and hence increasing the hydrodynamic efficiency of the fish. The majority of bony fish have thin, overlapping flexible scales with either a smooth edge (cycloid) or a toothed edge (ctenoid). Like trees, these fish scales form growth rings and the thickness and number of rings can help scientists determine the age and growth rate of a fish. Some fish have much harder, heavier and thicker scales (ganoid).

- **Fins** Protrude from the body surface and assist in movement, stabilising position, reproduction and protection. There are five main types of fins found in bony fish:
    - **Pectoral fins:** Found in pairs on either side of the body, just behind the operculum. Assist in turning, balance, stopping and swimming. Red Handfish (Figure 4.14a) have adapted their pectoral fins to walk while Flying fish (Figure 4.14b) use them to leap above the waves
    - **Caudal fin:** At the tail of the fish. The main source of power for propulsion. There are five main shapes, depending on the swimming style of the species (Figure 4.15). Rounded fins are found in relatively slow swimmers that can swim for long periods of time. Truncated fins are useful for ambushing prey as they allow the fish sudden changes in direction as well as providing quick acceleration. Forked fins are found in continuous swimmers. Lunate fins can maintain fast speeds for long durations. The last type is

> **KEY WORDS**
>
> **scales:** overlapping segments of bone covered by skin and mucus found on the outside of the fish
>
> **fins:** protrude from the body surface and assist in movement, stabilising position, reproduction and protection

Figure 4.14: Bony fish adaptations: **(a)** Red handfish; **(b)** Flying fish; **(c)** Hairy frogfish.

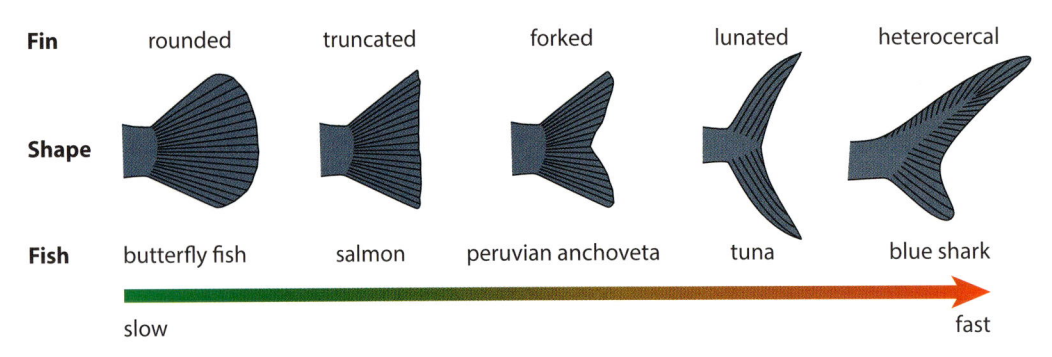

Figure 4.15: Types of caudal fin.

heterocercal shaped. This is the fastest tail fin however it is most commonly found in sharks rather than bony fish.

- **Pelvic fins:** Found in pairs, one on each side of the fish. They are found on the front of the fish so are also known as ventral fins. They assist with stability and can be adapted to assist with walking on, or sticking to a benthic substrate.
- **Anal fin:** Found on the ventral surface behind the anus/cloaca. They help stabilise the fish while swimming.
- **Dorsal fins:** Found on the back surface of the fish. There can be up to three dorsal fins. They assist with steering and balance, protecting the fish from rolling and enabling sudden stops and turns. They may also have spines that give protection against predators. Hairy frogfish (Figure 4.14c) use a spine on their dorsal fin as a lure to attract prey.

Bony fish also contain a variety of adaptations that can only be seen when we dissect a fish. As their name suggests, these internal features (Figure 4.13b) include a jaw and skeleton made of bone and cartilage. Many also contain a **swim bladder**, which is a specialised buoyancy organ. By adding or releasing gas between the swim bladder and the blood, the swim bladder allows bony fish to stay in midwater without the need to continuously swim.

> **KEY WORD**
>
> **swim bladder:** a buoyancy organ found in bony fish

Ecological importance of bony fish

The 27 000 known species of bony fish found in our rivers and oceans today are responsible for storing a significant proportion of marine organic nutrients in their tissue. When bony fish migrate, feed and reproduce they play a pivotal ecological role by linking the nutrient cycles of the different habitats they live in.

When bony fish excrete, they release nitrates, phosphates and other dissolved nutrients in a form that can be readily absorbed by primary producers. Primary producers are the nutrient and energy base of all marine ecosystems. Fish also play an important trophic link by linking the plankton eaten by planktivorous fish to higher order consumers in the food web. Not only are they a food source for an abundance of fish-eating (piscivorous) marine species, they also link the aquatic and terrestrial ecosystems. Dead fish that are washed up onto the shore transport and redistribute essential nutrients between the open ocean and coastal habitats.

One example of the ecological importance of bony fish are salmon species that migrate up river from the sea to spawn and die. During this salmon run, bears feast on the breeding stock (Figure 4.16). When the bears return to the surrounding woods, their faeces are important

Figure 4.16: Grizzly bear hunting a sockeye salmon.

source of nitrates to the soil. The salmon carcasses and eggs that remain in the stream contribute much-needed nutrients at the end of summer that help ensure many freshwater species survive winter. A reduction in salmon populations would jeopardise the productivity and survival of many other species. For this reason, salmon are considered keystone species; their abundance is indicative of the health and water quality of the whole wetland ecosystem.

The erosion of bony fish biodiversity is likely to have detrimental effects on land-based wildlife, including humans. If fish are harvested above sustainable levels then the resultant collapse of fish stocks will deprive us of an essential fatty acid and protein source in our daily diet.

Economic importance of bony fish

Throughout history, coastal communities have relied on harvesting and trading marine bony fish to provide nutrients and calories in our diet. Fish meat is an important source of protein and five essential amino acids that humans cannot synthesise. The liver of some fish, such as cod, contains oils that are often sold as nutritional supplements as they are rich in iodine, vitamin A and D. Russian sturgeon eggs are called caviar; they are an expensive delicacy in some countries. It is, however, not just ocean fisheries and their related service industries that provide income and employment. It is predicted that, in the future, fish farming will play an increasing contribution to our diet, especially if overfishing continues to deplete ocean stocks.

The non-edible parts of fish also have economic importance. They are rich in nitrogen and calcium phosphate. They are ground into fish meal for animal feed and fertiliser. The remaining oil can be used to create soap, candles, varnish and paint. The skin can be made into lanterns or turned into glue. The air-bladders can make a powder called isinglass, which is used in wine and beer making. The scales of fish can be used to create jewellery.

Other economic benefits from bony fish include recreational saltwater sport fishing; scuba diving and snorkelling by ecotourists; the catching and breeding of tropical fish for the pet industry; and the use of fish for scientific teaching and research.

CASE STUDY 4.1: THE ECOLOGICAL AND ECONOMIC IMPORTANCE OF PERUVIAN ANCHOVETA

Peruvian anchoveta are a species of anchovy fish that live for up to three years and can grow to be 20 cm in length. Anchoveta are filter feeders: water is taken in through the mouth and zooplankton is filtered out by the gill rakers which are bony extensions attached to gill arches. They are small forage fish found in the open ocean away from the seabed or the shore. A forage fish is a prey fish that is consumed by predators for food. Forage fish are an ecologically important part of the food chain as they provide food for:

- larger fish, such as tuna and salmon
- mammals, such as dolphins and whales
- sea birds, such as gulls and pelicans.

One important factor that controls the number of young Peruvian anchoveta surviving to maturity is the effect of El Niño events (introduced in Chapter 2). El Niño is a change in the trade winds in the Pacific Ocean that stimulate upwelling of cold, nutrient-rich waters into the warmer sunlit water above. During an El Niño year, the thermocline deepens, which effectively blocks the cooler water underneath from mixing with the warm water at the top. Lack of nutrients therefore limits the primary productivity in the sunlit zone, leading to reductions in the numbers of fish.

The Peruvian anchoveta fishery is the biggest single species fishery in the world and is of pivotal importance to the economy of local communities. In the 1960s, annual catches of anchoveta off the coast of Peru were more than 10 million tonnes per year. In 1971, the catch was 13.1 million tonnes. In 1972, the industry collapsed because of overfishing and the El Niño phenomenon. After the collapse of the anchoveta populations, the industry shifted to fishing sardines for several years until the waters cooled again and anchoveta numbers increased. There was another reduction in numbers during an El Niño event in the early 1980s, but by the mid-1990s the catch was back up to 12.5 million tonnes. In 2014, only 2.2 million tonnes were caught after the second fishing season was cancelled because of the El Niño phenomenon. It is not just the fishing industry that is affected by El Niño. Guano (excrement from sea birds) is an important fertiliser. When there are fewer fish, there is less food for the sea birds, which are their predators, and, therefore, less guano is produced.

> CONTINUED

Questions

1 Explain how a reduction in the nutrients in the upper layers of the ocean could lead to a decrease in the numbers of forage fish such as anchoveta.

2 Anchoveta feed on large zooplankton whereas sardines feed mainly on phytoplankton. Use this information to suggest why sardine numbers are less likely to collapse during an El Niño event.

3 Look at the graph in Figure 4.17. Suggest **two** years, other than 1971, that could have had El Niño events. Explain your answer.

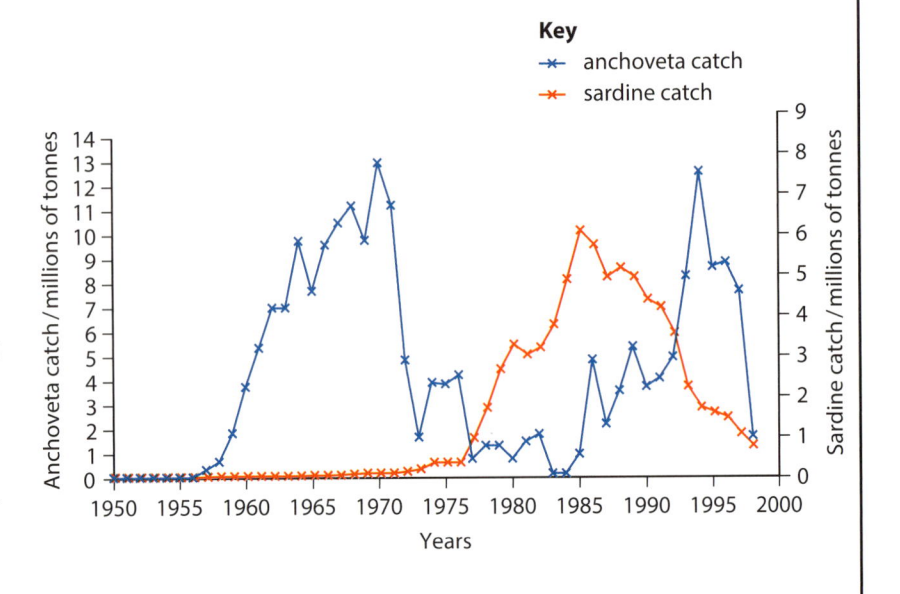

Figure 4.17: Anchoveta and sardine catches between 1950 and 1998.

Cartilaginous fish

The second main type of marine fish is the Class *Chondrichthyes*, which includes sharks, skates, rays and chimaeras. These are cartilaginous fish as their jaws and skeletons are made of cartilage only. Cartilage has less calcium in it, and is softer and more flexible, than bone. Most sharks have eight fins: two pectoral, one caudal, two pelvic, one anal and two dorsal. The caudal fin of many sharks is larger on the dorsal than the ventral side. This hetercercal shape (Figure 4.14) provides a greater surface area for muscle attachment on the dorsal side, which provides more speed and acceleration. In contrast, rays get their forwards thrust through use of their pectoral fins.

Cartilaginous fish also have a tough skin covered with unique tooth-like scales called **denticles**. These overlapping scales are all in one direction and, when rubbed the wrong way, give them their characteristic sandpaper-like feel. Denticles provide protection, as well as improving swimming efficiency by improving the streamlining. The lateral line in cartilaginous fish is not externally visible as it is under the skin.

Unlike bony fish, cartilaginous fish have a number of separate openings that help ventilate the gills. Sharks, skates and rays have five to seven pairs of **gill slits** just behind the head, plus a modified slit, called a spiracle, which lies just behind the eye. They take water in through the mouth, over the gills, and out via the gill slits. They can use two methods, known as 'ram ventilation' and 'pumped ventilation'. Cartilaginous fish do not have swim bladders and so to keep buoyant they must keep swimming in a forward direction.

Ecological importance of cartilaginous fish

Cartilaginous fish occupy a wide variety of marine habitats ranging from hunting in estuarine inlets and lagoons to cruising the continental shelf, and even diving deep into benthic waters to feast on whale falls. Their ecological niche is invariably one of a top predator, but there are also some cartilaginous scavengers and filter feeders.

> **KEY WORDS**
>
> **denticles:** a type of overlapping scales that provides protection and improved hydrodynamic efficiency in sharks
>
> **gill slits:** external openings from the gills through which water taken in at the mouth can pass back to the ocean

Cartilaginous fish play a pivotal ecological role with marine food webs. Their abundance is often linked to their evolutionary cousins, bony fish. For example, overfishing of bony fish, such as haddock in New England, led to an increase in cartilaginous fish including dogfish and skates. This increase is thought to be due to reduced interspecific competition between the two groups of fish. The decline of one fish group does not, however, always lead to a rise in the other. An example is when fishermen removed cartilaginous fish such as tiger sharks from tropical waters, hoping that this would lead to an increase in tuna catches. The opposite occurred, with a fall in tuna numbers and densities. This was believed to be because the absence of sharks led to less shoaling by tuna, and an increase in the abundance of other smaller predators of fish. The loss of cartilaginous fish can also detrimentally affect commercial shellfish stocks. For example, a decrease in sharks along the US Mid-Atlantic coast resulted in an increase in their prey, including the cownose ray population. The rays then decimated the bivalve species including oysters, scallops and quahog clams. As a result of this, the North Carolina scallop fishery collapsed and restaurants were forced to remove clam chowder from their menus.

The most significant ecological impact is arguably due to sharks as they comprise more than 500 of the approximately 1250 species of cartilaginous fish. An example is the blue shark (Figure 4.2) which was once one of the most common sharks with a large geographic distribution inhabiting temperate and tropical waters between Norway and New Zealand. It has large pectoral fins which allow it to conserve energy on its long migrate in search of food and mates. The fins are highly prized when caught either intentionally by shark finning operations or as bycatch in gillnet and longline commercial fisheries. When caught, the fins are cut off and kept, while the rest of the shark is often thrown back overboard as waste.

Through harvesting and loss of habitat, it is estimated that up to 20 million blue sharks are killed each year. This is especially alarming as sharks take a long time to reach sexual maturity and do not produce many offspring. This makes their recovery as a species from overfishing more difficult. As a result, some populations have fallen by 80% and the International Union for Conservation of Nature and Natural Resources (IUCN), have classified blue sharks as 'near threatened' with extinction.

As apex predators, the only threats blue sharks face are being fed on by larger sharks, such as great white and tiger sharks, and due to culling by man. Blue sharks feed on a wide variety of species including squid, cuttlefish, octopuses, lobster, shrimp, crab, bony fishes, small sharks and sea birds. Sharks play a crucial role in the ecosystem by promoting biodiversity through helping maintain a balance between the predator and prey species below them in the food web. As such, they are keystone species as they serve as an indicator of ocean health.

When shark populations are normal, they keep the prey population constant by removing weak and diseased individuals within a coral reef ecosystem (Figure 4.18). When sharks are over-harvested, the larger predatory fish, such as groupers, increase in abundance and feed more voraciously on the herbivores, such as yellow tang. This results in a drop in the abundance of primary consumers. With less herbivores, the algae that they graze on, increase their interspecific competition with coral, resulting in the reef becoming covered by algae.

Sharks also predate and play an important role in the control of invasive species, such as lionfish, which causes a significant decrease in the population of juvenile native fish. The loss of sharks can hence indirectly lead to the decline in the biodiversity of coral reef habitat.

Economic importance of cartilaginous fish

The declining global stock of bony fish has led to a surge in the commercial fishing of a range of cartilaginous fish species. Game fishing provides an even greater economic return as there is the additional economic benefits of the coastal communities charging tourists for charter boat hire, food and lodging. This intense harvesting is causing the reduction of many shark and ray populations and the reduction in these top-level predators may now be negatively affecting marine ecosystems.

Since ancient times, cartilaginous fish have been harvested for more than just their strongly flavoured meat. The gelatin-rich cartilaginous fins have been a culinary delicacy in China. Shark liver oil was originally harvested as a nutritional source rich in vitamin A. It is now more commonly used in preserving leather and wood, as a lubricant, in cosmetics, and for its range of medicinal properties from treating arthritis to cancer. The denticles provide an abrasive surface that is traditionally favoured in Japan for covering sword hilts. Shark leather is more durable than cowhide and can be

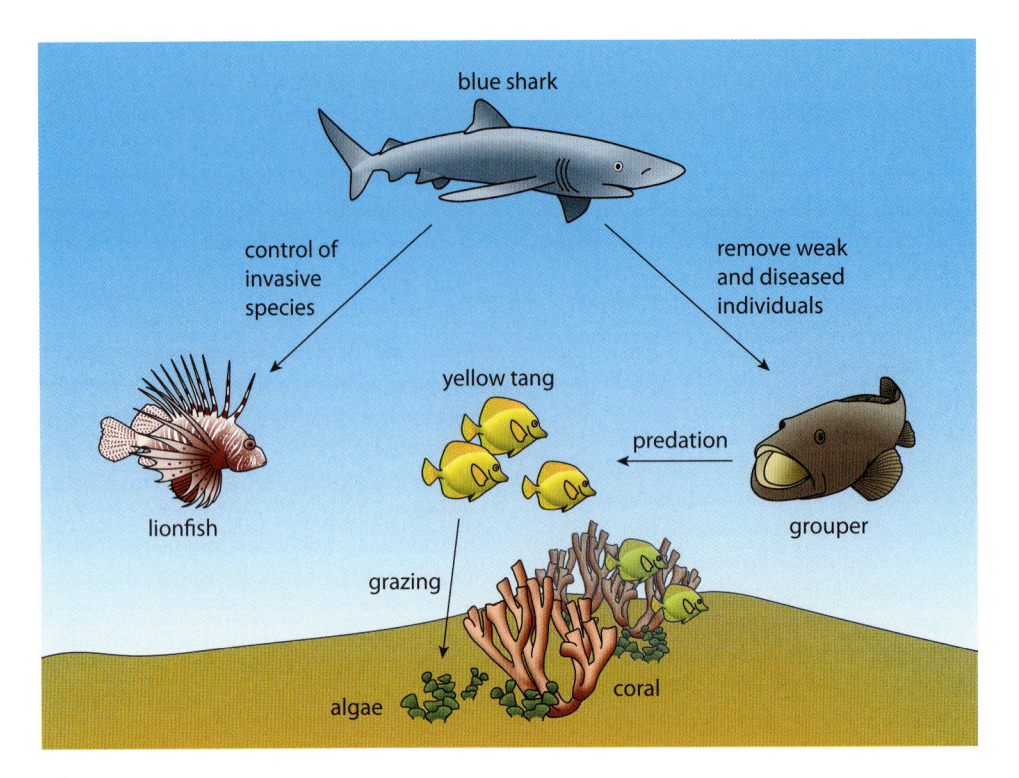

Figure 4.18: Blue Shark as apex predator in a coral reef.

used in the manufacture of boots, belts and wallets. In Greenland, some Inuit make rope from shark skin, while the Maori of New Zealand use shark teeth as earrings. Many indigenous cultures used the spines of stingrays as needles and spear tips, and the ancient Greeks and Romans used the electric shock of electric rays to 'cure' headaches.

In more recent times the commercial value of ecotourism has flourished. In the Bahamas, a reef shark when caught by a fisherman is worth US$ 50. In contrast, dive tourism and photography can generate US$ 250 000 to the local community. Similarly, one whale shark in Belize can bring in US$ 2 million over its lifetime. Diving with sharks and rays has also promoted a better understanding of the beauty of these creatures, as well as the ethical and biological importance inherent in their preservation and conservation.

Chordates

Bony fish and cartilaginous fish are both chordates (in the Phylum *Chordata*). All organisms in this phylum share common features at some point in their development (Figure 4.19). Some of these features are listed below.

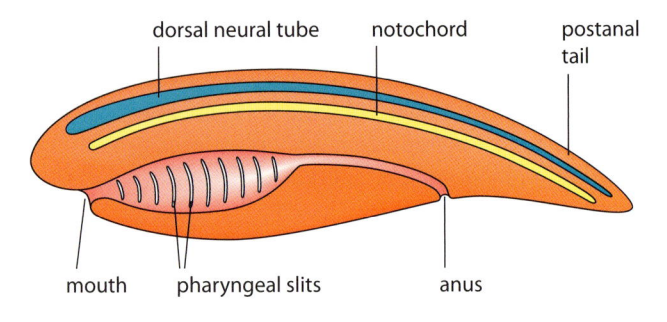

Figure 4.19: Common features of chordates.

Notochord is a flexible, rod-shaped organ that extends the length of the body and allows the body to bend during muscle contractions.

Dorsal neural tube is a tube-shaped organ that extends the length of the body. During development, the forwards (anterior) end becomes the brain while the rear (posterior) end becomes the spinal cord.

Pharyngeal slits link to the mouth cavity and the digestive system. In primitive chordates, they permit the release of water taken in by the mouth for filter feeding. In bony or cartilaginous fish, the pharyngeal slits develop into gill arches that support ventilation

4 Classification and biodiversity

across the gills. In most marine mammals and birds, pharyngeal slits are present only during embryonic development and develop into the jaw and inner ear bones.

Post-anal tail is mainly used for swimming and is located to the rear of the fish.

Macroalgae

As well as phytoplankton there are also much larger marine producers such as macroalgae, including kelp and seaweeds; and marine plants, such as seagrass. These organisms are all photoautotrophs: they make their own food (chemical potential energy) using light energy from the Sun.

Most macroalgae species have a similar structure that enables them to survive in the water of shallow seas and oceans (Figure 4.20). The whole body of the macroalgae is known as a thallus and has three main parts:

- **Holdfast** This is a strong, root-like structure that anchors the kelp to the seabed, preventing it from being moved by strong ocean currents or storms. It is for anchorage only and has no function in absorbing minerals.

- **Stipe** This is a long, tough, vertical stalk similar to the stem of plants. It extends from the holdfast and reaches up to the blades. It is very tough, to prevent breakage.

- **Blades** The blades are broad leaf-like structures that 'hang' in the water. They have a large surface area to absorb light and minerals.

Some macroalgae species also have **gas bladders** (also known as pneumatocysts) found underneath the blades. These act as floatation aids to keep the producer upright and the blade in the top of the photic layer to where there is increased light intensity for photosynthesis. Because many species live at depths where exposure to red light is restricted, they contain accessory pigments such as xanthophyll and fucoxanthin to absorb additional wavelengths of light.

Ecological importance of macroalgae

Macroalgae are particularly important in the intertidal (littoral) and subtidal (sublittoral) coastal habitats. One major underwater ecosystem is giant kelp forests (Figure 4.21) which are composed of brown macroalgae species. They require nutrient-rich clear water and a temperature of between 8 °C and 16 °C. When conditions are optimal, they have a very high rate of growth. One genus, *Macrocystus*, is able to grow up

Figure 4.21: Giant kelp forests.

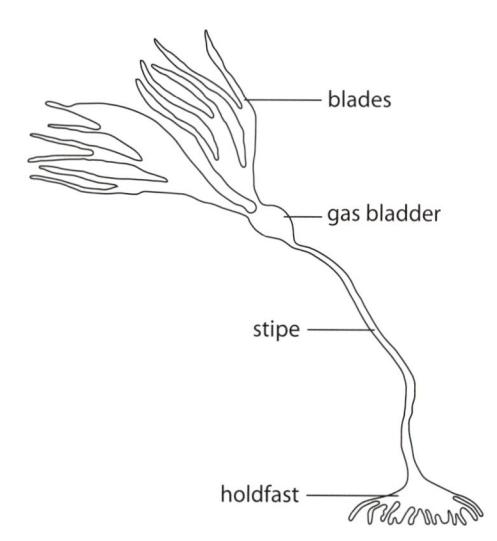

Figure 4.20: Kelp showing the features of macroalgae.

> **KEY WORDS**
>
> **holdfast:** strong, root-like structure that anchors the macroalgae to the seabed
>
> **stipe:** long, tough, vertical stalk similar to the stem of plants
>
> **blades:** leaf-like structures that 'hang' in the water and absorb light and minerals
>
> **gas bladder:** a gas-containing structure that provides buoyancy for some species of seaweed

to 0.5 metres a day and can reach lengths up to 80 m. Large kelp forests proliferate on continental shelves and serve as crucial habitats for a diverse range of fauna. Kelp also increases the productivity of the nearshore ecosystem by generating large quantities of detritus. Kelp forests are an important global marine ecosystem because they are the base of many food chains, generating vast species biodiversity.

CASE STUDY 4.2: THE IMPORTANCE OF SEA OTTERS IN MAINTAINING KELP FOREST ECOSYSTEMS

Kelp beds can be damaged by sea urchins, which are echinoderms that feed on kelp and detach them from their holdfasts that anchor them to their rocky substrate. Biotic factors that control sea urchin populations include predators such as sea otters, *Enhydra lutris*. The kelp forest food web (Figure 4.22) shows that the life in the ocean is, however, far more complicated than a simple food chain such as:

kelp → sea urchin → sea otter

In reality, many species, including abalone, crabs and herbivorous fish, feed on kelp. There is also a range of additional predators that feed on sea urchins, including starfish and larger bony fish (such as cod and sheepshead).

Predator–prey relationships are crucial for keeping a healthy balance of populations within the kelp ecosystem. Sea otters prey on sea urchins, and where sea otter populations have decreased, kelp density has also decreased because of a dramatic increase in the sea urchin population. If these predators did not protect kelp forests from damage by the sea urchins, kelp barrens would eventually form. This reduced productivity in the ecosystem would result in less chemical energy (food) for other species in the food web, causing a reduction in biodiversity.

Sea otters are a keystone species for kelp forests because many other populations are dependent on them. The loss of sea otters would lead to a significant decrease in overall biodiversity.

Reductions in sea otter populations can be caused by abiotic factors including climatic fluctuations (such as storms, the El Niño Southern Oscillation and global warming). Natural biotic factors can also negatively affect sea otter abundance. An increase

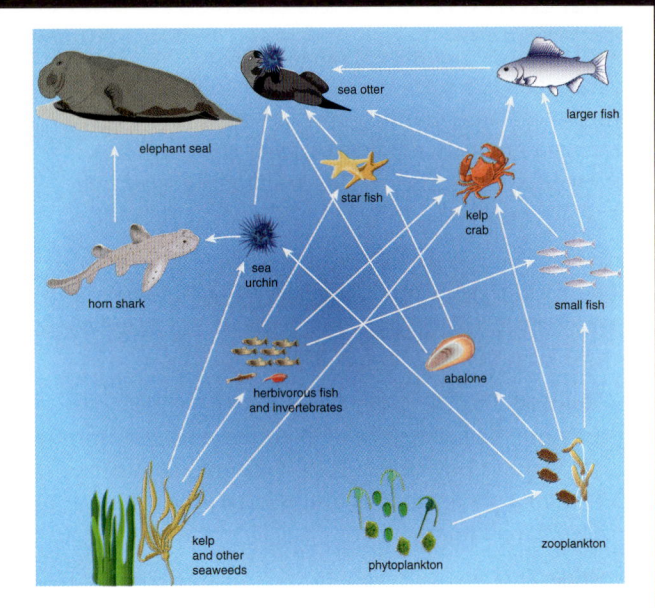

Figure 4.22: A kelp forest food web.

in killer whale numbers can result in increased predation on sea otters. Similarly, a decline in the populations of seals and sea lions may cause killer whales to switch their diets to include more sea otters.

Sea otter populations face a number of threats from humans. Sea otters often get caught in discarded nets and traps, which injure or kill them. Oil in the ocean from oil spills clogs sea otters' fur, decreasing the fur's ability to shield against cold water, leading to death by hypothermia. Polluted waters have also contributed to diseases in some sea otter populations. Hunting for fur historically had huge impacts on sea otter populations: European and North American fur traders hunted sea otters to the brink of extinction in the 1800s. Commercial fishing decreases the number of fish resulting in reduced food for the sea otters.

4 Classification and biodiversity

> **CONTINUED**
>
> **Questions**
>
> 1 Why do kelp forests only grow in shallow waters?
>
> 2 Explain what effect an decrease in kelp density could have on fish abundance.
>
> 3 Using the kelp ecosystem food web in Figure 4.22, suggest reasons for potential positive and negative affects that a decrease in the kelp density could have on the local abalone shellfish industry?

Economic importance of macroalgae

Humans have harvested macroalgae, such as kelp and seaweeds, for thousands of years. Depending on the species it can be harvested (Figure 4.23) in three different ways: attached to a substrate, free floating or cast up on the shore. Concerns, however, have been raised as to the impact of this wide-scale harvesting on the marine environment.

Despite production doubling since 2000, the demand exceeds the supply and many parts of the world, such as China and Japan, have begun commercial farming (mariculture). Macroalgal mariculture has grown to become an international industry with eight million tonnes produced annually and an estimated value of US$ 6 billion (£4.75 billion). Seaweed is seeded onto nets or ropes, which are then tethered in an area of lagoon that is not shaded, ideally with a temperature between 25 °C and 30 °C. After a period of growth, it is collected and hung out to dry. It is then used for a rich variety of products.

Figure 4.23: Harvesting of seaweed in the Philippines.

- **Cooking** Seaweeds have been used as food by coastal communities for years in many countries such as Japan, Korea, Iceland and Wales. In Japan, more than 20 species of seaweed are used as food and the red algae species *Porphyra* is dried to make sheets of nori, commonly used as the wrapping for sushi rolls. Nutritionally, seaweed is rich in protein, many vitamins and mineral salts, especially iodine, and is very low in fat.

- **Food industry** Seaweed is used as a source of biochemicals that are used to make solid gels and emulsifiers that hold food substances in suspension, including:

  - **Alginate:** a substance extracted from seaweed and used to form a gelatinous substance; it is used as an additive in many foods such as ice cream and has recently been used to make small gelatinous capsules that contain different flavours, like a synthetic caviar; alginate gel is also used in burns plasters and firemen's clothing

  - **Agar:** used to make vegetarian jellies and also the agar plates used frequently in microbiology to grow bacteria and test antibiotic resistance

  - **Carrageenan:** used to make food with a range of different textures, including chocolate milk drinks and milk chocolate bars, because it helps to hold the chocolate in suspension.

- **Cosmetics and herbal medicine** Seaweed extracts are often found in moisturising skin creams and herbal remedies for a range of conditions including arthritis, tuberculosis and the common cold.

- **Fertiliser** This is added as a rich source of nutrients to farmland.

- **Aquaculture** This is processed into pellets which can be used to feed abalone in aquaculture farms.

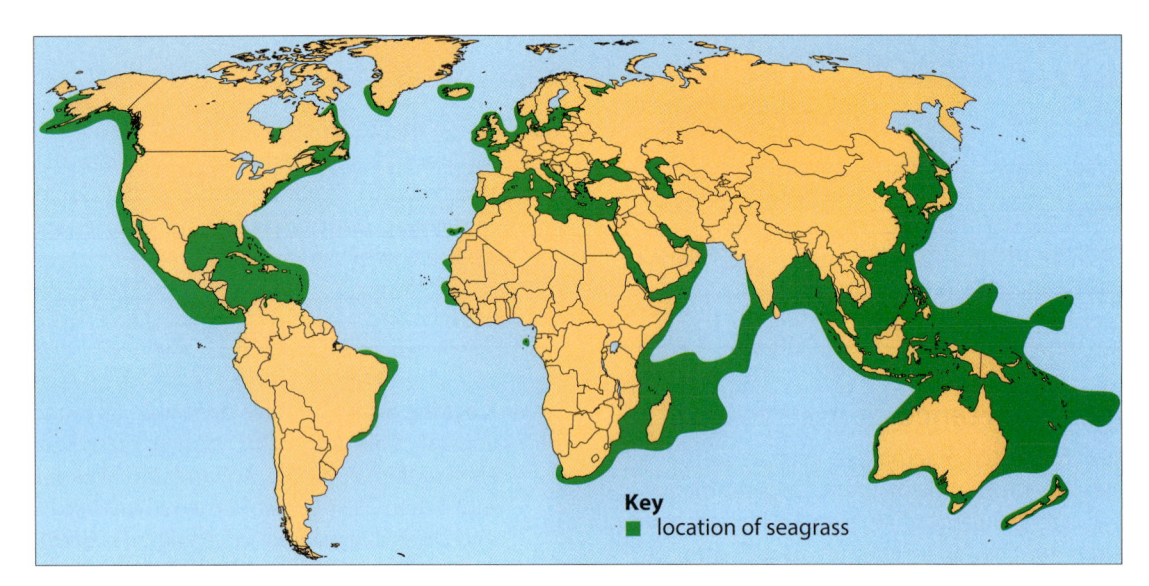

Figure 4.24: Location of seagrass beds.

Marine plants

Flowering plants are less common in estuarine and marine environments than they are in land-based (terrestrial) ones. Like other aquatic producers, they can come in three variants: floating, emergent and submergent.

Floating plants include the water cabbage, a type of floating herb found in the Brazilian wetlands at the mouth of the Amazon river.

Emergent plants are those that are rooted in the substrate and project above the water surface. Estuarine examples of these include the mangrove forest (that we will discuss in Chapter 5) and the herbs and shrubs that make up saltmarsh communities.

Submergent plants are rooted in the substrate but remain beneath the waterline. These include 72 species of seagrasses which can be found in large beds, called meadows, on the shallow continental shelf. They are the most common marine plants and will be the main focus of this section.

> ### KEY WORDS
> **root:** structure at base of plant that anchors it to the substrate and absorbs nutrients from the sediment
>
> **rhizomes:** a horizontal underground structure that enable seagrasses to reproduce asexually

Seagrasses, which are marine plants, are not to be confused with seaweeds, which are macroalgae. Seagrasses are flowering marine plants that form underwater meadows in shallow waters ranging from 4°C to 24°C (Figure 4.24). Seagrasses are, therefore, not found in subpolar regions and are also under threat from global warming.

Marine plants have many specific adaptations to life on the continental shelf.

They have well-developed **root** systems, with thick, horizontal **rhizomes** that lie up to 25 cm deep in the substrate (Figure 4.25). The root system anchors the seagrass into the seabed so that it is not moved by the shifting water currents and wave actions. The rhizomes also enable seagrasses to reproduce asexually.

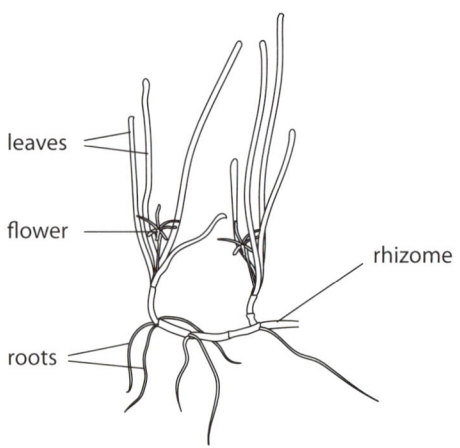

Figure 4.25: Seagrass showing the features of marine plants.

4 Classification and biodiversity

The **leaf** structure is unusual. It has an epidermis layer with chloroplasts (these are absent in the epidermis of most terrestrial plants) to maximise photosynthesis, no stomata, and a very thin waxy cuticle so that the leaf cells can obtain mineral ions directly from the water. Seagrasses have very few vascular bundles, as there is no need to transport water or minerals through the plant. The leaves are also very flexible so they do not get broken by water currents. The leaves and roots are physiologically adapted to seawater so that their cells are able to exist in saltwater without losing water by osmosis. They also contain a specialised tissue of 'air cells' within stems called aerenchyma. This tissue delivers air containing oxygen for aerobic respiration to all the submerged areas of the plant.

They are able to reproduce both sexually and asexually. When reproducing sexually, they produce **flowers** that release pollen that is carried in the water to other flowers.

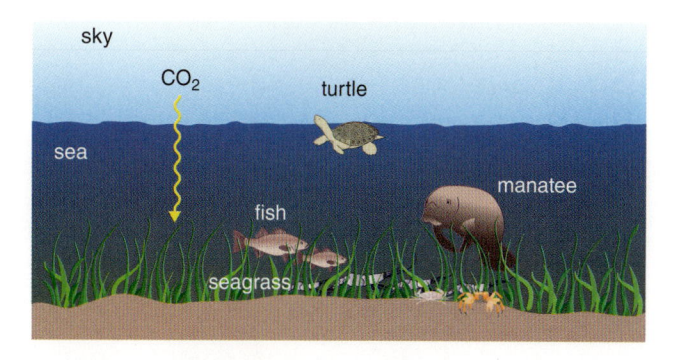

Figure 4.26: The ecological importance of seagrass meadows.

> ### KEY WORDS
>
> **leaf:** photosynthetic organ of plants
>
> **flower:** sexual reproductive organ of plants

Ecological importance of marine plants

Marine plants are the foundation of aquatic communities with a high biodiversity. Their sensitivity to water quality makes them important keystone species that can help indicate the overall health of coastal ecosystems. The different types of marine plants all share the ability to perform numerous crucial ecological roles in coastal areas.

Marine plants and phytoplankton are the dominant producers in estuarine habitats and are a direct source of food energy for marine primary consumers. For example, if a massive amount of seagrasses die, it will reduce the overall energy available for the consumers in the ecosystems. Consumers that rely on seagrass species are especially harmed. One such species is turtle grass, *Thalassia testudinum,* which is found in the Gulf of Mexico, Caribbean Sea and Bermuda, and is a vital food source for turtles, manatees (Figure 4.26) and herbivorous fish. Detritus from dead seagrass provides organic energy for worms, sea cucumbers, crabs, echinoderms and sea anemones. Some fish, such as seahorses and lizardfish, can be found in seagrasses throughout the year, while for many other vertebrate and invertebrate species the seagrass provide a nesting and nursery habitat for only their larval and juvenile stages. Bottlenose dolphins are often found feeding on fish, crabs and squid.

Seagrass meadows occupy less than 0.2% of the area of the world's oceans but hold about 15% of the ocean's total carbon. They also act as oxygen producers, increasing the dissolved oxygen. Seagrasses typically grow as long, thin leaves which help absorb wave motion and slow currents. Seagrasses further reduce turbidity and improve water clarity by trapping silt suspended in the water column. Their dense intertwined root systems bind the soft sediment reduce the stirring up of silt while filter-feeders, such as bryozoans, sponges and forams, help maintain the quality of coastal areas by absorbing the nutrient and heavy metal rich run off from land-based ecosystems before they can reach and damage more sensitive marine habitats such as coral reefs.

Research in India and Florida has suggested that conservation programmes for individual species within seagrass ecosystems can have mixed results. For example, when sea turtle populations are too low, seagrass dies off and is replaced by algae. To combat this, sea turtle conservation projects use turtle hatcheries to increase the local populations of sea turtles. (Figure 4.27). This in turn encourages good seagrass growth, increases the fertility of the seabed and helps disperse the seagrass. However, if turtle populations become too high, seagrass is overconsumed and dies off. Sharks play a key ecological role by consuming juvenile sea turtles but, in many parts of the world, shark numbers have plummeted due to overfishing. A seagrass conservation programme that focusses only on turtles and does not also protect the natural predators, such as sharks, can lead to further ecological damage due to an overabundance of populations of herbivores that eat seagrass. So, damaged seagrass habitats need a holistic

Figure 4.27: A sea turtle conservation project.

restoration programme to protect these ecologically sensitive natural refuges combining:

- turtle breeding and nesting protection
- a ban on shark fishing
- restricted fishing, aquaculture and coastal land use practices.

Economic importance of marine plants

It may appear that marine plants have less economic importance to humans than their terrestrial counterparts, as they care rarely used as a food source and cannot be harvested as easily. However, marine plant's main economic value should be measured through the industries that they support indirectly. As nursery grounds for marine invertebrates and vertebrates, for example, marine plants are the biotic cornerstone of the next generation of commercial and recreational fisheries. The habitats also provide incalculable economic support to coastal communities through their physical protection from weathering, erosion and flooding during storms. Traditionally, mangroves provided wood for fires and building, and seagrasses were used to insulate houses, weave furniture, thatch roofs, make bandages, fill mattresses and fertilise fields. More recently, ecotourism ventures which promote scuba diving to observe manatees are also becoming popular conservation adventure holidays.

Test yourself

3 Copy and complete Table 4.3 to show how each species is classified.

4 Purple seastar (*Pisaster ochraceus*) are an example of an echinoderm that is a keystone species in coral reef communities. Purple starfish are not top predators, because they are prey for sharks, rays and sea anemones. Purple starfish feed on a range of species, including sea urchins and mussels.

   a Explain the effect on the coral reef if purple starfish are removed.

   b Discuss why purple seastar can be considered a keystone species.

Taxonomic hierarchy	Crown of thorns starfish (COTS)	Antarctic krill	Blue shark	Peruvian anchoveta
domain		Eukarya		Eukarya
kingdom	Animalia		Animalia	
phylum		Arthropoda		
class	Asteroidea			Actinopterygii
order	Valvatida	Malocostraca	Carcharhiniformes	Clupeiformes
family	Acanthasteridae	Euphausiacea	Carcharinidae	Engraulidae
genus				
species				

Table 4.3: Classification of marine species.

4.3 Biodiversity

Biodiversity describes the degree in variation of organisms and ecosystems on Earth. Life evolved in the maritime environment and our global seas and oceans have an extremely high biodiversity. Biodiversity can be explored at three levels: **species diversity**, **genetic diversity** and **ecological diversity**. These three levels work together to describe the complexity of life on Earth. This is the first step to starting to understanding the importance of maintaining the biodiversity of marine environments.

> **KEY WORDS**
>
> **biodiversity:** a measure of the species, genetic and ecosystem diversity of different species
>
> **species diversity:** the abundance and richness of a species in a given place
>
> **genetic diversity:** the variety of forms of genes (alleles) within a species
>
> **ecological diversity:** the variation of ecosystems or habitats on a regional or global level

Types of biodiversity

Species diversity

Species diversity is a measure of the abundance and richness of a species in a given place at one time. Species abundance is the number of individuals per species. Species richness measures the number of species in an area. Coral reefs have many different ecological niches which are exploited by a multitude of different species, hence are one of the most species-rich areas on Earth. Other marine habitats, such sandy shores, have a far lower number of species.

Genetic diversity

Genes are made up of nucleic acids (DNA or RNA) and are the developmental code for life on Earth. The forms of genes are called alleles and they are responsible for both the similarities and the differences between species. Genetic diversity describes the variety of forms of gene alleles within a species. Each species has a set number of genes. Individuals within a species have their own particular gene allele composition. A population is all the individuals within one species in one area at one time, and each population has a different gene allele frequency. Genetic diversity within a species can be assessed by finding out the allele frequency per gene. Understanding the genetic biodiversity of different populations of a species is crucial as some may be inbred and have a smaller range of alleles. A reduction in the number of alleles may result in populations being less able to adapt when there are changes in the environment.

Ecological diversity

Ecological diversity is the variation of ecosystems or habitats on a regional or global level at one time. An ecosystem is a community of organisms (biota) and their interaction with the abiotic environment. An ecosystem can cover a large area, such as the Great Barrier Reef, or be as small as a hydrothermal vent. Measuring ecological diversity is however difficult because each of Earth's ecosystems merges into the ecosystems around it.

Importance of marine biodiversity

Marine ecosystems with a high biodiversity include kelp forests, seagrass meadows, mangroves and coral reefs. These habitats each provide crucial services to the coastal communities that they support.

Maintaining stable ecosystems

The more species there are, and the more evenly the number of organisms are distributed among the different species, the greater the species diversity. Ecosystems with high species diversity are considered important as they tend to be more stable and resistant to ecological change. The environment is a major factor influencing the biodiversity of a habitat. Environments that are either unstable or extreme tend to have a lower biodiversity than environments that are stable and not extreme. Stable ecosystems support a rich biodiversity which helps maintain the complex interactions between the community of organisms and the physical environment. Some common marine examples are coral reefs, rocky shores, hydrothermal vents, and reef slopes.

Coral reefs

Coral reefs occupy less than 1% of the ocean floor, but contain more than 25% of known marine life. This high biodiversity is the result of a stable and non-extreme environment that provides abiotic conditions that are close to optimum for the producers. A vibrant community of producers provides the foundation for long food chains and a diverse food web.

Rocky shores

Rocky shores are also stable, non-extreme environments. The rock provides a good attachment surface for molluscs and seaweeds, so there is less chance of the organisms being washed away. Rocky shores also provide protective habitats, such as rock pools and crevices. They are less porous than sandy shores so organisms are less prone to dying from drying out (desiccation). Rocky shores hence support a greater biodiversity than sandy shores.

Hydrothermal vents

Hydrothermal vents communities are located in an environment that is extreme because the abiotic conditions, including toxins, temperature, pH, hydrostatic pressure and light, are outside the zone of tolerance for most organisms. Because very few organisms are adapted to live in the extreme conditions, hydrothermal vents have a low biodiversity.

Reef slopes

Reef slopes are the steep, sometimes vertical, walls at the front (fore) of a reef. These fore-reef zones absorb most of the energy and damage from incoming waves and stormy seas. This means the sandy substrate of a reef slope is easily eroded by currents, waves and wind, and it is difficult for marine plants to grow there. Lack of biomass in primary producers and the usual loss of energy between trophic levels means that food chains are short and the environment cannot support species at higher trophic levels. The organisms that can successfully use the reef slope sand habitat include animals that burrow into the sand, such as worms, clams, sand fleas and crabs. Although the physical conditions are not extreme, they are constantly changing so the environment is described as unstable. Not many marine organisms are adapted to survive in such conditions, so biodiversity is low.

Protection of the physical environment

Ecosystems with a high marine biodiversity lead to increased protection of the coastal environmental. For example, the root systems of marine plants such as seagrasses and mangroves, stabilise the muddy substrate and so reduce the erosion of estuaries and mud flats during heavy storms. Similarly, fringing reefs of coral provide a physical barrier to the destructive action of waves during tropical storms. The reefs absorb the power of waves and storms before they hit the mainland. This protects the coastline (for example, sandy beaches) from damage due to weathering and erosion.

Climate control

The producers which underpin high biodiversity marine ecosystems play a pivotal ecological role for our planet as they regulate atmospheric increases in carbon dioxide concentration that can lead to climate change. An example is the high productivity of phytoplankton and seagrasses which results in them being able to store twice as much carbon dioxide per hectare as terrestrial rainforests. Photosynthesis by these carbon sinks helps reduce atmospheric carbon dioxide and the man-made effects of ocean acidification and global warming. A by-product of this process is the production of oxygen which is required by marine organisms for aerobic respiration.

Providing food sources

High biodiversity ecosystems include the primary producers which provide food and shelter for many other species in a vibrant food web. By doing so, they nurture the growth of the range of ocean species – such as macroalgae, crustaceans and fish – which humans depend upon as a staple part of our nutrition.

Source of medicines

Marine biodiversity is an exciting source of new medicinal drugs derived from marine plants, animals, fungi or bacteria. Figure 4.28 shows the proportional

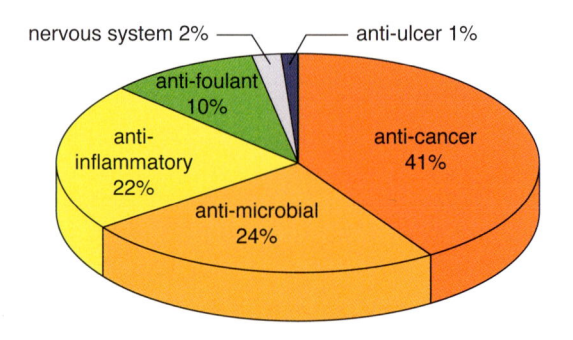

Figure 4.28: The use of beneficial chemicals derived from marine organisms.

uses of beneficial chemicals derived from marine organisms. Discoveries from our aquatic pharmacy that are currently undergoing medical trials include:

- a pain-relief drug harvested from marine cone snails
- schizophrenia medication from marine worms
- wound-healing drugs from corals
- anti-cancer drugs from a range of marine bacteria, bryozoans, fungi, tunicates and nudibranchs.

A variety of marine ecosystems have proven lucrative in the global hunt for new 'superdrugs'. The littoral zone of rocky shores in western North America are home to the giant keyhole limpet, *Megathura crenulata* (Figure 4.29). A protein extracted from this species, called keyhole limpet hemocyanin (KLH), has been proven to stimulate the immune system. KLH's immunotherapy properties have meant that it is in high demand to treat a range of autoimmune, inflammatory and infectious diseases. It is also being tested as a potential vaccine for skin, breast and bladder cancer. Over-harvesting of the species has, however, resulted in a significant decline in their populations and research is now focussing on the potential aquaculture of this pharmaceutically important mollusc.

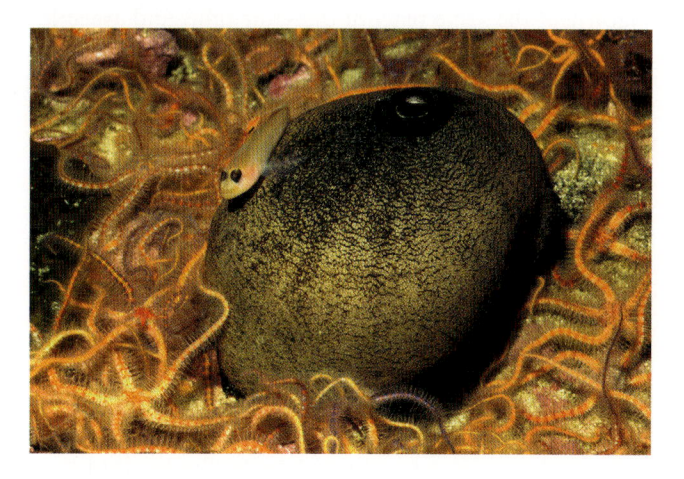

Figure 4.29: Giant keyhole limpet (*Megathura crenulata*).

Deep-sea trenches are the largest unexplored habitat on Earth. Marine scientists are searching a number of these ocean trenches either by deep-sea submarines or dropping a long coring device to the ocean floor. Researchers extract and test the bioactive compounds produced by these organisms for medicinal properties. *Dermacoccus abyssi* is a bacterium retrieved from sediment in the Mariana Trench. This organism produces dermacozines, a biochemical that may help protect against the parasite that causes African sleeping sickness.

Marine organisms that live closer to the surface can also be the source of pharmaceuticals. For example, three species of Australian sea sponges have been found to produce chemicals called chondropsins. The drug potential of chondropsins is related to their ability to inhibit certain enzymes that play a role in the development of bone cancer, Alzheimer's disease, viral infections, diabetes and cardiovascular disorders.

Test yourself

5 With reference to a mangrove ecosystem, define the following terms:
   a   species abundance
   b   species richness
   c   genetic diversity of mud crabs.

6 The giant keyhole limpet, *Megathura crenulata*, occurs in intertidal and sub-littoral waters along the rocky coast of Eastern Pacific ocean from Southern California in USA to the Baja California peninsula in Mexico. Explain the importance of maintaining the biodiversity of this habitat with regards to:
   a   medicine
   b   food
   c   climate stability.

4.4 Populations and sampling techniques

Humans have been trying to measure, describe and understand life on Earth for millennia. As our understanding has progressed, scientists have created a biological vocabulary to help describe the structure and interdependency of marine **ecosystems**. This section

> **KEY WORD**
>
> **ecosystem:** the living organisms and the environment with which they interact

will start by introducing some of the vocabulary that is key to sharing this knowledge: **habitat**, **niche**, **species**, **population** and community.

> **KEY WORDS**
>
> **habitat:** the natural environment where an organism lives
>
> **niche:** the role of a species within an ecosystem
>
> **species:** a group of similar organisms that can interbreed naturally to produce fertile offspring
>
> **population:** all the individuals of the same species that live at the same place and time

Life on Earth can be divided into subunits called ecosystems. An ecosystem is all the living organisms in an area plus the non-living environmental factors that act on them. Key examples of five marine ecosystems will be discussed in greater detail in Chapter 5: the open ocean, tropical coral reef, rocky shore, sandy shore and mangrove forest. The biological, chemical and physical parts of an ecosystem are linked by energy and nutrient flows that were explored in Chapter 3.

A habitat is the natural environment where organisms live. Habitats are areas in which organisms can find food, protection, shelter and a mate. Marine environments form a range of habitats in estuaries, on the shoreline and in shallow and deep ocean water. Estuaries are brackish areas where fresh and salt water mix. Sediments from streams often settle in estuaries, creating a number of important habitats where marine species can feed and breed. These habitats include swampy areas called wetlands, mangrove forests and salt marshes.

The habitat an organism occupies can be defined by where it lives and how it moves. For example, organisms that:

- drift in ocean currents (planktonic) include phytoplankton and zooplankton
- can actively swim (nektonic) include fish, marine reptiles and mammals
- live on the seabed (benthic) include starfish, crabs and sea cucumbers.

Some organisms cross from one habitat to another during their life cycles. For example, crabs and clams both start out as planktonic larvae but become benthic adults. Habitats are not always geographical (for example, parasitic worms live inside their host species).

A species is defined as a group of similar organisms that can interbreed naturally to produce fertile offspring. Endemic species are organisms that are found in only one area. For example, the Galápagos marine iguana only lives and hunts for food on the shores of the Galápagos Islands (Figure 4.30).

Figure 4.30: Galápagos marine iguana (*Amblyrhynchus cristatus*).

A population is all the organisms of the same species that live at the same place at the same time, and are able to reproduce. For example, the squat lobsters living off Otago, New Zealand, are a population. Similarly, all the salmon in the Atlantic Ocean make up the Atlantic salmon population. The number of individuals in any population often increases and decreases. Population increases are caused by reproduction or by new individuals joining the population area. Population decreases are caused by death or by individuals leaving the population area. The largest population that can be sustained by the available resources is called the carrying capacity. If some resources are less than optimal, or get completely used up, they are called limiting factors and result in reduced growth in the population. Limiting factors can be either biotic or abiotic. Biotic limiting factors include competition and predation. Abiotic limiting factors affect growth, survival and reproduction, and include living space, food, water temperature, pH and light intensity.

A community is an association of all the different populations of species occupying a habitat at the same time. An example is the mollusc community on a Californian rocky shore, which would include all the different species of molluscs living in this habitat. Biomes are communities that extend over large areas of the globe and are classified according to the predominant

4 Classification and biodiversity

vegetation. Marine biomes include intertidal, rocky, sandy and muddy shores, coral reefs and the seabed. Each biome has a characteristic community.

A niche is defined as the role of a species within an ecosystem. There are a variety of roles, or niches, that organisms perform in their aquatic environment. These were described in Chapter 3 and include producers, consumers, decomposers, predators and prey. The term niche also takes into account interrelationships with other organisms:

- **Feeding relationships** Both sperm whales and killer whales are top predators. Sperm whales predominantly consume squid, whereas killer whales consume a wider variety of prey, including elephant seals and baleen whales. These two species of whale therefore occupy different ecological niches.

- **Spatial relationships** Two species may have the same feeding relationships but occupy that niche in different parts of the ocean. For example, if a prey species is found throughout the water column, one predator may feed on it within the surface photic zone (where there is light) while another feeds deeper down in the aphotic zone (where there is no light).

- **Temporal relationships** Two species may have the same feeding relationships but occupy the niche at different times. For example, if a prey species is found in the same location throughout each day, one predator may feed at night (nocturnal) while another feeds in the daytime (diurnal).

Biotic and abiotic factors in marine ecosystems

The distribution and abundance of organisms in the marine environment are affected by both biotic and abiotic factors. The **biotic factors** of an ecosystem are the links between living organisms, and include the feeding relationships between producers, consumers and decomposers. These trophic level connections can be shown as food chains or food webs and include predator–prey relationships. The distribution of a predator is reliant on there being prey species for it to hunt, kill and eat. An example on a rocky shore is that predators such as oyster borers are reliant on the abundance of prey species, such as oysters, mussels and barnacles.

Other interspecies interactions that were discussed in Chapter 3 include the three main types of symbioses (an interaction between two different organisms living in close physical association): parasitism, commensalism and mutualism. Symbiosis means 'living together' and refers to two or more organisms from different species living in close physical association. The abundance of the hosts will directly affect the symbiont (for example, the growth rate of hard corals is far slower without mutualistic zooxanthellae).

Diseases are illnesses characterised by specific signs and symptoms and can be caused by pathogens such as viruses and bacteria. Diseases result in a decrease in a marine population's distribution and abundance. Florida is currently experiencing a widespread and lethal coral disease outbreak caused by stony coral tissue loss disease (SCTLD). This results in small colonies of hard corals dying within a few weeks, while larger colonies can take more than a year to perish (Figure 4.31). SCTLD was first sighted in 2014 and by 2019 had spread to affect nearly half of the stony coral species found on the Florida Reef Tract.

Competition is a biotic relationship between organisms that strive for the same resources in the same place. There are two different types of competition:

- **intra-specific competition**, which occurs between individuals of the same species (for example, two male fish of the same species competing for female mates in the same area)

- **inter-specific competition**, which occurs between members of different species (for example, predators of different species competing for the same prey).

Inter-specific competition can lead to overlap between ecological niches. The species that is less well adapted has access to fewer resources and is less likely to

> **KEY WORDS**
>
> **biotic factors:** the living parts of an ecosystem, which includes the organisms and their effects on each other
>
> **disease:** an illness characterised by specific signs and symptoms
>
> **intra-specific competition:** competition between individuals of the same species (for example, for food or a mate)
>
> **inter-specific competition:** competition between members of different species (for example, predator–prey.)

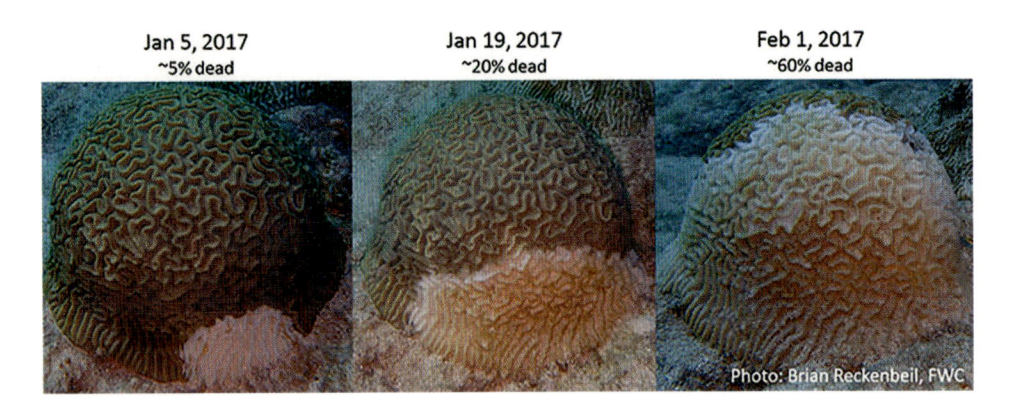

Figure 4.31: Destruction of a brain coral by stony coral tissue loss disease (SCTLD).

survive and reproduce: this could lead to the species becoming extinct. However, inter-specific competition more often leads to greater niche adaptations and niche specialisation. The fundamental niche is the niche of a species when that species experiences no competition with others. The fundamental niche can also be defined as the tolerance range for all important abiotic conditions, within which individuals of a species can survive, grow and reproduce. But all organisms are part of complex food webs, sharing the ecosystem with other species, and all competing for the same biotic and abiotic resources. As these resources are limited, this leads to inter-specific competition.

The competitive exclusion principle predicts that, in a stable ecosystem, no two species can be in direct competition with each other. If the niches for two species are identical, one species will die out as a result of inter-specific competition. For example, if an introduced species is added to an existing marine habitat then the new species may have the same niche as a native species (for example, two top predators feeding on the same prey at the same time in the same habitat). Inter-specific competition between the two species will occur, as they compete for this niche. One of the two species will be better at hunting the prey and, therefore, will thrive and increase in population size. The population of the other species will be less ecologically or reproductively viable, eventually dying out. Abiotic factors that affect the distribution abundance of marine organisms include:

- geological features include substrate type and shape of the seafloor (topography)
- physical features include temperature, exposure to air, wind and sunlight, wave action, tides, currents, hydrostatic pressure, water turbidity (murkiness), as well as light availability. The light available can be measured by both its brightness (intensity) and colour (wavelength).
- chemical features include pH, salinity, oxygen concentration, carbon dioxide concentration and nutrient availability (for example, nitrate/ phosphate concentration).

Each of the above biotic and abiotic factors can potentially reduce the growth, survival and reproductive success of organisms with marine ecosystems. If so, they are called limiting factors. In a deep sea hydrothermal vent, limiting factors include the lack of light, the acidic pH and the extremely high hydrostatic pressure and temperature.

The abiotic factors (the environment's geological, physical and chemical features; the non-living part of an ecosystem) of a marine ecosystem are the environment's non-living components. The hard coral species can only grow in the surface waters of reefs as they are limited by the need for low turbidity clear waters which allow light to penetrate for photosynthesis by the mutualistic zooxanthellae. Coral reefs are also limited to growing between 30°N and 30°S of the equator as they require warm waters. A reduction in sea level caused by either climate change or low tides can also kill coral. This is due to the polyps' inability to survive exposure to air. A lack of nutrients (such as calcium required for corallite) limits the polyps' ability to grow. An excess of nutrients, such as nitrate and phosphate ions in the run-off from land-based fertilisers, can also limit growth due to excessive algal growth that smoother the polyps (eutrophication). In contrast, soft corals are usually only found in deeper waters as they are out-competed by the faster growing coral species. The environment here is colder and darker, which results in a slower growth rate.

In a rocky shore ecosystem, the organisms that survive at high tide must be able to resist large changes in daily salinity and temperature due to the seawater becoming more concentrated on a hot summer day due to evaporation, while on a cold and rainy day, the salinity and temperature will plummet due to the influx of cold fresh water. The organisms must also be able to cling firmly to the rocky substrate in order to resist dislodging by wave action and tides.

Measuring marine biodiversity

The majority of all aquatic life in the world's oceans is thought to be unknown. Universities and research institutes use a range of scientific methods and statistical models to discover, sample and estimate this unknown biodiversity. In this section we will introduce how fieldwork techniques can be used to measure the fauna and flora within the littoral zone. We will also use maths skills to help us estimate population sizes and analyse the relationship between biotic and abiotic factors.

Mark–release–recapture

For mobile species where it is not practical to count all the individuals in the population, one approach to estimating the population size is by using the **mark–release–recapture** method. Using this approach, the population size can be estimated from as few as two visits to the study area, but increased accuracy is gained by more than two visits.

Estimation of the size of rocky shore populations of dog whelks can be made using the mark–release–recapture method. The molluscs are captured and all marked with a small dot of non-toxic waterproof paint. The number captured and marked is recorded. One to two days later another sample of the dog whelk population at the same location is taken and the total number captured on this second visit, both marked and unmarked, is counted. The number of marked individuals within this second sample is also recorded.

Numbered tags are another way of marking animals and these are commonly used for assessing fish, whale, turtle or shark populations. In addition to population estimates, the data from tagging can provide information on migration routes, feeding patterns, seasonal variation in numbers and birth and mortality rates. This data is useful for conservation scientists as well as those employed in managing the fishery industry.

All biological surveys are limited by their methodology. For example, the population estimate calculated by the mark–release–recapture method is based on a number of assumptions:

- Marked individuals are unaffected by the tagging process.
- Marked individuals disperse throughout the unmarked population.
- All animals have the same probability of being marked initially.
- Markings are not lost in the time between the two samples.
- The second sample is a random sample.
- The effects of emigration, immigration, mortality and recruitment are negligible.
- All marked animals seen in the second sample are reported.

KEY WORDS

mark–release–recapture: a method to estimate the population size of mobile species

Lincoln index: a mathematical equation that can use the mark–release–recapture data to estimate the population size

MATHS SKILLS 4.1

ESTIMATING POPULATION SIZE USING THE LINCOLN INDEX

The **Lincoln index** is one of a number of mathematical equations that can use the mark–release–recapture data to estimate the population size.

The Lincoln index uses the following formula and symbols:

$$N = \frac{n_1 \times n_2}{m_2}$$

where

N = estimate of population size

n_1 = number of individuals captured in first sample

n_2 = number of individuals (both marked and unmarked) captured in second sample

m_2 = number of marked individuals recaptured in second sample

> **CONTINUED**
>
> **Worked example**
>
> The mark–release–recapture method was performed on dog whelks found a rocky shore.
>
> The results were:
>
> n_1 = number of dog whelks captured and marked on the first visit: 120
>
> n_2 = number of dog whelks (both marked and unmarked) captured on the second visit: 200
>
> m_2 = number of recaptured dog whelks that were marked: 40
>
> Use the Lincoln index equation to estimate the total population size of dog whelks, N.
>
> $$N = \frac{n_1 \times n_2}{m_2}$$
> $$= \frac{200 \times 120}{40}$$
> $$= 600$$
>
> **Questions**
>
> 1. A biologist wants to estimate the size of a population of turtles on an island. He captures 20 turtles on his first visit, and marks their backs with red paint. Two weeks later he returns to the island and captures 25 turtles. Five of these 25 turtles have red paint on their backs. Using the Lincoln index equation, calculate the estimated population size.
>
> 2. Overfishing in Antarctica has resulted in a steep decline in Patagonian toothfish. Fishery scientists are monitoring the population size to see if it is recovering by using the mark–release–recapture method and the Lincoln index equation.
>
>   On their initial visit, the scientists caught and marked 100 specimens. When they returned on a second visit, they captured a total of 70 Patagonian toothfish. If the scientists estimated the population size was 700, how many of the recaptured toothfish were marked?

If any of these assumptions are not true, the accuracy of the predicted total would decrease.

Investigating distribution and abundance of organisms in the littoral zone

There are a number of methods that can be used to investigate the distribution and abundance of organisms in the littoral zone.

A **frame quadrat** is traditionally a plastic or metal square that sets a standard unit of area for study of the distribution marine organisms (Figure 4.32). They can be of any size but for most field work they are 10–100 cm in length. They are one of the most common tools used by marine ecologists and are best suited to estimate populations for sessile (immobile) marine species.

In marine ecology field studies, a **transect** is any rope marked at regular intervals. For rocky or sandy shore this may often be a 30–50 m tape measure. The regular interval can vary (for example, on a rocky or sandy shore this may be 2–5 m). Two common population sampling methods that use these tools are line transects and belt transects.

> **KEY WORDS**
>
> **frame quadrat:** a plastic or metal square that sets a standard unit of area for study of the distribution of marine organisms
>
> **transect:** a rope or tape marked at regular intervals that sets standard distances for study of the distribution of marine organisms

4 Classification and biodiversity

Figure 4.32: Frame quadrat.

Line transects are a quick way to record data on distribution of species; in other words, which species are present. The transect is placed in a straight line between two points in the direction of the environmental gradient you wish to study (for example, between the high and low tide mark on shore). In **continuous sampling**, any species that touches the line is recorded along the whole length of the transect. Alternatively, if **systematically sampling**, then the species presence is only recorded at regular intervals on the transect, say, every 0.5 m.

Belt transects are similar to the line transect method but give additional data on species abundance. A frame quadrat is placed at regular intervals on one side of the line and the frequency or percentage cover of organisms is recorded. You will investigate this method further in Core Practical Activity 4.2.

The belt transect method is an example of systematic sampling as samples are taken at fixed intervals along the transect. It is used to gather data on the distribution and abundance when investigating the zonation of marine species (dependent variable) along an abiotic gradient, such as exposure from high tide to low tide (independent variable).

In contrast, frame quadrats can also be used for **random sampling**. This is often chosen when the environment under study is fairly uniform or time is limited and the habitat size is very large (for example, a flat area of seagrass meadow). In the most basic random sampling method the quadrat is placed anywhere within the sample site. A more rigorous method is to generate a numbered grid of the sample site. A computer program is then used to select which squares to sample. This ensures that there is no observer bias in the selection of the sample locations.

When planning a field experiment to sample natural populations of organisms, it is crucial that we design an ethical and safe method. An **ethical method** is one that evaluates and chooses ways to protect the natural habitat under investigation. For example, an investigation that involves students snorkelling on a coral reef could elect for students to all access the reef from the beach in a single file to reduce the area damage by students walking over and damaging the coral. Designing a **safe method** involves identify potential hazards and then reducing their risk of occurring. For the coral reef study, this could involve checking the tides and weather forecast to plan the safest time for the sampling.

Test yourself

7   Explain what is meant by each of the following terms:
    a   population
    b   community
    c   species
    d   ecosystem.

8   Blue bat star (*Patiria pectinifera*) are a species of seastar that live in Japanese waters. They were marked with a branding iron as part of a mark–release–recapture method to estimate their populations near Japan. Suggest one positive and one negative effect of this marking process.

KEY WORDS

line transect: a sampling method involving counting of species that touch the transect

continuous sampling: samples are taken along the whole length of the transect

systematic sampling: samples are taken at fixed intervals along the transect

belt transect: a sampling method involving counting of species in frame quadrats placed adjacent to the transect

random sampling: samples are taken at random places within the sample site

ethical method: evaluates and chooses ways to protect the natural habitat under investigation

safe method: identifies potential hazards and then reducing their risk of occurring

CORE PRACTICAL ACTIVITY 4.2: INVESTIGATING THE DISTRIBUTION AND ABUNDANCE OF ORGANISMS IN THE LITTORAL ZONE

Introduction

The littoral zone of a rocky shore has distinct intertidal zones (for example, low tide, mid-tide, high tide and splash zones) where specific groups of organisms are found. The species commonly found in each zone are those that are best adapted to the abiotic and biotic conditions of that zone. Field work using a quadrat and transect line can be performed to investigate these zonation patterns. A typical quadrat for this habitat is a square approximately 50 cm in length with a marked grid of ten squares by ten squares. By collecting quantitative and qualitative data about the relative abundance of species between high- and low-tide marks, you can determine which organisms are found in each zone of a rocky shore (Figure 4.33). This method can also be used to study sandy and muddy shores.

Figure 4.33: Students taking a rocky shore transect of Buckleton's Beach, New Zealand.

Equipment

You will need:
- 30 m tape measure as a transect
- quadrat 50 cm in length
- species identification chart
- recording sheets in a waterproof folder.

Safety considerations

- Check weather forecast to ensure no storms or bad weather.
- Check tide times to ensure beach study at low tide.
- Complete a safety and risk assessment before starting the practical.

Before you start

1. Research either online or using a species identification chart (field guide) the organisms found on a rocky shore in your local area or elsewhere. In pairs, test each other to see if you can recognise and name them.
2. Discuss the difference between safe and ethical practices. As a group, name three of each and discuss together why they are a benefit.

Method

1. Look at local tide charts and time the field trip for one hour either side of low tide.
2. Lay out a tape measure to mark your transect route. The transect should be perpendicular to the water's edge, from high tide to low tide.
3. Use a quadrat to sample the rocky shore organisms.
4. Use a species identification chart to identify common organisms on your rocky shore. Choose four species to collect data for.
5. Choose the number of sampling points. For example, if you are doing a 20 m transect line, you may decide to take 11 quadrat samples – one for every 2 m, starting at high tide (0 m).

Recording data

- There are a number of ways to record your data. For each species you must use the same method for all the transect lines sampled. To be able to calculate averages, it is important to repeat the transect three to five times at different points along the rocky shore.

CONTINUED

- For large fauna (for example, chitons) the simplest method is to count the total number of organisms in your quadrat. Alternatively, if numbers are large (for example, periwinkles or barnacles), then an estimate can be made by counting the number in a quarter of the quadrat and multiplying this value by 4.
- For plant species (for example, seaweed) vegetation percentage cover can be estimated using the 10 × 10 quadrat grid. Alternatively, abundance can be recorded using the ACFOR scale:

  A = abundant (greater than or equal to 30%)

  C = common (20–29%)

  F = frequent (10–19%)

  O = occasional (5–9%)

  R = rare (1–4%)
- Abiotic data (for example, temperature, pH or salinity) may also be recorded along the transect line. You may wish to use a data logger probe for this.
- On your record sheet there should be a column for any features that may affect the abundance of species (for example, if the quadrat is in or near a rock pool or crevice).
- You may wish to record the height of each quadrat above low tide. The collected data can then be used to plot the topographical shape (profile) of the rocky shore.
- A sketch map of the rocky shore should also be drawn showing the position of your transect lines. This may be useful when comparing zonation patterns with different coastal characteristics (for example, more exposed versus less exposed to wave action).

School-based simulation

If you cannot get to a coastline, you can simulate the above method within your school. One way is to use a sports field or school gym. One side of the pitch is designated as high tide while the other end is low tide. Four sets of coloured cones, each representing a different littoral species, are then placed across the surface of the pitch. You can then complete the method above using a 30 m tape measure, as a transect, together with large 1 m × 1 m plastic-framed quadrats.

Alternatively, a table in a classroom can be used to represent a rocky shore. Four differently coloured self-adhesive stickers or paperclips can be scattered over the table to represent the four littoral organisms being sampled. You can use a miniature frame quadrat, such as 10 cm × 10 cm together with a 1 m ruler as a transect.

Results and analysis

Record your results in a table such as the example for a rocky shore shown in Table 4.4.

Figure 4.34 shows how a **kite graph** can be used to represent the distribution and abundance of each organism (y-axis) against the distance from low to high tide (x-axis). Note that the y-axis represents different methods of estimating abundance. For example, seaweed and periwinkles are both being measured in percentage cover, while mussels and barnacles are measured in number of specimens.

Species		Quadrat distance from high tide to low tide / m										
		0	2	4	6	8	10	12	14	16	18	20
periwinkles	% cover											
mussels	number											
barnacles	number											
seaweed	% cover											

Table 4.4: Rocky shore data.

KEY WORD

kite graph: a graph of the distribution and abundance of organisms in the littoral zone that allows zonation patterns to be easily seen

CONTINUED

The scale chosen for plotting abundance may also vary between each species and does not have to be the same. Kite graphs allow zonation patterns between organisms in the littoral zone to be easily seen. For example, in Figure 4.34, periwinkles are found most commonly towards high tide, mussels and barnacles are found most commonly in mid-tide, seaweed is most commonly found further towards low tide. Line plots of either profile or abiotic data can also be included at the bottom of kite graphs. This may be also useful when discussing reasons why an organism's niche may be at a certain zone on the littoral habitat.

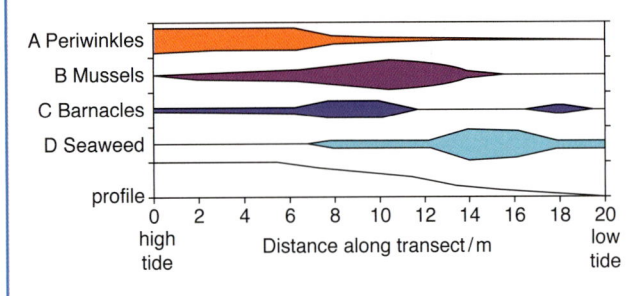

Figure 4.34: A kite graph representing zonation patterns on a rocky shore.

Evaluations and conclusions

1. Identify and describe each of the following:
   a. independent variable (variable that is changed)
   b. dependent variable (variable that is measured)
   c. control variables (variables that are kept constant).

2. a. When using a quadrat, suggest a time when the percentage cover for the species present may total to more than 100%.
   b. Quadrats can come in different sizes. It is important to ensure the correct quadrat is used in field work. Discuss the problems associated with using a quadrat that is either too large or too small.
   c. A common question asked by students is how far apart should quadrats be placed in a belt transect. Discuss this in a group and see if you can reach a recommendation.

3. a. For each of the three methods of measuring population size, state whether the data is quantitative or qualitative.
   b. Comparing quantitative data with qualitative data, suggest:
      i. **one** benefit of each method
      ii. **one** limitation of each method
   c. If the tide was coming in and the weather turning, suggest which method of measuring population size would be most appropriate.

4. Collate you class data from this activity. Analyse it to see what zonation patterns you found.

5. a. Look at the species that are found closest to high tide and explain adaptations that they have that allow them to survive here.
   b. Explain common adaptations shared by species that are located at low tide.

REFLECTION

After completing Core Practical Activity 4.2, think about these questions:

1. Discuss how the findings of this school-based investigation reinforce your understanding of the effects of tidal exposure on the zonation of marine organisms. What were the benefits and limitations of this practical approach?
2. What problems did you have carrying out this practical activity? How could you avoid them in the future?

MATHS SKILLS 4.2

CALCULATING BIODIVERSITY

There are a variety of ways to quantify the biodiversity of a marine community. The two main factors to consider are richness and evenness:

- **Richness** is the number of species in a community. The more species present in a sample, the 'richer' the sample. Richness does not take into account the population size of each species, so gives equal rating to those species that have very few, and those species that have many, individuals. One whelk therefore has as much influence on the richness of a rocky shore as 1000 barnacles. A community with many species is considered to be richer than a community with a lower number of species present.
- **Evenness** is a measure of the relative abundance of the different species making up the richness of an area by comparing the population size of each of the species present. A community dominated by one species is considered to be less diverse than a community in which several different species have a similar abundance.

A biodiversity measure that accounts for both species richness and species evenness is **Simpson's index of diversity (D)**. It can be calculated using the following formula and symbols:

$$D = 1 - \left(\Sigma\left(\frac{n}{N}\right)^2\right)$$

where Σ = sum of (total)

n = number of individuals of each *different* species

N = the total number of individuals of *all* the species

What do indices of biodiversity mean?

A low species index of diversity suggests that:

- there are relatively few successful species in the habitat
- the environment is extreme or unstable with relatively few ecological niches, and only a few species are really well adapted to that environment
- food webs are relatively simple
- a change in the environment would probably significantly reduce the biodiversity.

A high species index of diversity suggests that:

- There is a greater number of successful species and a more stable ecosystem.
- More ecological niches are available and the environment is less likely to be hostile.
- There are complex food webs.
- Environmental change is less likely to be damaging to the biodiversity of the ecosystem.

Species biodiversity may be used to investigate the biological health of a particular habitat. For example, a decrease in the biodiversity index of a coral reef indicates that something has had a negative effect on the reef's health (for example, an oil spill or overfishing), which marine ecologists and managers need to mitigate. Alternatively, an increase in the biodiversity index may signify that conservation efforts have been effective.

Worked example

Scientists who discovered a recent whale fall counted the species in Table 4.5. Use this data to calculate Simpson's index of biodiversity for this habitat.

Species	Number (n)
sharks	2
amphipods	8
whales	1
hagfish	1
crabs	3
total	$N = 15$

KEY WORDS

richness: the number of species in a community

evenness: a measure of the relative abundance of the populatrions of different species in an area

Simpson's index of diversity (D): a biodiversity measure that accounts for both species richness and evenness

CONTINUED

Organism	Number (n)	$\frac{n}{N}$	$\left(\frac{n}{N}\right)^2$
sharks	2	0.133	0.018
amphipods	8	0.533	0.284
whales	1	0.067	0.004
hagfish	1	0.067	0.004
crabs	3	0.200	0.040
Totals	N = 15		$\Sigma\left(\frac{n}{N}\right)^2 = 0.350$

Table 4.5: Whale fall data.

Putting the figures into the formula for Simpson's index of biodiversity:

$$D = 1 - \Sigma\left(\frac{n}{N}\right)^2 = 1 - 0.350 = 0.650$$

Questions

1 Calculate Simpson's index of diversity for the following data in Table 4.6 for a reef on the Baa Atoll in the Maldives.

Species	Number of individuals
whale shark	1
surgeon fish	12
butterfly fish	3
parrot fish	2
stingray	3
anemone fish	6

Table 4.6: Reef species data.

2 Calculate Simpson's index of diversity for the mangrove swamp data in Table 4.7.

Species	Number of individuals
mangrove crabs	82
water snake	2
manatee	1
grey snapper	8
loggerhead turtle	2
alligator	2

Table 4.7: Mangrove swamp data.

3 Calculate Simpson's index of diversity for the rocky shore survey data in Table 4.8.

Species	Number of individuals
barnacle	63
hermit crab	8
black nerita	33
sea slaters	55
periwinkles	22
rock snails	11
limpets	6

Table 4.8: Rocky shore survey data.

4 Two prospective marine reserve locations are being investigated for the release of captive-bred turtles. Site A has a Simpson's index of diversity of 0.821 while site B has an index of 0.411. Based on this information, suggest and explain which location is better suited as a marine reserve.

MATHS SKILLS 4.3

SPEARMAN'S RANK CORRELATION

While population sampling on a rocky shore you may observe that the distribution of an organism is linked to variations in an abiotic factor, such as time exposed above tide. Alternatively, two different species may seem to occur in the same littoral zone and you may consider if there could be a predator–prey association between them. The **null hypothesis (H_0)** is that there is no correlation between the two species. To test if there is any potential association, you first plot a **scatter graph**.

Three types of relationships are shown in Figure 4.35.

- In graph A, there is a positive correlation relationship: as x increases, y increases.
- In graph B, there is a negative correlation relationship: as x increases, y decreases.
- In graph C, there is no association: an increase in x is not linked to y.

If the scatter graph suggests there is a correlation, then you can use different types of correlation coefficient calculations to test the strength of the relationships between the distribution and abundance of species and abiotic or biotic factors. **Spearman's rank correlation** is commonly used in marine science to find out if there is a correlation between two sets of variables, when they are not normally distributed.

Correlations exist between −1 (perfect linear negative correlation), 0 (no correlation) and +1 (perfect linear positive correlation). In Figure 4.35, graph A is close to a perfect linear positive correlation, so it will have a correlation of just less than 1. The relationship in graph B is a negative correlation but it is not as linear, so it will have a correlation value between 0 and −1.

The Spearman's rank correlation coefficient (r_s) is determined using the following formula and symbols:

$$r_s = 1 - \left(\frac{6 \times \Sigma D^2}{n^3 - n}\right)$$

where

r_s = Spearman's rank correlation coefficient

ΣD^2 = sum of the difference between each pair of ranked measurements

n = number of pairs of items in the sample

The Spearman's rank correlation coefficient involves ranking the data for each variable and assessing the difference between the ranks. It can be used when you have collected either quantitative data (for example, distance from high tide, light intensity, number of

Graph A — positive correlation

Graph B — negative correlation

Graph C — no correlation

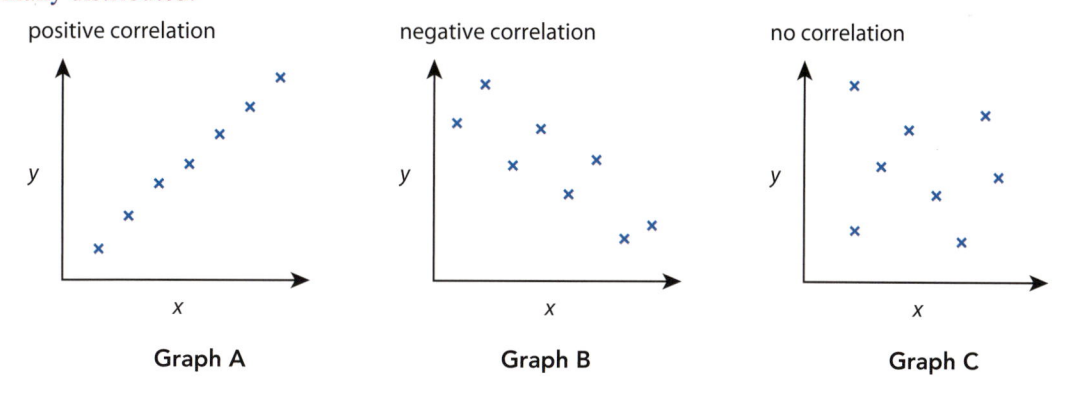

Figure 4.35: Types of scatter graph.

KEY WORDS

null hypothesis (H_0): there is no correlation between the two sets of variables

hypothesis: an explanation of an observation that can be tested through experimentation

scatter graph: when two sets of variables are plotted to indicate if there is a relationship between them

Spearman's rank correlation: a mathematical tool used to find out if there is a correlation between two sets of variables, when they are not normally distributed

CONTINUED

animals or percentage cover of plant species in quadrats) or qualitative data (for example, ACFOR abundance scale for animals plant species in quadrats).

Worked example

A marine scientist collecting rocky shore data wants to find out if there is a relationship between the distribution and abundance of two species (spp). The scientist sampled 10 quadrats and collected the data shown in Table 4.9.

Quadrat #	1	2	3	4	5	6	7	8	9	10
spp A % cover	0	1	2	10	8	9	11	7	4	3
spp B % cover	0	5	14	25	28	30	40	32	20	8

Table 4.9: Species percentage cover.

The first step is to draw a scatter graph either by hand or by using the graphing facility of a spreadsheet program. The results, shown in Figure 4.36, suggest that there may be a positive correlation.

To test the strength of this correlation, we calculate the Spearman's rank correlation coefficient.

First, we count the number of pairs of data sets in the sample. This is 10, as each of the 10 quadrats sampled contains one pair of data sets (one set for species A and one set for species B).

Next, we rank each data set for species A, and then rank each data set for species B. For example, for species A, the percentage cover in quadrat 7 is highest (11%), so we rank it 1 for species A. The next highest is in quadrat 4 (10%), so we rank this 2. For species B, the highest percentage cover is also in quadrat 7 (40%), so that is ranked 1 for species B, and so on.

Once we have ranked the data sets for both species, we calculate the differences in rank, D, by subtracting the rank of species B from the rank of species A. Each of these differences is then squared to give D^2.

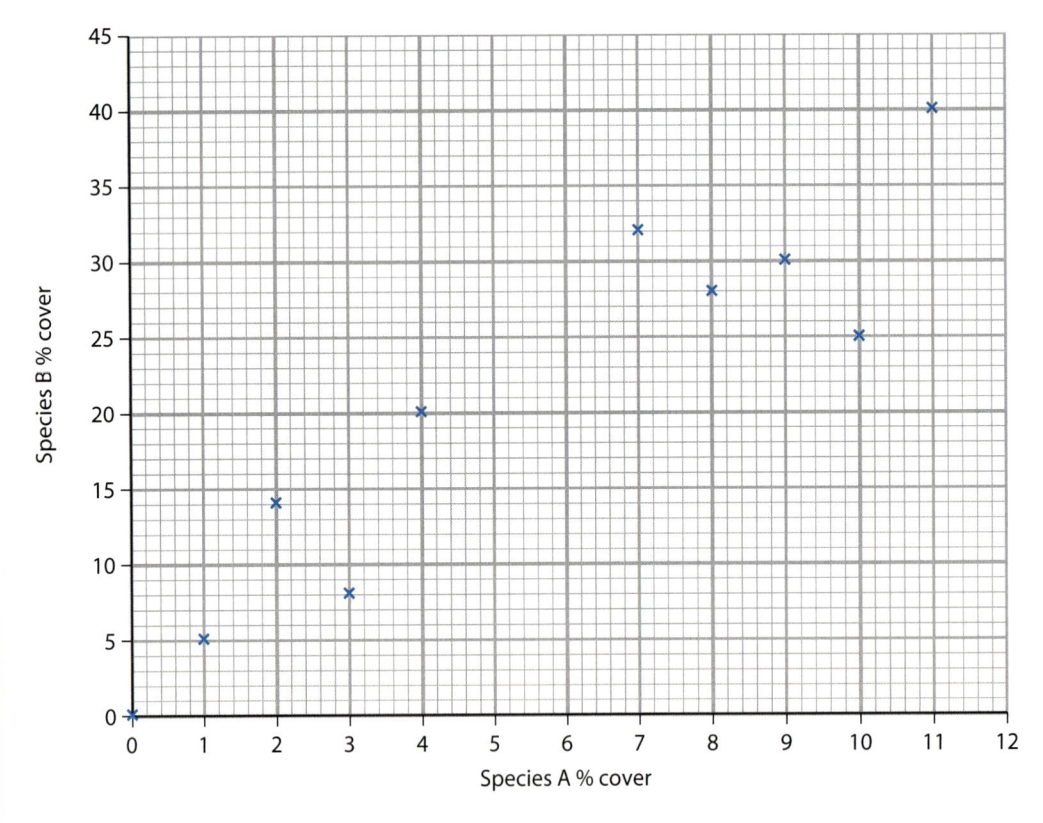

Figure 4.36: Scatter graph of percentage cover species A vs species B.

CONTINUED

Last, you add all the D^2 values to find ΣD^2. This is shown in Table 4.6.

Quadrat #	1	2	3	4	5	6	7	8	9	10
spp A % cover	0	1	2	10	8	9	11	7	4	3
spp A rank	10	9	8	2	4	3	1	5	6	7
spp B % cover	0	5	14	25	28	30	40	32	20	8
spp B rank	10	9	7	5	4	3	1	2	6	8
D	0	0	1	−3	0	0	0	3	0	−1
D^2	0	0	1	9	1	0	0	9	0	1
ΣD^2	21									

Table 4.10: Spearman's calculation table.

Substituting into this formula, we can calculate the Spearman's rank correlation coefficient:

$$r_s = 1 - \left(\frac{6 \times \Sigma D^2}{n^3 - n}\right)$$

$$= 1 - \left(\frac{6 \times 21}{1000 - 10}\right)$$

$$= 1 - \left(\frac{126}{990}\right)$$

$$= 1 - 0.13$$

$$= 0.87 \text{ (to two decimal places)}$$

To test if r_s is significant, we use Table 4.11 to compare our calculated r_s (0.87) with the **critical values of r_s** at 0.05 (5%) probability for $n = 10$ (0.65).

n	5	6	7	8	9	10	11	12	14	16
critical value r_s	1.00	0.89	0.79	0.76	0.68	0.65	0.60	0.54	0.51	0.51

Table 4.11: Critical values of r_s at 0.05 probability.

Because 0.87 > 0.65, we can conclude that the null hypothesis (that there is no correlation between the two species) is rejected.

We can, therefore, accept the **alternative hypothesis** that there is a significant correlation between the abundance of species A and species B on a rocky shore.

A correlation does not necessarily imply a *causal* relationship. For example, the number of species A and species B may have a positive correlation but this does not mean that there is a direct association (in other words, a change in

KEY WORDS

critical values of r_s: indicate when the calculated Spearman's rank is sufficient to suggest a correlation between the two sets of variables

alternative hypothesis: there is a significant correlation between two sets of variables

> **CONTINUED**

A does not *cause* a change in B, or vice versa). For example, there may be an independent abiotic or biotic factor that is causing both to occur in the same rocky shore littoral zone, such as tidal exposure time.

Questions

Marine science students decided to investigate if there was a correlation between the abundance of green turtles and the percentage cover of seagrass.

1. State a null hypothesis (H_0) for this field experiment.
2. Population samples were studied at eight sites and the results are recorded in Table 4.12. To test whether there was a correlation between the abundance of the two organisms, a Spearman's rank correlation was performed.
   a. Complete the ranking for seagrass in Table 4.12.
   b. Calculate ΣD^2
   c. Calculate r_s to three decimal places. Show your working.
3. Table 4.13 shows part of a Spearman's rank probability table. Use the critical values in Table 4.12 to state what the calculated r_s says about the relationship between green turtle and seagrass abundance.
4. Explain if the results prove that sea turtles cause a change in seagrass density.

Site #	Green turtle / number	Rank	Seagrass / % cover	Rank	D – rank difference	D^2
1	3	5	57			
2	0	8	52			
3	2	6	30			
4	12	2	20			
5	1	7	55			
6	6	4	34			
7	14	1	22			
8	9	3	25			

Table 4.12: Spearman's rank calculation table

N (number of pairs)		8	9	10	11	12
critical value, r_s	at significance level 5%	0.738	0.700	0.648	0.618	0.618
	at significance level 1%	0.881	0.883	0.794	0.755	0.727

Table 4.13: Spearman's rank (r_s) probability table.

4 Classification and biodiversity

PROJECT: A MARINE SKIT

In pairs, choose a marine organism that fascinates you or that you have seen recently in a local or international news article. Prepare a three minute dramatic performance to give in class on this species to cover the following areas:

- the species' classification
- ecological role of the species including its predators and/or prey
- economic value of the species
- human impact on the species
- conservation of the species.

Thinking about your project

Produce a written multiple choice test with five questions based on your presentation (one for each of the points above) to give to the class. Look at the results from the multiple choice tests and analyse which questions classmates failed to answer correctly. Reflect on how you could change your presentation next time to make it better.

Reflect on the other presentations made by your classmates:

- Which ones were the most informative?
- Where these the same ones you enjoyed the most?

Suggest three ways that you could you have improved your own presentation to make it more informative and interesting.

EXAM-STYLE QUESTIONS

1 Figure 4.37 is a biological drawing of a sea cucumber, one type of echinoderm.

Figure 4.37: Biological drawing of a sea cucumber.

a State **one** feature seen in Figure 4.37 that is characteristic of echinoderms. [1]

b State **one** feature from Figure 4.37 that is not characteristic of other echinoderms. [1]

c Sea cucumbers are considered to be a keystone species in the Galápagos Marine Reserve. State what is meant by a keystone species. [1]

d Describe the ecological importance of the planktonic larvae and adult sea cucumbers. [2]

143

> CONTINUED

> e Sea cucumbers are considered a delicacy in Asia and commercial fishing of sea cucumbers around the Galápagos Islands began in 1992. In 1999, a fishing season and minimum catch size were introduced but failed to prevent overfishing and the collapse of sea cucumber stocks in 2005. Predict the economic and social impact of this on the local community. [2]
>
> [Total: 7]
>
> 2 a Green crabs, *Carcinus maenas*, are an invasive species of crustacean now found in Maine, USA. State **two** characteristics of crustaceans. [2]
>
>   b Figure 4.38 shows the ecological interdependence of ocean temperature, green crabs and clams.

> Figure 4.38: The interdependence of ocean temperature, green crabs and clams.

>   i Describe the relationship between ocean temperature and the green crabs. [2]
>   ii Describe the relationship between the distribution of green crabs and clams and suggest an explanation for this. [3]
>
> [Total: 7]
>
> 3 Kelp are important marine producers often found growing in coastal waters in dense forests.
>   a i Explain how the gas bladders ensure rapid growth of the kelp. [2]
>   ii Explain the role of the holdfast. [1]
>   b State **two** uses from the harvesting of macroalgae such as seaweed or kelp. [2]

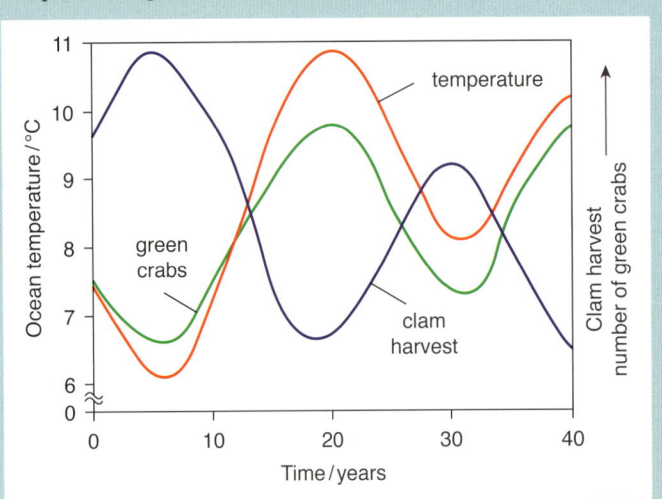

CONTINUED

    c In an area of sea off the coast of Scotland, sea urchins graze on kelp and are in turn eaten by sea otters.

        i Draw this food chain. [1]

        ii Fishing and pollution have caused a reduction in the population of sea otters in some areas. Predict how this could affect the abundance of kelp. [2]

        iii Suggest how and why a reduction in kelp density could affect future harvests of fish. [2]

                                                                                                                                                       [Total: 10]

4 **a** Describe **three** differences between the two species of seagrass in Figure 4.39. [3]

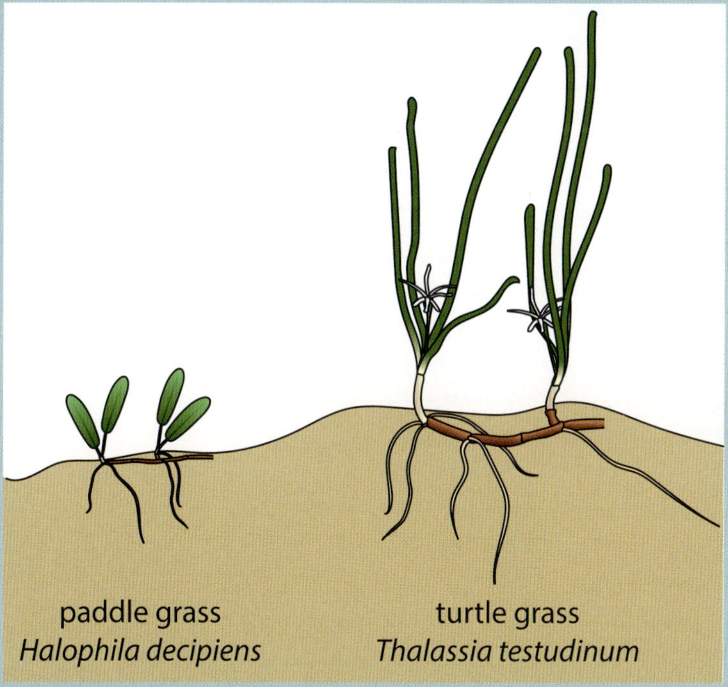

Figure 4.39: Two species of seagrass.

paddle grass
Halophila decipiens

turtle grass
Thalassia testudinum

    b Describe and explain the adaptations that seagrass possess to enable them to survive in their particular habitat. [5]

    c Tiger sharks live in the shallow coastal waters off Hawaii where they hunt, kill and eat sea turtles. Sea turtles, in turn, graze the seagrass beds. Predict the ecological impact of a collapse in the tiger shark population due to over fishing in the Pacific. [3]

                                                                                                                                                     [Total: 11]

CONTINUED

5   The predominant krill species is the Arctic ocean is the Northern krill, *Meganyctiphanes norvegica*. Figure 4.40 shows the trophic niche of krill in a food web for the Arctic.

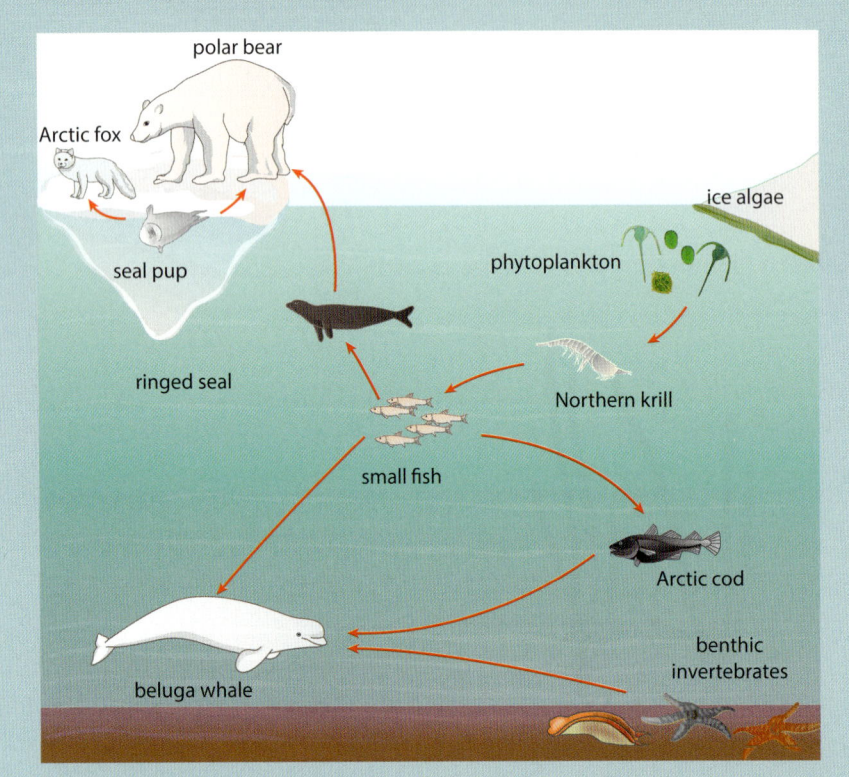

Figure 4.40: Arctic food web.

a   Beluga whales are hunted in Canadian, Alaskan, and Russian Arctic regions for their meat, blubber and skin. Explain how this could affect the population numbers of northern krill in the food chain: phytoplankton → northern krill → small fish → beluga whale. [2]

b   Predict the effect of global warming on northern krill. [3]

c   A study of the stomach contents of ringed seals found that they included a variety of invertebrate prey: 73 crabs, 55 clams, 47 snails, 32 amphipods and 18 northern krill.

   i   Calculate, to the nearest whole number, the mean of invertebrates in the seals' stomachs. Show your working. [2]

   ii Use Simpson's index of diversity (D) to calculate the biodiversity in the seals' diet.

$$D = 1 - \left(\Sigma\left(\frac{n}{N}\right)^2\right)$$

where: Σ = sum of (total)

n = number of individuals of each *different* species

N = the total number of individuals of *all* the species. [2]

CONTINUED

    iii A different population of ringed seal was found to have a higher species index of diversity. What does a high species index of diversity suggest about the habitat? [2]

[Total: 11]

6 Two rocky shores were sampled using quadrats. Transect lines from rocky shore A found 320 oysters, 335 whelks and 345 barnacles. Transect lines from rocky shore B found 20 oysters, 39 whelks and 941 barnacles.

  a What is the species richness for each rocky shore? [1]

  b Predict which rocky shore has the greatest biodiversity. [3]

  c Use Simpson's index of diversity (*D*) to calculate the biodiversity of rocky shore A. Show your working and give your answer to 3 d.p.

$$D = 1 - \left(\Sigma \left(\frac{n}{N} \right)^2 \right)$$

    where: Σ = sum of (total)

              n = number of individuals of each *different* species

              N = the total number of individuals of *all* the species. [2]

  d Simpson's index of diversity for rocky shore B is 0.113. **Justify** which rocky shore has the lower biodiversity. [1]

[Total: 7]

7 Describe a systematic sampling method to investigate the distribution and abundance of littoral zone organisms living between high tide and low tide on a rocky shore. [10]

[Total: 10]

8 Marine copepods are a type of zooplankton that feed on phytoplankton and are eaten by juvenile fish and other plankton-eating organisms (planktivores), including some whales. Many copepods are parasites of other marine organisms (for example worms and snails). Explain how biotic and abiotic factors influence the copepod population in a marine ecosystem. [10]

[Total: 10]

> **COMMAND WORD**
>
> **justify:** support a case with evidence / argument

SELF-EVALUATION CHECKLIST

I can:	See section...	Needs more work	Almost there	Ready to move on
understand the classification of species and binomial system	4.1			
construct and use simple dichotomous keys and make biological observations and drawings	4.1			
understand the role of phytoplankton as producers and zooplankton as consumers	4.2			
state the main features of typical adult echinoderms, crustaceans, bony fish, cartilaginous fish, macroalgae and marine plants.	4.2			
understand the ecological and economic importance of these marine organisms, including named examples	4.2			
explain the genetic, species and ecological biodiversity of marine environments	4.3			
understand the importance of maintaining the marine biodiversity	4.3			
explain the terms ecosystem, habitat, niche, species, population and community	4.4			
explain and identify biotic and abiotic factors in marine ecosystems	4.4			
describe sampling and field work methods and calculations used in the littoral zone and interpret different types of correlations	4.4			

4 Classification and biodiversity

EXTENDED CASE STUDY: EXPLORING THE SECRETS OF MARINE BIODIVERSITY

Scientists and engineers work together to design ingenious new ways to gather biotic and abiotic data needed unlock the ecological secrets of the deep blue ocean, and the organisms that live on its coastal fringes.

Robomussels

The Partnership for Interdisciplinary Studies of Coastal Oceans (PISCO) uses 'Robomussels' to monitor how abiotic factors could affect rocky shore biodiversity. Robomussels are data loggers that resemble and change temperature like real mussels (Figure 4.41). When glued onto a rocky shore, they can be used to record the temperatures of mussel beds. This data is being used to monitor and predict the effects of global warming.

Figure 4.41: Robomussel.

Autonomous Reef Monitoring Structures (ARMS)

A different approach is being taken by the Smithsonian's Global Marine Biodiversity Project. This project uses Autonomous Reef Monitoring Structures (ARMS), which are cubes containing a tier of plates that mimic the cracks and crevices of a reef. These devices are designed to be colonised by the small invertebrates and algae (cryptofauna) that inhabit the ocean floor rather than the better known vertebrate fauna. The ARMS is deposited on the ocean floor and left for one to three years. ARMS provide a standard method to quantify and compare biodiversity between global reef communities. Scuba divers have used ARMS to monitor shallow water reefs. With the use of submarines ARMS can also now be deployed on deep sea reefs to explore the role these deep reefs might play in the survival of shallow reefs. In time, scientists hope that ARMS can monitor the impact on reefs of ocean warming and acidification.

Super subs

Some of the most difficult marine habitats to explore are the Earth's deepest points, the deep sea trenches. Marine scientists have for some years been able to observe and sample the benthic sediment using remotely-operated vehicles (ROVs) or by dropping long coring devices from survey ships to the ocean floor.

An exciting recent development are super subs, capable of taking humans to the deepest parts of the oceans. The first dive to the Mariana Trench in the Western Pacific ocean took place in 1960 by US Navy lieutenant Don Walsh and Swiss engineer Jacques Piccard in a vessel called the Bathyscaphe Trieste. Movie director James Cameron then made a solo plunge half a century later in 2012 in his Deep Sea Challenger submarine. In May 2019, undersea explorer Victor Vescovo solo navigated his titanium submarine, DSV Limiting Factor (Figure 4.42).

Figure 4.42: Victor Vescovo's submarine, DSV Limiting Factor.

CONTINUED

Figure 4.43: The Five Deeps Expedition.

Vescovo became the first person to reach the very deepest part of the Mariana trench at a depth of 10 972 m. On his expedition he discovered three new species of marine animals: an amphipod, spoon worm and a pink snailfish. He also found evidence of potential plastic litter on the bottom, which shows that human waste may have reached the very depths of our ocean long before man did.

Vescovo and his team did not, however, stop in the Pacific. Their Five Deeps Expedition was the first to reach the deepest point in the each of the other oceans: the Puerto Rico Trench in the Atlantic, South Sandwich Trench in the Southern Ocean, Java Trench in the Indian Ocean, and Molloy Deep in the Arctic Ocean. (Figure 4.43) The submarine was accompanied by a research and exploration ship, the DSSV Pressure Drop, equipped with dry and wet laboratories together with a high-resolution multi-beam sonar capable of mapping the seafloor.

Additional scientific exploration was carried out by three seafloor landers called Flere, Skaff and Closp. The sub and landers both had video cameras and light as well as 'bio boxes' that could store geological and biological samples.

One of the key goals of the expedition, alongside discovering new benthic creatures, was to help understand different ecological niches and the adaptations and behaviours that help them survive in the hadal zone. The marine scientists also investigated the effect of frequent seismic activity on the diversity, size, age and reproduction of communities living in deep sea trenches.

A deep sea pharmacy

Deep sea vents may prove to be a source of new pharmaceutical drugs as they are inhabited by extremophile organisms with unique and unusual biochemistry, allowing them to survive in extreme temperatures, pressure and pH. Marine scientists are bioprospecting the benthic sediment by dropping a long coring device from survey ships to the ocean floor. Organisms in the sediment are pressure-sensitive and need high-pressure chambers to survive and grow in laboratories at sea-level. Researchers extract and test the bioactive compounds produced by these organisms for medicinal properties. Zebrafish are used to test new medicines as they have a similar physiology to humans. One such useful drug is from *Dermacoccus abyssi*, a bacterium retrieved from sediment in

CONTINUED

the Mariana Trench. This organism produces dermacozines, a new drug that may help protect against the parasite that causes African sleeping sickness.

Questions

1 Suggest why the Five Deeps Expedition tested the genetic connections between the biological samples taken from the five deeps.

2 The DSV Limiting Factor submarine was able to measure abiotic conditions found in each of the five different dive sites. Use the map in Figure 4.43 to predict if differences in temperature and pressure may result in a different biodiversity of organisms being found.

3 Marine scientific expeditions work in extremely remote locations far from land. Suggest what safety precautions a captain of a research vessel would need to take.

4 Suggest the benefits of a human-operated submarine to explore marine habitats rather than using an Autonomous Reef Monitoring Structures (ARMS) or a remotely-operated vehicle (ROV).

5 Six new species of marine sponges (A–F) were discovered in marine habitats. The sponges each produced different antibiotics against a drug-resistant bacterium.

In an experiment, a lawn of drug-resistant bacterium was grown on an agar plate (Figure 4.44). White discs containing the antibiotics from each sponge were placed on the bacterial lawn and left for 24 hours. The effect of each antibiotic was then measured by the radius of its inhibition zone. An inhibition zone is an area where bacteria cannot grow because of the production of an antibiotic. On Figure 4.44, the inhibition zone is the diameter of the clear zone around each disc (A–F).

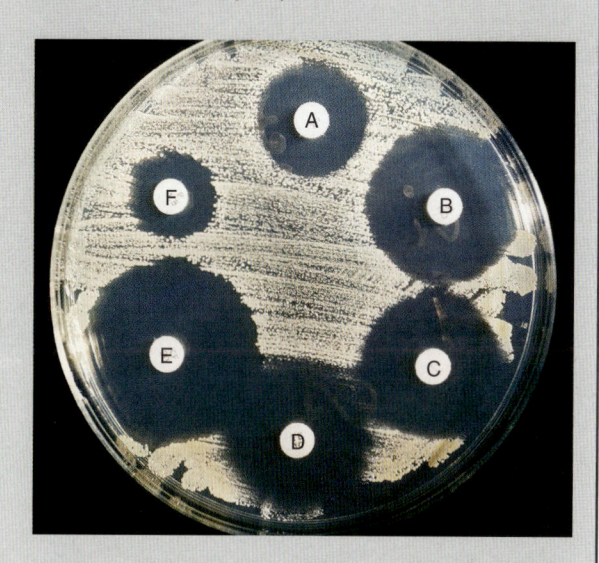

Figure 4.44: The effect of antibiotics produced by six new species of marine sponges (A–F).

a Describe a control variable for each of the antibiotic discs A–F that would help to ensure a fair test.

b Explain which marine sponge (A–F) is the most effective against the growth of this drug-resistant bacterium.

c Suggest reasons why medical researchers may elect to perform clinical trials using a number of the antibiotics found.

Chapter 5
Examples of marine ecosystems

LEARNING INTENTIONS

In this chapter you will learn how to:

- describe the World Ocean as an interconnected body of water encircling the globe and identify the depth zones within
- explain why the interactions between the ocean and the atmosphere are important
- discuss the structure and importance of both natural and artificial coral reefs relating to the economy, ecology of the planet and medical importance to humans
- discuss the abiotic and biotic causes and effects of reef erosion
- identify the different zones on a typical exposed rocky shore using abiotic factors and describe how those factors affect the distribution and abundance of organisms on the rocky shore
- explain, using named examples, the adaptations that organisms have for living in the different zones on a rocky shore and to living on a sandy shore

5　Examples of marine ecosystems

CONTINUED

- describe the sandy shore as an ecosystem with an unstable, shifting, porous substrate and explain why it has a relatively low biodiversity
- investigate the effect of particle size on the permeability of substrates
- outline the conditions required for the development of mangrove forest tidal ecosystem, the ecological and economical importance of these forests and the threats facing them
- explain how the red mangrove tree has developed multiple adaptations to the mangrove environment.

BEFORE YOU START

- With a partner, discuss how you would divide the deepest parts of the ocean up to make them easier to study. What abiotic factors would you use to create your study areas? Write out your plan to share with the class.
- Think about a rocky shoreline and a sandy beach. As a group, create a list of abiotic factors that make the rocky shoreline and sandy beach unique for the organisms that live there.
- Take one minute to sketch a coral reef from your imagination. Then label your sketch with one- or two-word descriptions of the abiotic factors you included (such as sunlight, water and temperature). What does this tell you about the environment that a coral reef needs to survive?
- As a class, look at a picture of a mangrove forest. Discuss and list the benefits the mangrove forest could provide for humans and marine organisms.

DISCOVERING THE DEEP

Oceans are a mixture of different habitats and ecosystems, each with their own environmental factors that determine what plants and animals can live there. From easily-explored coastal ecosystems, such as rocky shores, to the darkness of ocean trenches, the organisms that survive in ocean ecosystems have developed some remarkable adaptations; some may even help us in our own survival by providing the links to new medicines and cures to disease.

One of these remarkable adaptations is **bioluminescence**.

Multiple species of bacteria, squid, ctenophores (comb jellies) and fish use a chemical reaction between the protein luciferin and oxygen to generate light. Because the deepest parts of the ocean are so dark, light is often the only way these organisms can communicate. Some species use bioluminescence to locate a mate, avoid or distract predators, or as a lure for prey. Scientists have suggested that bioluminescence is such an essential part of life in the deep, it has evolved at least 40 different times within different classes of organisms.

Questions

1. Can you think of any organisms in land-based ecosystems that use bioluminescence for communication?
2. What other adaptations might organisms in the deep ocean have developed?

KEY WORD

Bioluminescence: the biochemical release of light by living organisms

5.1 The open ocean

One of the largest ecosystems on the planet is the marine (ocean) ecosystem. Nearly three-quarters of our planet is covered in oceans, with an average depth of about 3 688 m. The oceans contain, potentially, over a million different species. The open ocean is the part of the ocean away from the seashore and coastline.

The World Ocean

More than 70% of the Earth is covered in interconnected bodies of water called the **World Ocean**. The World Ocean helps Earth maintain its global temperature. It is a habitat to over 200 000 named species and many more unnamed species. Through these organisms, the World Ocean provides food for billions of people. Historically, the World Ocean was not recognised as a single body of water, but rather as five smaller oceans: the Arctic, Atlantic, Pacific, Indian and Southern Oceans. Looking at a modern map (Figure 5.1), however, shows that these oceans are interconnected.

The Pacific Ocean has a surface area of 165 250 000 km^2, covering approximately 33% of Earth's surface. It is the largest of the five oceans. The Pacific Ocean is divided into the North Pacific and South Pacific by equatorial currents. It is home to the deepest place on Earth, the Mariana Trench, which has a depth of 11 034 m.

The second largest of the major oceans, the Atlantic Ocean, has a surface area of 106 460 000 km^2, covering nearly 20% of the Earth's surface. The Atlantic Ocean forms an S-shape between the Americas to the west and Europe and Africa to the east. This ocean basin is divided by equatorial currents into the North Atlantic and South Atlantic oceans.

The third largest ocean, the Indian Ocean, lies in the area between Eastern Africa and Western Australia. It has a surface area of 73 440 000 km^2. The boundaries of the Indian Ocean are difficult to define, though, as there is some debate about where it meets the Pacific among the islands of the north and where it joins with the Southern Ocean to the south.

> **KEY WORD**
>
> **World Ocean:** the combination of all major oceans into one large, interconnected body of water that encircles the world's continents

Figure 5.1: Map of World Ocean.

The southernmost waters of the World Ocean are considered to be part of the Southern Ocean. The boundaries of the Southern Ocean circle Antarctica and continue northward to the 60°S latitude. The Southern Ocean is where southern circulation takes place, which is a vital set of currents that mix the nutrients of the bottom water within the global conveyor belt (see Chapter 2).

The Arctic Ocean is located around the North Pole and connects with several seas. It is the smallest and shallowest of the major oceans. However, due to its nearly constant cover of sea ice and its remote location, the Arctic Ocean is also the least studied of the oceans.

Zones of the open ocean

In order to appropriately identify where organisms live within the open ocean, scientists divided this region into five zones based, primarily, on light penetration (see Figure 5.2). Light penetration depends on the wavelength of the light and the turbidity (clarity) of the water. Longer wavelengths of light (such as orange and red) are quickly absorbed by the water and do not travel very deep into the ocean. Shorter wavelengths of light (such as blue and green) travel the furthest and reach the deepest depths. This is why divers need flashlights when diving below depths of 40 m. Without additional light, everything appears in shades of blue.

In ideal conditions, sunlight could travel up to 1000 m deep into the ocean. However, it is rare that there is enough light to perform photosynthesis below 200 m. For that reason, the first zone of the ocean only reaches from the surface to 200 m deep; it is called the **epipelagic zone**. This is the zone of the ocean with abundant productivity due to the high levels of light and nutrients.

Below the epipelagic zone is the **mesopelagic zone**. This zone of the ocean stretches from 200 m to 1000 m in depth. Organisms here typically have enough light to see, but not to perform photosynthesis. Because of the low nutrient levels and lack of oxygen within the oxygen minimum zone, organisms have specialised adaptations (for example, some species of bacteria use nitrates instead of oxygen to respire).

Below the mesopelagic zone is the **bathypelagic zone**. It stretches from 1000 m to 4000 m in depth. This zone is characterised by organisms that survive on the detritus and marine snow that fall from the epipelagic zone. Organisms here live in complete darkness and, therefore, many organisms are transparent and bioluminescent, such as jellyfish, squid and ctenophores (see Figure 5.3).

Below the bathypelagic zone, from 4000 m deep to just above the sea floor, is the **abyssopelagic zone**. Due to the unending darkness, this region is home to many species of blind and colourless animals. This zone of the ocean is also very cold due to its near freezing water temperatures (2–3°C).

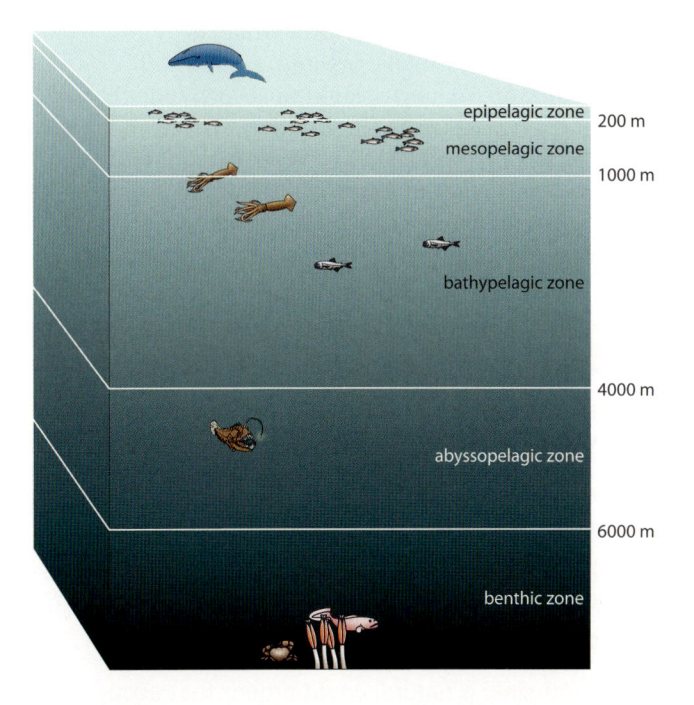

Figure 5.2: Zones in the open ocean based on depth and light penetration.

> **KEY WORDS**
>
> **epipelagic zone:** the zone of the ocean between 0 and 200 m deep which receives enough light for photosynthesis
>
> **mesopelagic zone:** the zone of the ocean between 200 and 1000 m deep which receives very little light
>
> **bathypelagic zone:** the zone of the ocean between 1000 and 4000 m deep which receives no sunlight
>
> **abyssopelagic zone:** the zone of the ocean between 4000 and 6000 m deep with near-freezing water temperatures and intense pressure

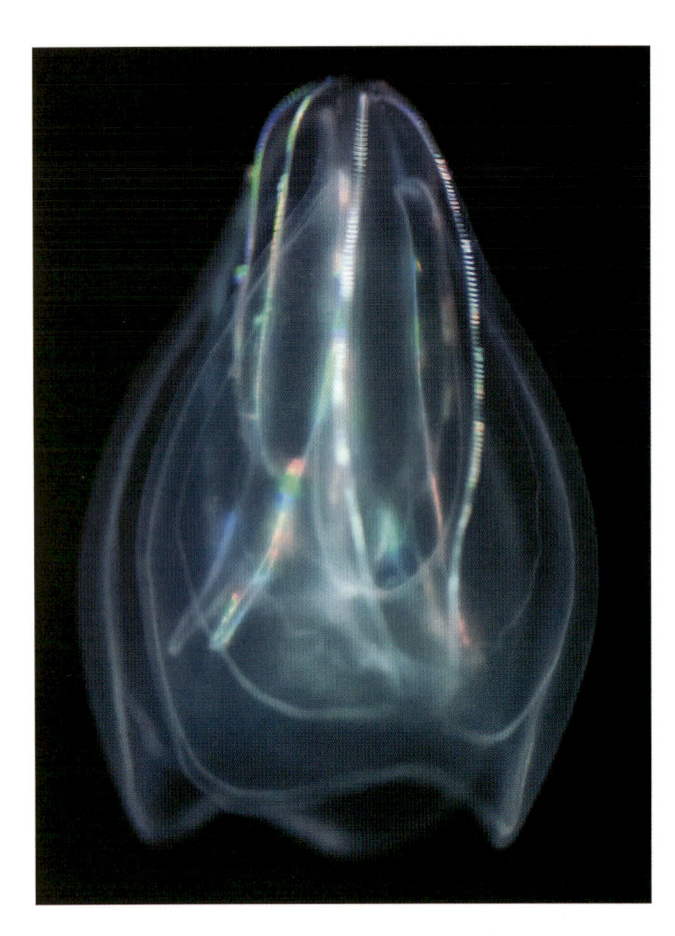

Figure 5.3: The sea walnut (*Mnemiopsis leidyi*), a ctenophore, displaying its bioluminescence within the bathypelagic zone.

The seafloor and the area immediately above it make up the **benthic zone**. Organisms found in this zone are called **benthos**. Benthos include crustaceans, echinoderms and polychaetes. In the open ocean, the benthic zone is always in complete darkness; however, the term 'benthic zone' generally refers to the bottom of a body of water. Therefore, in other coastal bodies of water, such as an estuary, the benthic zone may receive sunlight.

The importance of the ocean

The oceans provide many **ecosystem services**, or benefits, for humans. These include food production, maintaining biodiversity, and recreation – places we go to relax. However, when we look at interactions between the ocean and the atmosphere, we can see the World Ocean provides even more ecosystem services that are of vital importance to our survival as a species and a planet.

The World Ocean as a carbon sink

As you learned in Chapter 3, the carbon cycle is the movement of carbon molecules from their inorganic state to an organic state capable of being used by organisms. As part of the carbon cycle, carbon dioxide (CO_2) in the atmosphere will diffuse into the epipelagic zone of the ocean. Most of the carbon will be changed into something new. Producers will gather carbon dioxide to photosynthesise and create glucose. Corals and hard-shelled molluscs will take up the carbon to make their shells or skeletons. Finally, a portion of the carbon dioxide will mix with the water to create carbonic acid (H_2CO_3).

As organisms and chemical interactions change and use up the new forms of carbon, the atmosphere can continue diffusing carbon dioxide into the ocean. Since more carbon enters the ocean than leaves it, we refer to the ocean as a **carbon sink**. This makes the World Ocean a major component of carbon storage for our planet, especially as carbon dioxide levels have been rising in our atmosphere since the Industrial Revolution. As these levels continue to rise, the ocean continues to absorb more and more carbon dioxide, which can pose potential problems for ocean ecosystems.

The World Ocean as a source of oxygen

The epipelagic zone of the World Ocean contains billions of photosynthetic organisms known as phytoplankton. As phytoplankton absorb sunlight and carbon dioxide to create glucose, they also create oxygen gas (O_2) as a by-product. The oxygen is then released into the ocean and the atmosphere. Current estimates for how much atmospheric oxygen is produced by the ocean range from 50 to 85% depending on the season.

> **KEY WORDS**
>
> **benthic zone:** the lowest depth region in any body of water including the surface of the substrate
>
> **benthos:** the community of organisms found in the benthic zone
>
> **ecosystem services:** benefits people obtain from ecosystems, including food, flood regulation, climate control and water purification
>
> **carbon sink:** a natural environment that absorbs carbon dioxide from the atmosphere faster than it releases it

5 Examples of marine ecosystems

The World Ocean as a temperature buffer and global climate control

Water has a high specific heat capacity, so oceans can absorb large amounts of heat without changing temperature. The oceans store the heat energy when the atmosphere is too warm. And, when the atmosphere is too cold, the ocean can transfer heat to the atmosphere to warm it up again. In this way, oceans provide a crucial ecosystem service by regulating temperatures of areas near the coast. This is one reason why the weather in coastal areas tends to be milder during winter and summer than it is in landlocked regions.

Oceans are also able to regulate long-term climate conditions using the same methods. Scientists have noticed a correlation between the rise in greenhouse gases released into the atmosphere and the global rise in temperature. Our ocean temperatures have also been rising, but at a much slower rate due to the specific heat capacity of water. The oceans have been absorbing much of the excess heat energy and storing it to prevent even more drastic changes in our climate.

5.2 The tropical coral reef

Close your eyes and picture a coral reef in your mind. You probably think of warm, clear blue waters, and sunlight shimmering through the water. You see brightly coloured fish, corals of all shapes and sizes growing closely together, and maybe the occasional turtle or shark (Figure 5.4). Thinking of your imaginary coral reef and all the life that survives there, it may not surprise you to know that, globally, nearly 60 000 different species have been found living on reefs. Some scientists claim the more accurate estimate of the number of species that call coral reefs home is between one and nine million.

Coral classification and anatomy

All corals belong to a phylum of organisms called **cnidarians**. Organisms in this phylum are found in aquatic ecosystems, primarily marine, and capture food using stinging cells called **cnidocytes**. The presence of these stinging cells in corals indicates a close relationship with sea anemones and jellyfish.

Like anemones, corals live their entire adult life as **polyps**. Polyps are the sessile (non-moving) life stage of coral animals. Polyps may live individually or in giant colonies capable of building reefs. Polyps tend to look simple – just a cylinder of epidermal tissue with tentacles surrounding a mouth. They live attached to a rocky substrate, as seen in Figure 5.7.

The polyp's tentacles are used to capture prey and ward off predators. The tentacles are lined with cnidocytes. These cnidocytes contain organelles called **nematocysts**. Nematocysts are harpoon-like structures that contain a toxin. A coral polyp can deliver this toxin to its prey or predators. Once stung, coral polyps use the strand that connects the nematocyst to the cnidocyte to capture their prey. The prey is then brought to the mouth of the polyp which leads to a simple stomach, or digestive sac, made of tissue designed to secrete enzymes for digestion.

Coral attach to a rocky substrate using a **basal plate** at their base. Corals then form a cup-like **calyx** around themselves for protection. The walls of the calyx are

Figure 5.4: A Hawksbill sea turtle (*Eretmochelys imbricata*) swims over a coral reef in West Papua, Indonesia.

KEY WORDS

cnidarians: marine animals that capture food using stinging cells

cnidocytes: stinging cells that cover the tentacles of cnidarians

polyp: non-moving, cup-like life stage of cnidarians

nematocyst: the harpoon-like organelle inside of cnidocyte that contains toxin to be delivered to the prey

basal plate: lower part of the coral calyx that separates the polyp from the substrate

calyx: the stony cup in which a coral polyp lives its life

called the **theca**. When in a colony, corals connect their individual calyxes and create a stony skeleton made of calcium carbonate ($CaCO_3$).

Categories of corals

There are two major categories of corals: corals that build reefs (**hard corals**) and corals that do not build reefs (**soft corals**).

Figure 5.5: Staghorn coral (*Acrophora cervicornis*) is a type of hard coral.

Figure 5.6: The sea fan (*Gorgonia sp.*) is one example of a soft coral.

Hard corals are the reef-building group of corals, such as staghorn and brain corals. Within this group, the coral polyps live in colonies and always have a symbiotic relationship with **zooxanthellae** (Figure 5.7). These colonies begin when a single planktonic coral larva settles on a hard substrate. Once the larva has attached its basal plate, it goes through metamorphosis to become a coral polyp. If this original polyp survives and thrives, it will reproduce asexually through a process called budding. Budding happens when the initial polyp grows a clone of itself. As a result of this process, typically all polyps in a coral colony are genetically identical to the founder polyp. In order to cement themselves to the substrate, each polyp secretes calcium carbonate ($CaCO_3$) onto the substrate forming its calyx and thecae. When an older polyp dies, a new polyp will grow in its calyx, adding another layer of calcium carbonate beneath the basal plate for attachment. Eventually, this process creates a limestone skeleton that can form many different shapes and provides the framework of the coral reef. Because coral polyps are so tiny, it can take billions of polyps to form a reef.

Soft corals are flexible and do not create calcified stony skeletons; they use proteins for support instead. Soft corals resemble plants, trees or fans, and generally do not maintain a symbiotic relationship with zooxanthellae. Some examples of soft corals are sea whips, sea fans and gorgonians.

Coral nutrition

Hard corals would not be able to build reefs without their symbiotic relationship with zooxanthellae. Zooxanthellae are microscopic, single-celled dinoflagellates that live within the tissue of hard corals (Figure 5.7). Using carbon and other nutrients provided by the coral host, zooxanthellae perform photosynthesis to generate organic material that can then be passed on to the coral. Without the extra nutrition provided by zooxanthellae, corals would be unable to secrete enough calcium carbonate to build the skeleton of the reef. Depending on the conditions, zooxanthellae can provide so much food that, often, the coral can survive without eating. This type of symbiosis is an example of mutualism, since both species benefit.

Like soft corals, hard corals are still predators despite their relationship with zooxanthellae. Coral polyps use their tentacles filled with cnidocytes to filter out microscopic zooplankton floating in the water near them.

> **KEY WORDS**
>
> **theca:** the walls of the calyx
>
> **hard corals:** stony corals capable of reef-building that have a relationship with zooxanthellae
>
> **soft corals:** corals that do not build reefs and lack calcification
>
> **zooxanthellae:** symbiotic, photosynthetic dinoflagellates living within the tissues of many invertebrates

5 Examples of marine ecosystems

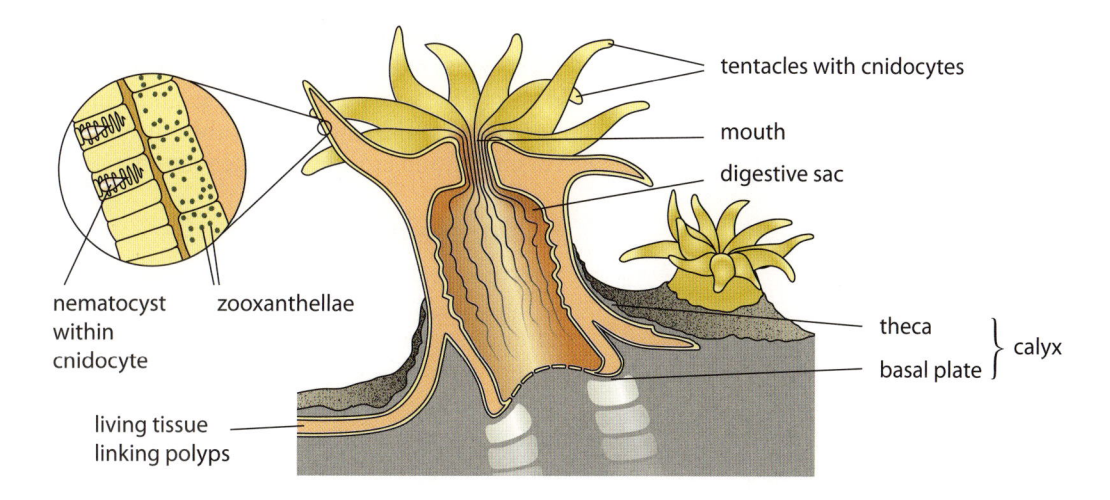

Figure 5.7: A cross-section of a generalised polyp.

Additionally, both hard and soft corals can gain nutrition through the process of diffusion. Microscopic pieces of dissolved organic matter are constantly floating through the ocean's waters. Corals absorb and use this organic matter to supplement the nutrients gained from the symbiotic relationship with zooxanthellae and predation on zooplankton.

Conditions required for tropical reef formation

When mapping out coral reef distribution (Figure 5.8), scientists can hypothesise which reefs will have the highest growth rates by evaluating the presence or

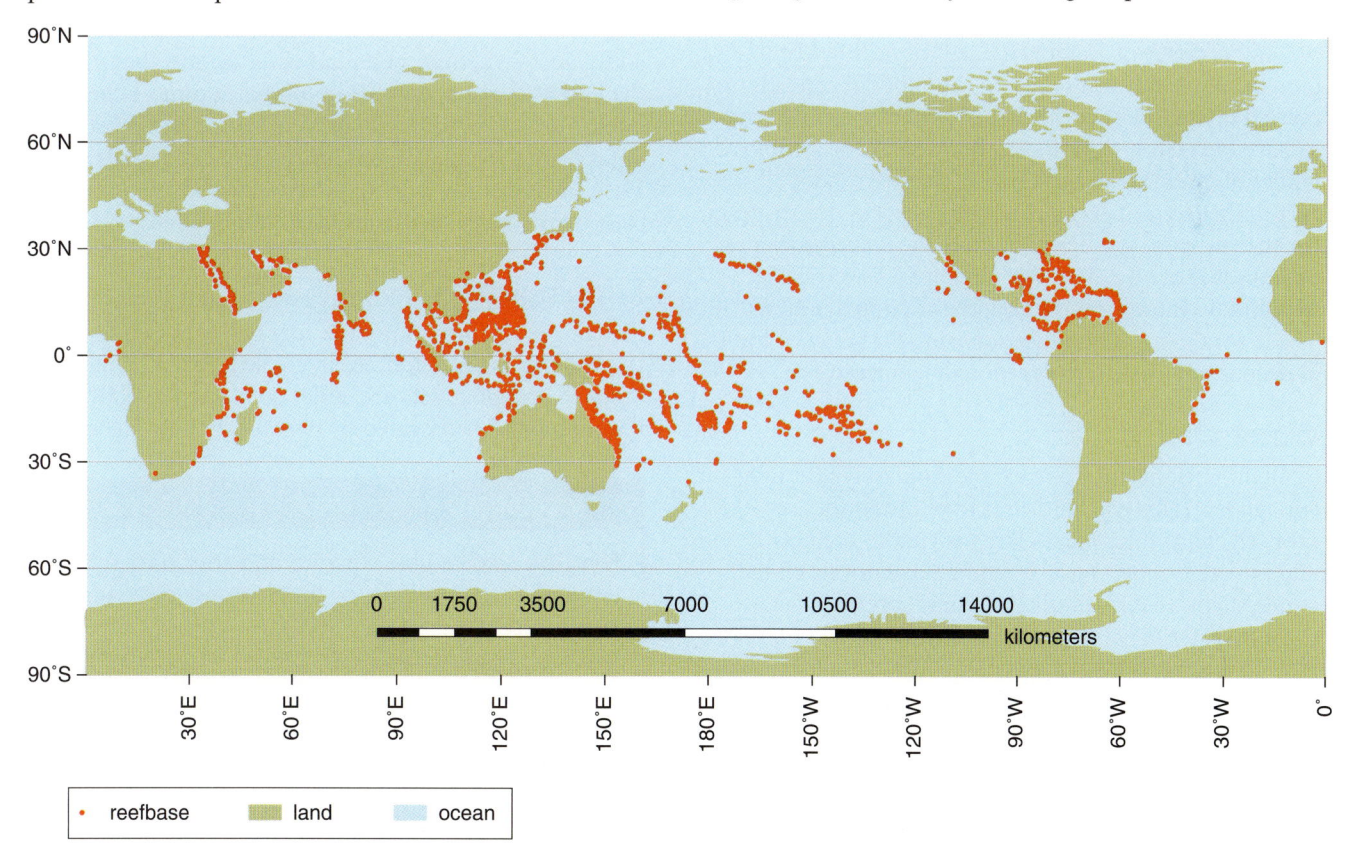

Figure 5.8: A map of the world's coral reefs.

absence of several key abiotic factors. Coral reefs are reliant on these factors – specifically an appropriate water temperature, water clarity and suitable depth – for healthy growth and colonisation. Coral reefs are most likely to be found in the tropics because these regions provide the greatest number of locations where all of these abiotic factors exist.

Water temperature

The most important physical factor for corals is temperature. Hard corals are limited to waters with temperatures ranging between 16 °C and 35 °C (61–95 °F). Corals growing in water with temperatures at either end of this range tend to be less healthy and grow less quickly than those in water of the preferred range of 23–25 °C (73–77 °F). Because of the warm temperatures needed for successful coral growth, you would expect to find coral reefs located exclusively in the tropics between 30° N and 30° S of the equator. However, some areas outside this zone, such as Florida and southern Japan, are also able to support healthy coral reefs. This is because there are warm water currents flowing along the continental shelf in those areas.

Water depth

A suitable depth of water is needed for healthy coral growth. While all corals grow in the subtidal zone, those present in areas within the first 20 m of the surface tend to have the fastest growth rate. Because of the symbiotic nature of coral's relationship with photosynthetic zooxanthellae, you do not find coral reefs in deeper water because there is insufficient light. If the seabed subsides, or sinks, the coral polyps will tend to grow vertically to maintain the appropriate depth for photosynthesis. Those corals that do not use zooxanthellae may be found in deeper waters with warm enough temperatures.

Water clarity

Sunlight must be able to reach the coral polyps at high enough levels for zooxanthellae to photosynthesise properly. Therefore, water clarity is vital to the health and growth of coral reefs. If sunlight cannot reach the coral polyps, the zooxanthellae cannot produce the organic material necessary for the coral to build up the reef. This reduces overall growth and potentially stresses the coral, which is why clear water without silt or an excess of nutrients is needed for rapid coral growth. An abundance of nutrients may lead to an algal bloom that can cloud the surrounding water and reduce light penetration.

Marine producers can also play a crucial role in reducing turbidity and maintaining water clarity. For example, the roots of mangrove swamps and seagrass beds stabilise the soft muddy substrate and reduce its stirring up and erosion by water currents.

Substrate and salinity

Substrate and salinity are also determining factors in the success of a coral reef. Corals must have an appropriate rocky surface for attachment. Coral larvae cannot attach to sand or other unstable materials, so the larvae tend to attach to denser materials that are less likely to move in the undersea currents. The basaltic rocks of undersea mountains and other hard surfaces along the continental shelf provide excellent attachment sites for the larvae. Corals are not adapted to freshwater or brackish (low salinity) conditions. For this reason, they do not do well near river mouths or other areas linked with fresh water or run-off flowing into the sea.

Types of reefs

Charles Darwin was the first scientist to catalogue the world's coral reefs. He both mapped and described all the reef structures he found while sailing aboard the HMS *Beagle* and wrote about his findings in his book *Coral Reefs*. Darwin outlined three fairly distinct types of reef: **fringing reefs**, **barrier reefs** and **atolls**. With further study, scientists have since added a fourth category of reefs – **patch reefs** (Figure 5.9).

Fringing reefs

Fringing reefs form along the edges of continental landmasses, islands and oceanic volcanoes in tropical regions. Fringing reefs are either connected directly to the shoreline or separated by narrow, shallow lagoons.

> ### KEY WORDS
>
> **fringing reef:** a reef close to and surrounding newer volcanic islands or that borders continental landmasses
>
> **barrier reef:** a reef separated by a lagoon from the land mass with which it is associated
>
> **atoll:** a coral reef somewhat circular in shape with a central lagoon
>
> **patch reef:** small, isolated reef usually located within the lagoon of a barrier reef

5 Examples of marine ecosystems

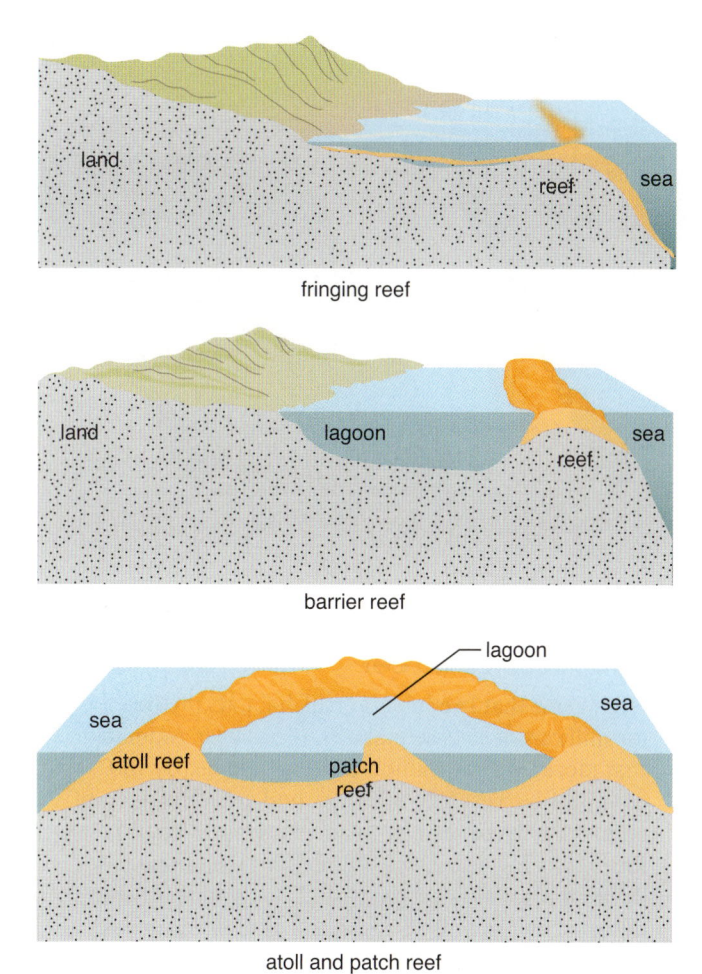

Figure 5.9: Different hard coral reef formations.

between the barrier reef and the shoreline. Portions of barrier reefs may have grown so that the water above is very shallow, making it dangerous for boats to travel over them.

Atolls

An atoll is a coral reef that develops as a ring around a central lagoon. Atolls vary in size from 1 to 32 km in diameter. Most atolls can be found in the tropical Indian Ocean and the west and central Pacific Ocean; they are rare in Caribbean and Atlantic oceans. Atolls vary drastically from fringing and barrier reefs in their location. Typically, atolls are found kilometres from any visible land in incredibly deep water, astounding the scientists of Darwin's day.

It was Charles Darwin, along with James Daly and Reginald Dana, who proposed the theory which solved the mystery of how atolls could develop so far from shore. The Darwin–Dana–Daly theory of atoll formation suggests that a fringing reef forms along the coastline of a newly formed volcanic island. As the reef grows and adds calcium carbonate to its coral skeleton, the island begins to subside, causing the reef to sink. This forces the coral polyps to grow vertically in order to stay at the ideal depth. As the reef grows upward and the island sinks down, a lagoon begins to form between the reef and the shore. The process continues for millions of years until all that remains is an atoll surrounding a lagoon with no island in sight (Figure 5.10).

Rocky shorelines are the best substrate for the initial placement of the larvae, but a soft bottom will do if there is at least one hard place for the initial coral larva to cement to before beginning the reef-building process. Fringing reefs are the most commonly seen and explored reefs because they tend to be easy to reach. This nearness to shore makes them vulnerable to excessive sediment, run-off containing pollutants and fresh water, and human disturbance.

Patch reefs

Patch reefs are the smallest of the reef types and they tend to grow vertically from the continental shelf or lagoon floor as an isolated formation within the lagoons formed by barrier reefs or atolls. The size of patch reefs can vary based on age and location, but they rarely have the vertical height needed to reach the water's surface. These reefs can provide crucial habitat for juvenile fish in the calmer waters within a lagoon.

Barrier reefs

Barrier reefs are similar to fringing reefs in that they lie along the shoreline of a larger landmass; however, barrier reefs are separated from land by deeper, wider **lagoons** and may be up to 97 km from the shore. Fringing reefs may even exist within the lagoon created

> **KEY WORDS**
>
> **lagoon:** a shallow, sheltered body of water with a soft sediment bottom

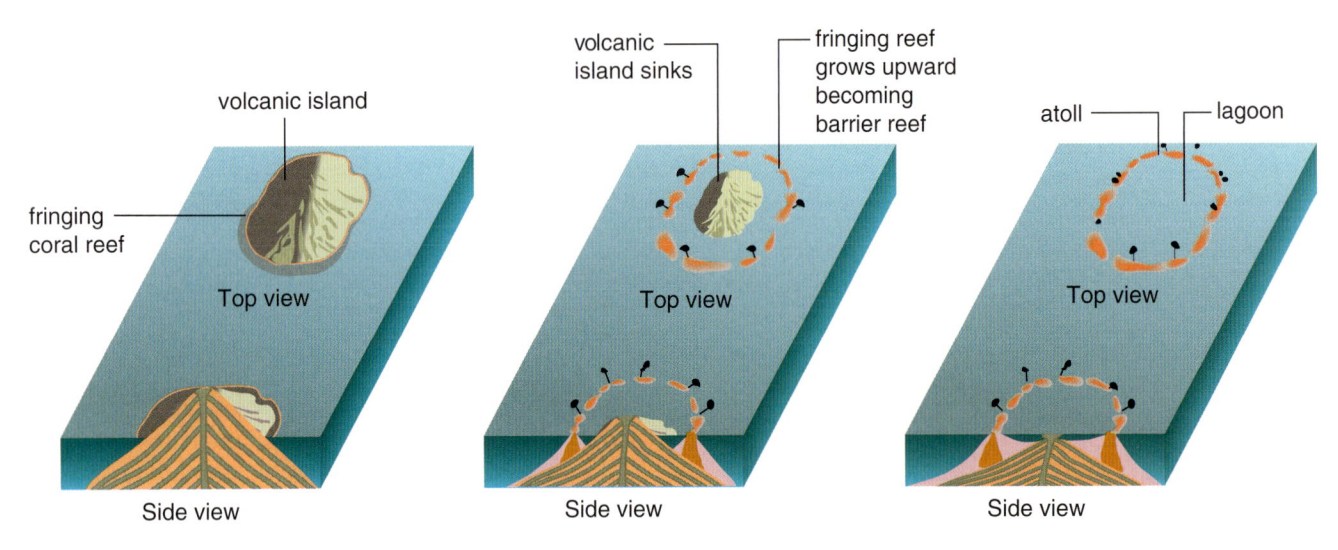

Figure 5.10: An aerial and side view of atoll formation.

The importance of coral reefs

Coral reefs, like the rest of the ocean, provide several key ecosystem services that are important for the planet. Probably one of the most important ecosystem services provided by coral reefs is the maintenance of biodiversity. Coral reefs rival the tropical rainforest in terms of providing habitat for different species increasing their biodiversity levels. While coral reefs only exist on less than 1% of the ocean floor, they are home to over 25% of all marine life. Through their biodiversity, coral reefs are able to provide other ecosystem services, such as protection of the coastlines, provision of food, provision of medicine and recreation through tourism.

Coastal protection

Coral reefs are not just beneficial in terms of biodiversity in the ocean – they are beneficial to onshore habitats. Coral reefs absorb, on average, 97% of the energy of waves coming into shore. Wave height is also reduced, on average by 84%. These reductions in wave energy and height have important implications for the shoreline. By reducing the oncoming wave energy, coral reefs are able to protect the shoreline from the erosion caused by strong waves. Preventing erosion of the shoreline and reducing wave height helps to protect anything on the shore from being damaged during storms or lost to sea as a result of erosion. Ecosystems that exist along the shoreline, such as mangroves, also benefit from reduced wave action and serve as nurseries for marine organisms.

Food from the reef

Organisms that live in coral reef habitats provide food for millions of people globally. It has been estimated that more than six million fishermen in nearly 100 countries harvest fish, molluscs and crustaceans from coral reefs. Even though the dependence on coral reefs for food is highest in coastal regions, the global fish demand also relies on reef fish. The coral reef fishing industry brings in US$6.8 billion globally each year.

Medicine from the reef

As pharmaceutical companies look to nature for inspiration, corals and other sessile animals are becoming more important. Because corals and anemones are sessile, they developed chemical methods of preventing predation. Scientists believe these chemicals may hold the cures for some of our most prevalent ailments such as cancer, arthritis and Alzheimer's disease.

Recreation and tourism

Coral reefs and the organisms that live there are beautiful, and they exist in serene tropical areas. So people travel the world to see a coral reef for themselves. It is estimated that coral reefs generate more than US$35 billion through tourism each year. That money comes in through jobs in hospitality, food service, boating, diving, and much more. Additionally, countries are spending money to improve their infrastructure to make tourists even happier, which in turn helps the people who live there year-round.

MATHS SKILLS 5.1

CALCULATING PERCENT CHANGE FOR DATA ANALYSIS

One mathematical method that scientists use to compare data change over time is calculating percent change. To calculate percent change, scientists need two sets of data – a 'before' and 'after', or 'original' and 'new'. There is a simple way to remember this method:

$$\text{percentage change} = \frac{(\text{new} - \text{original})}{\text{original}} \times 100 \, g$$

If your results give you a positive number, then there is a percentage increase. If your results give you a negative number, then there is a percentage decrease. If you have a percentage decrease, you must indicate this in your answer by stating it is a decrease *or* by including the negative symbol.

Worked example

Apo Reef, in the Philippines, is the world's second largest unconnected reef. In 2007, this reef became the country's second Marine Protected Area (MPA), with all fishing banned in the area. Prior to being reclassified, a survey was taken in 2006 of the percentage of hard coral coverage. Another survey was taken in 2007 to determine coral cover after Typhoon Caloy came through the area, and two others in 2010 and 2015 to check on the recovery process of the reef. This data has been collected for you in Table 5.1.

Year	Cover of hard corals / %	Change in coral cover / %
2006	51	n/a
2007	18	−64.7%
2010	35	
2015	42	

Table 5.1: Percentage of coral cover on Apo Reef before and after Typhoon Caloy and reclassification as an MPA.

We can use the data in Table 5.1 to calculate the percent change in coral coverage from before and after Typhoon Caloy. To do this we need to determine the 'new' coverage (18) and the 'original' coverage (51). Then we put the numbers into the formula.

$$\text{percentage change} = \frac{(\text{new} - \text{original})}{\text{original}} \times 100$$

$$= \frac{18 - 51}{51} \times 100$$

$$= -64.7\%$$

The negative result tells us there was a decrease of 64.7% coral coverage on the Apo Reef between 2006 and 2007.

Questions

1. Calculate the percentage change in coral coverage between 2007 and 2010.
2. Calculate the percentage change in coral coverage between 2010 and 2015.
3. Using the data you calculated, describe what has happened to the hard coral coverage in Apo Reef.
4. Suggest a reason why Apo Reef is recovering from Typhoon Caloy so quickly.
5. Describe one method scientists could use to conduct their survey.

Test yourself

1. What zones of the ocean have enough light for organisms to see each other?
2. Which abiotic and biotic factor(s) would be the most extreme if an organism lived in the benthic zone of the Pacific Ocean?
3. During which season(s) do you think the ocean would generate the most oxygen? Why?

Reef erosion

A healthy coral reef in a location where all physical factors are being met can expect to accumulate between 3 and 15 m of calcium carbonate every 1000 years. The largest of the hard coral species are the slowest growing, often only adding between 5 and 25 mm of calcium carbonate a year. The faster growing corals, such as staghorn corals, can add as much as 20 cm to their branches per year. According to current geological estimates, most modern coral reef systems are between 5000 and 10 000 years old. This slow growth rate of healthy corals is one reason why **reef erosion** can be so detrimental.

Causes of reef erosion

When a coral reef begins to lose more calcium carbonate each year than it accumulates, it is undergoing reef erosion. There are many causes of reef erosion, both biological and physical. Biological causes of reef erosion, often referred to as **bioerosion**, include the predation of coral by organisms such as the parrotfish, butterfly fish and the crown-of-thorns starfish. Physical causes of reef erosion include pH change, temperature change, physical damage and the presence of sediment.

Bioerosion

Both parrotfish and butterfly fish are predators of coral polyps among coral reefs. Butterfly fish tend to be specialists, eating only a few particular species of polyps. Parrotfish, on the other hand, are grazers that eat coral polyps in order to get to the zooxanthellae living within them. Parrotfish will use their beak-like teeth to bite off portions of rock or coral reef, which they swallow whole. Their bodies then digest the organic material (algae) located within the coral polyps and release the indigestible calcium carbonate as faeces. This process leads to an overall loss of calcium carbonate present on the reef, causing reef erosion.

The crown-of-thorns starfish has been a serious threat to corals in the Indo-Pacific region for the last 50 years. These coral predators have seen multiple population booms and may be the greatest cause of coral mortality on the Great Barrier Reef. There are several hypotheses about what causes an outbreak of crown-of-thorns starfish, but the most likely is nutrient-rich run-off as a result of the overuse of fertilisers, combined with the removal of predators through overfishing. These nutrients, primarily nitrogen and phosphorus, tend to cause plankton blooms where crown-of-thorns starfish larvae thrive. Without predatory fish to control the population of larvae, the larvae metamorphose into adult starfish and devour the reef.

Change in pH

For healthy growth in coral reefs, the ocean should be slightly alkaline, with a pH between 8.1 and 8.5. Waters with lower pH levels stress the corals and cause bleaching. (For a review of pH, see Chapter 1.) This is concerning, as there has been an average drop in pH for the World Ocean from 8.2 to 8.1 over the last 150–200 years.

Although this seems like a small drop in pH, scientists believe the process of **ocean acidification** is underway. . Many scientists attribute this process to an increase in atmospheric carbon dioxide. As higher levels of CO_2 enter our oceans through dissolution, higher levels of carbonic acid (H_2CO_3) are produced, lowering the overall pH of the ocean. This is having an abnormally large impact on coral reefs that use calcium carbonate in the manufacture of their skeletons. Ocean acidification prevents corals from absorbing much of the calcium carbonate they need to build their skeletal structures, halting reef growth and leading to skeletal loss.

> **KEY WORDS**
>
> **reef erosion:** when a coral loses more of its calcium carbonate skeleton per year than it gains
>
> **bioerosion:** reef erosion caused by living organisms
>
> **ocean acidification:** a process where the pH of the ocean is reduced over an extended period of time; generally attributed to a rise in atmospheric carbon dioxide

CASE STUDY 5.1: CROWN-OF-THORNS STARFISH ON INDO-PACIFIC REEFS

The crown-of-thorns starfish (*Acanthaster planci*) is a naturally occurring venomous predator found on coral reefs in the Indo-Pacific Ocean. This predator is an important part of the food web on these reefs. On healthy reefs, it tends to feed on only the fastest growing corals, such as staghorn and plate corals. It may seem that any coral predation is negative, but by feeding on these fast-growing corals, the crown-of-thorns starfish provides a mechanism for the slower growing coral species to develop into well-established colonies. This increases the coral biodiversity on the reef, which in turn provides more niches for other organisms to occupy, increasing the overall biodiversity of a reef.

However, the crown-of-thorns starfish has earned a bad reputation as a destroyer of reefs. There have been multiple instances over the last 50 years when masses of crown-of-thorns starfish have swarmed over hard corals that are centuries old and devoured all of the living tissue in their path, as seen in Figure 5.11 This behaviour is termed an 'outbreak'. The Great Barrier Reef Marine Park Authority defines as outbreak as a time when there is a high level of coral cover and 'there is roughly more than 15 starfish per hectare' on a given reef. Outbreaks of crown-of-thorns starfish have been cited as one of the most significant threats to the Great Barrier Reef. An outbreak may last over a decade as the crown-of-thorns starfish spread along the reef southwards.

Causes of outbreaks

Many studies have been conducted to determine what causes these outbreaks and it seems that multiple factors may be responsible. Large female crown-of-thorns starfish can produce up to 65 million eggs during the spawning season, but this is not unusual for invertebrates. Therefore, other causes must have a role in an outbreak. Initially, there needs to be an overall increase in certain limiting nutrients, particularly nitrogen and phosphorus, in the ecosystem. Generally, an increase in these nutrients is seen when fertiliser used on land is washed into the sea as run-off. When these nutrient levels are high, phytoplankton blooms provide more food for crown-of-thorns starfish larvae. As more larvae are well-sustained in this juvenile stage, an unusual number of larvae settle and metamorphose to become adult crown-of-thorns starfish.

However, as larvae and adults, crown-of-thorns starfish have natural predators. So, a second factor that must come into play for an outbreak to occur is a reduction in crown-of-thorns starfish predators. Not much is known about the larval predators, although many scientists hypothesise that corals themselves are the best predators of larval crown-of-thorns starfish. Adults are preyed on by giant triton snails (Figure 5.12), humphead Maori wrasse, starry pufferfish and titan triggerfish. When these animals are overfished for either food or aquaria, then the reef can become overwhelmed by starfish.

Figure 5.11 Multiple crown-of-thorns starfish work to devour a hard coral during an outbreak off Espirtu Santo Island, Vanuatu in 2019.

Figure 5.12 A giant triton snail attacks while a crown-of-thorns starfish tries to dine on a piece of the coral reef.

> CONTINUED

Outbreak on the Great Barrier Reef

In November 2017, an isolated outbreak of crown-of-thorns starfish was located along the Swain Reefs at the southern end of the Great Barrier Reef, approximately 250 km from the Queensland coast. This area of the reef is remote and difficult to reach, so scientists struggled to develop a plan to control the starfish and fund the project.

In February of 2018, a group of 25 volunteer divers were taken to the reef to try to cull the numbers of crown-of-thorns starfish. Over the course of the nine-day trip, the divers worked to inject the many starfish they found with bile salts in order to quickly and efficiently kill them. At the end of the trip they had killed a record-breaking 47 000 crown-of-thorns starfish from a single part of the reef. Scientists on-board the mission admitted that the problem was not solved with this single trip but were hopeful that the reef had a better chance for recovering.

Questions

1. Outline the causes of crown-of-thorns starfish outbreaks.
2. Describe how a loss of coral through reef erosion during a tropical cyclone may lead to an outbreak of crown-of-thorns starfish.
3. Explain how poor fishing practices and waste management are contributing factors to outbreaks of these starfish.
4. Explain when and how crown-of-thorns starfish can be beneficial to the coral reef ecosystem.
5. Do you believe it is ethical to cull crown-of-thorns starfish populations? Justify your response.

Change in temperature

Many studies have found a correlation between the rate of **climate change** and rising levels of carbon dioxide in our atmosphere as a result of fossil fuel use. Climate change has two primary impacts on ocean ecosystems: a rise in sea surface temperatures and a lowering of pH levels, as previously discussed.

Coral bleaching occurs when hard corals become stressed by environmental factors, particularly rising water temperature and reduced pH. This stress causes the coral polyps to reject their symbiotic zooxanthellae from their tissues. Because the zooxanthellae contain all the pigments that give the coral polyps their colour, the bright white calcium carbonate skeleton of the reef becomes visible. This change from yellows and browns to white is called bleaching, as seen in Figure 5.13. When corals are bleached, they do not add to their calcium carbonate skeletons, so reef growth stops. If the bleaching event lasts too long, the corals will die as a result of lack of nutrients and poor water conditions. There have been multiple mass bleaching events around the world since the mid-1990s.

Physical damage

Physical damage to reefs during low tide can be extensive. Corals need to be in subtidal regions – any exposure to air can be dangerous. During spring tides, the lowest of the tides can leave coral reefs exposed to the air, causing the corals to dry out (**desiccation**) or overheat. When the coral polyps die, they may be replaced with algae or slowly eroded by waves.

Hurricanes, typhoons and tropical storms can also cause extensive physical damage. Typically, the damage comes when: coral is broken by the high-energy waves that are

> **KEY WORDS**
>
> **climate change:** changes in global or regional climate patterns since the late twentieth century
>
> **coral bleaching:** whitening of coral that results from the loss of a coral's symbiotic zooxanthellae
>
> **desiccation:** the removal of moisture or drying out of an organism

5 Examples of marine ecosystems

Figure 5.13: A Double-saddle butterfly fish (*Chaetodon falcula*) feeds on a partially bleached coral on the Kaafu Atoll in the Republic of Maldives, Indian Ocean.

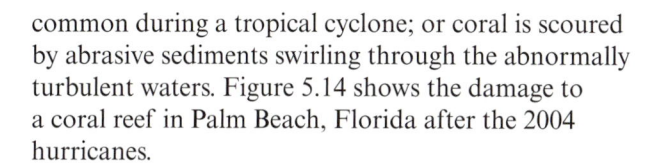

Figure 5.14: Coral reef in Palm Beach, Florida begins recovery after extensive physical damage caused by 2004 hurricanes.

common during a tropical cyclone; or coral is scoured by abrasive sediments swirling through the abnormally turbulent waters. Figure 5.14 shows the damage to a coral reef in Palm Beach, Florida after the 2004 hurricanes.

Corals can generally recover from hurricane damage. The time required for recovery is influenced by several factors, including:

- the amount of coral rubble remaining after the storm
- the sediment stirred up by turbulence
- the growth of algae competing for attachment surfaces within the reef
- run-off, which may bring toxins, lower the salinity of the water and increase nutrients, encouraging an algal bloom.

For example, Hurricane Hattie destroyed a 43 km stretch of barrier reef off the coast of British Honduras in 1961. At the time it was estimated that 80% of the Belize Barrier Reef was damaged by this storm. While the reef has since recovered, scientists at the time believed it would take between 25 and 100 years for the ecosystem to repair itself.

Humans are another source of physical damage. Tourists will step on corals or break off a piece to take home. Others will break pieces to sell or make into jewellery. Boats can destroy coral reefs by driving over shallow reefs or dragging their anchors through them.

For example, a single cruise ship destroyed 3150 km² of reef in Fiji in 2006.

Presence of sediment

An excess of small sediments, such as silt, causes water turbidity. Water turbidity reduces light penetration and prevents zooxanthellae from photosynthesising. Sediment in the water is also likely to settle on top of coral polyps. In small amounts, the polyps are able to use the mucus that covers their bodies to move and push off the sediment. However, after a hurricane or tropical cyclone, the sediment can pile on in large amounts, smothering the coral.

Effects of reef erosion

Coastal regions near reefs suffering from reef erosion are at a greater economic risk than those with healthy reefs. Healthy coral reefs help protect shorelines, boats and anchorages ([human] areas where people anchor their boats; [ecological] areas where sessile organisms attach to the substrate) by reducing wave action and erosion. Coastal properties and shores are at a greater risk of exposure to the damaging effects of waves, particularly during tropical cyclones. The loss of shoreline and greater damage by storm surges can cost human communities millions of dollars to repair. Areas without healthy coral reefs may even have to build expensive structures, called breakwaters (barrier built out into a body of water to protect a coast or harbour from the force of waves), to create calmer waters. The reduction in erosion, protected shorelines, and reduced costs of breakwaters and repairs means areas with healthy coral reefs have a significant economic advantage over those areas without. Reef erosion will also lead to a loss of money from reduced tourism and damage to the fishing industry. There will be less food for local populations and the potential loss of future medicines.

> **Note:** anchorages and breakwater are extension content, and are not part of your syllabus.

Artificial reefs

Rising economic costs are one reason many communities are creating **artificial reefs** off their coastlines. In addition to increasing biodiversity and ecological stability, artificial reefs provide many of the other benefits of healthy coral reefs.

Artificial reefs are human-made structures designed to recreate a coral ecosystem. Typically, these reefs are placed in areas that do not have an appropriate substrate for larval attachment. Many different materials have been used to create artificial reefs, including specially designed non-toxic concrete, sacks filled with sand, stone blocks and even sunken ships. The USCG *Duane*, a search and rescue ship for the United States Coast Guard from 1936 to 1985, was deliberately sunk off the Florida Keys in November of 1987 to create an artificial reef. Figure 5.15 is a current image of the bow (the front of the ship) of the USCG *Duane* covered in corals and sponges. Before sinking, the ship was overhauled to ensure no toxins (such as paints or oils) would seep from it into the marine environment. Since its sinking, the *Duane* has become a popular diving location to see reef fish and has been added to the US National Register of Historic Places.

Artificial reefs provide a physical structure for coral, sponges and algae to colonise. Once these sessile animals have become attached and begun to colonise, many different species of fish are attracted to the area. Generally, structures designed to become a reef, such as the reef balls seen in Figure 5.16, have open spaces and hiding places built into the design in order to better mimic the shape and structure of a natural reef. After several years, it should be impossible to tell that the reef was once an artificial construct. However, at the Cancun Underwater Museum in Mexico, British artist Jason de Caires Taylor has created an art installation with more than 500 sculptures of humans and everyday objects designed to become artificial reefs. Even as these artificial reef sculptures are colonised, they may retain some of their original identity.

Figure 5.15: The bow of the USCG *Duane*, a United States Coast Guard vessel that was purposely sunk to create an artificial reef.

Figure 5.16: Reef balls with implanted corals placed on the soft seabed to form an artificial reef in the Maldives.

> **KEY WORD**
>
> **artificial reef:** an underwater structure built by humans to mimic the characteristics of a natural reef

Unfortunately, not every attempt at creating artificial reefs has been successful. In some cases, these attempts have actually been detrimental to the local environment. Using materials like old tires or improperly cleaned vehicles can lead to toxic materials leaching into the environment. In some cases, adding new artificial reefs to an area can help invasive species, like the orange cup coral, spread to new regions. One goal of artificial reef installations, like the Cancun Underwater Museum, is to reduce the environmental pressures on natural reefs by tourists. However, interesting artificial reefs often increase the number of tourists to an area, creating an even greater pressure on both the natural and artificial systems.

Test yourself

4 Compare and contrast the growth of soft corals with that of hard corals.

5 State the abiotic factor linked most closely with the symbiotic relationship coral has with zooxanthellae. Explain your choice.

6 State and describe **three** major factors that lead to reef erosion.

7 Explain the role of artificial reefs in the preservation of shorelines.

5.3 The rocky shore

As discussed in Chapter 2, a rocky shore is any shoreline that has a rocky substrate but may vary in slope and composition of rocks. Living on a rocky shore is not easy. Organisms have a lot to contend with, including fluctuating temperatures, wave action and exposure to air based on the tides. Other factors that they adapt to are the slope of the shore, what type of rocks make up the substrate, whether the habitat is in a temperate or tropical region, and how much sunlight is available at any time during the year. It may, therefore, seem surprising that rocky shores are typically habitats with significant biodiversity (Figure 5.17).

Figure 5.17: A rocky shore tide pool rich with biodiversity.

Rocky shores provide habitat and stability to many species within the littoral zone. The rocky substrate provides many places for organisms to attach to, a necessity for survival in a place where waves can wash organisms and substrate away. Algae, barnacles, sea anemones and many species of mollusc make their home attached to the rocky surface. The need for safe anchorage makes space, not food or light, the main resource that organisms compete for in this ecosystem.

In order to reduce competition for space and adjust for changing abiotic factors, species in rocky shore ecosystems space themselves vertically on the rocks in a pattern called **zonation**. To determine the upper limit of a species' zone, scientists look for abiotic factors affecting survival: temperature tolerance and length of time the species can spend out of water before desiccation. To find the lower level of a species' zone, scientists look at biotic factors, particularly competition between other species and predation. The **intertidal zone** on a rocky shore can be divided into four major areas (Figure 5.18).

Splash zone

The **splash zone** is the area of the shore that is just above the high tide mark. During an average day, the organisms that live here are only 'sprayed' with seawater during high tide and left to dry out during the remainder of the day. Only during spring tides or storm surges will organisms here be submerged in water.

If you are looking for life in the splash zone, you may find a few salt-tolerant lichens clinging to the rocks amongst the periwinkles and limpets. Periwinkles are common snails that use their muscular foot to clamp

> **KEY WORDS**
>
> **zonation:** distribution of plants or animals into specific zones within an ecosystem based on a specific abiotic factor, like desiccation
>
> **intertidal zone:** area known as the seashore which is exposed at low tides and under water at high tides
>
> **splash zone:** area of a rocky shore that is just above the high tide mark and receives water through the splashing of waves

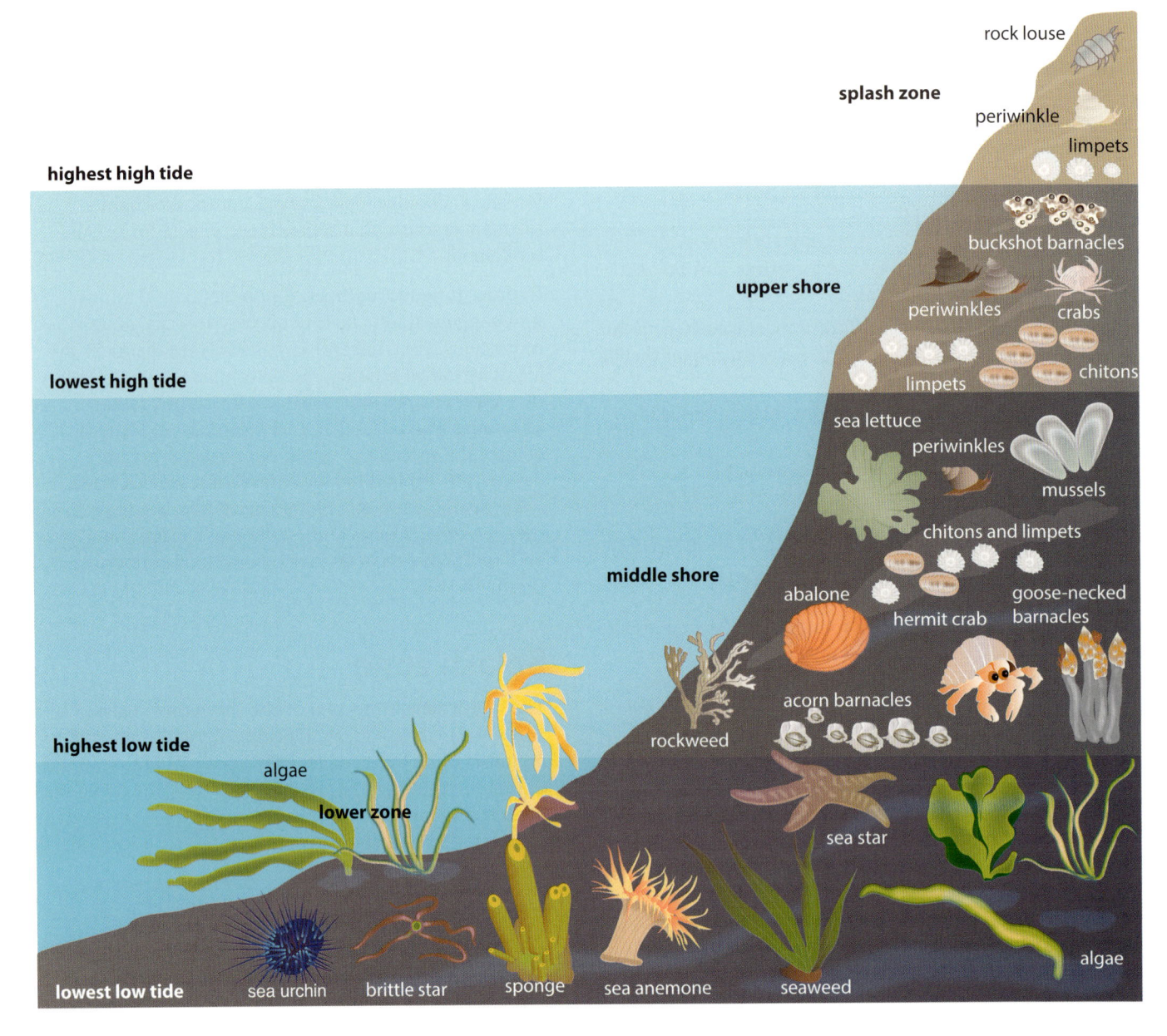

Figure 5.18: A diagram of the zonation patterns of common organisms found on a rocky shore in temperate regions.

onto rocks to prevent being swept away by waves. Many species of periwinkles can survive for days without food or water by closing themselves into their shell and storing just enough water in their gills for gas exchange. Limpets are flattened-looking snails that clamp their shell to a rock in order to seal in water during the driest parts of the day. This helps them maintain their temperature and perform gas exchange.

Upper shore

This portion of the shore is only submerged during high tides, so organisms here must be able to withstand long periods of time without water or food and drastic changes in temperature. These organisms risk desiccation during low tides. Additionally, the movement of the water as tides come in and out can be very powerful, so these organisms must be able to withstand that pull.

Typical organisms located in this zone include chitons, barnacles, limpets, periwinkles and channelled wrack. Chitons are another example of a mollusc with a muscular foot that is able to clamp down hard onto rocks to prevent waves from pulling them into the sea or predators from eating them. They are also able to trap water in their mantle during low tide to allow for gas exchange and temperature regulation. Channelled wrack is a type of algae that has developed many adaptations for survival, particularly desiccation, in the upper shore. Since these algae may have to survive up to eight hours without water, the fronds of the algae are curled to reduce water loss by evaporation, and they have channels within the frond designed to trap water at high tide. These algae are so good at surviving without water, they can lose nearly 90% of their water and rehydrate in 25 minutes.

Middle shore

The middle shore is exposed to air twice a day at low tide, so organisms must have a coping method to deal with desiccation, but not to the extent of those living in the upper shore and splash zone. These organisms do need to be able to survive while submerged for long periods of time, however, as they will be equally exposed to air and submerged underwater. Organisms in this zone include brown algae, barnacles, limpets, periwinkles and mussels.

Many species of barnacles, a type of crustacean, can be found in rocky shores. These animals cement themselves to a suitable substrate as larvae and then metamorphose into their adult form. When the tide is in, the water causes the barnacles to open their outer shell and extend their feather-like feet to filter feed on the incoming plankton. When the tide goes out, the barnacles close their shells to prevent desiccation and predation.

Blue mussels are another organism found in the middle shore. These mussels use byssal threads (silky, protein-based fibres produced by mussels for attachment to rocky surfaces.) – strong, silky fibres – to attach to rock faces in the middle shore. These threads help mussels hang on during tide changes when waves are crashing. Additionally, these molluscs are able to clamp their two shells shut, trapping water inside to prevent desiccation.

Lower shore

The lower shore is an area usually covered with water, except during the lowest spring tides. Organisms found here have very few adaptations for living outside water, so they dry out or overheat easily. Generally, the conditions in the lower shore are the most stable of those in the rocky shore community. Therefore, a greater biodiversity and abundance of organisms can be found here. Typical organisms found here include seaweed, algae, sea stars, sea urchins, sea anemones and oysters.

Tide pools

Within each of these zones, tide pools may exist. Tide pools form when seawater fills a particularly low spot in the rocks during low tides. Tide pools are important for organisms in the higher zones to survive because they create an area where they can cool down, carry out gaseous exchange and feed. However, the longer the tide is out, the warmer and saltier the tide pool becomes due to the shallowness of the water and evaporation. Lack of oxygen also becomes a problem because the increasing temperature and salinity force dissolved oxygen to leave the water and, at the same time, the organisms within the pool are using up the oxygen. Once the tide comes back in, the water in the tide pool is replaced and refreshed and ready to be used again.

Test yourself

8   Compare the abiotic factors of the splash zone with the upper shore of a rocky shoreline.
9   Explain what abiotic factors an organism living in a tide pool may have to adapt to.

5.4 The sandy shore

Sandy shore ecosystems have a unique set of factors for organisms to adapt to. The most challenging factor is the ever-shifting, **porous** substrate. Sandy shores are incredibly unstable, as a single wave or gust of wind can remove a lot of the fine sand that makes up the shore. Additionally, sandy shores do not hold onto water very well because they are porous. Both water and air easily

> **KEY WORD**
>
> **porous:** substrate with holes that allow for the passage of air and water

slip between the grains of sand through the spaces within the substrate. This means that, despite being well oxygenated, the sandy shore can become inundated at high tide, or completely dry at low tide, making desiccation a risk for the organisms that live here.

Sandy shores also lack places for attachment, so seaweeds cannot survive there. The only producers that may occur on a sandy shore are phytoplankton brought in by the tides.

Most organisms deal with these abiotic factors by living *in* the substrate rather than *on* the substrate. Organisms within a sandy shore community tend to be burrowers or infauna (organisms that burrow within a substrate), such as ghost crabs, cockles and other bivalves, and annelid worms, such as ragworms and lugworms. Lugworms (*Arenicola marina*) are marine annelids that burrow in the sand on European beaches. However, there are still biotic factors that influence these communities, such as predation and competition. Fewer rocks means fewer habitats and places to hide from predators such as shore birds. There are also fewer niches on a sandy shore due to the reduced number of food sources. Since the primary food source on a sandy shore is plankton and organic material washed in with the tide, most of the organisms on sandy shores are detritivores that collect organic material from between sand grains as they burrow. This causes competition between the few species of organisms that do live in the sandy shore.

These challenges explain why sandy shores tend to have low biodiversity compared to rocky shores. Generally, a sandy shore will have only a handful of different species within the sand grains, but they may be in great abundance. Each of those species has adaptations that help them survive in such an unstable ecosystem. For example:

Ghost crabs (*Ocypode cordimana*) dig deep burrows high on the shore above the high tide mark. These burrows may be 1 m deep in order to avoid the heat of the day. As the Sun sets, ghost crabs leave their burrows to travel to the water line and eat any detritus that washes up on shore. They are hard to spot because of their excellent sand-coloured camouflage. The ghost crab species live on Indian and Pacific beaches.

Lugworms (*Arenicola marine*) are marine annelids that burrow in the sand on European beaches. You can usually find a lugworm by looking for a pile of worm-shaped, sandy castings next to a small hole (Figure 5.19), Lugworms can make up to 30% of the biomass on a sandy beach. As such, lugworms are a popular food stuff among the predators on a sandy shore. Lugworms have adapted to this: their tail, the part of them most likely to be found in the sand, can be regrown if lost. They can sacrifice a piece of themselves to the predator and still survive.

Figure 5.19: A lugworm (*Arenicola marina*) poking out its burrow in search of detritus.

Razor clams (*Siliqua patula*) are a large bivalve that live on sandy shores along the Eastern Pacific Ocean. In order to avoid predators these clams bury themselves in the sand by forcing their muscular foot out of their shells to create a hole. They then quickly expand their shells to create more room for their body. Then the close their shells to create a sinking motion. This process is repeated until the clam has fully buried itself leaving only a tube called a siphon exposed in order to allow for gas exchange.

Test yourself

10 Why are rocky shores likely to have more biodiversity than sandy shores?

11 Suggest which adaptation may be most important to surviving on a sandy shore. Explain your reasoning.

5 Examples of marine ecosystems

CORE PRACTICAL ACTIVITY 5.1: INVESTIGATING THE EFFECT OF PARTICLE SIZE ON THE PERMEABILITY OF SUBSTRATES

Introduction

Permeability is how well water flows through the substrate or material making up the bottom of an ecosystem. Two main factors determine the permeability of a substrate: how well the particles making up the substrate fit together and the **porosity** of the substrate. Porosity is the amount of water a substrate can hold based on the amount of empty space within it. In order for water to flow through the substrate, there must be empty spaces to fill. The more tightly packed the substrate, the harder it is for water to flow through it.

Equipment

You will need:

- 9 × medium paper or plastic cups
- graduated cylinder (at least 100 cm^3)
- beaker (larger than 100 cm^3)
- marker
- push pin
- stopwatch
- calculator
- spoon
- water
- 2 × cups gravel
- 2 × cups soil
- 2 × cups sand
- paper towels

Safety considerations

Follow all laboratory safety rules as provided by your instructor.

Be careful not to poke yourself with the push pin.

Before you start

1. You will need to measure 100 cm^3 of water for this experiment. Which piece of apparatus would make the most accurate measurement: a graduated cylinder or a beaker? Why?
2. Look at the size of the grains for the three sediments provided and how they fit together. Based on these features, which substrate do you think has the largest pores?
3. Which substrate do you predict will have the highest permeability (fastest time for water flow)?

Method

1. Measure 100 cm^3 of water using the most suitable piece of apparatus.
2. Pour the 100 cm^3 of water into one of the cups.
3. Use the marker to mark the height of the water on the cup.
4. Pour the water carefully back into the graduated cylinder.
   a. If there is less than 100 cm^3 in the graduated cylinder when refilled, add the difference to bring it back to 100 cm^3.
   b. Use a paper towel to wipe out the cup.
5. Use the push pin to poke a hole in the bottom of the cup you just marked.
6. Fill the cup with sand up to the line you drew.
7. Hold the cup over the beaker to capture the water that will flow out of the hole.
8. Set the stopwatch for 60 seconds.
9. Pour the 100 cm^3 into the cup of sand and begin the stopwatch soon as the water hits the sand.
10. After 60 seconds, record the volume of water that was able to pass through the substrate in one minute in the appropriate column on a copy of Table 5.1.
11. Using a new cup, repeat steps 1–10 twice more with sand and three times each with gravel and soil. (You can also opt to carefully clean and dry the cup between each repeat.)
12. Calculate the rate of permeability for each trial using the following equation:

$$\text{rate of permeability} = \frac{\text{volume of water that passed through (cm}^3\text{)}}{\text{time (60s)}}$$

13. Calculate the means for both volume and rate of permeability for each sediment type.
14. Record all results in a copy of Table 5.1.

KEY WORDS

permeability: how well water flows through a substrate

porosity: how much water a substance can hold based on the empty space within it

> CAMBRIDGE INTERNATIONAL AS & A LEVEL MARINE SCIENCE: COURSEBOOK

CONTINUED

Results

Sediment type	Volume of water able to pass through the substrate in 60. seconds/cm³				Rate of permeability/cm³ s⁻¹			
	trial 1	trial 2	trial 3	mean	trial 1	trial 2	trial 3	mean
sand								
soil								
gravel								

Table 5.1: Results of investigation on permeability of substrate based on size.

Evaluation and conclusions

1. What units should be used to convey the rate of permeability?
2. Based on your data, which sediment type had the highest permeability? Did this support your hypothesis?
3. Based on your data, which sediment type had the lowest permeability? Explain why.
4. What features, other than particle size, of the sediments may have caused the rate of permeability to increase or decrease?
5. How do you think particle size featured into your results?

REFLECTION

After completing Core Practical Activity 5.1, think about these questions:

1. What do you think is the purpose of this experiment?
2. What other variables could be tested to validate your results? How would you test them?

5.5 The mangrove forest

Mangroves are salt-tolerant trees that prefer to live in coastal or estuarine environments between latitudes 25° N and 25° S. There are more than 110 species of mangrove, many of which are found in Indonesia where mangrove biodiversity is highest. These trees survive in saline habitats because of the lack of competition from other plants. Mangroves tend to form intertidal woodland habitats in these tropical and subtropical regions with other salt-tolerant plants that provide the basis for incredibly biodiverse communities of organisms.

Conditions for formation of a mangrove forest

Mangrove forests tend to grow in saltwater areas with a large tidal range where deposition is more frequent than erosion due to calmer waters with reduced wave action. This deposition will provide the sandy to silty sediment that will allow the **propagules**, or reproductive structures of mangrove trees, to embed in the sand and take root. As these are tropical and subtropical trees, the temperature of the region needs to be mild to warm year-round. Even the coldest month should not have an average temperature below 20 °C. Typically, mangroves will grow best in areas with healthy coral reefs offshore due to the protection provided by the reefs.

KEY WORD

propagule: a reproductive structure that detaches from the parent plant and is able to grow into a new individual

The red mangrove

All mangroves have adapted to life within a coastal or estuarine habitat by developing characteristics to compensate for the abiotic factors that are found there. Mangroves must contend with a high salt content in the water and a shifting, anoxic substrate. This section will focus on the red mangrove tree (*Rhizophora mangle*). The red mangrove is probably the most iconic species of mangrove due to its wide distribution throughout the globe and distinct root structure (Figure 5.20).

Figure 5.20: Red mangroves along a lagoon in Loango National Park in Gamba, Gabon.

Stability

The red mangrove's root structure is its most distinguishing feature. Prop roots (Figure 5.20) grow from the sides of the tree trunk and curve outwards toward the sediment. The intricate systems of roots earned red mangroves the name 'prop roots' because they primarily exist above the substrate and prop up the tree in the unstable and shifting sediment. By having multiple anchors in the sediment, each tree is less likely to be washed away during storms or incoming tides.

Oxygen absorption

Prop roots also help mangroves deal with the lack of oxygen in the substrate. Since the substrate is flooded with water twice a day for long periods of time, the underground roots of the mangrove are unable to extract the oxygen they need for cellular respiration. Without this oxygen, growth cannot happen, and the roots would rot, killing the tree. The prop roots, however, are above the water line and have special structures called **lenticels** that allow for gas exchange. The oxygen gained in this process is then sent where it is needed throughout the tree.

Salt exclusion

Red mangroves have two methods for living in saltwater. The first method begins at the roots, which have become nearly impermeable to salt because of an efficient filtration method. Some studies have shown that nearly 97% of salt present in the water is prevented from entering the roots. The salt that does enter the tree is pushed toward the leaves and accumulated there. When the leaf dies and falls off the tree, the salt goes with it. It was previously believed trees would use a 'sacrificial leaf', where red mangroves would deposit the excess salts in a particular leaf or two, but recent studies have shown that salt content is constant among all leaves on a tree, rejecting this hypothesis.

Viviparous reproduction

Red mangroves are one of a few plant species that use **viviparous reproduction**. In this reproductive strategy, the parent mangrove produces flowers which are fertilised to produce seeds. These seeds then continue to develop into a propagule (Figure 5.21) while still attached to the parent plant, rather than being released as in most plants. Once they have a reached the appropriate size, the long, green tubular propagule is released from the parent plant to float in the ocean.

Red mangrove propagules have an obligate dispersal (the amount of time a mangrove's propagule must remain in the water before it can propagate; varies among species.) period of 40 days. This means the propagules must float in the water for an additional 40 days while continuing to mature before they are ready to implant themselves in sediment. After the 40 days, the propagule needs to find an appropriate place to come ashore or 'strand'. Red mangrove propagules must be stranded for at least 15 days before the primary roots and initial leaves of a mangrove plant will develop. Red mangroves have the longest periods of obligate dispersal and obligate stranding of any mangrove species and they are also able to develop even if it has been an entire year since they have fallen from their parent tree. This means they

> **KEY WORDS**
>
> **lenticel:** a raised pore in the roots of a mangrove that allows gas exchange between the atmosphere and the internal tissues
>
> **viviparous reproduction:** [plants] a reproductive strategy where the seed develops into a young plant while still attached to the parent plant

Figure 5.21: A grouping of propagules dangle from a red mangrove (*Rhizophora mangle*) tree.

Figure 5.22: Illustration of red mangrove (*Rhizophora mangle*) demonstrating how prop roots retain sediments and act as a habitat for local species.

have the most time to spread as far away as possible and have the lowest rate of mortality amongst mangrove propagules.

> **Note:** obligate dispersal is extension content, and is not part of your syllabus.

Ecological importance of mangrove forests

The unusual design of prop roots allows them to perform multiple specific functions within coastal ecosystems in addition to the traditional purpose of tree roots (Figure 5.22). Because these roots provide a cage-like structure under the water at high tide and collect sediment, many organisms find a home among the roots. Algae, fish, oysters, sponges, crabs, barnacles and other crustaceans all live among mangrove roots, making mangrove a keystone species in this environment. In addition to those species that live within the root systems of mangroves their whole life, there are many fish species that only stay within the mangrove forest as juveniles. The mangroves act as a nursery for these fish and other animals by providing a safe place away from larger predators until they reach an appropriate size to return to the ocean.

Prop roots help prevent erosion by storms and reduce wave energy, similar to a coral reef. The prop roots slow the water energy and cause deposition of sediments within their cage-like structure. This allows the mangroves to build on the land behind and pull sediments from the water. This deposition action prevents sediments from being carried out to coral reefs and nearby seagrass beds, protecting them from sediment build-up. The presence of mangroves keeps both of these ecosystems healthy. These are just some of the reasons mangroves are protected in many countries and why they are being replanted in places in Indonesia.

Mangroves themselves are also a becoming a vital component in controlling atmospheric carbon levels. New research suggests mangrove forests are able to hold on to four times as much carbon as tropical rainforests, making them one of the most effective carbon sinks on Earth.

Not only do mangroves store excesses of carbon within their tissues, but they also add excess carbon to their soils. Some studies estimate that mangrove soil can hold over six billion metric tonnes of carbon in their soils. Using mangrove forests to reduce atmospheric carbon is one proposed solution to reduce climate change.

Economic importance of mangroves

The presence of a healthy mangrove forest provides many economic benefits to human communities. Island communities have used mangroves for centuries as a place to harvest fish and other marine life for food, gather timber to build homes and infrastructure, or to burn for fuel. Since mangroves act as a keystone species, they are responsible for much of the biodiversity of these regions. As mentioned, mangroves also provide natural protection for coastlines from erosion and storms. Mangrove forests also act as a sponge for floodwaters and a purification system for water. All these benefits come for free from the presence of a healthy mangrove ecosystem, but cost island nations vast amounts of money to recreate if mangroves are missing. Scientists estimate the worth of the ecosystem services provided by mangroves at nearly US$200 000 per hectare each year.

An added benefit to having a healthy mangrove forest is ecotourism. As with coral reefs, people want to see the biodiversity swimming in among the mangroves. The forests themselves are beautiful and, generally, more accessible to tourists, particularly those who are unable to SCUBA dive. Snorkelling, glass bottom boats, and forest hikes are all ways for people to enjoy the mangrove forest as a tourist. Bringing tourists to these new locations brings more money to these island nations. That money is then used to benefit the local people through employment and better infrastructure.

Threats to the mangrove forest

Unfortunately, despite the many benefits of mangrove forests, they have been under attack for generations. Researchers estimate 35% of the world's mangrove forests were destroyed between 1980 and 2000. Mangrove forests are threatened globally by temperature change, over-harvesting, storm damage and changes in the use of coastlines.

Climate change

As the climate changes, mangrove forests are likely to be impacted in a variety of ways. Increased temperatures, both atmospherically and in the water, may increase productivity. However, they will likely change local precipitation patterns, alter ocean currents, increase the number and ferocity of storms, and lead to sea-level rise. These factors will impact the salinity of the coasts where mangroves survive and lead to greater erosion. Rising sea levels will put existing prop roots underwater longer than they have adapted to, causing the trees to drown.

Over-harvesting

Mangrove trees have been used by people for firewood and timber for centuries. When people were taking just what they needed for their families, this was a sustainable practice that caused no overall harm to the forests. Recently, the populations of these regions have grown and the uses for harvested mangroves has grown to include the creation of charcoal, wood chips and pulp production for paper. The demand for mangrove wood has become unsustainable.

Storm damage

Storms carry powerful winds and strong waves with them. The waves and winds can destroy miles of mangrove forest along a coastline which will take years to recover. The damage is worse when the local coral reefs are not healthy because there is no longer a breakwater to calm the waves of the storm. The stronger waves are able to pull the sediment from the mangrove prop roots and wash away essential nutrients for the recovery of the forest.

Change in coastal land use

Many countries and local governments thought they could make more money by cutting down the mangrove forests and creating new infrastructure, such as tourist resorts or shrimp farms. Some believe mangroves are unproductive and foul-smelling. However, as shorelines begin to erode and land is lost on these island nations, more governments are rethinking this plan and beginning to replant the mangroves they removed.

Test yourself

12 People often refer to mangroves as a keystone species. How do the roots of the red mangrove support the idea that mangroves are a keystone species?

13 Explain how mangrove forests slow down climate change.

> PROJECT: MODELLING A MARINE ECOSYSTEM

Working with a partner, use a shoebox to create a scale model of one of the marine ecosystems discussed in this chapter. Your model should be three-dimensional and should include:

- abiotic factors that organisms must deal with in that ecosystem
- at least five organisms, including their common and scientific names
- a list of adaptations for each organism and how those adaptations increase survival in your chosen ecosystem.

You can base your model on a general version of the ecosystem (such as a coral reef) or choose a named habitat to model (such as the Great Barrier Reef). You will share your model with the class when it is finished.

Thinking about your project

What were some of the most interesting discoveries you made while working on this project?

What were some of the most challenging parts of this project, and what made them so challenging?

EXAM-STYLE QUESTIONS

1. **a** State and describe the relationship shared by the following pairs of organisms:
    - **i** coral polyps and zooxanthellae [3]
    - **ii** crown-of-thorns starfish and coral polyps. [2]
   b Describe each of the following reef types:
    - **i** fringing reef [2]
    - **ii** barrier reef [2]
    - **iii** patch reefs [2]
   c Sketch a diagram of an atoll. [3]

   [Total: 14]

2. Figure 5.23 shows mangrove crabs living among the roots of a red mangrove tree. Mangrove crabs can climb in the trees or burrow in the mud of the mangrove forest. They eat the decaying leaves of the mangroves that fall on the ground.

Figure 5.23: Mangrove crabs among roots of red mangrove tree.

CONTINUED

    a   State **one** adaptation mangrove crabs have for living in the intertidal zone. [1]

    b   Researchers used the mark–release–recapture technique to estimate the population density of mangrove crabs. A sample of 53 crabs was collected and a small drop of light coloured paint was placed on their carapace (upper shell). The marked crabs were released back into their mangrove habitat. After three days, a second sample of 75 crabs was collected from this area. Of those crabs collected, 25 were marked.

$$\text{estimated size of population} = \frac{N_1 \times N_2}{N_3}$$

where: N_1 = the number of individuals captured and marked

N_2 = the total number of individuals in the second sample

N_3 = the number of marked individuals in the second sample.

       i   Using the data provided above and the Lincoln index calculate the population of mangrove crabs in this population. [2]

       ii   The area of mangroves studied is 10 m × 10 m. Use your answer from part **bi** to calculate the mean number of mangrove crabs per square metre. [2]

       iii   Suggest **two** reasons why this method of population estimation may be inaccurate for mangrove crabs. [2]

    c   Mangrove forests are being deforested globally. Give **three** reasons why they are being cut down. [3]

[Total: 10]

3   **a**   Explain what is meant by the term *intertidal zone*. [1]

    b   Compare the physical factors affecting organisms living on a rocky shore to those living on a sandy shore. [4]

    c   **i**   Define the term *zonation*. [1]

       ii   Explain how the physical and biological factors of a rocky shore ecosystem contribute to vertical zonation of the organisms that live there. [4]

       iii   Name an example organism and describe its adaptation for survival in the upper shore of the rocky intertidal habitat. [2]

[Total: 12]

4   Biodiversity levels between ecosystems vary due to many factors.

    a   Suggest reasons for why the biodiversity on a sandy shore is different than that of a coral reef. [5]

    b   State and explain **two** processes that impact the shape of a sandy shore. [4]

    c   State **three** adaptations you would expect most organisms living on a sandy shore to share. [3]

[Total: 12]

> CONTINUED

5 a Outline **three** reasons why artificial reefs are beneficial to shorelines. [3]

   b In order to determine the best placement for artificial reefs, developers must take certain physical factors into consideration. Explain which factors are most important when determining placement of a coral reef for healthy growth. [6]

   c Most artificial reefs are now constructed from a pH-neutral cement material. Explain why scientists prefer this material to old truck tyres, abandoned planes and ships. [4]

   [Total: 13]

6 a Describe the habitat where you would expect to find mangrove trees. [3]

   b Identify **two** environmental challenges within the mangrove forest and explain an adaptation the red mangrove has for each. [4]

   c Explain how red mangroves benefit coastal ecosystems. [4]

   [Total: 11]

7 Figure 5.24 is a diagram of the open ocean.

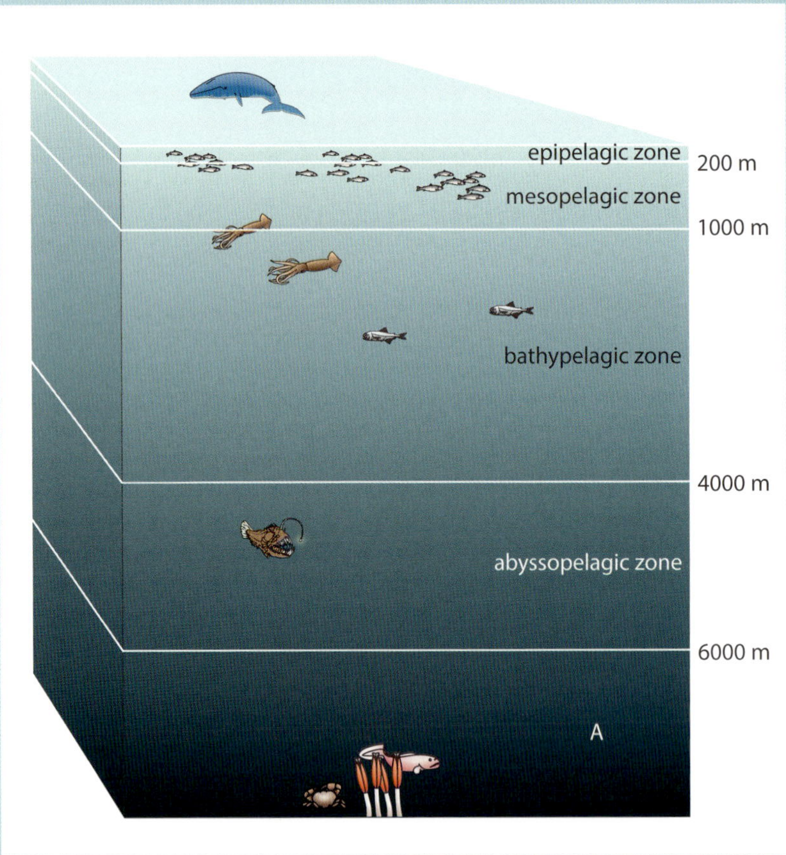

Figure 5.24: A diagram of the open ocean.

CONTINUED

    a Using Figure 5.24 state the **two** primary abiotic factors used to differentiate between the zones of the open ocean. [2]

    b Using named examples, give **two** adaptations organisms may have for living in the abyssopelagic zone. [2]

    c   **i** State the name of the zone labelled A in Figure 5.24. [1]

        ii Give **two** abiotic factors, other than lack of light, that organisms have to adapt to in order to live here. [2]

[Total: 7]

8 The World's Ocean is responsible for maintaining our planet in many ways. It accomplishes many of these goals through its interactions with the atmosphere.

    a Define the term *carbon sink*. [1]

    b Explain how El Niño events interfere with the World's Ocean's ability to function as a carbon sink. [5]

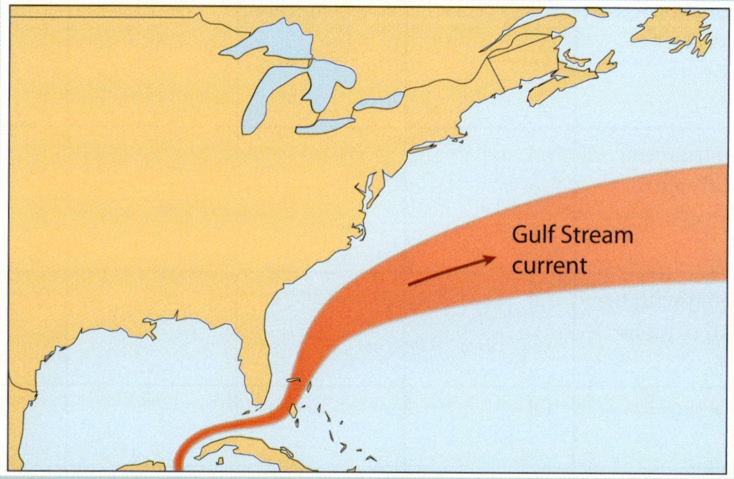

Figure 5.25: A diagram of the Gulf Stream.

    c The Gulf Stream (Figure 5.25) is a warm water current that flows from the Gulf of Mexico around the southern tip of Florida in the south-eastern United States up the eastern seaboard. Explain what impact this warm water current may have on the northern coastal states. [3]

[Total: 9]

9 **a** Outline the connection between increased carbon dioxide in the atmosphere and ocean acidification. [3]

    b Explain how limiting nutrients, such as nitrogen and phosphorus, can have both *positive* and *negative* impacts on coral growth. [6]

    c Suggest **one** reason why coral reefs are not usually found in upwelling areas. [1]

[Total: 10]

SELF-EVALUATION CHECKLIST				
I can:	See section...	Needs more work	Almost there	Ready to move on
describe the World Ocean as an interconnected body of water encircling the globe and identify the depth zones within	5.1			
explain why the interactions between the ocean and the atmosphere are important	5.1			
discuss the structure and importance of both natural and artificial coral reefs relating to the economy, ecology of the planet and medical importance to humans	5.2			
discuss the abiotic and biotic causes and effects of reef erosion	5.2			
identify the different zones on a typical exposed rocky shore using abiotic factors and describe how those factors affect the distribution and abundance of organisms on the rocky shore	5.3			
explain, using named examples, the adaptations that organisms have for living in the different zones on a rocky shore and to living on a sandy shore	5.3, 5.4			
describe the sandy shore as an ecosystem with an unstable, shifting, porous substrate and explain why it has a relatively low biodiversity	5.4			
investigate the effect of particle size on the permeability of substrates	5.4			
describe the mangrove forest as a tidal ecosystem featuring salt tolerant trees and other plants, together with other populations all interacting in the littoral zone of some tropical and subtropical coasts	5.5			
outline the conditions required for the development of mangrove forest tidal ecosystem, the ecological and economical importance of these forests and the threats facing them	5.5			
explain how the red mangrove tree has developed multiple adaptations to the mangrove environment	5.5			

EXTENDED CASE STUDY: GEOENGINEERING THE OCEAN

The ocean helps maintain our climate with naturally occurring ocean currents and biological processes. But, as **anthropogenic** levels of carbon in our atmosphere are increasingly linked to climate change, scientists are trying to think of new ways to use these naturally occurring processes in our favour. Many scientists believe the ocean's ability to act as a carbon sink can be increased through a process called **geoengineering**.

What is geoengineering?

Geoengineering is a relatively new field that aims to combine modern technology with the ancient natural processes of the Earth. In general, geoengineering is the intentional manipulation of the environment so that its processes are more efficient at reducing the impacts of climate change. The scale of geoengineering projects can be simple, such as painting rooftops white in order to better reflect sunlight, or complicated, such as sending thousands of tiny mirrors to float in orbit between the Earth and Sun (Figure 5.26). Additionally, many of these plans are controversial within the scientific community because they come with their own, possibly negative, side-effects.

Ocean fertilisation

The most common geoengineering plan related to our oceans relates to **ocean fertilisation**. Ocean fertilisation is the effort to dump iron filings, nitrates,

> **KEY WORDS**
>
> **anthropogenic:** caused by human activity
>
> **geoengineering:** intentionally manipulating environmental processes that affect the climate in order to reduce the impacts of climate change
>
> **ocean fertilisation:** the dumping of iron or other nutrients into the ocean in areas with low productivity to enhance growth of phytoplankton

Note: anthropogenic, geoengineering and ocean fertilisation are extension content, and are not part of your syllabus.

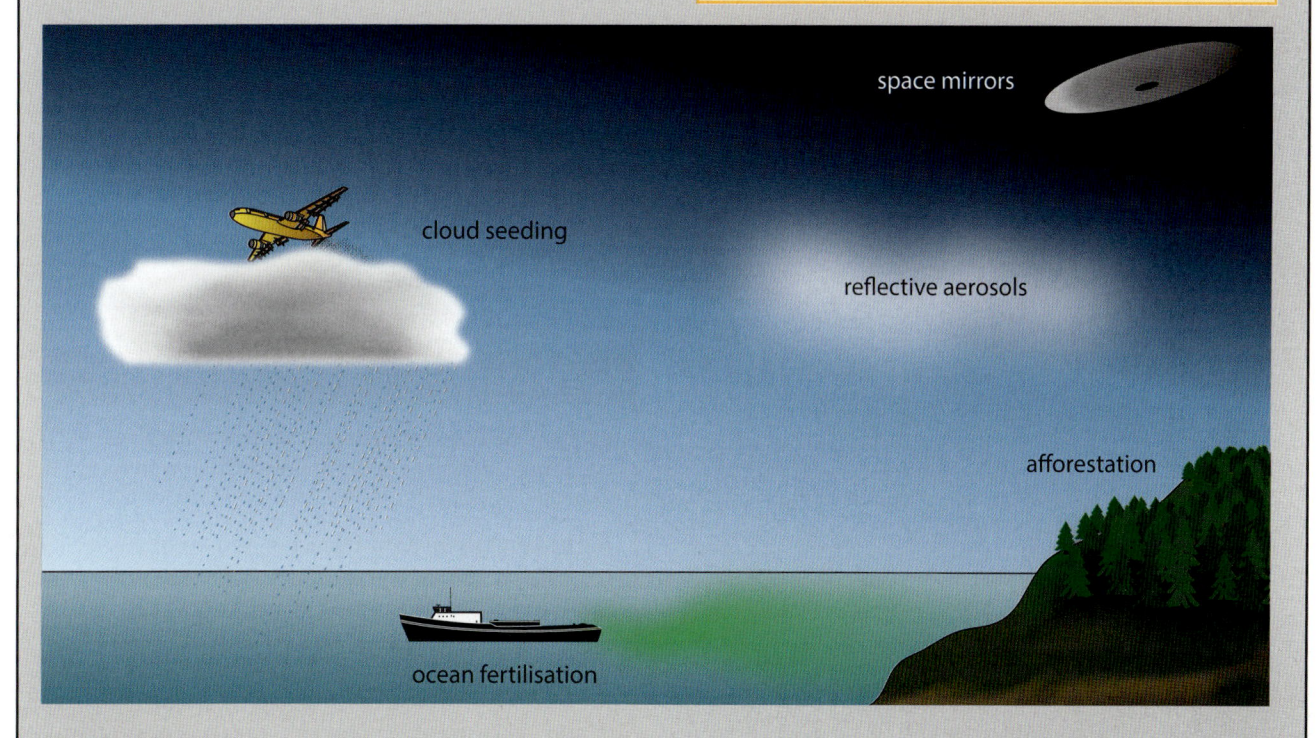

Figure 5.26: Illustration of different proposed methods of geoengineering to reduce the impacts of climate change.

CONTINUED

or other micronutrients into low productivity zones in our oceans. The goal is that the presence of these nutrients would encourage new and expanded growth of phytoplankton in areas with low levels of photosynthesis, thereby increasing the amount of carbon dioxide removed from our atmosphere. Eventually, these phytoplankton will die and sink to the ocean floor as marine snow. After sinking, the decomposition of the phytoplankton would lock the carbon that makes up their body into the seafloor where it can be stored for millions of years. The long-term storage of carbon within the seabed is one form of **carbon sequestration**.

Due to the simplicity of this process, multiple experiments with ocean fertilisation have already been carried out with varied results. Scientists from Planktos in the United States, Oceaneos Marine Research Foundation in Canada, Korea Polar Research Institute in South Korea and a co-effort sponsored by the Indian and German governments have all developed ocean fertilisation experiments that they plan to test. At least 13 ocean iron fertilisation experiments have taken place globally over the last three decades and more are on the way, particularly near Chile.

Potential impacts

Despite the positive impacts of removing excess carbon from the atmosphere by enhancing the ocean's ability to function as a carbon sink, many in the scientific community have begun to argue against ocean fertilisation. The proposed arguments are due to the unintended side-effects that have been reported during these experiments. In some cases, the food chain was strongly disrupted when iron was added to the system. After fertilisation, the phytoplankton communities in the regions that were fertilised saw a significant shift in population from algae to species of much larger, harder-to-digest diatoms. Since phytoplankton are the base of the food web, a reduction in edible species may cause a decline in the health and stability of the entire ecosystem.

In other cases, phytoplankton blooms were reported, leading to an overall decline in oxygen available for other marine species in the region. Also, adding excess nutrients may cause a **harmful algal bloom (HAB)** where the algae become overpopulated and release harmful toxins into the water. These toxins are dangerous to organisms in the environment and to any humans in the region.

Current results

Unfortunately, those experiments that have been conducted are not having the results that scientists hoped for. The amount of carbon that actually makes it to the seabed is significantly lower than expected – in some cases it is not even detectable. This is primarily because, with an increase in phytoplankton (a producer) we see an increase in consumers expanding the food web that is normally present in the region. Through consumption and respiration by consumers, most of the carbon that was removed from the atmosphere was released again or maintained within the food web.

Additionally, evidence exists that, by increasing the amount of iron in a region, there is a decrease in the amounts of other essential nutrients in the area. The excess of iron allows for the other essential nutrients to be used at a faster rate depleting their stores. This will directly impact those communities of phytoplankton and food webs that are down current from the fertilisation site and reduce the productivity in those regions. This could have major long-term implications for local fishery industries.

Questions

1. Create a flow chart to represent the intended results of geoengineering through ocean fertilisation.
2. Explain how increased levels of nutrients would decrease the rate of climate change.
3. Compare the potential benefits of ocean fertilisation with the potential risks. In your opinion, is this an idea worth pursuing? Justify your response.

KEY WORDS

carbon sequestration: long-term storage of carbon to mitigate global warming and avoid climate change

harmful algal bloom (HAB): when an excess of nutrients leads to overgrowth of marine plankton that release toxins into the water

Note: carbon sequestration and harmful algal bloom are extension content, and are not part of your syllabus.

AS & A Level Practical skills

LEARNING INTENTIONS

In this chapter you will learn how to:

- state the independent variable in an investigation and give the range of values it will take
- state the dependent variable in an investigation and describe how it will be measured
- list the control variables and explain how they will be controlled
- make scientific predictions and formulate hypotheses
- describe how apparatus must be set up during experimental work and give the steps in the practical procedure
- explain how to work ethically and safely during investigations
- present data in a single table of results which is large enough for all of your data and the results of any calculations
- present data in the form of clear and accurate charts, graphs or drawings
- identify any sources of error or anomalous results and suggest reasons for these
- make informed judgements on your confidence in your conclusions
- suggest improvements to a method in order to improve the accuracy of the results
- describe the patterns or trends in your results and give scientific explanations for these.

THE HISTORY OF THE SCIENTIFIC METHOD

The Ancient Greek philosopher Aristotle (384BC–322BC) is believed to be the first person who realised that it is necessary to take measurements in order to increase our knowledge. More than 2000 years have passed since he made this suggestion and scientific enquiry is still based on his idea. The philosophers and scholars who followed him added to his idea and refined it so that we now have a standard way to carry out scientific enquiry. In the Middle Ages, a monk named Roger Bacon (1214–1292) described a scientific method that he used to investigate nature. He made observations, formulated a **hypothesis** and carried out experiments. This sequence of events in scientific enquiry is probably familiar to most of us today. Galileo (1564–1642) has been called the father of modern science and he also contributed to the development of the scientific method. He began to standardise measurements so that experimental results could be checked by other people.

The scientific method requires a logical approach in order to collect measurable results. Measurements are taken in an experiment designed to test a hypothesis. The results will then be used to either support or contradict the hypothesis. Because experimental data are naturally variable there will often be uncertainties in the results. The level of uncertainty can be reduced by ensuring that large numbers of accurate measurements are taken. **Variables** other than the one being investigated should be kept constant or, if this is not possible, measured. If enough evidence is gathered to support a hypothesis, then it may become a **theory**.

Question

1. People often use the word 'theory' when they should use the word 'hypothesis'. Discuss, in groups, what you think the difference is between the words theory and hypothesis. Try to think of examples of each.

2. Think of an experiment you have carried out. List the variables in the experiment. Compare your list with other people and look for similarities. Discuss which variables appear most often, and the reasons for this.

KEY WORDS

hypothesis: an explanation of an observation that can be tested through experimentation

variable: a condition in an experiment that can be controlled or changed

theory: a well-substantiated explanation of an aspect of the natural world that has been repeatedly tested and confirmed through observation and experimentation

Introduction to practical skills

During your marine science course you will develop your practical skills by carrying out experiments and investigations which link to the theory you are learning. By the end of the course you should be able to plan experiments; present your observations and data clearly; evaluate both the method and the quality of your data; and draw appropriate scientific conclusions. These skills will be tested in Papers 2 and 4. You will be expected to apply them to unfamiliar practicals, as well as those which you have carried out in class. There are four main areas which you need to feel confident in:

- planning
- presenting
- evaluating
- concluding.

Experimental planning including making estimates, predictions and hypotheses

There are several steps in the scientific method that should be followed whenever an experiment is planned. It is important to remember that the scientific method is a process. Even if a hypothesis is supported, ideas can change in the future if new observations are made.

Defining the problem

In order to plan a successful investigation you need to be clear about the question you aim to answer. The first stage in the planning process is often making observations. Initial observations are often **qualitative** rather than **quantitative**. This means that they are descriptive rather than having an amount or numerical value. A hypothesis is then formulated to try and explain the observation. A hypothesis is one possible answer to the question 'why?'. At this stage a **prediction** can also be made. A prediction states what you think will happen in the experiment and is linked to the hypothesis. During an assessment you may be given the observation and expected to formulate the hypothesis and prediction using your knowledge of marine science. You might also need to give your prediction in the form of a graph rather than by describing what you think will happen. In this case, you should just sketch the shape of the graph you would expect to see.

After formulating a hypothesis and making a prediction, the next stage is to design an experiment to test your hypothesis. The experiment needs to produce quantitative data that can be evaluated and used to support or refute the hypothesis (submitting evidence that shows that a hypothesis is not correct).

All experiments involve variables: these are the conditions that can be changed. The **independent variable** is the one that is changed during the experiment and the **dependent variable** is the one that is measured.

A **control experiment** should normally be included in the investigation. The control group is treated in the same way as the experimental groups apart from the independent variable. This gives you results to use as a comparison. To obtain valid results, all variables other than the independent variable must be kept the same. If more than one variable is changed at the same time it would be impossible to say which one caused any changes in the measurements. The variables that are kept the same are the **control variables**. A control variable is any variable that could affect the dependent variable. Important examples to consider when deciding on the control variables are:

- temperature
- carbon dioxide concentration
- oxygen concentration
- pH
- light intensity
- light wavelength.

When using living organisms in laboratory experiments it is often impossible to make sure that every organism is

> **KEY WORDS**
>
> **qualitative data:** descriptive data about a variable (for example colour or behaviour)
>
> **quantitative data:** numerical data that gives the quantity, amount or range of a variable (for example, concentration of oxygen or number of eggs laid)
>
> **prediction:** a statement of the expected results in an experiment based on the hypothesis being tested
>
> **independent variable:** the variable being changed in an experiment
>
> **variable:** a condition in an experiment that can be controlled or changed
>
> **dependent variable:** the variable being measured in an experiment
>
> **control experiment:** a group within an investigation or study that receives exactly the same treatment as the experimental groups with the exception of the variable being tested
>
> **control variables:** variables that are not being tested but that must be kept the same in case they affect the experiment

identical. However, you can try to keep as many features of your organism the same as possible. For example, by using organisms of the same species, age, size and sex as well as choosing organisms which originated in the same place.

Obviously the factors listed above can only be controlled if they are not the independent variable and there may be other controls depending on the experiment being carried out.

It is much more difficult to control the variables in field-based experiments than in laboratory-based experiments. You cannot control the temperature or amount of light available on a seashore, for example. To help analyse the results, measurements should be taken of any variable that might affect the dependent variable. These are generally the same variables that would be controlled in the laboratory (for example, the pH or light intensity). These are measured at the same sampling sites as the dependent variable and recorded. Any trends or patterns in the results can then be related to changes in these measurements as well as to changes in the independent variable. You may also see these variables referred to as **confounding variables**. In laboratory experiments these are the variables that must be controlled so that they cannot affect the results. In field experiments they are normally just measured and recorded so that we can see any effect on the results.

Choosing appropriate techniques

Once you have decided on the dependent and independent variables in an investigation you need to choose the correct techniques to measure them

> **KEY WORD**
>
> **confounding variable:** a variable that could affect the independent or dependent variable and therefore the results of the experiment

EXAMPLE

You might observe that phytoplankton are found in the upper layers of the ocean.

The position of the phytoplankton is observed and its position in the ecosystem is described.

Your initial question might be:

Why are the phytoplankton observed in the upper layers of the ocean?

This would then lead you to make a hypothesis, such as:

Phytoplankton need light to grow.

Using this hypothesis, your prediction might be:

The more light phytoplankton are given, the more they will grow.

To test the hypothesis that phytoplankton need light to grow you would need to change the light intensity. This would, therefore, be the independent variable. You would then measure the growth of the phytoplankton at different light intensities. The growth would be the dependent variable and could be measured by counting samples of the cells under a microscope. You would need to have a control group which would be phytoplankton which are given no light.

Although you would be varying the light intensity you would keep the wavelength of light the same. The other factors which could affect the dependent variable (the growth of the phytoplankton) are likely to be the temperature and pH of the water. The carbon dioxide concentration could also have an effect but this is likely to remain constant during a short experiment. You would need a sample of phytoplankton taken from the same area at the same time and there would need to be the same volume of phytoplankton in each light intensity at the beginning of the experiment.

Now you try

1. A student observes that there are more algae growing in a fish tank in summer than in the winter. Suggest a hypothesis to explain this and predict the results of an experiment to investigate it.

2. State the dependent and independent variables in an investigation into the effect of light wavelength on the growth of algae.

3. Give **three** control variables for the experiment in question 2.

Practical skills

accurately. You will also need methods to control and to measure the other important variables.

In a laboratory-based experiment you will need to be able to describe how to control your key variables. Temperature is often controlled using a **water bath**. This can be as simple as a large container to which you add hot or cold water as necessary. There are also large, thermostatically controlled water baths which have heating units to keep the temperature within programmed limits. In either case you should also measure the temperature with a thermometer to ensure that it remains as constant as possible.

The pH can be controlled using a chemical called a **buffer**. This is a solution consisting of an acid and a base which remains at the same pH even if more acid or base is added to it.

The levels of carbon dioxide and oxygen are often controlled by making sure they are present in excess. This means that there is enough carbon dioxide and oxygen present that they will not become a limiting factor and affect the dependent variable. An excess of carbon dioxide is usually achieved by using hydrogencarbonate solution. Oxygen can be bubbled into the solution using an air pump.

> **KEY WORDS**
>
> **water bath:** a container of water heated to a given temperature which can be used to either vary or control the temperature
>
> **buffer:** a solution which can maintain a relatively stable pH

Light intensity is normally controlled by maintaining an equal distance from a light source. If this is the case, other sources of light must be removed as far as possible (see Practical 3.1 in Chapter 3). The wavelength of light is similarly controlled by using the same source of light (with the same wavelength) throughout an experiment. It is difficult to measure the wavelength of light, so once the light has been standardised we often just assume that it remains the same.

You then need to choose the correct equipment for your experiment. In any experiment, it is important to choose the equipment which will give you the most accurate results. For example, the correct equipment to measure a liquid is often a measuring cylinder; you should choose the smallest appropriate size. Measuring $8\,cm^3$ in a $10\,cm^3$ cylinder is more likely to be accurate than using a $200\,cm^3$ cylinder because it will be easier to read the correct value from the scale. For volumes of liquid that are less than $10\,cm^3$, a pipette or a syringe would be more accurate. Table P.1 shows some of the methods you need to be aware of to measure common variables. The actual volumes you choose will depend on the activity being carried out. If you are adding a stain to a microscope slide, for example, you will probably need less than $1\,cm^3$ of the solution. However, if you are adding water to a tank containing living organisms which you plan to investigate, you may need to measure in litres ($1000\,cm^3$).

You also need to consider safety and ethics. Safety means that you must think about the hazards and risks of your experiment. A hazard is something which could cause harm or damage to health, the risk is the chance of this damage happening and how severe the harm might be. Table P.2 shows some of the common laboratory hazards and the risks they pose.

Variable	Method for accurate measurement
temperature	thermometer – the most accurate are digital thermometers
pH	universal indicator or a pH probe
light intensity	often approximated using distance from the light source; you can also use a light sensor
volume	a measuring cylinder, pipette or syringe
mass	balance (you may have seen this referred to as weighing scales)
time	stopwatch
distance	for short measurements a ruler (in mm), for longer distances a tape measure (in metres)

Table P.1: Methods for accurate measurement of common independent, dependent or control variables.

Hazard	Risk	Precaution
corrosive chemicals	enters the eye or harms the skin	wear goggles to protect the eyes and gloves to protect the skin
glass equipment	it can break and enter the eye or cause cuts to skin	wear goggles and take care to keep glass equipment away from the edge of the bench to avoid breakage.
hot equipment	burns to the skin	take care with hot equipment, use tongs to hold hot glassware and avoid touching hot bulbs

Table P.2: Hazards, risks and precautions to consider when planning an experiment.

Ethics relates to how you treat other living organisms and avoid causing them harm. In any investigation which involves living organisms you must consider this in your planning.

When you have decided on your plan you need to be able to communicate it so that someone else could follow it. The idea behind this is that if your experiment is valid and reliable, someone else could follow your plan and obtain the same pattern of results. You will need to describe how the apparatus is set up which can be easiest to do using a labelled diagram. If you choose this option make sure you follow the rules for scientific drawing (see Chapters 4 and 6). You will also need to be able to put the steps into your plan into a logical order and write them out step by step.

> ### EXAMPLE
>
> You could be asked to plan an investigation into the distribution of a particular species of snail in the littoral zone on a rocky shore. The independent variable would be the part of the littoral zone. You could vary this by taking measurements in the low, middle and high tide zones. The dependent variable in this investigation would be the abundance of the snails which could be measured using the mark–release–recapture method (see Chapter 4). As this is a field experiment, there are few control variables, although you could make sure that the readings were taken at the same time of day, at the same time of year and in the same types of weather. You would also need to measure confounding variables which could include the temperature in each area.
>
> The most appropriate equipment might be a quadrat to choose the snails to be sampled in each area, as well as tape measures to measure out a grid for random sampling. If you are carrying out random sampling in this way you might also need a method to generate random numbers to use as coordinates. Try to avoid referring to a random number generator as it is a rather vague description. Instead you should be using the random number function on a calculator or a table of random numbers which can be found online. You would also need a thermometer to measure the temperature.
>
> As you are investigating the rocky shore the hazards are likely linked to rocks and the tides. The risks might include the chance you could slip and hurt yourself or get caught out by the tide coming in. It would be unethical to remove the snails from their original habitat or to mark them in a way which would affect their survival. You would need to ensure that each snail was marked using a method which could easily be removed, and then returned to where it was found.

CONTINUED

Now you try

1 Suggest the most appropriate equipment to accurately measure the following:

   a $86\,cm^3$ of water

   b $0.5\,cm^3$ of water

   c the mass of seaweed found in $1\,m^2$

   d the temperature of a sample of seawater.

2 An investigation is carried out into the effect of light intensity on the rate of photosynthesis in pondweed. Describe what the main hazards and risks are, and the precautions you would take to avoid those risks.

Determining number of measurements and/or observations to take

The final stage of the planning process is to choose the range and values of your independent variable, and how many readings to take at each value. Each reading is referred to as a replicate. In order to compare results effectively you should always aim to have at least five different values for your independent variable. This will enable you to see any trends in the results and to plot graphs if necessary. It is normally impractical to have more than ten different values as this would take too long to measure. So once you have chosen a range you need to choose between five and ten values which fit into your range. If possible these should be evenly spread, but it is not essential. The measurements need to be repeated.

To make sure that the results are **reliable** each treatment needs to be repeated. You can then calculate mean values for your measurements. This also allows you to identify any **anomalous** results that could affect your conclusions. Anomalous results are individual results that do not fit the pattern of the rest of the data. They may be caused by errors in measurement or difficulties in controlling the variables. It can be difficult to tell whether an anomalous result is due to natural variation within the variable being measured or genuine problems with the data. For this reason repeated readings are important to help to identify any anomalies by comparing them with the other readings taken at the same point in the experiment. During analysis of data, anomalous results are sometimes ignored and not used to calculate mean values. For this reason you should aim to include at least three readings at each value of the independent variable. This should enable you to tell which of the three (if any) is the anomaly.

KEY WORDS

reliable: results that can be replicated by other people

anomaly (anomalous): a result or observation that deviates from what is normal or expected; in experimental results, it normally refers to one repeated result that does not fit the pattern of the others

EXAMPLE

In an investigation into the effect of salinity on the freezing point of water the independent variable would be the salinity. The logical starting point would be fresh water and you would probably want a range of salinities in between fresh water (0% salt) and seawater (3.5% salt). You would need to choose between five and ten intermediate values between this range. Sensible choices of value for the salinity (as measured by %) could be 0.0, 0.5, 1.0, 1.5, 2.0, 2.5, 3.0 and 3.5. If there was not enough time for all of these readings then you could just choose five of the values to investigate as this would still give enough data to investigate the pattern.

Now you try

1 A student measured the freezing point of water at five different salinities. She took two readings at each salinity. Explain why it would have been better to take three readings.

> **CONTINUED**
>
> 2   In an investigation into the rate of photosynthesis at different light intensities, the independent variable (light intensity) was varied by moving a lamp different distances from the photosynthesising organism. Suggest a suitable range of values for this independent variable.
>
> 3   State the values which you would choose for the independent variable described in question 2.

EXPERIMENTAL PLANNING SUMMARY

Once a hypothesis and prediction have been made, an experimental approach to testing them must be planned. In order to obtain accurate results and to make valid conclusions, you should take the following steps.

1. Decide on the independent variable and the range of values to use.
2. List all the control variables that could affect the experiment and that must therefore be kept the same.
3. Decide how to keep the control variables the same.
4. Decide how many replicates to carry out.
5. Decide the timescale of the experiment.
6. Work out the hazards and risks which the experiment poses, and list the precautions you will need to take.
7. If working with living organisms, describe how you will work ethically to avoid harming them.
8. Plan which measurements to take of the dependent variable and which equipment to use to do so accurately.

Test yourself

1   Copy and complete Table P.3 to summarise the different variables in an experiment:

Type of variable	Description
independent	
dependent	
control	
confounding	

Table P.3: Types of variables.

2   Suggest **two** control variables for each of the following investigations:
   a   the effect of temperature on the growth of algae
   b   the effect of pH on the number of zooplankton
   c   the effect of light intensity on the growth of seagrass.

3   A student wanted to investigate the effect of temperature on osmosis in potato tissue by measuring the change in mass.
   a   Write a prediction for the results.
   b   State the independent variable and choose a range of values for it.
   c   State the dependent variable and describe how you will measure it.
   d   Give **two** control variables and explain how they will be controlled.

Presentation of data and observations

The results of any experiment must be clearly and accurately recorded. The best way to do this is often in a results table. However, in some cases a drawing can be more appropriate, particularly when examining biological organisms. It is often useful to present the results in the form of a chart or graph as this will enable you to identify trends in the data and see whether these support your hypothesis.

Recording data and observations in tables and other suitable forms

For experiments which involve taking measurements you need to record your results in a table. This should be drawn before the experiment begins and must have space to fit in all the data to be collected. It should be constructed using ruled lines and have a border around it so that it is easy to see your results. Normally, the independent variable is placed in the first column of the table. All the columns should have headings that describe the variables and state the units that will be used to measure them. If you are planning to carry out calculations using the data from your experiment you should also include columns in the table to show the results. Sometimes you will also need to add in a column to explain what an observation means. This might be where a colour change occurs (the observation) and you then need another column to record what that colour change shows you.

When recording your results you will also need to be careful that you record them with an appropriate **precision**. If you have been able to measure to the nearest 1 °C, for example, you cannot record a result as 64.563 °C as you are overstating the precision. The results of calculations should also be recorded to the same degree of precision. In practice this often means using the same number of decimal places for every result. So, if the answers to your calculations were 43.34221 and 37, you would record them as 43.3 and 37.0.

In some investigations there is no data to record in a table. Instead, drawings must be made to show what is present in the sample. This is often the case if you are investigating different types of cell, for example, or studying organisms which are found in different areas of the shore. In this type of practical activity there is no results table but you still need to show your observations clearly. Drawings should be large and drawn in pencil. Unlike an artistic sketch, you need to use a single unbroken line and avoid shading your drawing. You should show the outline of what you are looking at. Chapters 4 and 6 give you more details of how to produce an accurate scientific drawing.

> **KEY WORDS**
>
> **precision (in measurements):** the level of refinement in a measurement as shown by the number of significant figures given
>
> **precision (in experiments):** this refers to the closeness of the measurements to each other; precise measurements are close to each other and there is little spread about the mean

EXAMPLE

An experiment which requires a fairly complex results table is an investigation into the effect of surface area to volume ratio on the rate of diffusion in agar. In this example you would need to record the dimensions of your chosen shape; the surface area and volume (both calculated using the dimensions of the shape); the ratio (calculated using the surface area and the volume); the time taken for diffusion for each reading and an average time taken calculated from the different readings. This is a large amount of information to fit into a table and so you would have to make sure that it was big enough to see all of the data clearly. The independent variable is the surface area to volume ratio but unusually this will not go in the first column because it must be calculated from the size of the original shape. The data should also be recorded in the table in a logical order. In this example the most logical order is by size of the shape from the smallest to the largest. If you recorded your results in the order in which they were obtained (rather than in size order) it would be much more difficult to see any patterns which might emerge in the results.

Table P.4 shows how you might record these results for an experiment using cubes of agar.

The length of each cube in Table P.4 has been measured in mm. With an ordinary ruler it might be possible to measure to within 0.5 mm; however, it is unlikely that cubes of agar could be cut **accurately** enough to make this worthwhile. Each cube has, therefore, been measured to the nearest whole 1 mm.

> **KEY WORD**
>
> **accuracy:** ensuring that measurements are close to the true value

> **CONTINUED**

Length of cube side / mm	Surface area / mm²	Volume / mm³	Ratio	Time taken for cube to change colour / s			
				Trial 1	Trial 2	Trial 3	Mean
1							
2							
3							
4							
5							

Table P.4: A results table for an experiment investigating the effect of surface area to volume ratio on diffusion.

We need to remember the precision of our calculated values. In this experiment the surface area to volume ratio of the smallest cube is 6, and the ratio of the largest cube is 1.2. If you write 6 it could mean somewhere between 5.5 and 6.4 but recorded to the nearest whole number. To show that it is exactly 6 it should be written as 6.0. This means both answers (1.2 and 6.0) have been recorded to the same number of decimal places and, therefore, have the same precision.

Now you try

1. A student carried out an investigation into the rate of photosynthesis in pondweed and recorded his results in Table P.5. Identify the errors he has made in the presentation and recording of his results.

2. A student was measuring the width of limpets using equipment which can be read to the nearest 0.5 mm. The raw data for five limpets is:
66.5, 3, 72.1253, 49.2, 52.9
Rewrite it using the correct level of precision.

Distance from lamp / mm	Number of bubbles	Number of bubbles	Number of bubbles	Mean
0	102	105	111	106
200	76	74	92	80.666667
1000	12	21	15	16
600	35	38	41	38
400	56	62	52	56.6666667
800	19	23	21	21.2

Table P.5: A results table from a student investigating the effect of light intensity on the rate of photosynthesis by counting the bubbles released from pondweed in each minute.

Presenting data in the form of graphs and charts

Once you have obtained the results of an experiment it is often necessary to present these in the form of a graph. The most common types of graph you will need to use are **line graphs**, **histograms** and **bar charts**.

Drawing a line graph

Line graphs are useful to show the relationship between two **continuous variables**. A continuous variable is one which can take any value. Temperature, time, depth and salinity are all examples of continuous variables. With an accurate enough thermometer, for example, there are an infinite number of possible temperatures which can be measured. A temperature of 35.5554 °C is different from a temperature of 35.5555 °C. A **discontinuous variable** is one which can only take certain values. A good example in humans is our blood type. You can have type A, B, AB or O blood and there is no overlap between each type.

There are several things to remember when plotting a line graph. The first is that the independent variable must go on the x-axis (the horizontal one). The dependent variable goes on the y-axis (the vertical one). You should use a scale which means that you will use at least three quarters of the available space. This will prevent you from drawing a graph which is too small to see clearly. The larger your scale, the easier it is to see any patterns in the data. So if you have 20 units for each square of paper it will be harder to identify changes than if you have 1 unit to each square. Your scale also needs to be linear. This just means that the scale goes up in equal intervals on the axis of your graph. Although the scale must be linear it does not have to start at zero if this is not appropriate for your data.

The scale must also be sensible, that is it allows you to work out what the intermediate points on your graph represent. For example, if each square on the graph paper is worth 0.35 of a unit, it will be very difficult to read the values in between your plotted points. Generally, round numbers work best as we are able to count on through the graph, so you can have 1 square to 5 units, 100 units or even 1 000 000 units, as these are all easy to count. Similarly, you could have 1 square to every 0.1 unit or 0.01 if the data are very small numbers.

Both the x- and y-axis must be fully labelled with a description and units. These are normally the same as those in the results table. Sometimes at A-level you might have to plot two different dependent variables against the same independent variable. For example, if you were monitoring the temperature and salinity of the ocean you might want to show how they vary over the course of a year on the same graph. In this case you would have two y-axes (one on either side of the graph); one would be for temperature and the other for salinity. Time would go on the x-axis. You would plot one line showing how salinity varies with time using the salinity axis and another showing how temperature varies with time using the temperature axis. It is then important that you label the lines so it is clear which data is represented by each line.

Often in a line graph the points are joined together with straight lines, using a ruler. Sometimes a line of best fit can be used, although this does imply that you can predict the intermediate data between each of your points. For this reason, lines of best fit are not often used in experiments involving living organisms as they can be unpredictable. You must also remember that a line can be a straight line or a curve. Do not assume that a line of best fit is always a straight line.

Drawing a histogram or bar chart

Histograms and bar charts both involve drawing bars to a certain height to represent the data.

A histogram is normally used for frequency data; that is, something which has been counted. The independent variable is continuous and goes on the x-axis. The dependent variable is the number which have been counted (the frequency) which goes on the y-axis. Many of the techniques in Chapter 4 will lead to a histogram.

A bar chart shows the relationship between two variables, only one of which is continuous. In a bar chart there are gaps between the bars to show that it is discontinuous data.

> **KEY WORDS**
>
> **line graph:** a graph which is drawn to show the relationship between two continuous variables
>
> **histogram:** a graph which is drawn to show the frequency of one continuous variable
>
> **bar chart:** a graph which is drawn to show the relationship between one continuous and one discontinuous variable
>
> **continuous variable:** one which can take any value (for example, temperature, time, concentration)
>
> **discontinuous variable:** one which can only take certain values (for example, human blood type or eye colour)

EXAMPLE

An example of an investigation involving two continuous variables is the effect of light intensity on the rate of photosynthesis. Figure P.1 shows a line graph using the data for the experiment shown in Table P.5.

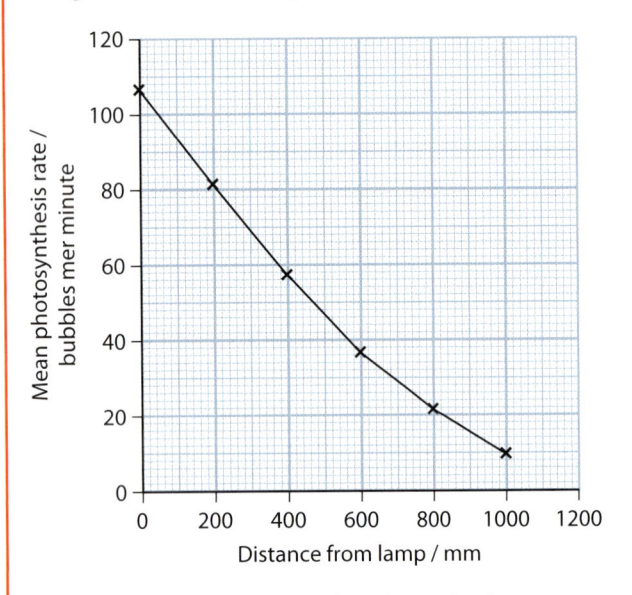

Figure P.1: A graph to show the relationship between light intensity and the rate of photosynthesis in pondweed.

In this investigation the independent variable is the distance from the lamp so it has been plotted on the *x*-axis. The dependent variable is the rate of photosynthesis, shown on the *y*-axis. In the graph shown in Figure P.1 the distance and photosynthesis rate both go up in increments of 20 but you do not have to use the same interval for both axes. You just need to ensure that both axes have linear scales.

The results of an investigation into the distribution of limpets in the littoral zone of a particular beach are shown in Table P.6.

This data can be plotted on a histogram. The distance is the independent variable and so will be plotted on the *x*-axis. The bars of the histogram should be drawn touching each other to show that distance is a continuous variable. The dependent variable is the average number of limpets which will be plotted on the *y*-axis. Figure P.2 shows a histogram drawn using this data.

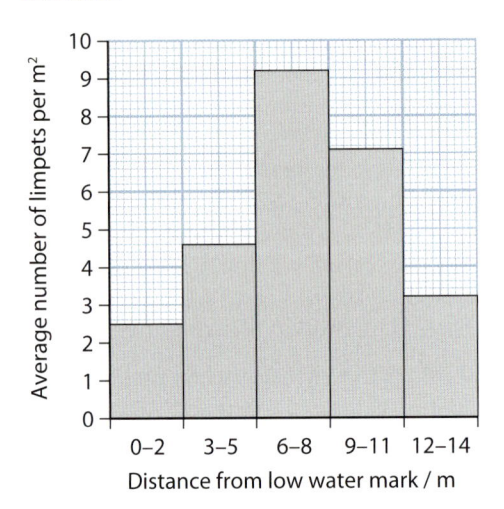

Figure P.2: A graph to show the distribution of limpets at different distances from the low water mark through the littoral zone.

However, if the limpet investigation had been carried out on five different beaches and the average number on each beach was found, then 'beach' would be the independent variable. There is no linear scale for beach; it is a discontinuous variable. The data for this investigation would, therefore, need to be plotted on a bar chart. The bars would have gaps between them to show that beach is a discontinuous variable.

Distance from low water mark / m	Average number of limpets per m^2
0–2	2.5
3–5	4.6
6–8	9.2
9–11	7.1
12–14	3.2

Table P.6: The average number of limpets found in different areas of the littoral zone.

CONTINUED

Figure P.3 shows a bar chart for the limpet investigation on five different beaches.

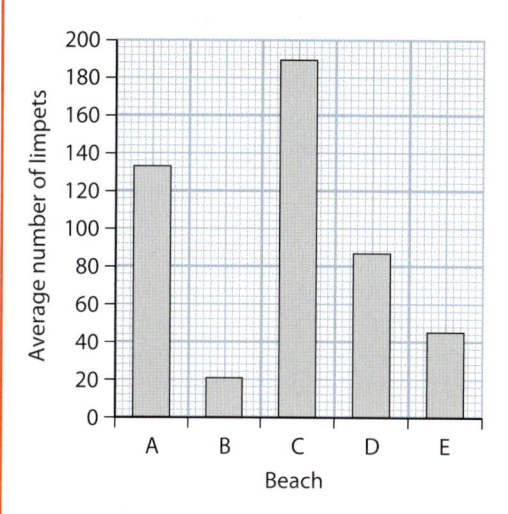

Figure P.3: A graph to show the average number of limpets found on five different beaches.

Now you try

1. Sort the following list of variables into continuous and discontinuous:

   type of shore, temperature, concentration of oxygen, blood group, colour of scales, windspeed, humidity, water potential, light intensity, species of plankton, trophic level

2. Suggest the correct type of graph for an investigation into:

   a the relationship between wavelength of light and photosynthesis

   b the relationship between speed of swimming and heart rate

   c the distribution of crabs on five different rocky shores

   d the relationship between distance from the low water mark and the numbers of algal species found.

GRAPH DRAWING SUMMARY

Once you have collected your data, you need to work out the best type of graph to draw. Follow these steps to make sure that it is plotted accurately:

1. Decide on the type of graph you need to draw. If both the variables are continuous it will be a line graph. If you have frequency data for different continuous categories it will be a histogram. If one variable is discontinuous it will be a bar chart.
2. Put the independent variable on the x-axis and divide it equally to make a sensible scale.
3. Put the dependent variable on the y-axis and divide it equally to make a sensible scale.
4. Give each axis a descriptive label with units. This can be taken from the results table.
5. If it is a line graph plot each point using a small ×. If it is a bar chart or histogram, draw the bars using a ruler. In a bar chart, the bars should have gaps between but in a histogram they should be touching.
6. Join the points of a line graph with a ruler unless you have been asked to draw a line of best fit. If it is a line of best fit then try to make sure there are the same number of your plotted points on either side of the line.
7. If there is more than one line on your graph then write a key or label each line to make it clear which is which.

Test yourself

4. Draw a table which could be used to record the results of an investigation into the effect of different concentrations of sucrose solution on plasmolysis in onion cells. Five concentrations will be used (measured in mol dm^{-3}) and the number of plasmolysed cells will be counted in three samples of 50 cells at each concentration. This will then be converted into an average percentage at each concentration.

5. Describe the graph you would draw for the experiment described in question 4 including the type of graph you would draw and which variable would go on each axis.

6. Describe the important things to remember if you had to draw one of the plasmolysed cells.

Evaluation of procedures and data

At the end of an experiment it is important to evaluate both your results and the procedure used to obtain them. This will enable you to identify any anomalous readings and suggest reasons for these as well as to improve the practical for the next time it is carried out.

Identifying the limitations and sources of error

It can be difficult to be certain about the results of experiments because the measurements will almost always vary to some extent. If an experiment is reliable, it can be repeated by other people and similar data obtained. This decreases the uncertainty about the results. Controlling all variables apart from the independent variable also reduces uncertainty because you know that only the independent variable could have altered the measurements. Finally, it is important to take all measurements as accurately as possible. This means choosing the most appropriate equipment to take the measurements and then reading the results properly. Despite taking these precautions there will often be sources of error in the experiment and you need to be able to identify the most important of these. This does not mean identifying mistakes that you made during the procedure, it means identifying unavoidable errors.

There are two main types of error which occur during practicals. These are **systematic** and **random errors**.

Systematic errors affect all of the results equally which means that your results will be less accurate. Systematic errors can sometimes result from difficulties in taking the reading from your equipment. It is often difficult to identify systematic errors in an experimental procedure because the pattern of your results tends to stay the same, but you should be aware that they can occur.

Random errors are caused by factors which vary from one measurement to another. They are often associated with difficulties in controlling variables such as temperature or light intensity. If these vary during the experiment it may affect your results but it will not affect each result in exactly the same way. It is also possible for a random error to be introduced if you have to decide when the end-point of an experiment has been reached. You would be unlikely to stop the experiment at exactly the same point each time.

After an experiment has finished you should be able to identify the random sources of error based on your experience during the procedure, and suggest any sources of systematic errors. You should also have been measuring your control variables as discussed in the planning section and this will enable you to see how effectively they were controlled. The smaller the differences in your measurements, the more effective the control. There may also be anomalous values in your data and you need to be able to identify these by looking for the ones which do not fit the pattern. Once you have identified any anomalies you will then need to suggest their causes. Most anomalies will be caused by errors or difficulties in controlling the variables.

At this point you should be able to evaluate the procedure and decide how confident you are in your conclusions. To evaluate the procedure you should go through any difficulties (for example in taking measurements or controlling variables), any errors

> **KEY WORDS**
>
> **systematic error:** a consistent error which affects each measurement in the same way, normally caused by faulty measuring equipment or difficulties in reading that equipment
>
> **random error:** an error in measurement which is caused by factors which vary from one measurement to another

caused by the difficulties and any anomalous results. If there were no difficulties and there are no anomalous results then your evaluation will of course be positive. This is also a good time to look at whether enough repeated readings were taken. If there are not enough replicates it can be difficult to know which result is anomalous. The more repeats there are, the more any result which does not fit will stand out.

After your evaluation you can also decide how confident you are in the conclusions made using your data. In general, the more accurate the measurements taken, and the less variation there is within repeated results, the more valid the conclusions will be.

A good conclusion will come from an experiment with the following features:

- Repeated readings are taken.
- Anomalous results are identified and explained.
- Sufficient measurements of the dependent variable are made to show a clear pattern,
- Other variables are controlled and recorded.
- The measurements of the variables are made accurately using appropriate equipment.

EXAMPLE

If you were measuring the growth of salmon by measuring their mass you would use a balance. If the balance was not calibrated correctly and added 5 g to each measurement, then it would look as though every salmon was 5 g heavier than the real mass. This would be a systematic error as the pattern of the results would remain the same but the average mass would be incorrect. You could also introduce a systematic error through reading the measuring equipment. If you were measuring the maximum width of the salmons' tails with a ruler you could probably read the ruler to the nearest millimetre. So, you might measure the width as 150.5 mm but it could actually be 150.3 mm or 150.4 mm.

During the experiment, the salmon being measured might be kept at the same temperature so that this did not affect their growth. However, the temperature will not be exactly constant; it will vary randomly above and below the set point. If you were controlling it manually by adding warmer or cooler water it would vary more than if there was an automatic system with a thermostat. The variation in temperature would introduce a random error into the results.

In the agar diffusion experiment which we looked at in the section on recording data, the time taken for the agar block to change colour is measured. For each block you have to stop the timer when it has completely changed. This is difficult to see and you might stop the clock a little faster or slower each time. This would therefore also cause a random error.

Now you try

1. Describe the difference between a random and a systematic error and give an example of each.
2. Explain what an anomalous result is.

Suggesting improvements

After you have identified the limitations and sources of error, you should be able to suggest improvements to the method to avoid the same problems in the future. The improvements will obviously depend on the limitations of the experiment but in general they tend to be one of the following:

- Improve reliability by carrying out more repeats. This makes it easier to see any anomalous results.
- Control variables more effectively or control more of the variables. More effective control is often by using a more accurate control method. If there were variables which were not controlled originally then you need to say how they could be controlled in future.
- Use more precise equipment to take measurements.
- Avoid human error by using objective scales rather than measuring by eye.
- Include more values of the independent variable so that you have a better idea of the pattern. This is particularly important if there is a sudden change in the pattern of your results between two points. More measurements taken between these two points would enable you to see exactly where the change happened.
- Sometimes there may be a completely different approach to measuring the same variable and you might plan an alternative method.

EXAMPLE

You might choose to investigate the rate of diffusion or osmosis at different temperatures. In this experiment, a more accurate control method would be to use a thermostatically controlled water bath to keep each temperature more constant. This will mean that each temperature will vary less and so there should be fewer random errors. If one of the difficulties in the experiment is reading the thermometer accurately, then you could use a digital thermometer which will give a precise reading of the temperature and increase the precision of the results.

If you were using the change in colour of an indicator to show when diffusion had taken place, you could use a colorimeter to measure the colour change. This would be an objective method and would reduce the random errors caused by judging the end point of the experiment by eye.

If you then measured the diffusion rate at five different temperatures and found a sudden increase between your measurements at 40 °C and 50 °C you would need to investigate further. An improvement would be to take measurements at 42 °C, 44 °C, 46 °C and 48 °C so that you could find out when the change happened. Otherwise, you would not know whether it took place at 40.1 °C or 49.9 °C.

An example of the use of alternative approaches is the two methods used to investigate osmosis in Chapter 6. One involves taking the mass of tissue and the other looks at the plasmolysis of cells but both would enable you to work out the water potential. If you carried out an experiment using one of the methods, a potential improvement would be to use the other and to compare the results to look for any anomalies.

Now you try

1. Suggest improvements which involve more accurate methods to measure each variable:

   a the temperature measured with a glass thermometer

   b the pH measured with universal indicator

   c the width of a crab using a metre ruler.

2. Table P.7 shows the results of an investigation in the growth of algae at different light intensities. State where you think more readings should be taken, giving your reasons why.

Light intensity / lux	Algal growth / number of cells	
	Reading 1	Reading 2
0	35	34
2000	47	49
4000	199	204
6000	238	234
8000	264	392

Table P.7: The results of an investigation into the growth of algal cells at different light intensities.

EVALUATION PROCEDURES AND DATA SUMMARY

1. Look at the pattern of your results and identify any readings which do not fit the pattern. These are anomalous results.

2. Identify any sources of error which may have caused the anomaly. If you have no anomalous results there can still be sources of error.

3. Check the measurements of your control variables to see how much these varied and whether they could have caused any anomalous results.

4. Evaluate the procedure and decide how confident you are in your conclusions.

5. Use your evaluation to suggest improvements to the procedure which would enable you to obtain more accurate, reliable and precise results in future.

Practical skills

Test yourself

7 Read through the plan for the experiment, shown below. Evaluate the method and describe your ideas to improve the procedure.

An investigation into osmosis in chicken eggs.

- Five chicken eggs were de-shelled by leaving them in acetic acid overnight
- The eggs were weighed using a balance and the mass of each was recorded
- Each egg was placed into a solution ranging from water to $2\,mol\,dm^{-3}$ sucrose solution (0, 0.5, 1.0, 1.5 and $2.0\,mol\,dm^{-3}$ solutions)
- The eggs were removed from the solutions after a day and the mass was recorded

8 Table P.8 shows the results of the egg experiment. Identify the anomalous result and explain what the next step in the investigation should be.

Concentration of sucrose/$mol\,dm^{-3}$	Initial mass of egg/g	Final mass of egg/g
0.0	56	65
0.5	62	43
1.0	52	58
1.5	61	53
2.0	54	42

Table P.8: The results of an investigation into the effect of sucrose concentration on osmosis in chicken eggs.

Analysis of data and making conclusions

Once the data have been analysed a conclusion can be drawn. This should be a statement describing the results and any patterns obtained. The data obtained during the experiment is used to illustrate each point. The trends and patterns in the results should then be explained and linked back to the prediction or hypothesis.

Display of calculations and reasoning

You will often have to carry out calculations during experimental work. The maths skills sections in each chapter will help you to do this. It is important to show your working and not just write down the answers. This will mean that someone else can see how you worked out your results.

You will also need to consider how many significant figures (s.f.) to give your answer to. Sometimes you will be told to use 2 or 3 s.f. If not, you should aim to use the same number as the least precise part of the calculation.

So, if you were to calculate 53 (2 s.f.) multiplied by 23245 (5 s.f.) you would give your answer to 2 s.f. to match the least precise part of the calculation (53).

$53 \times 23245 = 1231985$
$= 1200000$ (2 s.f.)

EXAMPLE

Chromatography is a technique which can be used to separate mixtures of pigments because they will all move a different distance on filter paper when dissolved in a particular solvent. An R_f value can be calculated to show the solubility of each pigment. If you carried out a practical to separate different photosynthetic pigments by chromatography (see Chapter 7) you would need to calculate the R_f values for each pigment. Table P.9 shows a sample set of results for this experiment.

To calculate the R_f values we use the formula:

$$R_f = \frac{\text{distance moved by pigment}}{\text{distance moved by solvent}}$$

Pigment or solvent	Distance moved/mm
solvent	67
1	15
2	40
3	65

Table P.9: Distances moved by three photosynthetic pigments and the solvent in a chromatography experiment.

> **CONTINUED**

The best way to show your working is to write this out and then to write out the calculation.

So, for pigment 1:

$$R_f = \frac{\text{distance moved by pigment}}{\text{distance moved by solvent}}$$

$$= \frac{15}{67}$$

$$= 0.2238806$$

$$= 0.22 \text{ (2 s.f.)}$$

Note, because both parts of the calculation have 2 s.f., the answer should also be given to 2 s.f.

Now you try

1. Carry out the remaining R_f calculations from Table P.9, showing your working in full.
2. State how many significant figures the results of each of the following calculations should be given to (you do not need to complete the calculations):
   a. 23×15.7
   b. 14.55×0.239
   c. 0.0045×75

Description of patterns and trends

You need to be able to describe the results of your own experiments in detail and summarise the key points, as well as the results of unfamiliar experiments. You might have to describe data which is given in the form of tables or graphs. In order to do this clearly you should follow these steps.

- Describe the overall pattern of the data and the relationship between the independent and dependent variables. You could also comment on any positive or negative correlations.
- Draw attention to any variability in the data (or lack of variability).
- Look for any changes in the pattern. This is easiest on a graph because you can look for changes in the gradient of the line. In a table you will need to look for sudden jumps in the data (for example, if the readings for the dependent variable were 23%, 25%, 27%, 82%, 94% you could point out the sudden increase between 27% and 82%).
- Quote figures from the table or graph to show the areas you are talking about.

> **EXAMPLE**

An example of a description is given here for Figure P.1 which shows the results of an investigation into photosynthesis at different light intensities.

As the light intensity decreases (and the lamp is moved further away from the pondweed) the rate of photosynthesis decreases and fewer bubbles are produced each minute. The gradient of the line is fairly constant which suggests that it is a linear relationship and that there is little variability in the data. There is a positive correlation between the light intensity and the rate of photosynthesis. At 0 mm the rate is 106 bubbles per minute and at 1000 mm the rate has decreased to only nine bubbles per minute.

Now you try

1. Describe the results shown in Figure P.3.
2. Describe the results shown in Table P.6.

Interpretation of data and observations

Throughout the course you will learn many different mathematical skills which will enable you to analyse and interpret your data accurately. The methods for all of the calculations you are required to learn are shown in the Maths Skills features in each chapter. You will often need to calculate the mean of a sample of data, but you could also be required to work out the mode, median, percentage, rate of reaction or magnification. These calculations will enable you to simplify the data and the range will help you to determine the variability.

Practical skills

As discussed in the evaluation section, the more variability in the data, the less confident you would normally be in your conclusions. At A-level you will also be expected to calculate the standard deviation and standard error which are more accurate ways to determine the variability in your results. You can also use the standard deviation or standard error to put error bars onto a graph to show the variability in the data. You will learn these techniques in Chapters 7 and 9.

The statistical tests you will learn (Spearman's rank at AS and chi-squared at A-level) will enable you to see whether there is a statistically significant relationship or difference in your samples. The key point to remember with these statistical tests is that for the results to be significant we need than a 5% probability that the results are due to chance. In other words, we need to be 95% certain that the changes in the dependent variable are caused by the changes in the independent variable. You learned Spearman's rank in Chapter 4 and you will learn about chi-squared in Chapter 9.

If you have plotted a line graph you may need to work out the gradient of the line to find out the rate of a reaction (see Chapter 9). Alternatively, you might be asked to use your graph to work out another value.

EXAMPLE

Osmosis can be investigated by measuring the mass of plant tissues at different concentrations. If you took several readings of the mass at each concentration you could calculate a mean value. Knowing that the mean of a sample is 25 g does not actually give you very much information. Knowing that the mean is 25 g and the range is 23 g to 26 g shows you that there is little variability in the data. Conversely, a mean of 25 g with a range of 2 g to 73 g would show a large variability and might suggest a problem with the method or help to identify an anomalous result.

A graph can be plotted to show the change in mass against the concentration. The point where there is no change in concentration must be the point where the tissue used has the same concentration as the solution surrounding it. For this reason, the x-intercept is used to find the concentration of this tissue. You can take this one step further by using another graph called a calibration curve to convert the concentration into a figure for water potential. You can practise these techniques in Chapter 6.

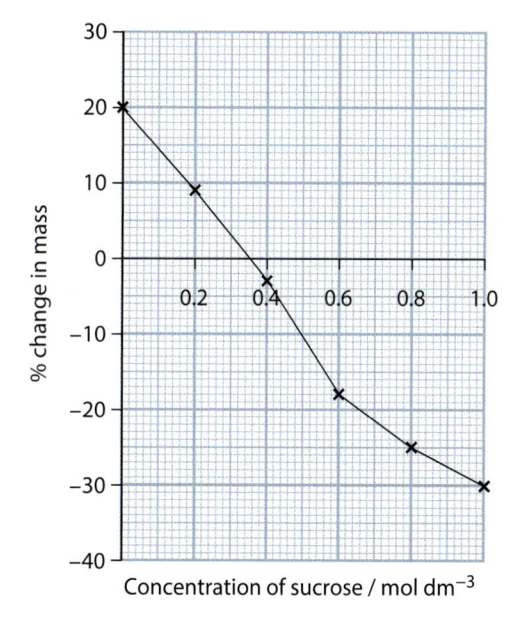

Figure P.4: The change in mass of carrot tissue left in different concentrations of sucrose solution for four hours.

Now you try

1. Figure P.4 shows the results of an experiment into osmosis in carrot tissue. Use the graph to work out the sucrose concentration of the carrot tissue.

2. Explain why a mean and a range is more useful than a simple mean for data analysis.

Making conclusions drawing on theoretical knowledge and understanding

The final stage in any experiment is to make and explain your conclusions. The conclusion should link back to the hypothesis and prediction made in the planning stage and should include a detailed scientific explanation of what has happened. If the results match the prediction, they support the hypothesis. If the results do not quite match the prediction, they do not support the hypothesis and it may need to be refined. If the results are completely different to the original prediction, they may be used to refute the hypothesis. This means arguing that the hypothesis is incorrect. You may then need to generate new questions by observing the data and making a new hypothesis that explains all of the data you now have. Alternatively, the original hypothesis may be refined to include the new observations.

You may also need to make further predictions or suggest questions which arise from the data you have been analysing.

A conclusion is simply a statement describing what the results of the experiment show. It will often follow on from the description of the graph or results table. You would then need to write a scientific explanation for your conclusion. The easiest way to make sure that you are explaining the results rather than describing them again is to start with the phase 'this is because' You then link back to your original hypothesis and state whether or not it is supported by the results. Finally, you need to add any further questions or investigations which could take place and make predictions for these. Sometimes you will be asked to write some of these sections rather than a detailed conclusion which includes every section.

> ### EXAMPLE
>
> In the previous section there was a description of Figure P.1. The conclusion to follow this description could be:
>
> *In conclusion the greater the light intensity in this experiment, the higher the rate of photosynthesis.*
>
> An explanation to go with the photosynthesis conclusion could be:
>
> *This is because the higher light intensities provided more light energy for photosynthesis so the rate increased and more oxygen was produced. Light must have been a limiting factor for photosynthesis.*
>
> Linking back to the original hypothesis and prediction gives us:
>
> *My hypothesis was that the light intensity would affect the rate of photosynthesis and I predicted that the higher light intensities would give the highest rate of photosynthesis. The prediction was correct and the results support my hypothesis.*
>
> Finally further investigations might be:
>
> *It would be interesting to increase the range of light intensities measured to find out when it ceases to be a limiting factor for photosynthesis and also what the lowest light intensity is which still produces bubbles. At 1000 mm the rate of photosynthesis was very low so I predict that there would be no photosynthesis if the light was more than 1200 mm from the pondweed. I would also like to use a light meter to measure the light intensity more accurately rather than measuring the distance of the lamp from the pondweed.*
>
> **Now you try**
>
> 1 Describe the relationship between the prediction and the results if those results support a hypothesis.
>
> 2 In a previous section you described Table P.6. Suggest a further question which could be investigated following on from these results.

ANALYSIS OF RESULTS SUMMARY

At the end of any experiment or if you are given some results you need to analyse them. Follow these steps to make sure you include all the important information.

1 Carry out any calculations which are necessary and show all of your working.

2 Use descriptive statistics such as the range, standard deviation or standard error to simplify your data, assess how variable the results are and decide how confident you can be in your conclusions.

3 If necessary test for correlation using Spearman's rank or test for goodness of fit using chi-squared and explain the statistical significance of your results.

4 Write a conclusion which describes the relationship between the independent and dependent variables.

5 Link back to your hypothesis and prediction and describe whether the hypothesis has been supported.

6 Explain the results using your scientific knowledge.

7 Suggest further questions which could be investigated and give your prediction for the results of these investigations.

Practical skills

Test yourself

9 Look back at Figure P.4 and write a conclusion and scientific explanation.

10 Look back at Table P.8 which gives the results of an investigation into osmosis in chicken eggs. State what you would calculate from these results and complete the calculation for the first row of data, making sure to show your working.

CASE STUDY P.1: INVESTIGATING BARNACLE DISTRIBUTION IN THE LITTORAL ZONE

A student made the observation that two species of barnacle appeared to be distributed unevenly on a rocky shore. She noticed one species (*Chthamalus stellatus*) living nearer the high water mark than the other (*Semibalanus balanoides*). She decided to investigate her observation and formulated a hypothesis. Her hypothesis stated that *Chthamalus stellatus* was more able to resist drying out than *Semibalanus balanoides* (Figure P.5)

She marked out a 50 mm² area just above the low-water mark and counted the number of each species that was present. She then repeated this at 5 m intervals from the low-water mark to the high-water mark at the top of the shore.

Her results are shown in Table P.10.

Distance from low water mark / m	Number of *Semibalanus balanoides*	Number of *Chthamalus stellatus*
0	12	0
5	9	8
10	11	0
15	6	0
20	0	10

Table P.10: Distribution of two species of barnacle on the shore.

The student concluded that her results supported her hypothesis. Some of the other students in her class were not sure and argued that there were problems with her results and with her method.

Figure P.5: Barnacles growing on rocks.

Questions

1 State the independent and dependent variables in this investigation.

2 Name a variable which the student could have controlled during the experiment

3 Give **two** confounding variables she could have measured and state the equipment needed to measure them.

4 Evaluate the results and the method and identify any anomalous results

5 Explain whether or not you think the student has made a valid conclusion and give your reasoning.

EXAM-STYLE QUESTIONS

1.
   a. Describe a laboratory-based experiment to test the hypothesis that light intensity affects the growth rate of algae. [6]
   b. Draw a results table which you could use to record your results. Include all the necessary column headings but do not fill in any results. [2]
   c. Sketch a graph to show what you would expect to see if the hypothesis in part a is correct. Label the axes but do not include a scale. [2]
   d. Explain the relationship you have shown in your graph. [2]

   [Total: 12]

2. An investigation into the growth of coral at different temperatures was carried out. Samples of coral were grown in the laboratory at different temperatures and the increase in surface area was measured in $cm^2\,week^{-1}$. The results are shown in Table P.11.

Temperature / °C	Increase in surface area / $cm^2\,week^{-1}$			Mean increase in surface area / $cm^2\,week^{-1}$
	Trial 1	Trial 2	Trial 3	
14	0.3	0.5	0.2	0.33
16	0.6	0.6	0.8	
18	0.8	0.9	1.1	0.93
20	1.4	0.1	1.3	1.35
22	1.6	1.5	1.8	1.63
24	1.7	1.4	1.8	1.63

Table P.11: Growth of coral at different temperatures.

   a.
      i. Calculate the missing mean for 16 °C. [2]
      ii. Identify the anomalous result in the table. [1]
   b. Plot a graph to show the relationship between the mean increase in surface area and the temperature. Use a ruler to join the points with straight lines. [5]
   c. Describe the pattern shown by the data in your graph. [2]
   d. The researchers devised the following hypothesis to explain the results:

   Coral grows faster at higher temperatures.

      i. Discuss the extent to which these results support the hypothesis. [2]
      ii. Give **two** factors that should have been controlled during the experiment. [2]

   [Total: 14]

Practical skills

EXAM-STYLE QUESTIONS – A LEVEL ONLY

3 Limpets are herbivorous marine snails which live on rocks in the littoral zone. When they are covered by water they are able to feed by scraping algae off the rocks with their tongues. They then clamp down on the rock to avoid drying out when the tide is out.

Plan a laboratory investigation which could be carried out to investigate the effect of the time the limpets are out of the water on their growth. You should include a hypothesis, the key variables, full details of the method, how you would analyse your results and how you will work safely and ethically. [12]

[Total: 12]

4 Fish meal is used as a protein rich food supplement for livestock. It is made from ground up dried fish. One of the world's biggest producers of fish meal is Peru which currently provides around 16% of the total production of fish meal. This began in the 1950s and there was a rapid expansion in the use and export of fishmeal made from Peruvian anchovetas. Table P.12 shows the number of fish meal plants in Peru as well as the global catch of anchoveta during this time.

Year	Number of fish meal plants in Peru	Annual global catch of anchoveta / million tonnes
1950	0	0.0011
1955	20	0.0663
1960	80	3.4
1964	150	9.8
1970	154	13
1973	151	1.7

Table P.12: Number of fish meal plants in Peru and the global catch of anchoveta during this time.

  a Plot a line graph to show the changes in the number of fish meal plants and the annual global catch of anchoveta between 1950 and 1973. You can plot the first two points for the annual catch as 0. [5]
  b Describe the changes in the global catch of anchoveta. [2]
  c Suggest a hypothesis using this data which could explain the changes in global catch of anchoveta between 1950 and 1970. [1]

[Total: 8]

SELF-EVALUATION CHECKLIST

I can:	See section...	Needs more work	Almost there	Ready to move on
state the independent variable in an investigation and give the range of values it will take	Experimental planning			
state the dependent variable in an investigation and describe how it will be measured	Experimental planning			
list the control variables and explain how they will be controlled	Experimental planning			
make scientific predictions and formulate hypotheses	Experimental planning			
describe how apparatus must be set up during experimental work and give the steps in the practical procedure	Experimental planning			
explain how to work ethically and safely during investigations	Experimental planning			
present data in a single table of results which is large enough for all of your data and the results of any calculations	Presentation of data			
present data in the form of clear and accurate charts, graphs or drawings	Presentation of data			
identify any sources of error or anomalous results and suggest reasons for these	Evaluation of procedures			
make informed judgements on your confidence in your conclusions	Evaluation of procedures			
suggest improvements to a method in order to improve the accuracy of the results	Evaluation of procedures			
describe the patterns or trends in my results and give scientific explanations for these	Analysis of data			

Chapter 6
Physiology of marine organisms

LEARNING INTENTIONS

In this chapter you will learn how to:
- recognise cell structures and outline their functions
- describe the fluid mosaic model of membrane structure and understand the semi permeable nature of membrane structure
- describe and interpret photomicrographs, electron micrographs and drawings of typical animal and plant cells
- make observations, drawings and magnification calculations from unfamiliar structures or specimens using the formula rate of magnification = $\frac{\text{image size}}{\text{actual size}}$
- describe and explain the processes of diffusion, facilitated diffusion, osmosis and active transport

CAMBRIDGE INTERNATIONAL AS & A LEVEL MARINE SCIENCE: COURSEBOOK

CONTINUED

- carry out practical investigations into diffusion, osmosis and water potential and explain the movement of water between cells and solutions with different water potentials
- understand that the raw materials and waste products of respiration must be moved to and from the surface of organisms
- understand how to calculate surface area : volume ratios and discuss the importance of this to biological processes
- describe gaseous exchange by simple diffusion, pumped ventilation and ram ventilation and relate an organism's method of gas exchange to its habitat and motility
- explain why marine organisms may need to regulate their water content and ion content, with reference to the composition of sea water and of body fluids
- explain the terms osmocoformer, osmoregulator, euryhaline and stenohaline and outline the process of osmoregulation in salmon.

BEFORE YOU START

- Draw a typical animal cell and a typical plant cell. Try to identify as many structures as possible and summarise their functions. List the structures that are found in both cells and those that are found only in plant cells. Compare your diagrams with other learners.
- Think about what you already know about how salinity can vary in different bodies of water and list as many factors that you know can affect it. You may have studied osmosis before. If you have, try to write down a definition and then think about how different salinities will pose challenges to marine organisms. Write down what you will think will happen if you:
    - put limp, dry lettuce into pure water for one hour
    - sprinkle pure sugar onto ripe strawberries
    - put red blood cells into pure water
    - put raw pieces of potato into pure water or very salty water.
- Think about what you already know about gaseous exchange in organisms (use yourself as an example). Write down:
    - the name of the gas that you remove from the air
    - the name of the waste gas that you release
    - how you carry out gaseous exchange and how your respiratory system is adapted to maximise this
    - list as many other methods of gaseous exchange that you have come across (not including lungs).

Compare your notes with other learners. The features that your respiratory system has to maximise gaseous exchange will be the same for every other method.

6 Physiology of marine organisms

> ### THE PHYSIOLOGICAL CHALLENGES FACED BY ORGANISMS IN THE MARINE WORLD
>
> The marine environment is a stable environment, but that does not mean it never changes. Temperature, oxygen concentration and salinity are three factors that can vary between different areas of water and over time. This means that marine organisms need to be adapted to cope with these variations. To be able to understand how marine organisms are able to live in their environments, we need to understand how their physiologies are designed. The physiology of all organisms is like a finely tuned machine in which all the parts work together in harmony.
>
> At the root of all physiology are the basic building blocks of life, cells. Multicellular organisms are made up of many different types of cell, all designed to play a role in their survival. Cells themselves are made up of smaller structures called **organelles**, all of which carry out specific functions for the cell to work. We need to understand the nature of the cells that organisms are composed of and how each cell structure plays its part.
>
> Human activity may be affecting the physical and chemical characteristics of our oceans. Global warming may be increasing their temperatures, changing their salinities and altering their oxygen levels. Pollution may be changing the ratios of solutes, and increased carbon dioxide levels may make oceans more acidic. We need to prevent our oceans from becoming more hostile to the organisms that live within them and predict the effects that uncontrolled pollution can have. If we are to be able to help marine organisms survive, we need to understand the way that their cells, tissue and organs work – this is why the study of marine physiology is so vitally important.
>
> **Question**
>
> 1. In what ways do changes to the physical and chemical nature of our oceans may make it difficult for marine organisms to survive?

6.1 General cell structure

A brief history of the cell

The first person to use the term **cell** was the English scientist, Robert Hooke (1635–1702). Hooke used one of the first light microscopes to look at thin slices of cork. In 1665, he observed that the cork was made up of tiny, repeated units that looked like the small rooms (or cells) that monks lived in (Figure 6.1).

As the quality of microscopes improved, and better methods of staining sections were developed, more details of cell structures were discovered. The Italian scientist, Marcello Malpighi (1628–1694) and English plant scientist Nehemiah Grew (1641–1712) both described the structures of plant tissues and made detailed drawings. The first animal cells were drawn

> **KEY WORDS**
>
> **organelle:** a specialised structure within a cell that has a specific function
>
> **cell:** the smallest structural unit of an organism that is capable of independent functioning

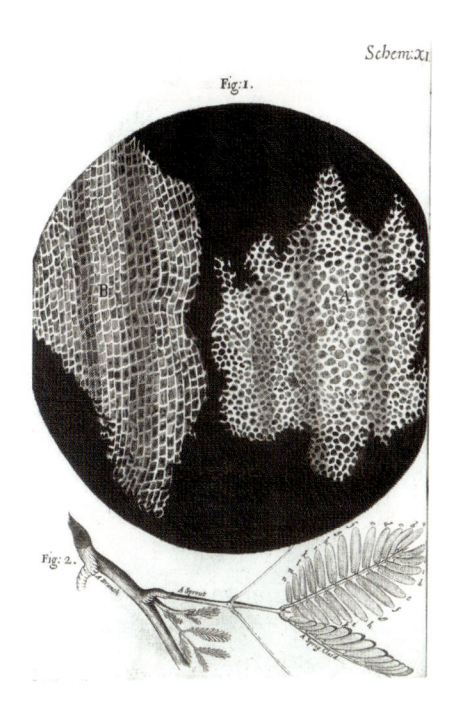

Figure 6.1: Robert Hooke's drawing of cork tissue.

and described by the Dutch microscoper, Antony van Leeuwenhoek (1632–1723) in 1676. He drew many, detailed diagrams of single celled organisms using a microscope that he designed himself (Figure 6.2).

Figure 6.2: A microscope used by Leeuwenhoek to observe cells.

Van Leeuwenhoek called the organisms 'animacules' and went on to identify the structures of sperm cells and red blood cells. It was only, however, in 1839 that two German scientists, Matthias Schleiden (1804–1881) and Theodor Schwann (1810-1882) proposed the cell theory that we know today. They realised that all living things are composed of cells and these cells are the smallest structural unit of an organism. Throughout the nineteenth and early twentieth centuries, improvements to the quality of microscopes and methods of preparing tissues led to discoveries of structures within cells which were called, organelles. These organelles included the **cell wall**, **cytoplasm**, **cell surface membrane**, **nucleus**, **chloroplast**, **mitochondrion** and **Golgi body**. All of these discoveries were made using **light microscopes**, which, as their name suggests, use light to see specimens. In 1931, the German scientist, Ernst Ruska (1906–88) developed the first **electron microscope**. The electron microscope was able to magnify images much more and show much more detail. Scientists were now able to see even more detail of cell organelles and start to unravel the functions of structures such as the **rough and smooth endoplasmic reticulum**.

> **KEY WORDS**
>
> **cell wall:** a layer that surrounds some types of cells and gives strength and support; plant cell walls are made of cellulose
>
> **cytoplasm:** all of the material, except for the nucleus, that is found within a cell
>
> **cell surface membrane:** a biological membrane that separates the internal contents of a cell from its external environment
>
> **nucleus:** membrane bound organelle that contains the genetic material of a cell
>
> **chloroplast:** the photosynthetic organelle in eukaryotes
>
> **mitochondrion:** (plural: mitochondria) the organelle in eukaryotes in which aerobic respiration takes place
>
> **Golgi body:** cell organelle that modifies proteins
>
> **light microscopes:** a type of microscope that uses visible light and glass lenses to magnify structures
>
> **electron microscope:** a type of microscope that uses electrons and electromagnets to magnify structures
>
> **rough and smooth endoplasmic reticulum:** a network of flattened sacs running through the cytoplasm or eukaryotic cells; molecules, particularly proteins, can be transported through the cell inside the sacs separate from the rest of the cytoplasm; ER is continuous with the outer membrane of the nuclear envelope

6 Physiology of marine organisms

Microscopes, magnification and resolution

Although there are many types of modern microscopes available, there are broadly two main types of microscope used today: light microscopes and electron microscopes.

- Light microscopes are the main tool used for looking at living cells and are the ones that you will find in your school laboratory. There are lots of different designs and they can usually give a maximum **magnification** of about ×1500. They use a visible light source to shine through specimens and focus the images using glass lenses (Figure 6.3).
- Electron microscopes are only used in research institutes. Instead of sending visible light through specimens, they send a beam of electrons. They can give magnifications of over ×200 000 and have a **resolution (resolving power)** of 0.2 nm.

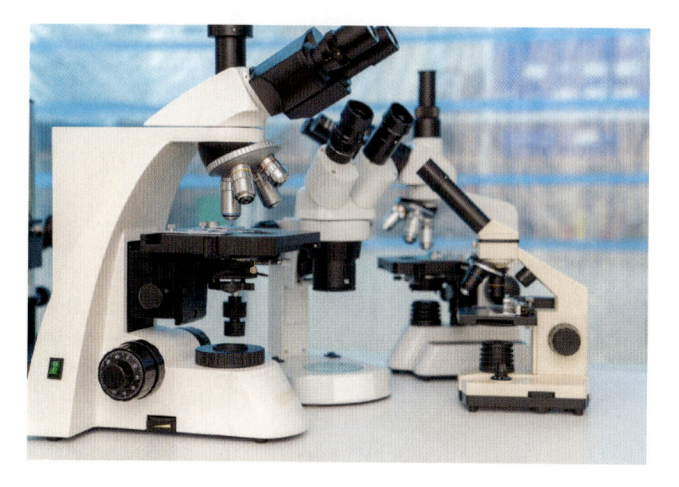

Figure 6.3: A range of light microscopes that are often found in laboratories.

Light microscopes

Light microscopes all require a source of light. This may be a bulb that is part of the microscope or a mirror that reflects light from another source into the microscope. Figure 6.5(a) shows the main parts of a light microscope and how it works. The specimen is placed on a slide which is then placed onto the stage. Light is focused through the specimen with a condenser lens. As light passes through the specimen, it is scattered and is then magnified and focuses by the objective and eyepiece lenses. We can look through the eyepiece or project the image onto photographic film to take a picture.

Resolution and magnification

The total magnification of the image is calculated by multiplying the magnification of the objective lens with the magnification of the eyepiece lens:

total magnification = magnification of objective lens × magnification of eyepiece lens

For example, the total magnification when using a ×4 objective lens and ×10 eyepiece lens would be:

$$4 \times 10 = \times 40$$

Most microscopes have a range of objective lenses that can be used to change the magnification power required.

To see different cell and tissue structures with a light microscope we use different stains. These stains bind to structures and give them different colours so that we can see them clearly. For example, the stain methylene blue binds to the nuclei of animal cells, while iodine will stain any starch-containing structures within plant cells black.

Resolution, or resolving power, is a measure of the smallest distance apart that two objects can be seen distinctly. A microscope that has high resolution can visualise the smallest structures within cells. The resolving power of microscopes depends on the **wavelength** of the light used (see Chapter 7 for a more detailed discussion on the wavelengths of light). The resolution of a microscope is roughly the wavelength of the light divided by two. This means that at best, the resolution of a light microscope is about 200 nm (0.0002 mm). To see smaller structures than this, we need to use something with a smaller wavelength.

> **KEY WORDS**
>
> **magnification:** the process of enlarging the size of an image
>
> **resolution (resolving power):** the smallest distance between two points that can be detected; it is a measure of the level of detail that can be seen
>
> **wavelength:** the distance between two corresponding points of a wave; different colours of light have different wavelengths

Electron microscopes

Electron microscopes, as shown in Figure 6.4, use a beam of electrons that are directed through the specimen. A beam of electrons behaves very much light a light ray but with a much smaller wavelength. This very small wavelength means that the resolution of electron microscopes can be less than 1 nm, much more than a light microscope, and the magnification can be up to ×200 000. Using an electron microscope is, however, much more difficult than a light microscope. Glass lenses cannot focus electron beams and so electromagnets are used instead.

Figure 6.5 shows how light and electron microscopes focus an image. Note that they both have three lenses, but the light microscope has glass lenses while the electron microscope has electromagnets. The image cannot be viewed directly and is displayed on a computer screen. Because electrons are particles, they would collide with air particles and so the specimen must be placed into a vacuum. Coloured stained cannot be used and so specimens are 'stained' with heavy metals such as lead or osmium that will deflect electrons. Sometimes, false colour electron micrographs are produced – these are not 'real' colours but have been enhanced to make it easier to see structures. Because specimens are treated harshly, they can be damaged or altered by the procedure. Electron microscopes are large, expensive pieces of equipment that can only be used by skilled operators. Table 6.1 compares the advantages and disadvantages of the two types of microscope.

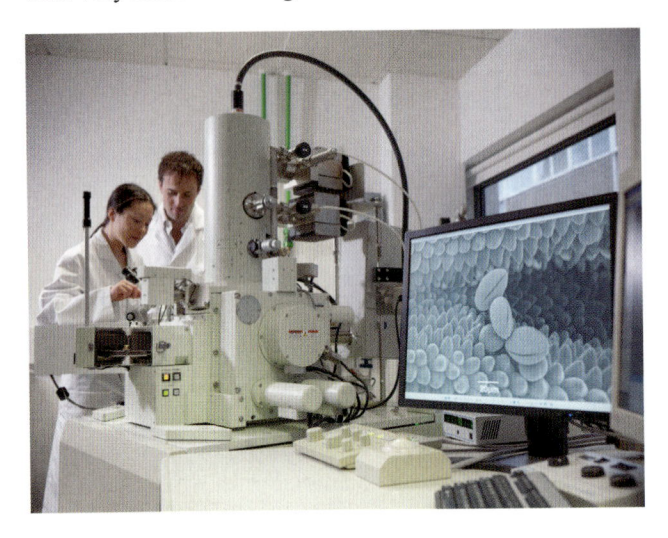

Figure 6.4: An electron microscope being used in a laboratory.

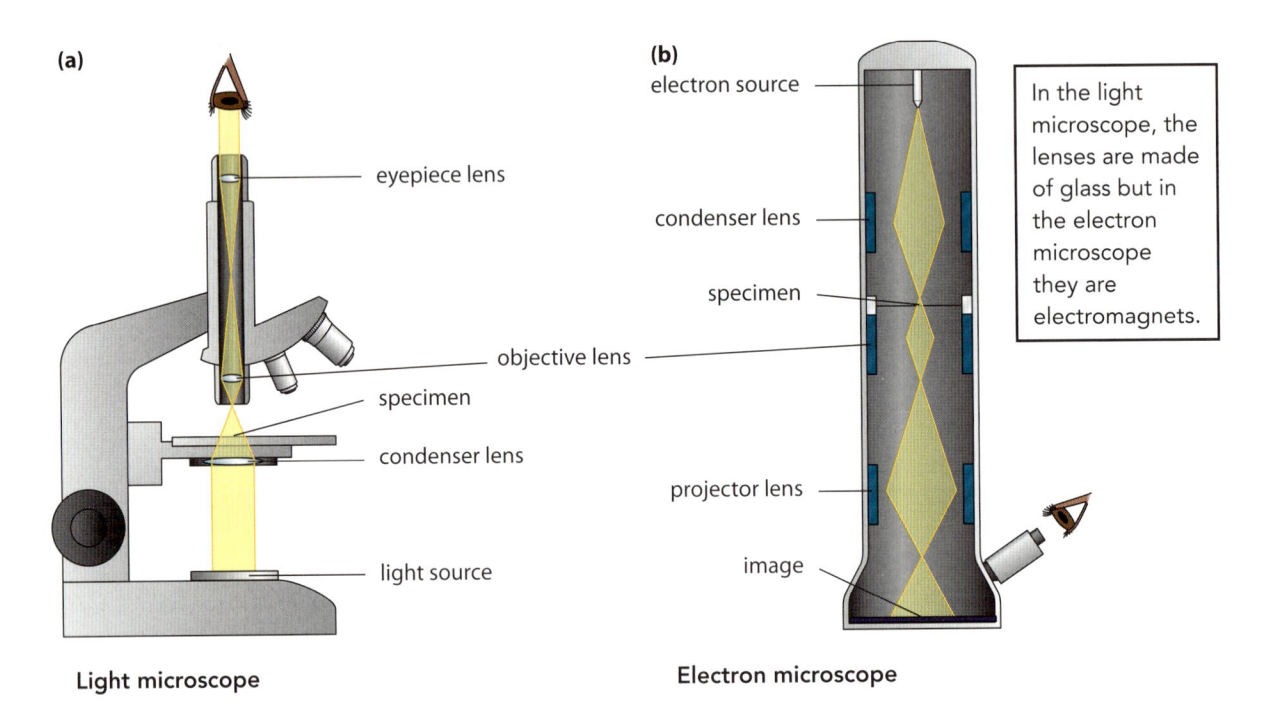

Figure 6.5: Comparing focusing with (a) a light microscope; and (b) an electron microscope.

In the light microscope, the lenses are made of glass but in the electron microscope they are electromagnets.

6 Physiology of marine organisms

Light microscope	Electron microscope
lower resolution	higher resolution
lower magnification	higher magnification
cheaper to purchase and run	expensive to purchase and run
portable	large (often takes up a room)
staining is less harsh	harsh treatment of specimens causes damage
living specimens can (sometimes) be used	living specimens cannot be used
colours are visible	no colour is visible
less skill is required	only skilled operators can use

Table 6.1: A comparison of the advantages and disadvantages of light and electron microscopes.

Cell organelle structures and functions

Micrographs are photographs taken using a microscope. A photomicrograph is a photograph taken when using a light microscope. An electronmicrograph is a photograph taken using an electron microscope. Figure 6.6(a) shows a photomicrograph of cells taken from a fish embryo. Several cells are clearly visible. The cell in the centre clearly shows the nucleus and cell surface membrane around the periphery. The cytoplasm, surrounding the nucleus, seems to show some structures but nothing distinct. Figure 6.6(b) shows a photomicrograph of a cell from *Elodea*, Canadian pondweed. The cell wall, nucleus, and chloroplasts are visible but, again, few other structures are clearly visible within the cytoplasm.

Figure 6.7(a) shows an electron micrograph of a mammalian liver cell; Figure 6.7(b) shows a drawing of it.

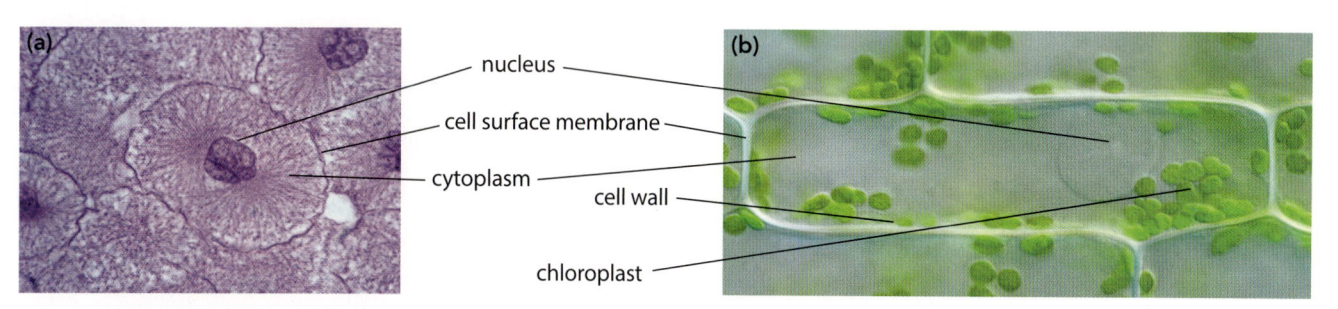

Figure 6.6: Photomicrographs of: (a) cells from fish embryo; (b) cells from *Elodea*, Canadian pondweed.

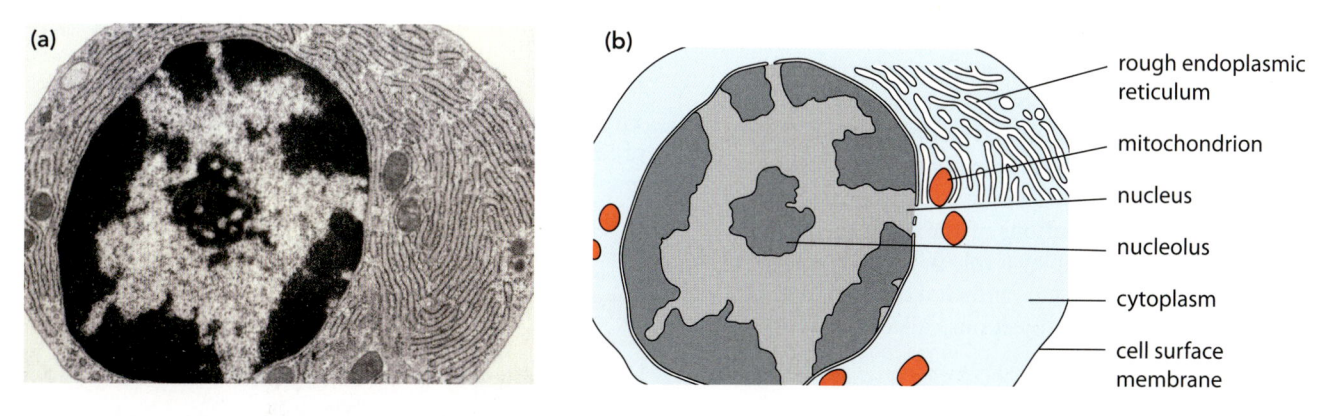

Figure 6.7: (a) Electron micrograph of a liver cell; (b) Diagram of a liver cell to show some of the organelles present.

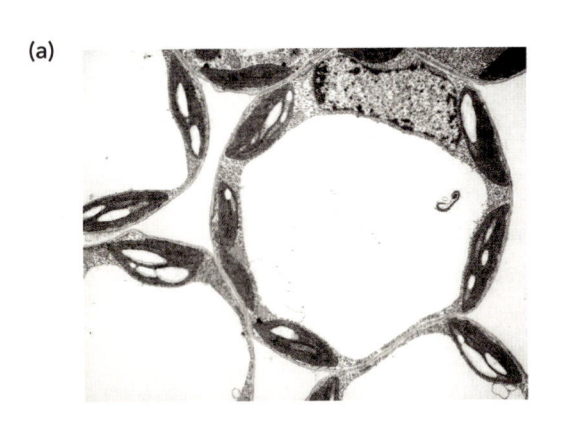

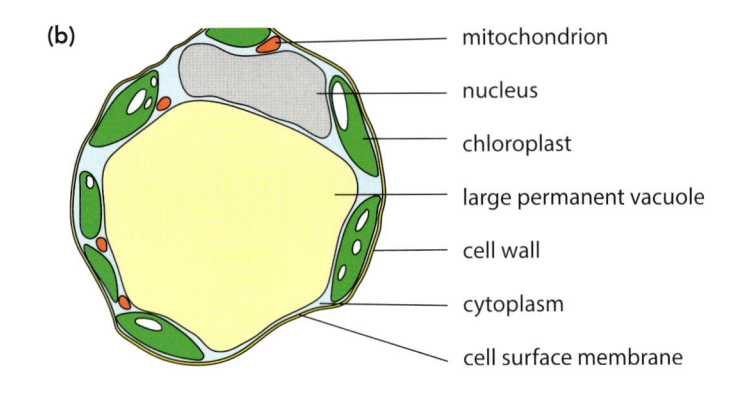

Figure 6.8: (a) Electron micrograph of a plant cell; **(b)** Diagram of a plant cell.

Many more organelles, such as mitochondria, rough endoplasmic reticulum (rER) and Golgi body are visible within the cytoplasm and we can see that the nucleus has a double membrane around it. Figure 6.8 shows an electron micrograph and drawing of a plant cell. The central vacuole, chloroplasts and nucleus are clearly visible. Mitochondria, chloroplast and nuclei all have a double membrane. Much more detail is shown inside the chloroplasts – they are not simply green 'blobs' but complex structures. The structures within cells are called organelles, and they have a range of structures and functions.

Cell surface membrane

There are many types of membrane within cells. Many organelles, such as the nucleus, chloroplast and mitochondrion are surrounded by membranes. Others, such as the Golgi apparatus and endoplasmic reticulum, are largely composed of membranes. The general properties of all cell membranes are very similar; we will look at this in more detail in Section 6.2. The membrane that runs around the outside of a cell is the outer cell surface membrane. It is the boundary of a cell with its exterior and, as a selectively permeable membrane, has a very important role in controlling the movement of substances in and out of the cell. It also plays an important role in receiving the instructions from other cells, such as binding to hormones. Some cells may have specialisations of the outer membrane. For example, cells that play a role in absorbing substances, such as the gut epithelial cell shown in Figure 6.9, have many projections called microvilli to increase the surface area.

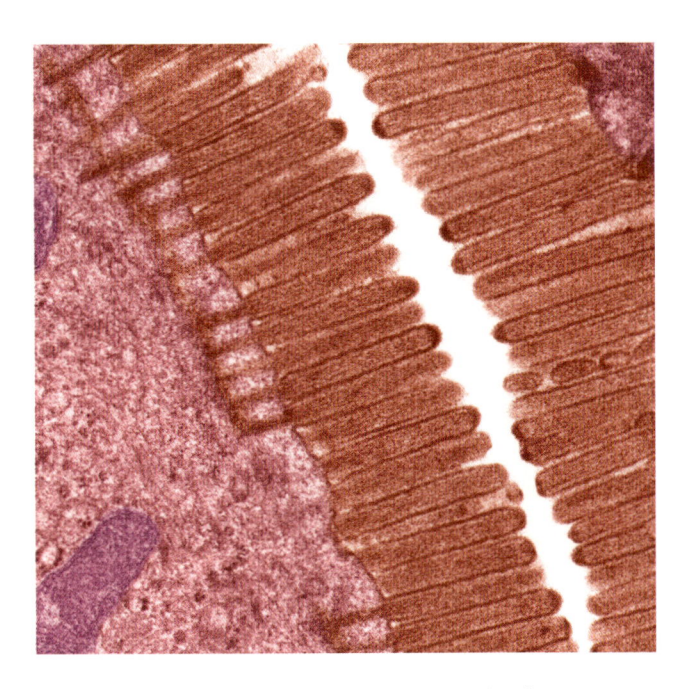

Figure 6.9: False colour electron micrograph of gut epithelial cell showing microvilli.

Nucleus

The nucleus in the cell is usually a very large organelle that is visible with both light and electron microscopes. It is present in both animal and plant cells and contains nucleic acids and proteins joined together as a substance known as **chromatin**.

> **KEY WORD**
>
> **chromatin:** DNA, RNA and protein, located within the nucleus of cells.

6 Physiology of marine organisms

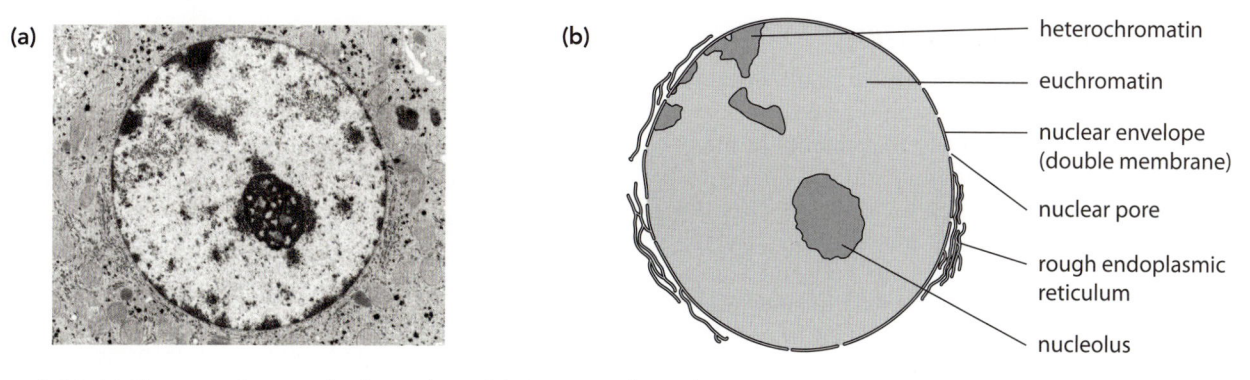

Figure 6.10: (a) Electron micrograph of a nucleus; (b) Diagram of a nucleus.

Electron micrographs show darker (heterochromatin) and lighter (euchromatin) areas within the nucleus. The areas of euchromatin are areas where genes are active. One or more dark **nucleoli** may be visible; these are areas where **ribosomes** are being synthesised. Ribosomes are very small organelles. They are found in all cells, including bacteria (although bacteria have ribosomes that are slightly smaller than those found in other organisms) and are made up of protein and RNA. The function of ribosomes is protein synthesis. Ribosomes are found free in the cytoplasm and also attached to the rough endoplasmic reticulum; in fact, it is the ribosomes that make the rough endoplasmic reticulum appear rough. The ribosomes that are attached to the rough endoplasmic reticulum produce secreted proteins. Cells that are involved in producing lots of proteins tend to have lots of ribosomes and lots of rough endoplasmic reticulum.

Rough and smooth endoplasmic reticulum

The first electron micrographs revealed that the cytoplasm was actually filled with a network of interconnecting membranes called the endoplasmic reticulum (ER). There are two forms that are distinguished by their appearance on the electron micrographs (Figure 6.11).

> **KEY WORDS**
>
> **nucleoli (singular nucleolus):** small circular areas inside the nucleus that produce RNA for ribosomes
>
> **ribosomes:** small organelles that are involved in the synthesis of proteins

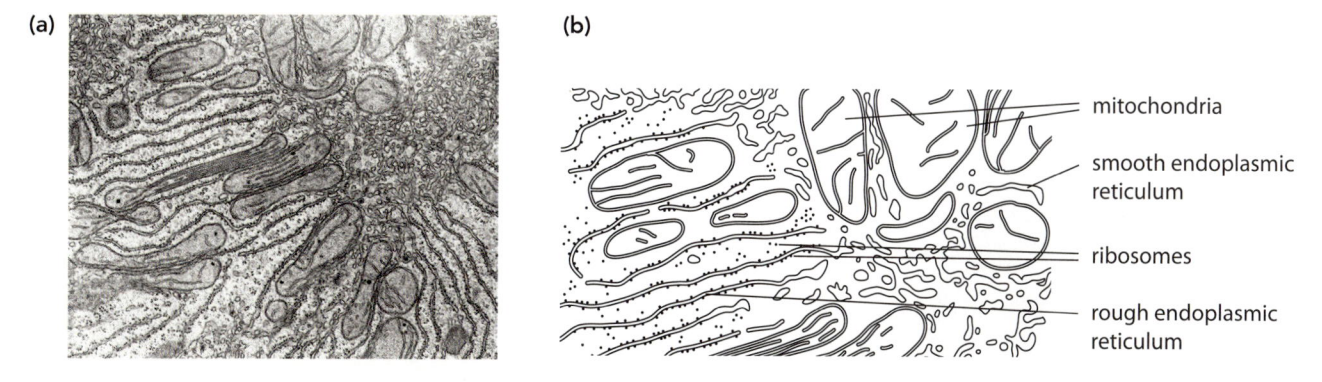

Figure 6.11: (a) Electron micrograph of rough and smooth endoplasmic reticulum; (b) Diagram of rough and smooth endoplasmic reticulum.

Rough endoplasmic reticulum (rER)

rER makes up the majority of the ER and it has many interconnected flattened membranes called **cisternae**. Its 'rough' appearance is due to the presence of many organelles called ribosomes on its surface. The function of the ribosomes is to synthesise proteins that are then folded and packaged up inside the rER. The proteins pass through the rER until they are 'budded off' in a ball of membrane called a **vesicle** than then moves to the Golgi apparatus. All proteins that are secreted, or released, by the cell are made in this way in the rER.

Smooth endoplasmic reticulum (sER)

sER is much less abundant in most cells and, as the name suggests, has a smooth appearance with no ribosomes. The structure is more 'tubular' than rER and it is not involved with the synthesis of proteins. Its main function is the synthesis of **steroid hormones** such as **oestrogen** and **testosterone** and so large amounts are found in cells such as testes and ovaries.

Ribosomes

Ribosomes are very small organelles. They are found in all cells, including bacteria (although bacteria have ribosomes that are slightly smaller than those found in other organisms) and are made up of protein and RNA. The function of ribosomes is protein synthesis. Ribosomes are found free in the cytoplasm and also attached to the rough endoplasmic reticulum; in fact, it is the ribosomes that make the rough endoplasmic reticulum appear rough. The ribosomes that are attached to the rough endoplasmic reticulum produce secreted proteins. Cells that are involved in producing lots of proteins tend to have lots of ribosomes and lots of rough endoplasmic reticulum.

Golgi body

The Golgi body, or Golgi apparatus, is composed of a series of parallel stacks of membrane pouches called cisternae (Figure 6.12). It has a three-dimensional structure so that the cisternae are connected with each other. It has a range of functions:

- It is involved in the chemical modification of proteins. This means that proteins have additional chemical groups, such as carbohydrates, added to them. All secreted and membrane proteins pass through the Golgi apparatus. It receives proteins that are packaged in vesicles from the rER on its flatter, cis, face. The vesicle membranes fuse the Golgi membranes and release the proteins. The proteins then pass through the cisternae and are modified before being released from the trans face in vesicles. The vesicles move to the cell surface membrane where they fuse with it and release

> **KEY WORDS**
>
> **cisternae:** flattened membranes of the Golgi body and endoplasmic reticulum
>
> **vesicle:** small structures that consist of fluid surrounded by a membrane; they are used for transporting substances around cells
>
> **steroid hormones:** steroid molecules that are used as hormones
>
> **oestrogen:** a steroid hormone that is the primary female sex hormone
>
> **testosterone:** a steroid hormone that is the primary male sex hormone

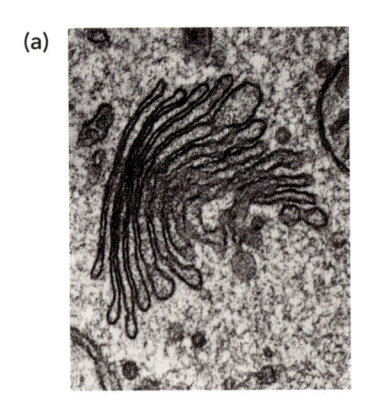

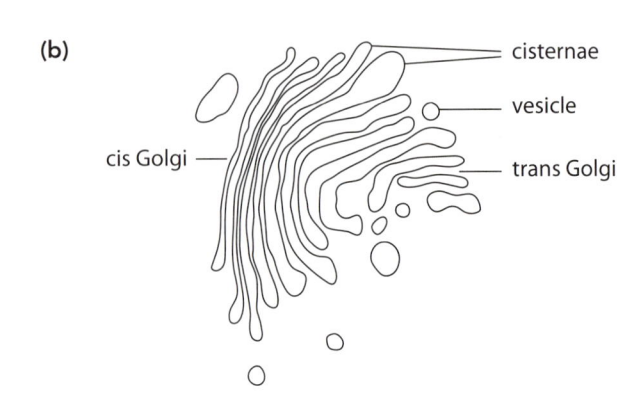

Figure 6.12: (a) Electron micrograph of Golgi body; (b) Diagram of Golgi body.

6 Physiology of marine organisms

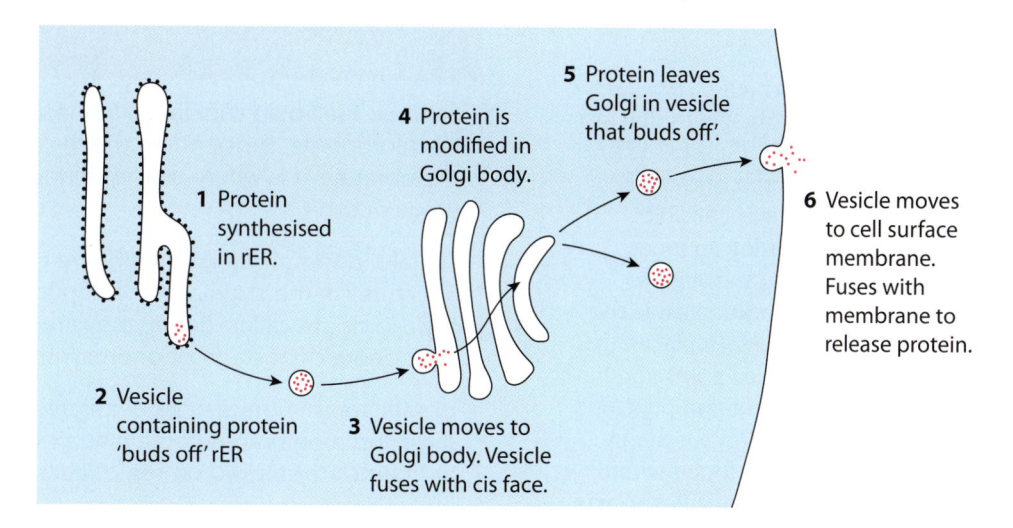

Figure 6.13: Synthesis and modification of secreted proteins in a cell.

the contents. Figure 6.13 shows the movement of synthesis of secreted proteins in a cell.

- It produces substances that are needed for plant cell wall synthesis.
- It produces organelles called **lysosomes**. These are small membrane spheres that contain digestive enzymes. Cells use them to digest substances that have engulfed and destroy old, damaged organelles.

Mitochondria

Mitochondria are organelles that are often called the 'powerhouses' of the cells. Their main function is the production of ATP by aerobic respiration in both animals and plants. You will consider the production of ATP in more depth in Chapter 7. Cells that have high energy requirements (for example, muscle cells) tend to have large numbers of mitochondria. Figure 6.14 shows the structure of a typical mitochondrion.

They have a cylindrical shape that is bounded by an outer membrane; this double membrane is similar to the nucleus and chloroplast. The inner membrane is folded into structures called **cristae** which are surrounded by an enzyme filled, fluid **matrix**. In the matrix are found ribosomes and a small, circular chromosome. The presence of ribosomes and DNA suggests that mitochondria were once independent organisms that lived symbiotically inside other bacteria. Eventually, they lost their independence and became mitochondria.

> **KEY WORDS**
>
> **lysosomes:** membrane enclosed organelles that contain digestive enzymes
>
> **cristae:** folds of the inner mitochondrial membrane; they are involved in aerobic respiration
>
> **matrix:** the fluid filled space within the inner mitochondrial membrane; it contains enzymes and sugars involved with respiration

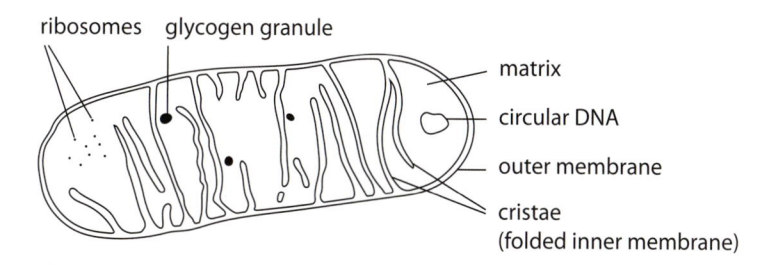

Figure 6.14: (a) False colour electron micrograph of a mitochondrion; (b) Diagram of a mitochondrion.

Chloroplasts

Chloroplasts are only found in plant cells. They carry out photosynthesis. They are large organelles that are easily visible with a light microscope (Figure 6.15) but, when seen with an electron microscope, their complex structure is visible. They have a double membrane surrounding them, enclosing an inner, liquid, **stroma** that contains enzymes and sugars. There is a massive network of membranes inside the stroma called the **thylakoid membranes**. In places, the thylakoids are arranged in stacks called **grana** and have a very large surface area. The grana contain pigments such as chlorophyll that trap light energy for use in **photosynthesis**. Starch grains are often found within the stroma and, similar to mitochondria, chloroplasts contain **DNA** and ribosomes. It is thought that, like mitochondria, chloroplasts were originally symbiotic bacteria that lost their independence.

Cell wall

Animal cells do not possess a cell wall. Although other organisms such as fungi and bacteria possess cell walls, while studying marine science you will only consider the **cellulose** cell walls found around plant cells. Plant cell walls are a very important structure and provide strength and support for the whole plant as well as preventing cells bursting due to inflow of water. The main component of the cell wall is the polysaccharide, cellulose. Cellulose is a polymer of a sugar called **β-glucose**. It is a very long, straight, linear molecule and

> **KEY WORDS**
>
> **stroma:** the liquid substance in the centre of chloroplasts, surrounding the thylakoid membranes; it is where the light independent stage occurs
>
> **thylakoid membranes:** membrane bound structures in the stroma of chloroplasts; stacks of thylakoids are called grana; they are where the light dependent stage of photosynthesis occurs
>
> **grana:** areas in the stroma of chloroplasts where thylakoid membranes containing photosynthetic pigments are stacked on top of each other
>
> **photosynthesis:** the process of using light energy to synthesise glucose from carbon dioxide and water to produce chemical energy
>
> **DNA (deoxyribonucleic acid):** the molecule that is used as hereditary material being passed onto subsequent generations; it contains the code for all the genes of organisms
>
> **cellulose:** an important component of plant cell walls which is made from many straight chains of glucose molecules held together by hydrogen bonds
>
> **β-glucose:** an isomer of the sugar, glucose; it is the monomer that cellulose is made up of

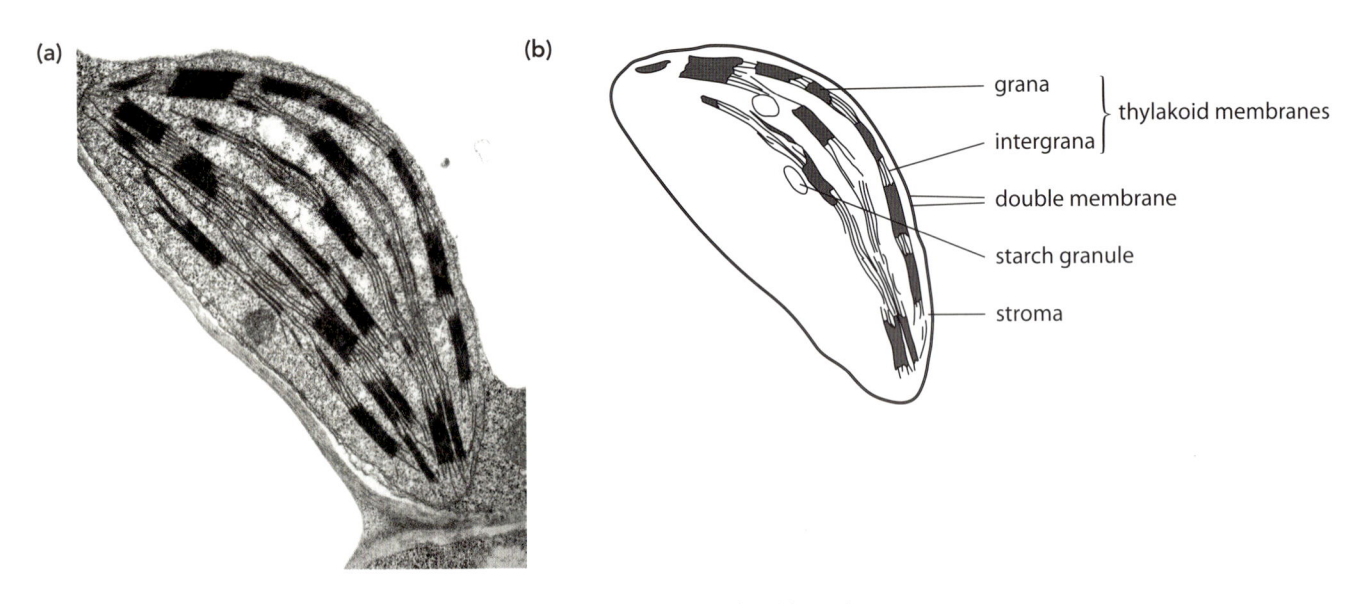

Figure 6.15: (a) Electron micrograph of a chloroplast; (b) Diagram of a chloroplast.

6 Physiology of marine organisms

(a)

cellulose fibre (50 nm diameter) made of many microfibrils

microfibril (10 nm diameter) made of 60–70 molecules

glycosidic bond

glucose ring structure – part of one cellulose molecule

hydrogen bond

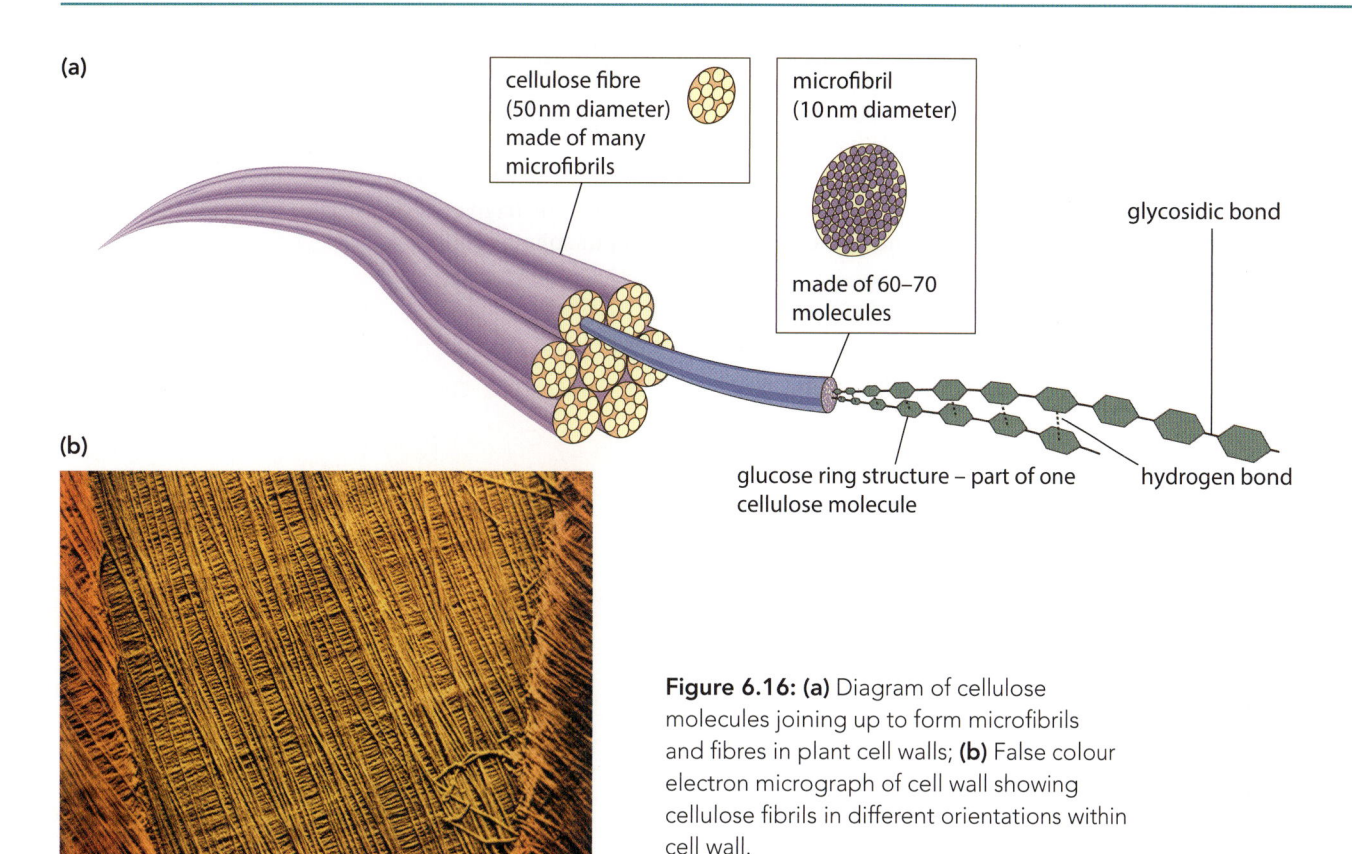

(b)

Figure 6.16: (a) Diagram of cellulose molecules joining up to form microfibrils and fibres in plant cell walls; (b) False colour electron micrograph of cell wall showing cellulose fibrils in different orientations within cell wall.

can form hydrogen bonds with other cellulose molecules (Figure 6.16). Many cellulose molecules bond together to form microfibrils, and many microfibrils bond together to form fibrils. Because so many cellulose molecules are bonded together in the fibrils, they are very strong.

The cell wall has several layers (shown in Figure 6.17):

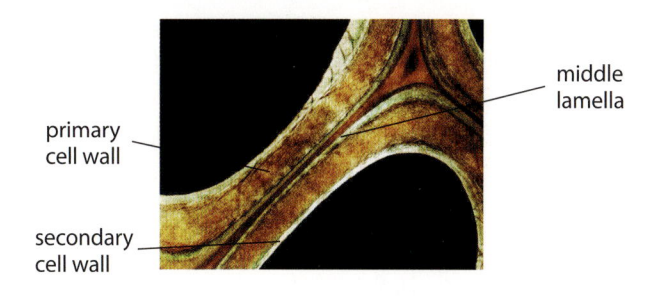

primary cell wall

secondary cell wall

middle lamella

Figure 6.17: Electron micrograph showing the structure of plant cell walls.

The **middle lamella** is the outer layer of a cell wall and is mainly composed of calcium pectate. Calcium pectate is like a glue which bonds plants cells to their neighbours. It is the substance that helps fruit jams to set.

The primary cell wall (the main layer in a plant cell wall; it is the first layer that is produced when plant cells are developing and is found under the middle lamella) is the first layer of cellulose fibres that form. They all wrap around in one direction and are mixed with other substances such as calcium pectate and hemicelluloses to make a firm wall.

The secondary cell wall (a layer of cell wall that is produced after plant cells have finished growing; it is the inner layer next to the cell membrane and may contain substances such as suberin) is the second layer of cellulose fibres that form. They are organised in different directions to the primary cell wall to give extra strength. In some species, extra substances such as lignin (wood) and suberin (cork) are added.

> **Note:** microfibrils, calcium pectate, primary and secondary cell walls are extension content, and are not part of your syllabus.

> **KEY WORD**
>
> **middle lamella:** a layer of pectin on the outside of plants cells; it cements neighbouring cells together

Large permanent vacuole

Many cells contain vacuoles. Vacuoles are fluid-filled sacs of membranes. But only plant cells have **large permanent vacuoles**. They are very large and can take up most of the volume of a cell (as can be seen on Figure 6.8). They are surrounded by a membrane called a **tonoplast**. They have a range of functions:

- Storage of **cell sap**, a fluid containing salts and sugars. The cell sap has a low water potential and so encourages water to enter the plant cell maintaining pressure within the cell. This cell pressure helps to keep the plant supported and upright.

- Storage of pigments, waste products and toxins. Pigments, such as those that give flowers colours, are often stored in vacuoles along with waste products. In some plants, chemicals stored in the vacuole are kept separate from chemicals in the cytoplasm. For example, when onion cells are broken, the enzyme allinase is released into the cytoplasm where it reacts with allinin to form allicin, a chemical which irritates our eyes and makes them water.

The structure of the cell surface membrane

Many organelles are surrounded by membranes. They play essential roles in the production of ATP by mitochondria and the harvesting of light energy by chloroplasts. The cell surface membrane is the boundary of the cell and controls the entry and exit of all molecules. Although the many types of membrane differ in their properties, they all share the same basic structure and composition. The model for the structure of membranes was proposed by Singer and Nicholson in 1972 and is called the **fluid mosaic model**.

Cell membranes are made up of three main types of molecule:

- phospholipids
- proteins
- cholesterol

Phospholipids are a class of lipids that consist of fatty acids, glycerol and phosphate; they are a major component of cell membranes.

Phospholipids

Figure 6.18 shows a phospholipid. They are molecules that are made up of a **glycerol** 'backbone' attached to two **fatty acid** (lipid molecules that are a major constituent of triglycerides and phospholipids) chains and a phosphate group.

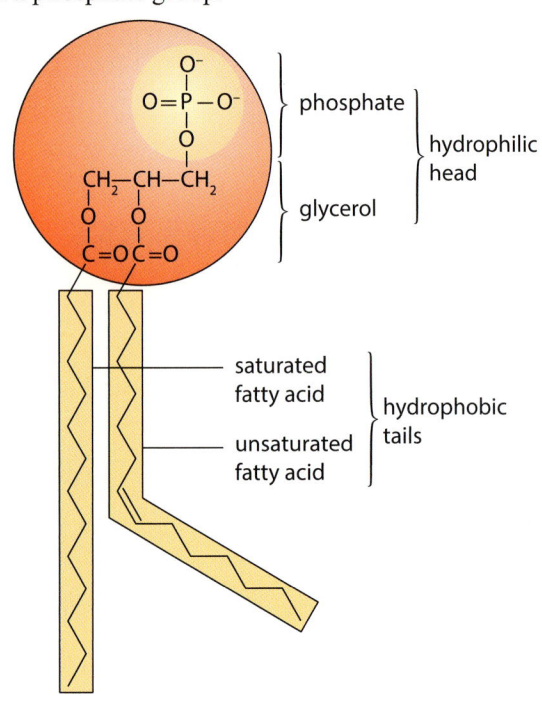

Figure 6.18: The structure of a phospholipid.

> ### KEY WORDS
>
> **large permanent vacuole:** a membrane bound organelle that is present in all plant and fungal cells; it contains cell sap
>
> **tonoplast:** the membrane found outside a large permanent vacuole in plant and fungal cells
>
> **cell sap:** the fluid located inside a large permanent vacuole
>
> **fluid mosaic model:** a model that explains the properties of cell membranes
>
> **glycerol:** a simple molecule that is a constituent of triglycerides and phospholipids

Note: phospholipids, fatty acid and cholesterol are extension content, and are not part of your syllabus.

6 Physiology of marine organisms

Fatty acids are long chain hydrocarbon chains that are uncharged and **nonpolar**. This means that they will not dissolve in water and are thus **hydrophobic** ('water hating').

Phosphate is a charged, polar molecule (when opposite sides of a molecule have contrasting electrical charges). This means that it will dissolve in water and is thus **hydrophilic** ('water loving').

Phospholipid molecules have an unusual property. Parts of them (the fatty acid tails) are uncharged and hydrophobic and do not want to enter water, whilst another part (the phosphate head) is charged and hydrophilic and does want to enter water. If phospholipids are mixed into water, the fatty acid tails move together to exclude water molecules and the phosphate heads sit on the outside, dissolved in the water. The structure they form, shown in Figure 6.19, is a micelle. Sometimes, several micelles can join together to form a phospholipid bilayer with the fatty acid tails on the inside and the phosphate heads on the outside. This phospholipid bilayer structure is the basis of all cell membranes.

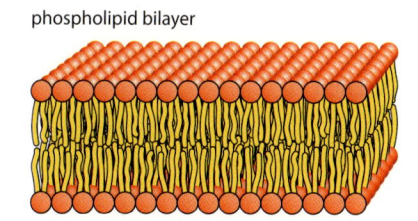

Figure 6.19: Phospholipids arranged as micelles and a phospholipid bilayer.

Proteins

All membranes are composed of very similar phospholipids. They differ due to the types of protein found within the phospholipid bilayer. There are many types of membrane protein with different functions and the naming can be confusing:

Intrinsic proteins

Intrinsic proteins (proteins that extend from one side of a membrane to the other) run through the phospholipid bilayer and are often used for transporting substances in and out of cells. Because the phospholipid bilayer has an uncharged, hydrophobic interior, water-soluble, hydrophilic molecules are unable to pass through it. To transport hydrophilic substances there are **carrier proteins** and **channel proteins** (these will be considered in more depth later in this chapter) through which they can diffuse, and active pump proteins which force substances against a concentration gradient. These transport proteins are usually very specific for particular molecules (for example, a glucose channel protein will only allow glucose through it). This means that the cell membrane is a highly selective barrier – only substances for which particular channels are present can pass through. Different cells will also have different transport proteins present.

Extrinsic proteins

Extrinsic proteins (proteins that are bound to the surface of membranes; they are found on one surface of the membrane) are only found on the outer or inner surface of the membrane and are often just 'anchored' in it. They have a range of functions. Some are receptor proteins for hormones to bind to, carrying a message to a cell. Some are molecules that bind to other cells so that they can recognise each other. Glycoproteins are proteins that have carbohydrates attached and are only found on the external side of the membrane.

> **KEY WORDS**
>
> **nonpolar:** molecules that do not have electric charge
>
> **hydrophobic:** substances that will not mix with water; they will not dissolve in water
>
> **hydrophilic:** substances that are attracted to water molecules; will dissolve in water
>
> **carrier proteins:** membrane proteins that are involved in the transfer of substances from one side of membranes to the other; they possess a specific binding site to which substances bind and change shape as the substance is moved across the membrane
>
> **channel protein:** membrane proteins that are involved in the transfer of substances from one side of membranes to the other; contain a pore through which substances will pass through

> **Note:** intrinsic and extrinsic proteins is extension content, and is not part of your syllabus.

Cholesterol

Cholesterol is small lipid molecule that has a role in maintaining the fluidity of the membrane. Cholesterol molecules are found between the fatty acid tails of the phospholipid bilayer (Figure 6.20). At low temperatures, it keeps the membrane fluid and at higher temperatures it prevents the membrane becoming too fluid.

The fluid-mosaic model

Singer and Nicholson's model (shown in Figure 6.20) proposed that the membrane is:

- a phospholipid bilayer
- proteins are embedded with the bilayer like the tiles in a mosaic (or like icebergs floating in the sea)
- the membrane is fluid (that is, the proteins are able to diffuse through the bilayer). The molecules are in motion and not totally static.

Drawing cells, calculating magnifications and interpreting diagrams

You will need to be able to identify organelles on photomicrographs and electron micrographs, calculate magnifications of diagrams and also use them to predict the functions of different cells and tissues from marine organisms.

Drawing cells

In Chapter 4, you will have learnt how to make good quality biological drawings of whole organisms. The same drawing rules apply when drawing cells and tissues:

Consistent drawing skills
• Only draw what you see.
• Use a sharp HB or 2H pencil.
• Draw guidelines with a ruler.
• Use unbroken, firm lines.
• Do not shade or sketch.
• Include scale bars and magnifications if appropriate.
• Print all labels.
• Give the diagram a title.
• Do not draw a diagram that is too small.

Figure 6.21 shows an example of how to draw a copy of a micrograph of an *Elodea* cell. When drawing individual cells, you should try to focus on a maximum of five cells of a particular type and show as much detail as possible in at least one of them. A cell is labelled as 'X'.

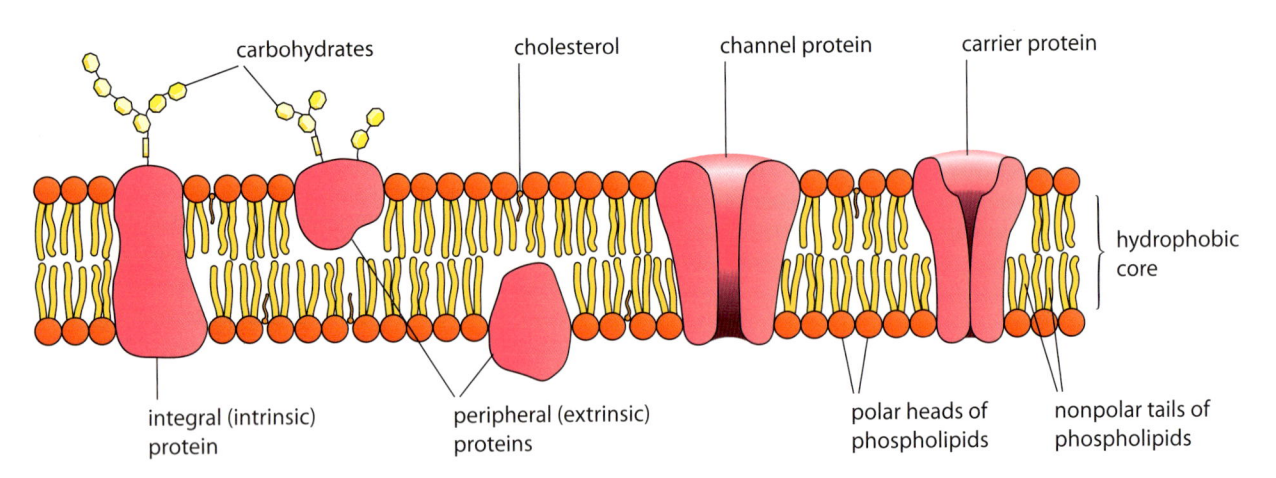

Figure 6.20: Diagram showing the fluid mosaic membrane model.

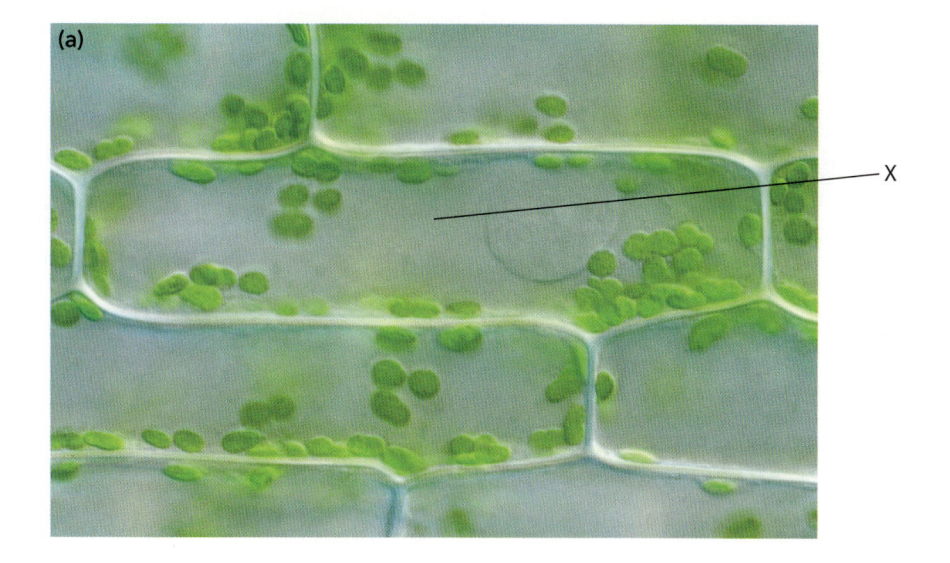

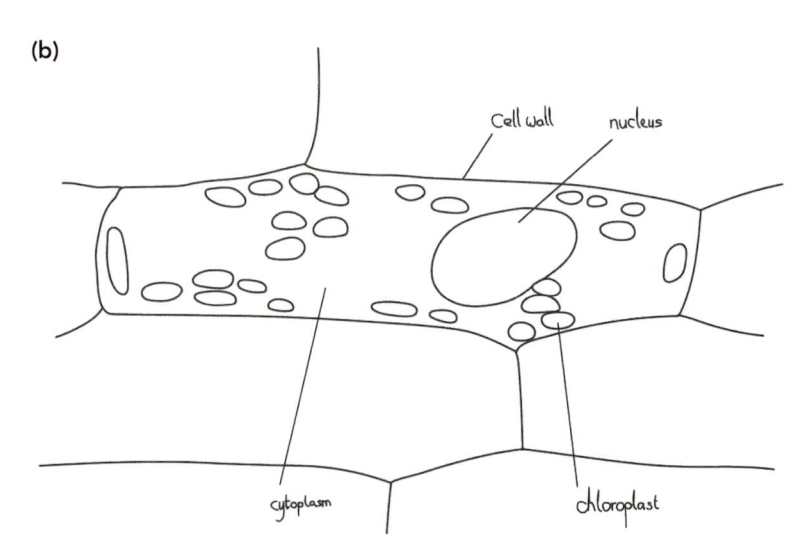

6 Physiology of marine organisms

Figure 6.21: (a) Photomicrograph of *Elodea* cells; (b) Student diagram of *Elodea* cell.

Calculating magnifications and the sizes of cells

You need to be able to calculate the magnifications of photomicrographs and electronmicrographs and use information given to you to calculate the actual sizes of structures.

This formula enables us to calculate magnifications:

$$\text{magnification} = \frac{\text{image length}}{\text{actual length}}$$

It is useful to remember this as a formula triangle in case you need to rearrange it to calculate the actual size of a cell or structure.

Where

I = image length

A = actual length

M = magnification

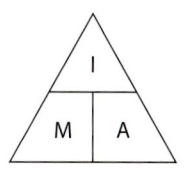

MATHS SKILLS 6.1

CONVERTING UNITS

The prefixes for units tell us their magnitudes in factors of 1000. For example, the units of length are:

1 megametre (Mm)	=	1000 kilometres (km)
1 kilometre (km)	=	1000 metres (m)
1 metre (m)	=	1000 millimetres (mm)
1 millimetre (mm)	=	1000 micrometres (μm)
1 micrometre (μm)	=	1000 nanometres (nm)

We use the same prefixes for all units (for example, 1000 g = 1 kg).

You will often need to convert from one magnitude to another. When calculating magnifications, the most common conversion that you will need to do is to convert from millimetres (mm) to micrometres (μm), or from micrometres to millimetres. Note that when you measure images, use millimetres rather than centimetres (cm).

To convert units from mm into μm, we need to multiple by 1000.

Worked example

0.02 mm is equivalent to $0.02 \times 1000 = 20\,\mu m$.

To convert μm into mm, we need to divide by 1000.

For example:

65.2 μm is equivalent to $65.2 \div 1000 = 0.0625\,mm$

Questions

1 Convert the following lengths into millimetres:
   a 150 m
   b 21.2 km
   c 0.003 km

2 Convert the following lengths into metres:
   a 250 mm
   b 50 μm
   c 270 nm

Calculating magnification from diagrams

To calculating the magnification of an image, you need to:

- measure the length of the image with a ruler
- ensure that you have the same units for the image length and the actual length
- use the formula for magnification by dividing the image length by the actual length.

For example, the cell labelled X in Figure 6.21 has an actual length of 81.8 μm. The image length of the cell on the photomicrograph is measured at 90 mm.

To convert the 90 mm actual length into micrometres, we multiple by 1000 to give us a length of 90 000 μm. So,

$$\text{magnification} = \frac{90\,000}{81.8}$$

$$= \times 1100$$

Calculating the actual length from diagrams when given the magnification

To calculate the actual length of a cell, we need to:

- measure the length of the image with a ruler (usually in millimetres)
- rearrange the magnification formula to calculate the actual length:

$$\text{actual length} = \frac{\text{image length}}{\text{magnification}}$$

For example, the mitochondrion labelled in Figure 6.14 has a magnification of ×40 000. The image length is 60 mm. So,

$$\text{actual length} = \frac{60}{40\,000}$$

$$= 0.0015\,mm \equiv 1.5\,\mu m$$

6 Physiology of marine organisms

Calculating the actual length from diagrams when given a scale bar

Sometimes, instead of giving the magnification of a diagram, a scale bar is placed on it (such as the one shown in Figure 6.22). To calculate the actual length of the structure accurately, we need to:

- calculate the magnification of the diagram by using the scale bar
    - measure the image length of the scale bar with a ruler
    - calculate the magnification of the scale bar by dividing the image length by the actual length (this is written over the scale bar); make sure that the units are the same for both lengths
- measure the image length of the structure with a ruler
- use the rearranged magnification formula to calculate the actual length,

$$\text{actual length} = \frac{\text{image length}}{\text{magnification}}.$$

For example, Figure 6.22 shows an electron micrograph of a diatom. The scale bar has an image length of 20 mm. The actual length of the scale bar is 25 µm, so the magnification is:

$$\frac{20\,000}{25} = \times 800$$

The image length of the diatom = 85 mm, so the actual length of the diatom is:

$$\frac{85}{800} = 0.10625\,\text{mm or } 106.25\,\mu\text{m}$$

Interpreting diagrams

You will need to able to examine unfamiliar pictures and drawings of cells and make your own conclusions about what you can see. For example, if a cell has many mitochondria, it suggests that it requires a lot of energy; if it has well developed rER and Golgi bodies, it will produce a lot of secreted proteins. Figure 6.9 shows a cell from the lining of the small intestine. It has many mitochondria and many microvilli present on the outer membrane. Both these observations suggest that the cell performs active transport of substances. There is a large surface area to absorb large numbers of molecules and many mitochondria to provide energy for the active transport.

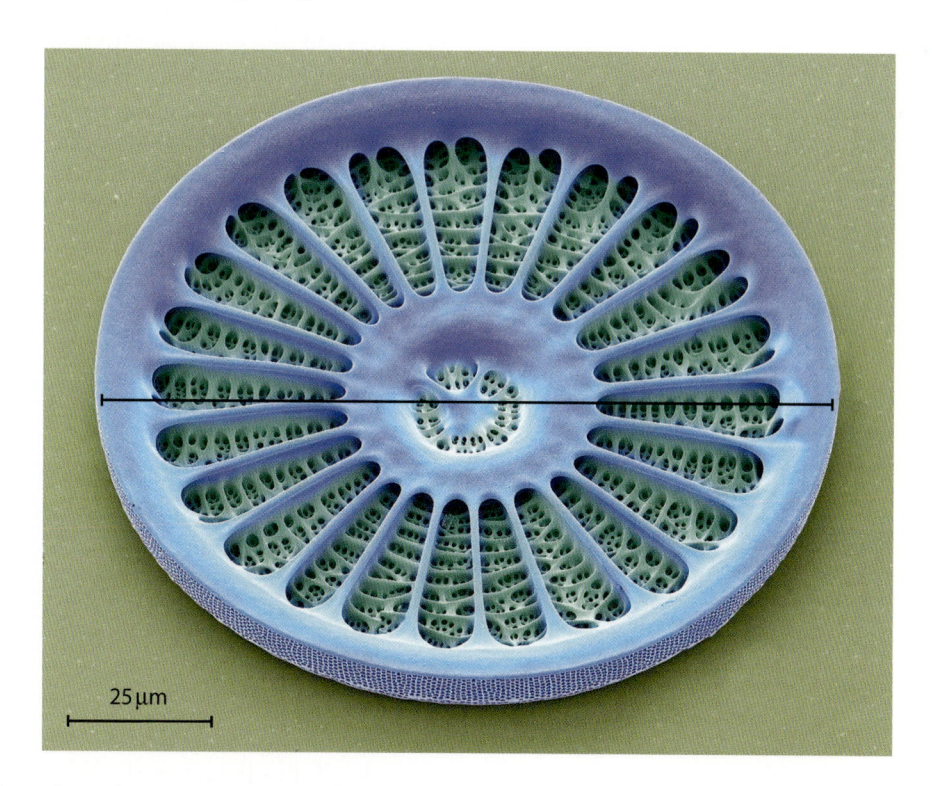

Figure 6.22: A false colour electron micrograph of a diatom.

CORE PRACTICAL ACTIVITY 6.1: DRAWING CELLS

Introduction

You will already have encountered how to draw whole organisms and parts of organisms. It is also important to be able to draw tissues and individual cells whilst viewing them through a microscope. This practical will help you to develop your drawing skills by looking at onion cells and leaf cells from pondweed. Once you have become confident at viewing tissues under a microscope, you will probably want to look at all sorts of other tissues and cells such as gills from fish, fish eggs and plankton. You can buy prepared slides of a range of marine organisms and it is always very interesting to look at samples of seawater or pond water under a microscope to see what you can find.

Before you start

1. You are going to look at plant cells with a light microscope. What structures do you think you will be able to see?
2. List the key drawing skills that need to be applied to biological diagrams.
3. How will the plant cells differ from animal cells?

Equipment

You will need:

- glass microscope slides
- glass coverslips
- microscope, ideally with an eyepiece lens of ×10 magnification and objective lenses of approximately ×4, ×10 and ×40. The microscope can have either a built-in light source or a mirror and external light source.
- iodine stain
- sterile cotton wool buds
- fresh pondweed such as *Elodea*
- plain paper
- HB or 2H pencils, sharpener and eraser
- ruler
- onion bulb
- forceps
- mounted needle
- tissue paper
- plastic dropping pipettes.

Safety considerations

- Concentrated iodine solution is harmful and may pose a risk to the environment. In dilute form it is classed as a low hazard, but care should be taken to wash off spills with water and wear eye protection.
- Care should be taken when using sharp forceps.
- Care should be taken when pressing down on the glass coverslip. Coverslips are very fragile and can easily break – the slide and coverslip should be wrapped in tissue paper before any pressure is applied.

Method

1. Cut open the onion bulb and remove some of the inner layers. Using the forceps, peel off a thin layer of epidermis tissue from one of the thick layers.
2. Cut a piece of the epidermis, about 1 cm² in size, and use the forceps and mounted needle to place it on the slide. Make sure that is not folded and is stretched out flat.
3. Use the dropping pipette to place a drop of iodine solution on the epidermis.
4. Gently lower a coverslip over the epidermis. Tap it down with the mounted needle, cover it and the slide with tissue and give it a gentle squeeze (not too hard so that the coverslip does not break) to remove any air bubbles.
5. View the section using the lowest power objective lens – you will need to focus it.
6. Change to the medium power objective lens and look carefully at the cells. You should be able to see cell walls and nuclei. You may be able to see cell surface membranes under the cell walls and nucleoli within the nuclei.
7. Using a sharp pencil, draw five adjacent cells on the blank paper. Label your diagram. Remember the drawing rules! Write the total magnification used next to the title, this will be the power of the objective lens multiplied by the power of the eyepiece lens (for example, 10 × 10 = ×100).
8. Try viewing the cells under high power. Repeat step 7, this time only drawing three cells.

> **CONTINUED**
>
> 9 Take a new microscope slide and place a small, fresh leaf from the pondweed on it – make sure the leaf is not folded. Place a drop of water on the leaf and then place a coverslip on top.
>
> 10 View the leaf under low power. You should be able to see cell walls and green chloroplasts. The cells have not been stained so the nuclei will probably not be visible.
>
> 11 Increase the magnification to medium power. Draw five adjacent cells.
>
> 12 Try viewing the cells under high power. Draw three cells.
>
> **Results**
>
> The results for this experiment should be a series of labelled diagrams. They should be large, drawn in pencil and labelled with ruled label lines. There should be no sketching.
>
> **Evaluation and conclusions**
>
> 1 Explain why it was important to make sure that the onion epidermis and leaves were not folded.
>
> 2 State the purpose of the iodine solution.
>
> 3 Compare the structures of the leaf and onion cells.
>
> 4 Explain why mitochondria, endoplasmic reticulum and ribosomes were not visible with the light microscope.

> **REFLECTION**
>
> After completing Core Practical Activity 6.1, review your diagrams with another member of your class. Discuss how accurate they are and how well you have stuck to the drawing rules.

Test yourself

1 Look at Figure 6.23.
   a Name the organelles labelled A, B and C.
   b State the functions of each of the labelled organelles.
   c State, with reasons whether the cell is an animal or plant cell.

2 Calculate the actual, maximum lengths of each of the organelles A, B and C in Figure 6.23.

3 Reflect on what you have learnt about the structure of the cell surface membrane. Explain the structure and function of each component.

Figure 6.23: False colour electron micrographs of cells, magnification ×4275.

6.2 Movement of substances

As we have already seen, one of the main roles of the cell surface membrane is to control the transport of different molecules across it. There are four main methods by which molecules are transported through cell membranes:

- **diffusion**
- **facilitated diffusion**
- **active transport**
- **osmosis**

Diffusion

Molecules are constantly moving in random directions. The energy of movement that they possess is known as **kinetic energy**. To understand diffusion, it helps if you look at a specific example (Figure 6.24). There is an uneven concentration of a molecule between two places, A and B. There is a **concentration gradient** between A and B, with a higher concentration in area A.

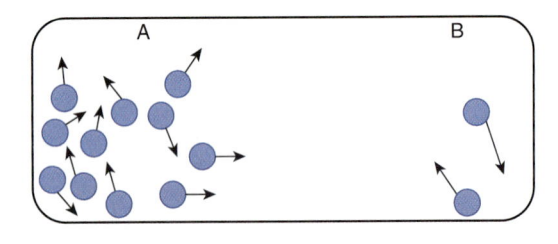

Figure 6.24: Net diffusion of particles from a high concentration to a low concentration. Particles move in random directions.

Because the molecules are all constantly moving in different directions, some of them will move from A to B. Because there are more molecules in area A, there is a higher probability that more of them will move from A to B than from B to A. There is a net diffusion of molecules from A to B. Eventually, the concentration in area A decreases and the concentration in B increases until the two areas are equal. When the two areas are equal, physical diffusion does not actually stop as the molecules are still moving.

The rate of movement in both directions is approximately equal so that the net rate of diffusion is zero (Figure 6.25).

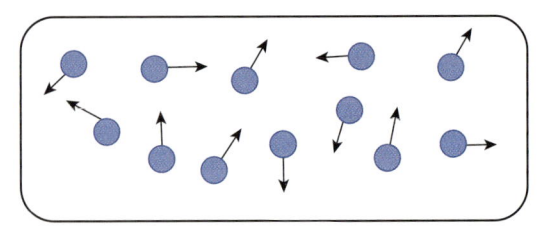

Figure 6.25: Particles are evenly spread and there is equal movement in both directions.

Diffusion is a **passive process**, requiring no additional input of energy, and is defined as the 'random net movement of particles from a higher concentration to a lower concentration'. It is a very important process by which many substances enter and leave the bodies and cells of organisms. Substances that are small and non-polar, such as oxygen and carbon dioxide, are able to diffuse through the phospholipid bilayer between the fatty acid tails.

> ### KEY WORDS
>
> **diffusion:** the random movement of particles (or molecules) from a higher concentration to a lower concentration (down a concentration gradient); it is a passive process, not requiring the input of energy
>
> **facilitated diffusion:** a process by which polar substances diffuse through cell membranes via carrier or channel proteins.
>
> **active transport:** the movement of molecules across a membrane from a region of lower concentration to a region of higher concentration; it requires the release of energy from ATP
>
> **osmosis:** the movement of water from a higher water potential to a lower water potential across a selectively permeable membrane.
>
> **kinetic energy:** the energy possessed by objects or particles due to movement
>
> **concentration gradient:** the difference in concentration of molecules between two regions
>
> **passive process:** processes that occur without use of additional energy

The diffusion of molecules in and out of cells and other tissues is affected by several factors, including:

- temperature
- concentration gradient
- distance moved
- surface area of exchange surface.

Temperature

Moving particles possess kinetic energy. As temperature rises, the kinetic energy of the particles rises so the particles move faster. If particles are moving faster, diffusion is faster.

Concentration gradient

A concentration gradient is the difference in concentration of a substance between two places, such as the difference in oxygen concentration between a muscle cell and the blood.

The steeper or higher the gradient, the faster the rate of diffusion. Molecules move in random directions and so if there are more molecules present, the probability of them moving in a particular direction becomes higher. If there are equal concentrations on both sides of a membrane, there is an equal probability of molecules moving in each direction so there is no net movement.

Diffusion distance

To ensure rapid diffusion, the distance that the molecules travel must be as small as possible. Cell membranes are all very thin, so the rate of diffusion across them is fast.

Surface area

Having a large surface area will increase the area over which diffusion can occur. Figure 6.9 shows a cell from the lining of the small intestine. The cell surface membrane is folded into many small projections called microvilli. These microvilli increase the surface area so that diffusion will be rapid.

Facilitated diffusion

Charged, hydrophilic molecules cannot pass through the hydrophobic fatty acid tails of the phospholipids. This means that they are unable to enter or leave cells by simple diffusion. They are, however, able to move along their concentration gradients through selective transport proteins. To facilitate something means to 'help it.' Facilitated diffusion is a type of diffusion by which charged, hydrophilic molecules can diffuse into cells through transport proteins. There are two types of transport proteins:

- **Channel proteins** – these are integral proteins that pass through the membrane. They have an inner pore through which water-soluble molecules can pass (Figure 6.26). They are selective (for example, a sodium ion channel will only let sodium ions flow through).

- **Carrier proteins** – these are also integral proteins that pass through the membrane. They bind to molecules on one side of the membrane and then change shape to move the molecule to the other side (Figure 6.26).

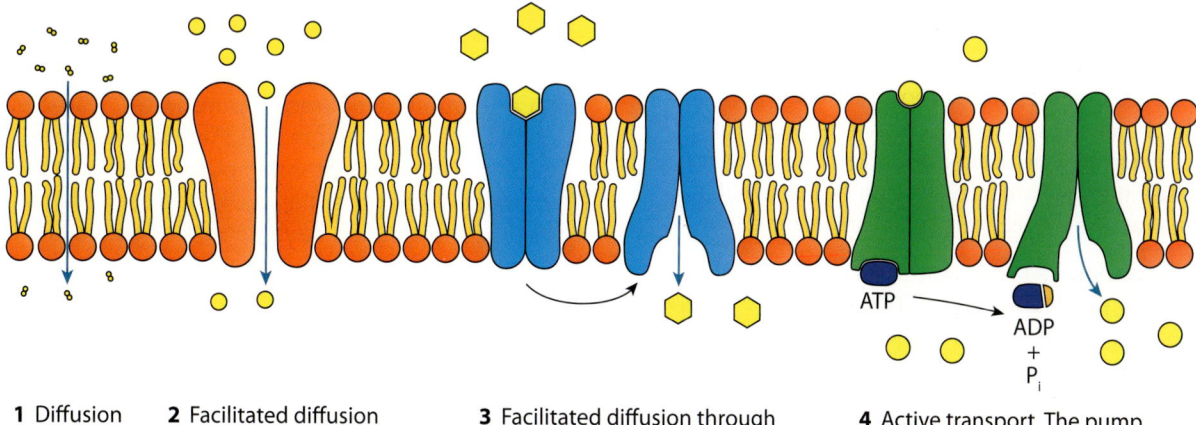

1. Diffusion
2. Facilitated diffusion through channel protein
3. Facilitated diffusion through carrier protein. The protein changes shape as the molecule enters.
4. Active transport. The pump protein uses energy from ATP to pump molecules against a concentration gradient.

Figure 6.26: Diagram showing the processes of diffusion, facilitated diffusion and active transport across a membrane.

Facilitated diffusion, like simple diffusion, is a passive process that does not require additional energy and will only move molecules down a concentration gradient. It is also affected by the same factors as diffusion: temperature, concentration gradient, distance moved and the surface area of the membrane. In addition, to these factors, the rate of facilitated diffusion can be affected by the number of channel and carrier proteins available. If there are too few membrane proteins, the rate of facilitated diffusion will be limited by this, despite the concentration gradient (Figure 6.26).

Active transport

Active transport is the pumping of substances (often ions) across a membrane by living cells against a concentration gradient. It is carried out by carrier proteins, often called pumps, that use the energy in ATP to move the ions against the concentration gradient.

Similar to facilitated diffusion, the carrier proteins bind to molecules on one side of the membrane. ATP then binds to the carrier protein and is broken down into ADP and phosphate, releasing energy. The energy is used to change the shape of the protein so that it moves the molecules across the membrane. The carrier protein will then return to its original shape so that it can repeat the process (Figure 6.26). Because it requires energy, it can only take place in living, respiring cells. Cells that do lots of active transport tend to have many mitochondria.

Osmosis

Osmosis is a process that is of vital importance to all organisms. It is a special form of diffusion that only applies to the movement of water molecules across membranes. Cell membranes possess water-specific protein channels called aquaporins. It is defined as the net movement of water molecules from a region of higher **water potential** to a region of lower water potential across a selectively permeable membrane.

Water potential is a measure of the potential energy of the water molecules in a solution. The more water molecules in a solution, the higher the water potential. If a solute such as salt is dissolved in the water, the proportion of water molecules in the solution decreases so the water potential falls.

In simple terms, the higher the concentration of solutes, such as salt in a solution, the lower the water potential. The highest water potential possible is that of pure water, which has a water potential of 0 kPa.

If you place two different salt solutions next to each other, separated by a selectively permeable membrane (Figure 6.27), water molecules will move from the weaker, more dilute solution to the more concentrated one.

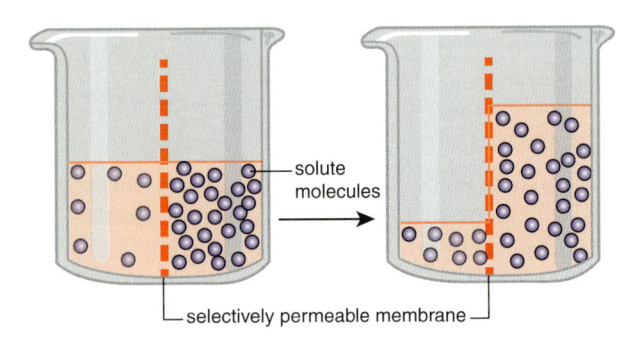

Figure 6.27: Movement of water by osmosis from a dilute solution to a concentrated one.

Certain terms are used to describe solutions that have higher or lower water potentials compared with the cells and body fluids of an organism.

- **Hypertonic** solutions have a lower water potential. They have a higher concentration of solutes and will tend to draw water out of cells.
- **Isotonic** solutions have a water potential that is equal to the cells. They have an equal concentration of solutes and will result in no net movement of water.
- **Hypotonic** solutions have a higher water potential. They have a lower concentration of solutes and will tend to pass water into cells.

KEY WORDS

water potential: the potential energy of water in a solution compared to pure water; water will move by osmosis from a higher water potential to a lower water potential; pure water has the highest water potential at 0 kPa; dissolving solute makes the solution have a more negative kPa

hypertonic: a solution that has a greater concentration of solutes compared to another solution

isotonic: a solution that has the same concentration of solutes compared to another solution

hypotonic: a solution that has a lower concentration of solutes compared to another solution

hypertonic   isotonic   hypotonic

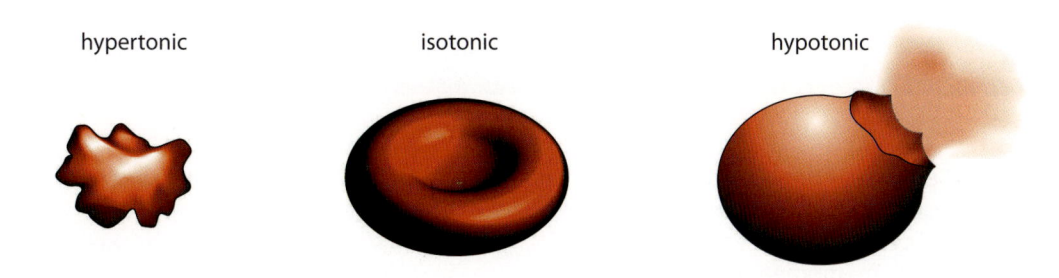

Figure 6.28: Diagram showing the effects of placing red blood cells into solutions of different salinities.

In living organisms, changing the salt concentration around cells can result in water entering cells or leaving them, causing extensive damage. Organisms such as plants and algae possess cell walls so if water passes into the cells, the cells will not burst. Animal cells, however, do not possess cell walls and if too much water passes into them, they will burst.

Osmosis in animal cells

Changes in salinity can have dramatic effects on animal cells. Animal cells do not have a cell wall and are only bound by the very fragile cell surface membrane. If they are placed into hypertonic solutions, water is drawn out of them by osmosis and they shrivel up, causing chemical reactions to stop and the cell will die. If they are placed into a hypotonic solution, they will absorb water by osmosis, swell and eventually burst. Figure 6.28 shows red blood cells that have been placed in hypertonic, isotonic and hypotonic solutions.

Osmosis in plant cells

Plant cells possess a strong cell wall around them which prevents them from bursting. If they are placed into hypotonic solutions, they will absorb water by osmosis. The large, permanent vacuole will expand and the cytoplasm swells so that the cell surface membrane touches the cell wall. The cytoplasm exerts a pressure on the cell wall called, **turgor pressure**. This turgor pressure gives plants support and strength to keep them upright. If the cells are placed into hypertonic solutions, they will lose water, the large permanent vacuole will shrink and the cell membrane peels away from the cell wall. When the cell wall peels away from the cell wall, there is no turgor pressure and the plant will lack support and wilt, unable to stay upright. Figure 6.29 shows plant cells that have been placed into hypotonic and hypertonic solutions.

hypertonic   isotonic   hypotonic

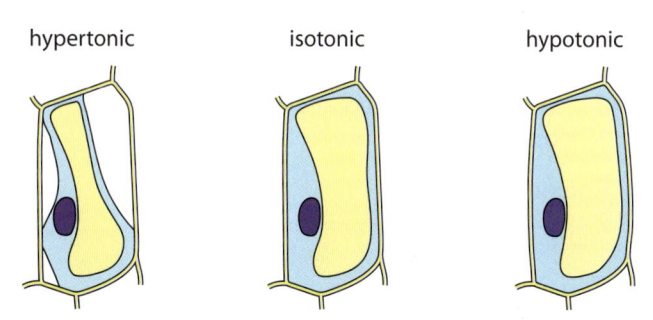

Figure 6.29: Diagram showing the effects of placing plant cells in solutions of different water salinities.

The osmometer

An osmometer (shown in Figure 6.30) is a simple piece of equipment that can be used to model osmosis. It consists of a glass rod with a bag tightly attached to its base. The bag is made from a substance called Visking tubing, a synthetic membrane that is selectively permeable. Visking tubing will only allow very small molecules, such as water, to pass through it and excludes larger ones such as sucrose. A solution of sucrose is placed into the apparatus and a dye can be added. The bag can then be lowered into solutions of different sugar concentrations. Water will enter or leave the bag through the Visking tubing, depending on the difference in water potential, and so the fluid in the tube will rise or fall.

> **KEY WORD**
>
> **turgor pressure:** the force within a plant cell that presses the cell membrane against the cell wall

CORE PRACTICAL ACTIVITY 6.2: INVESTIGATING TURGOR PRESSURE USING VISKING TUBING

Introduction

The cell wall around plant cells prevents the cells bursting when large quantities of water enter the cells by osmosis. When the cytoplasm and vacuole volume increases, the cell surface membrane presses on the cell wall. The pressure generated inside the cell that is resisted by the cell wall is called turgor pressure. When the cells in a plant are all turgid, they press on each other and provide the plant with support.

In this practical you will investigate how pressure increases within Visking tubing when water enters by osmosis.

Before you start

1. Will the syrup or sucrose solution have a higher or lower water potential than pure water?
2. What part of a plant cell does the sucrose solution inside the Visking tubing represent?
3. What factors could affect the speed with which osmosis takes place?

Equipment

You will need:

- syringe or pipette, $5\,cm^3$ or $10\,cm^3$
- a boiling tube
- a 20 cm long piece of Visking (cellophane) tubing, this should be soaked in water for 10 minutes before the experiment
- $100\,cm^3$ syrup or concentrated sucrose solution. The syrup mixture should be made by mixing $50\,cm^3$ golden syrup with $50\,cm^3$ distilled water. If sucrose solution is used, 100 g of sucrose should be dissolved in $100\,cm^3$ of warm water.
- boiling tube rack
- stop clock
- $100\,cm^3$ distilled water.

Safety considerations

Take care when handling glass pipettes.

Method

1. Carefully tie a knot in one end of the Visking tubing.
2. Use the syringe or pipette to place $3\,cm^3$ syrup or sucrose solution into the Visking tubing.
3. Make sure that there are no air bubbles in the Visking tubing and then tie a knot in the top of the tubing approximately 2 cm below the end of the tubing. This is shown in Figure 6.30(a).
4. Bend the Visking tubing and note down how much pressure feels to be inside the tubing. You only need to give a description of the pressure.
5. Wash the outside of the tubing with distilled water and place it into the boiling tube.
6. Fill the boiling tube with distilled water and leave for approximately one hour. This is shown in Figure 6.30(b).
7. Remove the Visking tubing and bend it again. Record how the pressure feels to have changed.

Results

Describe the pressure changes before and after placing the Visking tubing into the distilled water.

Evaluation and conclusions

1. Describe the changes in volume and pressure inside the Visking tubing.
2. Explain the effect of placing the Visking tubing into distilled water on the pressure inside the tubing. Refer to the terms: osmosis, water potential, selectively permeable membrane.
3. This experiment generated qualitative data – this means that it is descriptive rather than giving numerical answers. Suggest how you could have modified the experiment to give a quantitative determination of the amount of water that has passed into the Visking tubing.

6 Physiology of marine organisms

> **CONTINUED**
>
> 4 Suggest whether leaving the Visking tubing for longer than one hour would affect your results.
> 5 Plan an investigation, using the Visking tubing, to determine the effect of changing the concentration of sucrose solution inside the tube on the mass of water that enters the tubing. You should state the variables that you will change and the variables that you will keep constant.
>
> **Figure 6.30:** (a) Visking tubing containing syrup / sucrose solution and (b) Visking tubing placed inside boiling tube and surrounded by water.

> **REFLECTION**
>
> After completing Core Practical Activity 6.2, think about these questions:
>
> 1 How accurate was the method of determining turgor pressure? Why?
> 2 How can you use this as a model to understand the effects on plants when they are placed into solutions of different salinities?
> 3 Climate change could cause increased melting of glaciers, releasing more fresh water into some areas of ocean. Discuss with other students how this experiment could give an insight into how marine organisms could be affected by this.

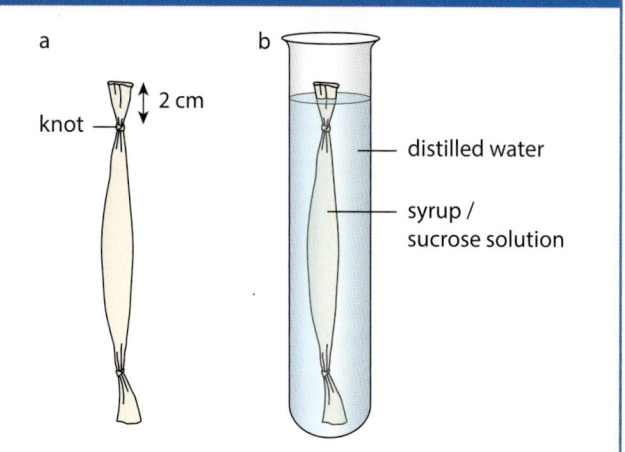

CORE PRACTICAL ACTIVITY 6.3: INVESTIGATING THE EFFECTS OF IMMERSING PLANT TISSUES (POTATOES) IN SOLUTIONS OF DIFFERENT WATER POTENTIALS

Introduction

We can investigate how the concentration of sucrose affects the mass of water that enters and leaves potato cells. Although potato is not a marine organism, investigating osmosis in potato cells will help your understanding of how osmosis occurs.

- When pieces of potato are placed into hypotonic solutions, water will enter the cells by osmosis and the pieces of potato will gain mass.
- When pieces of potato are placed into hypertonic solutions, water will leave the potato cells by osmosis and they will lose mass.
- When pieces of potato are placed into isotonic solutions, there will be no net movement of water in or out of the potato cells, and the mass of the potato will not change.

In this practical, you will place pieces of potato into different sucrose concentrations in order to estimate the concentration of sucrose solution that is isotonic to the solution in the potato cells.

CONTINUED

Equipment:

You will need:
- 6 × test tubes and bungs (foil caps can be used)
- 250 cm³ of 1 mol dm⁻³ sucrose stock solution
- one large potato
- scalpel
- balance.

Safety considerations

Take care when using a scalpel to cut the potatoes.

Before you start

1. What are the independent and dependent variables?
2. What variables need to be controlled?
3. Why does the masses of potato change when placed into different concentrations of sucrose solution?

Method

1. Use the scalpel to cut six equal rectangular cuboid pieces of potato with dimensions of 10 mm × 10 mm × 50 mm. Ensure that all are the same shape and that there is no peel on the sides.
2. Label the test tubes 0.0 mol dm⁻³, 0.2 mol dm⁻³, 0.4 mol dm⁻³, 0.6 mol dm⁻³, 0.8 mol dm⁻³ and 1.0 mol dm⁻³.
3. Make up 25 cm³ sucrose solutions in each of the test tubes as shown in Table 6.2.

Concentration of solution / mol dm⁻³	Volume of water / cm³	Volume of 1 mol dm⁻³ sucrose solution / cm³
0.0	25	0
0.2	20	5
0.4	15	10
0.6	10	15
0.8	5	20
1.0	0	25

Table 6.2: Making up the different concentrations of sucrose solution.

4. Dry each of the potato pieces, weigh them and record the mass. Place one piece of potato into each test tube and place the bung in the test tube.
5. Leave the potatoes for between two and six hours.
6. Remove the pieces of potato, dry them on tissue paper and measure their mass.

Results

1. Copy Table 6.3, enter your results and carry out the calculations. To calculate the percentage change, use the formula:

$$\text{percentage change} = \frac{\text{finish mass} - \text{start mass}}{\text{start mass}} \times 100$$

Concentration of sucrose solution / mol dm⁻³	Start mass of potato / g	Finish mass of potato / g	Finish mass – start mass / g	Change in mass / %
0.0				
0.2				
0.4				
0.6				
0.8				
1.0				

Table 6.3: Results table for the effects of sucrose solution concentration on mass of potatoes.

CONTINUED

Some of the percentage changes will be positive and some negative.

2 Plot a graph of *Concentration of sucrose solution*/mol dm^{-3} against *Change in mass*/%. Join the points with a ruler. The axes will need to look like those in Figure 6.31.

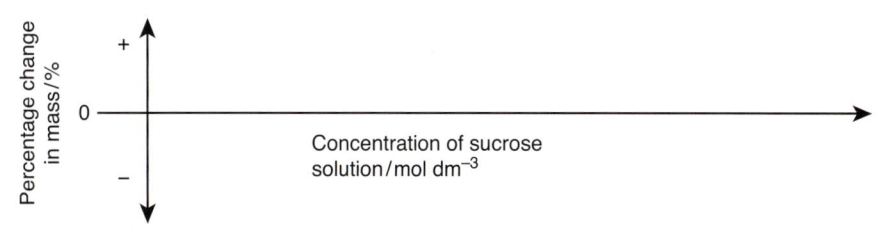

Figure 6.31: Axes with labels for showing your results.

Evaluation and conclusions

1 Describe and explain the effect of increasing sucrose concentration on percentage change in mass of the potatoes.

2 Use the graph to predict the concentration of sucrose that is isotonic to the potato cell cytoplasm. Do this by finding where the line crosses the horizontal (x-axis). This is the place at which there is no net movement of water in or out of the cells. Read the concentration of sucrose at this point. Label on the graph the range of concentrations that are hypotonic and hypertonic compared with the potato cell cytoplasm.

3 Explain why the pieces of potato were dried before weighing them.

4 Suggest why bungs are placed in the test tubes.

5 As an extension activity you can now find the water potential of the potato cells. The graph that you have plotted enables you to find the concentration of sucrose solution that is equivalent to the solute potential in the cytoplasm. To find the actual water potential, you need to convert the sucrose concentrations to water potentials using Table 6.4 and then plot a second graph of percentage change in mass against water potential. The point at which the line crosses the horizontal (x) axis is the water potential of the potato cells.

Concentration of sucrose solution/mol dm^{-3}	Water potential/kPa
0.0	0
0.2	−540
0.4	−1120
0.6	−1800
0.8	−2580
1.0	−3500

Table 6.4: Table to convert sucrose solution concentrations into water potential values.

> CAMBRIDGE INTERNATIONAL AS & A LEVEL MARINE SCIENCE: COURSEBOOK

REFLECTION

After completing Core Practical Activity 6.3, think about these questions:

1. How accurate do you think your measurements were? Why?
2. How can scientists use models like this one to build an understanding of how our oceans function?
3. Discuss with other students how this experiment helps you to understand the challenges faced by organisms that live in estuaries.

CORE PRACTICAL ACTIVITY 6.4: INVESTIGATING THE EFFECT OF IMMERSING PLANT CELLS IN SOLUTIONS OF DIFFERENT WATER POTENTIALS

Introduction

Changes in salinity can have drastic effects on marine organisms. An increase in salinity of the sea will lower the water potential of the seawater. A decrease in salinity of the sea will raise the water potential of the seawater. If a marine organism is unable to regulate the salinity of its own body fluids, changes to the water potential of the seawater can cause water to enter of leave its cells by osmosis. This investigation looks at the effects of changing the water potential of a solution on the movement of water in and out of onion epidermis cells.

Equipment:

You will need:

- an onion (red onions work best)
- distilled water
- 100 cm^3 of 1.0 mol dm^{-3} sodium chloride solution
- 6 × test tubes
- 1 cm^3 and 10 cm^3 pipettes or syringes
- iodine solution
- 6 × small glass dishes
- forceps
- scalpel
- microscope (with ×10 objective lens)
- microscope slides and coverslips.

Safety considerations

Take care when using sharp instruments such as scalpels and forceps.

Before you start

1. Identify the independent and dependent variables.
2. State why tissue from only one onion should be used.

Method

1. Label six test tubes: 0.3 mol dm^{-3}, 0.4 mol dm^{-3}, 0.5 mol dm^{-3}, 0.6 mol dm^{-3}, 0.7 mol dm^{-3}, 1.0 mol dm^{-3}.

CONTINUED

2   Use pipettes or syringes to make up the appropriate sodium chloride solution in each test tube. The volumes of water and sodium chloride solution are shown in Table 6.5. Ensure that you mix each solution thoroughly.

Concentration of sodium chloride solution / mol dm^{-3}	Volume of 1 mol dm^{-3} sodium chloride / cm^3	Volume of distilled water / cm^3
0.3	3	7
0.4	4	6
0.5	5	5
0.6	6	4
0.7	7	3
1.0	10	0

Table 6.5: How to make the concentrations of different sodium chloride solutions.

3   Label each of the six glass dishes with the concentrations of sodium chloride solution and transfer about 5 cm^3 of each solution to the appropriate dish.

4   Use the scalpel and forceps to peel away some of the thin epidermis tissue found between the layers of the onion. Cut six pieces of the thin epidermis tissue with the scalpel to a size of approximately 1 cm^2. Use the forceps to place one piece of onion epidermis into each of the sodium chloride solutions. Leave for between 20 and 30 minutes.

5   Using forceps, place each piece of onion epidermis tissue onto a different, labelled slide and place a drop of the appropriate solution on it. Add a drop of iodine solution and cover with a coverslip.

6   Observe the cells under the microscope with the ×10 objective lens. You may need to adjust the light intensity to see the cells better.

7   Select 20 cells for each concentration of sodium chloride solution and record how many of these cells have the cell surface membrane peeling away from the cell wall (see Figure 6.32). These cells are said to be plasmolysed.

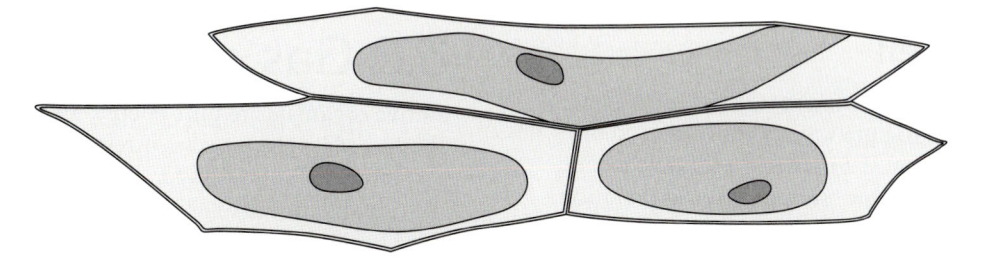

Figure 6.32: Diagram showing plasmolysed onion epidermis cells.

CONTINUED

Results

1. Copy Table 6.6, enter your results and calculate the percentage of cells that are plasmolysed at each concentration of sodium chloride solution.

Concentration of sodium chloride solution / mol dm^{-3}	Number of plasmolysed cells	Cells that are plasmolysed / %
0.3		
0.4		
0.5		
0.6		
0.7		
1.0		

Table 6.6: Results table for effect of sodium chloride solution concentration on onion cell plasmolysis.

2. Plot a line graph of *Cells that are plasmolysed / %* (y-axis) against *Concentration of sodium chloride solution / mol dm^{-3}* (x-axis). Join the points with straight lines.

Evaluation and conclusions

1. Describe the results shown by your graph.
2. Explain, by referring to water potentials and osmosis, the shape of your graph.
3. Read off your graph the concentration of sodium chloride solution at which 50% of the cells are plasmolysed. Do this by drawing a straight line from the vertical axis at 50% to your graph line and then drawing a straight line from this point down to the x-axis. This is the point at which we consider the water potential of the solution to be equal to that of the cells.
4. Identify sources of inaccuracy in the experiment.

REFLECTION

After completing Core Practical Activity 6.4, consider how the results of this experiment reflect the need for cell walls in marine algae.

Test yourself

4. Rearrange the following in order of increasing water potential: pure water, 2 mol dm^{-3} sodium chloride solution, 1.5 mol dm^{-3} sodium chloride solution, 0.2 mol dm^{-3} sodium chloride solution.
5. Draw a table to compare diffusion, osmosis and active transport (think about facts such as the direction of movement, the need for energy, the substances moved and the need for a membrane).

6.3 Gas exchange

Active organisms require energy, and this energy is released by the process of respiration. Aerobic respiration requires oxygen and produces waste carbon dioxide that needs removing. This means that organisms need to obtain oxygen from their environment and expel their waste carbon dioxide. **Gas exchange** is the term

KEY WORD

Gas (gaseous) exchange: the uptake of oxygen and release of carbon dioxide by cells or other surfaces we give to the uptake of oxygen and release of carbon dioxide. It can refer to the exchange of gases across the membrane of cells or across membranes that line tissues such as the lining of gills.

Factors affecting rates of gas exchange

Gas exchange takes place by diffusion so, as we have already discussed earlier in this chapter, there are several factors that can affect the speed at which it takes place:

- temperature
- concentration gradient
- diffusion distance
- surface area.

Temperature

As already explained in Section 6.2, increasing temperature will increase the rate of diffusion.

Concentration gradient

When cells are respiring, it is important to keep a higher concentration of oxygen outside the cells than inside. Respiration uses up the oxygen inside the cells rapidly, maintaining a low concentration inside. The result of this is that the oxygen concentration inside is kept lower than in the fluids outside the cells. There is always a difference in concentration between the inside and outside of the cell, so that oxygen diffuses into the cell. Carbon dioxide is being constantly manufactured inside the cell and is removed outside: the direction of the carbon dioxide gradient is the opposite of oxygen, ensuring a constant net diffusion out of the cell.

The maintenance of concentration gradients for gaseous exchange between blood and water is essential. Maintaining gradients is very important if diffusion is to be rapid, so organisms have evolved transport systems and ventilation movements to ensure delivery and removal of gases.

Marine organisms keep the concentration of oxygen in water higher than inside their blood by both moving the blood and by ventilation movements. Moving the blood brings fresh blood with a low oxygen concentration, and the ventilation movement brings fresh water with a high oxygen concentration.

Diffusion distance

As already stated in Section 6.2, for rapid diffusion, the diffusion distance should be very small. Gaseous exchange systems, such as gills, generally have very thin walls through which gases can diffuse rapidly.

Surface area

Most gaseous exchange organs, such as gills and lungs, have very large surface areas. If a surface area is large, the rate of gaseous exchange is high.

Gaseous exchange in marine organisms

Marine organisms have evolved a range of methods to ensure efficient gaseous exchange that take into account all the factors that affect rates of diffusion and the properties of water.

Water as a gaseous exchange medium

Carrying out gaseous exchange in water is more demanding than in air. The oxygen concentration in water is around 40 times lower than in the air, so gaseous exchange organs have to be highly efficient. The oxygen concentration is also highly variable and affected by both temperature and salinity, as shown in Figure 6.33. The higher the temperature and salinity, the lower the concentration of dissolved oxygen. Water is much denser and more viscous than air, so moving it through the body of an organism requires more effort. This means that organs such as gills have an inlet and outlet aperture, whereas lungs require only one aperture through which air is breathed in and out.

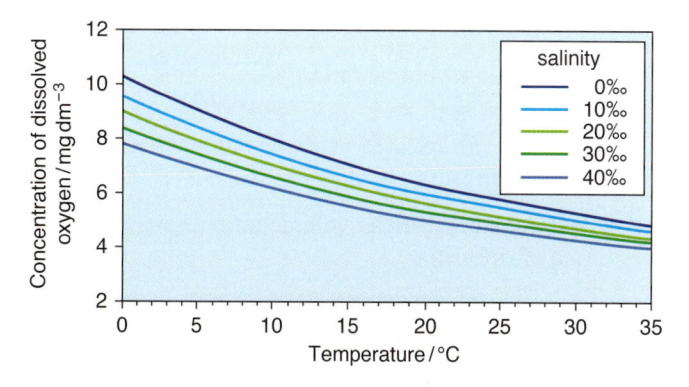

Figure 6.33: The effect of increasing temperature and salinity on the concentration of dissolved oxygen.

Size and shape of marine organisms and gaseous exchange

In order to maximise gaseous exchange, organisms need to have a large surface area. As the size of organisms increases, both the surface area and volume increase, but not in a proportional, linear relationship. If you take a cube and increase the length of each side, the increase in volume is proportionally bigger than the increase in surface area. This is shown in Figure 6.34, where it is clear that the increasing size of the cube results in a much steeper increase in volume than surface area.

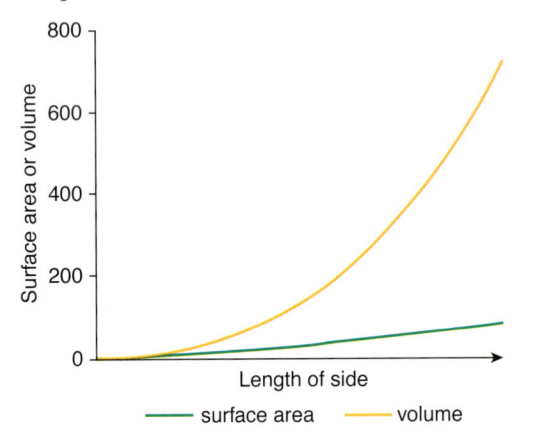

Figure 6.34: Effect of increasing the side length of a cube on the volume and surface area.

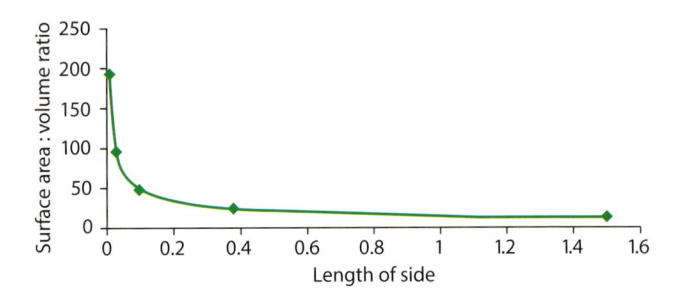

Figure 6.35: The effect of increasing side length of a cube on surface area : volume ratio.

In living organisms, having a higher surface area increases the rate of diffusion, but a higher volume tends to reduce the rate of diffusion as the distance to the centre of the organism increases. Larger organisms also have more cells so have a higher demand for oxygen. An index that takes into account both the surface area and volume of an organism is called the SA:Vol (**surface area : volume ratio**) and is calculated using the equation:

$$\text{surface area : volume ratio} = \frac{\text{surface area}}{\text{volume}}$$

- A higher surface area : volume ratio increases the rate of diffusion.
- A lower surface area : volume ratio decreases the rate of diffusion.

> **KEY WORD**
>
> **surface area : volume ratio:** an index that gives a relative measure of both surface area and volume; exchange organs generally have a very high surface area : volume ratio

As spherical or cubic shapes increase in size, the surface area : volume ratio decreases (Figure 6.35). This means that the rates of diffusion of substances through the surface is lower. Protrusions from the surface (such as the tentacles of sea anemones) help to increase the surface area. This increases the surface area : volume ratio, making diffusion faster.

The surface area : volume ratio of organisms affects their ability to carry out gaseous exchange. Very small organisms such as single-celled protozoa have high surface area : volume ratios so have a rapid rate of diffusion through their surface. They have no need for any specialised gaseous exchange organs as the surface area is sufficient for gaseous exchange and the diffusion distance is low. As the size of organisms increases, the surface area : volume ratio decreases and the surface of the organism is no longer sufficient for gaseous exchange. The distance from the outside of the organism to the centre over which gases would have to diffuse also becomes too great. Because of these problems, the majority of larger organisms have specialised gaseous exchange organs such as gills or lungs. Some larger organisms have shapes that increase the surface area and increase the surface area : volume ratio. Coral polyps and anemones have surface projections such as tentacles that increase the surface area : volume ratio.

The surface area : volume ratio is affected by both the overall size of an organism and its shape. More spherical organisms that minimise their surface area tend to have a low surface area : volume ratio, while those that are thinner with a very folded surface have a higher surface : volume ratio.

6 Physiology of marine organisms

CORE PRACTICAL ACTIVITY 6.5: INVESTIGATING THE EFFECT OF SURFACE AREA:VOLUME RATIO ON THE RATE OF DIFFUSION

Introduction

The surface area:volume ratio of organisms affects the rate of diffusion across their surfaces. Gas exchange organs all have a large surface area:volume ratio to maximise the amount of oxygen that can be absorbed. This practical shows the effects of changing the surface area:volume ratio of agar cubes on the rate of diffusion of acid. The agar contains an alkali and an indicator solution, cresol red. Cresol red is purple-red in alkaline conditions and yellow in acidic conditions. When blocks of agar are placed into hydrochloric acid, the acid diffuses into the agar and so the colour of the agar changes from red-purple to yellow. The rate of diffusion can be measured by measuring the time taken for the agar blocks to change colour completely. When there is no red-purple colour left, the acid has reached the centre of the agar block.

Equipment:

You will need:
- pink agar blocks
- scalpel
- 5 × test tubes
- stop clock
- test tube rack
- about 200 cm^3 of 2 mol dm^{-3} hydrochloric acid.

To prepare agar:
- Stir 10 g agar crystals into 100 cm^3 tap water and heat to boiling point.
- Add 5 cm^3 of 1% cresol red solution and 2 cm^3 bench (2 mol dm^{-3}) ammonium hydroxide.
- Pour the agar to a depth of 10 mm in plastic Petri dishes lightly smeared with a little oil, and when cool cut into blocks of 20 mm × 10 mm × 10 mm.

Safety considerations

Take care when heating the agar to dissolve it. Wear safety glasses throughout.
Hydrochloric acid and ammonium hydroxide are both corrosive. Wipe spills immediately and wash off any splashes on skin.
Cresol red is an irritant in eyes and on skin, and in the event of contact with eye or skin should be washed off.

Take care when using a scalpel.

Before you start

1. Identify the dependent and independent variables.
2. Identify variables that need to be controlled.
3. Consider how the shape of organisms affects rates of diffusion.

Method

1. Using the scalpel, cut a block of agar of dimensions 20 mm × 10 mm × 10 mm, as shown in Figure 6.36. Cut this block in half and reserve one half. Take the other half and cut this in half as shown in Figure 6.36, again reserving one half. Repeat this procedure, as shown in Figure 6.36, so that five agar blocks are produced.

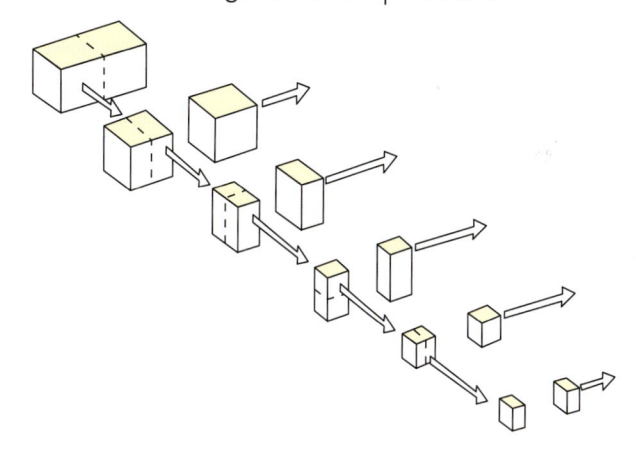

Figure 6.36: Flow chart for cutting agar blocks.

2. Fill each test tube with 5 cm^3 of 2 mol dm^{-3} hydrochloric acid.
3. Copy Table 6.7.
4. Place the largest block into a test tube and record the time taken for the agar block to change from pink to orange. Repeat this with all the blocks.
5. To ensure reliability, the experiment should be repeated two more times using fresh agar blocks.

243

CONTINUED

Dimensions/mm	Surface area/mm²	Volume/mm³	Surface area:volume ratio	Time taken for block to change colour/s			
				1	2	3	mean
10 × 10 × 10	600	1000	0.6				
10 × 10 × 5	400	500					
10 × 5 × 5	250	250					
5 × 5 × 5	150	125					
5 × 5 × 2.5	100	62.5					

Table 6.7: Results table for the effect of cube size on diffusion rate.

Results

1. Record all the data in the table and calculate the mean time taken for each size of block to change colour.
2. Calculate the surface areas, volumes and surface area:volume ratios of each block and record them in the table.
3. Plot a graph of *Surface area:volume ratio* (y-axis) against *Mean time taken for block to change colour* (x-axis).

Evaluation and conclusions

1. Describe the effect of increasing surface area:volume ratio on the time taken for the acid to diffuse into the blocks.
2. State whether or not the relationship between surface area:volume ratio and rate of diffusion is linear.
3. Explain why the agar blocks changed colour as the acid diffused in to them.
4. Identify any anomalies (values that do not seem to fit the pattern) in your results table. Suggest what could have caused these anomalies.
5. Identify any possible sources of error in the experiment.

REFLECTION

After completing Core Practical Activity 6.5, think about how you could relate the results of the experiment to the need for specialised exchange organs in larger organisms?

MATHS SKILLS 6.2

SURFACE AREA:VOLUME RATIOS, RATES AND REARRANGING FORMULAE

The shape and size of organisms affect their physiology. The surface area of an organism is the area taken up by its entire surface or skin. The volume of an organism is the amount of three-dimensional space taken up by its shape. There are different formulae used to calculate the surface area and volumes of shapes (Table 6.8).

Shape	Formula for surface area	Formula for volume
cube with side length a	$6a^2$	a^3
rectangular cuboid with side lengths of: w, l, h	$2(wl + hl + hw)$	wlh
cylinder with height, h, and radius of circular cross section, r	$2\pi r(r + h)$	$\pi r^2 h$
sphere of radius, r	$4\pi r^2$	$\frac{4}{3}\pi r^3$

Table 6.8: Surface area formulae for different shapes.

CONTINUED

Calculating volumes, surface areas and rates

It is important to be able to calculate the volumes and surface areas of several shapes, including the volumes of spheres, cylinders, cubes and rectangular cuboids. You also need to be able to calculate rates confidently and change units.

Worked example

Each of the 12 tentacles of a coral polyp approximate to the shape of a cylinder with length 0.75 cm and radius 2 mm.

a Calculate the surface area : volume ratio of each of the tentacles.

First, we need to calculate the surface area each polyp.

$A = 2\pi r(r + h)$

We need to convert all units to millimetres, so:

radius = 2 mm and length (height) = 75 mm

surface area = $2 \times \pi \times (2 + 75)$

surface area = $2 \times \pi \times 77 = 967.12$ mm²

Second, we need to calculate the volume of each polyp.

$V = \pi r^2 h$

volume = $\pi \times 2^2 \times 75$

volume = 942 mm²

Finally, we can calculate the surface area : volume ratio of each polyp.

SA : Vol = SA ÷ V

= 967.12 ÷ 942 = 1.0

b If the polyp takes in 15 mg of oxygen in 24 hours, calculate the rate of diffusion of oxygen into the polyp per square mm of polyp in milligrams of oxygen per square millimeter per hour.

To calculate the rate of diffusion per square millimeter, we firstly need to calculate the total surface area.

SA of one polyp = 967.12 mm²

SA of 12 polyps = 967.12 mm² × 12 = 11 605.44 mm²

We then need to calculate the amount of oxygen consumed in one hour.

In 24 hours, the polyp consumed 15 mg of oxygen.

In 1 hour, the polyp consumed 15 ÷ 24 = 0.625 mg oxygen; this means that the oxygen consumption is 0.625 mg h⁻¹

So, the rate of oxygen consumption per square millimetre is:

0.625 ÷ 11 605.44 = 0.000 0538 mg mm⁻¹ hr⁻¹

Note: This could be converted to 0.0538 µg mm⁻¹ hr⁻¹

Questions

Use the formulae in Table 6.8 to answer the questions.

1 A coral grows in the approximate shape of a sphere: calculate its mean rate of growth in cm³ month⁻¹ if its diameter changes from 50 cm to 58 cm in one year.

2 Determine the density of 75 tilapia fry in tilapia m⁻³ when placed into:
   a cubic tanks of side lengths:
      i   5 m
      ii 8 m
      iii 225 cm
   b rectangular cuboid tanks of dimensions:
      i   2 m × 3 m × 8 m
      ii 150 cm × 6 m × 2 m

3 Use the formulae above to calculate the surface areas of the following shapes:
   a cube with side length 5 cm
   b rectangular cuboid with dimensions of 6 cm × 6 cm × 12 cm
   c rectangular cuboid with dimensions of 6 cm × 2 cm × 36 cm
   d sphere with radius 8 cm
   e cylinder with cross sectional diameter of 4 cm and height of 8 cm.

> **CONTINUED**

4 Calculate the volumes of each of the shapes **a** to **e** above. Comment on the difference in the surface area : volume ratios of the two rectangular cuboids.

5 Surface area : volume ratio is calculated by dividing the surface area by the volume. Use your answers to questions **3** and **4** to calculate the surface area : volume ratios for the shapes **a** to **e**.

It is often necessary to rearrange formulae.

For example, the formula for the surface area of a sphere is:

$A = 4\pi r^2$

If we want to find the radius, we can rearrange the formula so that:

$r = \sqrt{(A/4\pi)}$

So, the radius of a sphere with a surface area of 160 mm² is

$r = \sqrt{(160/4\pi)}$

$= \sqrt{12.74}$

$= 3.57 \text{ mm}$

6 a Calculate the height of a cylinder with a radius of 3 mm and a total surface area of 250 mm².

b Determine the radius of a sphere with surface area of 400 cm².

7 A coral polyp has 32 cylindrical tentacles each with a radius of 2 mm and length of 10 mm.

a Calculate the total surface area of the tentacles.

The polyp was placed into 0.1 dm³ seawater with an oxygen concentration of 9.0 mg dm⁻³. After two hours, the oxygen concentration in the water had fallen to 7.5 mg dm⁻³.

b Calculate the total mass of oxygen taken up by the coral over the two-hour period.

c Calculate the rate of oxygen diffusion per mm² polyp membrane in mg mm⁻² h⁻¹.

Circulatory systems

The use of specialised gaseous exchange organs brings with it the problem of how to transport gases. Circulatory systems evolved as a method of delivering oxygen to all tissues. In fish, blood that transports oxygen is pumped through a network of arteries, veins and capillaries by a heart. As in humans, the red blood cells of fish contain the protein **haemoglobin**, which binds reversibly to oxygen in the gills to form **oxyhaemoglobin**. In areas such as muscles with low oxygen, the oxyhaemoglobin releases the oxygen for respiration. The blood also transports dissolved carbon dioxide from the tissues to the gills.

oxyhaemoglobin gills ⇌ haemoglobin + oxygen tissues

> **KEY WORDS**
>
> **haemoglobin:** protein that is found in red blood cells and transports oxygen around the body
>
> **oxyhaemoglobin:** formed when haemoglobin binds reversibly to oxygen in the gills

In a typical fish circulatory system such as that shown in Figure 6.37, blood travels in a particular route around the body.

- Blood passes through muscles and other body tissues in capillaries, the smallest blood vessels, and releases oxygen and gains carbon dioxide.

- Blood is then returned to the heart in veins.

- Blood is then pumped out of the heart in arteries towards the gills.

- As the blood passes through capillaries in the gills, it releases carbon dioxide into the water and gains oxygen.

- Blood leaves the gills in arteries and travels to the muscles in order to deliver oxygen and remove carbon dioxide.

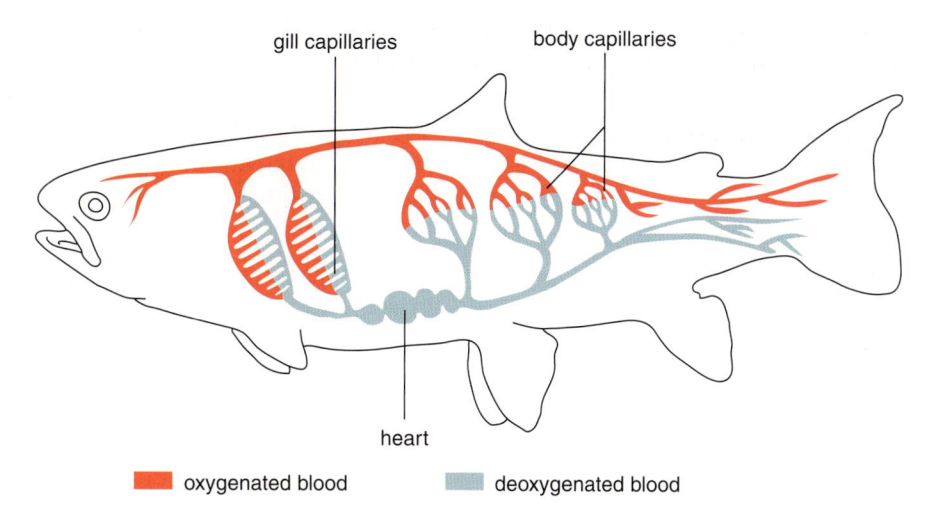

Figure 6.37: The circulatory system of a typical bony fish.

Very active fish, such as tuna, require rapid respiration in the muscles, so blood is pumped quickly to the muscles. The circulatory system of these active fish is very efficient and maintains a high rate of blood flow.

Fick's Law and gaseous exchange organs

Gaseous exchange organs follow a rule know as Fick's Law. This states that the rate of diffusion of a substance is proportional to the product of the surface area of the organ and the diffusion gradient divided by the diffusion distance.

$$\text{diffusion rate} \propto \frac{\text{surface area} \times \text{concentration gradient}}{\text{diffusion distance}}$$

Fick's Law enables us to predict the following common features of all gaseous exchange surfaces:

- a large surface area
- steep concentration gradients of oxygen / carbon dioxide
- short diffusion distances.

Specific examples of gaseous exchange methods

There are different methods of gaseous exchange adopted by different marine species. Here, we will look at the different methods seen in coral polyps, grouper and tuna.

Coral polyps

Coral polyps do not possess specialised gaseous exchange organs and all gaseous exchange takes place directly across the body surface by simple diffusion. The surface area : volume ratio of the polyp is sufficient because it has a large number of tentacles (Figure 6.38) and the thickness of the coral polyp epidermis is thin so that diffusion is rapid. Sometimes, polyps move their tentacles to generate water currents refreshing the

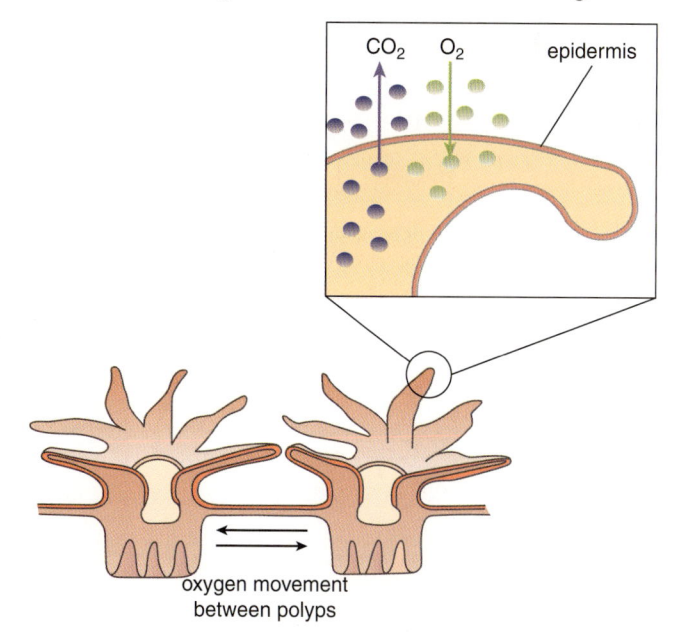

Figure 6.38: The structure of a coral polyp. The tentacles provide a large surface area and the epidermis is thin, reducing the diffusion path. Oxygen can move between polyps.

water around the polyp. This movement brings more oxygenated water into contact with the tentacles and maintains the diffusion gradients between the inside of the polyp and the water. Some coral polyps are able to pump oxygenated fluids between each other to ensure an even distribution of oxygen.

Grouper, tuna and the adaptations of fish gills

Bony fish, such as groupers and tuna, breathe by taking in water through the mouth, passing it over the gills and then forcing it out through gill openings (Figure 6.39). The gills are covered by a plate called an operculum (a thin bony flap of skin covering and protecting the gills) that can open and close. On either side of the head are four pairs of gill arches, which are bony structures supporting the gills. The gills themselves are made up of many **filaments**, on the surfaces of which are folds called **lamellae** that are arranged at a 90° angle to the filaments. The filaments and lamellae provide a very large surface area to maximise gaseous exchange. The lamellae are very thin and contain an extensive capillary network. Blood circulates through the capillary network and red blood cells pass through the capillaries very close to the external water, minimising the diffusion path. Pillar cells are found within the secondary lamellae, which help to slow the blood flow and press red blood cells to the surface of the lamella. Deoxygenated blood enters the gills through afferent arterioles and the oxygenated blood leaves through efferent arterioles to then travel to body tissues.

Fish of different species and ages have different gill surface areas according to their oxygen demand. Fast, active swimmers, such as tuna, mackerel and swordfish, have a high oxygen demand (and need to remove carbon dioxide rapidly) because the rate of respiration in the muscles is high. These fish have very large gill surface areas.

> **KEY WORDS**
>
> **filaments:** parts of gills that branch out from gill arches; they are sometimes called primary lamellae
>
> **lamellae:** addition branches of gill filaments that increase the surface area of the gills; they are sometimes called secondary lamellae

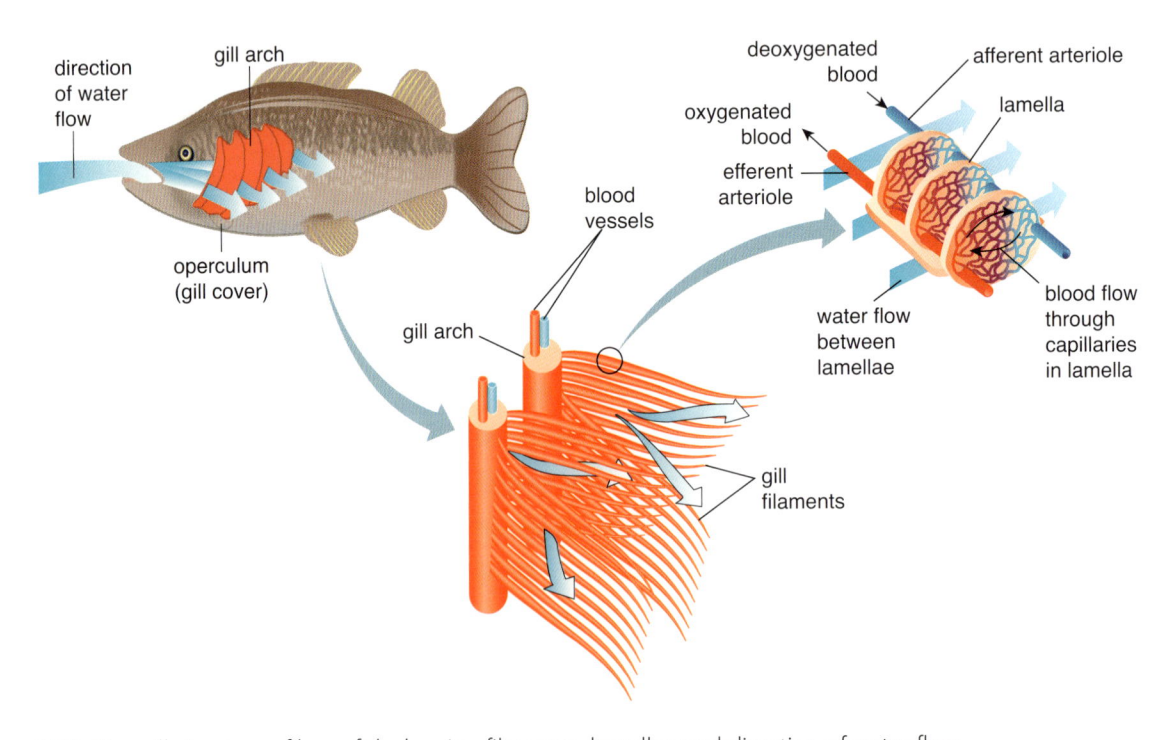

Figure 6.39: The gill structure of bony fish showing filaments, lamellae and direction of water flow.

6 Physiology of marine organisms

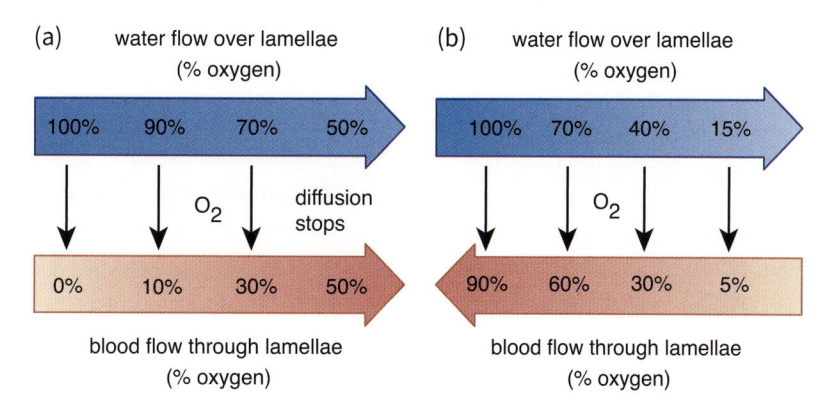

Figure 6.40: (a) A concurrent flow of blood and water; (b) A counter–current flow of blood and water.]

Less active fish, such as sole and plaice, which often stay stationary for long periods of time, tend to have smaller gill surface areas. These fish move in shorts bursts in order to evade predators or catch food. The energy for this is often obtained by anaerobic respiration so the oxygen demand is lower.

Counter-current exchanger

Blood flows through the capillaries in the secondary lamellae in the opposite direction to the water. This arrangement in known as a **counter-current** mechanism. It ensures that gaseous exchange is highly efficient because the diffusion gradient is maintained across the whole gill surface.

If blood and water flow in the same direction, in a concurrent flow (Figure 6.40a), the diffusion gradient occurs until an equilibrium point when the concentration of oxygen in the blood and water is equal. In a counter-current flow (Figure 6.40b), the diffusion gradient is maintained along the full length of the gill so that diffusion is more efficient. In this way, oxygen diffuses into the blood along the whole length of the gill while carbon dioxide diffuses out into the water along the whole length of the gill.

Ventilation movements

In order to maintain the diffusion gradients of oxygen and carbon dioxide, water is constantly passed over the gills. Two different processes are used by fish to ventilate the gills: **ram ventilation** and **pumped ventilation** (Table 6.9).

> ### KEY WORDS
>
> **counter-current (in gills):** a mechanism by which gas exchange in gills is made more efficient; water and blood flow in opposite directions to maintain the diffusion gradient across the length of the gill
>
> **ram ventilation:** ventilation of gills by swimming with the mouth open so that a constant flow of water passes through the mouth and over the gills; it only occurs when a fish is swimming
>
> **pumped ventilation:** ventilation of gills by the muscle action of the mouth pumping water over the gills; it can occur when the fish is stationary

Ram ventilation	Pumped ventilation
non-active pumping, saving energy	active pumping, using energy
can only occur when swimming	can occur during swimming and resting

Table 6.9: Differences between ram and pumped ventilation.

Ram ventilation

Fast-swimming fish, such as tuna and sharks, swim with an open mouth. As they swim, water is forced through the mouth, over the gills and out through the operculum or gill slits. There is no muscle contraction required by the muscles of the mouth and all the force for moving the water is generated by the forward motion of the fish. As no extra effort is made in pumping the water over the gills, energy is saved. One drawback is that fish that only use ram ventilation must keep swimming constantly in order to maintain a constant flow of water over the gills. Some fish species, such as tuna, can switch back and forth between ram and pumped ventilation depending on their speed of movement. As fish swim faster, using more energy in their muscles, the rate of water flow over the gills automatically increases so that the rate of gaseous exchange increases. The rapid flow of water generated by high-speed swimming could potentially damage the delicate gill structures. In order to prevent this damage, the gill arches are often reinforced or fused together in tuna species.

Pumped ventilation

The majority of fish actively pump water over their gills. This means that even when a fish is stationary, there is a constant flow of water over the gills. Fish that use this method, such as the grouper, use the muscles of the buccal cavity (mouth region), which requires energy so it can be energetically costly. The benefit of pumped ventilation, however, is that fish can continue to breathe when not moving so can remain in one place for extended periods of time. When the fish swim faster, the oxygen demand increases, and the rate of pumping also increases. Many species of fish will change the rate at which they ventilate their gills in response to different concentrations of oxygen in the water. Fish may also change the speed at which they ventilate in response to the concentration of oxygen in a habitat. Goldfish increase their rate of ventilation when in water with lower concentrations of oxygen.

When considering pumped ventilation, it is a good idea to remember:

- Water always flows from an area of higher pressure to an area of lower pressure.
- As the volume of a cavity increases, the pressure decreases, and vice versa.

Figure 6.42 shows the stages of water flow through the buccal cavity of a bony fish.

During inflow of water:

- The mouth opens.
- The volume of the buccal cavity is increased by muscle contraction and relaxation.
- This lowers the pressure inside the buccal cavity to below the external pressure.
- Water flows into the buccal cavity down a pressure gradient.
- The operculum closes as water tries to flow back across the gills.

During outflow water over the gills:

- The mouth closes.
- The volume of buccal cavity is reduced by muscle contraction and relaxation.
- Pressure inside the buccal cavity rises above the external pressure.
- Water flows over the gills and the operculum is forced open, allowing the outflow of water.

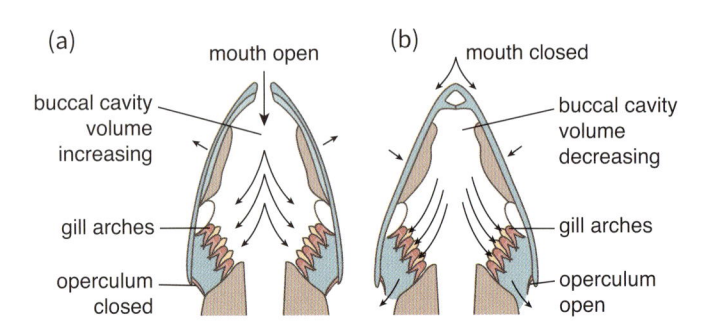

Figure 6.41: Movement of water across gills seen from above. **(a)** Mouth open, buccal cavity chamber increases in volume, water is drawn into the buccal cavity, operculum is closed; **(b)** Mouth closed, buccal cavity chamber reduces in volume, operculum opens and water flows over gills.

Gaseous exchange organs of different species all obey Fick's Law (Table 6.10).

Species	Gaseous exchange surface	Large surface area	Short diffusion path	Maintenance of diffusion gradient
coral polyp	body surface	large numbers of tentacles	thin epidermis on body surface	none, although tentacles may move
grouper	gill	gill filaments and secondary lamellae	thin epidermis on gills	blood flow through capillaries, pumped ventilation
tuna	gill	gill filaments and secondary lamellae	thin epidermis on gills	blood flow through capillaries, ram ventilation
shark	gill	gill filaments and secondary lamellae	thin epidermis on gills	blood flow through capillaries, ram ventilation

Table 6.10: Summary of how gaseous exchange organs of different species obey Fick's Law.

6.4 Osmoregulation

Marine organisms usually live in an environment with high salinity and low water potential. Although the concentration of most seawater is isotonic to body fluids, it still means that there is a danger of water loss from their bodies into the surrounding water. Some organisms are able to survive only in a narrow range of salinities and are classed as **stenohaline** species. Species such as salmon, which are able to tolerate a wide range of salinities, are classed as **euryhaline** species.

Osmoconformers

Osmoconformer organisms have an internal water potential of cells and body fluids that is equal to that of the surrounding water. This means that their fluids are isotonic to the water and there is no net gain or loss of water. The majority of osmoconformers are stenohaline invertebrates and are thus not resistant to major changes in external salinity.

Mussels are euryhaline osmoconformers and frequently live in estuarine areas where the salinity of the water may be very variable. They are able to survive there by using two methods.

- When salinity changes, mussels close their shells tightly to prevent the seawater coming into contact with their body tissue.
- They can increase and decrease the solute concentrations of their cells if the external salinity changes. The solute concentration is matched to the external water so that no net in- or out-flow of water occurs.

Despite some degree of control over osmoregulation, most mussel species tend to be restricted to a particular range of salinities. Some species are restricted to brackish waters of estuaries while others are restricted to the more saline waters of the sea.

Osmoregulators

Osmoregulators maintain a constant internal osmotic pressure that may differ from the environment they are in. The majority of bony fish species are stenohaline osmoregulators that can only live in a narrow range of salinities. They actively maintain a particular salinity in their cells and body fluids. Tuna are a typical example of a marine, stenohaline, osmoregulatory species.

> **KEY WORDS**
>
> **stenohaline:** organisms that cannot tolerate wide changes in the salinity of water
>
> **euryhaline:** organisms that can tolerate wide changes in the salinity of water
>
> **osmoconformer:** organisms that have an internal body fluid salinity that it is the same salinity as external water
>
> **osmoregulator:** organisms that regulate the internal salinity of their body fluids within a narrow range

Marine fish

In most seas and oceans, the water surrounding fish has a higher salinity (hypertonic) than the cells and body fluids. Water is drawn out of the body from the gills and skin by osmosis and salt diffuses into the body from the water. This constant loss of water could lead to dehydration, resulting in cell damage and death. In order to prevent excess water loss, marine bony fish carry out several processes:

- They constantly drink seawater to replace water that is lost by osmosis.
- Sodium and chloride ions are actively secreted by the gills. Specialised cells on the gill filaments have protein 'pumps' in their membranes that pump the ions into the water, which requires energy in the form of ATP.
- Magnesium and sulfate ions are actively secreted by the kidney into the urine.
- Reabsorption of water by the kidney produces a low volume of very concentrated urine.

These processes are summarised in Figure 6.42.

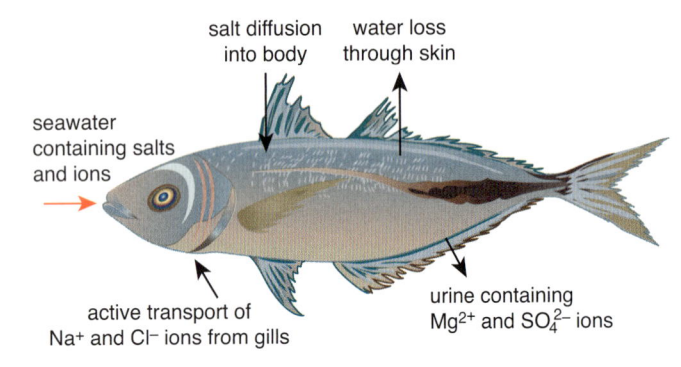

Figure 6.42: Osmoregulation by marine fish.

Fresh-water fish

Fish species that live in fresh water have the opposite problem to marine fish. Fresh water has a very low salinity and high water potential (hypotonic). Water constantly enters the body through the gills and skin by osmosis (Figure 6.43). In order to prevent excess water loss, fresh-water bony fish carry out several processes:

- They drink small amounts of water.
- The gills actively pump sodium and chloride ions into the blood and body fluid. Specialised cells have protein pumps that actively pump the ions from the external water to the internal body fluids. These pumps use ATP, similar to the pumps in marine fish.
- They produce large amounts of very dilute urine.

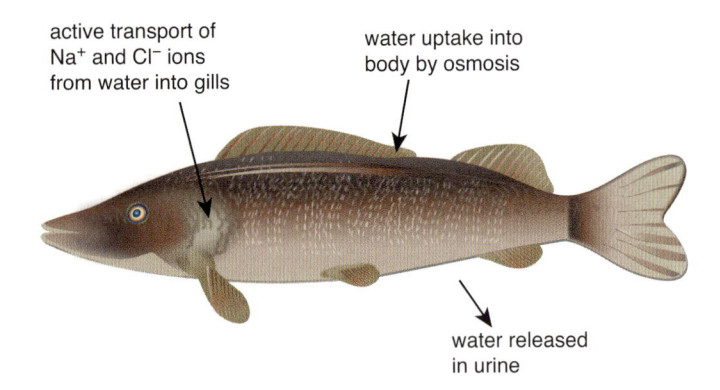

Figure 6.43: Osmoregulation in fresh-water fish.

Euryhaline fish

Euryhaline osmoregulatory species, such as salmon and eels, are able to live in a wide range of salinities, from the fresh water of rivers to the salt water of the oceans. They are able to change direction of ion pumping depending on the salinity of the surrounding water (Table 6.11).

	Salmon body fluid	Ocean water	Fresh water
solute concentration / %	1.0	3.5	<0.1

Table 6.11: Comparison of salinity in salmon body fluids, ocean water and fresh water.

When in saltwater, the surrounding water is hypertonic to their body fluids. Salts are pumped out of the gills and they drink water to replace the water that has been lost by osmosis.

When in fresh water, the surrounding water is hypotonic to their body fluids. The ion pumps move the salts in the opposite direction, taking salts into the blood.

CASE STUDY 6.1 THE LUNGFISH – FISH THAT CAN BREATHE AIR

Lungfish, as their name suggests, are fish that use a lung to breathe atmospheric air. The fossil record suggests that they were once very diverse and widespread but there are now only six known species on the planet. One species is found in Australia, one in South America and four in Africa (one of which is shown in Figure 6.44). They are large fish – the yellow, marbled Ethiopian species growing up to two metres in length. All lungfish species have large sacs, or lungs that extend from the mouth. The lungs are divided up into lots of small air sacs and have a rich blood supply along with a thin wall that separates the air from the blood. When their oxygen levels fall, the fish push their heads out of water so that they can breathe atmospheric air. One species, the Australian lungfish, in addition to a single lung, has gills, and can exchange gases when under and out of the water. All the other species have two lungs and have no functional gills, being totally dependent on breathing air for gas exchange.

All six species of lungfish live in water that often has low levels of dissolved oxygen and often dries up during hot seasons. The Australian lungfish is often found in small, isolated pools of water and surfaces every 40 to 50 minutes to breathe. Most other fish species suffocate and die when water becomes hot and begins to dry up. When rivers begin to dry up during the hot seasons in Africa, the African lungfish covers itself in a thick layer of mucus before burying itself in the mud of the river bed. They remain buried in the bed, sometimes for more than two years, in a dormant state until the rains come and the rivers flow again. While dormant, scientists have found that the cellular respiration rate of the lung fish drops to a very low level. Staying dormant to survive the hot, dry conditions is called estivation.

Questions

1. Explain how the lungs of lungfish are adapted to maximise gas exchange.

2. Suggest how having lungs enables the lungfish to survive in small pools of water during hot weather.

3. Discuss how the estivation of the African lungfish enables it to survive the dry period.

Figure 6.44: An African lungfish.

Test yourself

6 Explain why rapid respiration in a muscle cell would increase the rate of diffusion of oxygen from the blood into the cell and carbon dioxide out of the cell into the blood.

7 Global warming could lead to an increase in sea temperature and ice cap melting. Suggest and explain how this could affect the dissolved oxygen content of seawater.

8 Draw up a table to show the different methods of gaseous exchange used by coral polyps, tuna and grouper, and the advantages and disadvantages of each method.

9 Explain the following.
   a Highly active fish die more frequently than less active ones when the temperature of the water rises very high.
   b Gill parasites that eat away parts of the gill lamellae reduce the growth rate of farmed salmon.
   c If fish are removed from water, they suffocate as the gill lamellae collapse and stick together.

10 Summarise the osmoregulatory mechanisms a salmon uses as it moves from river water to the sea.

11 Suggest and explain why salmon that are grown in water with higher, hypertonic, salinities have lower growth rates than those grown in lower, isotonic, salinities.

PROJECT: BLOOD COLOURS

Many of us think that all organisms have blood that is red. The natural world is never that simple, though. There are red, blue, green and violet coloured bloods found in different species of marine organisms.

Carry out some research to identify the different pigments that produce these four different colours of blood in nature. You should include:

- the four different respiratory pigments
- the organisms that these are found in (including photographs)
- the function of these pigments
- the different properties of each.

Present your findings as a webpage to other students.

Thinking about your project

Produce a set of five quick questions for your audience about the webpage. This is a good guide to see how well the webpage explained your findings.

EXAM-STYLE QUESTIONS

1 a i **Explain** what are meant by the terms:
         osmoregulator
         osmoconformer
         euryhaline. [3]
      ii **Describe** how salmon maintain the water balance of their body fluids while swimming in salt water. [3]

COMMAND WORDS

explain: set out purposes or reasons / make the relationships between things evident/ provide why and/or how and support with relevant evidence.

describe: state the points of a topic / give characteristics and main features.

CONTINUED

b Figure 6.45 shows how the numbers of a mussel species and the salinity of the water change along a river, through the estuary and out into the sea.

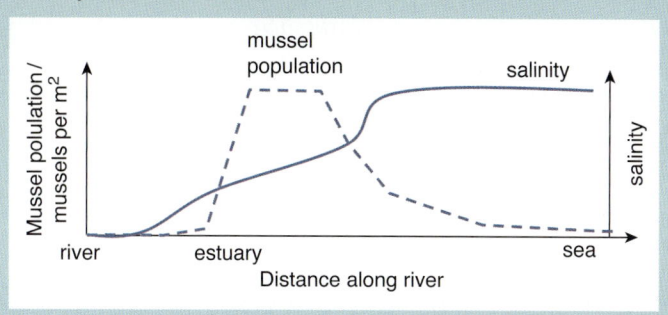

Figure 6.45: Changes in population of a species of mussel and the salinity of water along a riverbed into the sea.

    i Describe the changes in the mussel population and the salinity of water as the distance increases. [2]

    ii Suggest and explain the changes in mussel population. [4]

[Total: 12]

2 a i Complete the equation for aerobic respiration.

glucose + ... → .... + water [1]

    ii Use your knowledge of the marine environment and respiration to explain why fish species that are found in deeper areas of the ocean tend to have low activity levels and swim with short rapid bursts. [4]

b i Explain why small single-celled organisms do not possess specialised gaseous exchange organs. [3]

Fick's Law states that diffusion rate is proportional to the product of concentration gradient and surface area divided by the diffusion distance:

$$\text{rate of diffusion} \propto \frac{\text{concentration gradient} \times \text{surface area}}{\text{diffusion distance}}$$

    ii Use Fick's Law to explain how the gill system of the grouper is adapted to maximise gaseous exchange. [3]

[Total: 11]

3 a i Using named fish species as examples, compare the differences between pumped and ram ventilation. [6]

    ii Some species of fish use pumped ventilation when swimming at low speeds but switch to ram ventilation when swimming at high speed. Explain why the ability to switch between the two methods of ventilation is advantageous. [3]

COMMAND WORDS

suggest: apply knowledge and understanding to situations where there are a range of valid responses in order to make proposals.

compare: identify / comment on similarities and/or differences

> **CONTINUED**
>
> **b** During their life cycle, salmon live in both fresh and salt water. Use your knowledge of osmoregulation and osmosis to explain how salmon are able to live in both fresh and salt water. [6]
>
> [Total: 15]
>
> **4** Figure 6.46 shows an electron micrograph of a liver cell.
>
> **Figure 6.46:** Electron micrograph of a liver cell, magnification ×23 000.
>
> **a i** Draw a diagram of the area of the cell inside the box. [4]
>
>   **ii** **Calculate** the maximum length, in micrometres, of organelle C. [2]
>
> **b** **State** the names of organelles A, B and C. [3]
>
> **c** Explain the evidence in Figure 6.46 that suggests this cell produces large amounts of protein and has a high energy demand. [4]
>
> [Total: 13]

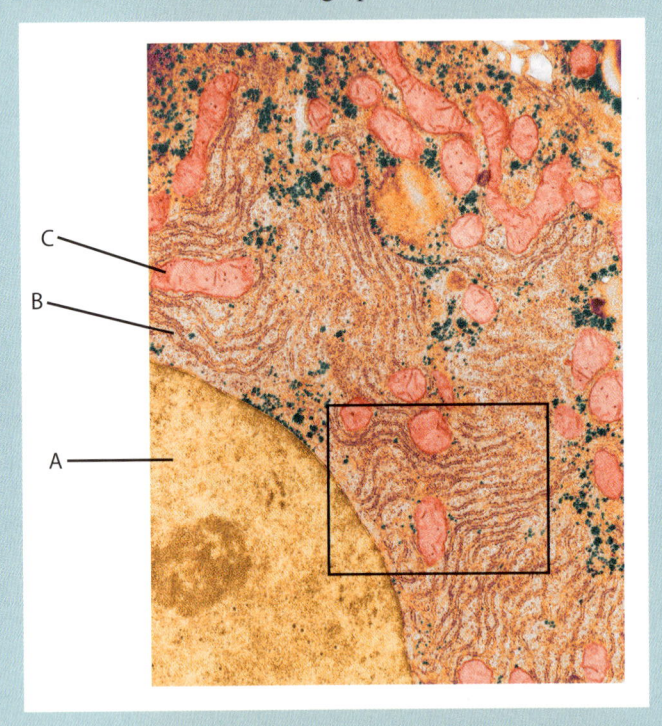

COMMAND WORDS

calculate: work out from given facts, figure or information

state: express in clear term

CONTINUED

5 The Baltic Sea is a North European sea that is attached to the North Sea. It is almost entirely surrounded by land and has only a small region between Sweden and Denmark where it connects to the North Sea.

Figure 6.47 shows the salinity of different areas of the Baltic Sea along with the distribution of some species.

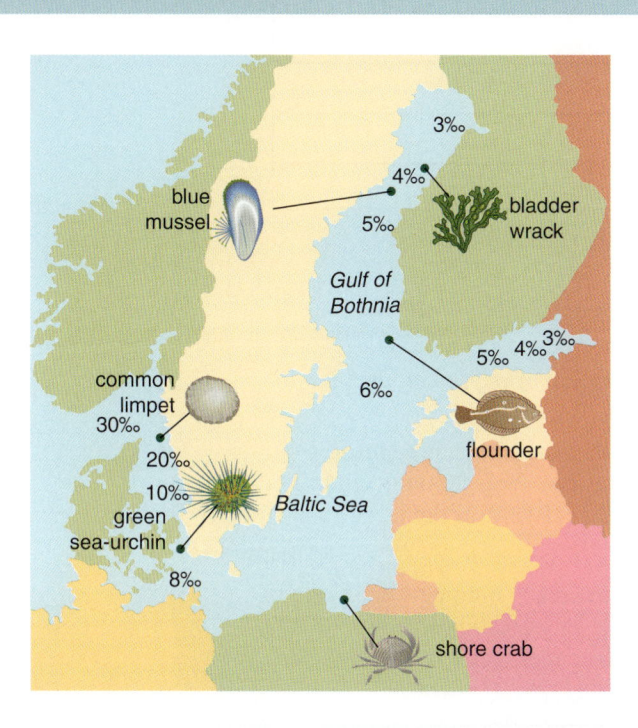

Figure 6.47: Salinity levels of different areas of the Baltic Sea and distribution of some of the species. Salinity is measured in parts per thousand (‰).

- **a i** Explain how temperature and river outflow can affect ocean salinity. [4]
- **ii** Suggest and explain a reason for the difference in salinity of the different parts of the Baltic Sea. [3]
- **b** The common limpet is an osmoconformer. Use your knowledge of osmosis to explain why the common limpet is not found in the Gulf of Bothnia. [3]

[Total: 10]

6 A student investigated the rate of oxygen use by salmon. A fish was placed in a 5 dm³ water tank with an oxygen probe.

The temperature of the water was maintained at 5 °C.

A reading of oxygen concentration in the water was taken every 2 minutes for 10 minutes.

CONTINUED

The results are shown in Table 6.12.

Time/min	Oxygen concentration/mg dm^{-3}
0	11.0
2	10.6
4	10.1
6	9.6
8	9.2
10	8.9

Table 6.12: Change in oxygen concentration over time.

a i Describe the change in oxygen concentration over the 10-minute period. [2]

   ii Calculate the mean rate of absorption of oxygen by the salmon between 0 and 6 minutes. [3]

b Plan an investigation into the effect of increasing temperature on the rate of uptake of oxygen by salmon. You should include a hypothesis and describe how you will analyse your data. [10]

[Total: 15]

7 A student investigated the effect of surface area : volume ratio on rate of diffusion. She cut cubes with different side lengths and recorded the times taken for dye to diffuse to the centre of the cubes. Table 6.13 shows her results.

Side length/cm	Surface area/cm²	Volume/cm³	Surface area : volume ratio	Time taken for dye to diffuse to centre of cube/s
0.5	1.5	0.125	12.0	25
1	6	1.000	6.0	50
2	24	8	3.0	100
3	54	27	2.0	155
4	96			350
5	150	125	1.2	475

Table 6.13: Effect of cube side length on time taken for dye to diffuse.

a i Calculate the volume and surface area : volume ratio for a cube with a side length of 4 cm. [2]

CONTINUED

    ii Plot a single line graph to show how increasing the side length of the cube affects both the time taken for the dye to diffuse to the centre of the cubes and the surface area:volume ratio of the cubes. Join your points with straight, ruled lines. [6]

    iii Describe the effect of increasing side length on the SA:Vol of the cubes. [2]

b Fish gills are composed of many lamellae. The lamellae are numerous and have a flattened, thin shape. Use Table 6.13 and your graph to explain the structure of the gill lamellae. [5]

[Total: 15]

8 Figure 6.48 shows three cells in a seagrass leaf. The water potential of each cell is shown.

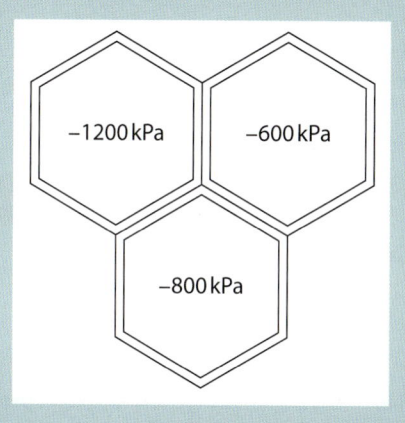

[Diagram: three hexagonal cells labelled −1200 kPa, −600 kPa, and −800 kPa]

Figure 6.48: Water potentials in three cells in a seagrass leaf.

a   **i** **Define** the process of osmosis. [2]

    ii Draw arrows on the diagram to show the movement of water by osmosis. [1]

    iii Seagrass cells are typical plant cells. Explain how the structure of the cells prevents them being damaged when placed in pure water. [3]

b Explain how structure of the cell surface membrane affects the movement of charged, polar substances across it. [5]

c A student placed investigated the transport of potassium ions into seagrass root cells. He placed the cells into a solution of potassium ions and recorded the movement of potassium ions into the cells. He repeated the experiment after the root cells had been treated with cyanide, an inhibitor of respiration. The results are shown in Figure 6.49.

> **COMMAND WORD**
>
> **define:** give precise meaning

CONTINUED

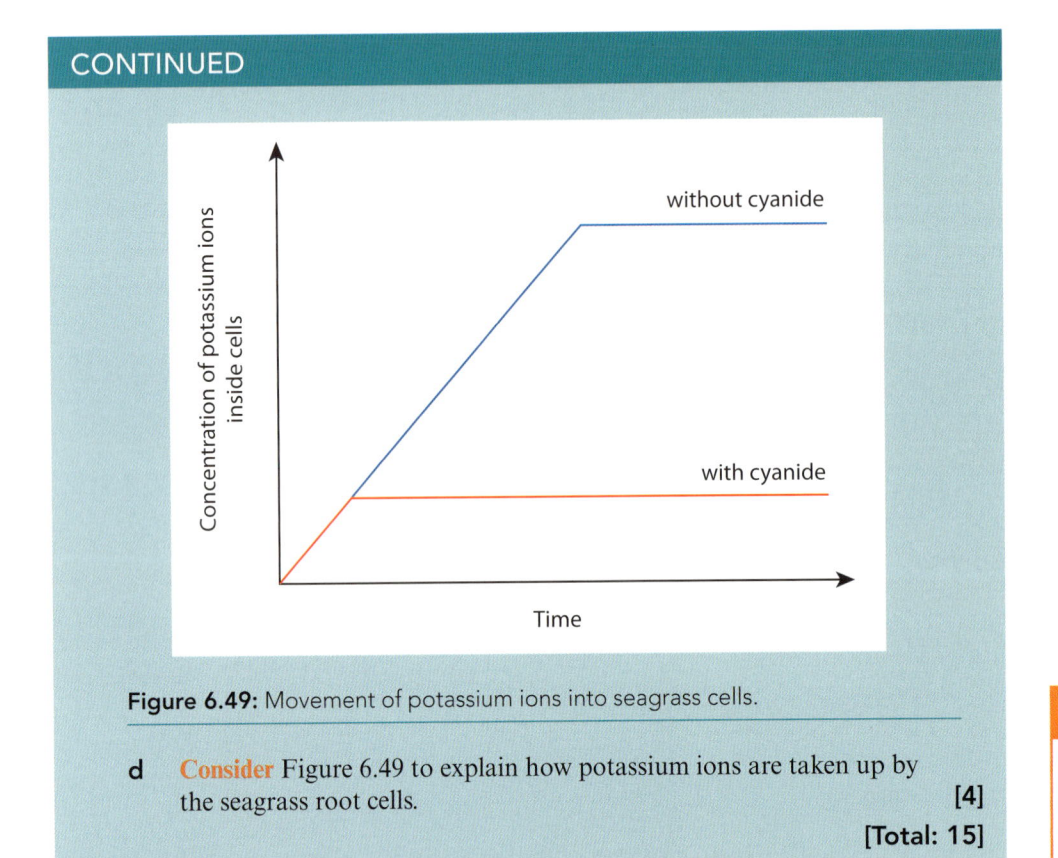

Figure 6.49: Movement of potassium ions into seagrass cells.

d **Consider** Figure 6.49 to explain how potassium ions are taken up by the seagrass root cells. [4]

[Total: 15]

> **COMMAND WORD**
>
> **consider:** review and respond to given information

SELF-EVALUATION CHECKLIST

I can:	See section...	Needs more work	Almost there	Ready to move on
recognise cell structures and outline their functions	6.1			
describe the fluid mosaic model of membrane structure and understand the semi permeable nature of membrane structure	6.1			
describe and interpret photomicrographs, electron micrographs and drawings of typical animal and plant cells	6.1			
make observations, drawings and magnification calculations from unfamiliar structures or specimens using the formula: magnification = image size / actual size	6.1			

CONTINUED

I can:	See section...	Needs more work	Almost there	Ready to move on
describe and explain the processes of diffusion, facilitated diffusion, osmosis and active transport	6.2			
carry out practical investigations into diffusion, osmosis and water potential and explain the movement of water between cells and solutions with different water potentials	6.2			
understand that the raw materials and waste products of respiration must be moved to and from the surface of organisms	6.3			
understand how to calculate surface area : volume ratios and understand the importance of this to biological processes	6.3			
describe gaseous exchange by simple diffusion, pumped ventilation and ram ventilation, and relate an organism's method of gas exchange to its habitat and motility	6.3			
understand why marine organisms may need to regulate their water content and ion content, with reference to the composition of sea water and of body fluids	6.4			
explain the differences between osmocoformer and osmoregulator regulator organisms	6.4			
explain the terms osmocoformer, osmoregulator, euryhaline and stenohaline, and outline the process of osmoregulation in salmon	6.4			

EXTENDED CASE STUDY: THE ARAL SEA, AN ECOLOGICAL CATASTROPHE

The Aral Sea (Figure 6.50) is a landlocked lake located in Central Asia on the border of Kazakhstan and Uzbekistan. In 1960, the Aral Sea was the fourth largest lake in the world, with an area of 67 499 km². It was a slightly saline lake with an average salinity of about 10 g dm^{-3} and was fed by two rivers, the Amu Darya in the south and the Syr Darya in the east. It was inhabited by at least 12 different fish species and more than 160 invertebrate species. Kazakhstan and Uzbekistan were part of the former Soviet Union, and in the early 1960s the Soviet government decided to divert the feeder rivers in order to build an enormous irrigation network. Over 20 000 miles of canals, 45 dams and more than 80 reservoirs were constructed in an effort to irrigate the desert region for agricultural purposes, particularly the production of cotton and wheat. The irrigation system was poorly constructed, with an estimated 75% of the water that was diverted lost as a result of leaks and evaporation.

By the mid-1960s, up to 60 km³ of river water was being diverted each year to the agricultural projects, rather than replenishing the Aral Sea. Between 1961 and 1971, the level of the Aral Sea fell by an average of 10 cm year^{-1}. The fishery industry of the Aral Sea began to suffer as stocks of the fresh and brackish water fish it depended on began to disappear.

As agricultural production increased over the rest of the twentieth century, the decrease in sea-level declined at a faster rate, averaging over 90 cm year^{-1} in the 1980s. In 1987, the continued loss of water led to the Aral Sea breaking up into two separate seas, the North (or Lesser) Aral Sea and the South (or Greater) Aral Sea. In 1991, Kazakhstan and Uzbekistan became independent nations but large-scale cotton production continued to drain the Aral Sea. By 1998, the combined area of the now two separate seas was 28 687 km², with more than an 80% decrease in volume. The salinity had risen to 45 g dm^{-3} (typical seawater salinity is around 35 g dm^{-3}). Many original fish, such as carp, and invertebrate species were completely extinct and were replaced by marine and euryhaline species, such as flounder, that were more adapted to the high salinity.

By 2004, the surface area of all parts of the Aral Sea had shrunk to 17 160 km², 25% of its original size (Figure 6.51), and a nearly five-fold increase in salinity had killed nearly all of the native species. Many of the introduced marine species were becoming extinct, unable to cope with the high salinity.

Soviet scientists and the Soviet government considered the loss of the Aral Sea a price worth paying for the mass production of cotton. They often cited the work of the Russian climatologist, Aleksandr Voeikov, who stated that the Aral Sea was a 'mistake of nature' and a 'useless evaporator'. Cotton is Uzbekistan's main cash crop. It produces more than one million tonnes per year and accounts for approximately 17% of Uzbekistan's exports. It is the sixth largest producer and second largest exporter of cotton in the world, and the cotton industry employs a significant proportion of the population. The cotton industry in Uzbekistan is, however, controversial. The industry is controlled by the government and a system of forced labour is used to harvest it, including children as young as nine.

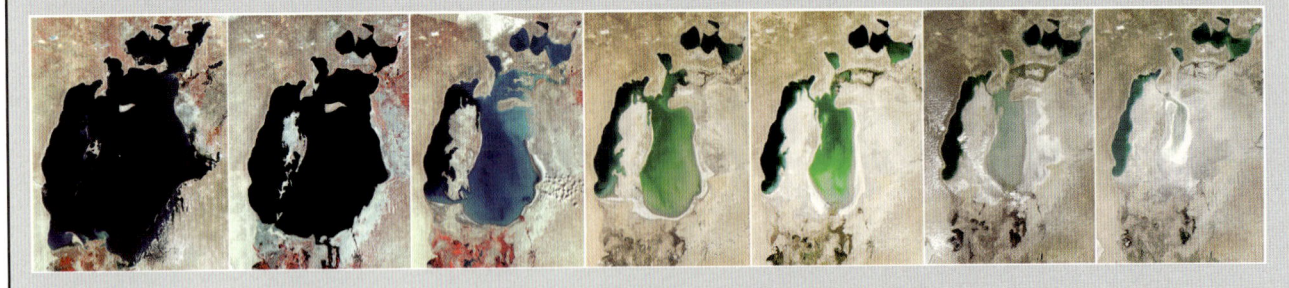

Figure 6.50: Satellite photographs showing the changes in the Aral Sea from 1973 to 2009.

CONTINUED

Some farmers are forced to grow cotton but the profits are often retained by the government. Because of alleged human rights abuses by the Uzbekistan government, several large clothing companies have stopped using cotton from Uzbekistan in their products.

North Aral Sea restoration project

In 2003, the Kazakh government began a project to restore the North Aral Sea. A large concrete dam was built in order to separate the North and South Aral Seas so that water from the north that still had river water flowing into it would not be lost to the south. The dam was completed in 2005 and since then the sea-level of the North Aral Sea has gradually increased, along with a fall in salinity, as shown in Figure 9.51. By 2006, the salinity had fallen to typical estuarine levels and some of the indigenous fish species began to reappear. Fisheries began to report a fall in numbers of marine species such as flounder. Ironically, this has led to a small loss in fishing revenue as people tended to prefer the taste of the marine species.

Sadly, the South Aral Sea has been abandoned to its fate. The dam prevents any overspill from the North Aral Sea entering it and, as a result, by 2007, the sea's area had shrunk to 10% of its original size, and its salinity in the remaining water had increased to over $100\,g\,dm^{-3}$. No fish at all now live in the South Aral Sea, and even marine species are unable to tolerate its high salinity. A few invertebrates that can tolerate extreme salinity survive there, but very little else.

Consequences of the destruction of the Aral Sea

The loss of the Aral Sea has had many consequences, both ecological and social.

Ecological. The South Aral Sea is now almost a 'dead sea'. No fish are left and few invertebrates. Species that depended on fish as part of the food chain are under threat. At one time more than 173 species of animal lived around the Aral Sea, including wild boar, deer, jackals and even tigers; there are now fewer than 38 species.

Human health. Toxic dust storms that contain a high proportion of salt are frequent in the area. This has led to respiratory, liver, kidney and eye diseases. Child mortality is high, at over 75 for every 1000 births. The loss of fish and food crops as a result of lack of fresh water and deposition of salt on the land has led to a loss of food, leading to malnutrition.

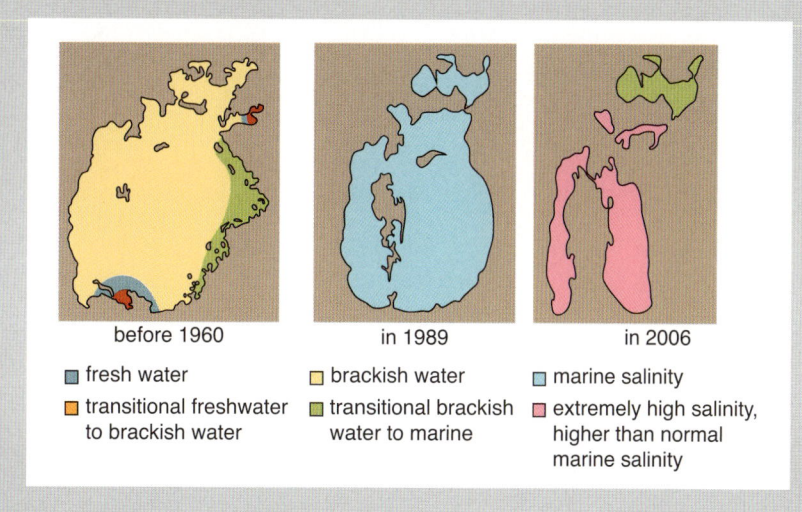

Figure 6.51: Changes in salinity of the Aral Sea over time.

> **CONTINUED**

Economic. The Aral Sea fishing industry, which once employed more than 40 000 people and accounted for a huge proportion of the total fish catch of the Soviet Union, has virtually disappeared. Wrecked fishing boats lie on the dried up land that was once covered by water. Unemployment is high, leading to poverty and population loss as so many people have left the area.

Questions

1. Summarise how human impact has led to the loss of the Aral Sea.
2. Explain the changes in salinity of the water over time as shown in Figure 6.51.
3. Explain in detail why stenohaline fresh-water fish have become extinct in the Aral Sea.
4. Explain how marine euryhaline fish were able to survive better in the Aral Sea.
5. Evaluate the impact of growing large quantities of cotton in Kazhakhstan and Uzbekhistan.

Chapter 7
Energy

LEARNING INTENTIONS

In this chapter you will learn how to:

- describe the nature of light as part of the electromagnetic spectrum
- explain the process and roles of photosynthesis in marine ecosystems
- describe photosynthesis as a two-stage process: light dependent and light independent
- describe and explain the functions of the structures in a typical chloroplast
- describe the role of primary and accessory pigments
- describe and use chromatography to separate and identify chloroplast pigments
- interpret absorption spectra of chloroplast pigments and action spectra for photosynthesis
- describe the effect of limiting factors of photosynthesis, including light intensity, wavelength of light, carbon dioxide concentration and temperature on the rate of photosynthesis
- investigate the effect of wavelength of light on the rate of photosynthesis
- describe and explain the function of chemosynthesis in hydrothermal vent food webs
- understand the process and functions of aerobic and anaerobic respiration.

BEFORE YOU START

- In Chapter 2 you learnt about hydrothermal vents. List reasons why photosynthetic organisms would not be able to live there.

- You will have studied photosynthesis, respiration and food webs in Chapter 3. Write down the basic word equations for photosynthesis and respiration and try to think of a list of all the factors that will affect their rates. Explain why photosynthesis in organisms such as seagrass is so important. If you can, compare your equations and factors with other groups. Discuss with each other why you think each factor will affect the rates.

- In Chapter 6, you learnt about the roles of the different organelles found in cells. Try to design a leaf or plant that would be able to photosynthesise as fast as possible. Think about how it will obtain all the raw materials. Explain your diagram to someone else.

THE FOUNDATIONS OF LIFE

Until around 2.45 billion years ago, there was very little oxygen gas in the oceans and atmosphere. Minerals, such as iron, were abundant and all life was anaerobic. Around this time – although the actual date is much debated – the first organisms that were able to photosynthesise evolved; they were tiny photosynthetic bacteria called cyanobacteria. These cyanobacteria lived in the oceans and gradually increased in number. They were able to trap the Sun's light energy and transform it into chemical energy by the process of photosynthesis. Oxygen and glucose are the products of photosynthesis and so, as the numbers of cyanobacteria increased, the amount of oxygen in the oceans increased. After about 1.85 billion years, the oceans became saturated with oxygen and it began to diffuse out into the atmosphere. This oxygen was absorbed by land surfaces. By about 0.85 billion years ago, the land surfaces became saturated with oxygen and the atmosphere began to fill. This massive increase of oxygen in the oceans and atmosphere is known as the Great Oxygenation Event.

The high levels of oxygen in the atmosphere seem to have had many effects. Metals, such as iron, became oxidised into minerals such as iron oxide (rust). Atmospheric methane was oxidised into carbon dioxide gas. Carbon dioxide is a weaker greenhouse gas than methane, and so as methane levels fell, the planet cooled, resulting in an ice age. There was also a huge increase in the range of biological life in the oceans and on the land. Aerobic organisms evolved, mitochondria became part of cells and aerobic respiration developed.

Photosynthesis is the key to all life on the planet. It is a process that has changed the nature of the Earth and the life on it. It could be argued that it is the most important chemical reaction on Earth.

Questions

1. Discuss whether you agree that photosynthesis is the most important chemical reaction on Earth.

2. Write down what you already know about how energy is fixed into food chains.

7.1 Photosynthesis

All food chains and food webs begin with organisms that can trap or fix energy and transform it into energy stored in organic chemicals such as carbohydrates. This ability to take inorganic molecules and use energy to create organic molecules is called **autotrophic nutrition**.

The roles of primary producers are to fix carbon and provide habitats for other organisms. Scientists have known about the role of photosynthesis in fixing energy into ecosystems for a long time, but it was only when scientists started exploring underwater in the 1970s that they discovered a different way of fixing energy. They found complex food webs around deep hydrothermal vents where there is no light. Analysis of the organisms in these vents showed that they depended on energy from the chemicals released by hydrothermal vents rather than light energy.

Producers also shape environments by fixing the substrate and providing shelters and nursery grounds (important habitats of oceanic water where young fish and other species find food and shelter from predators, such as mangroves) for other species of animal. Without producers in an ecosystem, there would be no food chain, very little atmospheric oxygen and a loss of habitat for many animals.

> **Note:** nursery grounds is extension content, and is not part of your syllabus.

The majority of primary productivity in the world's seas and oceans is the result of photosynthesis. It is the process by which green plants, photosynthetic **protoctists** such as **diatoms** and **dinoflagellates**, and photosynthetic bacteria such as cyanobacteria, gain their energy from sunlight. Organisms that transform light energy into chemical energy in the form of organic chemicals are the basis of most of the world's food webs. Without photosynthesis, there would be almost no way to bring energy into the planet's ecosystems, and life on Earth would be all but extinct.

Photosynthesis requires light energy to be trapped by pigments such as chlorophyll. This trapped energy is then used by producers to produce glucose and oxygen (as by-product) from carbon dioxide and water. The carbon dioxide is fixed into organic compounds and the energy from sunlight is transformed into chemical energy in the form of these organic compounds.

You will have already encountered the basic equation for photosynthesis in Chapter 3 as:

$$\text{carbon dioxide} + \text{water} \xrightarrow{\frac{\text{light}}{\text{chlorophyll}}} \text{glucose} + \text{oxygen}$$

For A level Marine Science, you also need to know the balanced chemical symbol equation:

$$6CO_2 + 6H_2O \xrightarrow{\frac{\text{light}}{\text{chlorophyll}}} C_6H_{12}O_6 + 6O_2$$

The cells of producers contain chloroplasts, the organelles that carry out photosynthesis.

> **KEY WORDS**
>
> **autotrophic nutrition:** the ability of an organism to make its own food by taking inorganic molecules and using energy to create organic molecules
>
> **protoctists:** a kingdom of organisms that are characterised by the presence of a nucleus and are distinct from plants, animals and fungi; it is a diverse group that includes unicellular and multicellular organisms and organisms with and without cell walls and chloroplasts
>
> **diatoms:** group of unicellular algae found in phytoplankton characterised by silica skeletons
>
> **dinoflagellates:** group of unicellular algae found in phytoplankton characterised by the presence of two flagella

Chloroplasts

We have already discussed the basic structure and functions of chloroplasts in Chapter 6. Different types of chloroplast are found in different species of producers, although they all have some common features. The structure of chloroplasts provides clues about their origins, which is thought to involve a process called endosymbiosis. All chloroplasts contain their own DNA and ribosomes and show structural similarities to a group of photosynthetic bacteria called **cyanobacteria**. It is thought that cyanobacteria were engulfed by other cells but were not broken down, so were able to live within these cells. Eventually, the cyanobacteria lost their independence and became chloroplasts.

The majority of green algae and plants have chloroplasts similar to the general structure shown in Figure 7.1.

Chloroplasts are covered with two membranes, one of which is probably a legacy of the original bacterial ancestor and the other a legacy of the ancestral host cell. Inside the chloroplast is an extensive network of membranes called thylakoids. These have stacked areas called grana, which contain the photosynthetic pigments. The thylakoid membranes are where light energy is trapped, and the extensive network ensures that a large surface area is exposed to the light. Surrounding the thylakoid membranes is a fluid called the stroma. This contains many chemicals and enzymes and is where glucose and other sugars are synthesised. The stroma also contains ribosomes, DNA and other substances, such as insoluble starch granules and lipid droplets.

The primary and accessory pigments found in producers

The thylakoid membranes contain a range of different pigments that absorb light. The **primary pigment** that is most important in photosynthesis is **chlorophyll *a***, but there are many other **accessory pigments**, including **chlorophyll *b***, the **carotenoids** and **xanthophylls**. The chlorophylls give most plants their green colour. Different species of producer often have different accessory pigments depending on their particular habitats, and this will be discussed later in this chapter.

> **KEY WORDS**
>
> **cyanobacteria:** group of photosynthetic bacteria found in marine and fresh water
>
> **primary pigment:** photosynthetic pigment that is directly involved with photosynthesis
>
> **chlorophyll (*a* and *b*):** green pigments responsible for light capture in photosynthesis in algae and plants
>
> **accessory pigment:** a pigment that is not essential for photosynthesis but that absorbs light of different wavelengths and passes the energy to chlorophyll *a*, such as chlorophyll *b*, xanthophylls and phycobilins
>
> **carotenoid:** a yellow, orange or red plant pigment used as an accessory pigment in photosynthesis
>
> **xanthophyll:** a yellow or brown plant pigment used as an accessory pigment in photosynthesis

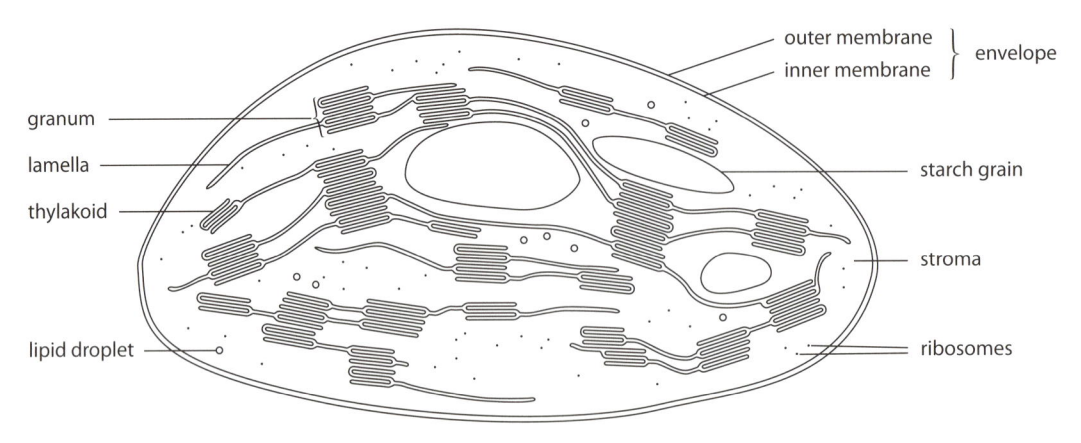

Figure 7.1: Diagram of a chloroplast found in typical green plants and algae.

7 Energy

We can separate and identify different pigments by carrying out **paper chromatography**. In chromatography, the pigments are extracted from the producers and dissolved in a solvent. The extract is then placed on a strip of chromatography paper and the wick of this placed into more solvent. As the solvent moves up the paper, the pigments dissolve and are carried up the paper. Pigments that are more soluble travel faster and so run further up the paper, as shown in Figure 7.2.

> **KEY WORD**
>
> **paper chromatography:** a technique used to separate substances by their solubility

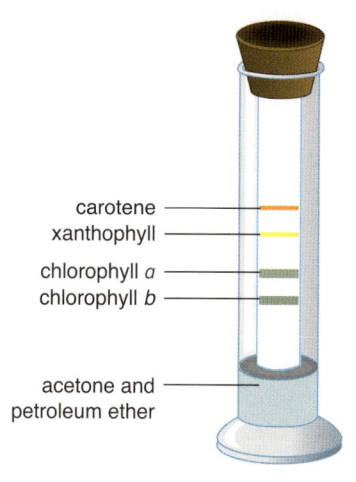

Figure 7.2: Separation of photosynthetic pigments by chromatography.

CORE PRACTICAL ACTIVITY 7.1: SEPARATING OUT PHOTOSYNTHETIC PIGMENTS BY CHROMATOGRAPHY

Introduction

There are many chromatography techniques that can be used to extract and separate out the photosynthetic pigments from marine algae, some more complex than others. This method can be adapted for different solvents. In this practical you will separate out the pigments from a green plant such as grass.

Equipment:

You will need:

- 250 cm³ beaker (or similar sized glass jar)
- very fine bore pipette or glass capillary tube
- about 10 g washed sand
- chromatography paper (such as Whatman's number 1), which should be cut into strips that are long enough to hang into the base of the beaker with the top folded
- 50 cm³ propanone
- 10 cm³ chromatography solvent (a 1 : 9 mixture of propanone to petroleum ether (boiling point 100–120 °C); the two substances are mixed in a ratio of one propanone : nine petroleum spirit, by volume)
- about 1 g of plant material (for example, grass or seaweed), which should be as fresh as possible
- scissors
- pestle and mortar
- pencil
- ruler
- splint or straw.

Safety considerations

Petroleum ether (boiling point 80–100 °C) is highly flammable, so no naked flames should be present. It is toxic to aquatic life and can have long-term effects on aquatic life so waste solvent should be collected and disposed of appropriately. It is toxic by inhalation or ingestion so should only be used in a well-ventilated area. It may cause drowsiness or dizziness if inhaled. It is an irritant so eye protection should be worn at all times.

Propanone is flammable and an irritant, so no naked flames should be present and safety glasses must be worn, particularly when grinding.

Capillary tubes are made of thin glass, which is easy to break and get in your eyes. Safety glasses should be worn, and care should be taken when handling them.

Before you start

1. List the primary and accessory pigments found in producers.
2. How will you identify each different pigment?

CONTINUED

Method

1. Using the scissors, cut up the grass or other producer into small pieces and place them into the mortar.

2. Add a few pinches of washed sand and, using the pestle, grind the grass until a pulp is produced.

3. Add between 4 and 8 cm^3 propanone and continue grinding until a dark green solution begins to form. If the solution is pale, add more grass and continue to grind. If the pulp has little free solution, add more propanone.

4. When a dark green solution of propanone is produced, leave the mixture to settle for about one minute. If a centrifuge is available, the propanone can be decanted into centrifuged tubes and the solid debris 'spun down' to remove it, leaving a very clear propanone solution.

5. Take the chromatography paper and draw a pencil line 20 mm from the base of the paper.

6. Using the fine pipette or capillary tube, draw up a small quantity of the pigment extract from the mortar and carefully make a spot in the centre of the pencil line on the paper. Dry the spot for a few seconds and repeat the process in exactly the same place. The aim is to place as much pigment in as small a spot as possible. If the paper is not allowed to dry, the solution will diffuse across the paper, making the spot too large.

7. Place a small amount of chromatography solvent into the beaker and suspend the chromatography paper into the solvent taped onto the splint or straw, as shown in Figure 7.3. It is essential that the solvent does not rise over the spot. The experiment should now be left until the pigments have separated.

8. When the pigments have separated clearly, use a pencil to mark the highest distance that the solvent has reached.

9. Remove the chromatography paper and leave it to dry.

R_f **values** need to be calculated to identify the pigments. The R_f value of a pigment is a measure of the distance it will move compared with the solvent. Each pigment has a specific R_f value for a particular solvent. To calculate R_f values, use a ruler to measure the distance that the solvent has moved from the origin and then measure the distance the centre of each spot of pigment has travelled.

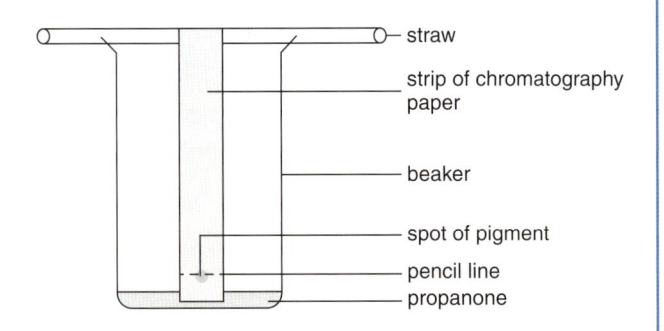

Figure 7.3: Setting up the chromatography paper in solvent.

The R_f value is calculated using the formula:

$$R_f = \frac{\text{distance moved by pigment}}{\text{distance moved by solvent}}$$

Use Table 7.1 of standard R_f values for pigments separated in propanone to identify each pigment.

Pigment	Colour	R_f value
chlorophyll *a*	green	0.45
chlorophyll *b*	blue-green	0.65
xanthophyll	yellow-brown	0.71
phaeophytin	grey	0.83
carotene	yellow	0.95

Table 7.1: R_f values for different pigments in propanone solvent.

KEY WORD

R_f **value:** the distance travelled by a substance on a chromatogram divided by the distance travelled by the solvent front

7 Energy

> **CONTINUED**
>
> **Evaluation and conclusions**
>
> 1 Use Table 7.1 to identify each pigment on your chromatograph.
> 2 Explain why you drew the line with pencil rather than ink.
> 3 Explain why the R_f values are not affected by the length of time that you run the experiment for.
> 4 Explain why having a longer piece of chromatography paper would make it easier to identify different pigments.
> 5 Suggest how the results would differ if different species of marine algae and seaweed were used.

> **REFLECTION**
>
> After completing Core Practical Activity 7.1, discuss with other learners how this experiment could be used to investigate how pigment concentrations change with different ages of algae.

Absorption and action spectra

Visible light is part of the **electromagnetic spectrum** which is shown in Figure 7.4. The visible part of the spectrum has wavelengths between 380 nm and 750 nm. Different colours of light have different wavelengths. 'White light' is a mixture of light of all the different visible wavelengths. The different pigments found in producers absorb light wavelengths of slightly different colours. The **absorption spectrum** of a pigment shows the amount of light of each wavelength that a particular pigment absorbs.

The absorption spectra of chlorophylls a and b and carotene are shown in Figure 7.5. The graph shows clearly the two peak areas of absorption of both chlorophylls around the blue and red ends of the spectrum. Most plants are green in colour because they reflect or transmit green light but absorb light in the red and blue areas of the spectrum. The overall absorption

> **KEY WORDS**
>
> **electromagnetic spectrum:** the range of frequencies and wavelengths of all types of electromagnetic radiation; the electromagnetic spectrum includes visible, ultraviolet and infra-red light, microwaves, X rays, radio waves and gamma waves
>
> **absorption spectrum:** a graph of the absorbance of different wavelengths of light by a compound such as a photosynthetic pigment

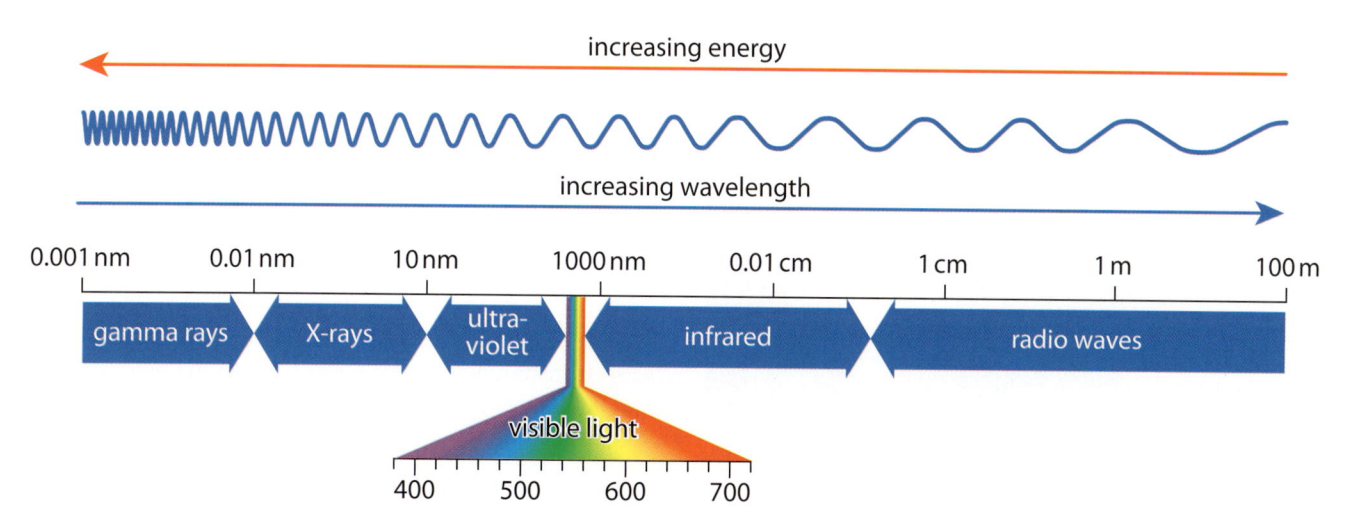

Figure 7.4: The electromagnetic spectrum showing the wavelengths of the different colours of visible light.

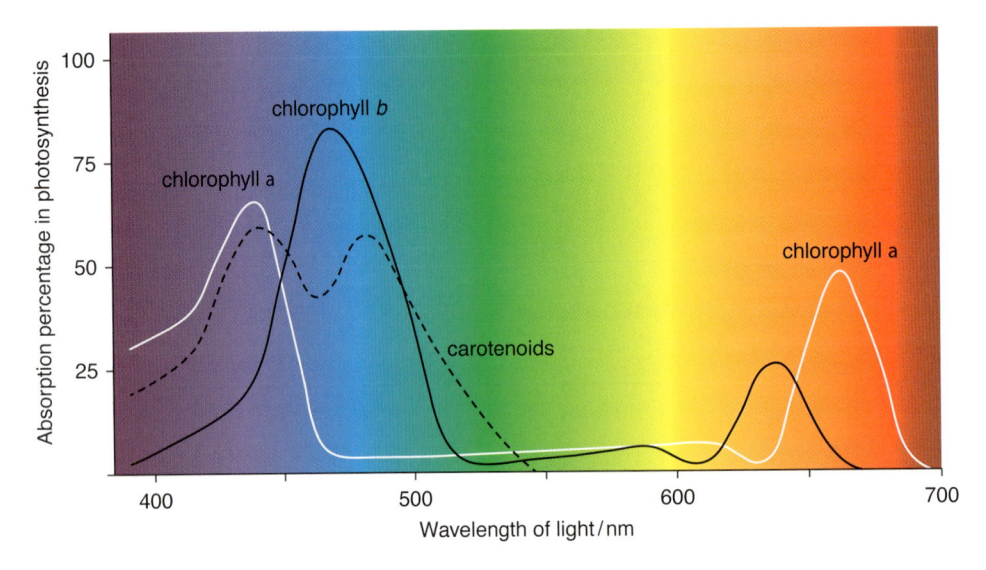

Figure 7.5: Absorption spectra of chlorophyll *a*, chlorophyll *b* and carotenoids.

spectrum of a particular producer will be the combined absorption spectra of all its pigments.

An **action spectrum** shows the actual effect of different light wavelengths on the rate of photosynthesis. It can be obtained by measuring the rate of photosynthesis of a producer at different light intensities. The shapes of action and absorption spectra are usually the same. This means that the light wavelengths used in photosynthesis are the same ones that are absorbed (Figures 7.5 and 7.6). Details of a simple practical for seeing this are given later.

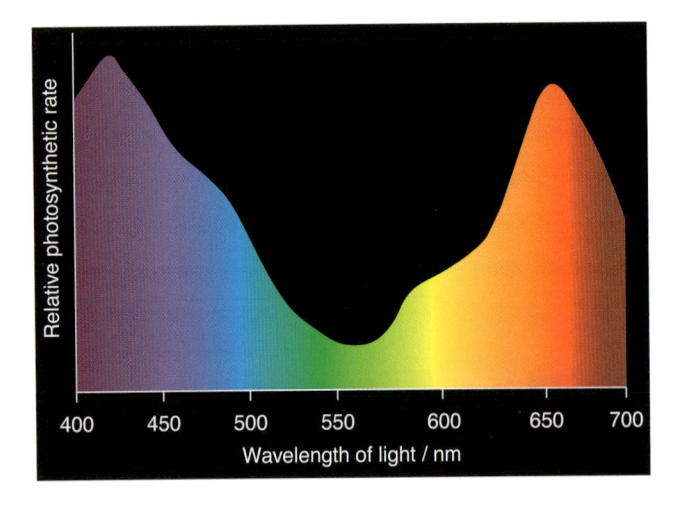

Figure 7.6: Photosynthetic action spectrum for a typical producer.

The pigments present in different species of marine primary producers are linked to the depth of water that they inhabit. Different light wavelengths penetrate to different depths in the water, so the wavelengths of light available to a particular producer depend on the depth it inhabits.

> **KEY WORD**
>
> **action spectrum:** a graph showing the effect of different wavelengths of light on a process, such as the rate of photosynthesis

Light penetration in water: wavelength and turbidity

There are two main factors that affect how deep in the water light can penetrate:

- the wavelength, or colour, of light
- the amount of particulate material, known as turbidity, in the water. (Turbidity is the level of transparency loss water has due to the presence of suspended particles in the water; the higher the turbidity, the harder it is to see through the water.)

Light wavelength

Light penetration is a measure of how far light will pass through water. Figure 7.7 shows the maximum depths to which different wavelengths of light penetrate. It also demonstrates that all wavelengths of light penetrate further in less turbid, open ocean waters than coastal waters.

Blue light reaches the deepest parts of the ocean, up to a maximum depth of about 200 m, while red light penetrates the least and is absorbed by the surface water within the first 10 m. Any producers living below 10 m only receive light from the blue and green areas of the spectrum. Chlorophylls a and b and carotene absorb very little light from the green area of the spectrum, which creates a potential problem. Red and brown algae are adapted to live in these depths, possessing accessory pigments such as xanthophyll and a group of pigments called **phycobilins**. Phycobilins are pigments that are bound to proteins, forming protein–pigment complexes called phycobiliproteins. There are several different phycobiliproteins. The main two phycobiliproteins are **phycoerythrin** and **phycocyanin**; their absorption spectra are shown in Figure 7.8.

These accessory pigments enable red and brown algae to absorb light from the yellow and green areas of the spectrum. This increases their rate of photosynthesis in depths where there is no red light. Red and brown algae with these pigments are able to compete and survive better at these depths than green algae, which lack these accessory pigments.

Turbidity

Large amounts of sediment, particles or even living organisms such as plankton, reduce light penetration because they reduce the **light intensity**, or brightness, of light. The cloudiness or clarity of the water is known as turbidity. Estuarine and coastal water generally has a greater turbidity than open ocean water, so light is less able to penetrate to lower depths (Figure 7.7). Light penetration can easily be measured by using a piece of apparatus called a Secchi disc. This is a white 30 cm circular metal or plastic disc attached to a rope. The disc is lowered into the water until it is no longer visible,

> **KEY WORDS**
>
> **light penetration:** the depth to which light can penetrate into a material
>
> **phycobilins:** a group a light absorbing pigments that are found in red algae and cyanobacteria; it includes phycoerythrin and phycocyanin
>
> **phycoerythrin:** a red accessory pigment that is frequently found in red algae
>
> **phycocyanin:** a blue-green accessory pigment that is found in some marine algae
>
> **light intensity:** a measure of the strength or brightness of light

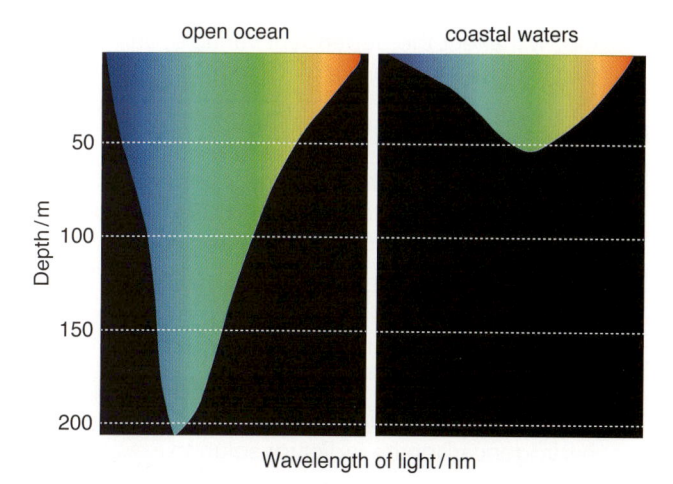

Figure 7.7: Penetration of different light wavelengths in clear ocean waters and turbid coastal waters.

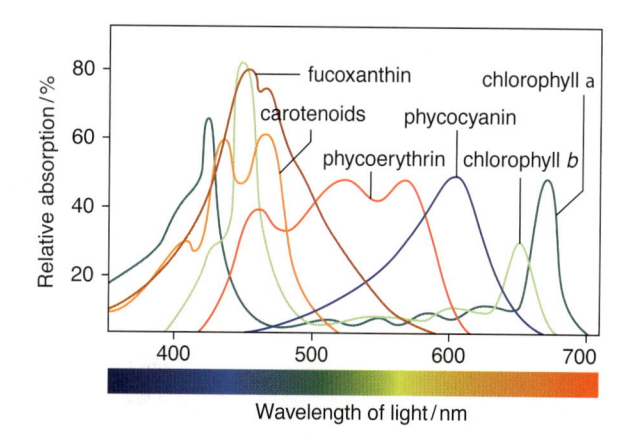

Figure 7.8: Absorption spectra of chlorophylls a and b, fucoxanthin (a xanthophyll found in algae), carotenoids, phycoerythrin and phycocyanin.

and the length of rope recorded. The disc is then raised and the length of rope when the disc becomes visible measured (Figure 7.9). An average distance is then calculated using the two values.

In areas of ocean with high turbidity and low light penetration, producers are less able to live at lower depths because they are unable to photosynthesise.

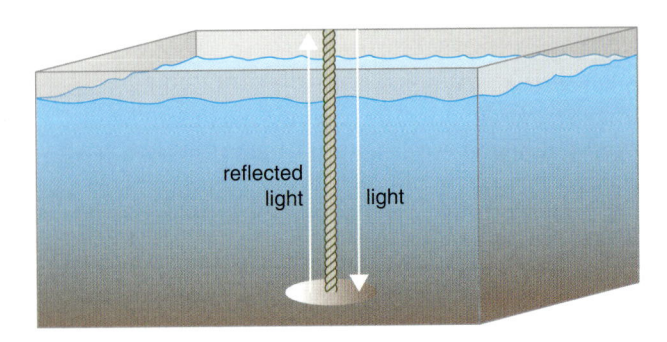

Figure 7.9: Use of a marine Secchi disc to detect water turbidity.

CORE PRACTICAL ACTIVITY 7.2: THE EFFECT OF LIGHT WAVELENGTH (COLOUR) ON PHOTOSYNTHESIS RATE

Introduction

The wavelength of light affects the rate of photosynthesis by a producer. In this practical, you will investigate how different wavelengths of light alter the rate of photosynthesis of an aquatic plant. The rate of photosynthesis of aquatic plants is easy to determine as they will release bubbles of oxygen at a rate that is dependent on the rate of photosynthesis. The pigments present in the plant you are using will affect the wavelengths (colours) of light that are absorbed and so affect the rate of photosynthesis.

Equipment:

You will need:

- fresh, healthy pondweed with good quality leaves; *Cabomba* is the best plant to use and is usually available from aquatic shops; if *Cabomba* is not available, *Elodea densa*, *Elodea canadensis* or *Chara* can be used (note, in some countries, some of these species may be considered to be invasive species and so will not be available)
- boiling tube
- bench lamp
- 250 cm³ of 1% sodium hydrogencarbonate solution
- coloured cellophane (red, blue, orange, yellow and green)
- boiling tube rack
- dissecting scissors.

Safety considerations

There is a risk of cold water being splashed onto the hot light bulb causing the glass to shatter, so safety glasses should be worn.

Before you start

1. Discuss the independent variable and how it could be changed.
2. Discuss the dependent variable and how it could be measured.
3. Discuss the control variables (other variables that will affect the dependent variable) and how they can be kept constant.

Method

1. Take an approximately 5 cm long piece of *Cabomba* with one cut stem and carefully cut the cut end of the stem at a 45° angle.
2. Place the *Cabomba* into the boiling tube with the cut end pointing upwards. It may be necessary to weigh the plant down with a paper clip.
3. Cover the plant entirely with 1% sodium hydrogencarbonate indicator solution.
4. Place the boiling tube in the boiling tube rack and place the lamp 10 cm away from the boiling tube.

CONTINUED

5. Switch on the lamp and switch off all other lighting in the room (there needs to be a reasonable gap between any other experiments going on and all the main lighting in the room should be turned off and any blinds or curtains drawn).
6. Leave the plant illuminated for 5 min; during this time check that it is producing a stream of bubbles from the cut end of the stem. The rate will vary between different plants.
7. Count the bubbles that emerge from the end of the stem for an appropriate period of time (for example, 1–5 min). If the stream of bubbles is rapid, use a shorter time period; for a slower stream of bubbles, increase the time. Record the number of bubbles and the time period.
8. Record the number of bubbles for two more time periods. There is no need to wait between readings.
9. Repeat the experiment after wrapping cellophane of different colours around the boiling tube. Each time the cellophane colour is changed, the plant will need 5 min to adjust to the colour of light.

Results

1. Copy Table 7.2 and enter your results, calculating the mean rates of bubble production.
2. Produce an appropriate graph of the results. You will need to decide whether to draw a bar chart or line graph.

Colour of light	Number of bubbles of oxygen counted	Time period	Rate of production of oxygen / bubbles min^{-1}
'white'			
red			
orange			
yellow			
green			
blue			

Table 7.2: Results table for effect of light colour on the rate of photosynthesis.

Evaluation and conclusions

1. Why was it important to wait 5 min before beginning a count with a new colour?
2. Describe and explain the pattern shown by your graph. Ensure that you include references to the absorption of light and the photosynthetic pigments.
3. Figure 7.10 shows a more accurate method of determining rate of photosynthesis. Explain why it would produce more accurate results than the method you have used.
4. Suggest how you could modify this experiment to investigate the effect of light intensity on rate of photosynthesis.

> **CONTINUED**

Figure 7.10: A photosynthometer (also called the Audus apparatus).

> **REFLECTION**
>
> After completing Core Practical Activity 7.2, think about the following: In the ocean, red light is absorbed by the surface water. Brown and red algae are adapted to survive in deeper water. Green algae, which generally possess the same pigments found in *Cabomba*, are largely restricted to the surface water. Consider how you could extend this experiment to investigate how these different types of algae are able to live at different depths.

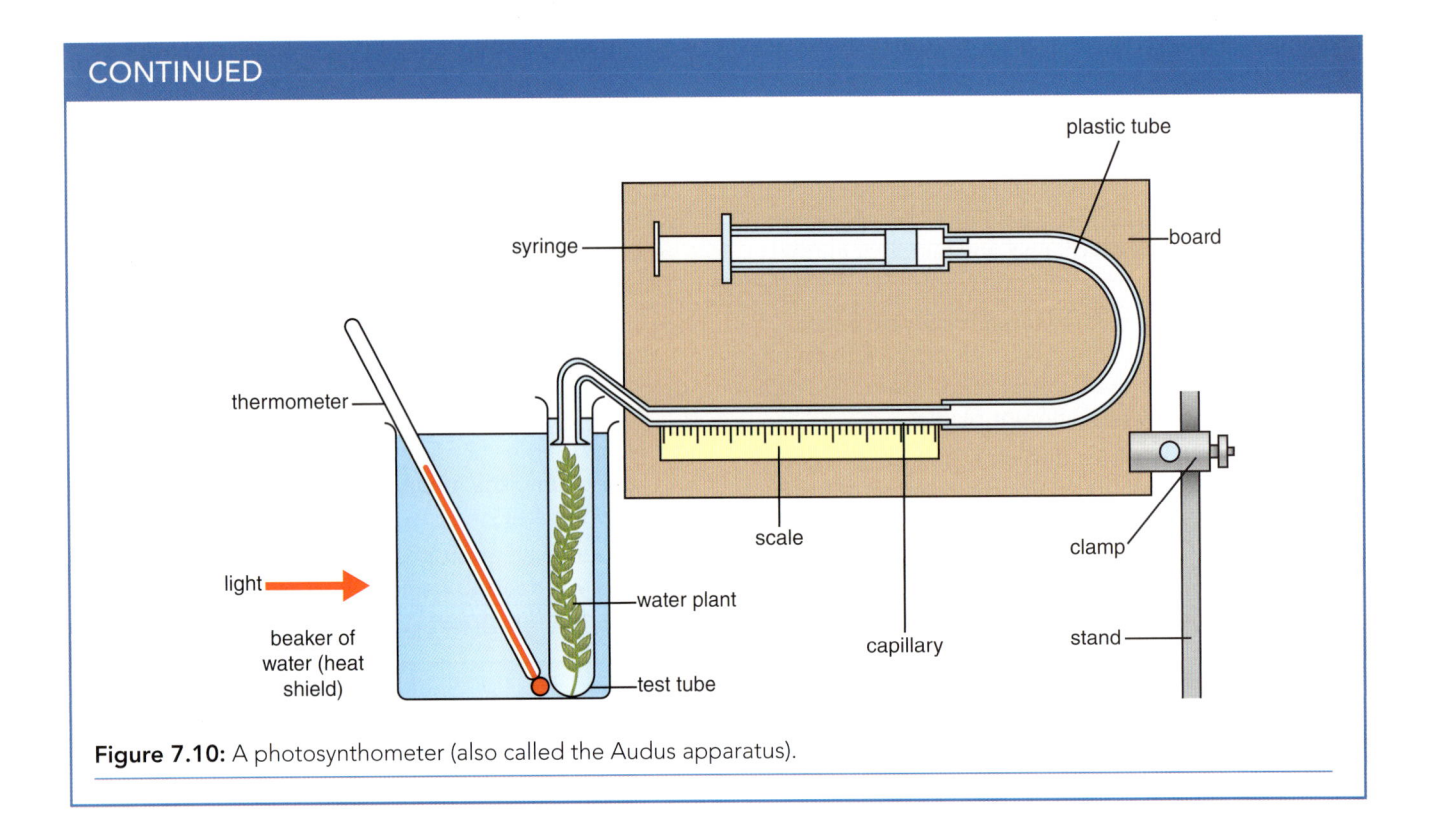

Stages in the process of photosynthesis

We have already looked at the basic equations for photosynthesis. In reality, it is a very complicated series of reactions that involves the trapping of light energy into a form it can be used to transfer to glucose. There are two main stages which have different functions:

- **light dependent stage**
- **light independent stage**.

Light dependent stage

The light dependent stage takes place in the grana of the thylakoid membranes. Its function is to trap as much light energy as possible and transform it to a form of chemical energy that can be used to make glucose. The grana contain primary and accessory pigments embedded in their membranes in clusters called **photosystems**. When chlorophyll *a*, the primary pigment,

> **KEY WORDS**
>
> **light dependent stage:** the stage in photosynthesis whereby light energy is harvested; occurs in the thylakoid membranes of chloroplasts and produces ATP and reduced NADP
>
> **light independent stage:** the stage in photosynthesis whereby carbon dioxide is converted into glucose by the Calvin cycle; occurs in the stroma of chloroplasts
>
> **photosystem:** a collection of photosynthetic pigments located in the thylakoid membrane; responsible for the absorption of light energy

absorbs light energy it undergoes **photoactivation**. The molecule loses an electron; in other words, it is oxidised (losing electrons: **oxidation**, gaining electrons: **reduction**). Because the electron loss was due to the trapping of light, we call this, **photooxidation**.

chlorophyll *a* → oxidised chlorophyll + electron

The energy from the light that was absorbed is 'carried' by the electron. The energy 'carried' by the electron is then used to create two substances in a series of complicated reactions:

- **adenosine triphosphate (ATP)** from **adenosine diphosphate (ADP)** + **phosphate (P_i)** (this is explained later in this chapter):

$$\left\{ ADP + P_i \xrightarrow{\text{energy from electron}} ATP \right\}$$

- reduced **nicotinamide adenine dinucleotide phosphate (NADP)** produced by an enzyme that takes oxidised NADP and adds the electron to it:

NAPD (oxidised) + electron ⇌ NAPD (reduced)

This means that the energy that came from the light has been transferred to electrons and ultimately to two energy rich molecules: ATP and reduced NADP.

After being oxidised, chlorophyll *a* has lost an electron and needs to replace it before it can repeat the process. It obtains electrons from water in a process called **photolysis**.

The term photolysis means splitting up using light. Water will naturally dissociate into oxygen gas, hydrogen ions (H^+) and electrons:

$$2H_2O \rightarrow O_2 + 4H^+ + \text{four electrons}$$

A common misconception is that shining light on water will make it undergo photolysis – this is not true. If more light is given to chlorophyll *a*, it will cause more electrons to be energised and released. This causes the chlorophyll *a* to 'grab' more electrons from water, driving the photolysis of water faster. This means that oxygen is produced as a by-product more quickly.

To summarise the light dependent stage:

- Its function is to harvest light energy and convert it into chemical energy.
- The energy is given to two molecules, ATP and reduced NADP.
- Photolysis of water provides electrons to replace those lost by oxidised chlorophyll *a*.
- Oxygen is released as a by-product of photolysis.

Light independent stage

The light independent stage is the second stage of photosynthesis. It is where the energy (ATP and reduced NADP) that has been harvested in the light dependent stage is used to make glucose by **carbon dioxide fixation**. It takes place in the stroma of the chloroplast. A complicated series of chemical reactions, called the **Calvin cycle** (Figure 7.11), is used to make glucose.

KEY WORDS

photoactivation: the activation of chlorophyll by light

oxidation: a chemical reaction in which an atom loses electrons

reduction: a chemical reaction in which an atom gains electrons

photooxidation: the loss of electrons due to the absorption of light energy.

adenosine triphosphate (ATP): an organic molecule that provides energy to drive many processes in living cells; when broken down into ADP (adenosine diphosphate) and phosphate (P_i), it releases energy for cellular processes

adenosine diphosphate (ADP): an organic molecule that when combined with phosphate (P_i) during respiration produces ATP

phosphate (P_i): a compound made from phosphorus and oxygen that is combined with ADP to form ATP

nicotinamide adenine dinucleotide phosphate (NADP): a molecule that is reduced during the light dependent reaction; reduced NADPH is then used in the light independent reaction to transform GP into TP

photolysis: the process of the breakdown of water into hydrogen and oxygen due to the effect of light during the light dependent reaction of photosynthesis

carbon dioxide fixation (carbon fixation): the conversion of inorganic carbon dioxide into organic compounds such as glucose

Calvin cycle: the series of reactions that occur during the light independent stage of photosynthesis; it converts carbon dioxide and other substances into glucose

During the Calvin cycle, carbon containing molecules are converted through a range of different forms. Although you do not need to learn the names of all the different intermediate compounds shown in Figure 7.11, it will help your understanding to see the whole process.

The stages in the Calvin cycle are:

- Carbon dioxide is combined with a sugar called **ribulose biphosphate (RuBP)**. RuBP is a sugar with five carbon atoms and two phosphates. The enzyme that joins these two things together is called **rubisco** (ribulose biphosphate carboxylase oxygenase – just learning rubisco is fine).
- Joining carbon dioxide (one carbon atom) with RuBP (five carbon atoms) makes a sugar with six carbon atoms – this is very unstable and breaks down into two sugars with three carbons called glycerate phosphate (GP). (GP is intermediate compound produced in the Calvin cycle from the combining of carbon dioxide and RuBP).
- GP is converted into a different sugar (with three carbons) called triose phosphate (TP) (intermediate compound produced in the Calvin cycle from the reduction of GP; it is used to produce glucose and reform RuBP) by using the energy from ATP and NADPH.
- Some of the TP is used to make glucose while the rest is used to make a new sugar called ribulose phosphate (RuP) (intermediate compound in the Calvin cycle that is phosphorylated by ATP to produce RuBP). RuP is a five-carbon sugar with one phosphate.
- The RuP is given another phosphate by more ATP to make RuBP. The RuBP can then repeat the Calvin cycle with fresh carbon dioxide.

Tip: Some of the chemicals have long and complex names. It is fine to use abbreviations such as NADP, DNA and ATP.

> **KEY WORDS**
>
> **ribulose biphosphate (RuBP):** an organic molecule that is used in the light independent stage of photosynthesis; combined with carbon dioxide as part of the Calvin cycle
>
> **rubisco:** enzyme that is involved in the first step of the Calvin cycle; it catalyses the reaction between carbon dioxide and RuBP

Note: intermediate compounds in Calvin cycles and glycerate phosphate (GP) are extension content, and are not part of your syllabus.

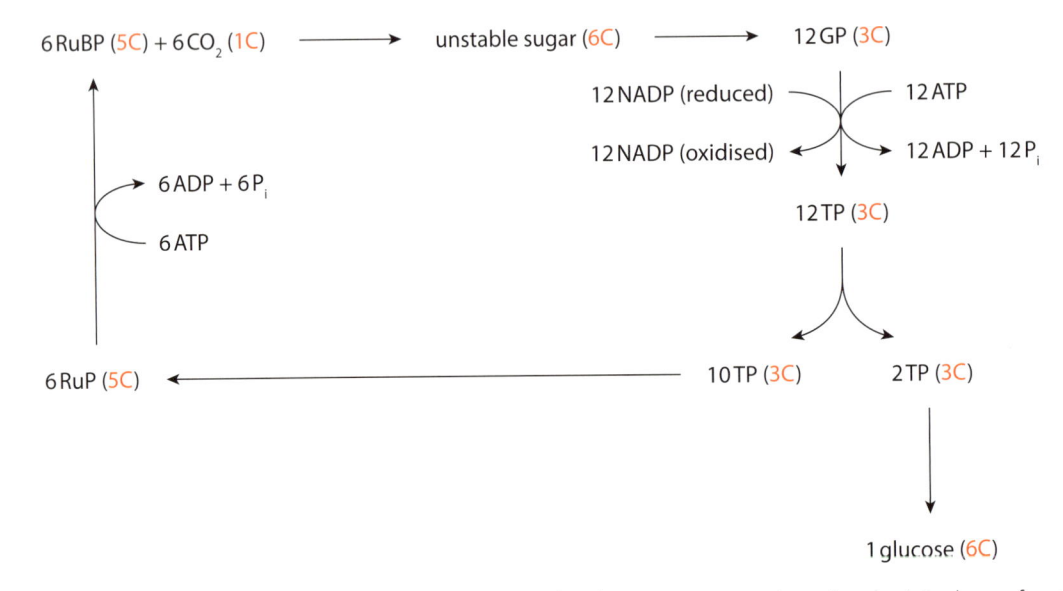

$6\,\text{RuBP (5C)} + 6\,CO_2\,\text{(1C)} \longrightarrow \text{unstable sugar (6C)} \longrightarrow 12\,\text{GP (3C)}$

12 NADP (reduced) / 12 ATP
12 NADP (oxidised) / 12 ADP + 12 P_i

12 TP (3C)

6 ADP + 6 P_i / 6 ATP

6 RuP (5C) ← 10 TP (3C)   2 TP (3C) → 1 glucose (6C)

Figure 7.11: The Calvin cycle. Numbers in red are the number of carbon atoms in each molecule. It is shown for six carbon atoms so that the equations balance.

7 Energy

To summarise the light independent stage:
- It uses the energy from ATP and reduced NADP that were produced in the light dependent stage.
- The enzyme rubisco combines carbon dioxide with RuBP.
- It fixes carbon dioxide and makes glucose.
- The energy from light ends up in the glucose.

The glucose that is produced can be used to make a whole variety of organic molecules. It is directly used to make carbohydrates such as starch and cellulose. It is combined with mineral ions, such as nitrates, to make molecules such as amino acids.

Limiting factors, productivity and photosynthesis

Productivity and depth of water

There are three distinct zones in marine waters that relate to the depth of light penetration and productivity. The upper layer of water, where there is high light penetration, is called the euphotic zone. This zone may extend to about 200 m in clear water or only about 5 m in turbid water. Producers are able to photosynthesise effectively in this zone. Below the euphotic zone is the disphotic zone, often referred to as the twilight zone. This zone has some blue light but at a low intensity and ranges from between 15 m in highly turbid water to 1000 m in very clear water. No producers are found here, despite the presence of some light. Below the disphotic zone is the aphotic zone, where less than 1% of the surface light reaches. There are no producers here that use photosynthesis as a method of primary productivity. The zones are shown in Figure 7.12.

To understand why there are no producers in the disphotic zone, despite the presence of light, you need to consider the processes of photosynthesis and respiration.

If you look at the basic equations for photosynthesis and respiration, it becomes clear that they are exact opposites.

Photosynthesis: $6CO_2 + 6H_2O \rightarrow C_6H_{12}O_6 + 6O_2$

Respiration: $C_6H_{12}O_6 + 6O_2 \rightarrow 6CO_2 + 6H_2O$

Photosynthesis builds up glucose, which has energy from light locked into it. The glucose is converted into other compounds, such as starch and protein, which are used for storage and growth. Respiration releases the energy in the glucose by oxidation.

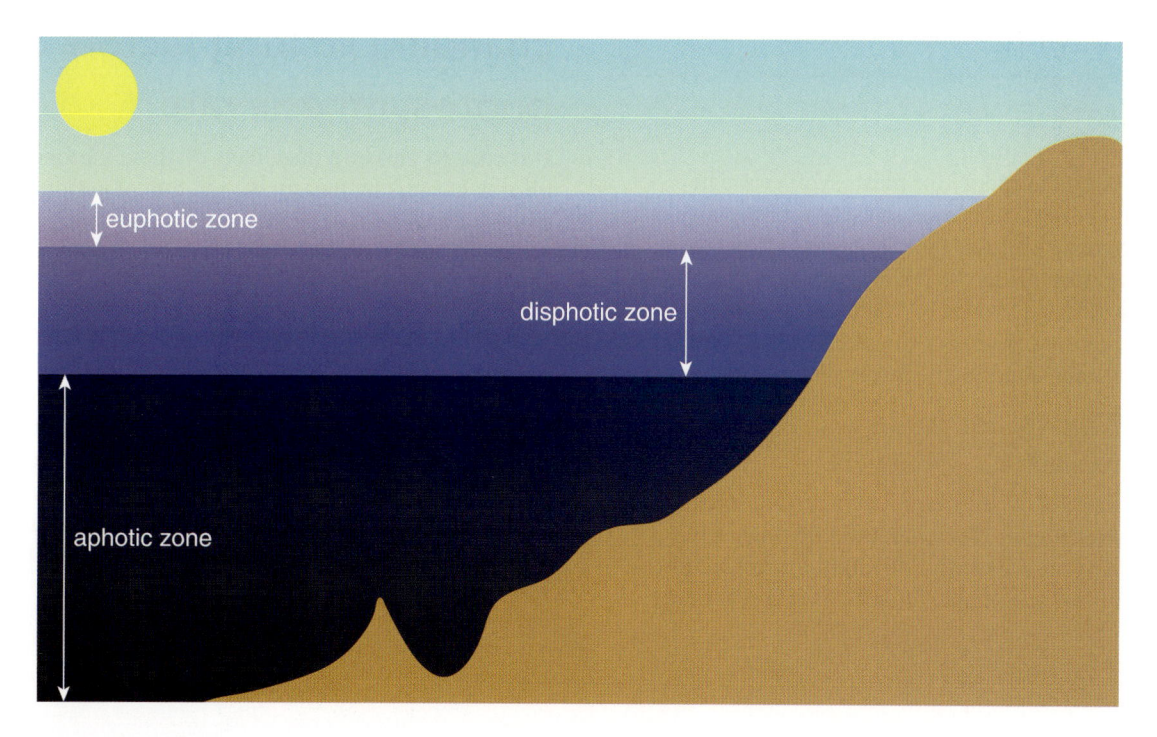

Figure 7.12: The euphotic, disphotic and aphotic zones of the ocean.

Factors affecting the rate of photosynthesis and the law of limiting factors

Several external factors affect the rate of photosynthesis, including:

- light intensity
- light wavelength
- temperature
- carbon dioxide concentration.

As these abiotic factors affect the rate of photosynthesis, they affect the distribution of marine producers. In order to maximise photosynthesis, a plant must be exposed to sufficient light intensity of appropriate wavelengths, must be kept at a relatively warm temperature and must be supplied with sufficient carbon dioxide and water. In practice, the factors that are in the least supply restrict the rate of photosynthesis: this is the law of **limiting factors**.

> **KEY WORD**
>
> **limiting factor:** the one factor, of many affecting a process, that is nearest its lowest value and hence is rate limiting; photosynthesis rate is usually limited by light intensity, temperature and/or carbon dioxide concentration

Light intensity

Light provides the energy for photosynthesis. The more light energy that is available, the more energy can be used to make glucose. Light energy is absorbed by chlorophyll and this harvested energy is used to combine carbon dioxide with water to make sugars. The higher the light intensity, the faster the rate of photosynthesis. This can be measured by the increasing rate of oxygen production.

Light wavelength

As you have already seen, producers contain pigments that absorb the light. Depending on the pigments present, different wavelengths of light are absorbed. Most producers are unable to absorb certain colours of light, such as green. Many contain accessory pigments, such as phycoerythrin, phycocyanin and xanthophyll, which enable them to absorb additional light wavelengths.

Temperature

A suitable temperature is essential to maximise the rate of photosynthesis. Carbon dioxide and water molecules are combined by the action of enzymes. These molecules constantly move in random directions and react when they collide with each other. As the temperature rises, kinetic energy (the energy of movement) increases, so they move faster. Faster moving particles collide more frequently, so photosynthesis becomes faster. If the temperature rises too high, the enzymes denature, causing the reaction to slow down to almost zero.

Carbon dioxide concentration

Carbon dioxide and water are the essential raw materials for photosynthesis. If they are in short supply, the rate of photosynthesis is reduced. If their concentrations increase, they collide more frequently with the enzymes involved in photosynthesis, and the rate of photosynthesis increases. In practice, water is not considered to be a limiting factor because it is rarely in short supply.

Measuring the effects of changing limiting factors on photosynthesis rate

It is easy to measure the effects of these factors on photosynthesis by measuring the rate of production of oxygen by an aquatic plant such as *Cabomba*.

A typical experimental setup is shown in Figure 7.10. The water plant is placed into a boiling tube in a solution of sodium hydrogencarbonate, which provides a source of carbon dioxide for photosynthesis. The cut end of the stem is arranged below a capillary tube so that oxygen produced by photosynthesis collects in the tube. The plastic tube and capillary are also filled with sodium hydrogencarbonate. The tube containing the plant is placed into a water bath and a light source is placed next to it. The beaker of water prevents the lamp heating up the plant.

When oxygen has been collected for a set period of time, the syringe is used to draw up the bubble of oxygen and line it up against the scale so that the length of it can be measured. The limiting factors can be changed using methods shown in Table 7.3.

Limiting factor	Method of altering factor
light intensity	set light source at different, measured, distances from plant
light wavelength	place coloured filters in front of light source
temperature	change temperature of water bath and measure with thermometer
carbon dioxide concentration	alter concentration of sodium hydrogencarbonate solution

Table 7.3: Altering different limiting factors.

Figure 7.13 shows how you can present the effects of changing limiting factors.

Figure 7.13(a) shows the effect of increasing light intensity and temperature on the rate of photosynthesis of a producer. Over section X of the graph, the rate of photosynthesis increases as the light intensity increases at both 5 °C and 15 °C. This means that over these light intensities, the light intensity must have been the limiting factor.

At Y on the graph, increasing the light intensity at 5 °C has no more effect on the rate of photosynthesis as the graph has now levelled off. This means that light is no longer a limiting factor and something else must be. Increasing the temperature to 15 °C from 5 °C increases the rate of photosynthesis, so at point Y temperature must be the limiting factor.

In Figure 7.13(b), you can see that increasing the concentration of carbon dioxide has a similar effect as increasing the light intensity on the rate of photosynthesis.

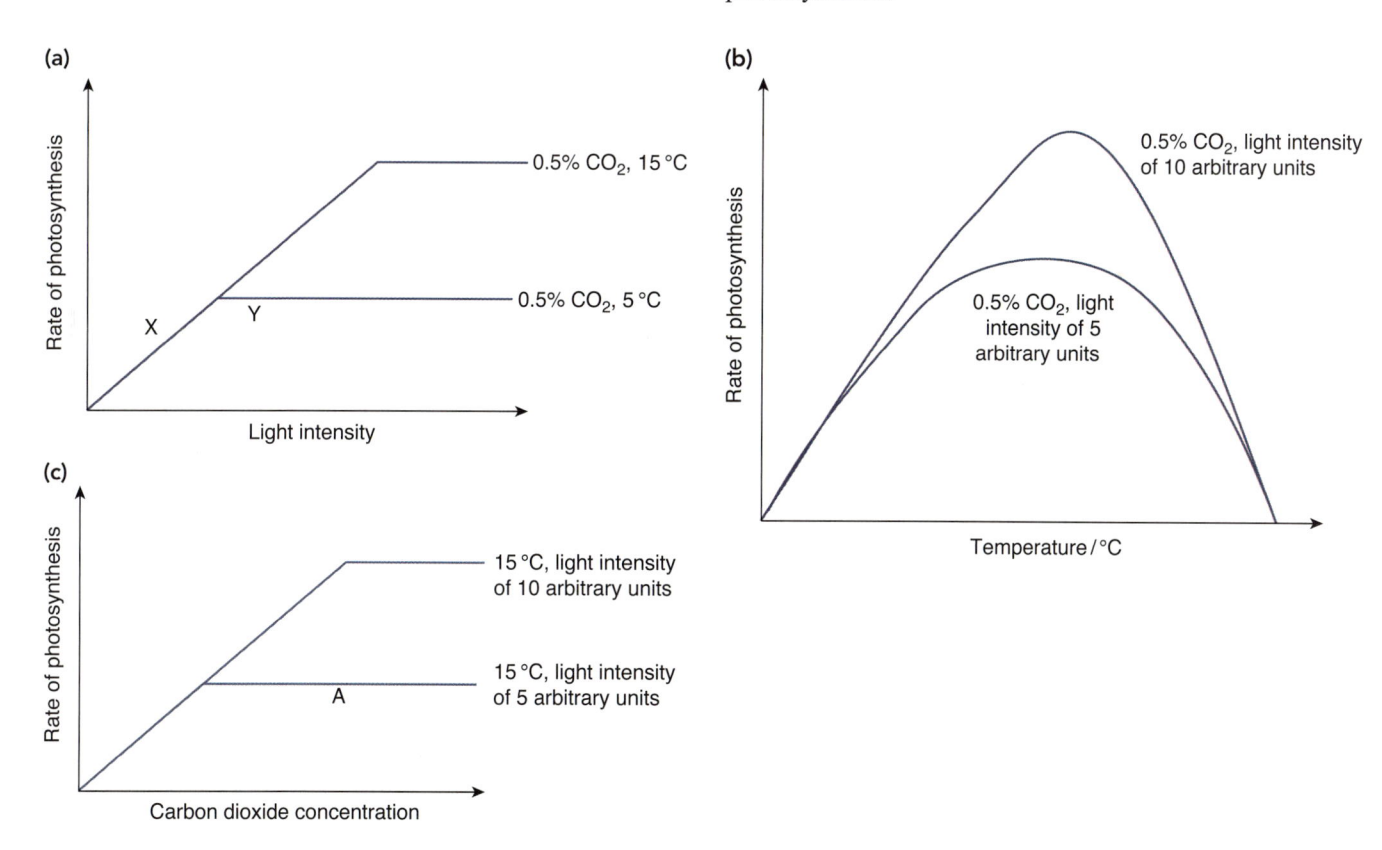

Figure 7.13: The effects of increasing (a) light intensity, (b) temperature and (c) carbon dioxide concentration on the rate of photosynthesis.

The effect of increasing temperature gives a slightly different shaped graph (Figure 7.13c). As the temperature increases, the rate of photosynthesis increases until another factor limits the rate of photosynthesis. If the temperature continues to rise, however, the rate of photosynthesis eventually drops. Causes enzymes to **denature**.

> ### KEY WORD
>
> **Denature:** the loss of shape of enzymes, resulting in a loss of activity; usually the result of heating to a high temperature

An understanding of limiting factors can help you understand how producer growth increases under certain climatic conditions. For optimal growth, marine producers require a high light intensity for a long period of time, high carbon dioxide levels and a warm temperature. Phytoplanktonic blooms often occur when these conditions are optimal and primary productivity increases rapidly. These phytoplanktonic blooms underpin many food chains: marine species, such as whales, have migration patterns that ensure their arrival at a particular location at the time when the blooms occur to maximise productivity.

CASE STUDY 7.1 THE USES OF SEAWEEDS

Humans have harvested seaweed for thousands of years. Some of the reasons for harvesting and farming them are obvious, but there are many others that you would not guess. These include:

Food

Seaweeds have been used as food by coastal communities for years in many countries such as Japan, Korea, Iceland and Wales. In Japan, over 20 species of seaweed are used as food and the red algae species *Porphyra* is dried to make sheets of nori, commonly used as the wrapping for sushi rolls. Nutritionally, seaweed is rich in protein, many vitamins and mineral salts, especially iodine, and is very low in fat.

Gels and emulsifiers

Seaweed is used as a source of three substances that are used to make solid gels and emulsifiers that hold food substances in suspension: alginate, agar and carrageenan. Alginate is extracted from seaweed and is used to form a gelatinous substance. It is used as an additive in many foods such as ice cream and has recently been used to make small gelatinous capsules that contain different flavours, like a synthetic caviar. Alginate gel is also used in burns plasters and firemen's clothing. Agar is used to make vegetarian jellies and also the agar plates used frequently in microbiology to grow bacteria. Carrageenan is used to make food with a range of different textures, including chocolate milk drinks and milk chocolate bars, because it helps to hold the chocolate in suspension.

Cosmetics and herbal medicine

Seaweed extracts are often found in moisturising skin creams and herbal remedies for a range of conditions including arthritis, tuberculosis and the common cold.

The demand for seaweed has led to the development of seaweed farms in many parts of the world, such as China and Japan. Seaweed is seeded onto nets or ropes, which are then tethered in an area of lagoon that is not shaded, ideally with a temperature between 25 °C and 30 °C. Figure 7.14 shows various depths at which seaweed might be planted. For environmental reasons, spraying fertiliser on the water is not recommended.

Questions

1. Explain how the increased demand for seaweed gathered from natural sites could cause environmental problems.

2. Explain why seaweed grows best in the water depth shown in Figure 7.14(b).

3. Using your knowledge of the compensation point, suggest why *Eucheumia* grown in very deep, warm water (30 °C) dies rapidly.

4. Explain why use of fertilisers is discouraged when growing seaweed.

> 7 Energy

CONTINUED

(a) totally submerged (b) just under surface (c) exposed above surface

Figure 7.14: Depths at which seaweed might be planted.

Test yourself

1 Explain what is meant by the terms *absorption spectrum* and *action spectrum*.
2 In 1882, Theodor Engelmann carried out an experiment to investigate the effect of light wavelength on the rate of photosynthesis of the filamentous alga, *Spirogyra*. He placed a filament of the alga on a microscope slide with some aerobic bacteria that moved towards areas of higher oxygen concentration. He used a prism to illuminate the algal filament with different wavelengths of light and then observed the movement of the bacteria.
   a Suggest why aerobic bacteria that move towards oxygen were used.
   b State what the production of oxygen by the chloroplasts shows.
   c Explain the results shown in Figure 7.15.
3 Explain why a diver's red watch would appear black in deeper water.
4 It has been suggested that it is energetically very costly to produce phycoerythrin and phycocyanin. Suggest why algae found at the surface do not contain these pigments.
5 Explain why coastal waters have lower light penetration than open ocean.
6 Suggest why an average distance is calculated for visibility of the Secchi disc rather than relying on the distance it immediately becomes no longer visible.

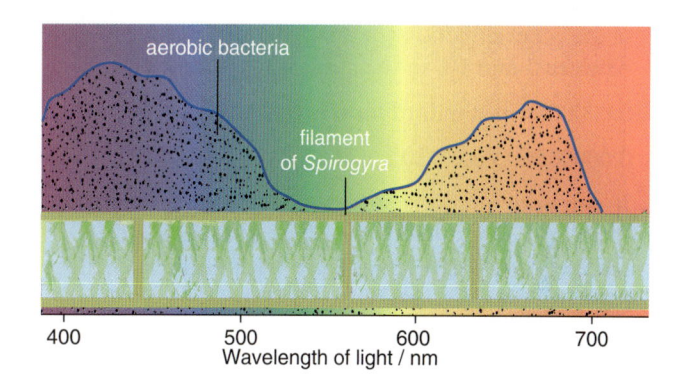

Figure 7.15: Results from Englemann's experiment showing which parts of the algal filament the aerobic bacteria have migrated towards.

7 Use Figure 7.11 to explain what would happen to the quantities of GP, TP and RuBP if a plant is placed into the dark.
8 Produce a table to summarise the substances that are used and produced in both the light dependent and light independent stages.
9 Use your knowledge of limiting factors to explain why plants die when placed in a warm greenhouse in winter when day length is short.
10 Suggest and explain why increasing the turbidity of water could lead to a reduction of ecosystem productivity.

MATHS SKILLS 7.1

STANDARD FORM AND DECIMAL PLACES

Standard form is a useful way of writing down very big or very small numbers. A number in standard form is always written in the form of:

$A \times 10^n$

where A is a number between 1 and 10 and n is the number of places a decimal point needs to move.

Worked examples

750 000 000 is the same as $7.5 \times 10 \times 10 \times 10 \times 10 \times 10 \times 10 \times 10 \times 10$

It is written in standard form as 7.5×10^8

An easy way of working this out is to count how many 'jumps' the decimal point must make to the left to get to a number between 1 and 10. In this case, eight:

$750\,000\,000.0 \rightarrow 7.5 \times 10^8$

When the number is very small, the decimal point moves in the other direction (to the right) to get to a number between 1 and 10, so the index is negative.

0.0000056 in standard form is 5.6×10^{-6}

$0.0000056 \rightarrow 5.6 \times 10^{-6}$

If you need to add or subtract two numbers in standard form, it is easiest to convert them first into ordinary numbers and then change them back into standard form. For example:

$3 \times 10^4 + 6 \times 10^5 = 30\,000 + 600\,000 = 630\,000$, which is the same as 6.3×10^5

If you want to multiply and divide numbers in standard form there are rules to follow:

- To multiply, you add the powers.
- To divide, you subtract the powers.

$(3 \times 10^3) \times (6 \times 10^4) = (3 \times 6) \times (10^{(3+4)}) = 18 \times 10^7$, which is the same as 1.8×10^8

$(9 \times 10^4) \div (3 \times 10^2) = (9 \div 3) \times (10^{(4-2)})$, which is the same as 3×10^2

The number of decimal places a number is given is the number of places after the decimal point. The number 5.621 has three decimal places.

If, for example, you are asked to give a number to two decimal places, you may have to round the number: 6.372 to two decimal places is 6.37.

If you are asked to give a number to a certain number of decimal places, you may have to add zeroes after the decimal point: 0.2 to two decimal places is 0.20.

In experimental results tables you need to have a consistent number of decimal places, and you should always use the number of decimal places your equipment was capable of measuring to.

Table 7.4 compares two presentations of the masses of four mussels.

Mass of mussel/g	Mass of mussel/g
5.35	5.35
5	5.00
5.2	5.20
5.35	5.35

Table 7.4: Setting up results tables to the correct number of decimal places.

The column on the right is correct because each value has been given to two decimal places.

Questions

1. a Write the following in standard form:
      i   35 000 000   iii 45 000
      ii 0.0000352   iv   0.00000000435
   b Work out the following:
      i $(3 \times 10^5) + (6 \times 10^6)$
      ii $(1.2 \times 10^{-2}) + (1.1 \times 10^{-3})$
      iii $(2.3 \times 10^3) \times (1.2 \times 10^2)$
      iv $(4 \times 10^3) \times (3 \times 10^4)$
      v $(6 \times 10^6) \div (3 \times 10^3)$

2. a Round the following to two decimal places:
      i   0.3267   iii 1.378
      ii 1.234   iv   3.599
   b Present the following lengths of juvenile groupers in a table; they were measured with a ruler that had 1 mm increments: 10.3 cm, 12 cm, 4.56 cm, 5 cm, 7.6 cm.

7.2 Chemosynthesis

Most of the primary productivity on the planet is due to photosynthesis. There is, however, another method of fixing energy and carbon into food webs. Chemosynthesis (the production of organic compounds by bacteria or other living organisms using the energy derived from reactions with inorganic chemicals) is a method of autotrophic nutrition that does not use light as a source of energy for carbon fixation, but instead uses the chemical energy of dissolved substances.

In 1977, a team of US scientists led by Jack Corliss was investigating hydrothermal vents around the Galápagos Islands. Hydrothermal vents, which are discussed in Chapter 2, are located at the very bottom of the sea and so have unique conditions.

The lack of light means that it is impossible for photosynthesis to fix carbon into the ecosystem. While diving in the Alvin research submersible, the scientists noticed that the hydrothermal vents had many organisms living around them and discovered a new species of giant tubeworm called *Riftia* (Figure 7.16).

Figure 7.16: A hydrothermal vent with *Riftia* growing around it.

Riftia is only found around hydrothermal vents and can survive in high concentrations of hydrogen sulfide. These tubeworms can grow to over 2m in length with a diameter of 4 cm. When specimens of *Riftia* were brought back to the laboratory, it was found that they have no gut and instead have a cavity called a **trophosome** (Figure 7.17). The US scientist, Colleen Cavanaugh, recognised that the presence of sulfur crystals in the trophosome along with symbiotic bacteria meant that there were bacteria that were fixing carbon by chemosynthesis. The feathery plumes take in oxygen, carbon dioxide and hydrogen sulfide in the water. The large trophosome contains symbiotic, sulfur bacteria that use chemosynthesis to fix carbon dioxide. The outer tube is a hard, protective coating and there is a circulatory system to transfer nutrients around the body.

Since the first discovery of chemosynthetic bacteria at hydrothermal vents, several other species have been found which can use chemical energy from substances such as hydrogen sulfide, methane, hydrogen and iron salts.

The commonest chemosynthetic bacteria found at hydrothermal vents is **Endoriftia**. This species lives symbiotically in the trophosome of *Riftia*. Because *Endoriftia* lives inside *Riftia*, the relationship is called endosymbiosis. The bacteria produce glucose and other organic molecules, such as amino acids, which *Riftia* feeds off. In return, *Riftia* ensures the bacteria get a constant supply of raw materials for chemosynthesis.

Endoriftia uses energy from hydrogen sulfide to fix carbon and produce glucose. Although you will not need to learn the equation for this form of chemosynthesis, it is interesting to compare it to the equation for photosynthesis.

chemosynthesis: $12H_2S + 6CO_2 \rightarrow C_6H_{12}O_6 + 6H_2O + 12S$

photosynthesis: $6H_2O\ 6CO_2 \rightarrow C_6H_{12}O_6 + 6O_2$

> **KEY WORDS**
>
> ***Riftia:*** giant tube worm found around hydrothermal vents.
>
> **trophosome:** organ found inside some organisms that contains symbiotic bacteria.
>
> ***Endoriftia:*** symbiotic bacterial species that is found in the tube worm, *Riftia*.

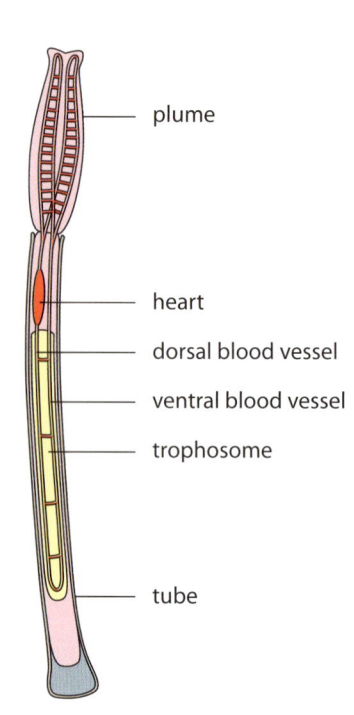

Figure 7.17: The anatomy of *Riftia*.

The two processes have similarities and differences:

Similarities	Differences
• both require a source of hydrogen (hydrogen sulfide or water) • both require carbon dioxide • both produce glucose	• the source of hydrogen is different (hydrogen sulfide or water) • chemosynthesis produces water and sulfur; photosynthesis produces oxygen • chemosynthesis uses hydrogen sulfide as an energy source; photosynthesis uses light as an energy source

The actual food webs found at hydrothermal vents are not fully understood. There are many other organisms present, including predators such as vent crabs and zoarcid fish (Figure 7.18) which may consume *Riftia*. What is definite, however, is that *Endorifitia* is the producer for the food web and *Riftia* is the primary consumer. When hydrothermal vents cease to release minerals ions into the water, *Riftia* soon die, and when that happens, the rest of the ecosystem disappears.

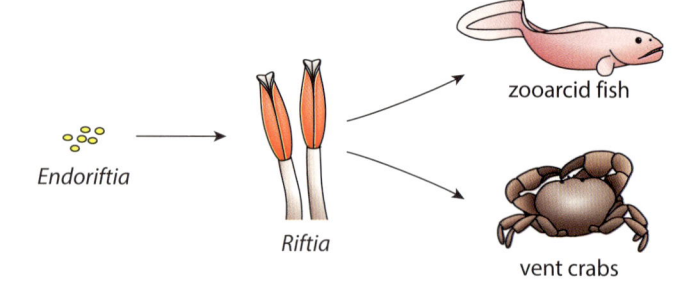

Figure 7.18: Possible food web for hydrothermal vent community. *Endoriftia* are producers. *Riftia* feed off *Endoriftia* and so are primary consumers. Vent crabs and zoarcid fish consume *Riftia* are so are secondary consumers

Test yourself

11 Explain why the trophosomes of *Riftia* contains crystals of sulfur.

12 Explain why *Riftia* and *Endoriftia* are said to have a mutualistic relationship.

MATHS SKILLS 7.2

SIGNIFICANT FIGURES AND WHEN TO USE THEM

Any measurement has some uncertainty in it, and it does not make sense to give values to a level of accuracy that could not have actually been measured. If you measure the length of a fish with a metre ruler, it is not sensible to give a measurement of 23.34235 cm. The ruler could realistically only measure with any accuracy to 23.3 cm. The number of figures used that makes sense is called a significant figure.

In Maths skills 7.1, you looked at using the correct number of decimal places in calculations and tables. When you are asked to give numbers to a certain number of significant figures, it is similar to using decimal places. It is common for people to mix up significant figures and decimal places. There are certain rules to remember when using significant figures.

- All non-zero digits are significant, which means that 34 has two significant figures while 21.325 has five significant figures.
- Zeros between non-zero digits are significant. For example, 2045 has four significant figures: 2, 0, 4 and 5.
- In a number with a decimal point, trailing zeros (those to the right of the last non-zero digit) are significant. For example, 0.0034500 has five significant figures: 3, 4, 5, 0 and 0 (the two zeroes to the right of the number five).
- In a number without a decimal point, trailing zeros may or may not be significant. For example, 2300 may have four significant figures: 2, 3, 0 and 0. However, it may be considered to only have two significant figures if it is the product of another number that has been rounded up or down. For example, the raw (actual) result may have been 2311; if this is rounded to two significant figures it will be 2300.
- Leading zeros are never significant. For example, 0.0000346 has three significant figures: 3, 4 and 6.

Worked example

You can compare the numbers of decimal places and significant figures. An example of 98.766 is shown in Table 7.5.

Number	Decimal places	Significant figures
5	98.76600	98.766
4	98.7660	98.77
3	98.766	98.8
2	98.77	99
1	98.8	100

Table 7.5: Difference between decimal places and significant figures for the value 98.766.

The easiest way to determine the number of significant figures is to use scientific notation.

For example, the number 7500 in scientific notation is 7.5×10^3. This is quoted to two significant figures. The number 0.00006751 is the same as 6.751×10^{-5}. This is quoted to four significant figures.

When carrying out calculations using different numbers, the rule is that the final answer should only be quoted to the same number of significant figures as the least accurate measure.

For example, $23.450 \times 1.31 = 30.7195$

30.7195 should be written to three significant figures because the least accurate input number is 1.31, which is three significant figures. The correct answer is, therefore, 30.7.

1. a Determine the number of significant figures that are used in the following numbers:
   - i 34.501
   - ii 3.050
   - iii 0.000340
   - iv 6400

   b Write the number 674.13 to 1, 2, 3 and 4 significant figures.

2. Calculate the following to the correct number of significant figures:
   a 432.00×22
   b $32.31 \div 7.2$
   c 6.002×213

7.3 Respiration

Respiration is the release of energy from organic molecules. It occurs in every living cell of an organism and is a fundamental property of life. There are two main types of respiration: **aerobic respiration** and **anaerobic respiration**.

> **KEY WORDS**
>
> **aerobic respiration:** the release of energy from glucose or another organic substrate in the presence of oxygen; the waste products are carbon dioxide and water
>
> **anaerobic respiration:** the release of energy from glucose or another organic substrate in the absence of oxygen; animals produce lactate as a waste product while plants and fungi produce ethanol and carbon dioxide

Aerobic respiration

During aerobic respiration, energy is released from glucose by oxidation, producing carbon dioxide and water as waste products. Aerobic means that the process uses oxygen. It is the complete combustion of glucose; the chemical and word equations for this are:

$$C_6H_{12}O_6 + 6O_2 \rightarrow 6CO_2 + 6H_2O$$

glucose + oxygen → carbon dioxide + water

The energy that is released is used to form a key molecule called adenosine triphosphate (ATP), which is shown in Figure 7.19. Aerobic respiration occurs in the mitochondria within cells.

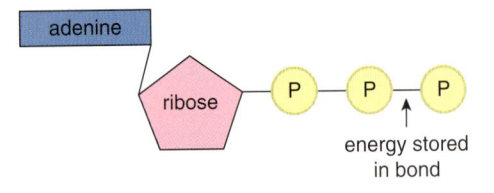

Figure 7.19: The structure of ATP.

> **Note:** Structure of ATP is extension content, and is not part of your syllabus.

An ATP molecule is made up of three main parts:

- a nitrogenous base called adenine, which is also found in DNA and RNA
- a carbohydrate sugar called ribose
- three phosphate groups.

Energy is 'stored' in the bonds between the phosphate groups, in particular between the second and third phosphates, as shown in Figure 7.20. When a cell carries out a process that needs energy, such as muscle contraction or active transport, ATP molecules are used. The bond between the second and third phosphates is broken, releasing energy that is then used to power the process. What remains is a molecule with two phosphates called adenosine diphosphate (ADP) and a free phosphate. To reform the ATP, cells respire to release energy from glucose and then use this energy to add the phosphate back onto the ADP, as shown in Figure 7.20.

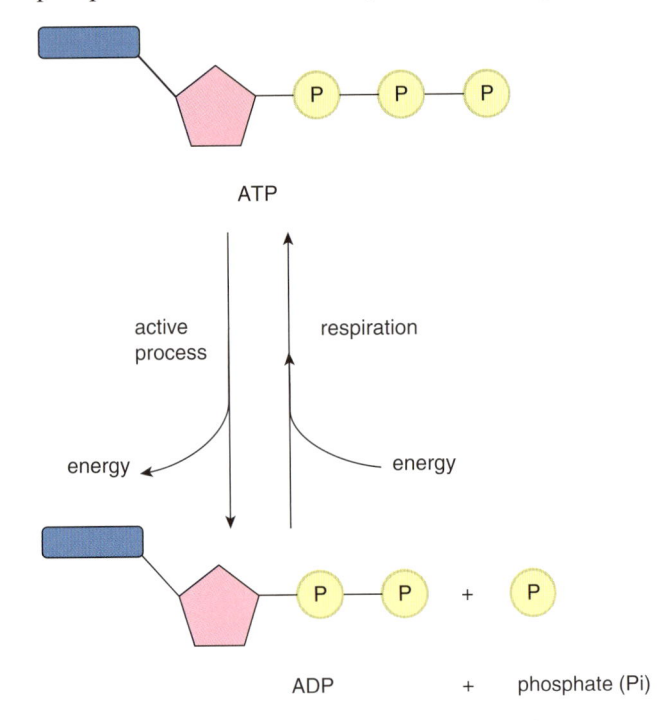

Figure 7.20: The production and breakdown of ATP.

The levels of ATP in a cell hardly change even if a cell is more or less active. This means that the faster a cell is using up ATP (for example a muscle cell in a fish), the faster the cell must respire to regenerate the ATP. Aerobic respiration is an efficient process, releasing enough energy from one molecule of glucose to produce up to 38 molecules of ATP (although this does depend on the cell type).

In active animals, it is essential to supply oxygen and glucose to the cells as quickly as possible and to remove one of the waste products of respiration, carbon dioxide. It is also important that the temperature of an organism is optimal, as respiration is affected by temperature. Like photosynthesis, the process of respiration is a series of chemical reactions that are brought about by enzymes. As the temperature increases, the rate of respiration increases because molecules collide with each other and enzymes more frequently. If the temperature rises too high, enzymes denature and the rate of respiration falls rapidly, as shown in Figure 7.21.

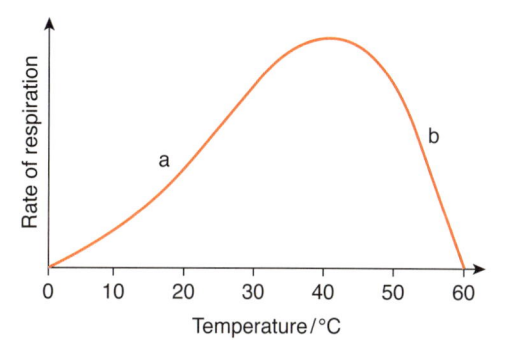

Figure 7.21: The effect of temperature on the rate of respiration. (a) As the temperature increases, the rate of respiration increases as molecules and enzymes collide more frequently. (b) As the temperature continues to increase, the rate of respiration falls steeply as the enzymes denature.

Anaerobic respiration

Cells can continue to respire in the absence of oxygen using a process called anaerobic respiration. This is the incomplete combustion of glucose and only generates two molecules of ATP from one molecule of glucose. The products are different in animals, plants and fungi (Figure 7.22).

> **Note:** pyruvate and additional information regarding anaerobic respiration are extension content, and are not part of your syllabus.

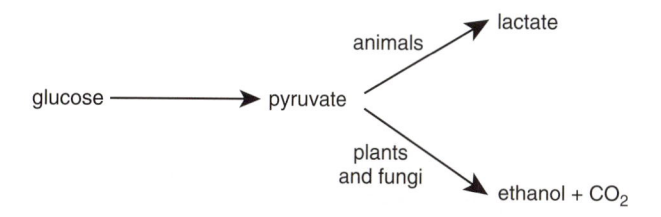

Figure 7.22: Summary of anaerobic respiration in different organisms.

In animals, glucose is first broken down into a carbohydrate called pyruvate (intermediate sugar that glucose is broken down into during respiration), which is then converted into lactate, also known as lactic acid. Lactic acid changes the pH of cells and, as a result, other cell processes eventually begin to stop. The lactic acid is removed from the cells and reconverted back into glucose.

In plants and fungi, the glucose is again broken down into pyruvate, but this is then converted to ethanol and carbon dioxide.

The first stage of aerobic respiration is also the breakdown of glucose into pyruvate, and this occurs in the cytoplasm of cells. If oxygen is present, the pyruvate moves into cell organelles called mitochondria, which complete aerobic respiration. If oxygen is absent, the pyruvate is converted into lactate or ethanol and carbon dioxide in the cytoplasm. Cells that are very active and have a high energy demand, such as the red muscle cells of tuna, have many mitochondria to produce large amounts of ATP.

Test yourself

13 Draw a table comparing aerobic and anaerobic respiration.
14 Explain why cold-blooded marine organisms tend to be less active in winter.

CASE STUDY 7.2 RED AND WHITE MUSCLES IN FISH

Fish have two distinct muscles types: red muscle and white muscle. The distribution of the muscle types in a tuna is shown in Figure 7.23.

The two muscle types have different functions. These different functions are reflected in their composition.

Red muscle is for continuous swimming. The muscle is red because it contains large quantities of a red, oxygen-binding pigment called myoglobin. Myoglobin is very similar to haemoglobin, the oxygen-transporting molecule found in red blood cells. The muscle also has a high fat content, many mitochondria and a rich blood supply.

CONTINUED

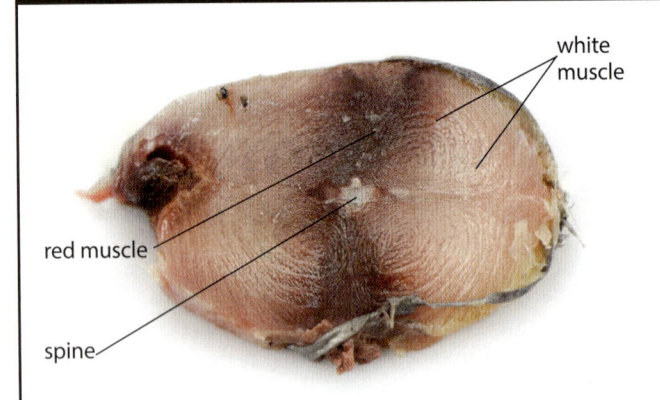

Figure 7.23: Cross-section through tuna showing muscle types.

White muscle is for rapid bursts of swimming such as catching prey by surprise or escaping predators.

It can perform very strong contractions but can only be used for short periods of time. There is no myoglobin present, fewer mitochondria, a low fat content and fewer blood vessels.

Different fish species have different proportions of the two muscle types. Tuna and swordfish have a high proportion of red muscle, while less active fish such as plaice and cod have far more white muscle. In salmon, the proportions change at different stages in the life cycle. While in the open ocean, the proportion of red muscle is high. When the salmon begin their migration, there is a large increase in the proportion of white muscle.

Questions

1. Using your knowledge of anaerobic and aerobic respiration, explain the roles and structure of the two muscle types.

2. Explain why tuna have such a high proportion of red muscle.

3. Suggest why salmon alter the proportion of the two muscle types when beginning their migration into rivers.

MATHS SKILLS 7.3

ANALYSING DATA

When you carry out scientific investigations, you often repeat experiments to improve reliability.

Repeating experiments allows you to identify anomalies and then calculate mean values. Identifying anomalies with biological data can be difficult and it is not often clear whether a value is anomalous or just part of natural variation. If a data point seems clearly anomalous, the general rule is to not include it when calculating the mean and, if possible, try to repeat the experiment.

We say that a measurement is *repeatable* if we can repeat the experiment using the same method and equipment and still get the same results. The measurement is considered *reproducible* if another person can repeat the experiment and get the same results.

Calculating mean values is very simple. All the values are added together after discarding anomalies and then divided by the number of values added together.

Worked example 1

Fifteen samples of zooplankton were taken from an area of ocean. The number of zooplankton per cm^3 of water were determined for each. The values were:

254, 269, 325, 295, 275, 315, 301, 258, 295, 321, 52, 245, 342, 295, 375

There is quite a large range between the maximum and minimum values. The lowest value, 52, seems very different compared with the other values, so would appear anomalous and would be ignored when calculating the mean. The wide range in values could otherwise be the result of variation in the samples.

7 Energy

> **CONTINUED**
>
> The mean number of zooplankton per cm³ =
>
> $$\frac{(254 + 269 + 325 + 295 + 275 + 315 + 301 + 258 + 295 + 321 + 245 + 342 + 295 + 375)}{14} = 297.5\text{, which can be rounded up to 298}$$
>
> The *range* for the values is expressed as the lowest to the highest value (with anomalies excluded), which in this example is 245 to 375. The range can also be expressed as the difference between the lowest and highest value; in other words, 375 − 245 = 130 zooplankton per cm³.
>
> ### Question
>
> 1. Calculate the means and ranges for the following series of data, discounting anomalies:
>   a. Oyster spats were collected on 12 oyster cages, and the numbers found in each cage were:
>   45, 72, 53, 65, 98, 2, 65, 98, 58, 97, 101, 45
>   b. The numbers of eggs spawned by eight female salmon were:
>   3525, 2974, 3198, 4872, 2956, 3542, 4100, 2954
>
> ### Worked example 2
>
> Mean values are useful, but they do not always tell us the whole story. For example, two different experiments were both run twice. The repeat values for one experiment were 14 and 16 and for the second experiment were 30 and 0. The mean value for both experiments is the same, 15. The raw data, however, suggests that the data is more complex. It is often useful to determine how much spread there is about the mean value. This calculation is called the standard deviation. The higher the standard deviation, the greater the spread of the values about the mean (Figure 7.24). For a normal distribution:
>
> - Approximately 68% of all values lie within a range of the mean ± 1 standard deviation.
> - Approximately 95% of all values lie within a range of the mean ± 2 standard deviation.
>
> To calculate the standard deviation, *s*, you use the formula:
>
> $$s = \sqrt{\frac{\Sigma(x - \bar{x})^2}{n - 1}}$$
>
> Where
>
> x = each measurement
>
> $\bar{x}$ = mean
>
> $\Sigma(x - \bar{x})^2$ = sum of all the $(x - \bar{x})^2$ values
>
> n = number of measurements

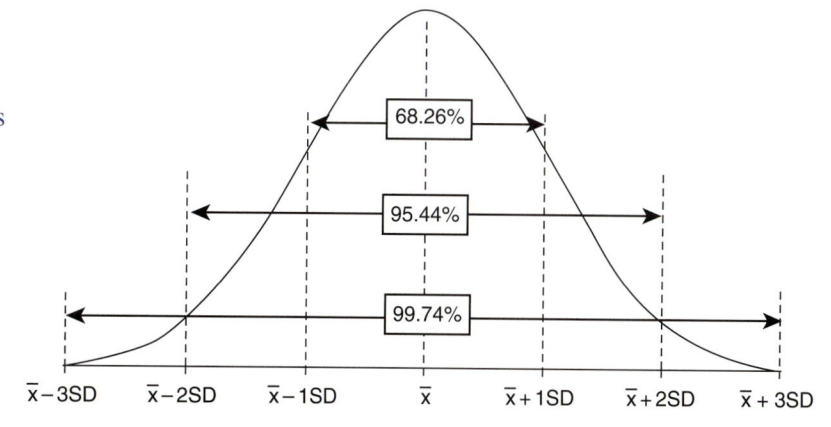

Figure 7.24: Normal distribution showing standard deviation from mean.

CONTINUED

Question

2 Calculate the standard deviation for the measurements shown in Table 7.6.

Measurements (x)	(x − x̄)	(x − x̄)²
27	(27 − 30.9) = −3.9	15.21
32		
29		
35		
25		
37		
31		

Table 7.6: Standard deviation table.

The mean of the measurements,

$$\bar{x} = \frac{(27 + 32 + 29 + 35 + 25 + 37 + 31)}{7} = 30.9$$

a Complete Table 10.9.
b Calculate the $\Sigma(x - \bar{x})^2$ by adding all of the $(x - \bar{x})^2$ values together.
c The number of values (n) is 7. Divide your value for $\Sigma(x - \bar{x})^2$ by $(n − 1)$.
d Calculate the standard deviation by finding the square root of this number.
e 68% of the values lie between $\bar{x} \pm 1 \times$ standard deviation. Calculate this range.
f 95% of the values lie between $\bar{x} \pm 2 \times$ standard deviation. Calculate this range.

Worked example 3

You can use standard deviations to compare mean values in an investigation. For example, the mean numbers of deep sea shrimp in two areas were compared. Area A had 25 shrimp per m² of water while area B had 15 shrimp per m² of water. If we look only at the means, area A seems to have more shrimps per m².

If you then take into account the standard deviations, you can see by how much the two areas really differ. In this example, the standard deviation for area A is 3 and for B is 4.

95% of values will lie between mean ± 2 × standard deviation, so

for area A, 95% of values lie between 25 ± (2 × 3)

= 19 to 31

for area B, 95% of values lie between 15 ± (2 × 4)

= 15 ± 8

= 7 to 23

There is an overlap of the two ranges: some of the higher repeated values for area B are higher than for area A. This means that the means are different but we cannot be totally confident that all parts of area A have more shrimps than area B.

Question

3 Use standard deviation to determine whether or not there is a clear difference between the mean numbers of groupers per square km of two reefs, as shown in Table 7.7. Calculate the mean, standard deviation and the ranges within which 95% of values lie.

Repeat	Number of grouper per square kilometre of reef	
	region A	region B
1	32	18
2	35	19
3	21	12
4	25	24
5	32	27
6	38	19
7	21	18
8	24	27
9	19	18
10	31	12

Table 7.7: Difference in grouper numbers from two reefs.

7   Energy

> **PROJECT: THE ADAPTATIONS OF DIFFERENT ALGAE**
>
> Carry out research on how different named species of red, green and brown algae are adapted to their habitats. Give at least one named example of a red, green and brown alga, and consider:
>
> - where the species live (for example, intertidal zones, open sea, deep sea, shallow rock pools)
> - what challenges their particular habitats pose (for example, available light wavelengths, shifting substrates, moving water, exposure)
> - how each species is adapted to its habitat.
>
> You should present your findings as a slideshow.
>
> **Thinking about your project**
>
> Think about what you thought was good about the content of your presentation and what could have been developed further. Then, ask a member of your audience to do the same. Compare your views with the member of the audience.

EXAM-STYLE QUESTIONS

1   **a**   Explain how the depth and location of a body of ocean water affects the rate of photosynthesis of marine primary producers. **[9]**

   b   Describe and explain the potential consequences on the marine environment of allowing unrestricted run-off from fields into a river estuary. **[6]**

   [Total: 15]

2   An experiment was carried out into the effect of temperature on the rate of photosynthesis of a seaweed.

   The seaweed was placed into a boiling tube containing saline with sodium hydrogencarbonate (a source of carbon dioxide gas) and the boiling tube placed into a water bath as shown in Figure 7.25.

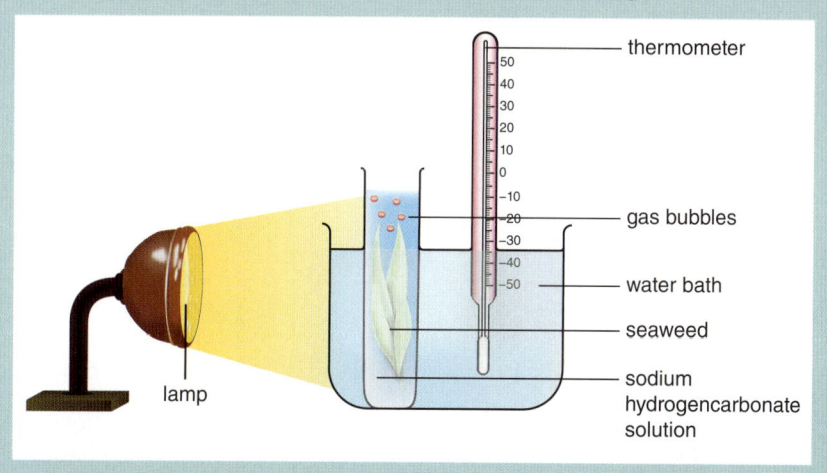

Figure 7.25: Apparatus to investigate the effect of temperature on photosynthesis of seaweed.

CONTINUED

The temperature of the water bath was set at 5°C and a lamp was placed 5 cm away from the beaker. The seaweed was left for 5 min. The seaweed was seen to produce bubbles of gas. The number of bubbles of gas was counted for 5 min.

This was repeated for different temperatures at intervals of 5°C up to and including 45°C.

- **a** State how the composition of gases in the bubbles differs from atmospheric air. [2]

  The results of the experiment are shown as a graph in Figure 7.26.

- **b i** Suggest what factor may limit the rate of photosynthesis between X and Y on the graph. Explain your reasoning. [2]
  - **ii** Suggest what factor may limit the rate of photosynthesis between Y and Z on the graph. Explain your reasoning. [2]

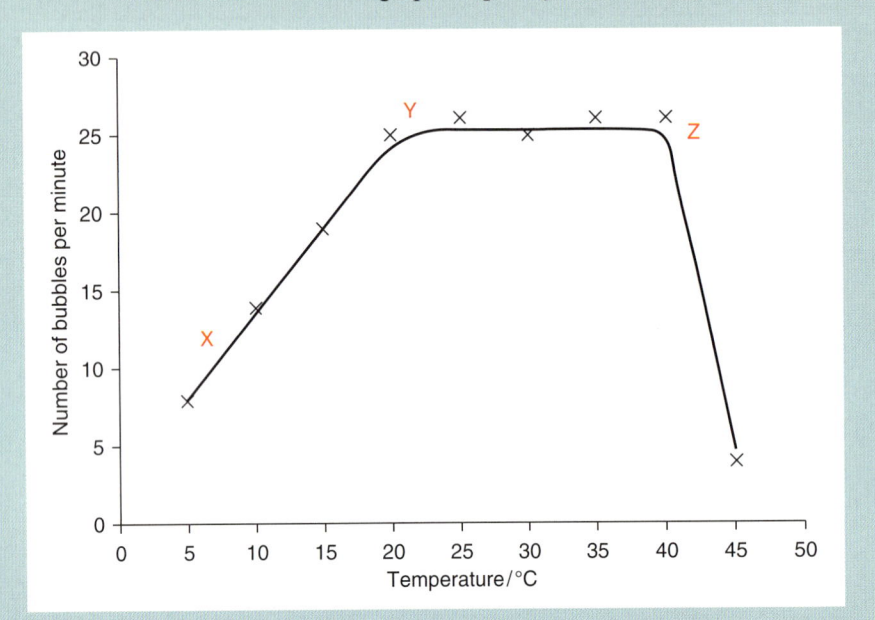

Figure 7.26: The effects of increasing temperature on the rate of photosynthesis of seaweed.

- **iii** *Sketch* a graph like the figure above to *predict* the effect of increasing temperature at a lower light intensity. [2]
- **iv** Explain the change in rate of photosynthesis between 40 and 45°C. [2]

- **c** It has been suggested that seaweed could be farmed in an intensive system using artificial lights and heaters. Suggest and explain the optimal temperature that a seaweed farmer would use based on the light intensity used in this experiment. [2]

[Total: 12]

COMMAND WORDS

sketch: make a simple freehand drawing showing the key features, taking care over proportions

predict: suggest what may happen based on available information

CONTINUED

3 Tilapia are often grown in aquaculture systems. An experiment was carried out to investigate the effect of temperature on the respiration rate of male tilapia. A male tilapia was placed into a tank of salt water and the temperature set at 10 °C. An oxygen probe was placed into the water and the oxygen concentration of the water measured every 15 min for 3 h. This was repeated with a different male tilapia at a temperature of 20 °C. The results are shown in Table 7.8.

Time / min	Oxygen concentration of water at 10 °C / mg dm^{-3}	Oxygen concentration of water at 20 °C / mg dm^{-3}
0	9.2	9.3
15	8.9	8.4
30	8.7	7.9
45	8.5	7.3
60	8.2	6.4
75	7.9	5.6
90	7.5	5.0
105	7.2	4.7
120	6.9	4.4
135	6.6	4.1
150	6.4	3.7
165	5.9	3.4
180	5.7	2.9

Table 7.8: Effect of temperature on oxygen uptake by male tilapia.

a **i** State **two** factors that should have been controlled in the experiment. [2]

ii Suggest how the reliability of the experiment could have been improved. [1]

iii Calculate the mean rate of oxygen decrease over the 3 h period for both temperatures in mg dm^{-3} h^{-1}. [2]

iv Describe and explain the effect of increasing temperature on the rate of oxygen consumption of the tilapia. [3]

Table 7.9 shows the effect of increasing temperature on concentration of dissolved oxygen in seawater.

Temperature / °C	0	5	10	15	20	25	100
Oxygen solubility / mg dm^{-3}	14.6	12.8	11.3	10.2	9.2	8.6	0.0

Table 7.9: Effect of temperature on oxygen concentration.

CONTINUED

b   Use Tables 7.8 and 7.9 and your own knowledge to explain why intensive aquaculture of tilapia in warmer countries requires the provision of additional oxygen. [4]

[Total: 12]

4   Chemosynthesis is a method of autotrophic nutrition used by some species of hydrothermal vent bacteria.

   a   i   Give the name of **one** substance that is used as a source of energy in chemosynthesis. [1]

       ii   Give the name of the organic molecule produced by both photosynthesis and chemosynthesis. [1]

   b   i   Explain, with reference to the bacteria and *Riftia*, the meaning of the term symbiosis. [4]

       ii   Explain why chemosynthesis is the method of production around hydrothermal vents. [2]

[Total: 8]

5   a   Complete the chemical symbol equation for aerobic respiration. [2]

.... + ... → $6CO_2 + 6H_2O$

   b   A scientist decided to carry out an investigation into the effect of temperature on the rate of respiration of mussels. She decided that the rate of production of carbon dioxide bubbles was a suitable method to measure the rate of respiration.

Plan a valid experiment to investigate the effect of temperature on the respiration rate of mussels. Your plan should:

- include a clear statement of the hypothesis
- identify the key variables
- include full details of the method
- describe how you would analyse your results
- be safe and ethical. [12]

[Total: 14]

6   a   i   State the name of the enzyme that combines carbon dioxide with ribulose biphosphate (RuBP) during the light independent stage. [1]

       ii   State the location of the light independent stage. [1]

       iii   Explain how the light dependent stage of photosynthesis harvests light energy. [5]

   b   The light independent stage in photosynthesis was investigated. Marine algae was placed into sea water and illuminated with a lamp. After one hour, the lamp was turned off and the algae kept in darkness for another hour. The levels of GP and TP were monitored throughout the experiment. The results are shown in Figure 7.27.

COMMAND WORDS

give: produce an answer from a given source or recall / memory

identify: name / select / recognise

CONTINUED

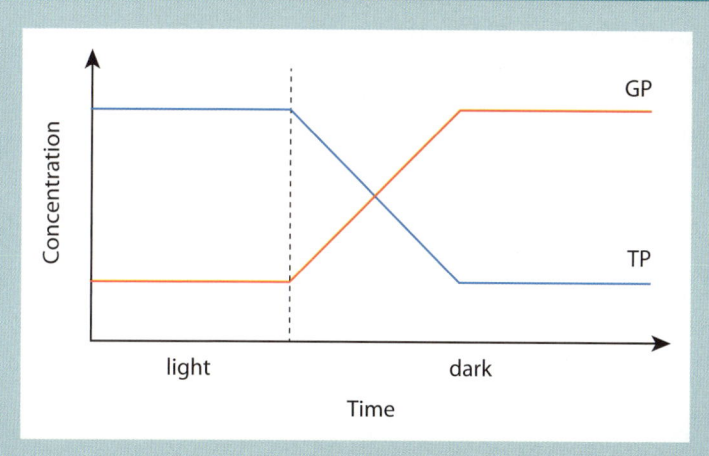

Figure 7.27: Effect of light and dark on GP and TP concentrations.

Explain the changes in concentrations of GP and TP shown in Figure 7.27. [5]

[Total: 12]

7 a Describe how chromatography can be used to identify the pigments present in a species of marine algae. [5]

b A student investigated the effect of light wavelength on the rate of photosynthesis of three different species of algae. He measured the rate of oxygen production of each species of algae when illuminated with red, green and blue light. Each condition was repeated five times and the mean rate of photosynthesis and standard deviation were calculated.

The results are shown in Table 7.10.

Species of algae	Mean rate of photosynthesis / mm³ oxygen produced per min		
	red light	green light	blue light
Species A	12.2 ± 3.5	2.5 ± 1.1	16.4 ± 2.1
Species B	10.1 ± 4.2	8.2 ± 1.5	
Species C	12.4 ± 3.3	1.2 ± 0.2	15.2 ± 3.1

Table 7.10: Effect of light wavelength on the rate of photosynthesis of two species of algae.

The results for species B when placed in blue light were:

$18.2 \, mm^3 \, min^{-1}$, $17.6 \, mm^3 \, min^{-1}$, $16.8 \, mm^3 \, min^{-1}$, $17.2 \, mm^3 \, min^{-1}$, $18.1 \, mm^3 \, min^{-1}$

i Calculate the mean rate of photosynthesis for species B when placed under blue light.

Give your answer to the correct number of significant figures. [2]

CONTINUED

ii Use the equation for standard deviation to calculate the standard deviation for the mean rate of photosynthesis for species B when placed under blue light. [3]

Standard deviation, $s = \sqrt{\dfrac{\Sigma(x-\bar{x})^2}{n-1}}$

Where

x = each measurement

$\bar{x}$ = mean

$\Sigma(x-\bar{x})^2$ = sum of all the $(x-\bar{x})^2$ values

n = number of measurements.

iii The student concluded that species B was a species of algae that lives in deeper water than species A and C. **Evaluate** this conclusion, using Table 7.10, your answers to parts **bi** and **bii** and your own knowledge to **justify** your answer. [5]

[Total: 15]

8 Table 7.11 shows the effect of light intensity on the rate of oxygen production by two species of marine algae.

Light intensity / arbitrary units	Rate of oxygen production / $cm^3 h^{-1}$	
	Species A	Species B
0	−6.2	−2.4
5	−1.0	4.5
10	3.2	8.9
15	6.9	12.2
20	12.8	12.3
25	18.9	12.3

Table 7.11: Effect of light intensity on rate of oxygen production by marine algae.

a i Plot a line graph to show the effect of light intensity on rate of oxygen production by both species of algae. Join your points with ruled, straight lines. [6]

ii Compare the effects of changing light intensity on the rate of oxygen production on the two species. [4]

b i Explain the effect of increasing light intensity for Species A. [4]

ii **Analyse** the information in Table 7.11 to explain the effect of increasing light intensity from 15 arbitrary units to 25 arbitrary units for Species B. [3]

c Consider the information in Table 7.11 to suggest which of the two species of algae is adapted to live in turbid water. [2]

[Total: 19]

COMMAND WORDS

evaluate: judge or calculate the quality, importance, amount, or value of something

justify: support a case with evidence / argument

analyse: examine in detail to show meaning, identify elements and the relationship between them

SELF-EVALUATION CHECKLIST

I can:	See section...	Needs more work	Almost there	Ready to move on
describe the nature of light as part of the electromagnetic spectrum	7.1			
explain the process and roles of photosynthesis in marine ecosystems	7.1			
describe photosynthesis as a two-stage process, light dependent and light independent	7.1			
describe the light dependent and light independent stages of photosynthesis and how they interact with each other	7.1			
describe and explain the functions of, the structures in a typical chloroplast	7.1			
describe the role of primary and accessory pigments	7.1			
describe and use chromatography to separate and identify chloroplast pigments	7.1			
interpret absorption spectra of chloroplast pigments and action spectra for photosynthesis	7.1			
describe the effect of limiting factors of photosynthesis, including light intensity, wavelength of light, carbon dioxide concentration and temperature on the rate of photosynthesis	7.1			
investigate the effect of wavelength of light on the rate of photosynthesis	7.1			
describe and explain the function of chemosynthesis in hydrothermal vent food webs	7.2			
understand the functions of aerobic and anaerobic respiration	7.3			

EXTENDED CASE STUDY: MARINE ALGAL BLOOMS AND RED TIDES: NATURAL CAUSES, POLLUTION AND GLOBAL WARMING

Algal blooms are rapid, extensive growths of phytoplankton and are common events that occur in the world's seas and oceans. Some of these blooms are so large that they become visible from space. There are many causes: some are natural, seasonal events, while others may be the result of human interference.

A harmful algal bloom (HAB) is an algal bloom that has a negative impact on other organisms, often because of the production of toxins. HABs have been known to cause harmful effects on several species, but in particular marine mammals, turtles, sea birds and predatory fish. In the spring of 2004, at least 107 bottlenose dolphins died off the coast of Florida because they had ingested contaminated menhaden fish with high levels of an algal toxin called brevetoxin. This toxin is produced by the dinoflagellate *Karenia brevis*, which frequently causes 'red tides' in the Gulf of Mexico. Manatees have also been killed as a result of consuming seagrass contaminated with brevetoxin.

Examples of common harmful effects of HABs include:

- the production of neurotoxins killing fish, sea birds, sea turtles and marine mammals
- human illness or death via consumption of seafood contaminated by algal toxins (see Table 7.12)

Condition	Symptoms in humans	Toxins	Affected organisms	Some causative algae
amnesic shellfish poisoning	abdominal cramps and diarrhoea, neurological symptoms including dizziness, short-term memory loss, respiratory difficulty and coma	domoic acid	scallops, mussels, some edible crab species	*Pseudo-nitzschia pungens*
ciguatera fish poisoning	diarrhoea, vomiting and abdominal pain, muscular aches, dizziness, sweating, numbness and tingling of the mouth and digits, paralysis and death	ciguatoxin, maitotoxin	grouper, snapper, barracuda, mackerel	*Gambierdiscus toxicus*
diarrhetic shellfish poisoning	diarrhoea, nausea, vomiting, abdominal cramps and chills, rarely fatal	okadaic acid	oysters, mussels, scallops	*Dinophysis spp.*
neurotoxin shellfish poisoning	diarrhoea, dizziness, aches, breathing difficulties	brevetoxins	shellfish, manatees, dolphins, sealions	*Karenia brevis*
paralytic shellfish poisoning	tingling, numbness and drowsiness, fever, rash and staggering	saxitoxins	shellfish, salmon, whales, menhaden, sea otters, sea birds	*Alexandrium spp.*
cyanobacteria poisoning	rashes, allergies, liver disease, effects on nervous system, possible link to neurodegenerative disease	cyanotoxins (including BMAA)	predatory fish, birds, otters	*Lyngbya spp.*

Table 7.12: Some of the effects of algal toxins.

CONTINUED

- suffocation of organisms with gills because of blockage with algae
- death of organisms because of the loss of oxygen after decomposition of dead algae.

The Gulf of Maine often experiences blooms of the dinoflagellate *Alexandrium fundyense*, an organism that produces saxitoxin, the neurotoxin responsible for paralytic shellfish poisoning. Seasonal blooms of *Pseudo-nitzschia*, a diatom known to produce domoic acid, the neurotoxin responsible for amnesic shellfish poisoning, occurs around California's Pacific coast. Many blooms of cyanobacteria have been recorded, along with poisonings of animals and humans eating shellfish that have accumulated the associated cyanotoxins. One cyanotoxin, BMAA (an altered amino acid), is a powerful neurotoxin and research is now being carried out to determine if it is an environmental cause of some human neurodegenerative conditions such as Parkinson's and Alzheimer's diseases. Because of their negative economic and health impacts, HABs are carefully monitored by organisations such as the National Oceanic and Atmospheric Administration (NOAA). The NOAA uses weather conditions and known seasonal changes together with known human pollution events to predict the formation of algal blooms, so that measures such as the banning of shellfish fishing can be put into place. Research on preventing HABs and how to clear them quickly is also carried out. In the Gulf of Mexico, NOAA's HAB Forecasting System uses satellite imagery, information about water conditions gathered by weather buoys, and observations from fieldworkers to map blooms and predict how and when they will spread.

Causes of HABs

Some HABs are caused by natural events such as the sudden upwelling of nutrients because of a change in water currents or water temperatures. HABs in the Gulf of Mexico have been reported since the time of early explorers, suggesting they are a natural phenomenon. The growth of marine phytoplankton is generally limited by the availability of nitrates and phosphates. Natural HABs are often predictable currents. Other factors, such as iron-rich dust influx from large desert areas such as the Sahara, are thought to play a role in causing HABs. Some algal blooms on the Pacific coast have been linked to natural occurrences of large-scale climatic oscillations such as El Niño events. Coastal water pollution caused by agricultural run-off from rivers and increases in seawater temperature have also been suggested as possible contributing factors to HABs.

Seasonal occurrences resulting from coastal upwelling, a natural result of the movement of certain ocean in some parts of the world has, however, been linked with increased nutrient release as a result of human interference.

Some specific examples of HABs are given below.

- *Lingulodinium polyedrum* naturally produces brilliant displays of bioluminescence in warm coastal waters. They have been seen in southern California regularly since at least 1901.
- In 1972, a red tide was caused in New England by a toxic dinoflagellate, *Alexandrium (Gonyaulax) tamarense*.
- The largest algal bloom on record was the 1991 Darling River cyanobacterial bloom in Australia, which affected over 1000 km of the Barwon and Darling Rivers.
- In May 2005, a major HAB led to the temporary suspension of fishing for shellfish in Maine and Massachusetts, leading to a big loss in revenue and also affecting the tourist trade.
- In 2009, Brittany, France, experienced recurring algal blooms caused by the high amounts of fertiliser released into the sea as a result of intensive animal farming. This even caused lethal gas emissions that led to one case of human unconsciousness and three animal deaths.
- In 2010, a major phytoplanktonic bloom occurred in the North Atlantic due to release of iron in ash from the eruption of an Icelandic volcano.
- In 2013, over 19 000 tonnes of sea lettuce algae was removed from beaches around Qingdao in China. The bloom was the size of Connecticut and ended up costing more than $100 million in cleaning costs and loss of fish as a result of suffocation by oxygen loss.

CONTINUED

- In 2014, *Myrionecta rubra* caused a major HAB on the south-eastern coast of Brazil.
- In 2014, blue-green algae caused a bloom in the western basin of Lake Erie, poisoning the Toledo, Ohio, water system.
- In 2016, a HAB occurred in Florida resulting in the closure of several beaches.
- In October 2017, an extensive red tide caused by *Karenia brevis* occurred around south-west Florida. The levels of *Karenia brevis* were only declared to have fallen to normal ocean levels in February 2019. Dead manatees and dolphins thought to have been poisoned by the algae were found at various times washed up on beaches.

Questions

1 Explain why an algal bloom of *Karenia brevis* led to the death of dolphins and manatees in Florida.

2 Suggest how HABs can lead to reduced oxygen in water resulting in the death of fish.

3 Explain why government agencies will often ban fishing of shellfish when algal blooms are sighted. Also explain the short- and long-term effects of algal blooms on the fishing industry.

4 Explain how farming practices could lead to HABs in marine environments.

5 Using your knowledge of limiting factors, explain why increased atmospheric carbon dioxide could cause an increase in the frequency of HABs.

Chapter 8
Fisheries for the future

LEARNING INTENTIONS

In this chapter you will learn how to:

- describe the life cycles of different species of marine organism
- explain why organisms have different stages in their life cycles
- explain the need for the sustainable exploitation of fisheries
- describe the impact of different modern fishing technologies
- understand the information that is needed to decide how best to exploit fishes sustainably
- describe the different methods that can be employed to ensure that fishing is sustainable
- explain the sociological and economic impacts of restrictions on fishing and unrestricted fishing
- describe the methods that can be used to replenish depleted fish stocks
- describe the general methods of aquaculture and the specific methods used to produce salmon, mussels and shrimp
- describe the principal requirements and explain the impacts of successful aquaculture.

BEFORE YOU START

- Discuss with other learners the reasons why fish stocks are reducing.
- Many marine organisms have life cycles with larval stages. A tadpole is a larval form of a frog. It has a different physical appearance, has different food and may live in a different habitat. Suggest why it may be an advantage to have a larval stage such as a tadpole.
- Write down as many methods of commercial fish harvesting that you can think of. Try to think about which ones are the most sustainable.
- Write down as many species of fish and shellfish that you think may be produced in aquaculture. You could research this by asking your local fishmonger where they obtain their fish.

FISHING FOR THE FUTURE

Since ancient times, humans have harvested many species from the seas and oceans. Until the beginning of the twentieth century, this harvesting of marine stocks was not particularly efficient, and, with a lower human population and less advanced transportation networks, the majority of fishing was sustainable. Throughout the twentieth century and beyond, however, an ever-increasing global population has seen the demand for protein-rich marine organisms rise dramatically. As technology has improved, boats and fishing equipment have become increasingly sophisticated. This has led to plundering of the world's oceans, resulting in a serious decline of species. In recent years the need to control our fishing has been recognised and we have begun to try to reverse the trend of ever-decreasing stocks and we have turned to methods of **aquaculture** to satisfy the demand for marine products.

To help preserve the stocks of fish for our children and grandchildren, it is essential to understand not only the technology we use, but how organisms reproduce. All life on the planet is driven to reproduce. All organisms have evolved **life cycles** and reproductive methods that solve particular problems associated with their ecosystem and environment. Some organisms provide no parental care but produce thousands of offspring (a female Atlantic herring can carry up to 50 000 eggs, for example) in the hope that maybe one or two will survive to breed. Some organisms produce only a few offspring but nurture and guard them in an effort to improve their chances of survival to breeding age. Which reproductive strategy a particular species uses is nature's solution to a particular environmental problem.

Our oceans are reaching the point of no return. If we fail to act, we will not only destroy the oceans but also the future of our descendants.

Questions

1. To what extent do you believe that our descendants will not be able to make a sustainable living from harvesting the oceans?
2. How does the harvesting of food from marine sources differ from how most of our food is produced?

KEY WORDS

aquaculture: the rearing of aquatic animals and plants for human consumption or use

life cycle: the different stages that a species passes through during its life

8.1 Life cycles

The life cycle of an organism is a description of all the stages that an organism goes through in its life. It shows the different forms that occur, the breeding cycle and the habitats for each stage.

Simple and complex life cycles

There are two main types of life cycle:

- Simple life cycles, where there are no major different stages, or **larval forms**, and **metamorphosis** does not take place.
- Complex life cycles, where there are several different stages and forms of organism; the different stages may include different larval forms and each stage occurs in different habitats.

Most marine organisms (other than marine mammals, birds and reptiles) have life cycles that are complex and consist of several stages. This means that the majority have larval forms of some description. Larvae are immature forms of animals that often live in different habitats to the adults and may also have different food sources. Many marine organisms, such as the giant clam, are **sessile** as adults. This means that they are attached to a substrate and do not move freely. Sessile species often have a free-swimming, or **non-sessile**, larval stage to help them to settle in different locations. When the larvae settle, they undergo metamorphosis, a process by which they change into a different form.

> **KEY WORDS**
>
> **larval forms:** the immature form of animals that undergo some metamorphosis, often having different food sources and habitats to avoid competition with the adults
>
> **metamorphosis:** the changing of an organism from one form to another, such as the changing of a larval stage into an adult
>
> **sessile:** when an organism is attached to a substrate and is therefore immobile
>
> **non-sessile:** when an organism is free moving (not attached to a substrate)

Advantages and disadvantages of larval stages

If an organism has several larval stages, there must be some form of benefit to the survival of the organism. Advantages include less competition for food, and distribution:

- **Less competition for food.** Often, larvae occupy a different niche or region of ocean compared with the adults. This means that the adults and larvae are not competing for the same food. Zooplankton is made up of many larval forms, some of which eat phytoplankton while others eat other zooplankton. Some species have several larval stages, each of which may exist in a different area and eat a different food source.

- **Distribution.** Where adults are sessile (fixed to a substrate), a larval stage offers the possibility of moving to another area. The adult giant clam *Tridacna gigas* is usually securely attached to the substrate, but the larvae are free to move in the ocean. When they settle to become an adult, the larvae are often situated away from the parent, which reduces competition with the parent. It also means that the species is more resistant to extinction if a disease, predator or catastrophic event (such as a volcanic eruption) affects one area. If some of the offspring live elsewhere, they may survive.

There are, however, also disadvantages:

- There will almost inevitably be less parental care so there is a higher risk of mortality.
- Larval stages tend to be small and free floating, and as a result may be more susceptible to predation and environmental stresses such as pollution and temperature change.
- Distribution across different areas does not necessarily mean that there will be a suitable substrate or food source in each area. Many larvae will be lost and simply die because they end up in an inhospitable area.

Examples of life cycles of marine organisms

In order to understand the advantages and disadvantages of different life cycles, it is useful to look at specific examples of a simple life cycle and a complex life cycle.

A simple life cycle: the bottlenose dolphin

The common bottlenose dolphin, *Tursiops truncates*, like all marine mammals, has a simple life cycle with no larval forms. Figure 8.1 shows the life cycle of the bottlenose dolphin. Mating occurs during a distinct breeding season when male dolphins compete for access to females. Males fight with each other and protect groups of females from each other. After mating, offspring develop inside the uteri of females for a gestation period of about 12 months. Most females only give birth to one dolphin at a time but, occasionally, they give birth to twins. The young, known as calves, stay with their mothers for up to eight years. The females feed the young with milk for at least 18 months, but calves have been known to suckle occasionally for up to eight years. Females become sexually mature between the ages of 5 and 13 years and males between 9 and 14 years. As adults, the males will usually live alone or in small groups, occasionally joining larger groups. Females breed between every two and six years and tend to live in larger, social groups, along with the young, immature dolphins. Although the very young feed on milk from their mothers, dolphins of all ages have a very similar diet of fish and molluscs such as squid. By living with their mothers for several years, young dolphins are protected from predators, have a regular source of food, bond socially with other dolphins and learn how to survive as adults. Table 8.1. summarises the life cycle of the bottlenose dolphin.

Stage	Habitat	Advantages	Time duration
young	ocean	protection from predators social bonding provided with milk, enables learning of survival skills	1.5–8 years
adult	ocean	reduces aggression between males group living offers protection complex hierarchies occur within groups	from 8–9 years, up to 60 years

Table 8.1: Summary of life cycle of bottlenose dolphin.

A complex life cycle: shrimp (a typical crustacean life cycle)

Crustaceans tend to have very complex life cycles with many different larval stages. There are hundreds, possibly thousands, of different species of shrimp, many of which have different life cycles. There are certain common themes, however, that occur in the life cycles of all shrimps, so the general principles are given here. Shrimps are decapod crustaceans and are closely related to lobsters and crabs. They are of significant commercial interest, both when fished and farmed. Shrimp farming has led to renewed interest in their reproductive behaviour.

Adult, sexually mature shrimp live in deeper ocean waters (Figure 8.2). Breeding seasons vary from species to species, and breeding may be triggered by a mixture of water temperature and lunar phases.

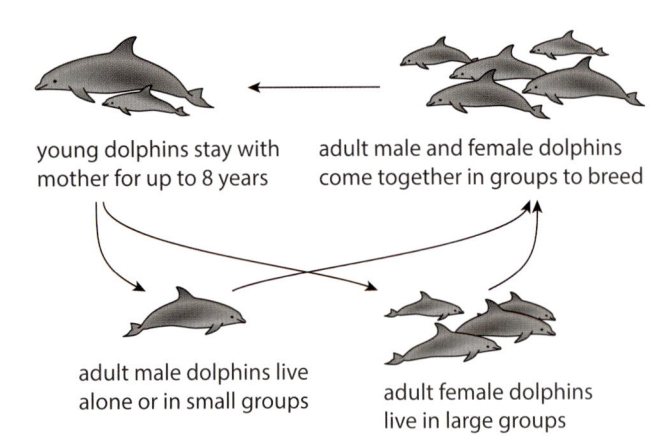

Figure 8.1: The life cycle of the bottlenose dolphin, a typical marine mammal.

8 Fisheries for the future

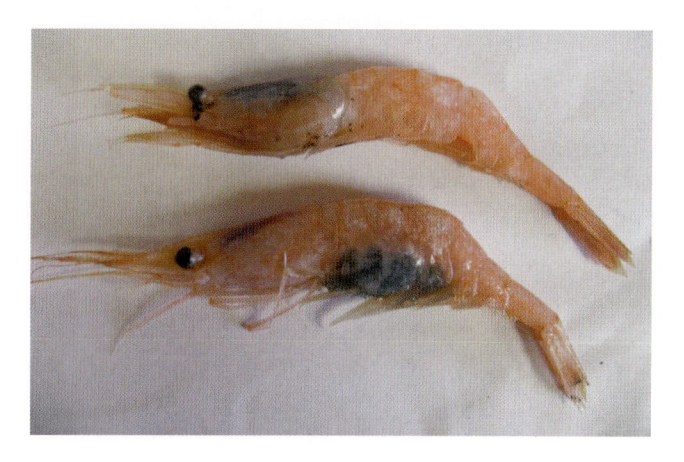

Figure 8.2: Adult shrimp; the lower shrimp has eggs attached.

Sex determination is not fully understood in most crustaceans. Some species initially develop as males for two or three years and then become females; in other species, the sexes are fixed for their entire lives.

Individual male and female shrimp mate with each other in deep ocean water (Figure 8.3). During mating, the male attaches a pouch of sperm called a **spermatocyst** to the underside of the female. As eggs are released by the female, sperm is released onto the female from the spermatocyst so that they are fertilised externally. This is a far less wasteful process than **broadcast spawning** (during which gametes are randomly ejected into the water), so fewer eggs need to be produced by a female, typically between 900 and 3000. In some species, such as the pink shrimp, *Pandalus borealis*, the fertilised eggs remain attached to the female until they hatch five or six months later. Other species, such as the tiger prawn, *Penaeus monodon*, release the fertilised eggs into the water.

A larva called a nauplius hatches from the egg and moves to the surface waters, where it feeds on plankton. The nauplius larvae are characterised by appendages on their heads that are used for swimming, and the

> **KEY WORDS**
>
> **spermatocyst:** a pouch used to transfer sperm from male shrimp to females
>
> **broadcast spawning:** the release of gametes freely into the water where they undergo fertilisation

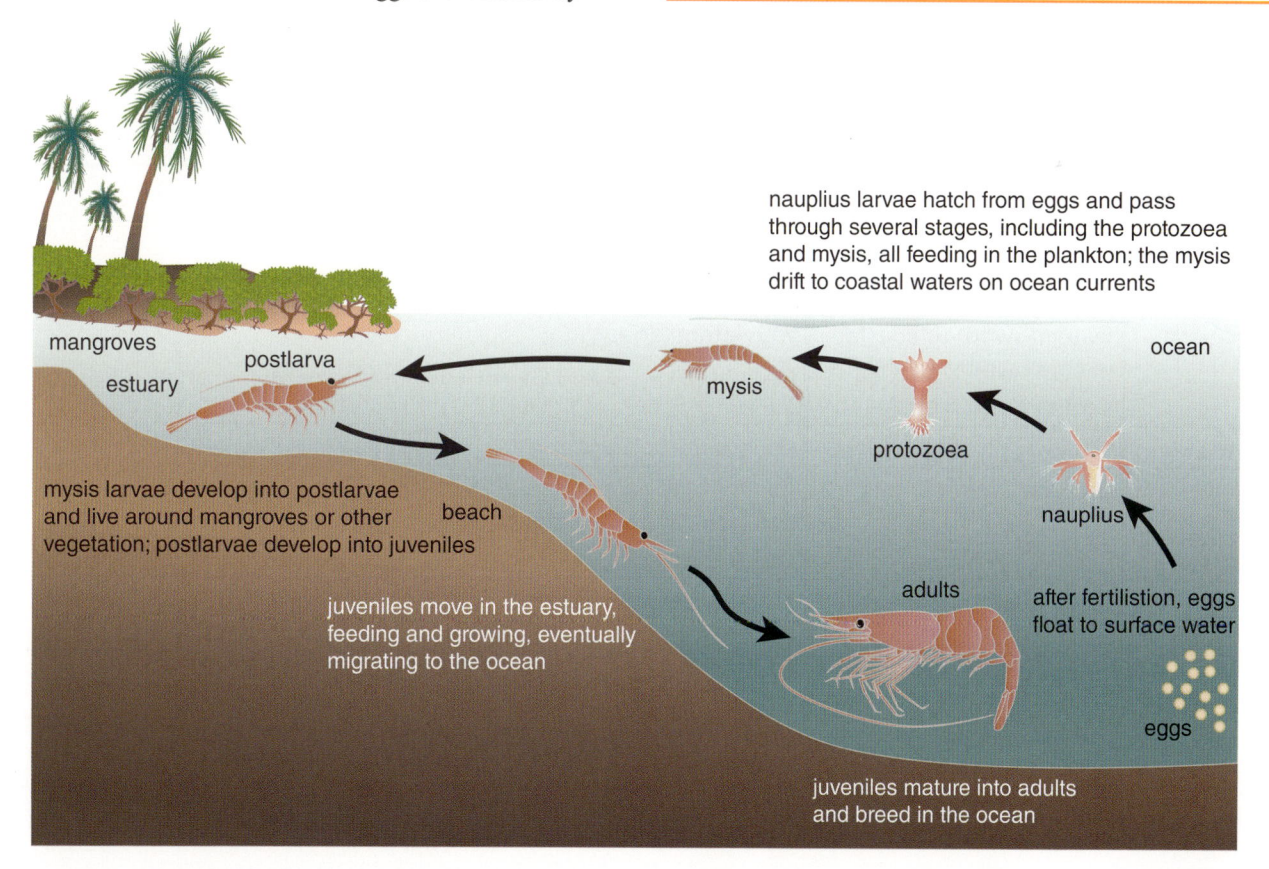

Figure 8.3: The life cycle of shrimp.

presence of a simple eye. After some time feeding in the plankton, they metamorphose into a different larval stage called a **protozoea**. The protozoea larva continues to feed on plankton and passes through several moults of its exoskeleton as it grows to eventually produce a larger, more typically shrimp-like, larva called a **mysis**. The mysis larvae are carried on ocean currents towards the coast and settle in nutrient-rich areas such as mangrove swamps, estuaries and bays. They move to the estuary floor and feed on detritus and small organisms, and metamorphose into a **postlarva**, which resembles a small adult shrimp. These postlarvae tend to move to the shallow estuarine waters, where they become increasingly carnivorous before growing into **juvenile** shrimps. The juvenile shrimps move into the deeper estuarine waters in search of larger prey (often being cannibalistic) and more detritus. When the juveniles approach adult size, they begin to migrate back out to the deep sea, where they become sexually mature adults and begin to breed. The life cycle is summarised in Table 8.2.

> **KEY WORDS**
>
> **protozoea:** the second-stage larva of crustaceans such as shrimp; typically planktonic, these larvae pass through several forms as they grow
>
> **mysis:** the later larval form of crustaceans; shrimp mysis larvae drift to coastal areas
>
> **postlarva:** the stage in the shrimp life cycle produced by metamorphosis of the mysis larva
>
> **juvenile:** the stage of life cycle that is not sexually mature

Stage	Habitat	Advantages	Time duration
fertilisation	deep sea	abundant food for adults and plenty of potential mates	about 6 months
nauplius	planktonic in surface waters	abundant food in plankton and not in competition with later stages distributed by ocean currents	a few days
protozoea	planktonic in surface waters	abundant food in plankton and not in competition with later stages distributed by ocean currents	a few days to weeks
mysis	planktonic in surface waters, swept to coastal waters by ocean currents settle in estuaries	abundant food in plankton and not in competition with later stages distributed by ocean currents	a few days to weeks
postlarvae	shallow estuarine waters	abundant food and shelter from predators	1–2 months
juvenile	estuaries, migrate into ocean	abundant food and shelter from predator and not in competition with larvae and adults larger than postlarvae so less vulnerable	1–2 months
adult	deep ocean areas	abundant food and mates and not in competition with younger stages and unlikely to cannibalise them	1–5 years

Table 8.2: Summary of the life cycle of shrimp.

The importance of different stages in the life cycles of sessile and non-sessile organisms

Some adult organisms, such as the giant clam, are permanently attached to a substrate and are said to be sessile. By having a sessile stage, it generally means that fertilisation must occur outside the body and occur by the random release of male and female gametes into the water. To colonise new areas, a separate, larval form is required that can move freely in the water until a suitable substrate is found for it to colonise. Other adult organisms, such as salmon, have no sessile stages in their life cycles but still have several distinct stages that enable them to survive. Each stage often has a different habitat and food so that adults and juveniles are not competing with each other. For predatory species such as tuna, it is important to keep younger stages away from the adults who would be quite happy to eat their own offspring.

In short, having different stages within a life cycles gives the following benefits:

- enables sessile organisms to colonise new areas
- reduces competition for food and habitats between younger and older individuals
- reduces the risk of cannibalism by older organisms.

Fertilisation methods

If the cycle of life is to continue, it is essential to ensure that gametes (sperm and eggs) meet. The fusion of sperm and eggs is called fertilisation. There are essentially two options for fertilisation:

- **external fertilisation**, which occurs outside the body
- **internal fertilisation**, which occurs inside the body.

External fertilisation

When gametes are released outside the body for fertilisation, there is some degree of uncertainty about them meeting. In order to try and improve the chances of successful fertilisation, most species have adapted their physiology or behaviour in a specific way.

Most marine organisms use external fertilisation. Organisms such as giant clams use broadcast spawning, where gametes are released into the water. It is pure

> **KEY WORDS**
>
> **external fertilisation:** when gametes such as sperm and eggs are released and fuse outside the body
>
> **internal fertilisation:** when gametes such as sperm and eggs fuse inside the body of a parent

chance whether one gamete meets another, and there is little, if any, choice of mate. Broadcast spawning can be a highly wasteful process because there may be no suitable mates nearby. This means that the majority of eggs and sperm simply drift away in the water currents or are eaten by predators. To compensate for the inefficiency of broadcast spawning, many species release massive numbers of eggs and sperm (up to half a billion eggs from one giant clam, for example). Gamete release is synchronised with other individuals by using chemical signals in the water to help ensure that fertilisation occurs. Tuna maximise the chances of fertilisation by aggregating in the same area to simultaneously release gametes.

So why does such an inefficient and seemingly random process exist? The answer is that the potential for so many fertilisations between so many different individuals can generate great genetic diversity, which is important for evolution.

Shrimp and salmon also use external fertilisation but produce far fewer eggs. In both cases, efforts are made to reduce the loss of gametes. Salmon pair up and make redds or nests in gravel, where they deposit the eggs. The sperm are released directly onto them. Male shrimp stick packages that contain sperm onto hairs on the females' bodies. This means that as eggs are released, sperm are already present. The methods used by salmon and shrimp help to make fertilisation far more likely, but there are costs to these adaptations. Individuals need to physically find each other and pair up. Unlike broadcast spawning, each individual has fewer partners so there is less genetic diversity. This means that species with fewer partners tend to have complex methods of mate choice to make sure individuals choose the 'correct' partner with which to mix their genes.

Internal fertilisation

Internal fertilisation requires one organism to introduce its gametes inside another so that fertilisation can take place inside the body. This means that there is a far higher probability that fertilisation will occur. As animals evolved on land and became less dependent on water, internal fertilisation became more important because externally released gametes would dry up and be lost. Gametes can drift and swim in water, so external fertilisation is more likely to be successful if they are released in aquatic environments than into air or onto land. Marine mammals such as whales and dolphins are ancestors of terrestrial mammals (they are thought to be related to the group of animals that include hippos) and use internal fertilisation. Male whales, like all mammals, have a penis for introducing sperm into the female vagina. Once deposited in the vagina, the sperm swim up to the fallopian tubes and, if an egg has ovulated, they may fertilise it. During the breeding season, female whales become fertile and, along with the males, migrate to breeding grounds. Complex courtship routines occur between the sexes and the females choose males to mate with. Most whale species are not monogamous, and both sexes will mate with several different partners during one breeding season. In an effort to gain a competitive advantage, male whales make large quantities of sperm to try and displace a previous male's sperm. If successful fertilisation occurs, a female whale will become pregnant with one calf fathered by one of the males in the breeding group.

Sharks are unusual among fish because they use internal fertilisation. The male shark has special adaptations called claspers, which are modified pelvic fins. A tube runs through the claspers through which sperm are ejected. During mating, the male inserts one of the claspers into the female shark's reproductive cavity, called a cloaca, and ejects sperm through the clasper. Internal fertilisation is beneficial for sharks for two main reasons. Some sharks live solitary lives, or live in single-sex groups until the breeding season, and do not often come across a potential mate. It is, therefore, essential that sharks try to ensure reproductive success by actively transferring the gametes from the male to female. Most species of shark invest a large amount of parental care in their offspring to help ensure their survival.

Parental care

Evolution by natural selection has created two opposing reproductive strategies for passing on genes to the next generation: the *r*-strategy and the *K*-strategy.

r-strategy

Many marine organisms produce millions of offspring and simply release them without any care or additional nourishment other than a yolk sac or nutrients in the egg. The survival of these offspring relies on chance; mortality rates are high and possibly less than 1% of them will

> **KEY WORDS**
>
> *r*-strategy: producing large numbers of offspring while providing little parental investment
>
> *K*-strategy: producing few offspring but providing a large amount of parental investment

survive. A giant clam may produce half a billion eggs in a breeding season but only one or two may actually survive. There is even the risk that none will survive.

K-strategy

The alternative approach is to produce fewer offspring and invest more energy in nurturing them. It would be impossible to guard and nurture half a billion offspring, but if there are far fewer offspring, it is feasible to make the effort to feed and defend them. However, there is still the risk that with only one or two offspring none will survive.

Examples of parental care

Tuna

All species of tuna are *r*-strategists and have a very similar life cycle. A female bluefin tuna can produce up to 25 million eggs every year, of which only a fraction will ever survive to become an adult tuna. No care is given to the larval stages, which have to take their chance within the plankton of the oceans.

Male and female tuna migrate to spawning grounds in the Atlantic and Pacific oceans and Mediterranean Sea at certain times of year. The breeding seasons vary for each species and may also depend on the water temperature of the spawning grounds. There are two separate populations of Atlantic bluefin tuna that either gather in a region of the Mediterranean near the Balearic Islands between May and July, or in the Gulf of Mexico between April and June. Pacific bluefin congregate in distinct spawning grounds in the north-west Philippine Sea and the Sea of Japan between April and August (Figure 8.4). By congregating in the same areas, it increases the likelihood of successful mating and means that genetically different tuna breed together, increasing genetic diversity.

Recent research using tagging has shown that tuna, like salmon, return to the spawning ground in which they themselves were spawned. Males and females swim together during spawning, which generally occurs at night. During spawning, many females release eggs into the water while males release sperm. This is called broadcast spawning because eggs and sperm from many individuals

8 Fisheries for the future

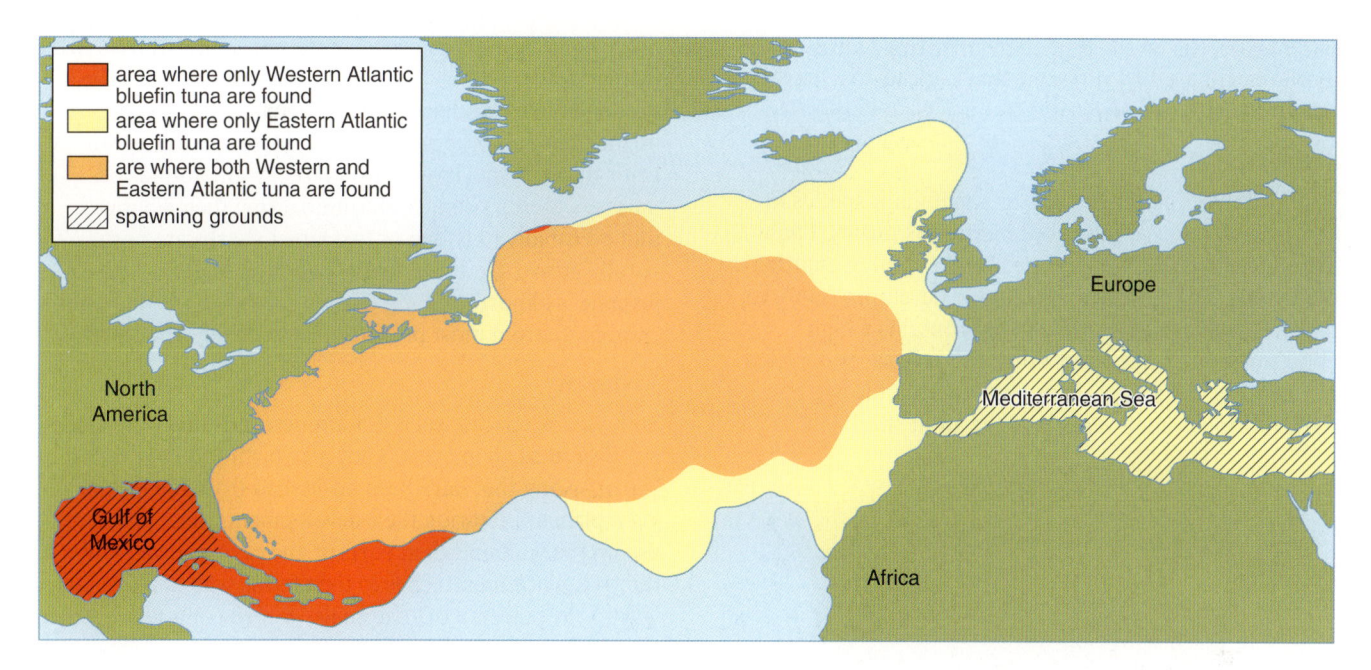

Figure 8.4: The ranges of the two groups of Atlantic bluefin tuna and their spawning grounds.

are in the water together. The random, external fertilisation results in increased genetic diversity, although many eggs are lost. The fertilised eggs, which are buoyant because of the presence of oils, float just beneath the surface of the water, where many are eaten by predators.

Each female can produce vast numbers of eggs, depending on their size; a five-year-old female bluefin tuna releases about five million eggs in a year whereas a 20-year-old female can release up to 45 million. Such huge numbers are produced because the majority will fail to fertilise or be eaten as eggs or larvae.

Larvae hatch after about two days and live in the planktonic surface waters, where they feed on the larvae of all species. They have disproportionally large heads and jaws to enable easy feeding (Figure 8.5). The larvae remain in the spawning grounds, growing rapidly, until they reach a certain size, when they move out into the open ocean feeding grounds. These juvenile fish tend to school together to avoid predators. Different species reach sexual maturity at different ages, typically between four and eight years of age, at which point they will migrate to the spawning grounds to mate.

Whales

Whales are *K*-strategists. As mammals, they are viviparous animals, meaning that the offspring develop inside the mother. The developing calf is located in the mother's uterus and obtains its nutrients from her blood via the placenta and umbilical cord. Different whale species have different gestation periods, ranging from 10 months for the humpback whale to 16 months for the sperm whale. Only one calf is born at a time and it is protected and nurtured by its mother, taking from milk from her mammary glands for between four and 11 months. The calves often remain with their mother or in family groups until they become sexually mature, which can be anything from two to five years, depending on the species. Some species, such as the sperm whale, are known to share 'babysitting' duties within their family groups and older calves will sometimes help raise the younger ones.

Sharks

Shark species use a range of reproductive strategies, but most are considered to be *K*-strategists because a lot of

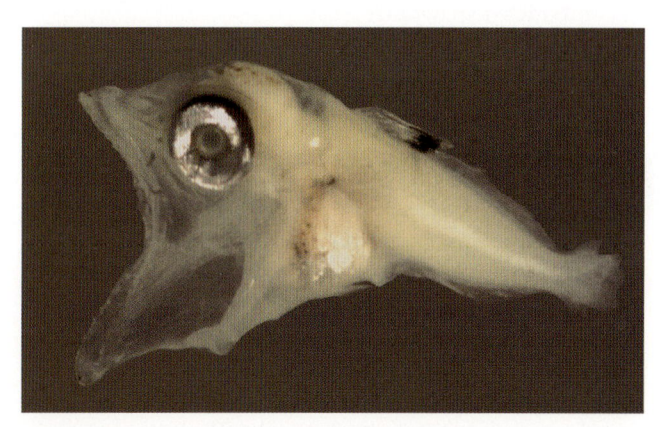

Figure 8.5: Tuna larva, showing its large mouth and head region.

parental care is invested in a few offspring. Three main methods are used by different shark species: oviparity, ovovivparity, and viviparity.

Oviparity

After fertilisation, the females of some shark species lay characteristic eggs often called mermaid's purses. These are attached to rocks or seaweeds and are often guarded by the female. The egg cases contain the developing embryo, which is attached to a yolk sac that contains a high concentration of nutrients. When the yolk sac is depleted of nutrients, the young shark hatches from the egg case as a fully formed, small version of the adult shark.

Figure 8.6: A single shark egg, 'mermaid's purse'

Ovoviviparity

Some sharks produce live young. In many cases, the eggs are fertilised internally in the female's body and then carried inside her until they hatch, eventually passing out as live young. There is a good supply of oxygen inside the mother and, by being inside her body, there is little chance of the young being eaten by predators. While inside the body of the female, they develop inside their egg cases using a yolk sac for nutrition. Some juvenile sharks are brooded inside the mother's body for longer in order to be protected for longer. This means the young need a further food supply. Thresher and porbeagle shark juveniles eat unfertilised eggs (oophagy) that are continuously ovulated by the mother so that they are born at a larger size. The sandtiger shark and grey nurse shark take this a stage further, with embryophagy or intrauterine cannibalism. Prior to birth, the developing sharks swim around the mother's uterus killing and cannibalising their siblings so that eventually only one or two larger sharks are born. A fully grown sandtiger shark is about 2.5m long; the juvenile is almost 1m long when born so is large and strong enough to avoid most predators immediately after birth.

Viviparity

Some shark species, such as hammerheads and bull sharks, are classed as viviparous. They give birth to fully formed live offspring that have been nourished from the mother via a placenta. During their development, these embryos use up the yolk and then parts of the egg covering, and the yolk placenta attaches to the uterine wall in a similar way to the placenta of mammals. A cord containing blood vessels, similar to an umbilical cord in humans, enables blood transport to and from the placenta. The developing shark is able to pass waste products into the mother's blood and gain nutrients such as glucose and amino acids for growth from the mother. When born, these sharks are fully developed and can swim away from their mother to live independently straight away.

Test yourself

1. List **two** advantages and **two** disadvantages of having a larval stage in a life cycle.
2. Suggest why young dolphins spend an extended period with their mothers.
3. Outline why sessile organisms, such as the giant clam, require different larval forms.
4. State **one** advantage and **one** disadvantage of broadcast spawning.
5. Summarise the differences between r- and K-strategies, giving named examples of marine organisms for each.

CASE STUDY 8.1: THE STRANGE LIFE CYCLE OF THE CERATOID DEEP-SEA ANGLER FISH

Life in the darker, deeper parts of the ocean is not easy. The pressure of the water is exceptionally high, there is no light and very little life. Fish that live at great depths may only encounter prey and mates very rarely, so need to ensure that when they do, these encounters are successful.

Some forms of deep-sea angler fish have adapted to these conditions by having a very unusual life cycle.

The male and female fish are very different from each other. The female fish are large, rather ferocious-looking fish with large mouths and teeth, so that any food they encounter is easily caught. Some species have a bioluminescent lure with which they attract other fish and squid. If a meal only passes by once a month, it is essential that it is caught. They also have large ovaries that can produce large numbers of eggs.

CONTINUED

The male angler fish are very different. They are very small and have only very rudimentary mouthparts and a poorly developed gut. Their small size means that they need little energy to move around, but they do have extremely well developed olfactory organs and testes. These tiny male fish can sense chemicals released from the females and swim towards them. When they encounter a female they attach themselves to her with their mouth and become a parasitic organism (Figure 8.7).

A blood supply grows from the female into the male so he simply becomes a part of her body, nourished by her blood supply. Once attached, he remains part of her body for as long as she lives, and in essence becomes an attached sperm-manufacturing organ that the female always has near. Female angler fish often have several of these parasitic males attached to them.

Questions

1. **a** Explain why the male angler fish is small and does not require a fully formed gut.

   b Explain why it is important that the female fish attracts food towards itself and has well-developed mouthparts.

2. Suggest why this life cycle is a good strategy for the angler fish in the deep oceans.

3. Suggest the benefit to the female of having more than one male angler fish permanently attached.

Figure 8.7: A female angler fish with two attached parasitic males.

8.2 Sustainable fisheries

Sustainable fishing is the harvesting of a particular species so that it will still be present in years to come. It is important that we maintain fish stocks at healthy levels for many reasons, including:

- conservation, to preserve biodiversity in order to maintain food webs
- ethics, to ensure that future generations have food that they can harvest.

The **maximum sustainable yield (MSY)** is a key term often referred to in sustainable fishing. The MSY is the rate of fishing that can be carried out without reducing the fish population. If the MSY is exceeded, populations will fall. This can be illustrated by the history of cod fishing in the North Sea.

Sustainable cod fishing in the North Sea

The North Sea is a region of the east Atlantic Ocean bordered by many European countries (Figure 8.8). Fishing fleets in the region had harvested fish for hundreds of years without any major effect on fish stocks.

KEY WORDS

sustainable fishing: fishing up to the maximum sustainable yield so that future fish stocks are not at risk of being depleted

maximum sustainable yield (MSY): the intensity of fishing that can be carried out without reducing future populations

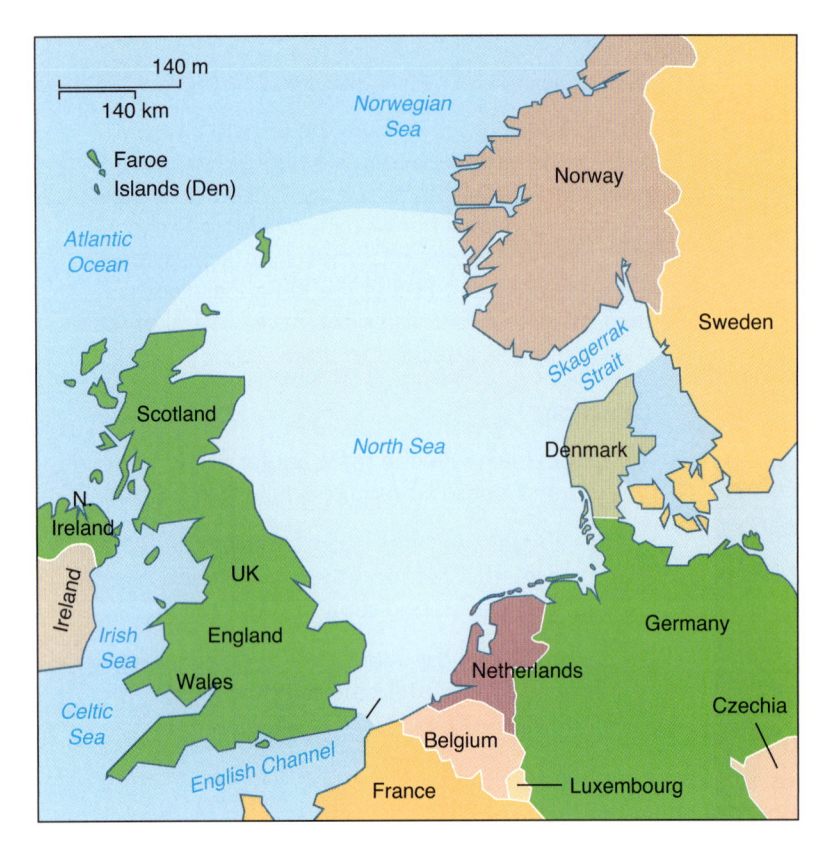

Figure 8.8: Northern Europe and the North Sea.

In the 1960s and 1970s there was a sudden, unexplained increase in populations of certain species, including cod, haddock and whiting. This event, together with EEC subsidies, led to heavy investment in new boats and equipment by fishing fleets. Under the CFP, fishing of the North Sea for whitefish and herring was carried out at unsustainable levels throughout most of the 1970s and 1980s. There were few restrictions on size or age of catch, and young and immature fish were often taken as well as older, sexually mature fish. The eventual consequence of this was a collapse of many of the fish stocks in the 1980s.

North Sea cod dropped to a level that indicated that it was being fished to extinction. Figure 8.9(a) shows the dramatic fall in cod stocks during this period. The average length of cod caught also decreased, indicating that the number of older fish in the population had fallen and increasingly younger fish were being taken. This trend is shown in Figure 8.9(b).

In 1970, the European Economic Community (EEC), now known as the European Union (EU), created a common fisheries policy (CFP). This declared that fish and coastal waters, apart from small zones around each country, would become a communal resource for all of the EEC. The CFP also created a subsidy system whereby if the price of fish fell, fishing fleets were given money to make up the shortfall.

In the 1990s, the EU issued national fishing quotas in an effort to reduce the overfishing. For political reasons these quotas were still in excess of what was required to save cod stocks. By the early 2000s, after carrying out more surveys of cod populations, scientists called for a ban on cod fishing in the North Sea to allow stocks to recover. At the same time, the CFP was reformed, and more focus was placed on protecting fish stocks for the future and preventing overfishing. Despite the scientific evidence, a ban was not implemented but a big reduction in quotas was agreed.

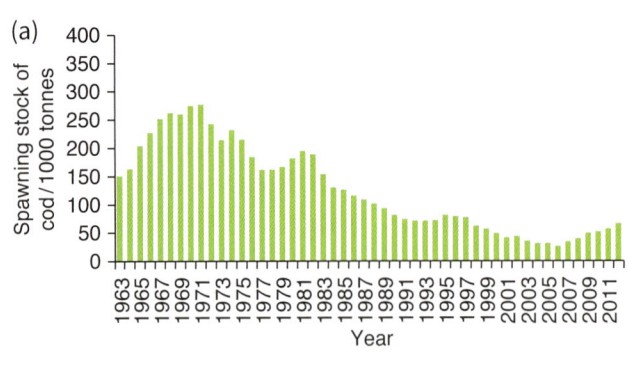

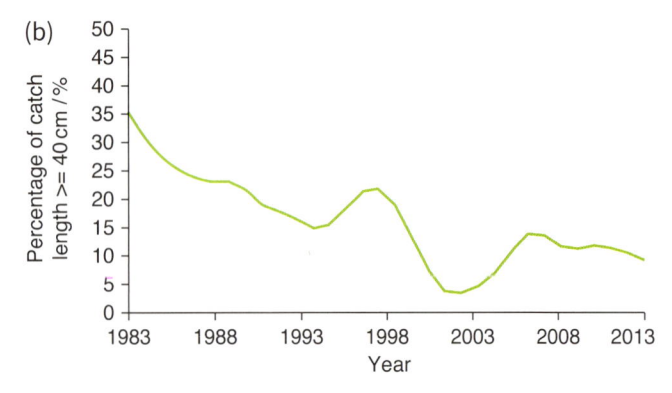

Figure 8.9: Graphs showing (a) changes in spawning stock of cod and (b) the percentage of cod caught that were longer than 40 cm.

Other measures taken included a reduction in the numbers of days that fishing was allowed and a ban on fishing during breeding seasons.

The much stricter quotas seem to have worked to some extent and, by 2015, fish stocks had begun to recover. In 2017, the Marine Stewardship Council (MSC) certified that North Sea cod stocks had risen to a sustainable level. Cod caught from the North Sea, along with cod from Icelandic waters and the Barents Sea, now carries the MSC certification of sustainability. But we still need to be very cautious: stocks are nowhere near the high levels of the 1970s, and quotas and restrictions on boat-days, fishing seasons and fishing areas need to be considered carefully if true long-term, sustainable fishing in the North Sea is to be achieved.

The impacts of modern fishing technology

Over the last 50 years fishing technology has developed significantly. The methods employed now are highly efficient, which means that we are in danger of fishing well beyond MSYs. However, the use of improved technology does not have to result in a negative effect on our oceans. We can design equipment with less focus on ensuring high catches and more on sustainability. Innovations have been made that can help prevent the capture of juveniles and non-target species. Some of the impacts fishing technologies have had will be discussed below.

SONAR

SONAR (**so**und **na**vigation) is the method usually used to find fish. Boats either carry a transducer (Figure 8.10) in the hull or drag one under water. The transducer emits sound waves that are reflected by air in the swim bladders of fish like an echo, and this echo is detected by the SONAR system. The fish-finder measures the time interval between emitting the pulse and the pulse rebounding back to the detector. It will take a shorter length of time for sound to return from a fish that is close compared with one that is further away. Information from the SONAR is transmitted to a monitor to provide a visual representation of the fish underwater. Modern SONAR is now so effective that it shows the exact depth of fish and can identify the type of fish. Some SONAR works horizontally enabling ocean areas around a boat to be scanned for shoals.

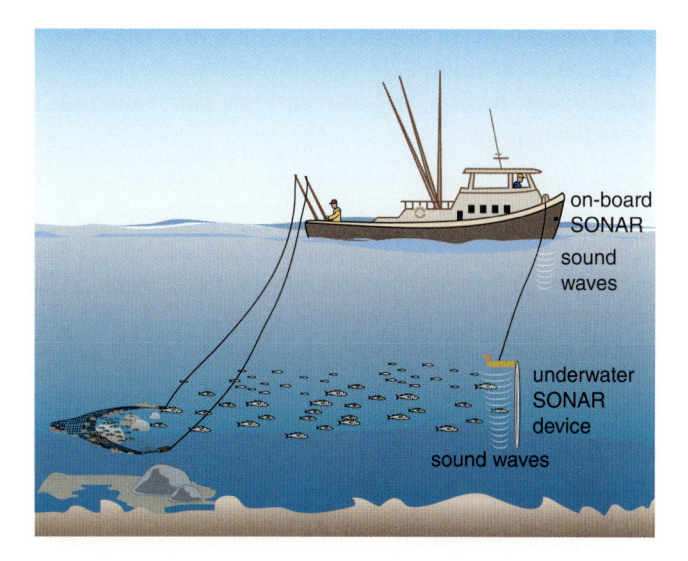

Figure 8.10: SONAR used on a trawler to identify fish.

Before the use of SONAR, identifying fish shoals relied on trial and error and the skill and expertise of the fishers. Experienced crews knew where fish shoals tended to congregate or looked for signs such as pods of dolphins and feeding sea birds. The use of SONAR means that fishing crews can constantly scan for shoals and then efficiently take the fish. This has placed a strain on fish stocks because it is easier to find rare shoals and more time can be spent harvesting the fish than looking for them.

Purse seine fishing

A seine is a fishing net that hangs vertically in the water with its bottom edge held down by weights and its top edge buoyed by floats. A **purse seine** (Figure 8.11) is a type of seine net that can be drawn shut at the bottom to capture fish. It is made of a long wall of netting framed with a float line that floats on the surface,

> **KEY WORDS**
>
> **SONAR:** a method that is used to detect underwater objects by the reflection of sound waves
>
> **purse seine:** a seine net used to capture pelagic shoals of fish; it has a series of ropes that are used to close it and trap the fish before hauling them on board

and a weighted lead line that sinks. Purse rings hang from the lower edge of the gear, through which run a purse line made from steel wire or rope. This is used to close the net.

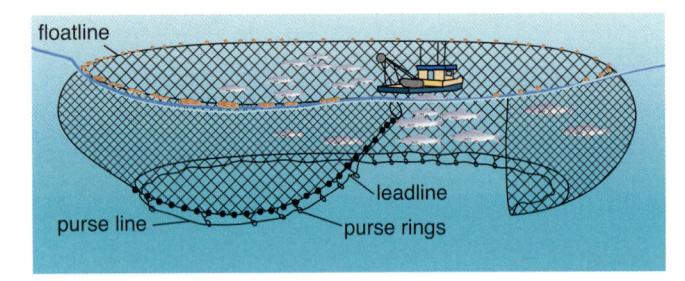

Figure 8.11: Purse seine fishing.

Purse seining is an efficient method for catching **pelagic** fish such as herring and mackerel and can be sustainable when used on a small scale. As net sizes have increased, however, it has been used to take large numbers of fish on an industrial scale (Figure 8.12). This is a problem if fish have vulnerable stocks, and it also takes many non-target species, known as **bycatch**. Purse seines are often used to capture skipjack tuna and bluefin tuna, both of which have seen dramatic population falls. When capturing skipjack tuna, many other species, such as yellowfin tuna, dolphins, turtles, sharks and rays, are also trapped and killed. Fishers in the Mediterranean wait in spawning areas where bluefin tuna aggregate during the breeding season and trap large numbers using purse seine nets. This practice has led to the collapse of Atlantic bluefin stocks.

Figure 8.12: Purse seine net being hauled on board a trawler.

Benthic trawling

Benthic trawling uses a large net with heavy weights that is dragged across the seabed, scooping up everything in its path. It is used to catch organisms such as shrimp, sole, flounder and ray, which live on the seabed. Two weighted, wooden or steel otter boards drag along the seabed disturbing sediments and keeping the net open (Figure 8.13). The net has an open front end, and the captured fish collect at the rear of the net, the cod end. Benthic trawling is possibly the most environmentally damaging method of fishing routinely practised. It has been likened to ripping up a forest to pursue and catch a deer.

Dragging the net across the seabed dislodges most of the organisms in its path, breaks coral reefs and severely damages seabed ecosystems. The damage caused by benthic trawling to a coral reef is clearly shown in

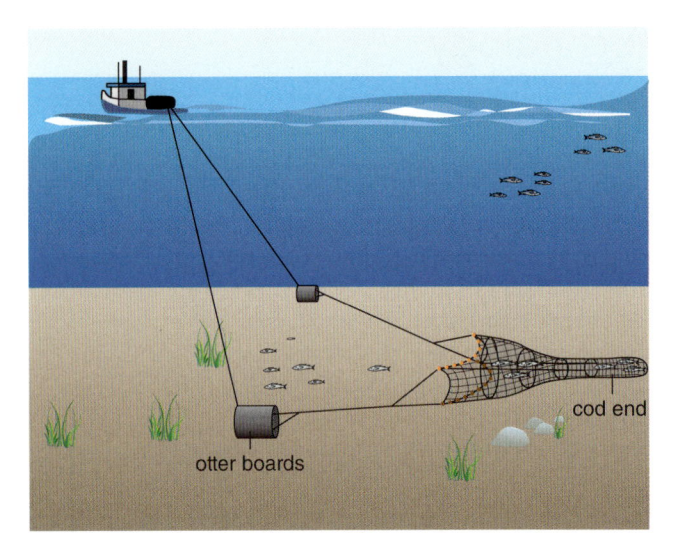

Figure 8.13: Benthic trawling, dragging a net along the seabed.

KEY WORDS

pelagic: zone of open ocean or sea water that is not close to the seabed or shore

bycatch: species, caught by fishing, that are not target species

benthic trawling: a fishing method that drags a net along the seabed; wooden boards at the front of the net keep the net open and stir up the seabed, causing damage

8 Fisheries for the future

Figure 8.14: the coral has been smashed to pieces and the reef is no longer capable of functioning as an ecosystem.

Benthic trawling is not selective and up to 90% of a trawl's catch may be bycatch; that is, non-target organisms. Many of the species caught are of little commercial value and are thrown back overboard already dead or dying. Scientists have estimated that in the Gulf of Mexico, for every pound of shrimp caught, between four and ten pounds of marine resources are thrown away. Shrimp trawls in Panama routinely discard more than 80% of their catch. Juvenile fish of many species are often caught, and in the Caribbean and Gulf of Mexico many juvenile snapper, mackerel and porgy are caught when shrimping. The capture of juvenile fish affects fish populations of target and non-target species, reducing yields for the fishing industries. In Indonesia, increased use of benthic trawling has led to a 40% reduction in catches by local, traditional fishers. In other areas, such as Guinea, benthic trawlers have caused physical damage to other boats and equipment.

Tourism is also affected by benthic trawling. Damage to the seabed affects the populations of many species that tourists come to see, such as turtles, coral reefs and sharks.

Benthic trawling is now banned by many countries. The Indonesian government has banned it in an effort to improve catches and income for local fishers. It has also been banned in a 23 000 square mile area of the Atlantic Ocean from North Carolina to Florida, to protect deep-sea coral reefs after it was found that 90% of an area of reef had been destroyed by benthic trawls. The New Zealand government has banned benthic trawling in many ecologically sensitive areas, in particular around hydrothermal vents.

Factory ships

Factory ships are large fish-processing ships. They are designed to exploit areas of ocean far from land and can be at sea many weeks before returning to port. Some factory ships, such as stern trawlers, collect large amounts of fish that is then processed onboard. Others ships act as freezer 'motherships'; other trawlers bring their catch back to the factory ship each day, where it is processed and frozen. The introduction of large factory ships has meant that more fish can be taken on one trip. It has also opened up rich fishing grounds in distant, previously unexploited areas. The Japanese, Korean and Russian fishing fleets have many factory ships and trawl areas such as the south Atlantic Ocean. The use of industrial factory ships has also caused conflict with local fishers who have seen their industries threatened by falling catches.

The original idea for factory ships came from whaling; whalers would sail into distant waters hunting whales and processing them as soon as they were caught. This brought many species of whales to the brink of extinction during the twentieth century. Only one whale factory ship now exists, MV *Nisshin Maru*, which is the mothership for the Japanese whaling fleet.

Regulating sustainable fishing

It is inconceivable for all global fishing to be banned and all fish products to be produced by aquaculture. A realistic aim is to ensure that fishing is sustainable and does not put future stocks at risk. In order to

Figure 8.14: Seabed **(a)** before and **(b)** after benthic trawling.

achieve sustainable fishing, certain data need to be collected about the fish populations. When the health of the populations has been determined, restrictions for preventing overfishing can be put into place and monitoring and enforcement can be carried out.

Information required for sustainable fishing

Scientists are employed by governments to determine the health of fish stocks and set safe harvesting quotas that will not cause them to fall. Estimating current and predicting future stocks is not easy and scientists must consider several factors in order to recommend accurate quotas.

Figure 8.15 shows a simple population dynamic model for fish stocks. Whether a population increases or decreases depends upon the rate that new fish enter a population (recruitment) and the rate at which fish leave the population. New fish are recruited by reproduction or immigration, while fish leave as a result of mortality or emigration. If fish leave a population faster than they enter, the population will decrease, and vice versa. If fishing is to be sustainable, fewer fish must leave than enter.

Recruitment

The number of juvenile fish surviving to a particular stage and entering a population is called the **recruitment**. The exact stage that a fish must be at to be classed as successfully recruited into a population varies from species to species and according to who is doing the survey. Most authorities consider this is to be when fish have reached a size when they can be caught and counted in nets.

Recruitment depends upon several factors, such as **fecundity**, age of **reproductive maturity**, growth and habitat dependency.

- **Fecundity**

Fecundity is the reproductive rate of the fish and is measured by the number of gametes produced in a set time. It is a measure of fertility. Many species have high fecundity, producing millions of gametes, but only a fraction of these survive to be recruited into the population.

- **Age of reproductive maturity**

Age of reproductive maturity is the control of maturity in fish is complex and there is variation both within and between different species. The age of fish plays an important role in many species. This is complicated by growth rates, masses, population densities and ratios of males and females. There is some evidence that

> **KEY WORDS**
>
> **recruitment:** the arrival of new organisms in a population; for fish it is often considered to be the stage at which fish have reached an age when they can be caught in nets
>
> **fecundity:** the rate of reproduction of organisms; in fish the rate of egg production is often considered as a measure of fecundity
>
> **reproductive maturity:** the time when an organism is able to reproduce sexually

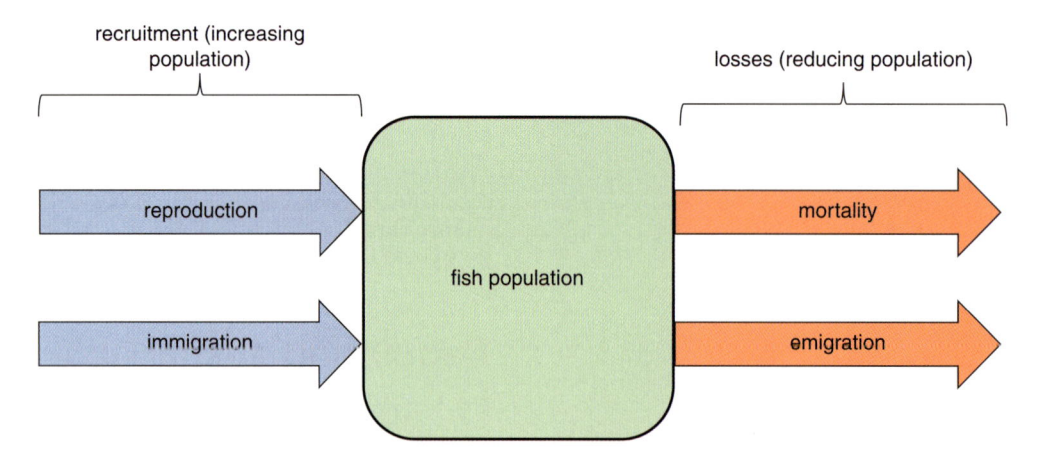

Figure 8.15: Factors affecting fish populations.

overfishing can lower the average age of reproductive maturity. The effect of this could be that younger, smaller fish become mature, produce fewer gametes, and overall recruitment falls. Species of fish that take many years to reach reproductive maturity will generally result in slower growing populations. Some species may need many years to re-establish healthy populations after a significant drop in number.

- **Growth**

The growth rate of fish is the speed at which the length or mass increases. Fish are considered to have been recruited into a population once they have reached a certain stage of development. Growth rates can vary as a result of many factors, such as food availability, temperature, oxygen levels and species of fish. Some species are naturally slow growing, while others grow rapidly. A slow-growing species will generally have a lower rate of recruitment. As already stated, growth rate can also have an impact on age of reproductive maturity and some species only start breeding once they have reached a particular size.

- **Habitat dependency**

Many species of fish have complex life cycles with different stages of development that require different habitats. In Chapter 7, the life cycles of salmon and grouper were described. Both of these species require a range of different habitats for different stages of their life cycle. If one of these habitats is lost, the life cycle is disrupted, and recruitment reduced.

Mortality

The rate of mortality is the rate at which the fish are dying. There are two types of **mortality rate**: natural mortality and fishing mortality.

> **KEY WORD**
>
> **mortality rate:** the death rate; natural mortality is the death rate arising from natural causes, while fishing mortality is the death rate caused by fishing

- **Natural mortality**

Fish populations are subject to the normal causes of mortality, such as predation, disease, lack of food and even chance events such as volcanic eruptions. Large numbers of predators and low amounts of food will directly reduce populations, but other factors can have indirect effects. Predator and food availability can depend on weather conditions, other food web changes, diseases, El Niño and human influence. This means that natural mortality rates can vary from year to year. Because there are so many variables, trying to create a predictive model for population change is almost impossible.

The climate influences how much energy enters a food web by affecting phytoplankton productivity. Phytoplankton growth depends on photosynthesis so is affected by light intensity, carbon dioxide levels and temperature. It also depends on mineral ion concentrations, often from upwelling currents. Human influences such as agricultural run-off and sediment can also have effects.

Diseases can suddenly affect populations. The spread of disease can be increased by high population densities so larger population sizes can appear to fall rapidly.

The majority of fish and shellfish have high fecundity, producing many gametes. The natural attrition rate for larval forms and juveniles is, however, very high. Despite having a high reproductive potential, very few fish are actually recruited into populations.

- **Fishing mortality**

The death of fish as a result of fishing activities is called fishing mortality. It is not simply the number of fish that have been harvested and sold, but includes bycatch, discarded fish and other deaths caused by fishing. The number of fish actually harvested is relatively easy to assess from records of fish sold. Losses as a result of discards and bycatches are more difficult to assess because they rely on reports by fishers and scientific experiments. Fishing industries and scientists often disagree on estimates of bycatch and discards. Because fishers are stakeholders in the industry; they may not feel it is in their short-term interest to report high fishing mortalities. This can lead to reduced estimates of populations and reduced future quotas. An accurate estimate is important for the long-term health of the industry, as unsustainable fishing puts future stocks at risk.

Sustainable fishing models

A simple approach to determining how many fish can be harvested at any one time is that, in order to be sustainable, the population must not be reduced below previous levels. Recruitment in any year must be equal to or greater than the sum of natural mortality and fishing mortality:

recruitment ≥ natural mortality + fishing mortality

If recruitment is lower than the sum of natural mortality and fishing mortality, then the population will fall and the fishing is unsustainable.

In reality, the setting of sustainable fishing quotas is more complicated than this. Predicting the natural mortality is almost impossible and it needs to be measured frequently by scientific surveys. The fishing mortality also has to be as accurate as possible, using scientific methods and not based simply on market sales of fish, which may underestimate discards and bycatch. The age and size profile of populations needs to be considered. Immature fish, despite being recruited, will not have reproduced so, if they are caught too early, will not contribute to the overall future of the population. Bluefin tuna farming has been problematic in this respect. Juvenile tuna are captured before reproducing and then taken to tuna 'farms'. This means that fish are lost before they have bred so stocks fall. Sudden events that can affect breeding and natural mortality also need to be considered, such as volcanic eruptions and El Niño.

Methods to ensure sustainable fishing

In order to ensure that there are stocks of fish for the future, action needs to be taken by national governments to regulate fishing practices. Fish do not respect national boundaries, and there are many areas of our oceans that lie beyond the jurisdiction of any nation. To deal with this problem, intergovernmental agreements have been made by agencies such as the Food and Agriculture Organization (FAO) of the United Nations.

Restriction by season

Prohibiting fishing during certain times of year is frequently used to protect stocks. Seasonal restrictions are often linked with area restrictions: bans are imposed on fishing in certain areas at certain times of year. The reasons for seasonal bans include the following.

- Preventing fishing for a period of time enables fish to grow, reach larger sizes and be recruited into the population.
- Restrictions often coincide with breeding seasons, to enable fish to spawn and prevent overfishing when fish have aggregated for breeding. Fishers found that catches were higher at certain times, usually when fish aggregated for breeding. Fishing efforts used to be increased at those times and had a very negative effect on stocks by disrupting breeding and overfishing the adult population.
- Restrictions in areas where juveniles are maturing improves their chances of reaching maturity. Many marine organisms have complex life cycles with different stages living in different habitats. In the Gulf of Mexico, shrimp fishing is regulated in this way: fishing seasons are set so that larval and juvenile shrimp are not fished when in coastal areas or in the process of migration out to sea. This allows shrimp to move to open water and grow larger, improving yields for the fishing industry.
- Seasonal restrictions are not only for the benefit of the target fishery organism. Some fishing restrictions in the Caribbean are set to coincide with the migration and breeding of turtles, which can be caught by accident. In some areas, fishing is closed during annual passages of whales and dolphins.

Fishers may object to seasonal restrictions because they reduce the period during which they can work. There is a risk that fishers will then catch other species to make up for the shortfall, which can lead to exploitation of other species. They may also overfish at other times of year to compensate for the lost revenue. If the reasons for the restrictions are explained, however, fishers will often support seasonal (and area) closures in order to help improve fish stocks and secure their long-term future. In many cases they will help prevent boats fishing illegally and help monitor the catch. If local fishers support the bans, it can help to reduce the expense of surveillance of boats and catches.

Imposing restrictions on fishing grounds that span more than one nation requires intergovernmental cooperation. A ban will not work if only fishers from one nation comply, and this can create conflict between fishing fleets. Georges Bank is a fishing ground near New England that is fished by both the US and Canadian fishing fleets. In the 1970s and 1980s it became clear that fish stocks were under severe threat of overfishing. The US and Canadian governments worked together to impose seasonal and area restrictions in an effort to help restore fish stocks. Despite worries about the threat to their main source of income, the majority of fishers had noticed a fall in their catch and supported the action. They worked with the regulators to put the restrictions in place so helping to restore the stocks of target species.

The advantages and disadvantages of using seasonal restrictions are summarised in Table 8.3.

Restriction by setting quotas

The most basic measure that can be taken is the allocation of specific quotas of fish that may be harvested each year. The aim is to restrict the number of fish taken to let stocks recover. National regulators set an overall quota that may be harvested within a set period of time and then share this allocation between the commercial fishers. These allocations may be used by the fishers or sold on to others. Despite their obvious value and apparent simplicity, implementing quotas is problematic because there are many different fishing vessels and checking catches is not easy. The first use of quotas by the EU for North Sea and Mediterranean fishing was not successful and over-fishing continued illegally in many countries. The quotas also inadvertently encouraged the discarding of dead fish back into the sea if a landing was over its quota. Quotas are, however, very important in regulating how many fish may be harvested each year based on the MSY. In practice, regulators now tend to set quotas and use methods of restriction to achieve those quotas. The advantages and disadvantages of setting quotas are summarised in Table 8.4.

Restriction by licensing

In many countries, boat owners must apply for a commercial fishing licence or permit. This enables regulators to control the number of boats that are permitted to fish each year. The licence system also enables regulators to stipulate the maximum boat and engine sizes, fish quotas, permissible fishing gear and number of boat-days the licensee is entitled to. Modern licences are now used in conjunction with sophisticated satellite monitoring and are held in electronic form as well as on paper. This new style of e-licence means that boats can be rapidly identified and their permitted catches checked to help identify vessels that are acting in broach of regulations. All licences can be revoked if the holder is not adhering to the rules and fines may be issued. Using a licence system can, however, be costly. Licences need to be issued, checked and some form of monitoring needs to be carried out to ensure that fishers do not break the rules. The advantages and

Advantages of seasonal restrictions	Disadvantages of seasonal restrictions
• allow breeding of fish • reduce fishing intensity at a time when fish aggregate in specific areas • reduce overall intensity of fishing, allowing growth of populations • reduce negative effects on non-target species • relatively easy to implement	• reduce the value of catch for local fishers • may encourage fishers to take excessive amounts of fish at different times of year to compensate for the loss of other seasons • may encourage fishers to take other species of fish • can cost money to patrol and monitor fishing at all times of year

Table 8.3: Advantages and disadvantages of seasonal restrictions.

Advantages of setting quotas	Disadvantages of setting quotas
• ensure that fish are only taken up to the MSY allowing populations to be maintained • ensure long-term sustainability of catches • give a clear indication of fish stocks	• difficult to monitor • can encourage the illegal dumping of dead fish • may be based on incorrect data

Table 8.4: Advantages and disadvantages of setting quotas.

Advantages of restriction by licensing	Disadvantages of restriction by licensing
• enable ministries to regulate fishing intensity • make it easy to identify illegal fishing boats • are a simple way to identify how many boats are permitted in an area	• do not actually stop illegal fishing unless they are checked • require monitoring systems and a governmental agency to issue them

Table 8.5: Advantages and disadvantages of restriction by licensing.

disadvantages of restriction by licensing are summarised in Table 8.5.

Restriction of location

Areas of sea may be closed for fishing, or restrictions placed on the type of fishing or number of boats that can be used. No-take zones are often set up where fishers are not able to take any fish. Restricting fishing in certain locations reduces the number of fish caught, thus increasing populations. The closure of areas that are known breeding grounds or nursery areas for juveniles helps secure recruitment into the general population. The reasons for restricting fishing within certain locations include the following.

- Allowing depleted populations to recover. It can also help increase populations that are not in the restricted area. In Norway, it was found that banning lobster fishing in protected areas increased populations of lobster in neighbouring areas as well. Some marked lobsters were found to have migrated hundreds of miles away from the protected areas.
- Preventing fishing in a particular breeding or nursery area. Fish aggregate in particular areas to spawn so banning fishing in these areas allows successful breeding. Areas such as mangroves are often nursery grounds, so banning fishing in them allows juveniles to reach adult size.
- Reducing bycatch and damage to other species. Ecologically sensitive areas such as coral reefs, seagrass meadows and mangroves often have bans on fishing to prevent damage to the complex food chains that exist in these areas. They act as a refuge for populations of fish, shellfish and other species.

Refuge zones are often set up as part of general conservation measures, such as the development of **marine protected areas (MPAs)**. MPAs serve as general protectors of biodiversity and, as refuge zones, allow fish to reproduce without threat. The fish then migrate to other areas, increasing the populations of those areas. MPAs and general conservation are discussed further in Chapter 9.

In theory, creating areas where fishing is restricted is a simple tool, as long as fishers respect the restrictions and they can be enforced. If fishers can be convinced of its value to their long-term viability, they will often regulate the areas themselves.

There can be problems, however. Areas that are fished by fleets of different nationalities require intergovernmental agreements across national boundaries. Surveillance and monitoring of an area may be required, and this can be expensive. In the large Phoenix Island Marine Reserve, an MPA around the republic of Kiribati, an illegal shark-fishing vessel reduced shark populations to near-zero levels at one atoll in the early 2000s. In such large MPAs, monitoring and enforcement is very expensive, particularly for countries with a low gross domestic product (GDP) (a measure of a nation's total economic activity). Another risk of creating protected areas is that fishers may target and over-exploit other areas instead, thus moving the overfishing problem to a different area. The advantages and disadvantages of restrictions on location are summarised in Table 8.6.

> **Note:** The gross domestic product theory is extension content, and is not part of your syllabus.

KEY WORD

marine protected area (MPA): an area of ocean or coastline where restrictions have been placed on activities; the levels of restriction may vary, some may be no-take areas where no fishing is permitted, others may allow some fishing, some may ban all access to unauthorised people, while others may allow restricted access

Advantages of restrictions on location	Disadvantages of restrictions on location
• create areas where fish populations can recover and increase • cause population increases in the restricted areas that 'spill over' into other areas, causing a general population increase • reduce bycatch and damage to other species • relatively easy to set up	• fisheries may lose profits • fisheries may begin to damage other areas • expensive surveillance and enforcement is required • can cause disputes within the fishing industry

Table 8.6: Advantages and disadvantages of restriction on location.

Restriction of method

Certain fishing methods are far more damaging than others. Restrictions may be placed on which methods are permitted at different times of year and in different areas.

Table 8.7 summarises the environmental effects of different fishing methods. The use of nets when purse seining (Figure 8.11) and benthic trawling (Figure 8.13) can have potentially major impacts on fish stocks. Both methods can take large numbers of fish at any one time, and if not used carefully do not discriminate between adult and juveniles and other species. Regulating mesh sizes can help reduce the catch of smaller, juvenile fish and smaller non-target species but

Fishing method	Example target species	Effect on target species	Effect on non-target species	Effect on habitat
purse seine	mackerel, tuna, herring, sardines	risk of overfishing mesh size restrictions can reduce catch of juveniles	loss of tuna, turtles and dolphins	low impact on habitat
benthic trawl	plaice, sole, rays	risk of overfishing mesh and net size restrictions can reduce catch of juveniles and prevent overfishing	severe impact on other species very non-selective method of harvesting	severe impact on seabed, damaging reefs and habitats
rod and line	tuna, swordfish	lower risk of overfishing less intensive than using nets	low risk of bycatch	little or no impact on habitat
long-lines	tuna, hake, cod, swordfish	medium risk of overfishing if lines are not long and have few hooks	demersal long-lines are a sustainable method if lines are secured to the seabed away from sea birds and turtles demersal long-lines can catch and kill sharks pelagic long-lines catch and kill sea birds, turtles, sharks and other non-target species	some impact on habitat

Table 8.7: A summary of the environmental effects of different fishing methods.

is not perfect. Theoretically, setting larger **minimum mesh sizes** should allow smaller fish to slip through the net. When fish gather at the cod end of a trawl, however, they are crowded together, and juveniles may not be able to reach the mesh where they could pass through to escape.

Purse seine fishing can be sustainable when used carefully but only when a shoal of target fish has been located. It should be used with turtle escape devices and dolphin deterrents. Almost all methods of benthic trawling are unsustainable, severely reducing stocks of target and non-target species and damaging habitats. Many fishing regulators have now placed restrictions on benthic trawling because of its potential to cause damage.

Rod and line fishing (often called pole-and-line) is used for catching pelagic predator species such as tuna and swordfish Figure 8.16. It is a much more sustainable method than using nets. As it is less efficient than net

> ### KEY WORD
> **minimum mesh size:** the smallest permitted size of the holes in fishing nets

> **Note:** demersal is extension content, and is not part of your syllabus.

Figure 8.16: Pole-and-line fishing for tuna around the Maldives.

fishing, fewer fish are caught so there is less impact on populations. If bait is used selectively, there is little risk of bycatch and there is almost no impact on the habitat. Many regulators ban all methods other than rod and line fishing for tuna.

Long-line fishing is a controversial method. Two types are practised, demersal (or bottom; region of sea close to seabed; demersal fish live on or close to the seabed) long-line fishing and pelagic long-line fishing (Figure 8.17). In both methods, large numbers of baited hooks hang on long lines. In demersal long-lining, the

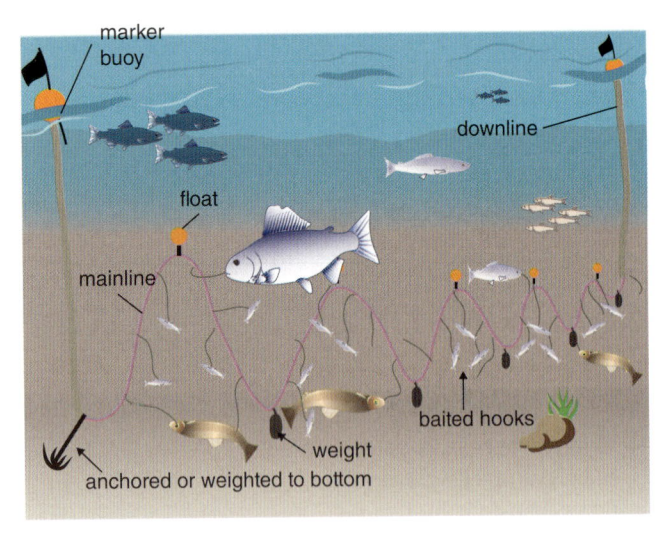

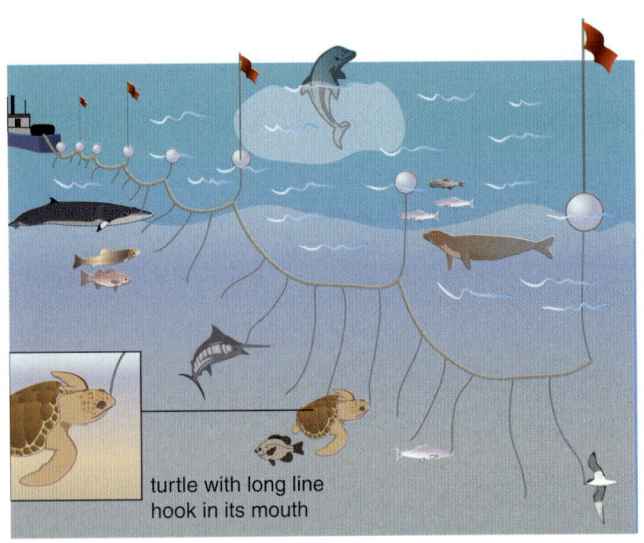

Figure 8.17: Long-line fishing methods: **(a)** demersal and **(b)** pelagic. Pelagic long-line fishing can cause the deaths of turtles, sea birds and sharks.

8 Fisheries for the future

Advantages of restricting fishing methods	Disadvantages of restricting fishing methods
• over-exploitation of target species by reducing net sizes and using less efficient methods such as rod and line fishing • bycatch by restricting the use of benthic trawling and pelagic long-lines and setting minimum mesh sizes • catch of smaller, immature fish by setting minimum mesh sizes	• more labour-intensive methods, such as rod and line, are required • can be resistance from fisheries • there is a cost to enforcing them

Table 8.8: Advantages and disadvantages of restricting fishing methods.

lines are weighed down at the seabed between marker buoys and left to catch fish such as cod. This method, as long as the lines are carefully secured, are not too long, do not have too many hooks, and the bait is carefully selected, is a sustainable method. The use of pelagic long-lines is much more damaging. When used to catch fish such as tuna, the lines are towed behind boats in the surface water. Lines can stretch for hundreds of metres and have many hooks. Unfortunately, the bait not only attracts tuna but many other species, such as sharks, sea turtles and sea birds. Pelagic long-lining is not a sustainable method, although research is being carried out into methods of weighting the hooks to take them out of the range of sea birds and turtles and making bait unappetising to non-target species. The advantages and disadvantages of restricting fishing methods are summarised in Table 8.8.

Restrictions on the size of fish that can be retained

If fish are removed from a population before they have reproduced, populations decline rapidly. Determining accurately whether a fish is reproductively mature is almost impossible while at sea, so a basic measure of whether or not it has reached reproductive maturity is its size. Large fish are more likely to be older and to have already had at least one breeding season. Many national and supranational regulators set minimum sizes for the fish and shellfish that may be kept. Fish need to be measured at the point of catch and thrown back into the sea immediately if they are undersize. This requires a quick measurement of length (usually the end of the snout to the end of the tail). Table 8.9 shows the minimum sizes for some North Sea fish. One of the problems with setting minimum sizes is that the fish may have already been killed or damaged by the time they are measured. Enforcing restrictions on fish size is costly and requires spot checks on fishing vessels, landings on the quayside and also the markets for undersize fish. What should be done with dead undersize fish is a difficult question. These fish are often discarded into the sea and not added to the quota of fish landed, and are a hidden cause of fish mortality. It is better to ensure that undersize fish are not caught in the first place. The advantages and disadvantages of setting minimum fish sizes are summarised in Table 8.10.

Species of fish	Minimum landing size / cm
bass	42
cod	35
dover sole	24
haddock	30
hake	27
herring	20
whiting	27
plaice	27

Table 8.9: Minimum sizes of North Sea fish.

Advantages of setting minimum fish sizes	Disadvantages of setting minimum fish sizes
• immature fish are returned to the sea to breed, increasing populations • fish stocks increase • very successful for lobsters and crabs which are returned to the ocean alive if undersized	• the enforcement of fish size restrictions is costly • damaged and dead fish are returned to the sea, which may not be included in the landing quota

Table 8.10: Advantages and disadvantages of setting minimum fish sizes.

Restriction of fishing intensity

If we are to ensure that fishing is sustainable, there needs to be regulation of how many fish are caught. Harvesting of fish needs to be below the MSY. Setting quotas for fish landings to ensure that we harvest below the MSY may seem simple, but in practice it is difficult to enforce and monitor. As already discussed, imposing quotas has, at times, led to dumping of dead fish that have been caught over quota, and these dead, undeclared fish are a hidden cause of fish mortality. Illegal catches are estimated to amount to between 11 and 26 million tonnes of fish annually. Rather than stipulating how many can be caught, it can be easier to control the intensity of fishing by restricting factors such as the number of boats in a fleet, boat sizes, engine sizes, number of boat-days and fishing gear sizes.

Restricting the number of boats in a fishing fleet will help prevent overfishing but has to be carried out in conjunction with other control measures. One factory ship can take many more fish than three small inshore trawlers, so not only does the size of the fleet have to be controlled, but also the size of individual boats. Engine size is another factor, as larger engines allow trawlers to reach more distant fishing grounds and move between fishing grounds more quickly in order to exploit more stocks. The aim of regulating boat numbers, sizes and engines is to create a system that ensures there is a fair allocation for all fishers in a fleet.

Restricting the size of nets and the lengths of lines used will help prevent overfishing. Less fishing intensity reduces the intensity of effort, so more trawls need to be carried out to achieve the same catch. Rod and line fishing is far less intensive than using nets, and in many parts of the world, such as the Maldives and Seychelles, this method is encouraged.

The number of days that boats are able to fish is also often restricted. Each fishing vessel owner is allocated an annual number of boat-days for fishing. Fishers need to keep detailed boat logbooks that can be inspected by regulators, stating the times they have been out at sea. One disadvantage of setting boat-days is that if trawlers are at sea for days without a reasonable catch, they will have used their boat-day allocation but at a loss.

Restricting fishing intensity requires regulation by governments and needs to be done in a way that does not disadvantage any particular fishers. In some countries, such as Indonesia and Malaysia, restrictions on fishing intensity have benefitted medium- and small-scale fisheries by reducing the share of large companies. The number of licences and permissible boat numbers and sizes needs to be evaluated annually depending on fish stocks, which requires constant scientific monitoring and enforcement. Care also has to be taken not to suddenly increase fleet capacity in a year when stocks are large, but then have to reverse this when stocks are lower, causing unemployment. Some regulators such as the EU operate subsidy systems to help fishers when fleet sizes need to be reduced. This has caused problems when subsidies have been spent on fewer, larger vessels with more equipment. The advantages and disadvantages of restricting fishing intensity are summarised in Table 8.11.

Monitoring

If restrictions are placed on fishing, they need to be monitored and enforced fairly. Illegal fishing needs to be prevented, so the best way of maintaining a restriction is if fishers are in agreement with the measures being taken. Most fishers want to be able to continue to harvest fish in the future. They will often be open to measures taken to protect stocks, as long as they are

Advantages of restricting fishing intensity	Disadvantages of restricting fishing intensity
• less fish are harvested, increasing stocks	• there is a possibility of unemployment and loss of earnings for fisheries and local communities
• careful restrictions on boat and engine sizes can help small- and medium-scale fisheries	• it can be expensive to monitor and enforce, and may require subsidies for boats that are no longer used
• licensing can help monitoring of boat numbers and make enforcement easier	
• it is easier to regulate than simply setting quotas, which are difficult to monitor	• different years require different-sized fleets, causing fluctuations in employment and income each year

Table 8.11: Advantages and disadvantages of restricting fishing intensity.

involved in the decision making and their needs and views considered. Fishers who are in agreement with restrictions will self-monitor and help to police and report transgressions. Rather than imposing what may seem to be draconian measures on the fishing industry from remote governmental organisations, a more successful policy is to bring all parties together for discussions. In order to monitor restrictions, several methods are available.

- **Air and sea patrolling**

The area covered by fishing boats can be very large so monitoring can be difficult and costly. Coastguards and fishery inspection teams use low-flying aeroplanes and surface boats to observe fishing boats randomly. If aerial observers are concerned about the activity of a particular boat, they will radio for a surface boat with boarding crew, who will intercept the ship. Aerial and sea patrols are useful because they can spot unusual activity, and can watch for boats that seem to be at sea too frequently. They are, however, expensive and it is impossible to cover large areas of ocean. Even if ships are seen breaking fishing laws, it can be difficult to obtain evidence. If a crew knows that it has been spotted, excess catch or gear can be disposed of before inspectors arrive. The advantages and disadvantages of air and sea patrolling are summarised in Table 8.12.

- **Satellite tracking**

The majority of ships use the Automatic Identification System (AIS), which is a satellite communication method originally used for maritime safety and security. It uses navigation and communication satellites so that ships can 'talk' electronically to each other and with authorities on shore. It broadcasts information such as vessel identification data, position, course and speed. Fishing regulators now use AIS as part of a vessel detection system (VDS) as it can transmit real-time information about the activities of each ship. If a ship is causing concern, air and sea patrols can be sent out with inspectors to obtain further information. The full integrated inspection system is shown in Figure 8.18.

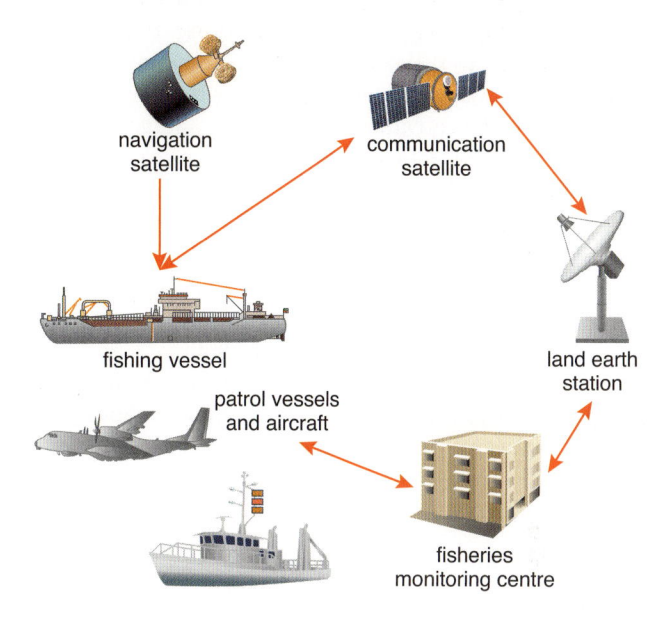

Figure 8.18: The integrated vessel management system (VMS) for monitoring fishing activity.

As part of satellite monitoring, electronic logbooks send information via satellite to the regulators so that real-time data of catches made at sea can be seen immediately.

Satellite monitoring makes it possible to carry out surveillance in areas of ocean that are too distant for air and sea patrols. It also means that ships are visible at all times, even in the dark.

A project called Global Fishing Watch is being developed that brings together satellite technology with the internet. It is the product of a technology partnership between Sky Truth, Oceana and Google. Its aim is to use AIS to show all trackable fishing activity

Advantages of air and sea patrolling	Disadvantages of air and sea patrolling
- monitor 'real-time' fishing	- there is a high financial cost
- place observers on boats with little warning	- trained staff are required
- work together as a team	- they cannot cover all fishing areas
	- they can be spotted, and ships may then discard evidence

Table 8.12: Advantages and disadvantages of using air and sea patrols.

in all the oceans on the planet. The information will be available via a website and open to the general public.

While satellite monitoring is a highly effective method, it cannot totally replace human monitoring. Fishing boats and catches still need to be checked by inspection teams once a boat has been identified as needing further investigation. The advantages and disadvantages of using satellite tracking to monitor fishing are summarised in Table 8.13.

- **Inspection of catch and fishing gear**

In many countries, owners of all licensed fishing boats have to keep detailed logbooks as a form of self-monitoring. In the US and EU, paper logbooks are gradually being replaced by electronic logbooks for ease of use and instant data access. These new e-logbooks instantly transmit information about catch weights via satellite links to regulators. The e-logbooks contain details such as:

- the number of hours spent at sea
- the number of hours spent fishing
- the fishing grounds and coordinates where fishing took place
- the catch taken from the sea before discards
- the catch taken after discards
- the catch that was landed on the quayside
- the catch that was sold at market.

In some countries, regulators ask to see logbooks as part of a system of random spot checks, and logbooks are submitted at regular intervals.

Catch inspections also take place. Inspectors may arrive without notice before a boat sets sail and observe fishing practices during a trip. They also travel to fishing grounds in fisheries support vessels to make spot checks on fishing boats and ensure that the logbook records are correct. Catches are checked on the quayside after unloading and again at markets. Inspectors often examine the size of fish on sale in fish markets and note any that are undersized and the boat from which they came. All fish sold now have a record of where and when they were caught, and by which ship, so it is easy to trace back to where they were fished. Fishing gear is also inspected to ensure that it is legal. When inspectors work with fishers and help them to fish legally, it generates an open, realistic picture of what is happening on ships. When inspectors are considered to be remote and punitive, they are mistrusted and some fishing practices remain hidden. The advantages and disadvantages of inspecting catches and fishing gear are summarised in Table 8.14.

Advantages of satellite tracking	Disadvantages of satellite tracking
- rapidly transfers information about fishing boats to regulators - gathers detailed information about boats - can reach all areas of the ocean at all times - can gather data about catches as soon as they are taken	- it can be costly - not every boat has the technology - it does not replace manual inspections, which still need to be carried out

Table 8.13: Advantages and disadvantages of using satellite tracking.

Advantages of catch and gear inspections	Disadvantages of catch and gear inspections
- self-monitoring with licences, which encourages ownership of fishing regulation by the fishers - random checks, which allow quotas and fishing methods to be monitored - fish records, which means that it is easy to trace illegally caught fish back to a particular ship	- records may be falsified - if inspectors are present on a ship, fishing practices may be modified - they are expensive to carry out - fisheries may distrust the inspectors

Table 8.14: Advantages and disadvantages of inspecting catch and fishing gear.

8 Fisheries for the future

- **Catch per unit effort**

The catch per unit effort (CPUE) is a measure of how much fishing effort has gone into harvesting a particular catch. It is a measure of the abundance of a target species and is calculated by dividing the total catch by the effort used to harvest it:

$$\text{CPUE} = \frac{\text{fish catch}}{\text{fishing effort}}$$

Fish catch is easy to measure from ships' logbooks and fish markets. The concept of fishing effort is, however, much harder to standardise and different authorities use different measurements. Factors that may be taken into account for fishing effort include:

- days spent fishing
- size of engines
- size of boats
- number of traps set.

In order to be consistent when comparing CPUE from year to year, the same measurement of fishing effort must always be used.

CPUE can be used as a monitoring tool to assess the health of fish stocks and whether tougher restrictions need to be enforced.

- If CPUE decreases, it indicates that either the catch is decreasing and/or the effort needed to harvest the catch is increasing. This would suggest that fish stocks are decreasing.
- If CPUE increases, it indicates that either the catch is increasing and/or the effort needed to gain the harvest the catch is decreasing. This would suggest that fish stocks are increasing.

If scientific surveys estimate that a fish population is low and a fishing company consistently declares a high CPUE, it may be that they have been underestimating their fishing effort and more investigations will be undertaken. In this way, CPUE can be used to monitor fishing vessels as well as the health of fish stocks. The advantages and disadvantages of using catch per unit effort (CPUE) to assess fishing are summarised in Table 8.15.

> **KEY WORD**
>
> **catch per unit effort (CPUE):** a measure of fish abundance calculated from the catch size divided by the fishing effort

Enforcement

In order to ensure that fishers follow restrictions and report their catches and activity accurately, there are several possible methods of enforcement (Table 8.16). The procedures and penalties for fisheries found breaking the law vary between different countries. The EU has instigated a points system whereby penalty points are added to fishing licences after committing offences. As transgressions are logged, more points are added to the licence. When a certain number of points is reached, a range of penalties is imposed. Some of the penalties that different countries use for breaking fishing laws include:

- bans on fishing for stated periods of time
- imposition of fines
- confiscation of boats and fishing gear
- imprisonment.

Advantages of using CPUE	Disadvantages of using CPUE
- easy to assess because data are readily available	- fishing effort is very difficult to standardise
- simple measure of stock abundance and changes can be easily monitored	- it is a very basic measure and changes in CPUE may be caused by natural population fluctuations
- can be used as a starting point for further investigations if there are concerns about fishing practices	

Table 8.15: Advantages and disadvantages of using catch per unit effort (CPUE) to assess fishing.

Enforcement method	Advantages	Disadvantages
bans	- deterrent - prevents overfishing for a period	- may be hard to enforce - small fisheries may lose all income
fines	- deterrent - loss of money to equate to any extra gained from illegal fishing	- may not affect very large fishery businesses - may cause poverty to small fisheries and lead to unemployment
confiscation of boats and equipment	- deterrent - prevents overfishing for a period	- may not affect very large fishery businesses - may cause poverty to small fisheries and lead to unemployment
imprisonment	- deterrent - prevents overfishing for a period	- may lead to loss of career and future, resulting in unemployment and poverty

Table 8.16: Methods for enforcing fishing restrictions.

Penalties are designed to act as deterrents. They also help fishers that work within the law see that they are not losing out to those who fish illegally. Minor infringements are often punished by short bans and fines. Fishers that who are repeat offenders, and those guilty of major infringements, can be punished more harshly, including long bans, the confiscation of their boats and fishing gear, and even imprisonment. These measures will cause a major loss of income and could lead to the complete loss of their livelihood. Similar to monitoring, it is best if regulators work with the fishers to advise and help them to work within the law and educate them about the need for sustainability. If penalties are too severe for genuine mistakes, people could lose their livelihoods and their whole future could be at risk. There has to be an awareness that larger fishing companies can cope with harsher penalties that could ruin small and medium-scale companies. Table 8.16 summarises the methods that can be used to enforce fishing restrictions.

Consumer-oriented tools

A major factor in ensuring that fishing is sustainable is consumer awareness. Consumers are becoming increasingly interested in the origin of their food, how it is obtained and how environmentally friendly it is. Tuna that has been caught by pole-and-line, a dolphin friendly method, is now often labelled as such to inform consumers. Environmental groups and government agencies often have publicity campaigns in the media to increase consumer awareness of the need to conserve fish stocks. There are many organisations that issue guidelines to consumers and put ratings on different products to advise on sustainability. Unfortunately, having so many different organisations offering 'accreditation' for different products can be confusing for consumers. The criteria that each organisation uses to classify food as sustainable can vary, meaning that a fishery may be classed as sustainable by one organisation but not another. Some of the current organisations accrediting seafood include: Marine Stewardship Council, Ocean Wise, SeaChoice and Seafood Watch.

If consumers choose to buy seafood that has been harvested using sustainable, environmentally aware methods, those fisheries will make more profit and expand. In theory, companies that continue to use unsustainable methods will not sell as much produce so will reduce in size. However, food that is certified as sustainable also often carries a price premium to cover the additional costs of lower intensity harvests. Unfortunately, not all consumers are prepared to pay more for food that has been harvested in a sustainable way. Bulk buyers of food, such as restaurants, workplaces and hospitals, may not always make informed choices, and processed products such as fish meal may be used. Table 8.17 illustrates some of the advice given by four different groups for different North American species and methods of fishing. The advantages and disadvantages of consumer-oriented tools are summarised in Table 8.18.

8 Fisheries for the future

Fish species and location	Marine Stewardship Council	Ocean Wise	Seafood Watch	SeaChoice
sablefish by hook and line – British Colombia	🟢	🟢	🟢	🟢
halibut by hook and line – Alaska	🟢	🟢	🟢	🟢
sockeye salmon – British Colombia	🟢	🟢	🔶	🔶
halibut by hook and line – British Colombia	🟢	🟢	🔶	🔶
haddock by hook and line – Atlantic Canada	🟢	🟢	🔶	🔶
haddock by bottom trawl – Atlantic Canada	🟢	🟢	🔶	🔶
lobster by trap – Atlantic Canada	🟢	🔴	🔶	🔶
spiny dogfish by long-line – British Colombia	🟢	🔴	🔶	🔶
shrimp by bottom trawl – Atlantic Canada	🟢	🔴	🔶	🔶
scallop by dredge – Atlantic Canada	🟢	🔴	🔶	🔶

Table 8.17: Consumer advice from four different organisations for North American seafood.

Advantages of consumer-oriented tools	Disadvantage of consumer-oriented tools
• consumers are advised on sustainable food and make informed decisions • market forces in crease production of sustainable seafood rather than unsustainable methods	• it only works where consumers are informed • several bodies offer accreditation and there may be conflicting advice • not all consumers are prepared to pay more for sustainable food • large-scale buyers, such as workplaces and restaurants, may not engage with the schemes • industrial, processed products such as fish meal may not be included

Table 8.18: The advantages and disadvantages of using consumer-oriented tools.

Table 8.19 summarises the advantages and disadvantages of the principal methods used to protect fish stocks.

Tool for maintaining fish stocks	Advantages	Disadvantages
restriction by season	<ul><li>allows breeding time for fish</li><li>may require intergovernmental cooperation</li><li>cost of implementation</li><li>reduces fishing intensity at a time when fish are aggregated in specific areas</li><li>may face hostility from fisheries</li><li>reduces overall intensity of fishing, allowing growth of populations</li><li>short-term loss of money from reduced catches</li><li>reduces effect on non-target species</li><li>relative easy to implement</li></ul>	<ul><li>may require intergovernmental cooperation</li><li>can have high implementation costs</li><li>may face hostility from fishers</li><li>can cause short-term loss of money from reduced catches</li></ul>
restriction by quota	<ul><li>ensures that fish are only taken up to the MSY, allowing populations to be maintained</li><li>ensures long-term sustainability of catches</li><li>gives a clear indication of fish stocks</li></ul>	<ul><li>difficult to monitor</li><li>can encourage the illegal dumping of dead fish</li><li>may be based on incorrect data</li></ul>
restriction by licensing	<ul><li>enables ministries to regulate fishing intensity</li><li>makes it easy to identify illegal fishing boats</li><li>simple way to identify how many boats are permitted in a area</li></ul>	<ul><li>does not actually stop illegal fishing unless licences are checked</li><li>requires monitoring systems and a governmental agency to issue them</li></ul>
restriction of location	<ul><li>creates areas where fish populations can recover and increase</li><li>population increases in restricted areas extend into other areas, causing a general population increase</li><li>reduces bycatch and damage to other species</li><li>relatively easy to set up</li></ul>	<ul><li>fisheries may lose profits</li><li>fisheries may begin to damage other areas</li><li>expensive surveillance and enforcement are required</li></ul>
restriction of method	<ul><li>prevents over-exploitation of target species by reducing net sizes and using less efficient methods such as rod and line fishing</li><li>prevents bycatch by restricting use of benthic trawling, pelagic long-lines and setting minimum mesh size</li><li>prevents catch of smaller, immature fish by setting minimum mesh sizes</li></ul>	<ul><li>more labour-intensive methods such as rod and line are required</li><li>resistance from fisheries</li><li>cost of enforcing</li></ul>

Table 8.19: The advantages and disadvantages of methods for protecting fish stocks.

8 Fisheries for the future

Tool for maintaining fish stocks	Advantages	Disadvantages
restrictions of size of organism	• immature fish are returned to the sea to breed, increasing populations • fish stocks increase	• enforcement of fish size restrictions is costly • damaged and dead fish are returned to the sea, which are not part of the landing quota
restrictions on fishing intensity	• fewer fish are harvested, increasing stocks • careful restrictions on boat and engine sizes can help small- and medium-scale fisheries • licensing can help monitoring of boat numbers and make enforcement easier • easier to regulate than simply setting quotas, which are difficult to monitor	• possibility of unemployment and loss of earnings for fisheries and local communities • expensive to monitor and enforce, may require subsidies for unused boats • different years require different-sized fleets, changing the employment and income status each year
monitoring	• help fisheries detect fishing intensity • help fisheries detect illegal fishing • enable catches to be checked to enforce quotas	• very costly to impose • illegal fishers may find areas that are difficult to patrol • non-patrolled areas become overfished • leads to a poor relationship between fishers and governments
enforcement	• acts as a deterrent against illegal fishing • impounding fishing gear stops illegal fishing allowing fish stocks to recover • encourages legal fishing is a better option	• fines and imprisonment can lead to loss of livelihood and poverty for families • can lead to a poor relationship between governments and fishing areas
consumer-oriented tools	• consumers are advised on sustainable food and can make informed decisions • market forces increase production of sustainable seafood rather than unsustainable methods • publicity campaigns raise awareness and get the general public involved	• only works where consumers are informed, does not affect industrial fish products such as fish meal • several bodies offer accreditation and the advice may conflict • not all consumers are prepared to pay more for sustainable food • large-scale buyers such as workplaces and restaurants may not engage • processed products such as fish meal may not be included

Table 8.19: The advantages and disadvantages of methods for protecting fish stocks. *(continued)*

MATHS SKILLS 8.1

COMPARING DATA

Catch data from trawlers are often presented as 'mass of fish landed'. However, when comparing data from year-to-year or from area-to-area, simply stating the mass of fish landed is not enough. To make data comparable, you need to take into account variables such as time, number of boats, boat-days and size of fishing ground.

Worked examples

Three fishing areas have released data about haddock catches:

- Area A: a total catch of 624 000 tonnes of haddock over three years.
- Area B: a total catch of 470 000 tonnes of haddock over two years.
- Area C: a total catch of 435 000 tonnes of haddock over five years.

If you just look at the raw data, you cannot make a fair comparison. You need to take into account the time period over which the catch was gathered to obtain a mean annual catch. This is calculated by dividing the catch by the number of years it was gathered over:

- Area A mean catch per year: 624 000 ÷ 3 = 208 000 tonnes year^{-1}
- Area B mean catch per year: 470 000 ÷ 2 = 235 000 tonnes year^{-1}
- Area C mean catch per year: 435 000 ÷ 5 = 87 000 tonnes year^{-1}

From the mean annual catch rates, it looks like fishing ground C has a much lower yield than the other two grounds. This lower yield could be due to lower fish stocks, a smaller fishing ground or simply less fishing effort.

Measuring the area of a fishing ground is not easy but you can get an approximation by looking at the water surface area in km^2. If you want to compare the health of fish stocks in different fishing areas, the fishing effort is usually considered. Larger areas will generally have more boats, so have higher fishing efforts. Fishing effort is difficult to measure but the concept of boat-days is usually used (although some authorities use boat sizes and engine capacities).

You now divide the mean annual catch by the number of boat-days. This is the CPUE.

The number of boat-days for each fishing area is:

- Area A: 2000 boat-days
- Area B: 2200 boat-days
- Area C: 1500 boat-days.

The CPUE value for each fishing area is:

- Area A CPUE: 208 000 ÷ 2000 = 104 tonnes year^{-1} boat-day^{-1}
- Area B CPUE: 235 000 ÷ 2200 = 107 tonnes year^{-1} boat-day^{-1}
- Area C CPUE: 87 000 ÷ 1500 = 58 tonnes year^{-1} boat-day^{-1}

When looking at fishery data, you also often need to compare trends in two or more sets of data. Different data sets may have very different units of measurement or may have very different magnitudes. Rather than plotting two separate graphs, it is helpful to use the same x-axis but two different y-axes.

Figure 8.19 shows the changes over time in the amount of groundfish brought to market in New England and the market values of these groundfish. The two measures have different units so use different y-axes. The left y-axis is the mass of fish and the right y-axis is the market value. Always take care when using these types of graph to read values from the correct y-axis.

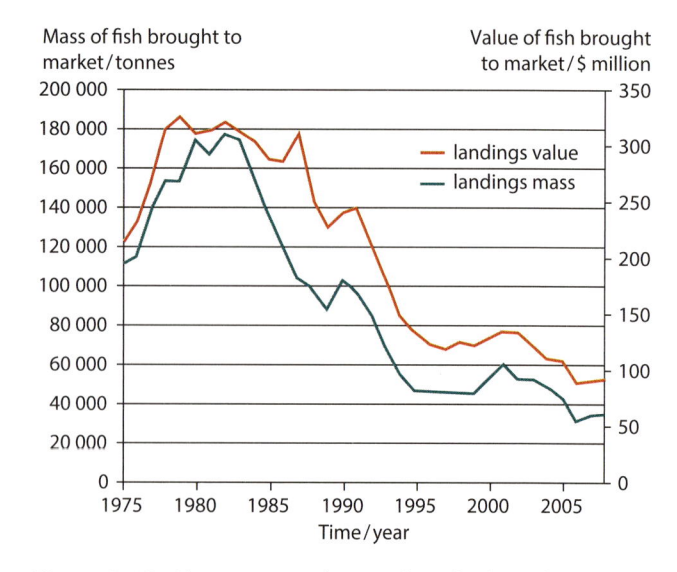

Figure 8.19: Change in market stock and value of stock of New England groundfish between 1975 and 2010.

CONTINUED

Year	Total annual catch/×1000 tonnes	Number of fishing boats in fleet
1985	125	70
1990	105	72
1995	85	74
2000	80	75
2005	65	60
2010	70	55
2015	65	45

Table 8.20: Total annual catch and number of fishing boats between 1985 and 2015.

Follow the steps below to draw a line graph of the data in Table 8.20.

- On the left-hand side, draw a y-axis, select a continuous scale, and label it *Total annual catch/×1000 tonnes*.
- Draw an x-axis with a continuous scale and label it *Year*.
- On the right-hand side, draw a second y-axis, select a continuous scale and label it *Number of fishing boats in fleet*.
- Using the left-hand y-axis, plot the points for the total annual catch and join them with straight, ruler-drawn lines.
- Using the right-hand y-axis, plot the points for the number of fishing boats in the fleet and join them with straight, ruler-drawn lines. Use a different style of line (for example, use different colours or dots and dashes).
- Add a key for the lines.

Questions

1 Calculate the CPUEs for the following sets of data.
   a A catch of 365 000 tonnes over six years with a fishing intensity of 2135 boat-days.
   b A catch of 275 000 tonnes over three years with a fishing intensity of 3282 boat-days.

2 Determine the fishing effort in boat-days that would be required to produce the following CPUE and total catches:
   a CPUE = 25 tonnes year^{-1} boat-day^{-1}; mean annual catch = 168 000 tonnes year^{-1}
   b CPUE = 15 tonnes year^{-1} boat-day^{-1}; mean annual catch = 125 000 tonnes year^{-1}

3 Check that the graph you drew for the worked example looks like the one provided in the answers.

Sociological impacts of fishing policies

Fishing regulations have major impacts on the fishers, who are the principal stakeholders in the industry. However, it is not only the direct employees who are affected. In some areas, fishing is the main industry that supports the local economy, and large service industries develop around it. Boat yards, fishing gear manufacturers and repairers, transport services, shops and other services can all be under threat if a fishing company closes. The local economy of an area is like a food chain, with the fishing industry filling the role of producer and the other industries being ultimately dependent on it. If the fishing industry fails, all the other industries are affected, which can result in unemployment, poverty and the loss of a whole community.

If restrictions are placed on fishing activity, this can lead to loss of revenue and unemployment in the short term (Table 8.21). A reduction in fleet size and fishing intensity would cause a sudden reduction in employment within the industry, and less money in the local economy. Protecting fish stocks could, however, be essential for securing the long-term future of fishing and employment in the area. In order to help local communities after reductions in the fishing intensity, governments need to help. They, along with local planners, need to explore ways of encouraging the development of alternative businesses and finding financial support.

	Restrictions	No restrictions
short term	• reduced fishing intensity • fewer boats • increased unemployment • reduced earnings	• continued high intensity fishing • continued employment • no reduction in earnings
long term	• sustainable future fishing • ensures future employment and income	• fish stocks collapse • total loss of fishing industry • mass unemployment and loss of income

Table 8.21: Long- and short-term sociological effects of restricted and non-restricted fishing.

If no restrictions are placed on fishing activity, in the short term the fishing industry would continue to generate revenue and the local economy would not suffer. However, in the long term fish stocks will begin to fall, and if fish stocks collapse completely there would be no fishing industry, leading to mass unemployment, loss of income and poverty. The economic future of the whole area could be in serious jeopardy.

Placing restrictions on fishing is not intended to punish the fishing industry. If used carefully and correctly, they are a way of securing its future. It is important, however, that governments and fishing regulators work with the industries and develop a strategic plan to safeguard employment and prosperity in affected areas.

Rehabilitation of stocks

When fish stocks have fallen, restrictions on fishing may not be enough to ensure that populations become fully rehabilitated. In the North Sea, restrictions have helped improve the numbers of cod and haddock, but they are still far from the levels of 50 years ago. Other methods can be employed to try to increase the numbers of fish, such as replanting mangroves, building artificial reefs and introducing cultivated stock to the wild.

Replanting mangroves

Mangrove forests are areas of rich biodiversity and exceptional ecological importance. They prevent coastal erosion and act as nursery grounds for large numbers of fish and crustacean species. Between 1980 and 2005, it was estimated that the global area covered by mangroves fell by about 20%, from 188 000 km^2 to 125 000 km^2. The majority of mangroves were cleared for shrimp farming, industrial development, housing, tourist resorts and agriculture. This has led to problems with coastal erosion and a reported reduction in wild fish and crustacean stocks.

Over the last ten years, there have been efforts in many countries, such as Guyana, Philippines, Indonesia and Malaysia, to rehabilitate areas of mangrove forest (Figure 8.20). Early attempts at replanting mangroves in Indonesia were not always successful. However, many lessons were learnt about the conditions needed, such as water depth and methods of rooting, and it was realised that it is essential to involve local communities in the projects. Mangrove rehabilitation is expensive, and this has made it difficult for many less economically developed nations. In an effort to help, other countries, such as Canada, the USA and the UK, along with charitable organisations have helped provide funding. Restoring mangrove forests and their areas to their

Figure 8.20: Replanting mangrove as part of a restoration project in Grenada.

former state will take many years if they have been very badly damaged. There are some signs of success, however, with fishers in the Philippines and Guyana reporting increased catches of fish and shellfish after mangrove reconstruction.

Building artificial reefs

Coral reefs are natural habitats for a rich diversity of marine life. They act as refuge areas for many fish species and help to increase populations. Artificial reefs have been successfully constructed in areas of the Mediterranean Sea for many years in an effort to increase fish stocks. Fishers have known for a long time that good catches are found around these artificial reefs, and many have now been built to improve the fishing industry. A range of materials have been used, including concrete blocks, old ships, cars and even old military tanks. The reefs certainly do increase fish stocks but care needs to be taken to make sure that the materials used are non-toxic, do not threaten shipping and do not damage other habitats.

Introduction of cultivated stock into the wild

The highest mortality rate during the life cycle of most marine species occurs in the period between egg and adult. Theoretically, if fish are bred and raised to a later stage by aquaculture, these fish could then be released back into the wild to help rehabilitate wild stocks. This practice has been used for many years to increase wild salmon populations in Alaska. Large numbers of king salmon are raised in tanks and then released into rivers to help to keep stocks high. There has to be strict regulation, however, as there are several risks.

- Released fish need to be disease free. Raising fish by aquaculture requires high stocking densities, which means there is a high risk of disease transfer. Aquaculture fish are often vaccinated and treated with medicines, but wild fish are not. Aquaculture fish can transfer diseases to the wild fish.

- Care has to be taken to not affect the gene pool in the wild. Fish that are raised in aquaculture may be from a particular genetic strain and can become inbred. If large numbers of these fish are released into the wild, it can affect the gene pool of wild fish and cause genetic weaknesses.

- Cultured fish may outcompete the wild fish. In Norway, it was discovered that many salmon caught by anglers from rivers and the sea were not wild salmon but escapees from farms. The escaped salmon were also found to feed more ferociously than wild salmon and they may have had other ecological impacts. There is concern that the salmon that are often thought of as wild in many North American fisheries are actually mainly cultivated salmon. The true, wild salmon may be decreasing in number.

- The number of fish released needs to be carefully regulated. Too many could affect other food chains that exist in the wild and outcompete other organisms.

Table 8.22 summarises a variety of methods that can be used to increase the numbers of fish.

Rehabilitation method	Advantages	Disadvantages
• replanting mangroves	• increases fish stocks • acts as nursery ground for many species • reduces costal erosion	• financially costly • requires research and skilled workers • may not grow successfully if not planted correctly
• building artificial reefs	• increases fish stocks • increases biodiversity of marine species	• may have harmful chemicals • may damage other habitats
• releasing cultivated fish	• increases fish stocks	• may affect gene pool of wild fish • may introduce disease • may affect other food chains

Table 8.22: Advantages and disadvantages of different methods for rehabilitating fish stocks.

CASE STUDY 8.2: SALMON HATCHERIES IN NORTH AMERICA

The first recorded instance of breeding salmon in hatcheries for release into the wild was in Canada in 1857. The aim was to increase wild populations and introduce salmon to new areas. This practice soon spread into the USA and Alaska and became a common method for reversing the trend of falling salmon populations. In 1938, the US government provided money for the construction of large-scale hatcheries to replace salmon spawning grounds that were blocked or flooded behind dams. More than 80 hatcheries were built in the Columbia River basin alone, and throughout the US more and more salmon hatcheries appeared. Washington State, USA, has more than 24 salmon breeding centres that raise millions of Pacific salmon for release every year (Figure 8.21). These fish are vital to the sport-fishing industry in Washington State which is worth more than US$850 million per year. It has been estimated that between 70% and 90% of 'wild salmon' caught by recreational and commercial fishers are in fact salmon that have been initially bred in captivity and released.

Figure 8.21: Coho salmon hatchery.

Between the 1950s and early 1970s, scientists found evidence that releasing hatchery salmon was harming wild salmon populations. It now seems clear that the process has had major ecological and genetic impacts on wild salmon populations. There has been a reduction of genetic diversity in salmon populations, altered behaviour of fish, and ecological imbalances. Some scientists consider that the release of salmon has caused more harm than good to native salmon populations and this could be irreversible. In the 1990s, there was a sharp decline in the price of salmon because of a succession of high catches. This sharp decline caused many salmon fisheries to go out of business. It may be that, by trying to increase the harvest, the policy of releasing extra fish has led to the decline of the industry.

Environmental groups have become increasingly concerned with the volume of artificially raised salmon that have been released into the wild. In 2004, the Hatchery Review Group issued a new set of guidelines for hatcheries. The document contained more than 1000 recommendations for improving the industry. Some of the main recommendations include:

- closing substandard hatcheries
- limiting the number of hatchery fish released
- putting in place safeguards for the genetic health of wild stocks and preventing the spread of infectious disease.

There are now strict guidelines on checking fish for disease before release. Hatcheries can only release eggs from local wild salmon and may not transport eggs or fish around the area.

Questions

1. Explain the environmental and economic reasons for releasing salmon bred in hatcheries.
2. State why many salmon fishing companies went out of business in the 1990s. Suggest one other factor that may have contributed.
3. Summarise the risks to the environment that releasing the salmon could cause.

Test yourself

6. Draw and complete a table to summarise the negative effects of purse seining, benthic trawling and factory ships on fish stocks and habitats.

7. Explain how the following factors could affect the amount of fish that can be safely harvested without affecting future populations of fish stocks:
   a. migration of large numbers of predator species into an area
   b. reduced age of sexual maturity of the fish
   c. reduced fecundity of the fish.

8. a. Population of cod is estimated at 325 000 in one year. The recruitment is estimated to increase the population by 15% year^{-1}. The death rate is estimated to be 10% year^{-1}. Calculate the number of fish that could be harvested without reducing the population below existing levels.
   b. Explain why it is useful to estimate both number and mass of fish when assessing fish stocks.

9. Explain why reducing the number of boats in a fleet may actually help secure employment in the future.

10. Compare and contrast the effectiveness of replanting mangroves and the introduction of cultivated fish in order to rehabilitate fish stocks.

11. Explain how the following could be monitored.
    a. Illegal shark fishing far from land in the mid-Atlantic Ocean.
    b. Concerns about the size of fish being sold by a fishing business.
    c. Concern about the fishing methods being employed by a group of inshore trawlers.

8.3 Marine aquaculture

It is estimated that the global population of humans reached one billion in 1804 and, 123 years later, it reached two billion. 33 years later it reached three billion and, by 1999, it reached six billion. Current projections suggest that the global population will reach eight billion sometime around 2030, and this ever-increasing human population needs more and more food. As the years have gone by, the increased demand for food from our oceans, along with more efficient fishing methods, has led to a dramatic reduction in many species of fish. The oceans alone cannot meet the consumer demand for fish so it has become increasingly important to use methods of aquaculture to farm fish. However, we have to be aware that aquaculture, if not regulated carefully, can have adverse effects on environments and human communities.

Extensive and intensive aquaculture

In order to produce fish and shellfish successfully by aquaculture, there are several requirements.

- **Food source:** there must be sufficient food to maximise growth.
- **Oxygen:** the water must contain sufficient oxygen for respiration.
- **Clean water:** waste must be removed before it becomes toxic.
- **Space:** with more predatory species, there must be sufficient space to prevent cannibalism.
- **Separation of ages and sizes:** with predatory species, smaller fish must be kept away from larger fish.
- **Disease prevention:** large numbers of a single species encourage the spread of disease, so methods of prevention and control must be used.

Aquaculture is usually carried out using one of three systems (Figure 8.22).

- **Cages:** organisms are placed into nets or cages within open, natural water (Figure 8.22a). The natural water flow flushes waste out of the cages and brings oxygen and some natural food into the cage. Molluscs such as mussels are often grown on free ropes in the water (Figure 8.22b).
- **Ponds:** organisms are placed into specially dug outdoor ponds (Figure 8.22c). The ponds may be made out of a range of materials, such as earth or concrete, and may be totally or partially separated from natural water. In some cases, they are simply areas of coastal water separated by ditches. Raceway ponds are a particular type of shallow pond that extend over a large area and are often used for the production of shrimp.
- **Indoor tanks:** species are placed into plastic or metal indoor tanks (Figure 8.22d). They are isolated from natural water and water is pumped in. Waste water is passed through filtration systems.

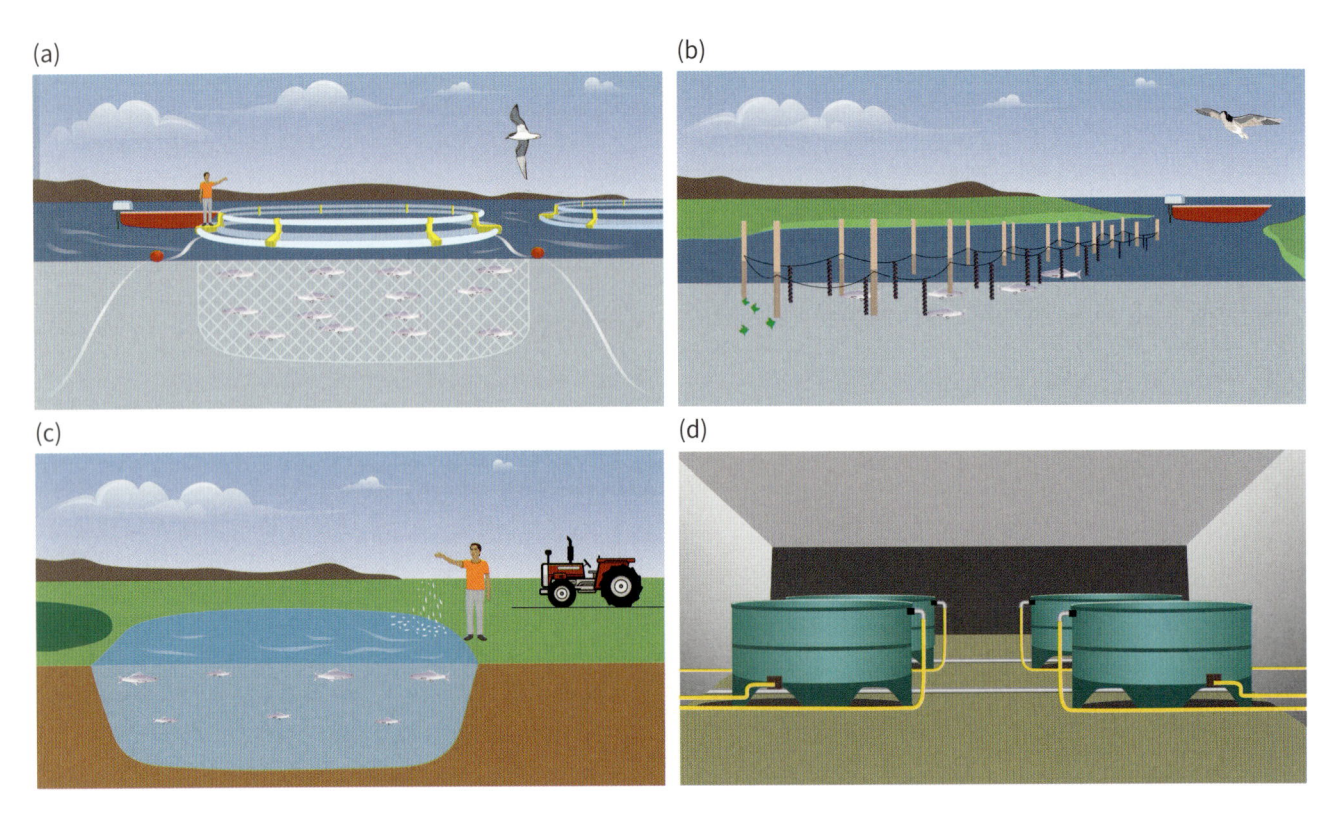

Figure 8.22: Basic methods of aquaculture: **(a)** a cage system, where the cage is placed into open water; **(b)** hanging mussels on ropes in open water; **(c)** a pond, where fish are placed in a specially dug pond that can be made of earth or synthetic substances such as concrete; **(d)** indoor tanks, where fish are totally separated from natural water.

Aquaculture is broadly divided into two main types based on the amount of 'effort' used: **extensive aquaculture** and **intensive aquaculture**.

A fully extensive method relies totally on the natural productivity of a body of water with no artificial feeding or maintenance. The water provides all food, oxygen and waste removal.

A fully intensive method requires much more capital investment and ongoing maintenance, with feeding regimes, an artificial oxygen supply and water filtration.

> **KEY WORDS**
>
> **extensive aquaculture:** aquaculture that uses little technology, low stocking densities and no artificial feeding
>
> **intensive aquaculture:** aquaculture that uses intensive methods such as high stocking densities and artificial feeding to maximise production

Intensive aquaculture is often carried out in closed containers rather than open water.

The method used depends on factors such as the demand for the fish, the requirements of a particular species and the level of investment that is available. The two systems have different effects on the environment, depending on the methods used. In practice, most methods of aquaculture lie somewhere between the two extremes.

Extensive aquaculture

Extensive aquaculture is less labour intensive and usually requires less capital investment. Fish and shellfish are grown in the ocean, lakes or rivers rather than in tanks, and in fully extensive systems there is no use of additional fertilisers or artificial feeding. Stocking densities are kept low. The capital investment required to set up an extensive system is usually low, as are the day-to-day running costs.

Productivity tends to be lower than in intensive systems because the food available is dependent on natural productivity, and oxygenation and waste removal are dependent on natural water flow. However, the low food usage and low stocking densities help reduce the threat of disease and pollution. There is little human involvement other than stocking and harvesting fish, so there is some risk of water pollution and disease due to waste accumulation. Fish that grow well in fully extensive systems tend to be very hardy. For example, tilapia can live in a range of salinities and can tolerate high waste accumulation and low oxygen levels.

There are both marine and fresh-water extensive systems for a diverse range of species, such as carp, tilapia, tuna, salmon and shrimp. The methods for each may vary. For example, some use a simple pond that is stocked with fish, while others rely on placing cages or nets filled with fish into an area of natural water. Figure 8.22(b) shows mussels and clams growing on ropes in an estuary, where they feed on the natural food present in the water.

Tilapia are often produced by extensive methods on rice farms. Fish are released into the channels of water where rice grows. They feed on floating plants such as duckweed, eliminating plant competitors. They require little maintenance, although it could be argued that the fertilisers given to the rice encourage the growth of weeds upon which the tilapia feed.

Intensive aquaculture

Intensive aquaculture requires much more human input. Stocking densities are high and frequent feeding is carried out. In tanks and ponds, water filtration systems are used to remove waste, and an oxygen supply is necessary. High stocking densities encourage the spread of disease so pesticides and antibiotics are frequently used. Productivity is high, although this can be reduced by high setting up and running costs and losses as a result of disease. The cage method, pioneered in Japan, is often a semi-intensive method that uses natural water but with intensive feeding and monitoring of the water quality. Care must be taken with these forms of semi-intensive methods in natural water because they can cause pollution. Food that is not consumed may fall through the cages, causing eutrophication. Pesticides and antibiotics can be released into the water, and pests that grow within the cages can be transferred to wild organisms. The fish and shellfish may also escape into the natural water.

Extensive and intensive methods are compared in Table 8.23.

Specific examples of aquaculture

Many different species of fish and shellfish are produced by aquaculture. Although there are certain general principals of aquaculture common to producing any species, each species often has its own particular requirements. The specific methods used in the aquaculture of salmon, mussel and shrimp are discussed below.

Salmon aquaculture

The origins of salmon aquaculture date back to the late nineteenth century when small salmon hatcheries, where salmon are bred, were developed in Europe and North America. These very small-scale attempts to breed salmon in captivity were the starting point for what is now a multibillion-dollar industry. Since 2018, over two million tonnes of salmon are produced by aquaculture every year, the majority of which is produced in Norway, Chile, Canada and Scotland, where cool coastal waters provide

Feature	Extensive	Intensive
feeding	natural food with no additional feed	frequent addition of artificial food
stocking density	low	high
start-up costs	low	high
running costs	low	high
management	low	high
productivity	low	high
risk of disease	low	high
use of pesticides / antibiotics	low	high

Table 8.23: Extensive and intensive methods.

Salmon production method	total mass of salmon each year / tonnes		Change in mass / tonnes
	2007	2014	
from wild	2587	2319	−268
from aquaculture	1 378 874	2 326 288	947 414
total	1 381 461	2 328 607	947 146

Table 8.24: Change in mass of salmon produced between 2007 and 2014.

ideal conditions. The industry is dominated by a handful of large multinational companies and there are concerns as to the impact on the environment and the wild salmon fishing industry. Three main species of salmon, Atlantic salmon, coho salmon and chinook salmon are produced, along with rainbow trout. Table 8.24 shows the change in amount of Atlantic salmon that is caught from the wild or produced by aquaculture between 2007 and 2014, according to the FAO. The mass that is taken from the wild has decreased but the mass produced by aquaculture has almost doubled.

Salmon aquaculture uses both intensive and extensive methods. The key stages, shown in Figure 8.23, are:

- preparation of brood stock
- spawning
- hatching
- nursery tanks
- growing out in sweater
- harvesting.

Preparation of brood stock

Brood stock fish are selected from open water cages in the sea. Males and females that seem to be of strong genetic quality are selected. These are placed into freshwater tanks or cages in autumn for a period of about two months during which they are fed with high-protein food to increase egg and sperm production. Males are females are usually kept in separate tanks. In some highly intensive aquaculture projects, fish are brought into reproductive season by manipulating the hours of light or injecting the fish with hormones.

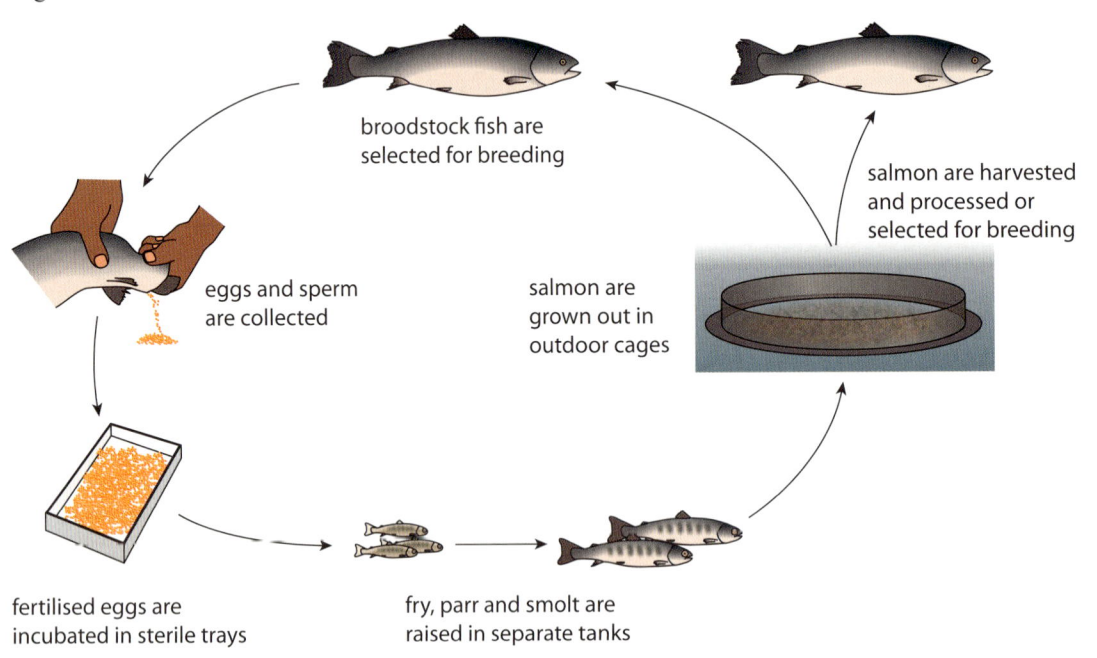

Figure 8.23: Stages in salmon aquaculture.

8 Fisheries for the future

Spawning

When the salmon are ready to breed, the females are carefully taken from the water and 'stripped' of their eggs (shown in Figure 8.24). The fish is held carefully, and light pressure applied to its abdomen so that the eggs are ejected into a bowl of water. A male fish is then taken and sperm (known as milt) ejected onto the eggs by applying light pressure to the abdomen. The eggs are then left to fertilise, are disinfected and then placed into trays of clean freshwater. Unfertilised eggs are removed as they could cause bacteria to grow.

Figure 8.24: Extracting eggs from salmon.

Hatching

The trays of eggs are left in freshwater at a temperature of less than 10 °C, usually in the dark. At the bottom of the trays are placed small stones or matting to recreate the conditions normally found in a 'redd' in the riverbed (see salmon lifecycle in this chapter). The trays are monitored by staff and as soon as hatchlings, called **alevins**, are seen to move to the surface of the water, food is added to the surface.

Nursery tanks

When the alevins develop into small fish, called **fry**, they are transferred to larger tanks and fed more frequently. The fry are grown in enclosed systems with recirculating fresh water and conditions, such as temperature, can be manipulated to change growth rates. In the wild, salmon fry develop into larger freshwater fish, called **parr**, that live in rivers. The parr live and feed in rivers for between six months and three years, after which they migrate to estuaries where they change into a **smolt**. Smolt gradually become adapted to the saline conditions of the ocean, and then migrate into the ocean to become adults where they live for up to four years. In aquaculture, when fry become parr, they are placed into either larger tanks or placed into outdoor cages located in freshwater bodies. When the parr become smolt they may also be raised in large, enclosed tanks or in lake cage systems.

Growing out in seawater

When smolts reach a size of around 100 g, they are checked to see if they have become tolerant to seawater, and then transferred to open sea cages systems. The cages are large nets suspended into the sea, anchored to the seabed and with platforms around them so that workers can feed, inspect and harvest the fish. Several cages are often grouped together to make it easier to raise the fish, as shown in Figure 8.25. The natural water currents remove waste, maintain salinity and bring oxygen.

Figure 8.25: Salmon cages in open water.

> ### KEY WORDS
>
> **alevin:** the first larval form of salmon; they possess a yolk sac and remain within the gravel nests or redds
>
> **fry:** the early, small larval stage of many fish, including salmon
>
> **parr:** salmon stage between fry and smolt; lives in rivers and has markings along sides of body that act as camouflage
>
> **smolt:** form of salmon that occurs when parr lose their markings while in estuaries; they are adapted for marine life by being silver in colour and elongated in shape

Food is provided for the fish regularly and consists of high-protein pellets supplemented with fish oils. As salmon is largely carnivorous, the food pellets tend to be produced from other fish catches. This can lead to overfishing of other species to provide food for the salmon. Feeding is now often automated and controlled to prevent overfeeding and pollution. The temperature of the water needs to be ideally between 6 and 16 °C and the fish are usually stocked up to a density of about $20\,kg\,m^{-3}$. Fish are kept in cages according to age so that their sizes are similar. Antibiotics, pesticides, fungicides and other substances may be added to reduce the spread of disease and to give the salmon meat the characteristic pink colour, pigments are added to the food pellets.

Harvesting

Salmon are typically harvested after about two years of growing out in seawater. They are carefully moved into holding pens before being transported to a slaughter area where they are stunned, bled and processed. Some adults are retained as brood stock for the next generation of fish.

Mussel aquaculture

Like salmon aquaculture, mussel aquaculture has a long history beginning in France during the thirteenth century. Nearly 200 000 tonnes of mussels are produced by aquaculture every year. A range of different systems are used but most have similar methods.

Mussels reproduce by broadcast spawning and external fertilisation. Sperm and eggs are released into the water and are fertilised. The fertilised eggs develop into free swimming **trochophore** larvae which in turn develops into **veliger** larvae. These veliger larvae eventually settle onto a substrate, where they metamorphose into small mussels called **spats**. The spats then develop into sessile, adult mussels.

The stages in mussel aquaculture (shown in Figure 8.26) are:

- seeding of ropes
- growing-out
- harvesting and processing.

> ### KEY WORDS
>
> **trochophore:** the first larval stage of molluscs such as giant clams and oysters; they move using cilia and are planktonic
>
> **veliger:** the second-stage larva of molluscs, characterised by the presence of a vellum organ used for feeding and movement, and a shell
>
> **spat:** larval form of bivalve molluscs that settles and attaches to substrate

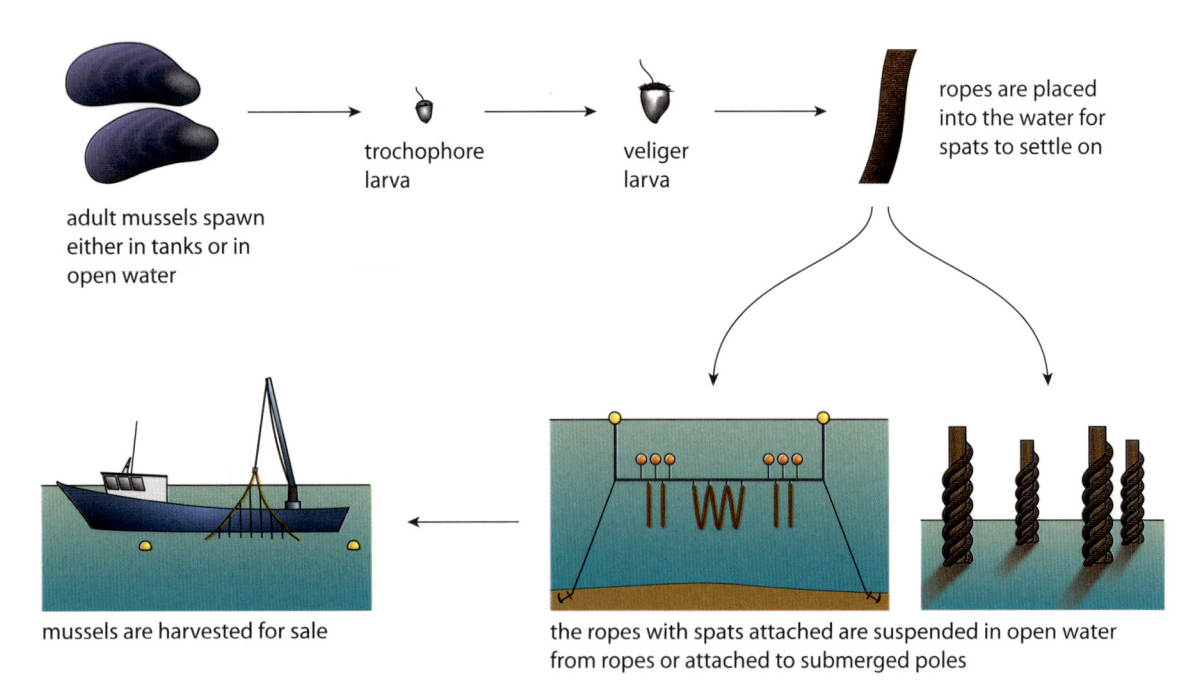

Figure 8.26: Stages in mussel aquaculture.

8 Fisheries for the future

Seeding of ropes

Ropes made from coconut fibre or 'socks' made from cotton are seeded with mussel spats. This is often carried out by using naturally produced spats by hanging the rope or socks into the sea around mussel beds, or adult mussels in the aquaculture project. Recently, some companies have begun to culture mussel larvae in tanks. Adult mussels are kept in tanks and fed with algae. Light and temperature is manipulated to induce spawning and the larvae are then fed for 13–15 days. Ropes are then placed into the tanks to enable the spats to settle on them. When the spats reach about 1 mm in size, they are transferred on the ropes to nursery tanks where they are fed until reaching a size of 6–10 mm. The ropes are then placed outdoors into the sea for growing-out.

Growing-out

The ropes or socks are placed into the coastal waters. A variety of systems are used, including:

- long-line (rope) method, where each rope or sock is hung from a long line that is suspended from the surface by buoys (Figure 8.27)
- Bouchet method, where the ropes are coiled around wooden poles that are embedded in the seabed
- raft method, where ropes are hung beneath a floating platform; different stages of mussel are grown using this method so that seeding of ropes and socks may be carried out simultaneously with growing-out.

Harvesting and processing

Mussels are grown for between 12 and 15 months after which they are harvested. They are often harvested by hand or by using hydraulic lifting devices. After harvesting, they are washed, cleaned and separated from each other before being packaged for sale. They may be kept in cleaning plots for two weeks after harvest during which time they expel mud and grit.

Shrimp aquaculture

Shrimp have been farmed in China and South-East Asia for hundreds of years using extensive, low-density methods. Juvenile shrimp were often trapped in saltwater ponds or the waters around mangrove forests. Food was supplied naturally by the water currents, which also removed waste and brought in fresh oxygen. In the late twentieth century, the global demand for shrimps increased, leading to the development of intensive and semi-intensive methods of aquaculture around the coastlines of Asia and Central and South America. A range of methods are now used, from fully extensive to highly intensive (Figure 8.28), in the farming of two main species of shrimp, the Pacific white shrimp and the giant tiger prawn. All the methods have some general procedures and particular stages in common.

Figure 8.27: Mussels growing on ropes.

Breeding and hatcheries

Before the 1980s, most shrimp farms relied on the collection of shrimp postlarvae from estuaries. This put pressure on wild stocks, and methods have now been developed to breed shrimp within the aquaculture farms. The shrimp are bred in indoor hatchery tanks and, after hatching, the larvae are fed initially on algae and later on zooplankton and brine shrimps. Disease outbreaks are common and difficult to contain, so antibiotics and pesticides are often included in the feed. All tanks are routinely rinsed with disinfectant. Despite these measures, there is still a high mortality rate of larvae.

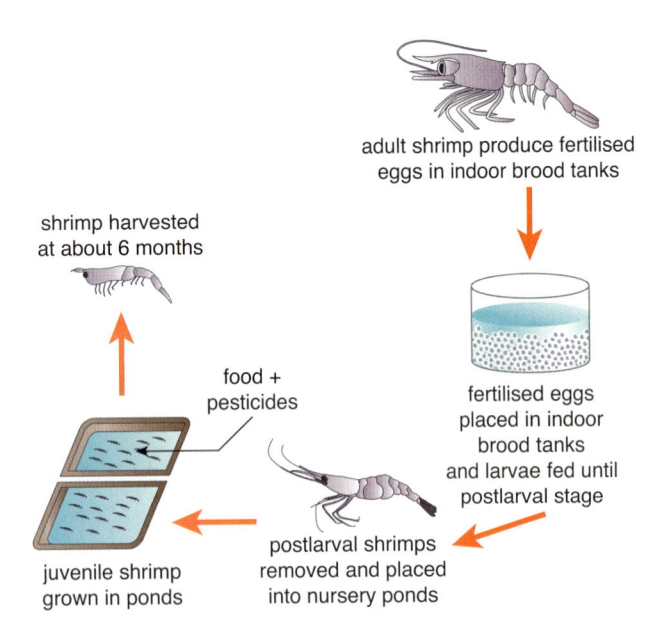

Figure 8.28: The stages of intensive shrimp aquaculture.

Nursery

Postlarval shrimps are transferred into separate long, shallow, rectangular tanks called raceway ponds. There is continuous water flow through the tanks and the shrimp are fed on a high-protein diet for approximately three weeks, before being transferred into grow-out ponds. The water temperature and salinity of the raceway ponds are gradually adjusted to that of the grow-out ponds to enable the shrimp to acclimatise.

Grow-out ponds

The juvenile shrimp are transferred into grow-out ponds, where they are fed for 3–6 months until they reach marketable size. Harvesting is performed by either draining the ponds or fishing with nets. A variety of pond structures are used, ranging from blocked off areas of coastal water, fields flooded with water to concrete walled tanks.

Depending on the farm, shrimp farming uses extensive, semi-intensive and intensive farming methods, especially for grow-out ponds.

Extensive systems

Extensive systems require low investment, are usually located on a coastal or mangrove area, and stock shrimp at low density. In their simplest form, they are areas of coastal water or mangrove roots surrounded by a ditch or netting. Water is refreshed by the sea and the shrimp feed on naturally occurring organisms. Rather than breeding the shrimp, they are often obtained by trapping wild larvae within the ponds. Yields tend to be low, but production costs and the technical skill required are also low, and because stocking densities are low the risk of disease is low.

Semi-intensive methods

Semi-intensive methods are more separated from the coastal water and do not rely on the tide for water flow. Pumps are used to move fresh water, often from the sea, and remove the waste water (Figure 8.29). The shrimp are stocked at higher densities so require additional food, although the natural growth of food is also encouraged. Productivity is higher than in extensive farms, but production costs are higher.

Figure 8.29: A semi-intensive method of shrimp aquaculture, using a pumping system to bring fresh seawater into the ponds and release waste water into the sea.

Intensive methods

Intensive methods, at fully intensive shrimp farms, isolate the shrimp from the marine environment. The shrimp are usually bred on the aquaculture site or bought in from suppliers, and are stocked at high density. Water is constantly circulated by pumps and filtration systems, and oxygen is supplied by aerators. Because of the high stocking densities, disease outbreaks are common so pesticides and antibiotics are frequently used. Feeding is intensive and uses artificially manufactured high-protein feedstocks. Productivity is high but is coupled with a high initial capital investment, high running costs and a need for skilled technicians.

Most studies estimate that about 55–60% of all shrimp farms worldwide are extensive farms, 25–30% are semi-intensive and the remaining 20–10% are intensive farms.

Requirements for the long-term success of aquaculture projects

It is a simple rule of business that if any business continues to make a financial loss, it is not sustainable. Aquaculture ventures are set up for different reasons, including:

- the conservation of fish stocks
- the re-establishment of stocks in the environment
- providing a food source for populations that lack protein in their diets
- to make a profit, either for small, local businesses or large international companies.

In every case, if an aquaculture venture operates at a major financial loss, it will not be able to continue.

To be successful, all aquaculture ventures have basic requirements: which are outlined below.

Availability of stock

There must be a source of juvenile organisms to provide the stock. This can be achieved by:

- keeping brood-stock adults, which provide a source of young offspring
- buying in fertilised eggs or larvae from other companies that produce them
- removing juveniles from the wild and bringing them into the aquaculture.

Most ventures aim to keep brood stock or buy in fertilised eggs, which requires capital outlay, as breeding tanks and more technically demanding methods and equipment are required. The majority of fully intensive farms breed their own stock and will often sell a proportion on to smaller producers. Breeding the stock on site also benefits the wild population, as removing juveniles from the wild can have devastating effects on the wild populations.

Availability of clean water

In order to reduce mortality rates caused by disease and accumulation of toxins, it is essential that the water is cleaned and replaced regularly. In extensive systems, natural water movements are used. This is not a problem for species that are grown in cages in open water but for species that are in semi-landlocked ponds, tidal movements can limit the population densities. In intensive farming, when tanks are not connected to a natural water source, constant running water is needed. At the same time, a filtration system is required to remove waste.

Availability of feed

Fully extensive systems use food provided naturally by the water. For example, in extensive shrimp farming, the tide brings water carrying food substances into areas partially sealed off from the coastal water. In semi-intensive systems, the growth of live food may be encouraged. Fertilisers are added to water to stimulate the growth of the phytoplankton that giant clam spats feed on. In fully intensive farming, fish and shellfish are stocked at high densities so food has to be added in order to maximise **growth rates**. The extra food can come from environmentally sustainable and relatively inexpensive sources. Protein pellets made from waste food (such as fish-processing trimmings) are often used to feed carnivorous species. Other sources of food can be environmentally damaging and costly. The aquaculture of predatory species such as bluefin tuna requires large quantities of fish and shellfish, which are usually removed from the environment, damaging wild stocks. If the feed fish are farmed, the financial costs of the venture rise. Highly active predatory species are particularly costly to feed because they need food from relatively high trophic levels.

> **KEY WORD**
>
> **growth rate:** the speed of growth of a population in terms of numbers or size of individual fish

Efficiency of use of feed

In extensive aquaculture, the feeding is natural so that there is no waste. In intensive systems, it would be financially inefficient and environmentally damaging to overfeed. An optimal strategy for feeding is needed on intensive farms. If fish and shellfish are underfed, growth rates will not be optimal and, in predatory species, cannibalism can occur. If feeding is excessive, food is wasted, which increases costs and causes pollution. Most farms tend to operate a little-and-often policy in order to reduce wastage, by constantly monitoring growth rates.

It is also important to control the type of food. Food that is highly indigestible will produce larger amounts of faecal waste and, because less is absorbed into the organism, slower growth. The addition of easily digested and absorbed substances, such as protein and fat, is a common practice in order to increase productivity.

Availability of labour

Any aquaculture venture requires a labour force. Extensive systems generally do not require a great deal of human input other than setting up the initial site, minimal maintenance and harvesting. As the level of intensive practice increases, there is a higher requirement for both numbers of people to work on the site and level of technical skill. A fully intensive system will need to employ people in different areas of the venture, such as breeding, maintenance, harvesting, feeding and processing. As a venture grows, more people are needed and with that comes the need for tiers of management and organisation. Complicated systems require skilled, trained staff, and this training can be carried out locally or at special training centres run by multinational aquaculture companies.

Disease management

The high-density populations that are produced in aquaculture, particularly in highly intensive systems, encourages the growth and spread of parasites and pathogens. Antibiotics are frequently added to tanks in order to suppress the growth of bacteria, which is financially costly and can affect the environment. Fungicides and pesticides are also added and, in intensive systems that are sited in natural water, these can be lost into the environment. Vaccines are often added to help fish such as groupers develop immunity to certain viral conditions. Nursery tanks in particular must be scrubbed and washed out with disinfectants because eggs and early stage larvae are particularly vulnerable to infection. In shrimp aquaculture, the mortality rate of early embryos can reach 60% as a result of infections such as white spot disease (Figure 8.30) unless strict precautions are taken. The costs of chemicals required to reduce disease can be high but this is generally outweighed by the cost of losing an entire harvest of a species.

Figure 8.30: Shrimp with white spot disease, a common infection found in shrimp aquaculture.

Availability of location

Extensive aquaculture ventures require an area of natural water that is easily accessible and suitable for the species being produced. There must be appropriate food present, a suitable substrate and water at suitable temperatures. Tropical species need warmer conditions while those from colder regions of the world need cooler temperatures. Most small, extensive systems in developing nations do not have a major impact on the environment and the land is not classed as premium. However, as farms expand, more space is required and more coastal habitats such as mangrove regions are removed. In more developed nations, in particular where tourism is a major part of the economy, the land may be premium and expensive to buy, increasing the amount of capital needed for aquaculture.

Intensive systems require far more support and are costly to build. Larger areas of land need to be purchased and more ponds and tanks constructed alongside pumping stations and water filtration units. Storage facilities for food and equipment are required. If harvests are large, processing facilities are needed on the site. Electricity needs to be installed, along with good transport links such as roads and rail links. One advantage of many highly intensive systems is that, by using separate tanks and ponds, they are less dependent on the natural condition of the water. The conditions of the tanks can be controlled according to the demands of the particular species being produced. For example, a species such as grouper can be produced in a location that is naturally cooler than the optimum for grouper growth by placing the fish in heated tanks. However, the cost both in terms of capital investment and maintenance is high so the product must be able to be sold for a high price.

Market demand

Figure 8.31 shows how the global demand for marine products has risen since 1950 and is predicted to continue to rise until 2050. Harvesting fish from natural stocks in the world's seas and oceans is no longer sufficient to meet the rising consumer demands for fish and shellfish. Aquaculture is needed to fill the gap between what is taken by fisheries (which, because of quotas and falling fish stocks, may decrease). However, if aquaculture ventures are to be sustainable in the long term, there must be continued, sufficient consumer demand for the products. As already discussed, if a venture is to be a long-term success, the profits must exceed the start-up and running costs. Like any other product, aquaculture obeys the commercial laws of supply and demand. If the demand for a product is high, the price for that product will tend to be high and bring higher profits. Prices do not, however, remain constant, and if production exceeds the demand (especially as more aquaculture ventures are developed) the prices will fall, reducing profit margins. Highly intensive systems that produce one product are often at risk from falling prices and need to ensure that the market demand is sufficient to meet operating costs.

Many aquaculture ventures now produce more than one product (for example by integrated production), so that if the demand for one species falls, profits may be generated from another.

Access to market

When an aquaculture venture is set up, it must have easy access to fish markets. This requires a transport network, which may include road, rail and air transportation. In most of the ventures set up in developing nations, the products are primarily produced for export. Fish and shellfish spoil rapidly, so they must be transported soon after harvest. Some larger businesses process the food at source and then export it as frozen food. Other businesses chill or freeze whole fish once harvested. There is a high demand for live fish in Asia, so aquaculture sites need facilities for packaging live fish and shellfish in chilled water. Refrigeration units and ice plants are needed, along with fresh, clean water. Road networks must be able to transport the products rapidly to airports, which are often situated close by. The need for efficient transport means that ventures are often too costly to set up in remote areas of developing nations without government intervention to build an efficient network. Building transport networks, however, may cost the environment in terms of pollution and loss of land.

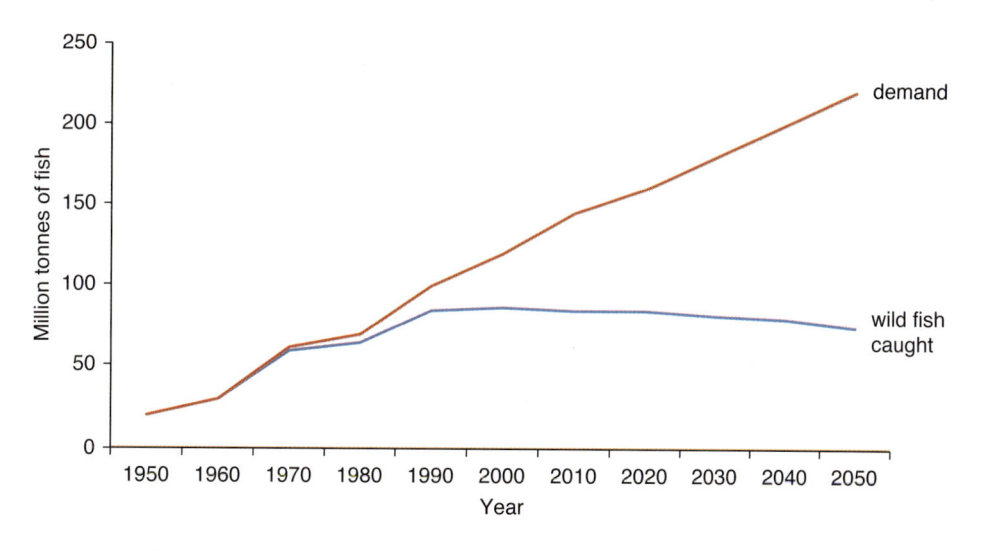

Figure 8.31: The demand for fish and the fish harvest. The growing gap between the two will have to be filled by aquaculture. Predicted demands and catches are shown for years 2020 to 2050.

Return on investment

If a business is to remain viable, it must be able to generate a profit over the long term. It is accepted that a new aquaculture venture may operate at a loss for the first few years because of initial start-up costs. Loans may be required to purchase equipment, stock, feed and other items, and paying back these loans can affect profits for several years. All ventures need a business plan in order to ensure they meet the necessary costs and are able to reinvest money into updating and expanding the business. As businesses age, equipment such as water pumps and filtration units require maintenance, which incurs more cost. Any successful aquaculture venture will have to consider the replacement and updating of equipment over time.

Large-scale aquaculture ventures are vulnerable to economic changes both within a nation and globally (Figure 8.32). If the currency of a particular country rises in value in world markets, a farm selling tilapia from that country will find its product harder to sell internationally as it becomes more expensive for other countries. Likewise, if a currency falls, it is easier to sell and export. A weak currency is not always good for production: raw materials that have to be bought in from other countries become more expensive.

Large multinational aquaculture companies are able to regulate production in the different countries they operate, but small- and medium-sized businesses are more vulnerable to world economic events. If the world economy goes through a period of weakness, there may be less money to buy premium brands such as bluefin tuna. On the other hand, if less money is available there may be more demand for less expensive products, such as tilapia.

Principal impacts of aquaculture

Aquaculture projects can have major ecological, sociological and economic impacts on the local area. Unless precautions are taken, they can result in severe damage to the surrounding ecosystems.

Environmental impacts

One of the aims of aquaculture is to make up the shortfall in fish and shellfish between global demand and what can be harvested from the seas. By reducing what is taken from the seas, the stocks of fish and shellfish should be protected and allowed to increase.

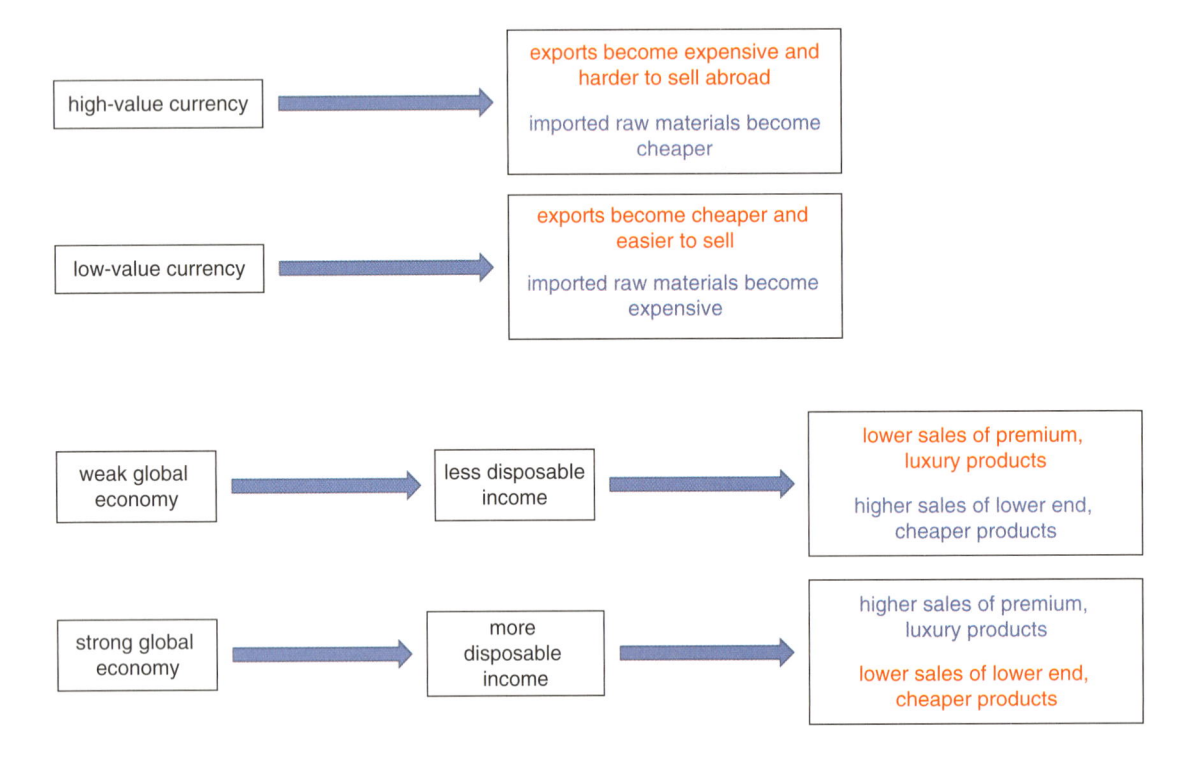

Figure 8.32: Effects of currency and economic conditions on the sale of goods.

This means that the environment can benefit from aquaculture. If not set up carefully, however, aquaculture can cause extensive damage to habitats, which are often delicate and ecologically important areas.

Factors that must be addressed to ensure environmental sustainability include:

- habitat destruction
- over-exploitation of feedstocks
- pollution
- introduction of **invasive species** and the escape of cultured stock
- spread of disease
- competition for resources
- reduction in the exploitation of native stocks.

> **KEY WORD**
>
> **invasive species:** species that have become established in an area that is not their normal habitat due to human activity

Habitat destruction

Building a new aquaculture venture will inevitably lead to land development. Even extensive systems may lead to the loss of habitats. For example, if an area of mangrove forest is sealed off from the sea to culture shrimp, it may lead to the loss of mangroves or other coastal habitats. Intensive systems that use cage methods or raceway ponds are often built in coastal areas. Intensive shrimp farming (Figure 8.33) has led to the loss of large areas of mangrove forest, resulting in a loss of biodiversity. Many coastal areas are already under threat from tourist resort development and further losses could lead to the extinction of many species. Indoor tank systems are less likely to damage fragile coastal ecosystems but still cause habitat loss because of their construction.

Overexploitation of feedstocks

Intensive farming of fish and shellfish requires a large quantity of food. In many cases, such as bluefin tuna farming, the food is harvested from the oceans. Bluefin tuna is a highly active, top predator so requires intensive feeding. Sardines, mackerel, other fish and squid are harvested from the sea and fed to the tuna. The harvesting of these species may lead to a fall in their populations and further effects on food chains.

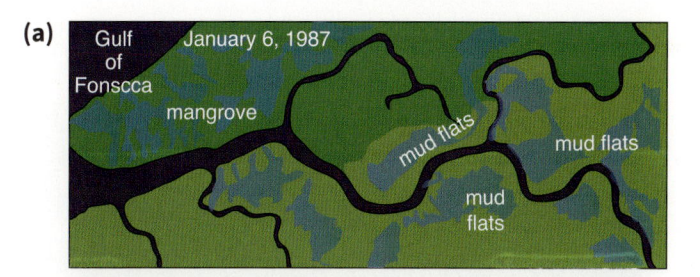

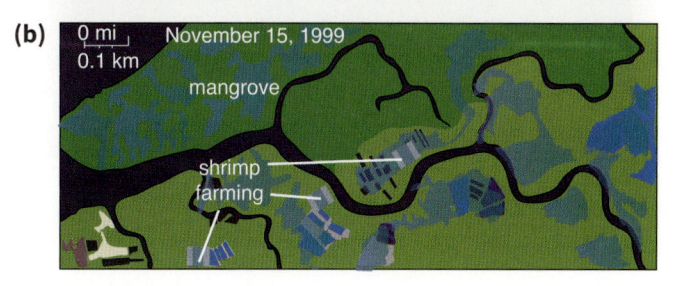

Figure 8.33: Effects of shrimp farming on areas of mangrove forest and mud flats in Nicaragua between **(a)** 1987 and **(b)** 1999.

Pollution

There are many types of pollution that can occur as a result of aquaculture. Extensive systems are less polluting because there is little to no additional feeding and there is less use of pesticides and other chemicals. Intensive systems, particularly cage systems in open water, have the potential to release large quantities of pollutants, including the following.

- Waste food that is not consumed and faecal waste: these can cause eutrophication (Chapter 9), leading to oxygen depletion in the water as a result of microbial decay. This has happened in the Philippines as a result of tilapia farming (Figure 8.34).
- Fertilisers that have been added to encourage plant growth: these can leach into the water and cause eutrophication.
- Pesticides that have been added to kill parasites: these can pass into the water and kill native species or generate resistance in native species.
- Antibiotics and antifungals that have been added to kill bacteria and fungi: these can also pass into the water and affect the natural bacteria and fungi.

Closed systems where fish and shellfish are grown in sealed tanks require filtration units before waste water is released into the sea. Open-water cage systems are more difficult to control and procedures are needed to

Figure 8.34: Eutrophication in the Philippines caused by waste from tilapia farming.

avoid over-feeding, overuse of chemicals and excessive production of waste.

Introduction of invasive species and cultured stock

Invasive species are species that are not native to a particular area. Aquaculture has often resulted in the introduction of invasive species, when cultured organisms escape into the wild. The impacts of invasive species are varied. In South-East Asia, introduced species such as tilapia and common carp have established populations that have brought socio-economic benefits in terms of dietary protein and money. But the same species can have a negative environmental impact.

In Cambodia, the population of the native bronze featherback fish (*Notopterus notopterus*) has declined in rivers and lakes as the invasive Nile tilapia populations have increased. In Laos, the decline of the native prawn and a native snail species has been linked to the introduction of invasive species. If introduced species have no natural predators, their populations will increase unchecked and they have the potential to over-consume prey species and outcompete native species.

Invasive species may bring diseases with them that escape and adversely affect native species. In Thailand, three fish diseases have entered the country with introduced fish. The viral white spot disease that infects shrimp is thought to have been introduced by imported shrimp larvae.

Spread of disease

Intensive farming tends to rely on stocking fish and shellfish at very high densities. Keeping large numbers of one species at a high density encourages the development and spread of disease, so aquaculture can provide a breeding ground for disease. It is estimated that up to US$6 billion is lost annually by disease in aquaculture. If open-water cage systems used, there is a risk that the diseases will spread to natural populations. One notable example is that of parasitic sea lice, which feed on salmon skin, mucus and blood and can kill the fish. Recent research in British Columbia suggests that sea lice infestation resulting from farms will cause local pink salmon populations to fall by 99% within four generations.

Waste water from tank systems is filtered and disinfected, and pesticides, fungicides and antibiotics are frequently used to reduce the spread of disease. Fish must be continuously monitored for the presence of disease and treated accordingly. White spot disease affecting shrimp is one of the most damaging diseases, and it is estimated that the early death of shrimp has cost over US$2 billion. Research into remote, rapid DNA diagnosis of the disease is being carried out to help to reduce its effects.

Competition for resources

The development of an aquaculture venture requires many raw materials from the local environment. If the venture is inland, away from major water bodies, large quantities of water need to be provided. Diverting large volumes of water to the venture can create competition within the local environment and with businesses such as traditional crop farms that need water for irrigation. If large quantities of water are taken from lakes and rivers, the water levels will drop, plant growth around the margins can be reduced and the ecosystem disturbed.

A large intensive aquaculture farm can potentially buy such large quantities of fertiliser and other raw materials that local farmers are unable to meet their needs. This can ultimately lead to loss of crops.

Intensive shrimp farming in ponds requires a considerable amount of fresh water to maintain the pond water at the optimum salinity for shrimp growth. Typically, this involves pumping water from nearby rivers or groundwater supplies, and this can deplete local fresh-water resources. Furthermore, if aquifers are pumped excessively, saltwater seeps in from the nearby sea, causing salinisation and making the water unfit for human consumption. For example, in Sri Lanka, 74% of people living in coastal shrimp farming areas no longer have ready access to drinking water. Shrimp farming can also cause increased soil salinity in nearby agricultural areas, leading to declines in crops. In Bangladesh there have been reports of crop loss because of the salinisation of land around shrimp farms.

Reduction in the exploitation of native stocks

One of the principal reasons for increasing production of fish by aquaculture is to reduce the exploitation of wild fish stocks. If more fish is raised by aquaculture to meet consumer demand, it should help to preserve wild populations. There is not a great deal of conclusive data to suggest that aquaculture alone is enabling wild fish populations to increase. If it used along with measures such as restrictions on fishing as part of a combined strategy to reducing fishing intensity it has the potential to satisfy consumer demand without depleting stocks.

Social and economic impacts

Aquaculture ventures can have positive and negative impacts on local people. They can bring employment, wealth and food, but may also cause loss of traditional fishing jobs, land and other species that are used as food. If not practised in an ethical, sustainable way, local communities may receive very few of the benefits of aquaculture.

All aquaculture ventures have an impact on local labour forces and social systems. If an area used to develop an aquaculture venture has a limited population, new people are brought into the area and will often settle there, requiring more housing and other infrastructures. Labour costs will fluctuate according to supply and demand. In areas where there are few industries and few opportunities for employment, labour costs will be cheap. In areas where there is competition for employers, labour costs are high and this increases the cost of the products.

An aquaculture business can have many short- and long-term social and economic impacts on the local population. If it is to be successful and socially sustainable, all possible outcomes need to be considered.

Positive outcomes

Increased employment opportunities are particularly important in areas with low employment and few opportunities for people to work and train. A successful business can provide higher incomes for local people and the opportunity for people to be trained in skills that can be transferable to other employment sectors. There can be improved employment prospects not only in the primary aquaculture business but also in secondary services such as transport, housing construction, food businesses and retail. As a business grows, it employs more people, many of whom may move into the area and require housing and will also buy goods and services from local businesses.

In areas with low wealth, the development of an aquaculture business that generates more money from exports can increase local wealth. Increased wealth can raise the standard of living for local people. For this to happen, however, the money must reach all parts of the local community.

If a major aquaculture venture is planned, local people may benefit from an improved infrastructure, such as increased road and rail links. If money from the venture is invested in a growing local community, better facilities, such as housing, schools and medical services, can be developed.

In regions where malnutrition is high, the development of aquaculture ventures may offer a cheaper and more abundant source of food that is rich in protein and several vitamins. This requires the venture to be used for local food production rather than exporting all the products.

Negative outcomes

Despite employing more people in the sector, some aquaculture ventures can actually cause more unemployment. Local fishing industries can become less cost effective and unable to compete with the lower prices of farmed products. If an intensive system is built, then smaller, less efficient extensive farms may close because they cannot compete. Intensive farms that use food that is taken from the sea may impact upon local fish stocks and so reduce the yield of fisheries.

If a large aquaculture production site is built, more people may move into the area and bring more wealth. The increased wealth of one group of people may lead to a rise in local prices that results in food and goods becoming too expensive for locals.

An aquaculture venture can also put pressure on housing. It may use building land, reducing the land available for housing (and raising the price of building land). If more people are attracted into an area, there will be a higher demand for housing and, as a result, many could be unable to afford houses because of increasing prices. If a population grows too rapidly without careful planning, the infrastructure is placed under strain. Schools, roads, medical care, sewerage and water supplies become inadequate and, if not improved, this can lead to social problems.

When one employment sector becomes dominant in an area and there is a shortage of labour, other, less attractive, industries may suffer a decline. There will be competition between different sectors for sufficient staff which may cause some businesses to close because of higher wage demands. Industries that may be perceived as old fashioned may be less able to attract staff and could go out of business. When traditional businesses begin to close, local traditions can be lost. If aquaculture becomes the only business in an area, it could become a major problem if it fails in the future. This is often a problem with larger international companies, who will open and close businesses in different parts of the world according to profitability at a particular time.

If a venture is to be sustainable, the local population should benefit from it. Intensive systems that do not benefit a local population are less likely to be sustainable.

Imagine a situation where a large international company buys an area of coastal water and begins to farm shrimp:

If the company employs few local people, exports the produce and does not allow profits to benefit the local area, it will not be popular. It is unlikely to be sustainable in the long term. Local people will not feel any loyalty to the company.

If the company has a well-designed aquaculture system, employs local people, produces food for local people as well as export, and puts profits into the local area, it will be highly regarded. Local people will benefit from the company and become stakeholders in its success. This should prove to be more sustainable in the long term.

Minimising the negative effects of aquaculture

A poorly planned aquaculture venture can have many negative impacts on the environment and the local human population. In order to reduce the overall impact, extensive planning is needed. Certain precautions should be taken, including:

- reducing pollution
- using resources sustainably
- preventing escape
- conserving habitats
- minimising social impacts.

Reducing pollution

For tanks and ponds that are physically separated from the natural water, there must be a source of clean water and removal of waste water. The waste water will carry with it waste food and faecal waste, together with any chemicals such as pesticides that have been used. There is also a risk of infectious organisms and pests from the tanks being released into the natural water. Figure 8.35 shows an aquaculture plant with a water purification system. The water is passed through a series of tanks that remove inorganic wastes such as carbon dioxide, nitrates and ammonia. Solid waste is allowed to settle out in other tanks and then passed into anaerobic digesters to produce methane gas, which can be used as an energy source.

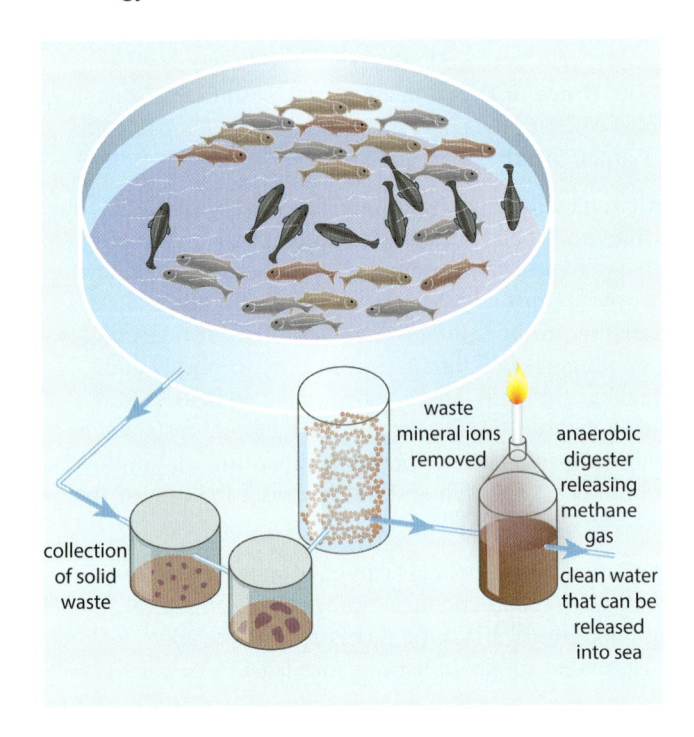

Figure 8.35: A water purification system to recycle water for aquaculture.

Reducing pollution from open-cage systems is more difficult because they are not physically separated from the natural water. Where fish are kept in cages in estuaries and coastal waters, it is important not to overfeed them as uneaten food can pass into the water and cause pollution. Care has to be taken to treat infections and parasite infestations before they can spread to wild populations, but treatment chemicals should not be used excessively to reduce leakage into the local water. Recently, integrated multi-trophic aquaculture (IMTA) systems have been developed (Figure 8.36). Fish are kept in open-water cages and detritus feeders such as lobsters and crabs are grown underneath. The detritus feeders consume the excess food and faeces from the fish. Filter-feeding molluscs such as mussels are grown on ropes in order to remove particulate waste in the water, and seaweed is grown in order to extract excess mineral ions from the water. These systems reduce pollution and also generate more profits by growing several different products.

A company in the Netherlands called *Happy Shrimp* uses waste from its shrimp farms to grow vegetables. The shrimp are fed on algae and bacteria as well as on aquaculture feed containing a high proportion of plant protein. They are cultivated in greenhouses that are heated in an environmentally sustainable way, and no shrimp juveniles are extracted from the wild.

Figure 8.37 illustrates a practice called integrated rice culture, where tilapia are grown in rice fields. The fish control weeds and pests and the faeces they produce fertilises the rice plants.

Not using high stocking densities helps to reduce the spread of pests and diseases and the use of chemical pesticides and antibiotics.

Using resources sustainably

Harvesting marine species, both plant and animal, to use as aquaculture feed is not a sustainable practice. Populations of species such as herring and sardines

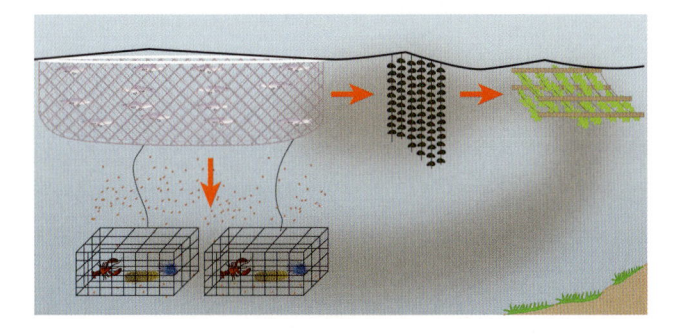

Figure 8.36: Integrated multi-trophic aquaculture (IMTA). Waste from the cage falls through to feed detritus feeders such as lobsters, sea urchins and sea cucumbers. Mussels and other molluscs are grown on ropes to remove small particulate matter, and seaweeds remove mineral ions such as nitrates and phosphates.

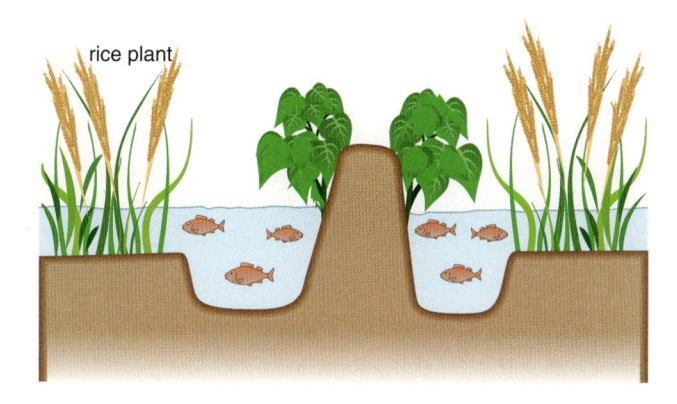

Figure 8.37: Integrated rice culture. This system puts tilapia into rice fields where they reduce weed numbers.

have declined in some parts of the world where they have been heavily fished for use in the aquaculture industry. Recently, plant species such as soybeans, barley, corn and peas have been used successfully to make feed pellets for herbivorous and omnivorous fish and shellfish. Carnivore species such as tuna are problematic because they require large quantities of other fish and fishmeal to feed on. They also need a source of omega 3 oils. Using the fish trimmings from fish-processing plants to make high protein and oil feed pellets is a possible sustainable source of feed for carnivorous species.

Inland aquaculture sites that require a water source need to recycle the water they use back into rivers and lakes rather than simply disposing of it through sewers. The water should be cleaned, filtered and, if necessary, desalinated before being released.

Preventing escape

If species, particularly invasive species, escape from aquaculture, they can have an impact on the ecology of the area. Food chains can be disrupted, and native species may be outcompeted by the escaped organisms. Escaped tilapia have caused the decline of native fish species in many parts of the world, including Nevada and Arizona in the United States, and in Madagascar and Nicaragua. Farmed species should be isolated from natural waters by using either tanks or closed pools. Where cages are used, there should be strong netting with an appropriate mesh size. The production of invasive species in cage systems that are in contact with natural water should be discouraged.

Conserving habitats

Figure 8.33 shows the loss of mangrove forest to the development of shrimp farms. Careful planning is needed before aquaculture sites are built, in order to minimise the loss of coastal habitats. Research should be undertaken into the likely effects on local ecosystems, and no aquaculture should be permitted in marine reserves.

Minimising the social impacts

The development of a new aquaculture site has the potential to bring many benefits to a local community. It can provide employment, increased standards of living and a high-protein food at a low price. However, if not planned carefully there will be little benefit to the local community. Existing industries such as fisheries may fail, inflation may occur increasing the cost of food, all the products may be used for export so that none is available locally, the area may become polluted and land lost. Care should be taken that existing industries are not affected and that the venture brings money into the local area so that the local community benefits. If local people become stakeholders in the venture, it will become a far more sustainable concern and will be more successful in the long term. Responsible employment will ensure that the needs of the workforce are met so that they are not exploited with low wages, and health and safety should be of paramount importance.

Test yourself

12 State whether the following aquacultures are extensive, semi-intensive or intensive.
    a Seabass grown in cages that are placed into the ocean. Natural food is brought in by tidal movements, although some extra food is added.
    b Mussels grown on ropes. The mussels are hung in estuaries but no artificial feeding is carried out. No antibiotics or pesticides are used and the yield is low.
    c Halibut raised in indoor tanks. Water is recirculated by pumps and is purified. The stocking density is high so feed is frequently added, as are pesticides and antibiotics.
    d Clams grown in cages. The clams are placed into open water and monitored. Most feeding is natural because of the flow of the water, but if growth rates are low artificial feed is added.
13 Compare the use of tanks with open-water cages in aquaculture.
14 Explain why intensive shrimp farming may be harmful to the environment.
15 Explain why aquaculture feed is often highly digestible and supplied frequently in small amounts rather than adding large amounts at any one time.
16 Summarise the possible negative effects that aquaculture can have on the environment.
17 Explain how integrated multi-trophic aquaculture methods reduce the pollution generated by aquaculture.

MATHS SKILLS 8.2

FREQUENCY TABLES, PIE CHARTS AND HISTOGRAMS

When you are collecting data about numbers of individuals in different categories, it is best to collate them in a frequency table. Pie charts are circular charts that show proportions easily. A histogram is a form of bar chart that is used to display frequency data when the independent variable is continuous.

Worked example

The variation in mass of 25 salmon was investigated after one year of aquaculture. The data are shown in Table 8.25.

Mass / g			
1260	1760	2100	2275
1265	1765	2050	2280
1525	1800	2125	2450
1525	1850	2075	2575
1600	1865	2165	
1605	1875	2200	
1700	1950	2255	

Table 8.25: Mass of 25 salmon after one year of aquaculture.

> 8 Fisheries for the future

CONTINUED

To determine the frequency of different categories, a frequency table needs to be made. If large amounts of data are being processed, it is useful to use a tally chart, as shown in Table 8.26.

To create a pie chart, you need to calculate the angles that each category will represent. To do that, you need to determine the percentage of the total for each category.

For example, five of the salmon have a mass in the range of 1501–1750 g. As there are 25 fish, the percentage of fish that have a mass between 1501 g and 1750 g is:

$$\frac{5}{25} \times 100 = 20\%$$

To determine the angle required for the pie chart, you need to calculate 20% of 360°:

$$\frac{20}{100} \times 360 = 72°$$

The rest of the percentages and angles for the salmon are shown in Table 8.27. The angles should all add up to 360°.

The pie chart can then be drawn using a protractor, and should look like Figure 8.38.

Histograms are very similar to bar charts but are used when the *x*-axis shows continuous data and the *y*-axis shows frequency. The bars in histograms touch, unlike bar charts, in which the bars are separate from each other. The category intervals for the bars should ideally be equal.

The histogram for the salmon data is shown in Figure 8.39.

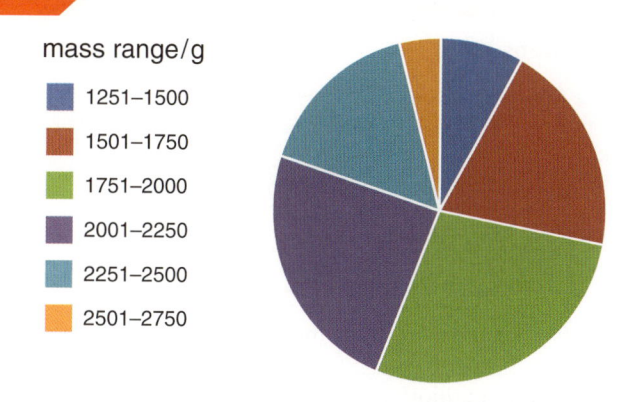

mass range/g
- 1251–1500
- 1501–1750
- 1751–2000
- 2001–2250
- 2251–2500
- 2501–2750

Figure 8.38: Pie chart showing the frequencies of different masses of salmon after one year of aquaculture.

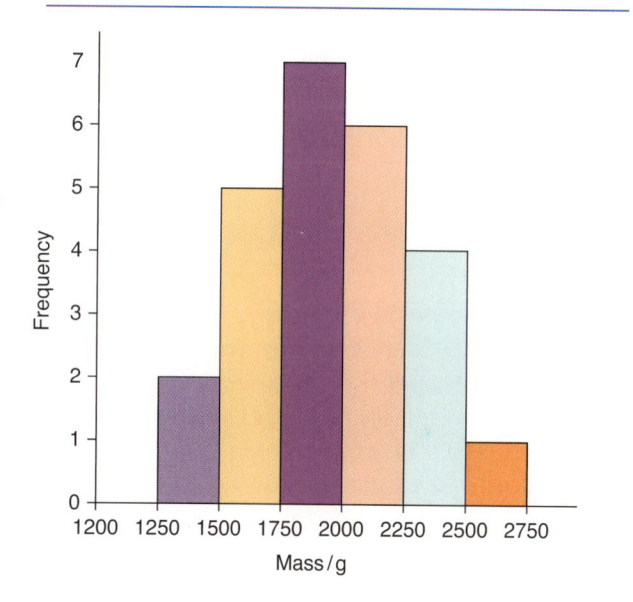

Figure 8.39: Histogram showing the frequencies of different masses of salmon after one year of aquaculture.

Mass range categories	Tally	Frequency	Percentage in category/%	Angle on pie chart/°
1251–1500	||	2	8	29
1501–1750	⁄⁄⁄⁄⁄	5	20	72
1751–2000	⁄⁄⁄⁄⁄ ||	7	28	101
2001–2250	⁄⁄⁄⁄⁄ |	6	24	86
2251–2500	||||	4	16	58
2501–2750	|	1	4	14

Table 8.26: Tally chart and frequency table showing the masses of 25 salmon after one year of aquaculture.

CONTINUED

Questions

1 An aquaculture company earns profits for five different products, as shown in Table 8.27.

Product	Profit / (USD$)
grouper	150 000
lobster	125 000
crab	25 000
scallops	75 000
seaweed	10 000

Table 8.27: Profits for five different products.

Display the profits for the products in the form of a pie chart.

2 One hundred tilapia were split into two tanks, which were placed at different temperatures for four months. The masses of the tilapia were measured and frequency categories determined. The results are shown in Table 8.28.

Mass category / g	Tilapia kept at 15 °C	Tilapia kept at 20 °C
251–500	6	1
501–750	13	4
751–1000	21	15
1001–1250	8	18
1251–1500	2	8
1501–1750	0	4

Table 8.28: Effect of temperature on tilapia masses.

Draw histograms to display the two sets of data.

PROJECT: MARKETING SALMON AQUACULTURE

Produce a brochure for an aquaculture company to market their ethically produced salmon to consumers. The salmon is grown in open water tanks placed in the estuaries in a less economically developed nation. Around the aquaculture project are areas of important marine biodiversity.

In your brochure you should include:

- a description of the process of aquaculture for the salmon
- how the company has minimised the risks to the environment
- how the company is working with local people to ensure that it is a successful project for the local economy.

Thinking about your project

To assess your project, you could ask people to comment on how likely they would be to buy salmon on the basis of the information you have given them. They could give a score out of 10 for each of the following:

- ethical product
- environmentally sustainable
- quality of product.

EXAM-STYLE QUESTIONS

1. **a** **i** Explain what are meant by the terms *internal and external fertilisation*. [2]

    Table 8.29 shows the mean number of fertilised eggs and mean number of offspring that survive to adulthood for one breeding cycle of giant clams and sperm whales.

species	mean number of fertilised eggs	mean number of offspring surviving to adulthood
giant clam	354 000 000	5.3
sperm whale	1	0.9

    Table 8.29: Survival rates of giant clam and whale fertilised eggs.

    ii Calculate the percentage of fertilised eggs that survive to adulthood for the giant clam and the sperm whale. [2]

    iii Explain how parental care strategies determine the number of eggs produced and number of fertilised eggs surviving to adulthood. [3]

    b Sandtiger sharks give birth to live young. In the uterus of the mother there are many fertilised eggs that develop into embryos. The embryos actively feed off other embryos until only one or two are left to be born. Suggest and explain how this reproductive strategy is beneficial to the sandtiger sharks. [4]

    [Total: 11]

2. **a** Compare simple and complex life cycles. [2]
   b **Outline** the life cycle of shrimp. In your answer, explain the advantages of the different stages. [10]

   [Total: 12]

3. **a** Suggest, giving explanations, the effects of mangrove loss on shrimp populations. [6]
   b **Discuss** the uses of replanting mangroves and releasing cultured stocks to replenish the populations of marine organisms. [8]

   [Total: 14]

4. Scientists have found that there are two discrete populations of Atlantic bluefin tuna. The populations overlap in the central Atlantic Ocean and then return to spawning grounds in either the Mediterranean Sea or the Gulf of Mexico. Each tuna always returns to the same spawning ground.

    a Suggest, giving explanations, why it is advantageous for the tuna to spawn in only two spawning grounds. [3]
    b Tuna use broadcast spawning as a method of fertilisation. This means that many tuna aggregate together and simultaneously release gametes into the water. Suggest and explain **one** advantage and **one** disadvantage of broadcast spawning. [2]

COMMAND WORDS

outline: set out main points

discuss: write about issue(s) or topic(s) in depth in a structured way

> **CONTINUED**
>
> c Figure 8.6 shows a tuna larva. Its skin and eye are silver and shiny.
>
> Suggest how the tuna larva is adapted to enable it to survive. [2]
>
> [Total: 7]
>
> 5 Giant clams release a chemical into the water called SIS, which synchronises gamete release from other clams. A scientist investigated the effect of different concentrations of SIS on the release of gametes.
>
> Ten giant clams were placed into a marine tank and exposed to a concentration of 2% SIS. The number of clams that released gametes within 2 s was recorded. The experiment was repeated with different concentrations of SIS, each time using different clams. The results are shown in Table 8.30.
>
> | Concentration of SIS / % | Number of clams that released gametes within 2 s |
> |---|---|
> | 0 | 0 |
> | 2 | 1 |
> | 6 | 1 |
> | 14 | 2 |
> | 22 | 8 |
> | 28 | 9 |
> | 36 | 9 |
>
> Table 8.30: Effect of different concentrations of SIS on release of gametes by giant clams.
>
> a i Plot a line graph of the effect of concentration of SIS on the release of gametes by giant clams. [4]
>
> ii Describe the effect of an increasing concentration of SIS on the release of gametes by giant clams. [2]
>
> b i Suggest **two** variables that the scientists would need to control. [2]
>
> ii The scientists concluded that 22% is the minimum concentration that the giant clams respond to. Explain whether this was a correct conclusion. [1]
>
> iii Suggest why the scientists only counted the clams that responded to the SIS within 2 s. [1]
>
> c Suggest and explain the advantages of the response by the clams to increasing concentrations of SIS. [2]
>
> [Total: 12]

CONTINUED

6 Catch per unit effort (CPUE) is defined as the catch in a year divided by the fishing effort. It is often used as a tool to determine whether fish stocks are healthy.

Fishing effort was measured in number of boat-days, which is the total of number of days during which fishing took place.

Table 8.31 shows the changes in CPUE for two species of North Sea fish, cod and pollock, over a period of 10 years.

Year	CPUE / tonnes boat-day^{-1}	
	Cod	Pollock
2000	55	64
2001	32	62
2002	25	54
2003	12	49
2004	8	45
2005	9	24
2006	15	21
2007	18	15
2008	22	14
2009	25	12

Table 8.31: Change in CPUE for cod and pollock in North Sea over a 10-year period.

- **a** **i** Plot a graph to show the changes in CPUE of cod and pollock over the 10-year period. [5]
  - **ii** Calculate the percentage change in CPUE for cod between 2000 and 2004. [2]
  - **iii** Compare the changes in CPUE for both species. [3]
- **b** In an effort to conserve stocks, restrictions on fishing effort for cod were introduced in 2005. Discuss the conclusion that the restrictions have helped the health of populations of North Sea fish. [4]

[Total: 14]

7 If fish stocks are under threat, restrictions are often used to help protect populations.
- **a** **i** State **three** types of restriction that can be used to preserve fish populations. [3]
  - **ii** Explain short- and long-term sociological effects of fishing restrictions on a coastal area where fishing is the major industry. [4]

CONTINUED

b In 2003, restrictions on scallop fishing were introduced in a coastal area of Australia in an effort to protect the population. The restrictions included a reduction in the number of boats that could fish and a reduction in the number of scallops that each boat could harvest.

Table 8.32 shows the effect on the mean annual profits made by fishing for the scallops per boat.

Year	Mean annual profit per boat per year / AUS \$ / USD \$ boat^{-1} year^{-1}
2001	4500 (AUS\$) / 2753 (USD\$)
2002	3700 (AUS\$) / 2264 (USD\$)
2003	4800 (AUS\$) / 2937 (USD\$)
2004	4700 (AUS\$) / 2878 (USD\$)
2005	5100 (AUS\$) / 3126 (USD\$)
2006	5300 (AUS\$) / 3249 (USD\$)
2007	5300 (AUS\$) / 3252 (USD\$)

Table 8.32: Annual profit per boat per year in Australian dollars (AUS\$) and United States dollars (USD\$) from scallop fishing.

　　i Describe the impact of the restrictions on the profits made from scallop fishing. [2]

　　ii Suggest and explain reasons for the effect of the restrictions on the mean annual profits made per boat. [4]

[Total: 13]

8 Different methods of fishing have different impacts on habitats and other non-target species organisms.

　a i Describe the negative impacts of benthic trawling. [3]

　　ii Explain why purse seine fishing is often replaced by rod and line fishing. [3]

In an effort to investigate the effects of fishing on the age profile of a population of cod, scientists sampled fish in 1985 and 2005. The percentage of fish in different age groups was determined in both years.

The scientists sampled the cod for the same lengths of time and using the same equipment each year.

The results are shown in Figure 8.40 and Table 8.33.

8 Fisheries for the future

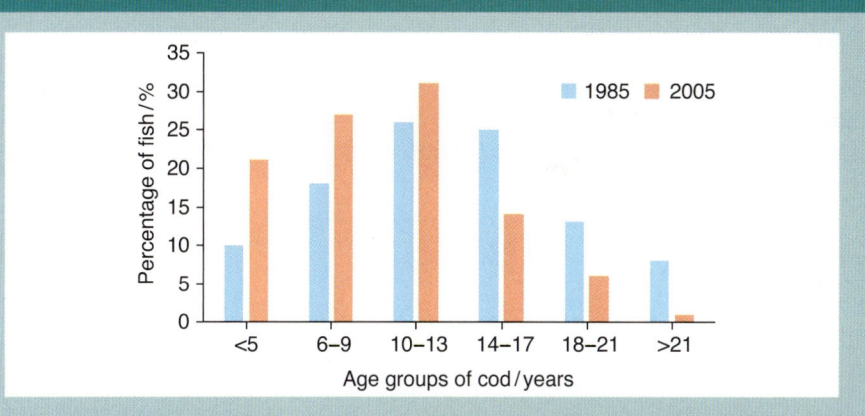

CONTINUED

Figure 8.40: Graph showing percentages of cod in different age groups in 1985 and 2005.

Year	Total number of fish sampled
1985	2524
2005	1414

Table 8.33: Sample sizes of fish in 1985 and 2005.

b i Calculate the difference in the numbers of fish sampled in the 10–13 age group between 1985 and 2005. [3]

ii Describe and explain the differences in the cod populations between 1985 and 2005. [3]

iii The scientists recommended that a range of fishing restrictions needed to be imposed. One of the recommendations was that there should be an increase in the minimum mesh size used in the nets. Explain how increasing the minimum mesh size could improve the health of the population. [2]

[Total: 14]

9 a Describe the differences between extensive and intensive aquaculture. [3]

b Figure 8.41 shows an enclosed aquaculture system used for growing grouper.

Figure 8.41: Tank aquaculture system used for producing grouper.

CONTINUED

    i Explain the purpose of the bubbler. **[2]**

    ii Explain why fresh water is pumped through the tanks. **[2]**

    iii Suggest and explain the effects on the environment that could occur if the filtration tank that waste water passes through before release was removed. **[5]**

    [Total: 12]

10 Figure 8.42 shows the map of a coastline where a new intensive shrimp aquaculture facility is proposed.

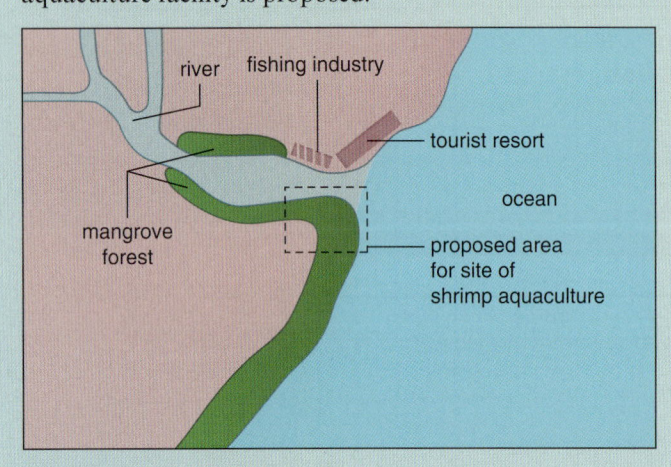

Figure 8.42: Map of coastal area where shrimp aquaculture venue is proposed.

    a Suggest and explain the negative consequences of developing the aquaculture venture. **[6]**

    b Suggest and explain what the company should do to minimise negative effects on the local community. **[5]**

    c Bluefin tuna is a carnivorous species of fish that is often produced by aquaculture. Explain why it is less sustainable to farm large carnivorous species rather than herbivore species such as carp. **[3]**

    [Total: 14]

11 a Outline the stages involved in the aquaculture of mussels. **[4]**

    b Explain the factors that a local government would need to consider before approving the development of a sustainable aquaculture venture for salmon. **[9]**

    [Total: 13]

12 The demand for fish is increasing as the global human population increases. Harvesting fish from the seas will be increasingly unable to meet the demand for fish in the future.

Table 8.34 shows the demand for fish since 1970 and the predicted demand up to 2050. It also shows the quantity of fish that may be harvested from the sea.

CONTINUED

Year	Demand / million tonnes	Harvest from sea / million tonnes
1970	60	60
1990	80	70
2010	140	80
2030	180	85
2050	220	80

Table 8.34: Changes in demand for fish and harvest of fish between 1970 and 2050.

a i Plot line graphs on the same axes of the demand for fish and fish that may be harvested from the sea. [5]

ii The difference in the total demand for a year and what may be harvested is the mass of fish that will have to be produced by aquaculture.

Calculate the mass of fish that will have to be produced by aquaculture in 2050. [1]

b Different types of fish feed are more or less digestible. This means that fish may be able to absorb them more or less efficiently, so growing more or less rapidly and producing more or less faecal waste.

Plan an experiment that would produce valid data to investigate the effect of different feed types on the rate of tilapia growth and faeces production. In your plan, you should include a hypothesis and draw the table in which you would record your results. [9]

[Total: 15]

SELF-EVALUATION CHECKLIST

I can:	See section...	Needs more work	Almost there	Ready to move on
describe the life cycles of different species of marine organism	8.1			
explain why organisms have different stages in their life cycles	8.1			
explain the need for the sustainable exploitation of fisheries	8.2			
describe the impact of different modern fishing technologies	8.2			

CONTINUED

I can:	See section...	Needs more work	Almost there	Ready to move on
understand the information that is needed to decide how best to exploit fishes sustainably	8.2			
describe the different methods that can be employed to ensure that fishing is sustainable	8.2			
explain the sociological and economic impacts of restrictions on fishing and unrestricted fishing	8.2			
describe the methods that can be used to replenish depleted fish stocks	8.2			
describe the general methods of aquaculture and the specific methods used to produce salmon, mussels and shrimp	8.3			
describe the principal requirements and impacts of successful aquaculture	8.3			

EXTENDED CASE STUDY: SUSTAINABLE ROCK LOBSTER FISHING IN WEST AUSTRALIA

The coastal waters off the state of Western Australia (Figure 8.43) contain rich stocks of fish and shellfish. Commercial fishing companies operate in the area and it is very popular with recreational fishers. Commercial fishing, including pearling and aquaculture, contributes around one billion dollars to Western Australia's economy each year. It also provides direct employment for 5000 people, plus many more in-linked industries. Commercial fishing is based mainly on small family businesses, and 85% of commercial fishing activity is conducted in remote coastal communities. Over the years, Western Australia has been considered to be an example of excellent practice for the regulation of sustainable fisheries. It has achieved this by careful implementation of several policies.

Methods employed to ensure sustainable fishing

An integrated fish management programme is used so that the state government works with representatives from commercial fisheries, recreational fishers and scientists. Fish management programmes are discussed by all stakeholders to produce quotas and policies that are fair for everyone.

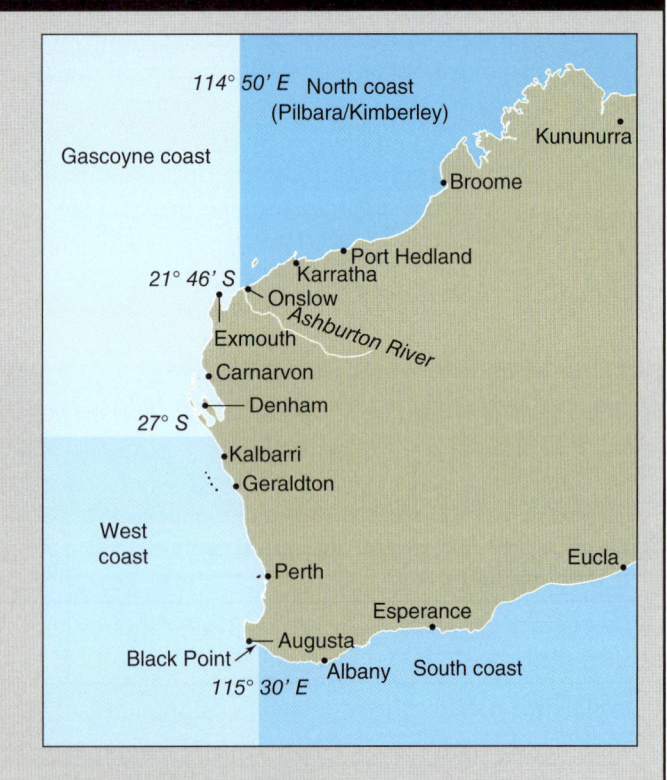

Figure 8.43: Western Australia, showing marine bioregions.

CONTINUED

Western Australia operates a very strict licensing policy for both commercial and recreational fishers. Fishing licences must be purchased, and the revenue raised from the sale of licences is used to pay for the development of sustainable fishing projects and sustainable aquaculture. Projects have included the building of artificial reefs and fish-attracting devices, the restocking of prawns, mulloway and barramundi, training programmes, research projects and surveillance programmes.

There are strict rules and regulations for recreational fishing:

- Only certain areas may be fished.
- Fish that are kept and not returned must be above a certain size.
- There are limits on the number of each species that can be kept.
- Certain fishing gear is not permitted.
- At some times of year fishing is prohibited in some areas.

There are also strict rules and regulations for commercial fishing:

- Restrictions on the number of licences issued, gear restrictions, seasonal closures and limits on total fishing time.
- Quotas to limit the quantity of fish that can be landed.
- Permanent and temporary area closures to protect important habitats.
- Specific measures to protect juvenile or breeding fish (such as size limits and seasonal and area closures).
- Nearly all boats carry AIS as a part of the VMS.

The measures taken to safeguard the future of Western Australia's fish and shellfish have proved to be some of the most effective in the world and are an example of good practice. Efforts to safeguard one species in particular, the western rock lobster, are seen as a good model for other species.

The western rock lobster

In the wild, western rock lobsters (Figure 8.44) can live for up to 20 years and grow to sizes of over 5 kg. They mature at around six or seven years of age. They are a very commercially important species and were initially exploited at the end of the Second World War, when small fisheries were set up to produce canned lobster for soldiers. The lobsters were caught by using baited lobster traps.

Figure 8.44: Western rock lobster.

Throughout the 1950s, lobster fishing expanded rapidly, with many more mechanised boats being used.

By the early 1960s, lobster populations were beginning to decline, and the average size of lobster caught was also decreasing. In 1963, the first restrictions on lobster fishing were introduced. No more new fishing licences were issued, and restrictions were placed on the number of lobster traps allowed on each boat.

Legislation controlling lobster fishing has continued to evolve and current measures include:

- restricted access to fishing grounds
- minimum legal size of 76 mm in length
- closed season from 01 July to 15 November each year
- escape gap of 54 mm in all pots to allow escape of smaller lobsters
- ban on taking spawning female rock lobsters and those in a pre-spawning condition
- annual quotas based on population estimates; if catch per unit effort is low, quotas are reduced
- maximum holding of 150 lobster pots per boat
- constant scientific surveys to assess numbers of juvenile lobsters in order to predict future stocks.

> **CONTINUED**

Recruitment of lobsters varies enormously and is affected by many natural factors, including the strength of the winds and water currents. Scientists have managed to produce a population model that takes into account many biotic and abiotic factors. This helps to predict future populations and set fishing quotas. Lobster fishing is actively managed. Before 2008, a period of very low juvenile settlement was recorded so that fishing effort reductions were introduced for the 2008–2009 season. Trap numbers and fishing periods were limited and the number of vessels decreased from 460 to 294 over two years. The reduced fishing effort was associated with an overall increase in profit compared with what would have been achieved if all 460 vessels had still been operating at the previous effort levels. After the restrictions, commercial catch rates improved and rock lobster egg production moved to record-high levels. The success of the measures, both environmentally and economically, has pleased both the scientists and the fisheries. By working together they have developed a model for sustainable fishing that can be copied elsewhere.

In recognition of its success, the West Coast Rock Lobster Managed Fishery was the first fishery in the world to be certified as ecologically sustainable by the Marine Stewardship Council. The state of Western Australia continues to work hard to promote sustainable fishing methods. It monitors and controls all fishing in its waters and carefully implements restrictions that take into consideration both the industry and the long-term health of fish populations. It continues to fund research: new lobster pots have been designed to prevent sealion pups getting trapped in them. Continuing and extensive consultation, in addition to a long-term science programme, has resulted in the western rock lobster being one of the best managed fisheries in the world.

Questions

1. Explain why the integrated management system that regulates fishing in Western Australia makes the regulation more effective.
2. Explain how **three** of the general commercial fishing rules help to preserve fish stocks.
3. Suggest how biotic and abiotic factors can affect the population of the lobsters.
4. Suggest why putting restrictions on lobster fishing has actually resulted in an increase in profits.
5. Make a summary of the reasons why the fisheries management by the state of Western Australia is considered an example of good practice for others to follow.

Chapter 9
Human impacts on marine ecosystems

LEARNING INTENTIONS

In this chapter you will learn how to:

- describe the effect of human activities on marine water quality, organisms and food webs
- explain the process of bioaccumulation
- describe the production of microplastics, the impacts associated with them and ways to limit their release
- explain the natural and enhanced greenhouse effects
- describe the evidence for global warming and be able to evaluate the evidence for and against it being caused by human activity
- describe the impacts of global warming on the marine environment
- describe and explain the causes and effects of ocean acidification
- investigate the effect of pH on the loss of mass of mollusc shells

> CAMBRIDGE INTERNATIONAL AS & A LEVEL MARINE SCIENCE: COURSEBOOK

CONTINUED

- explain the need for the conservation of marine ecosystems
- explain the roles of organisations such as the IUCN in marine conservation
- describe the threats posed by invasive species
- discuss a range of strategies for conserving marine species.

BEFORE YOU START

- Plastics are a major threat to the marine environment. With a time limit of five minutes, list as many types of plastic that you encounter in everyday life that could end up in the oceans. Write down three other human activities that are damaging to the marine environment and the problems that they may cause. Compare your list with other learners.

- In Chapter 3 you will have learnt about the carbon cycle. Draw out a diagram of the carbon cycle and identify the processes that decrease and increase atmospheric carbon dioxide. Discuss how human activity could affect these processes, and the effects that this could have on atmospheric carbon dioxide levels.

REPAIRING THE DAMAGE WE HAVE DONE TO OUR OCEANS

All species alter the environment around them. The changes inflicted on the environment by one species in particular, however, far outweigh all other species. That species is ours: *Homo sapiens*.

Human activities, particularly during the twentieth and twenty-first centuries, have had a major impact on marine ecosystems. Food webs have been disrupted, habitats destroyed, and biodiversity lost, along with changes to the physical and chemical nature of the water. A range of agricultural and industrial activities have affected the ecosystems of our oceans directly by altering the properties of the water and adding poisons, and indirectly by global warming. Some of our activities, such as the sinking of ships for wreck diving, can increase biodiversity; while others, such as the release of mercury, have a negative impact.

We are the dominant species on the planet and, as such, have a responsibility to maintain the ocean ecosystems for the future. If we are to remedy this and stop further damage, we need to think of ways of conserving species and their habitats. **Conservation** is often easy in theory but more difficult in practice. If conservation projects are to be successful, they need careful consideration and the support of local people. Projects that could affect local and national economies need to ensure that people retain employment and have the opportunity to improve their living standards. **Ecotourism** is an increasingly popular way of making conservation pay, but it needs careful regulation and a responsible approach from all concerned. If ecotourism is managed carefully, it is a valuable method from which the environment and local people benefit.

Questions

1 Why is the conservation of marine ecosystems important?
2 Do we really need to conserve marine species?

KEY WORDS

conservation: the protection of plants, animals and other organisms along with their habitats from extinction

ecotourism: sustainable tourism that is associated with an appreciation of the natural world and that minimises damage to the environment; it can benefit both environment and local populations

9.1 Ecological impacts of human activities

Various human activities can have an impact on marine water quality, habitats, organisms and food webs. In this section we will discuss human activities and their impacts, and what can be done to minimise their impacts.

The oil industry

Oil is the main source of fuel for ships, cars, trucks and aeroplanes around the world. It is a mixture of many different compounds, including gasoline, diesel, kerosene and bitumen. It was formed millions of years ago and is the remains of the anaerobic decomposition of marine organisms as phytoplankton and zooplankton. Over time, these remains became buried under layers of sediment and subjected to heat and pressure, resulting in their conversion into crude oil. Crude oil is the product of living organisms, but many of the chemicals within it are toxic.

Oil from deep deposits is brought to the surface by drilling on land or at sea on oil rigs. It is then transported in large oil tankers to refineries where different fuels are produced. The exploration, drilling, transport and use of oil causes many environmental issues.

Exploratory drilling and setting up offshore oil platforms

In order to identify oil reserves, survey ships map the seabed by emitting high decibel explosive impulses. The noise from these surveys has been reported to kill fish eggs and larvae, and damage the vibration detection mechanisms of fish. Damaged fish are less able to escape predators and are often unable to find mates. Whales and other fish divert from their normal migration routes.

Drilling through the seabed releases toxins such as benzene, zinc and arsenic into the water. These can pass through food chains due to **bioaccumulation**. Disrupted sediment can block the gills of invertebrates and fish, causing suffocation. Sediment can also block the light in the water, reducing phytoplankton productivity. The fragile seabed habitat can be physically damaged, resulting in organisms being dislodged and killed.

Oil spillage

Oil spills can be caused by leakage from oil tankers or drilling sites. Oil spillage may be a major, sudden event, such as the *Deepwater Horizon* disaster in 2010, caused by the explosion of an oil rig in the Gulf of Mexico. Such sudden spills release vast quantities of oil into the sea that then spread quickly onto coastlines (Figure 9.1). Continuous leakage from drilling sites or tankers is also a problem, leading to an on-going flow of oil into the sea.

Figure 9.1: Relief workers shovel oiled sand into plastic bags at Grand Isle State Park, Louisiana, June 5, 2010.

Oil spills can ruin entire ecosystems in oceans and on coastlines. They can take many years to clean up; they are very costly, both financially and environmentally, and the clean-up operations can sometimes cause as much damage as the oil spill. Since the transportation of oil began in the twentieth century, there have been many spillages and it is estimated that every year more than 880 000 gallons of oil are released into the water from drilling operations alone.

Marine oil spills have a range of effects, some of which are discussed below.

Oil toxicity

Crude oil contains many chemicals that are toxic when ingested by marine organisms. After the *Deepwater Horizon* explosion in 2010, many organisms were

> **KEY WORD**
>
> **bioaccumulation:** the accumulation of substances, such as pesticides, or other chemicals in an organism

poisoned, including dolphins, turtles, bluefin tuna and sea birds. Dolphins were found to have sustained serious damage to their lungs and fish larvae had undergone mutations.

Physical damage to organisms

When whales and dolphins come to the surface to breathe, oil can cover their blowholes and enter their lungs, damaging the tissue or causing suffocation. Oil can also get into the animals' eyes, potentially damaging vision. When oil reaches coastal water, it can prevent hatchlings and juvenile turtles from surfacing to breathe. Fish, especially pelagic fish such as bluefin tuna, can take in oil through their mouths, damaging their gills.

Sea birds, such as pelicans, become covered with oil when diving into oily water to feed (Figure 9.2). Once birds are covered with oil, they are unable to fly, making feeding and escaping predators impossible. Their natural buoyancy and insulation from cold are also lost, causing death by drowning or hypothermia. When oil washes up onto beaches, nests and eggs get covered, often killing the chicks and causing adult birds to abandon the nesting areas. Some birds exposed to crude oil show hormonal changes that disrupt breeding.

Figure 9.2: Oil-coated pelicans after the *Deepwater Horizon* oil spill.

Furred marine mammals, such as sea otters and seals, often get coated in oil. The fur then loses its insulating properties and as a result the animals can die from hypothermia.

Effects on food webs and productivity

Oil on the surface of the water reduces light penetration, decreasing phytoplankton productivity. Because of its toxic effect, oil also kills organisms from different trophic levels, causing food chains and webs to become unbalanced.

Damage to coastal ecosystems

Water currents drive oil spills onto coastlines and beach areas, resulting in a thick coating of oil on sand and rocks. This poisons and suffocates coastal organisms and can kill plants, including mangroves. The loss of mangroves is particularly damaging to ecosystems because mangrove roots anchor soil and prevent coastal erosion. Mangroves are nesting areas for many birds and the water around their roots is a nursery ground for many marine species. Rocky beach animals such as crabs and sea anemones are often killed and seaweeds are lost.

Sun and wind turn oil into a hard, asphalt-like substance that eventually breaks up and is washed away. On sandy beaches, oil can sink through to lower layers of sand, causing contamination that can last for years. Nesting sites for birds and turtles can be destroyed, leading to the loss of many breeding seasons. If an oil spill coincides with the hatching of turtle eggs, a whole generation can be lost. It can take many years for established food webs to recover, and sometimes it is impossible because erosion of the substrate results in habitat loss.

Damage caused by cleaning-up oil spills

Oil does not dissolve in water so tends to aggregate as a slick across the water surface. The natural movement of the sea breaks up the oil into smaller droplets, which then fall down through the water column to the seabed or spread further afield. Some methods, such as the use of booms to collect surface oil, do not affect the environment. Many other methods have environmental consequences.

Controlled burning of the surface oil involves igniting it by adding accelerants. This can only be carried out in calm weather and generates large quantities of smoke and air pollution, including sulfur dioxide gas, which causes acid rain.

Dispersants are sprayed onto the oil, helping to break it up into smaller droplets so that it is scattered. This helps prevent the oil contaminating coastlines but does not remove it. Corexit, a frequently used dispersant, is toxic to plankton and other marine organisms. Recent evidence suggests that it passes through food chains, accumulating and harming top predators such as dolphins and birds. Many dolphins seem to have been poisoned in this way after the *Deepwater Horizon* disaster and there have been reports that plankton biomass in the Gulf of Mexico has been reduced. Dispersants cause oil to sink to the seabed where, because of the cold, it persists for a long time, slowly leaking toxins into the water. Filter-feeder organisms such as mussels and oysters concentrate the dispersant in their bodies when they collect dead organic matter.

Oxygen dead zones

When oil sinks to the seabed, it is decomposed by bacteria that use it as a source of energy. The Gulf of Mexico contains many microbes that consume the natural seepage of oil from rocks. After the *Deepwater Horizon* disaster, these bacteria appeared to be one of the main processes by which the oil was broken down and removed. However, if large quantities of oil are released, the bacteria increase in number and their high rate of respiration removes oxygen from the ecosystem. This produces dead zones where most organisms are unable to live. Recent research suggests that the oxygen levels in some areas of the Gulf of Mexico were reduced dramatically after the *Deepwater Horizon* spill.

Indirect effects of the oil industry

When oil is burnt, it produces many waste gases, including carbon dioxide and sulfur dioxide. Carbon dioxide is a greenhouse gas and has potential effects on **global warming** and ocean acidification.

> **KEY WORD**
>
> **global warming:** the observed and projected increases in the average temperature of Earth's atmosphere and oceans due to an enhanced greenhouse effect

Sulfur dioxide dissolves in rainwater to produce sulfuric acid. This fall as acid rain on land and sea. On land, acid rain is known to cause deforestation and loss of fish from fresh-water lakes. High quantities of acid rain at sea have the potential to lower the pH of seawater, affecting the physiology of marine organisms such as coral reefs and bivalve molluscs. Table 9.1 summarises the effects of the oil industry on marine ecosystems.

Factor affected by oil industry	Effects of oil contamination
water quality	<ul><li>toxins such as heavy metals (for example, mercury and arsenic) released from drilling</li><li>oil emulsion in water column</li><li>loss of oxygen in water</li><li>surface coated with oil reducing light penetration and oxygen dissolution</li><li>oil affects surface tension of water</li><li>presence of many toxic hydrocarbons</li><li>presence of dissolved, toxic dispersants</li><li>increased acidity due to acid rain and carbon dioxide</li><li>high turbidity causing less light penetration</li></ul>
habitat	<ul><li>physical damage to seabed from exploration and drilling</li><li>coverage of beaches and coast areas with oil</li><li>loss of reefs and nesting sites</li><li>loss of mangroves, leading to coastal erosion and loss of nursery sites</li></ul>
organisms	<ul><li>reduction in biodiversity</li><li>loss of phytoplankton</li><li>loss of all species at all trophic levels due to ingestion of toxic oil, suffocation, loss of insulation, breeding</li></ul>
food webs	<ul><li>food webs disrupted at all levels</li><li>loss of producers reduces energy available</li><li>loss of top predators causes increases in some prey</li><li>overgrowth of decomposer bacteria</li></ul>

Table 9.1: Effects of the oil industry on marine ecosystems.

Agriculture

The effect of mineral ions such as nitrates and phosphates on algal blooms and producer productivity is discussed in Chapter 8. Using fertilisers on fields close to coastal areas and rivers can cause algal blooms in the sea. Overgrowth of algae can then lead to the establishment of dead zones in the sea, where oxygen is very low and virtually no life is present. This process is called eutrophication and consists of several stages (Figure 9.3).

- To maximise crop yields, farmers often add inorganic fertiliser to their fields. This dissolves in rainwater and runs off into rivers. The loss of the fertilisers into the rivers is called leaching.
- The rivers develop high concentrations of mineral ions, which are carried into estuaries and seas. These mineral ions encourage the overgrowth of phytoplankton, known as algal blooms.
- The overgrowth of algae produces a population that over-competes for light so many organisms die and sink down to the seabed.
- Decomposer bacteria break down the dead phytoplankton and respire at a high rate, reducing the concentration of oxygen in the water.
- The low oxygen concentration in the water leads to the death of aerobic organisms by suffocation.

The loss of organic matter, such as animal faeces or dead plant material, into rivers and seas also provides decomposer bacteria with nutrition and can lead to oxygen depletion. Dead zones can be catastrophic for sessile marine organisms such as mussels and oysters, and can affect coastal communities that rely on such organisms for their economy.

Not only is fertiliser and dead organic waste passed into the sea from agriculture, but pesticides, herbicides and fungicides may also be lost into the water. These substances can poison marine organisms and may accumulate along food chains, killing top predators.

In a recent investigation, the effect of agriculture on algal blooms in the Gulf of California was carried out. The Yaqui Valley is a 225 000-hectare area of Mexico where intensive farming is practised. The whole valley is fertilised and irrigated, causing excessive run-off of fertiliser into rivers, and eventually into the Gulf of California. Satellite images of water in the gulf were analysed between 1998 and 2002. It was found that in each year there were four periods when fertiliser was added to the wheat and, in each case, an algal bloom of up to 570 km^2 would appear in the Gulf of California days after the fertiliser was added. Table 9.2 summarises the effects of agriculture on marine ecosystems.

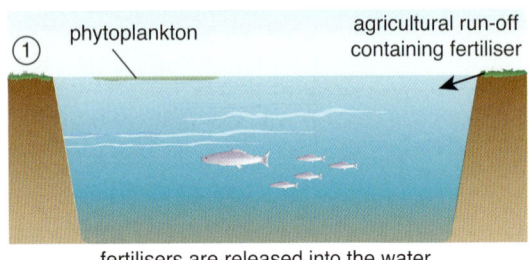

① phytoplankton / agricultural run-off containing fertiliser
fertilisers are released into the water

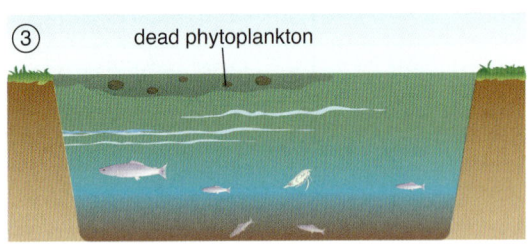

② thick bloom of phytoplankton
the fertiliser causes a thick bloom of phytoplankton in the water

③ dead phytoplankton
phytoplankton die due to lack of light and fish begin to die

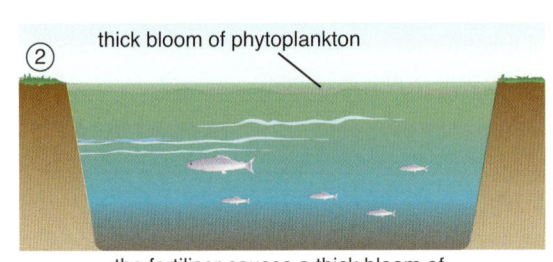

④ lack of oxygen causes death of fish and other organisms creating a dead zone

Figure 9.3: Stages in the eutrophication of a body of water.

9 Human impacts on marine ecosystems

Factor affected by agriculture	Effects of agriculture
water quality	- increase in sediments from run-off - increase in mineral ions such as nitrates and phosphates from fertilisers - reduced oxygen in water due to decomposition of organic waste and dead plants - increased algal blooms - possible increase in dissolved pesticides - increased turbidity due to sediment and algal bloom leading to reduced light penetration
habitat	- large quantities of algae can wash up on shores - dead organic matter can accumulate on the seabed
organisms	- reduction in biodiversity due to low oxygen - loss of many species, especially those that require higher levels of oxygen in water - some species die due to escape of pesticides into water - poisoning of some species by algal toxins
food webs	- food webs disrupted at several levels - loss of pelagic predator fish species due to low oxygen - over-growth of phytoplankton causing algal blooms

Table 9.2: Effects of agriculture on marine ecosystems.

Renewable energy installations

We have been dependent on fossil fuels for over a century. The large-scale combustion of fossil fuels is very polluting and may be one of the causes of global warming. As we have become more aware of the risks posed by burning fossil fuels, the search for cleaner, renewable energy sources has intensified. The marine environment offers several options including wind turbines, wave power devices and tidal turbines.

> ### KEY WORD
>
> **renewable energy:** energy that is taken from sources that are naturally replenished quickly (for example, sunlight, wind and tides)

Wind turbines

Many wind farms, such as the one shown in Figure 9.4, have been built in coastal areas to generate electricity. Wind turbines offer a clean, renewable way of producing electricity, and since it is usually very windy out at sea, placing them there makes it likely that they will generate electricity all year round. Wind turbines do, however, pose some risks to the marine environment. Installing them requires drilling into the seabed and securing the turbines with concrete. Benthic organisms such as corals or sponges may be damaged or lose their habitats. The loss of these organisms could affect complex food webs. Chemicals that may be toxic may leak out from metal or concrete and these could enter food chains. The main risk posed by wind turbines is likely to be to birds. There have been suggestions that birds may

Figure 9.4: A coastal wind farm.

alter their migration routes and flight paths to avoid large wind farms and there is a risk of collision with the turbines. The turbines also generate a small amount of underwater noise due to vibrations; this could potentially alter the behaviour of mammals such as whales and dolphins that have sensitive hearing.

Wave power devices

Large moving, floating platforms can be used to generate electricity from the constant movement of waves (Figure 9.5). As the waves move, the platforms move up and down, and this movement, is used to generate electricity. Like wind turbines, this method is generally very clean, renewable and does not release pollutants. The main threat to marine organisms is the risk of collision, particularly for marine mammals. Seals could use them as hauling out platforms and birds may nest on them. Some studies in Sweden have suggested that the platforms may act as fish aggregation devices, encouraging small fish to live under them. This could attract larger predators and disrupt existing food webs.

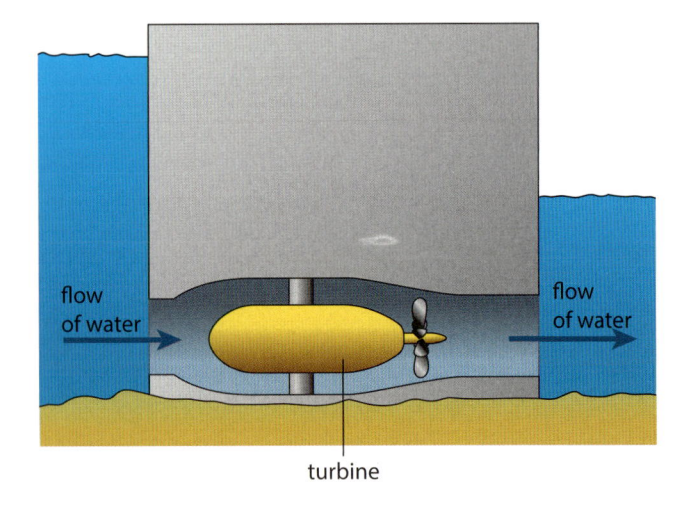

Figure 9.6: A tidal power electricity generator. Water moves past the turbine with the tidal current.

in Figure 9.7, rely on the construction of a concrete barrage structure. Building barrages can have many negative impacts on the marine environment. Species may lose their habitats, and if the barrage is close to an estuary, salinity may be altered. Marine mammals such as seals that often live in estuaries can be particularly badly affected. As there is less overall movement of water around the barrage, water turbidity decreases. The additional light can lead to algal blooms, affecting the balance of organisms throughout food webs. Barrages across estuaries can also lead to the accumulation of sediment behind the barrages.

Figure 9.5: Wave power devices floating on the sea.

Tidal barrages and turbines

There are several methods that can be used to harness the power of tides, all of which work to convert tidal energy into electrical energy. They all contain turbines which spin in response to the tidal movement of water in and out of coastal areas or estuaries (Figure 9.6). Many, such as the La Rance tidal-turbine in France, shown

Figure 9.7: The La Rance barrage in France.

Factor affected by renewable energy installations	Effects of renewable energy installations
water quality	- installation of wind turbines may stir up sediment
- chemicals may leak from concrete used to install wind turbines
- tidal barrages may cause build-up of sediment around estuaries
- tidal barrages may cause reduced turbidity in seawater
- tidal barrages around estuaries may affect the salinity of river and/or sea water
habitat	- wind turbines may damage the seabed
- tidal barrages may prevent migrating species returning to rivers
- tidal barrages may affect the habitats of mammals such as seals
- tidal barrages may cause silting up of estuaries
organisms	- birds may collide with wind turbines
- wind turbines may affect the migration patterns of some species
- tidal barrages may affect migration of species and destroy the habitat of species such as seals
- tidal barrages may cause algal blooms
- wave power devices may damage mammals due to collision
food webs	- loss of birds and large mammals may cause an increase in prey species
- wave power devices may act as fish aggregating devices
- tidal barrages may result in a loss of predators such as seals in estuaries

Table 9.3: Effects of renewable energy installations on marine ecosystems.

Recently, more research has been carried out on tidal turbines that do not require barrages and so do not have many of the associated negative impacts. Tidal fences and small, floating turbines do not block estuaries or coastal water and are desinged to allow sediment to flow through. Their main negative impact is the chance of physical damage to fish or mammals that try to swim through the turbines. Modern versions have protective coats around the turbines to prevent fish entering and sensors that stop the turbines when mammals are detected in the area. Table 9.3 summarises the effects of renewable energy installations on marine ecosystems.

Sewage disposal

Sewage is water that carries waste materials. It is usually channelled through plumbing pipes and a series of underground sewers. In most developed nations, sewage is sent to water treatment plants where it is cleaned by removing toxins and organic material before being released into lakes, rivers and the sea. In many countries, however, there is little or no purification of the water before it is released back into natural water bodies. There are several different sources of sewage.

Domestic sewage is waste water generated by human residences. It carries faeces, urine, washing water and laundry waste. Waste water from large institutions such as hospitals and schools may come under this category if it is similar to domestic waste water. It is usually channelled through underground sewers.

> **KEY WORD**
>
> **sewage:** liquid and solid waste material such as waste water or urine

Surface run-off is rainwater that runs over the ground, picking up particulate matter and dissolving mineral ions as it flows. It may carry sediment and mineral ions such as nitrates and phosphates.

Industrial waste water is liquid waste generated by factories that is washed into the sewerage system, although technically it is not defined as sewage. Companies have a duty to avoid releasing hazardous waste directly and should ensure that water is treated before release. Industrial waste water may contain substances such as detergents, heavy metals and pesticides, which pose a risk to living organisms.

Untreated sewage poses several risks to the marine environment because of its content (Table 9.4).

Factor affected by sewage	Effects of sewage
water quality	- increase in sediments reducing light penetration - increase in detergents and toxins from waste water - increase in toxins from run-off water - reduced oxygen concentrations due to decomposition - altered mineral ion concentrations - presence of harmful microbes
habitat	- sediment settling on seabed
organisms	- reduction in biodiversity - loss of many species due to low oxygen levels, especially organisms with higher oxygen demands - loss of species due to infection by harmful microbes
food webs	- disrupted at several levels by toxins and detergents - loss of predators due to infection

Table 9.4: Effects of sewage on marine ecosystems.

Faeces and other organic wastes provide a source of food for decomposer bacteria. If large quantities are dumped into the water, it has a similar effect to agricultural run-off, resulting in an increase in bacterial populations in the water. The bacteria respire rapidly, reducing the oxygen in the water so that other organisms die by suffocation.

If sewage contained only purely organic waste, it could be used as a fertiliser. However, it can contain chemicals including detergents, fertilisers and toxins. Detergents often contain phosphates, which can promote eutrophication and have been linked with algal blooms. Detergents also contain chemicals called surfactants, which reduce the surface tension of water. Surfactants are toxic to aquatic life, persist in the environment and have been found to break down the protective mucus layer that coats fish, making them vulnerable to parasites and bacteria. Medicinal drugs taken by humans can pass into the sewerage system in human urine and affect marine organisms. Steroid hormones from contraceptive pills may have altered the ratios of male to female fish around sewage outflow pipes, although this research is controversial.

Untreated sewage can contain pathogens such as viruses that can affect marine organisms, particularly mammals. In 2015, large numbers of grey seal pups off the Welsh coast died from infection with campylobacter bacteria, which cause human gastroenteritis. The infected seals had symptoms consistent with human gastroenteritis and it is thought they were infected from sewage.

Refuse disposal

Marine **refuse** is made up of discarded objects from coastal areas and ships. Typical examples include waste from beach users, waste from sewers, shipping debris and fishing waste such as old lines and nets. It is estimated that more than 10 000 containers are lost every year from ships during storms, with one notable event occurring in 1992 when a cargo of yellow plastic toy ducks were lost in transit from Japan. These ducks

> **KEY WORD**
>
> **refuse:** material that has been discarded

have been found all over the world and are known as the 'friendly floatees'. Their movements have helped reveal the path of the world's ocean currents (Figure 9.8).

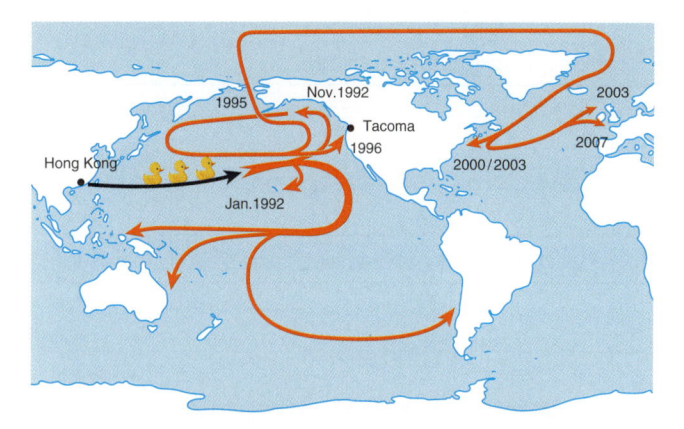

Figure 9.8: Ocean currents shown by the movement of a lost cargo of plastic ducks.

The majority of litter found in the seas is plastic, is not biodegradable and may persist for thousands of years. Exposure to sunlight and constant wave action breaks the plastics up into small microparticles that float in the surface waters of the sea. Ocean currents move the microparticles and concentrate them in 'garbage patches'. The Great Pacific Garbage Patch is a collection of marine debris in the north Pacific Ocean that is created by ocean currents (Figure 9.9). There are also larger pieces of debris and even old, floating computer screens have been seen. About 80% of the debris in the Great Pacific Garbage Patch comes from land-based activities in North America and Asia. The remaining 20% comes mainly from shipping, the majority of which is discarded fishing nets, which are particularly hazardous to wildlife. It takes about six years for refuse from North America to reach the Great Pacific Garbage Patch, while refuse from Japan takes about a year. Most other ocean garbage patches are located in the centre of gyres (Figure 9.9).

Refuse has several potential negative effects upon the marine environment. Sea birds, turtles, mammals and fish can become entangled in old fishing nets, fishing lines and other objects, causing them to drown, become more susceptible to predation, or die from starvation. Refuse can physically damage animals, killing them directly or wounding them, leading to infection and incapacity.

Many animals that live on or in the sea consume refuse by mistake, because it can look similar to their natural

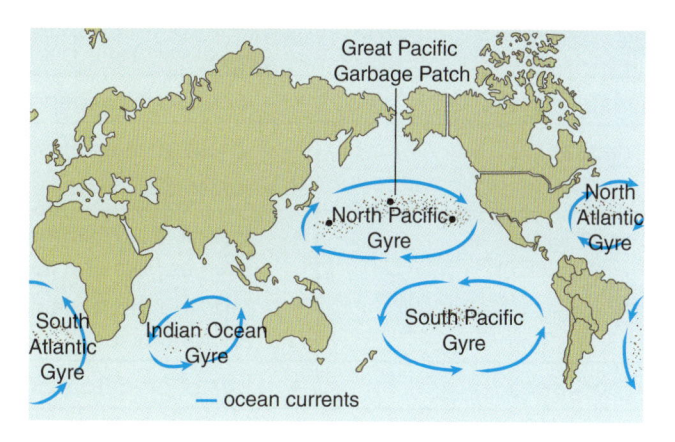

Figure 9.9: The location of five ocean gyres where refuse has accumulated.

prey. Plastic can become stuck in the digestive system of animals, blocking the passage of food and causing death by starvation or infection (Figure 9.10). Tiny floating plastic particles resemble zooplankton, which are eaten by animals and then travel up the food chain. Loggerhead sea turtles often mistake plastic bags for jellyfish, and albatrosses sometimes mistake plastic resin pellets for fish eggs, which they feed to their chicks.

Figure 9.10: The body of albatross showing ingested refuse.

Many plastics absorb toxins from the water which can be then be ingested by marine organisms. This, and other effects of plastics, will be discussed later in this chapter.

Microparticles of plastic in the water reduce the penetration of sunlight so reduce the rate of photosynthesis by phytoplankton, reducing primary productivity. If producers such as phytoplankton have a reduced biomass, there is less energy entering the food web. Table 9.5 summarises the effects of sewage and refuse on marine ecosystems.

Factor affected by refuse	Effects of refuse
water quality	- increase in suspended microparticles of plastics making water turbid
habitat	- refuse such as plastic damaging habitats - refuse and microparticles blocking upper water habitats
organisms	- loss of fish, mammals, birds and turtles due to physical damage from refuse such as nets and ingestion - reduced phytoplankton due to reduced light penetration caused by microparticles
food webs	- loss of predators due to physical damage by refuse and ingestion of refuse

Table 9.5: Effects of refuse on marine ecosystems.

CASE STUDY 9.1: DUMPING NEW YORK'S SEWAGE INTO THE NORTH-WEST ATLANTIC

Until 1992, the sewage of New Jersey and New York was collected and the solid parts were allowed to settle out in tanks. The resulting semi-solid sludge was then placed onto sewage ships that sailed out to sites in the north-west Atlantic and dumped into the sea. One such site was located 106 miles out to sea at a depth of 2500 m. It is estimated that between 1986 and 1992, about 42 million tonnes of wet, untreated, sewage sludge was dumped there.

A survey of the seabed at the site was carried out in the late 1980s. Oxygen levels in the water around the site were extremely low, and high concentrations of toxic metals such as cadmium and mercury, along with organic compounds, were found in the sediment. Sea urchins and sea cucumbers in the area were analysed for concentrations of radioactive isotopes of carbon, hydrogen and sulfur, which are very rare in the marine environment but are found in human faeces. The animals had high concentrations of these isotopes, indicating that substances from the sewage were entering the food chains. Traces of one potentially harmful bacterium that causes food poisoning were also found in the sediment.

During the time that the sewage was being dumped, there were several algal bloom events in the sea around New York. Cases of food poisoning were recorded in people who swam in the sea or visited the beaches and refuse such as used syringes was found washed up on beaches. Some shellfish beds died because of pollution and lack of oxygen, and others were often closed for fishing because of worries about the presence of pathogens. Beaches were shut for days each year because of harmful microbes.

The sewage dumping was stopped in 1992, after which the seabed at the dumping site began to change rapidly. Oxygen levels increased and species of organisms that require higher oxygen levels appeared. The waters around New York improved, with more species of fish present and much more biodiversity. Algal blooms still occur, but the beaches are much cleaner, are rarely closed and are safer for bathers. The fisheries have also benefitted with higher catches and less frequent closure of the oyster beds.

Questions

1. Explain why the oxygen levels were low at the base of the dumping site.
2. Explain how the radioactive tracers show that substances from the sewage were entering the food chain.
3. Suggest why the presence of mercury in the sewage sludge could be a problem for fisheries.

Desalination plants

The rapid increase in the human population over the last hundred years has brought with it increased demands for fresh water. Farming requires large quantities of fresh water, and the higher standards of living that people demand necessitates fresh water for things such as golf courses and swimming pools. The high demand for fresh water cannot be met in many parts of the world by natural sources alone, so increasing numbers of desalination plants have been built to extract fresh water from seawater.

Desalination plants can cause several problems to marine ecosystems (Table 9.6). Most of these problems are linked to the effluent that is released. There are two main types of desalination plant: distillation plants that boil seawater and collect fresh water by condensation, and reverse osmosis plants that pump water at high pressure through membranes to remove the salt. Both types generate similar pollutants that affect the water quality.

> **KEY WORD**
>
> **desalination plants:** industrial facilities that remove salts from seawater to manufacture fresh water

High salinity brine

Desalination plants release a very concentrated salt solution (brine) back into the sea. The brine from distillation plants is also very hot. It has a high density so sinks to lower depths and increases the salinity of the water there. Organisms that are osmoconformers are often killed by osmotic water loss, and even many osmoregulatory species are unable to survive. When the water temperature is high, it can kill organisms by causing overheating or can affect organisms' respiration rate. The productivity of phytoplankton is reduced by higher salinity and higher temperatures, and this reduces the energy available to food webs. Higher temperatures also reduce the solubility of oxygen, causing organisms to suffocate. The higher salinity can affect water currents because it alters natural haloclines.

Pollution due to waste chemicals

Chlorine is added to water in desalination plants to prevent the growth of algae within the machinery. Waste chlorine in the effluent water can be highly toxic

Factor affected by desalination plants	Effects of desalination plants
water quality	- increase in salinity as salt is dumped into water - toxic cleaning agents released into water - toxic heavy metal ions released from corrosion - acids and alkalis released from cleaning equipment - detergents released from cleaning fluids - increased sediment in water from pumping of waste water - reduced oxygen content - raised water temperature - altered haloclines due to higher density of saline water
habitat	- physical damage to seabed from release of water - loss of phytoplankton due to high salinity and temperature - agitation of sediment
organisms	- reduction in biodiversity - loss of many species, especially sessile osmoconformers such as shellfish, because of higher salinity, toxins and heat - loss of smaller organisms and eggs into the desalination plant
food webs	- food webs disrupted at several levels - loss of producers due to salinity change - loss of many sessile osmoconformers, such as molluscs, reducing food for higher trophic levels - loss of planktonic larvae and eggs lowers populations

Table 9.6: Effects of desalination plants on marine ecosystems.

to organisms in the sea. Heavy metals such as copper, iron, nickel and chromium are known to leak from the equipment into the waste water. These metals tend to aggregate in sediment on the seabed, where they are taken up by filter-feeding organisms and pass through food chains, accumulating in the body tissues of top predators. Desalination plants are cleaned every 3–6 months using harsh, toxic cleaning solutions that are often acidic or alkaline. When released, these solutions can poison marine organisms and alter the pH of the water, affecting their physiology.

Sediment movement

The outflow from desalination plants may agitate the seabed when pumped out at high pressure. This dislodges sediment, which can reduce light penetration for producers and damage the gills of fish and invertebrates.

Direct risks to organisms

In addition to the problem of water pollution, there is a risk that organisms are taken into the desalination plant with the seawater. To prevent fish and other species being sucked into the plant, filters are placed on inflow tubes, but smaller organisms, including planktonic larval forms, will still be drawn in. To reduce loss of plankton, only deeper water should be used. Harvesting water during spawning times can also remove eggs and larvae from the water column, reducing the populations of some species.

Fishing practices

In Chapter 8, you will have considered the effects of fishing practices on the stocks of fish. Fishing practices can also lead to direct damage to the marine environment. Two examples of factors that can have major negative effects on the marine environment are dredging and blast fishing.

Dredging

Dredging is the process of physically gathering up sediment from the bottom of shallow areas of sea. It is

> ### KEY WORD
>
> **dredging:** the removal of material from ocean and river beds

often used to keep shipping routes open but is also used when building the foundations for new structures or to harvest sand or minerals. There are several methods of dredging: suction dredging, mechanical dredging and water-injected dredging.

- **Suction dredging:** Specialised dredging ships carry giant suction tubes that operate like very strong vacuum cleaners (Figure 9.11). As the ships move through the water, they suck up the sediment from the seabed through tubes and deposit the sediment into large metal tanks on the ship or neighbouring barges, to be deposited later in other areas. Some suction dredgers use cutting equipment that breaks up the rocky seabed and dislodges underwater obstacles.

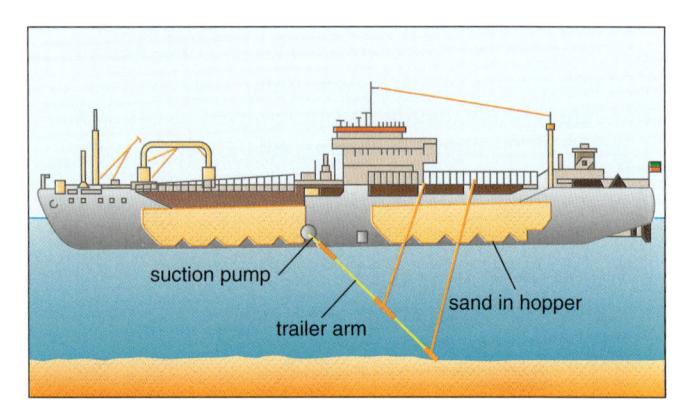

Figure 9.11: A typical suction dredger: sediment is taken from the seabed and stored in the hull of the ship.

- **Mechanical dredging:** Bucket dredgers carry a series of buckets on a rotating belt that scrape the seabed. They can be carried on ships and in some cases are strong enough to cut through coral. Clamshell dredgers use a large mechanical grab that can be lowered into the water in order to remove sediment.
- **Water-injection dredging:** Ships have large hosepipe-like structures that force water along the seabed. This dislodges the sediment, scattering it out of shipping lanes.

All forms of dredging can have negative impacts. The physical nature of the process has the potential to damage the seabed and sessile organisms and generate sediment.

Physical damage to benthic communities

All forms of dredging involve removal of the seabed. This obviously has the potential to destroy coral reefs and dislodge sessile organisms such as oysters and mussels. Breeding grounds for fish can be affected, and estuarine environments may become uninhabitable for species that prefer sandy seabeds with high levels of sediment. The loss of many filter-feeding organisms can have an effect on food webs, because they are a food source for other organisms. If the population of filter feeders decreases, organic waste that is washed down rivers is not removed and decomposes, resulting in loss of oxygen. It can take several years for communities to recover from dredging, particularly when the rocky seabed has been extensively altered.

Sediment release

Stirring up the sediment from the seabed causes an increase in water turbidity. Light penetration is reduced, lowering the productivity of producers so that less energy is available to the food web. Coral can become covered in sediment, reducing the amount of light available for zooxanthellae. Sediment can cover organisms that live over the seabed, getting caught in their delicate gill structures and eventually causing suffocation. Sessile organisms can become totally smothered so that they are unable to obtain sufficient oxygen or food. The sediment can also interfere with the spawning of fish and shellfish by killing eggs and sperm: in many countries dredging is prohibited during spawning seasons. In some cases, however, there have been reports that limited dredging has caused an increase in populations of shellfish such as oysters, mussels and even edible crabs, suggesting these organisms may benefit from some agitation of the water.

The effect of dredging on oxygen levels in the water is unpredictable. If sediment is released into the water, it has the potential to increase the rate of bacterial decomposition and thus reduce oxygen levels in the water. The release of nitrates and phosphates can cause eutrophication, which will also reduce oxygen levels. In some cases, however, the removal of large amounts of organic waste that has accumulated from sewage and rivers actually reduces the rate of decay so increases the oxygen levels.

Release of chemicals from sediments

Sediment from harbours and estuaries often contains toxins such as heavy metals ions, oil, tributyltin (TBT), PCBs and pesticides from shipping and coastal activities. These chemicals are embedded in the sediment and are dislodged when dredging is carried out. Some substances are directly toxic to marine organisms and also accumulate through food chains, harming top predators. If sediment is dumped into other areas of the sea, chemicals can seep out in those areas. Careful planning is needed before dumping sediment, to minimise damage to other communities. Table 9.7 summarises the effects of dredging on marine ecosystems.

Factor affected by dredging	Effects of dredging
water quality	increase in sediment reducing light penetration
	increase in heavy metals and toxins
	possible change in oxygen concentrations
habitat	physical damage to seabed from scraping
	destruction of reefs
	destruction of shellfish breeding grounds
	sediment covers areas of seabed
organisms	reduction in biodiversity
	loss of coral and sessile reef organisms
	loss of sessile shellfish beds, such as oyster, due to physical damage or smothering with sediment
	possible loss of species due to lack of oxygen
	possible increase in algal blooms due to release of mineral ions
food webs	food webs disrupted by loss of lower trophic levels such as coral and molluscs
	loss of higher predators due to loss of lower levels
	possible increase in algal blooms

Table 9.7: Effects of dredging on marine ecosystems.

Blast fishing

Blast fishing is one of the most damaging methods of fishing. Dynamite or other, often home-made, explosives are thrown into the water and ignited. The shock wave produced stuns or kills fish which are then collected. It is a highly indiscriminate method of catching fish and will kill any creatures in the area. Blast fishing poses one of the greatest threats to coral reefs, the effects of which are shown in Figure 9.12. It can take more than 15 years for a reef to recover from a single blast, and multiple blasting can reduce them to rubble from which they will never recover. Coral reefs are areas of high biodiversity and provide habitats for many species – their destruction leads to a loss of many species and affects food webs. Not only is blast fishing harmful to marine organisms and coral, it often results in the accidental death or injury of fishers. By destroying the habitats and complex food webs around coral reefs it could also threaten fish catches in the future. It is a highly inefficient method, and it is estimated that only one in ten of the fish stunned float to the surface, the rest sink to the bottom to decay.

> **KEY WORD**
>
> **blast fishing:** the use of explosives to catch fish

Figure 9.12: Area of coral reef near Sabah destroyed by blast fishing.

Despite global attempts to ban the practice, blast fishing still occurs in parts of the world. It is difficult to patrol and requires enforcement along with education programmes for fishers. In Tanzania, where blast fishing was used extensively, a joint operation between government agencies and people who live in fishing villages has successfully led to a massive reduction in this practice. Funding was provided to increase the number of patrol vessels and encourage the villagers to monitor fishing practices. People who were caught blast fishing were prosecuted and given harsh fines. Restricting the sales of explosives and fertilisers (that can be used to make explosives) has also been a successful way of reducing blast fishing. In other areas of the world, such as Indonesia and the Philippines, governments are now increasing patrols and working hard to educate fishers about the dangers. Surveillance methods such as the use of military technology to detect underwater explosions are now used throughout South East Asia. The most successful methods combine the use of patrols and monitoring with the involvement of local communities and education. Table 9.8 summarises the effects of blast fishing on marine ecosystems.

Factor affected by blast fishing	Effects of blast fishing
water quality	increase in turbidity due to sediment release
	release of toxic chemicals from explosives
habitat	destroys coral reefs which act as a habitat for many species
	destroys seabed
organisms	kills large areas of corals and other sessile organisms
	kills fish and other species indiscriminately
	very harmful for all marine organisms in the area causing extensive loss of biodiversity
food webs	very damaging to food webs due to loss of corals, nursery grounds, prey and predator species

Table 9.8: Effects of blast fishing on marine ecosystems.

9 Human impacts on marine ecosystems

The bioaccumulation and biomagnification of toxins

Chapter 3 discusses how energy passes through food chains. Similarly, toxins eaten at low trophic levels in a food chain are often passed from one organism to another, eventually ending up in top predators. Toxic heavy metals are released into the oceans from a range of human activities. Mercury is released from the combustion of fossil fuels. Tin is released in the form of a compound called tributyltin oxide (TBT) from the use of antifouling paints.

When organisms ingest toxins that are not excreted from their bodies, the toxins accumulate as they eat more of them; this process is called bioaccumulation. As the toxins pass along the food chain, the concentration found in the bodies of the organisms tends to increase with each trophic level: this process is known as **biomagnification**. Toxins that do not break down or are not flushed out of an organism's body tend to undergo biomagnification along food chains and can reach dangerously high levels in top predators.

Figure 9.13 shows a simple marine food chain. If each phytoplankton picks up $0.001\,\mu g$ of a toxin and each zooplankton consumes 100 phytoplankton, then the zooplankton gain 100 doses of $0.001\,\mu g$ of toxin ($0.1\,\mu g$ of toxin) each. Each anchovy consumes 100 zooplankton, gaining $10\,\mu g$ ($100 \times 0.1\,\mu g$) of toxin. Each herring eats 100 anchovies, gaining 1 mg of toxin, and the tuna eats 100 herring, gaining a massive 100 mg of toxin.

The organisms most affected by toxins tend to be top predators, and this is a problem not just for the marine organisms. Many of the species harvested for human consumption, such as tuna and shark, can contain high concentrations of toxins such as mercury.

Mercury accumulation

During the 1950s, animals in the seaside town of Minamata on Kyushu Island in Japan began to exhibit

> **KEY WORD**
>
> **biomagnification:** the increasing concentration of a substance, such as a toxic chemical, in the tissues of organisms at successively higher levels in a food chain

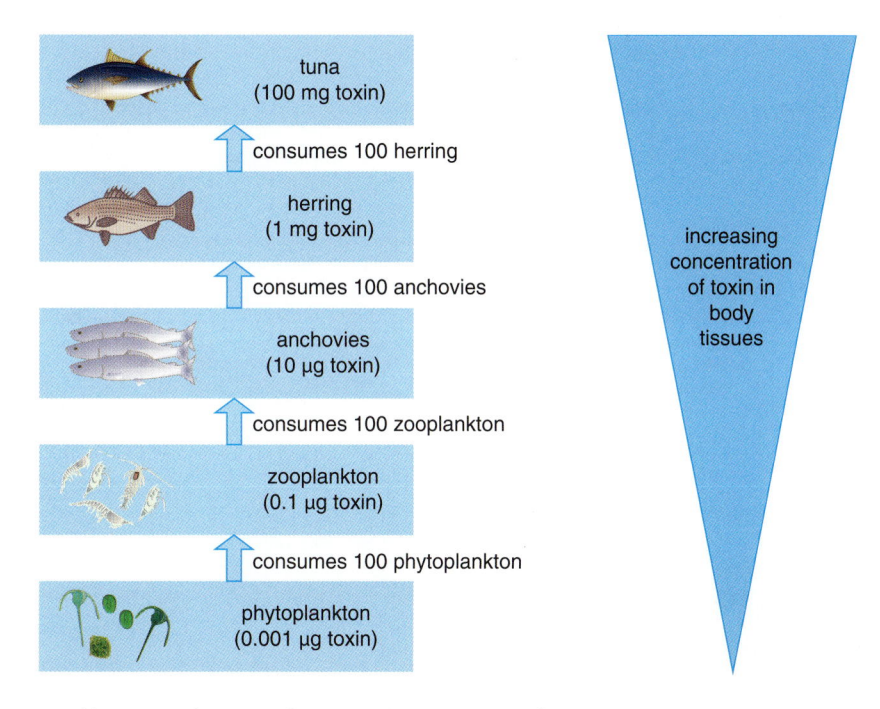

Figure 9.13: The process of biomagnification of a toxin along a marine food chain.

a series of strange behaviours. Cats developed nervous tremors, convulsions and screamed loudly, and birds fell out of the sky or tress without warning. Doctors were treating humans with tremors, seizures and other neurological symptoms. An enquiry was launched, and it was found that an industrial company called Chisso Corporation had been discharging heavy metal waste including mercury into the sea. The mercury had formed methylmercury, a highly toxic form of mercury, which had accumulated in the marine food chain. Humans and animals had consumed marine food that contained the methylmercury.

Methylmercury is present at very low concentrations in seawater but is absorbed by algae at the start of food chains. It is not excreted, but remains in the bodies of organisms, especially the liver, fatty tissues and muscles, and is passed along the food chain, increasing in concentration at each trophic level (Figure 9.14). Many fish and shellfish contain methylmercury in their bodies, and species that are long-lived and top predators – such as tuna, shark, swordfish and marlin – tend to have the highest concentrations. Methylmercury is a neurotoxin and caused the symptoms seen in the animals and humans of Minamata Bay.

The US Food and Drug Administration (FDA) advises that the risk of mercury poisoning from eating fish and shellfish is not a health concern for most people. However, certain seafood can contain levels of mercury that can harm unborn babies or young children, because of their small body sizes.

The FDA advice is that young children, pregnant women and women of child-bearing age can safely eat two or three portions of fish or shellfish a week. Good choices of fish and shellfish include salmon, shrimp, pollock, tuna, tilapia, catfish and cod. Fish that are best avoided are tilefish (from the Gulf of Mexico), shark, swordfish and king mackerel. The FDA also advises that white tuna should only be eaten once a week.

Mercury gets into the oceans from three main sources:

- 30% from human industries, mainly coal and oil burning and gold mining
- 60% from flooded land and forest fires, often as a result of human activities
- 10% from natural sources, such as volcanic activity and leaching from rocks.

In an effort to reduce emissions of mercury into the marine environment, countries such as Japan and the USA began to regulate industries in the 1970s. To reduce the global emissions requires international collaboration, and on 19 January 2013, 140 countries signed a treaty called The Minamata Convention on Mercury. This treaty represents a global commitment

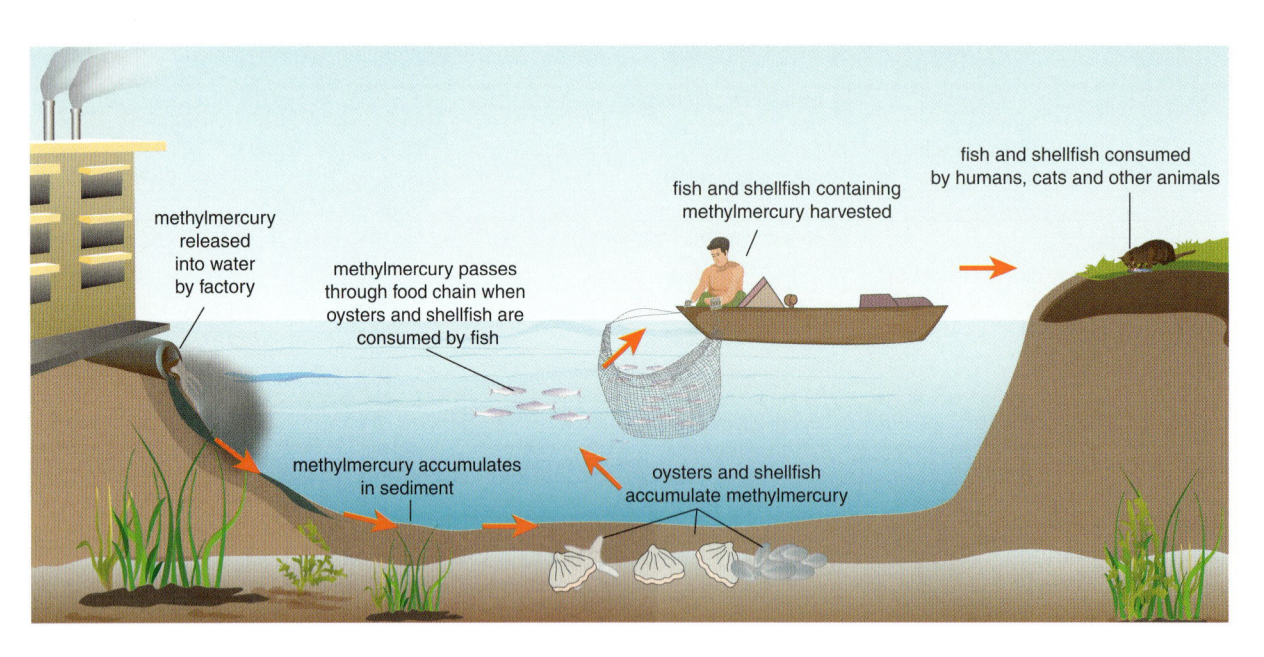

Figure 9.14: The transfer of methylmercury to humans and shellfish.

to protecting human health and the environment from mercury. It took three years of meetings and negotiations before the convention was signed but provides hope for the future.

Tributyltin (TBT)

When any physical structure is placed into the sea for any length of time, organisms attach to it and begin to create a community. This attachment is called biofouling. A diverse range of organisms – such as barnacles, molluscs, tube worms, seaweeds, sponges and many others – biofoul ships (Figure 9.15). This causes increased drag in the water for ships, leading to increased fuel use, which is estimated to cost the global shipping industry up to US$1 billion each year. The increased fuel use leads to increased output of carbon dioxide and sulfur dioxide, potentially contributing to global warming and acid rain.

Figure 9.15: Biofouling of a ship's hull with a range of marine organisms.

TBT is an anti-fouling chemical that was developed in the 1950s. It was added to paint used on the hulls of ships and other structures. It is highly effective but leaks out of the paint into the water. Once in the water, it attaches to sediments and sinks to the seabed, where it can remain for up to 30 years.

TBT is highly toxic for many species of marine organisms, often at very low concentrations. Besides the biofouling species it is targeted at, it has far reaching effects on other organisms as a result of bioaccumulation. It enters food chains at lower trophic levels, through organisms such as barnacles and molluscs, and then passes upwards. TBT concentrations increase in organisms as it moves through the food chain, eventually poisoning top predators such as tuna, dolphins and sea otters. Specific effects of TBT include:

- altered invertebrate development, such as deformities in oysters and the masculinisation of dog whelks, which results in fewer fertile females so reducing the population

- reduced immune response; for example, high concentrations of TBT have been recorded in the livers of top predators such as tuna, sea otters and dolphins, which has reportedly led to their deaths from infection because of a weakened immune response.

Because of its harmful effects on the environment, there have been efforts to ban the use of TBT. The International Convention on the Control of Harmful Anti-fouling Systems is an International Maritime Organisation (IMO) treaty that bans the use of TBT by all nations that sign up to it. By 2015, 71 nations, representing more than 85% of global shipping, had signed the treaty, but there are still reports of the illegal use of TBT in many areas and monitoring the ban is not easy.

Plastics and microplastics

One of the biggest threat faced by the marine environment is due to plastics. Every year, more than 300 million tonnes of plastic are produced, and it is estimated that over 10 million tonnes of this finds its way into the oceans. More than 80% of refuse in the oceans is plastic. So, where does the plastic come from? It is blown from rubbish tips, washed into the seas during storms, deliberately dumped from industrial factories, thrown from ships or illegally discarded directly into the water. It poses a range of problems for marine organisms. Species can become entangled in it, drowning or starving to death, or being severely injured. It is frequently ingested causing death due to internal blockages or poisoning due to the toxins it contains. We have now found that in the oceans, plastic breaks down into **microplastics** that enter food chains and may now even be poisoning us. Traces of microplastics are now being found in our food and even bottled water.

Microplastics

Microplastics are small pieces of plastic that are found in ocean water. They are defined as being less than 5 mm in length and are classified as either **primary microplastics** or **secondary microplastics**.

> **KEY WORDS**
>
> **microplastics:** plastic particles that are less than 5 mm in diameter
>
> **primary microplastics:** microplastics, such as beads found in cosmetics, that are released directly into water
>
> **secondary microplastics:** microplastics produced from the breakdown of larger pieces of plastic

Figure 9.16: Plastic nurdles found on a beach.

Primary microplastics

Primary microplastics are tiny pieces of plastic that are already less than 5 mm in size when released into the ocean. They are usually from clothing or are components in cosmetics such as certain types of skin lotion.

Primary microplastics are released directly into the sea. They are often placed into cosmetics and cleaning liquids as abrasives and so they enter the water via drains. Nurdles are tiny microbeads of plastic that are used as the building blocks with which to make plastic objects in industry. These nurdles (Figure 9.16) are the form in which plastics are transported around the world before being processed and so many of them accidentally become released into rivers and seas through waste pipes or spillage.

Secondary microplastics

Secondary microplastics are tiny pieces of plastics that have been produced from the breakdown of larger pieces of discarded plastic, such as plastic bags or drinks bottles.

Secondary microparticles are produced by the breakdown of larger pieces of plastic. Several factors affect the speed at which plastic breaks down into microparticles. These factors include ultraviolet light (UV), wave action, wind, oxygen concentration and temperature. UV light from the Sun affects the chemicals in the plastic so that the plastic breaks up more easily into small pieces. The effect of light on plastic is known as photo-degradation. Vigorous wave action and higher wind speed both increase the rate of physical weathering. The evidence for the effects of temperature and oxygen is not as well researched but it is thought that both warmer temperatures and higher oxygen concentrations increase the rate of breakdown (Figure 9.17). Plastics will generally breakdown faster in the surface waters of tropical oceans that are well illuminated, stormy and warm. Plastics that sink to colder, anoxic, lower depths tend to breakdown much more slowly.

The impacts of plastics on the marine environment

As already discussed in this chapter, plastic refuse can have many negative impacts on the marine environment. Some of these impacts are discussed below.

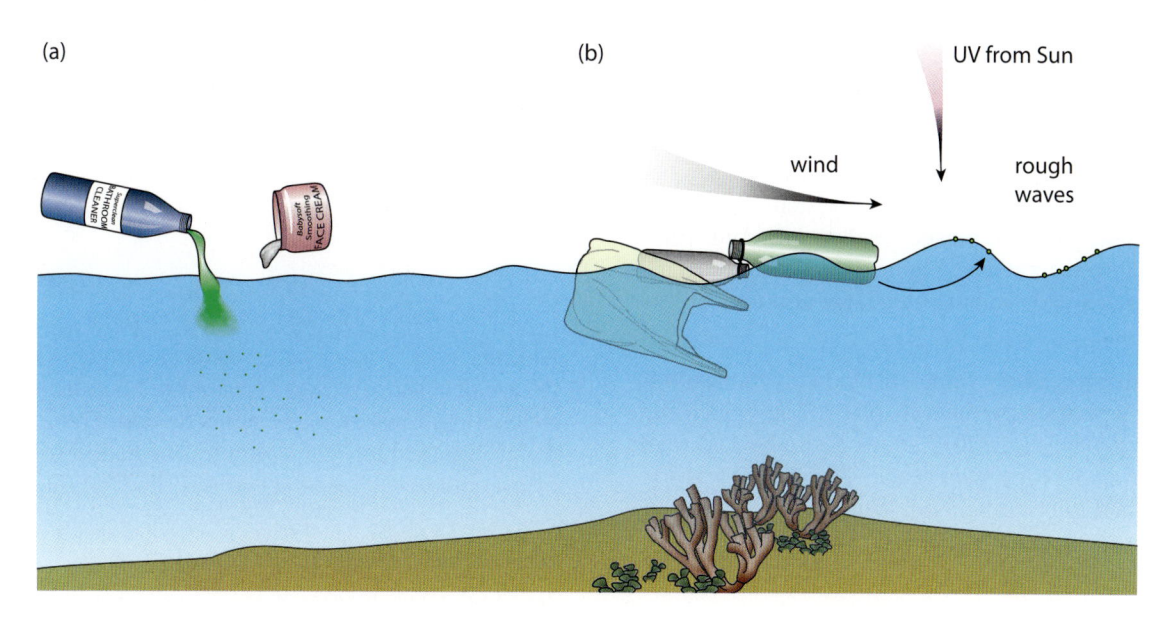

Figure 9.17: Diagram summarising the release of (a) primary and (b) secondary microplastics.

Uptake and transfer of microplastics and food chains

We have already defined microplastics as pieces of plastic that are less than 5 mm in length. These microplastics can be broken down into even smaller pieces, called nanoplastics. These particles float in the surface waters of the ocean and can be taken in by zooplankton when they feed, or can become lodged in their gills. Some of the plastic passes through the plankton and is released in faeces, but some accumulates inside their bodies. The plastic is then passed along food chains and will undergo bioaccumulation so that top predators end up with large amounts of plastic inside their bodies. Because we harvest some fish species that are at the top of food chains, there is a major risk that microplastics can reach us. Nanoplastics can pass across the blood–brain barrier, through the gut wall and across the placenta (possibly affecting unborn children). In 2018, a study found that microplastic was detected in the faeces of eight humans. Although it is not clear where the plastic came from, and the sample size was very small, it does show that there is a potential risk to us. It may be that our excess dumping of plastic into the marine environment is not only poisoning the oceans but also us.

The absorption of toxic compounds and risk to organisms including humans

There are many potentially toxic compounds present in seawater, many of which have been released by human activity. Many of these toxic compounds are hydrophobic, nonpolar molecules and so stick to plastic microparticles. This causes plastic microparticles to 'soak up' toxins and concentrate them. When marine organisms consume the plastics, they also consume the toxic compounds that are bound to them. Some of these toxic compounds include:

- polychlorinated biphenyls (PCBs) – these can affect reproductive ability, hormones and the immune system of organisms
- bisphenol A (BPA) – this can affect thyroid activity and can lower sperm production.

The plastic accumulates a mixture of toxins that can bioaccumulate along food chains and reach humans. Many of the compounds that have been detected are known to have negative health effects.

Ingestion of plastics by marine organisms

Marine organisms can also be damaged if they consume larger pieces of plastic refuse. Plastic can cause physical blockages in the gut and respiratory systems. Seabirds often mistake pieces of plastic for their prey and will also feed it to their chicks. Figure 9.9 shows the remains of an albatross that had ingested large amounts of plastic refuse.

Turtles are particularly vulnerable to being damaged by consuming plastics, particularly plastic bags which they mistake for jellyfish. In 2017, a sick goose-beaked whale was found on a Norwegian beach. The animal was so ill that it had to be euthanised. When scientists carried out a post mortem, 30 plastic bags were found to be blocking its gut.

Entanglement of marine organisms

Large pieces of plastic refuse can physically damage marine organisms. Fish, turtles, birds and marine mammals can become trapped in nylon ropes and nets (often called **ghost nets**) that have been discarded from fishing vessels (Figure 9.18). If the organisms are unable to move, they can suffocate, drown or starve to death. Even if they escape, they are often severely injured and so become easy prey for predators or die from infections. It is thought that up to half a million marine mammals die every year due to ghost nets.

> **KEY WORD**
>
> **ghost nets:** fishing equipment that has been lost from boats but still traps and kills organisms

Figure 9.18: Turtle entangled in nylon netting.

Limiting the release of plastics

The world has now woken up to the problem of marine plastic. There are several steps that we can take to try to prevent further damage and reduce the damage we have already done. Steps can be taken at different levels of society:

Intergovernmental agreements

Nations meet to make agreements on reducing the release of plastic. Because oceans are bounded by many different nations, everyone needs to help. The effects of plastic dumped into the ocean by one nation will be felt by everyone.

National government policies

National governments can introduce measures such as banning the use of plastic bags, introducing bag and plastic bottle taxes, encouraging more use of biodegradable plastic, providing better refuse collection services and recycling facilities, placing more bins around coastal areas and enforcing laws to prevent the discarding of plastics. Tax incentives can be introduced for companies who reduce plastic packaging and single-use plastic cups and bags.

Individual consumers and local groups

We, as consumers, can all make a difference. Reducing our use of plastic by measures such as not using disposable drinks cups, plastic straws, excessive packaging, reusing shopping bags and ensuring that we do not allow litter to reach the sea. Local conservation groups often meet to collect litter from beaches and raise awareness by holding meetings and publicity events. If one million people stopped using one plastic drinking straw per week, that would be 52 million fewer plastic straws discarded each year.

MATHS SKILLS 9.1

STATISTICAL TESTS – CHI (χ^2) SQUARED

Statistical tests are a tool to help us understand how different or similar groups of data are or can help us to see significant patterns. We can look at data and see differences, but it is hard to say for sure whether there is a real difference. The chi-squared test is a simple test that can determine if there are statistically significant differences between data.

Worked examples

The total catch from two fishing grounds is shown in Table 9.9.

Fishing ground A has a higher catch, but we need to use the chi-squared test to see if the difference between the catches from the two areas is significant.

Fishing ground	Total catch of cod/tonnes
A	376
B	340

Table 9.9: Catch of cod from two different fishing grounds.

Step 1: We first formulate a null hypothesis (H_0). A null hypothesis always states that there is no expected difference between the categories. So, in this case:

'There is no difference between the catch in fishing ground A and fishing ground B.'

Step 2: We now set up a chi-squared table:

The Observed column (O) contains the raw data.

The Expected column (E) contains the data that would be expected if the null hypothesis was true. We can calculate this by effectively sharing out the total amount of fish caught equally between the two fishing grounds:

$$\frac{(376 + 340)}{2} = 358$$

We then calculate (O − E) for each fishing ground and enter the answer in the table.

We then square this value to calculate $(O − E)^2$ and enter this in the appropriate column.

Next, we divide each of these values by the appropriate value of O and enter this in the appropriate column.

Step 3: We can now calculate the chi-squared value using the formula:

$$\chi^2 = \sum \frac{(O - E)^2}{E}$$

Where

χ^2 is the chi-squared value

O is the observed values

E is the expected values

The Σ symbol is a Greek capital S and stands for 'sum of.' This means that we need to add together all the $\frac{(O - E)^2}{E}$ values in the table. So, for out example here:

$$\chi^2 = 0.905 + 0.905 = 1.810$$

Step 4: Now that we have our value for chi-squared, we can use a chi-squared table (Table 9.11) to

Fishing ground	Observed (O)	Expected (E)	(O − E)	$(O - E)^2$	$\frac{(O - E)^2}{E}$
A	376	358	376 − 358 = 18	324	(324 ÷ 358) = 0.905
B	340	358	340 − 358 = −18	324	(324 ÷ 358) = 0.905
					$\Sigma \frac{(O - E)}{E} = 1.810$

Table 9.10: Chi-squared calculation table.

> **CONTINUED**

determine if there is a significant difference between the two fishing grounds.

First, calculate the number of degrees of freedom using the formula:

degrees of freedom = number of categories − 1

So, for our example, there are 2 − 1 = 1 degree of freedom.

We now look along the row for the correct number of degrees of freedom.

The critical value for whether we reject or accept our null hypothesis is at the P<0.05 column.

If our calculated value of chi-squared is greater than the critical value for P<0.05, we reject our null hypothesis and state that there is a significant difference between the fish catches. This means there is a probability of less than 0.05 (or 5%) that the difference between the two areas is due to chance.

If our calculated value of chi-squared is less than the critical value for P<0.05, we accept our null hypothesis and state that there is no significant difference between the fish catches. There is a probability of greater than 0.05 (or 5%) that the difference between the two areas is due to chance.

For our example, the critical value is 3.841 and our calculated value of chi-squared is 1.81. This is not greater than the critical value, so we do not reject the null hypothesis – there is no significant difference between the two catches.

Table 9.11 also shows that there is a higher level of significance at P<0.01. If the calculated value of chi-squared is greater than this (6.635), there is probability of less than 0.01 (or 1%) that the difference is due to chance.

Questions

1 Use Table 9.11 to decide whether the following calculated values of chi-squared suggest that there is a significant difference.

   a   7.9 with four degrees of freedom
   b   5.8 with two degrees of freedom
   c   10.7 with six degrees of freedom.

Degrees of freedom	Chi-squared (χ^2) distribution							
	Area to the right of critical value							
	0.99	0.975	0.95	0.90	0.10	0.05	0.025	0.01
1	—	0.001	0.004	0.016	2.706	3.841	5.024	6.635
2	0.020	0.051	0.103	0.211	4.605	5.991	7.378	9.210
3	0.115	0.216	0.352	0.584	6.251	7.815	9.348	11.345
4	0.297	0.484	0.711	1.064	7.779	9.488	11.143	13.277
5	0.554	0.831	1.145	1.610	9.236	11.071	12.833	15.086
6	0.872	1.237	1.635	2.204	10.645	12.592	14.449	16.812
7	1.239	1.690	2.167	2.833	12.017	14.067	16.013	18.475
8	1.646	2.180	2.733	3.490	13.362	15.507	17.535	20.090
9	2.088	2.700	3.325	4.168	14.684	16.919	19.023	21.666
10	2.558	3.247	3.940	4.865	15.987	18.307	20.483	23.209

Table 9.11: Chi-squared critical values table.

CONTINUED

2 Table 9.12 gives the number of dog whelks found on rocky shores facing north, south, east and west. Carry out a chi-squared test to determine if there is a significant difference in the number of dog whelks on the different shores.

Aspect of rocky shore	Number of dog whelks
north	235
south	205
east	165
west	175

Table 9.12: Numbers of dog whelks found on different rocky shores.

a Formulate a null hypothesis.
b Draw a chi-squared table and calculate the value of chi-squared.
c Calculate the number of degrees of freedom.
d Use your value of chi-squared and the critical values table to determine whether there is a significant difference between the different shore.

Test yourself

1 Explain **three** ways in which animals may be harmed directly by oil spills.

2 Use the following words to complete the sentences.

   bioremediation, bacteria, dispersants, droplets, respiration, temperature

   One method for protecting the coast from oil spills is to spray on _____.
   This causes the oil to break up into smaller _____ and sink to the seabed.
   Once it has sunk, _____ begin to break down the oil.
   The _____ at the seabed is low so that the rate of bacterial _____ is slow.
   This means it can take many years for the oil to be removed by this process of _____.

3 List human activities that can cause:
   a reduced oxygen content of water
   b accumulation of toxins through food chains
   c increased turbidity in the water.

4 Suggest **two** measures that could be taken to reduce the effects of pollution from:
   a agriculture
   b sewage
   c refuse.

5 Explain why it is recommended that pregnant women do not eat top predator fish such as swordfish.

6 Outline why TBT has been used on ships and explain why there are campaigns for it to be banned.

7 Outline the differences between primary and secondary microplastics.

8 Explain why the consumption of microplastics by plankton is a risk to humans.

9.2 Global warming and its impact

One of the indirect consequences of the oil industry is the production of large volumes of carbon dioxide gas as a result of burning fossil fuel. Increased atmospheric carbon dioxide may be leading to an **enhanced greenhouse effect** and increase in global temperature, which could pose many problems for our oceans.

KEY WORD

enhanced greenhouse effect: an elevated and imbalanced greenhouse effect caused by human activity

Greenhouse effect

The **greenhouse effect** is a natural phenomenon and is not wholly the result of human influence. Short wavelength solar radiation penetrates through the Earth's atmosphere and warms the planet when it hits the surface. Some of this radiation is reflected as longer wavelength infrared light. Some of this longer wavelength infrared light passes back through the atmosphere into space, but some of it is reflected back to Earth by certain greenhouse gases (Figure 9.19). The **greenhouse gases** in the Earth's atmosphere include carbon dioxide, methane, water vapour, chlorofluorocarbons (CFCs) and nitrous oxide.

> **KEY WORDS**
>
> **greenhouse effect:** the heating of the atmosphere due to the presence of carbon dioxide and other gases; these gases prevent infrared radiation being re-emitted into space
>
> **greenhouse gases:** gases such as carbon dioxide and methane that prevent infrared radiation being released into space

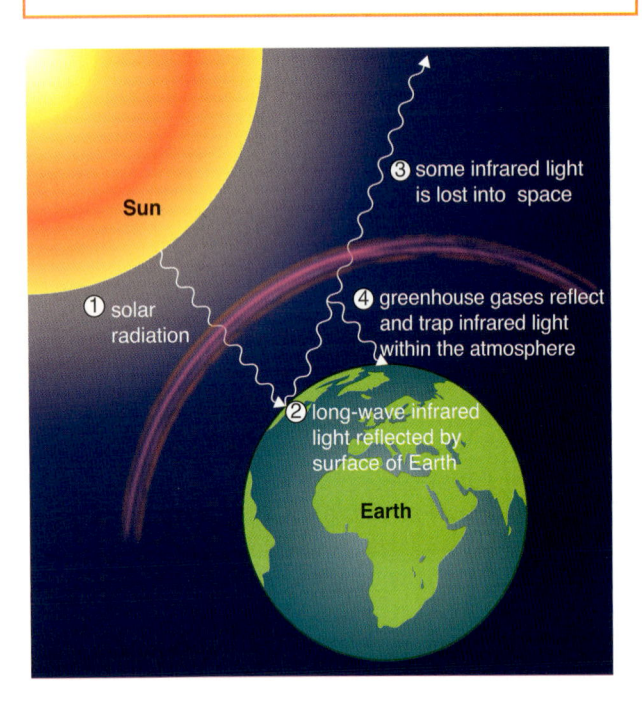

Figure 9.19: The role of atmospheric gases in the greenhouse effect.

This natural greenhouse effect maintains the Earth's ambient temperature within the range required for life.

All the greenhouse gases, apart from water vapour, are generated by both natural and human activities. During the twentieth and twenty-first centuries, the increasing global population and increased burning of fossil fuels has caused an increase in the production of these gases. This has led to an imbalance in the carbon cycle, with too much carbon dioxide being released into the atmosphere and too little removed. It is believed that if the Earth's atmosphere contains more greenhouse gases, the amount of infrared light trapped within the atmosphere will increase, resulting in an enhanced greenhouse effect and global warming.

Evidence for global warming

It is difficult to prove that human activities that produce greenhouse gases lead directly to global warming. There is, however, a lot of evidence to indicate that the amount of greenhouse gases in the atmosphere has increased and that the average global temperature has also increased.

Increasing global temperatures

Four main institutions have monitored average global temperatures, the NASA Goddard Institute for Space Studies (GISS), the UK Meteorological Office, the NOAA National Climatic Data Center and the Japanese Meteorological Agency. These institutions set a baseline average temperature and then determine how far the average temperature for a particular year deviates from the baseline. This value is called a temperature anomaly. The baseline used is slightly different for each agency. Figure 9.20 shows the temperature anomalies determined by each agency since 1880. It is clear that, despite small variations, the overall trend indicated by all of them is upwards.

Increasing levels of atmospheric carbon dioxide

Since 1958, the atmospheric concentration of carbon dioxide has been monitored by observatories on the Mauna Loa volcano in Hawaii. Figure 9.21 shows the change in atmospheric carbon dioxide since then. It is clear that there is an overall upwards trend. Each year shows a seasonal increase and decrease in carbon dioxide levels as a result of changes in the rate of photosynthesis through the year.

9 Human impacts on marine ecosystems

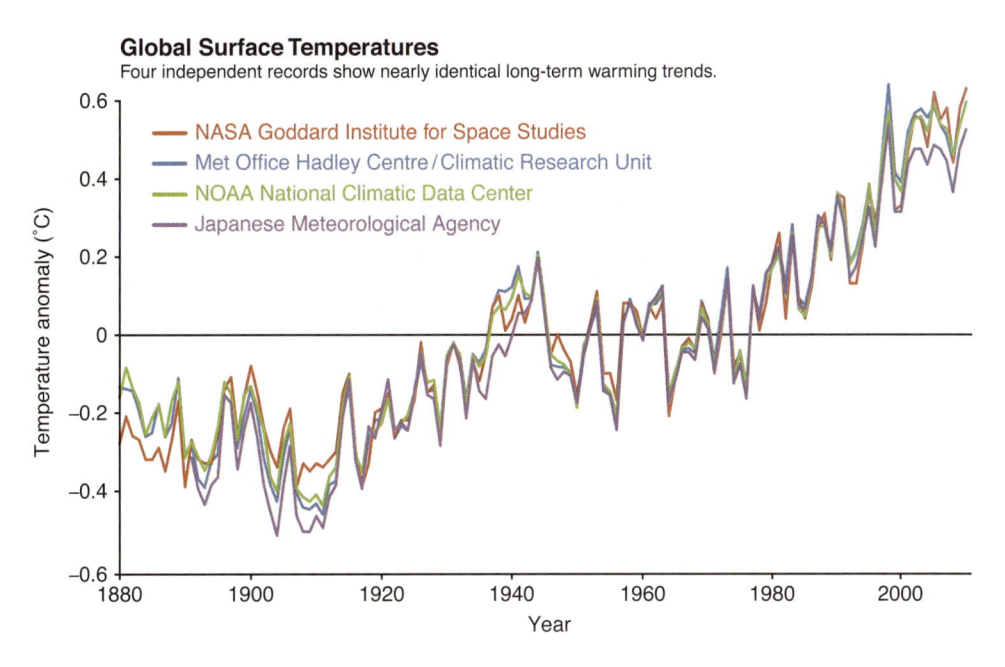

Figure 9.20: Change in global temperature between 1880 and 2000.

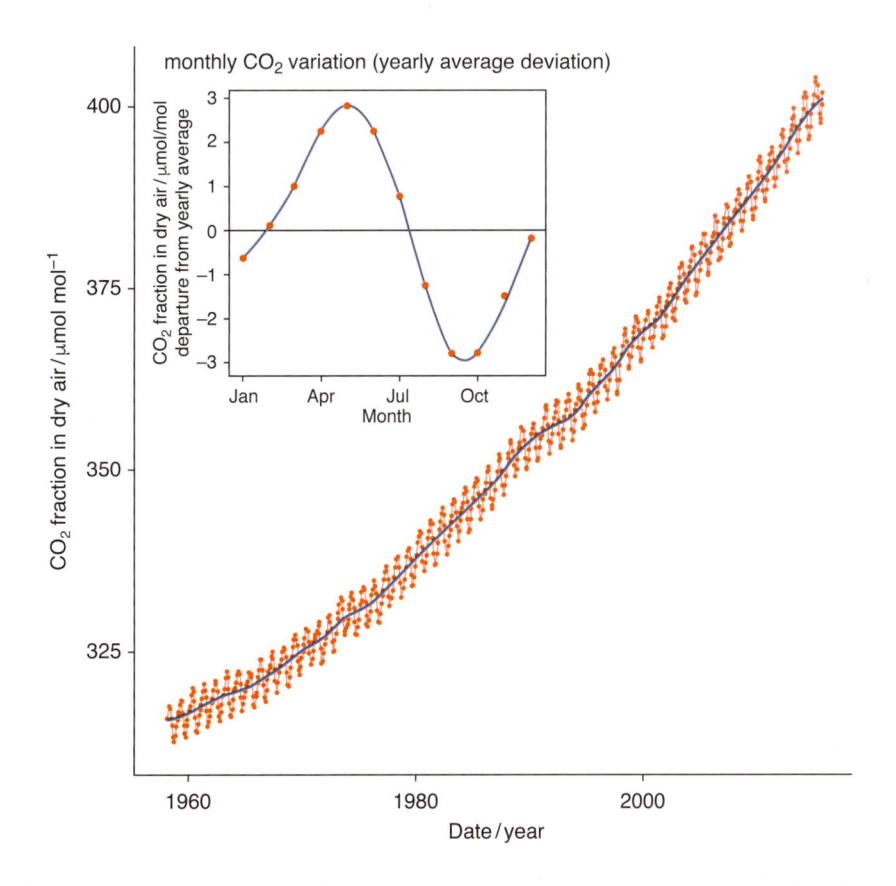

Figure 9.21: Change in atmospheric carbon dioxide levels from 1958 measured on Mauna Loa, Hawaii.

It is possible to analyse atmospheric carbon dioxide concentrations from much earlier time periods by analysing ice cores. Ice cores are cylinders of ice drilled out of an ice sheet or glacier, which can be up to 3 km deep. The oldest ice core records from Antarctica extend back for eight hundred thousand years. Within the frozen ice core are small bubbles of air that were trapped when the ice froze. These bubbles can give us a direct measure of the gas composition at different periods of time. It is also possible to determine the temperature at the time of deposition by analysing other gases. Figure 9.22 shows that carbon dioxide and methane concentrations remained stable over much of the past one thousand years, but increased rapidly during the twentieth century.

If you look at older ice core data, the results can seem confusing. Figure 9.23 shows that there have been periods of high and low carbon dioxide concentrations. Temperatures also show fluctuations through colder and warmer periods. What is clear, however, is that carbon dioxide and temperature fluctuate together and show a positive correlation.

Some people think that the fluctuations over time show that the current global warming is simply part of a natural cycle of heating up and cooling down and that it is nothing to do with human activity. What we must not forget, however, is that the current global increases in carbon dioxide, methane and temperature are all linked with a period of industrialisation, and that the steepness of the increases now seen is almost without precedent.

Melting of ice and sea-level rises

One of the possible effects of global warming is the melting of ice, both at sea and on land. The Arctic sea ice stretches to its minimum extent each September, after the warm summer. Satellite images show that the minimum extent of the ice has been getting less each year.

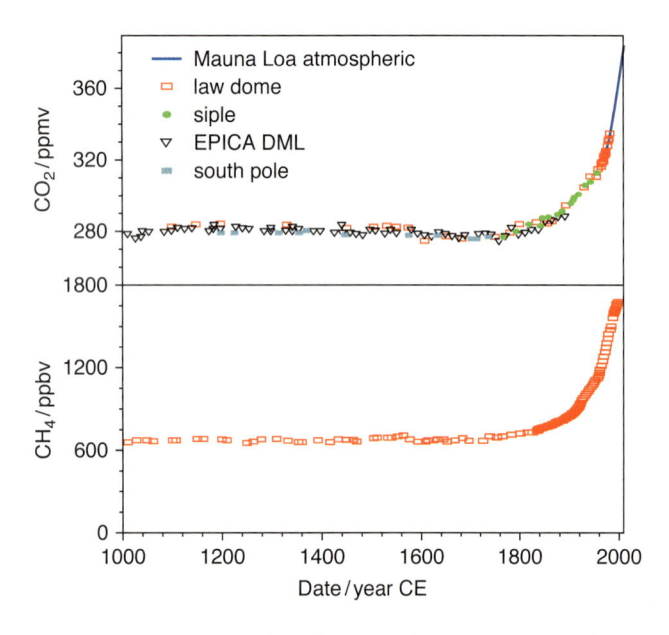

Figure 9.22: Ice core data showing changes in atmospheric carbon dioxide and methane between 1000 and 2000 CE.

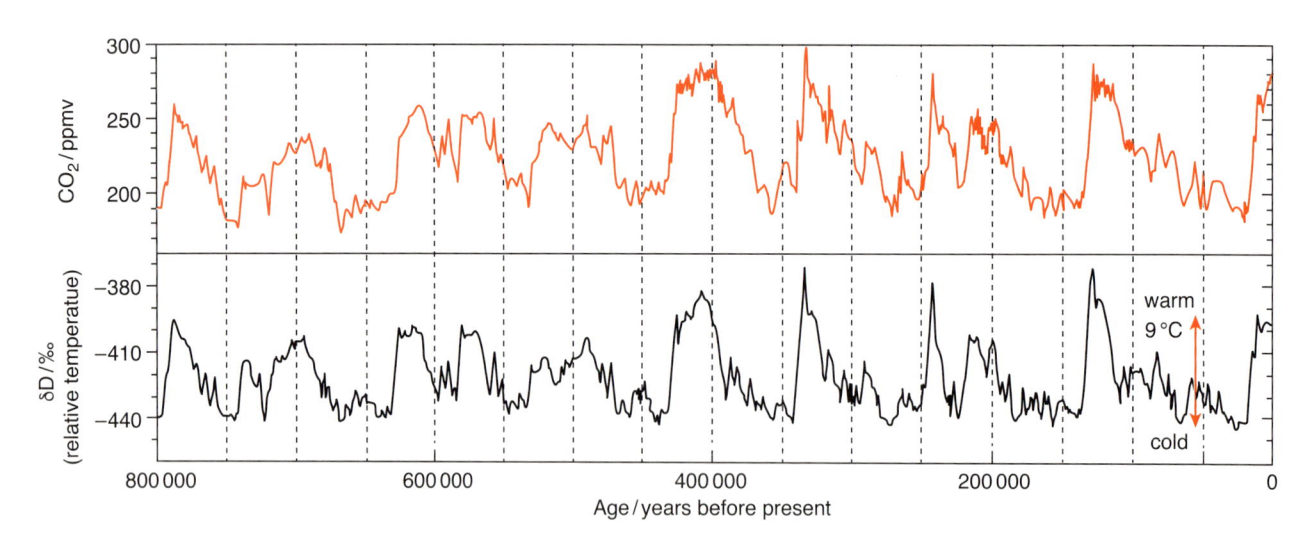

Figure 9.23: Ice core data showing fluctuations in carbon dioxide and temperature over 800 000 years.

9 Human impacts on marine ecosystems

Figure 9.24 shows that the mass of land ice in the Antarctic ice sheet has lost about 134 billion tonnes of ice per year since 2002, while the Greenland ice sheet has lost an estimated 287 billion tonnes per year. The graphs show that the mass of ice is decreasing each year.

As ice melts and the water enters the oceans, it causes an increase in sea-levels. In the last century, the global sea-level rose about 17 cm but the rate over the first decade of the twenty-first century has been nearly double that.

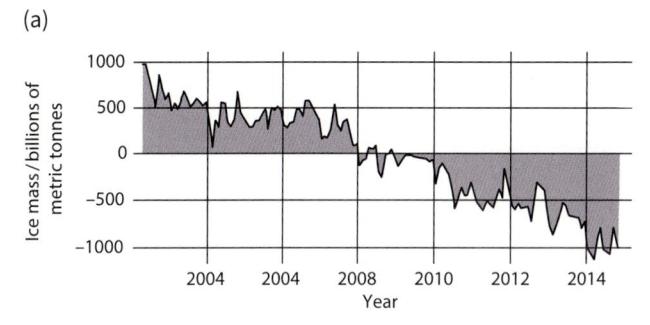

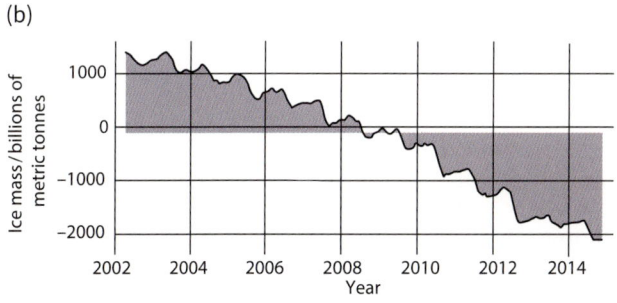

Figure 9.24: Changes of mass of ice in (a) Antarctic and (b) Greenland ice sheets since 2002. The baseline is set for an average between 2008 and 2010.

Climate change

As the global temperature has risen, there have been noticeable effects upon our climate. There are reports of changes in the seasons, with winters in the Northern Hemisphere ending earlier and the volume of snow decreasing. The ranges of some organisms are changing, with species such as barracuda and Pacific cod being found in more northerly latitudes. There have been more extreme weather events, such as major storms and floods. Many species of plant have flowered earlier in the year, and animals have emerged from hibernation earlier. In Canada, the mountain pine beetle, which consumes pine trees and is normally killed off by cold winters, is spreading further northwards as the winters become warmer.

Possible alternative theories

Despite the evidence suggesting that global warming is occurring, and that it is in large part now due to human activity, it is very difficult to prove. Critics often point out several problems with the evidence.

- Carbon dioxide levels and temperature do show a positive correlation, but it is difficult to show if one causes the other. If the planet is warming, the solubility of carbon dioxide in the oceans decreases, so carbon dioxide is released into the atmosphere increasing the atmospheric concentration.

- Ice core data shows that the planet goes through periodic heating and cooling cycles and that the same occurs with carbon dioxide levels. We may be in a natural cooling cycle.

- Some recent temperature measurements have conflicted with the current model of global warming, suggesting that the rate of temperature increase has slowed.

- Global temperature may correlate with solar activity rather than carbon dioxide concentrations. Comparisons of historic global climate warming and sunspot activity suggest a correlation. However, data comparing the solar energy reaching the planet with the global temperature indicates no significant correlation.

Impacts of global warming

Global warming could have many far-reaching consequences for our oceans and marine communities. There are already indications that some ecosystems are under threat.

Melting of ice sheets

Satellite images have demonstrated that the Arctic sea ice is at much lower levels than in the past and that the land ice sheets of Antarctica and Greenland are in retreat. The release of vast quantities of fresh water into the ocean could have many consequences.

Increase in sea-level

The rate of sea-level increase has doubled over the last decade and, if temperatures continue to rise, will increase further. Low-lying land will be far more prone to flooding, resulting in coastal erosion and loss of both human and animal coastal communities. Coastal soils will become more saline, affecting plant growth and the growth of crops. Many low-lying atolls could disappear altogether, causing species extinction and leaving people without a home.

Reduction in seawater salinity

The release of large amounts of fresh water would lower seawater salinity. This would harm osmoconformers, which can only tolerate narrow ranges of salinity. It could also affect breeding, as eggs and sperm are sensitive to changes in salinity. The world's great ocean currents are generated by differences in water density as a result of variations in temperature and salinity. If the salinity falls in the Arctic and Antarctic regions, the direction of these currents could change.

Habitat loss

The ice sheets of the Arctic and Antarctic are an important habitat for many organisms. If the ice melts, especially in the Arctic where there is no land under the ice sheet, organisms such as polar bears, which rely on the ice, will lose their habitat.

Acidification of the water

Carbon dioxide is an acidic gas that dissolves in water. As the concentration of carbon dioxide in the atmosphere increases, so does the acidity of the oceans. It is estimated that the pH of oceanic surface water is now 30% more acidic than in the eighteenth century. Acidification of water is a problem for organisms such as corals, molluscs and sea urchins, which secrete calcium carbonate to build skeletons and shells. When water is very acidic, the shells, skeletons and coral reefs erode. We will look at this in more detail later in this chapter.

Increased water temperature

The oceans absorb a lot of thermal energy (heat) and there are reports that the mean water temperature has increased. This temperature rise could have many direct and indirect effects on marine life.

Coral bleaching

Increased water temperatures can cause corals to eject their zooxanthellae, as described in Chapter 5. This results in a whitening of coral, called coral bleaching. (whitening of coral that results from the loss of a coral's symbiotic zooxanthellae). When coral lose the zooxanthellae they lose a significant proportion of their nutrients. If they do not recover from bleaching they eventually die. As they are areas of very high biodiversity, the loss of coral reefs affects many other organisms. Complex food webs are disrupted and habitats lost which could lead to the extinction of many other species.

Changes in ranges and distribution of organisms

As waters warm, the habitat a particular organism lives in may no longer be suitable, but other areas may be. Warm-water fish could extend their ranges further towards the poles and then come into competition with other species in these areas. Original species could become extinct as a result of competition with the new invasive species. Food sources may die out, leaving predators little to feed on. Krill is important for many ocean food chains and reproduces at a lower rate when in warmer water.

Phytoplankton productivity

Photosynthesis rates increase at higher temperatures, so there may be an increase in productivity of algae. Any increase, however, may be counterbalanced by changes in acidity and salinity which will negatively affect primary productivity

Harmful algal blooms releasing toxins and causing anoxic areas

As you will have read in Chapter 6, many species of algae can release harmful toxins. Over production of algae can lead to over competition for light, leading to the death and decay of the algae. Microorganisms that are decomposers and decay the algae respire at high rates, leading to a loss of oxygen in the water.

Changes in global circulation of sea currents

Ocean currents are the product of differences in density of water. The density of water is influenced by salinity and temperature. If the oceans increase in temperature, the density gradients would be disrupted, altering ocean currents.

Animal physiology

The majority of marine animals, other than birds and mammals, are cold-blooded and have a body temperature that is the same as the water. If their body temperature rises, processes such as respiration will increase, raising the demand for food and oxygen in the water.

Changes to breeding seasons

Breeding seasons are regulated by many things including day length, lunar periods, tides and temperature. If temperatures rise, some organisms may breed earlier, causing their offspring to mature at the wrong time. Many spawning seasons and migrations are timed so that the organisms arrive at locations when food sources increase. If different species' breeding seasons become out of phase with each other, there is a risk that food chains would be very badly affected.

Effects of climate change

Global warming may already be causing the climate to change. The last 20 years has seen an increase in severe weather episodes such as storms and hurricanes. Increases in storms can cause physical damage to reefs and coastal areas, breaking coral and stirring up sediments from the seabed. Coastal areas such as estuaries will experience more flooding from high tides, leading to increased salinity of land. Inland storms can increase run-off, which brings more mineral ions and sediment down to the coast. The sediment could smother estuarine organisms and the mineral ions contribute to eutrophication.

Test yourself

9   Draw up a two-column table to summarise the evidence that global warming is occurring. Use the column headings 'factor' and 'source of evidence'.

10 Use these words to complete the sentences below:

   extinct, ranges, food webs, bleaching, salinity, sea-levels

   Global warming could have serious consequences for our oceans.

   An increased temperature could lead to the _____ of organisms changing which may bring them into conflict with other species.

   As a result of this, species may become _____ and that could have effects on other organisms in _____.

   Acidification of the water and increased temperatures could cause coral _____.

   In addition, ice sheets could melt, raising _____ and reducing the _____ of the water which could kill organisms that cannot osmoregulate.

9.3 Ocean acidification

In Chapter 3 you will have investigated the carbon cycle and its importance to the marine environment. The combustion of fossil fuels may cause an increase in the concentration of atmospheric carbon dioxide, resulting in an enhanced greenhouse effect. This increased concentration of atmospheric carbon dioxide can also have an impact on ocean acidity with potentially serious consequences for the marine environment.

The carbon cycle and the ocean

Carbon dioxide is a very soluble gas that dissolves in ocean water and moves between the oceans and atmosphere by diffusion. There is about 50 times more carbon dioxide dissolved in the oceans than the Earth's atmosphere and so the oceans act as a 'sink' for carbon dioxide. If more atmospheric carbon dioxide gas is produced, the bulk of it is 'soaked up' by ocean water. When carbon dioxide diffuses into water, it produces a weak acid called carbonic acid (H_2CO_3). This carbonic acid dissociates into hydrogen carbonate ions (HCO_3^-) and hydrogen ions (H^+), making the solution acidic.

$$CO_2 + H_2O \rightleftharpoons H_2CO_3 \rightleftharpoons H^+ + HCO_3^-$$

Many marine organisms manufacture structures out of calcium carbonate ($CaCO_3$). The hard structure of coral reefs is made of calcium carbonate, as are the shells of many marine molluscs. These species take carbonate (CO_3^{2-}) ions and calcium (Ca^{2+}) ions from the water and combine them to make solid calcium carbonate. If the water has a high concentration of hydrogen (H^+) ions, and is thus acidic, the hydrogen ions will react with the carbonate ions to form more hydrogen carbonate ions (HCO_3^-).

$$CaCO_3 \rightleftharpoons Ca^{2+} + CO_3^{2-}$$
$$CO_3^{2-} + H^+ \rightleftharpoons HCO_3^-$$

Combustion of fossil fuel and ocean acidification

It has been estimated that the acidity of the oceans has increased by around 25% since the start of the industrial revolution, falling from pH 8.2 to its present-day level of pH 8.1. The oceans absorb approximately 20 million tonnes per day of carbon dioxide produced from human activities – this is about one third of the total carbon dioxide produced. Although the oceans can 'buffer' the excess carbon dioxide produced by us, preventing it accumulating in the atmosphere, there is a cost:

- An increase in atmospheric carbon dioxide leads to an increase in the amount of carbon dioxide entering the oceans, increasing the concentration of carbonic acid.

- This leads to a decrease in pH due to an increase of hydrogen ions.

- The hydrogen ions react with carbonate ions to produce more hydrogen carbonate ions.
- The concentration of carbonate ions in the water decreases.
- The concentration of carbonate ions available for marine organisms to build structures with decreases.
- Calcium carbonate is lost from coral reefs and mollusc shells as carbonate ions are released into the water.

The concentrations of the different ions are balanced in an equilibrium. If the concentration of one of them changes, the balance of all the other ions changes. Increasing carbon dioxide levels in the oceans are causing ocean acidification which is reducing the amount of carbonate ions available for coral to build reefs and molluscs to build shells. Calcium carbonate from the reefs and shells also dissolves into the water weakening the structures. Figure 9.25 shows how carbon dioxide dissolves into ocean water and affects calcium ion deposition.

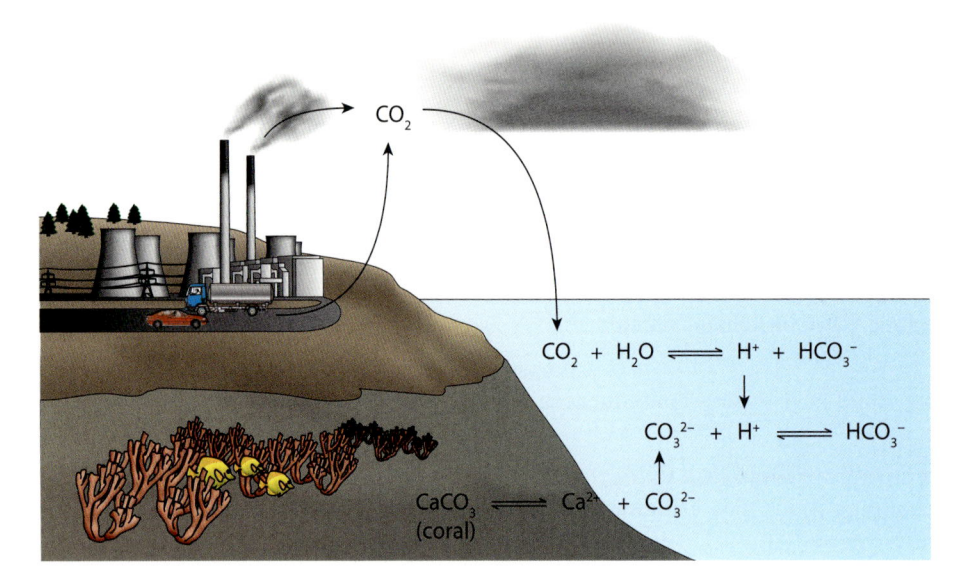

Figure 9.25: Effects of increasing carbon dioxide and ocean acidification on coral.

MATHS SKILLS 9.2

MEASURING GRADIENTS OF STRAIGHT LINES AND CURVES

You need to be able to use line graphs where the x-axis represents time to determine the rate of change of a variable. For example, Figure 9.26 shows the mean increase in mass of a group of farmed salmon over a period of six months. A line of best fit has been drawn through the points and the relationship is linear over the six month period. This means that the rate of increase is the same over the time period. You can calculate the mean rate of growth by determining the gradient of the line.

To calculate the gradient of the line, draw a triangle anywhere on the line of best fit, as shown in Figure 9.26.

gradient of a straight line = $\dfrac{y}{x}$

In this case, the gradient of the line = $\dfrac{y \text{ grams}}{x \text{ months}}$

So, this is a rate of *increase* in mass.

CONTINUED

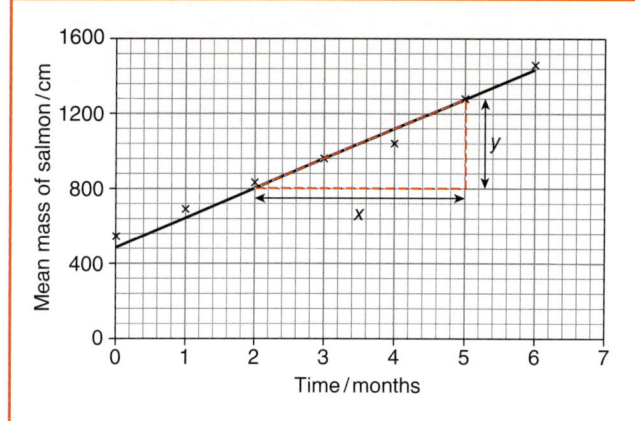

Figure 9.26: Calculating growth rate of salmon.

The graph shows that in the period between two months and five months, the mean increase in mass was:

$y = 1280\,g - 800\,g = 480\,g$

The time period, x, equals 5 months – 2 months = 3 months

$\dfrac{y}{x} = \dfrac{480}{3}$

$= 26.7\,g\,month^{-1}$

If a graph does not show a linear relationship, and the rate of increase or decrease changes, you need to draw a tangent to the curve in order to calculate the gradients at different points. For example, Figure 9.27 shows the increase in length of farmed tilapia over a 10-month period. It is clear that the curve of best fit is steepest at the start from month 0 up to month 2, and that it gradually levels off to a plateau as time increases.

In order to calculate the gradient at a particular point, use a ruler to draw a line with the same gradient as the curve at that point. You can now calculate the gradient of the tangent at the point.

For this example, the gradient at one month is:

$\dfrac{y_1}{x_1} = \dfrac{(25\,cm - 6\,cm)}{(2\,months - 0\,months)}$

$= \dfrac{19}{2}$

$= 9.5\,cm\,month^{-1}$

At 6 months, the rate of growth is:

$\dfrac{y_1}{x_1} = \dfrac{(63\,cm - 47\,cm)}{(8\,months - 4\,months)}$

$= \dfrac{16}{4}$

$= 4.0\,cm\,month^{-1}$

Questions

1 The population growth of oysters in two estuaries is shown in Figure 9.28.

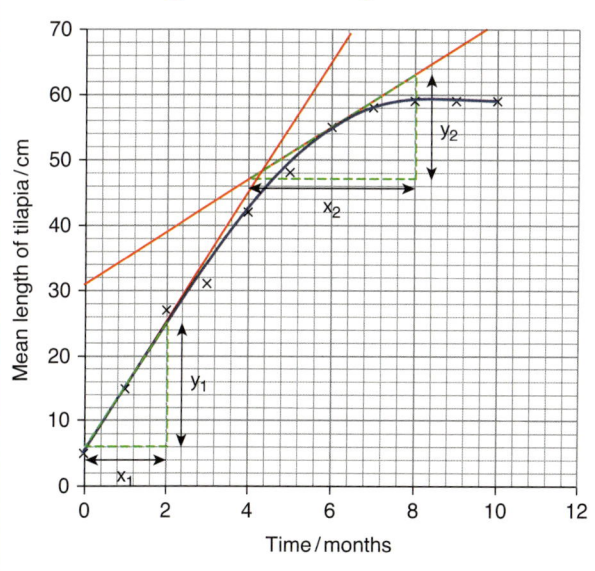

Figure 9.27: Calculating growth rate of tilapia with a variable growth rate.

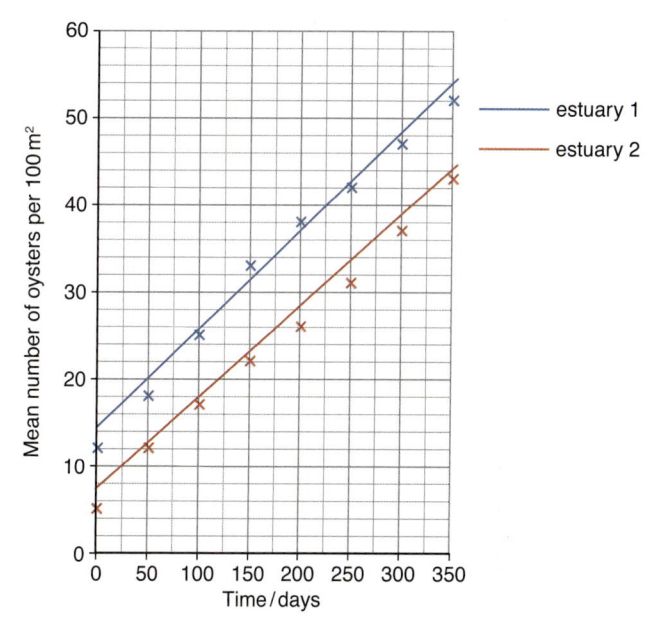

Figure 9.28: Growth of oyster populations in two estuaries.

> **CONTINUED**
>
> Use the graph to calculate and compare the rates of growth of the two oyster populations over the 350-day period.
>
> 2 The growth rates of a group of genetically engineered salmon was compared with a group of non-genetically engineered salmon. The mean mass of each group of salmon was determined at regular intervals over a period of 750 days. The results are shown in Table 9.13.
>
>   a Draw a graph to compare the growth rate of the two groups of salmon. Make sure that your axes are linear and that you draw two curves of best fit.
>
>   b Calculate the rates of growth of each group of salmon by drawing tangents to the lines at:
>
>   i 250 days
>
>   ii 550 days.
>
> | Time / days | Mean mass of genetically engineered salmon / g | Mean mass of non-genetically engineered salmon / g |
> |---|---|---|
> | 0 | 0 | 0 |
> | 250 | 500 | 275 |
> | 350 | 1000 | 450 |
> | 450 | 1500 | 550 |
> | 500 | 2000 | 800 |
> | 550 | 2500 | 950 |
> | 600 | 3200 | 1100 |
> | 650 | 4200 | 1700 |
> | 700 | 5000 | 2100 |
> | 750 | 6000 | 2900 |
>
> **Table 9.13:** Comparison of growth rates of genetically engineered and non-genetically engineered salmon.

CORE PRACTICAL ACTIVITY 9.1: INVESTIGATING THE EFFECT OF LOSS OF pH ON MOLLUSC SHELL MASS

Introduction

If atmospheric carbon dioxide levels continue to increase, more carbon dioxide will diffuse into the oceans. This could lead to an increase in ocean acidity. As we have discussed in this chapter, an increase in acidity could damage coral reefs and the shells of marine molluscs. This investigation models the effect of different pH values on the mass of mollusc shells.

Equipment

You will need:
- balance
- 100 cm^3 measuring cylinder
- 250 cm^3 beakers (or similar containers)
- 4 × mollusc shells (such as snail, mussel, cockle, oyster)
- 250 cm^3 distilled water
- 250 cm^3 0.1 mol dm^{-3} acetic acid (vinegar can be used)
- 250 cm^3 0.1 mol dm^{-3} hydrochloric acid
- 250 cm^3 0.1 mol dm^{-3} carbonic acid (this can be made by bubbling exhaled air through a straw into water – use universal indicator paper to check that the pH reaches between four and five)
- universal indicator paper.

CONTINUED

Safety considerations

Wear eye protection when handling acids. If acid comes into contact with skin, wash it off with water.

Before you start

1. Explain why acidity could lead to loss of shell mass.
2. State the independent and dependent variables.
3. List variables that need to be controlled.

Method

1. Label four beakers: water, acetic acid, hydrochloric acid, and carbonic acid.
2. Weigh four shells and record their masses in a copy of Table 9.14.
3. Place one shell in each beaker and cover each with the appropriate solution.
4. Use the Universal Indicator paper to determine the pH of each solution. Record each pH in the table.
5. Leave the beakers for 24 hours.
6. Remove each shell with a pair of forceps, dry with tissue paper and re-weigh them. Record the mass in the table. Replace the shells into the appropriate solutions.
7. Repeat step 6 after seven days.

Results

1. Use the formula to calculate the percentage change in mass of shells after 24 h and 7 days.

$$\text{percentage change} = \frac{(\text{start mass} + \text{finish mass})}{\text{start mass}} \times 100\%$$

Record your answers in a copy of Table 9.14.

2. Draw a bar chart to show the percentage change in masses of the shells after 24 h and 7 days.

Evaluation and conclusions

1. Describe the effects of the different solutions on the percentage change in mass of the shells.
2. Explain the effects of different acidities on the percentage change in mass of the shells.
3. Explain why the percentage change in mass was calculated rather than simply change in mass.
4. Suggest how the experiment could be modified to determine the maximum rate of decrease in mass of the mollusc shells. You will need to explain how you will analyse your results.
5. Give one variable that was not controlled and explain how it could have affected the results.

Solution	pH	Mass of shells / g			Percentage change	
		start	24 h	7 days	24 h	7 days
water						
acetic acid						
hydrochloric acid						
carbonic acid						

Table 9.14: Results table to show effect of acid on mollusc shell mass.

REFLECTION

After completing Core Practical Activity 9.1, discuss how the findings of this investigation reinforce your understanding of the effects of ocean acidification on marine organisms.

Test yourself

11 Explain why the pH of ocean water falls when more carbon dioxide is dissolved in it.

9.4 Conservation of marine ecosystems

If we are to repair the damage already done to the marine environment and stop further damage, we need to think of ways to conserve species and their habitats. Conservation is often easy in theory but more difficult in practice. If conservation projects are to be successful, they need careful consideration and the support of local people. Projects that could affect local and national economies need to ensure that people retain employment and have the opportunity to improve their living standards.

Conservation: what it is and why it is necessary

Most people are aware of at least one example of a conservation project, (for example to conserve areas of rainforest, or to prevent a species such as the blue whale from extinction). Formally defining conservation, however, is actually quite difficult. It is best thought of as an ethical philosophy, the main aim being the maintenance of the health of the natural world. Many things are included in conservation, such as the Earth's habitats, biodiversity (a measure of the species, genetic and ecosystem diversity of different species), fisheries, energy and non-renewable resources. In the preceding chapters you will have read about the human impact on fish stocks and our marine habitats. The aim of conservation is to prevent further damage, and in some way begin to rectify it. The people who try to protect nature are called conservationists. They have many roles and many types of people are involved. Some of these roles include:

- carrying out scientific research on how humans are affecting the planet and suggesting methods for protecting it
- raising awareness of conservation issues with the general public, businesses and governments
- carrying out practical conservation projects, such as the replanting of mangroves.

Why we need conservation

There are many arguments for conserving species and habitats, four of which are discussed below.

Ethical reasons

We are currently in the grip of a mass global **extinction** of species. There have been mass extinctions in the past (Figure 9.29), but the current mass extinction is different. In the past, mass extinctions have been caused by sudden, cataclysmic events. The extinction of the dinosaurs at the end of the Cretaceous period, for example, is thought to have been caused by an asteroid collision. And the Ordovician–Silurian extinction, about 440 million years ago, was probably due to the formation of massive glaciers. This glaciation caused much of the world's water to turn to ice and sea-levels fell dramatically. The eruption of super-volcanoes is thought to be the cause of other extinctions.

> **KEY WORD**
>
> **extinction:** the loss of a species from the planet; some species may be extinct in the wild but still present in zoos

Figure 9.29 shows how the rate of extinction shows a positive correlation with the human population. It is estimated that, if we do nothing, our activities will have led to the extinction of almost half of the world's current species by the year 2100. At present, we are the dominant species on the planet and have a moral duty to stop the damage that we are causing.

Future generations

We are the custodians of the planet for our future generations. Our activities now will shape the world of the future. If large areas of habitat continue to be lost, we will deprive our future generations of the opportunity to witness the beauty of nature. Their only knowledge of the beauty of coral reefs or unusual species will be through textbooks or films. There are already many species, such as the dodo and the Tasmanian tiger, that now only exist as drawings or

9 Human impacts on marine ecosystems

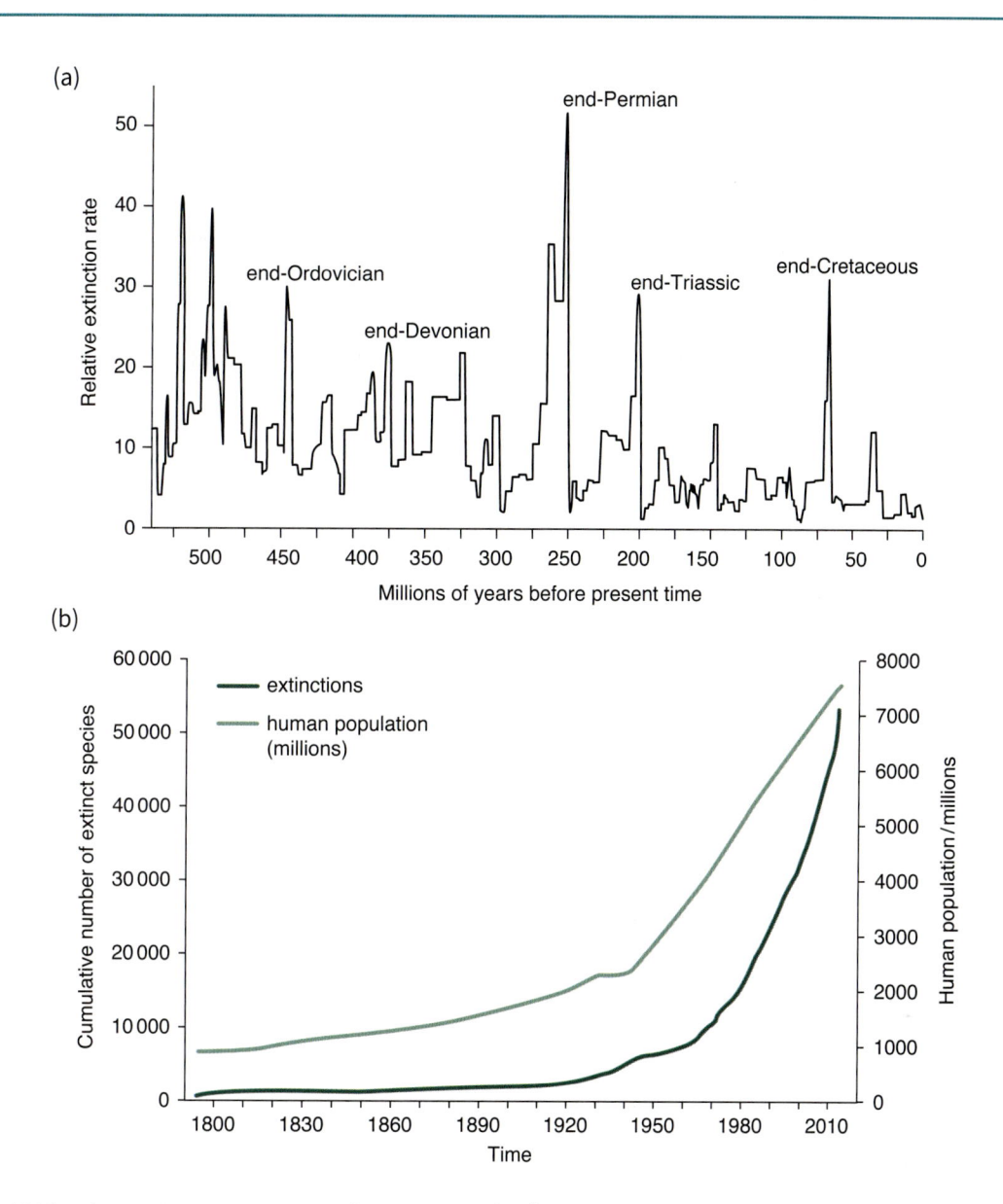

Figure 9.29: (a) The change in extinction rate, showing periods of mass extinction. The peaks represent periods of mass extinction; (b) The change in human population and number of species becoming extinct since 1800.

museum specimens. If we continue to allow extinctions, many more species will become simply a page in a book or an image on a screen.

Our planet also provides our food and many other resources such as oil. If we use all the fish in the seas and all the non-renewable energy sources without finding alternatives, there will be nothing left for future generations. If we have no food, we will soon be on the road to extinction ourselves.

Preserving ecosystems

An ecosystem consists of many species of interacting organisms and their habitats. Organisms are highly dependent on each other in many ways. They provide food for each other, can transport each other from place to place, and can provide and alter habitats for each other.

Food webs are complicated interactions between organisms, and if one species is lost from a food web, other trophic levels are affected. Some species are keystone species and have particularly important roles in maintaining ecosystems (see Chapter 4). If these keystone species are lost, the ecological effects are massive. For example, salmon feed in the oceans, obtaining their energy from a food chain based on phytoplankton. When the salmon migrate up rivers to breed, they are eaten by inland species such as bears and birds of prey. This means that the energy for many inland food chains comes ultimately from phytoplankton in the oceans. If salmon do not migrate, the energy for these food chains is lost.

Kelp forests are areas of rich biodiversity. Figure 9.30 shows part of the food web in a kelp forest. Sea otters eat sea urchins, which in turn eat kelp. If sea otters numbers fall, the sea urchin population would increase and the amount of kelp would decrease.

Some species depend on others for distribution. Barnacles attach themselves to humpback whales, so travel across oceans to spawn in different places. If humpback whales became extinct, barnacles would lose their distribution network.

Parrotfish live around coral reefs eating old coral. They grind up coral and release sand in their faeces that helps make sandy beaches and small islands. They also rasp away algae from the surface of the coral and remove sponges, helping to preserve the reefs. If parrotfish become extinct, the reefs would become overgrown with algae and sponges.

Benefits for ourselves

Our oceans provide us with many things that improve our lives, and more than 350 million jobs depend on them. We have harvested the oceans for food for hundreds of years, and they have enriched our lives for recreational purposes. People are attracted by the beauty and diversity of the marine world. Diving, recreational fishing, whale watching, sailing and just the pleasure of sitting by the sea all form part of our enjoyment.

Marine organisms can also provide us with medicines. Organisms found on coral reefs have formed the basis of drugs for asthma, arthritis, lung cancer and skin cancer. Scientists suspect that there are many more potential drugs yet to be discovered.

If we allow biodiversity to fall and habitats to be destroyed, we will lose a food source, a place of enjoyment and the potential to treat many diseases.

Human activities that have resulted in a need for conservation

Our activities over the past 100 years have placed pressure on many species, causing their populations to fall. Habitat loss due to a range of human activities, such fishing, industry, tourist development and mining, has had a major impact. Intensive fishing has led directly to the reduction of many commercially valuable species and has affected many non-target species, which have been caught as bycatch and affected by changes in the food chains.

The impact of human activities on biodiversity can be considered from two points of view: loss of habitat and direct effects on species.

Habitat loss

Many marine habitats are under threat. If a habitat is damaged, the species that live there and depend on it

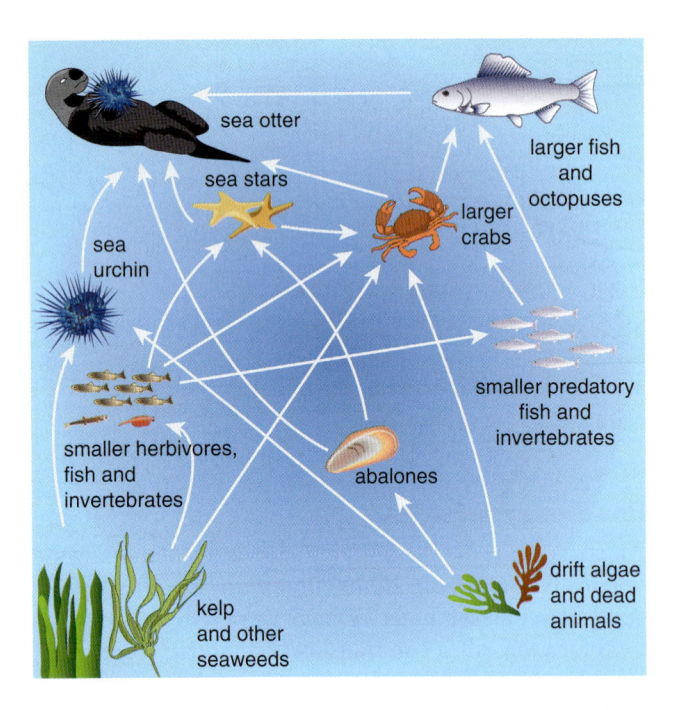

Figure 9.30: A complex food web that exists within a kelp forest. Sea otters are at the top of the food web and their numbers affect the diversity of the other species.

will be threatened with extinction. Large areas of coastal habitats have been lost all around the world to make way for aquaculture ventures, tourist resorts, marinas and industries. Any loss of habitat will negatively affect the species that live there, but this is easiest to understand when considering specific types of habitat. Mangrove forests, coral reefs and seagrass meadows all support high biodiversity and are under threat because of human activity.

Mangroves

Mangrove forests around the world are under severe threat (Figure 9.31). They are important habitats, acting as nursery grounds for many species, preventing coastal erosion, reducing wave energy and acting as a carbon dioxide sink. The United Nations Food and Agriculture Organization (FAO) estimates that approximately 150 000 hectares of the world's mangrove forests are lost every year. Since 1960, Thailand has lost more than half of its mangrove forests. In the Philippines, mangroves have declined from an estimated 448 000 hectares in the 1920s to only 110 000 hectares by 1990, and in Ecuador up to 50% of the nation's mangrove forest has been lost.

Figure 9.31: Mangrove deforestation in South-East Asia.

Mangrove loss is caused in various ways. Shrimp farming has had a devastating effect, with large areas being removed to make way for aquaculture businesses (Chapter 8). Many mangrove areas have been dug up for easier boat access and to build tourist resorts. Pollution from industrial waste, oil spills and agricultural run-off and climate change have also destroyed many areas.

Coral reefs

Coral reef areas are extremely important areas of biodiversity that help to maintain fish stocks of many species and play an important role in preventing coastal erosion. A survey in 2008 stated that the planet's coral reefs were in a critical state and estimated that already:

- 19% of the world's reefs had been lost
- 15% were seriously threatened with loss within the next 10–30 years
- 20% were under threat of loss within the next 20–40 years.

Many human activities have negative impacts on coral reefs. Benthic trawling physically wrecks coral and other fishing practices, such as the use of dynamite, break and shatter it. In many countries, coral has been mined to use as a building material. Irresponsible tourism has caused physical damage by boats and diving, and damage caused by the sewage and refuse released from tourist resorts. Toxic pollutants from industry, sediment from dredging and agricultural run-off can all cause eutrophication, which also damages coral.

The main threat to coral may be from climate change because of the increased emission of greenhouse gases. Corals cannot survive if the water temperature is too high or the pH is too acidic. High atmospheric carbon dioxide levels cause an increase in both these factors and this seems to have led to increased coral bleaching in many areas.

The state of coral in Australia's Great Barrier Reef is monitored carefully. Between 1985 and 2012, coral cover was found to have declined from 28.0% to 13.8%. Suggestions for the causes of this decline include climate change, storm damage (possibly a result of climate change) and high populations of the predatory crown-of-thorns starfish.

Seagrass meadows

Seagrass meadows are, like mangroves and coral reefs, very important habitats with high biodiversity. They provide food and shelter for many species and are the primary producers for many food webs. They also stabilise the substrate and act as carbon sinks. In 2009, a research project demonstrated that, since 1980, seagrass has been lost at a mean rate of $110 \, km^2 \, year^{-1}$. It has also been estimated that 29% of the area covered by seagrass has disappeared since recording began in 1879.

The principal causes of seagrass loss are related to human activity (Figure 9.32). Destructive fishing practices, boat propellers, anchors and coastal development for industry and tourism cause direct and immediate seagrass loss. Pollution from industry and oil spills has killed large areas. High levels of sediment from

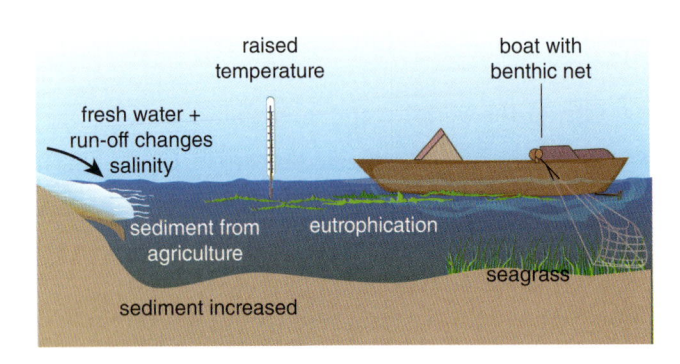

Figure 9.32: Activities that threaten seagrass.

agricultural run-off and dredging are also damaging, as they reduce light penetration in the water, reducing photosynthesis. Irrigation of agricultural land with fresh water that runs into the sea has killed seagrass by causing changes in salinity. Overfishing of predators such as sharks has caused increases in populations of herbivores that eat seagrass.

Invasive species may also have affected seagrass meadows. It is estimated that at least 56 non-native species, primarily invertebrates, non-native seagrasses and seaweeds, have been introduced to seagrass beds. These species have been introduced through shipping and aquaculture and have outcompeted or consumed native seagrasses. Increasing water temperatures as a result of climate change are also thought to be placing areas of seagrass under pressure.

Overfishing and hunting

The negative effects of overfishing species have been discussed in Chapter 8. The hunting of many species such as bluefin tuna and cod has led to collapses in their populations to almost unsustainable levels. In the twentieth century, whaling was responsible for bringing many species of whale close to the point of extinction. Figure 9.33 shows the estimated population of blue whales through the twentieth century. Before the onset of industrial whaling, the population was estimated to be around 275 000 animals. By 1964 the global population had fallen to between 650 and 2000. This catastrophic fall was due almost entirely to unrestricted hunting and a global ban on hunting blue whales was brought into effect in 1965. The population of blue whales has gradually begun to recover but, as they breed slowly, it will take a long time for them to recover to previous levels.

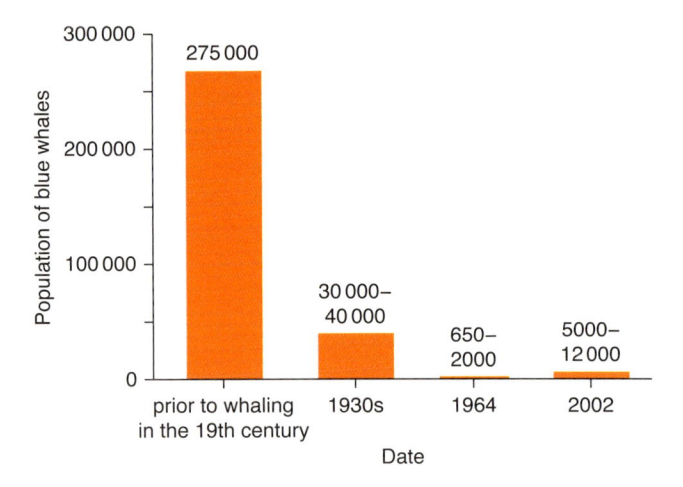

Figure 9.33: Change in populations of blue whales in the twentieth century.

As well as reducing the populations of species by specifically targeting them, human activity has accidentally affected many other species. Certain fishing methods, such as pelagic long-lining, purse seining and benthic trawling have a high risk of bycatch (see Chapter 8). Other non-target organisms, such as dolphins, turtles and sea birds, are often trapped. Collisions with boats have led to the deaths of organisms, particularly large mammals such as whales and manatees. When examined carefully, scars due to propeller damage can often be seen on the sides of these animals.

Pollution and refuse

Every day, large quantities of different pollutants are released into the water.

- Toxins such as mercury and TBT accumulate through food chains, killing top predator species.

- Fertilisers and sewage can cause eutrophication, lowering oxygen concentrations and suffocating organisms.

- Coastal industries have released heavy metal ions into the water along with their effluent.

- Sewage can contain toxins, and its decomposition leads to oxygen loss.

- Aquaculture produces large amounts of waste that can contain toxins and minerals that lead to eutrophication.

- Tourist resorts in coastal areas can release large amounts of sewage, and refuse such as plastic, into the sea. Large amounts of plastic from ships,

coastal communities and tourist resorts have killed thousands of sea birds, marine mammals and turtles as a result of ingestion and entanglement.
- Oil spills from container ships and oil platforms has poisoned and suffocated many species and damaged coastlines, and may persist for many years.
- Increased carbon dioxide emissions leading to global warming have directly affected many species. Increased sea-levels, increased temperatures, changes to salinity and pH, along with food chain effects, have the potential to cause catastrophic effects.

Coastal development

Tourist resorts have been built on crucial habitats such as nesting sites and migration routes, and boat trips can damage coral reefs. They can also release refuse and sewage into the sea. Cluttered, busy beaches hinder the movement of turtles along beaches when laying eggs and the movement of hatchlings from eggs to sea.

In Costa Rica in 2015, tourists gathered on beaches to see olive ridley sea turtles migrate from the sea up the beach to lay eggs. Unfortunately, there were so many tourists that the turtles were deterred from leaving the sea, and egg laying was prevented.

The role of the International Union for the Conservation of Nature (IUCN)

In 1964, the IUCN established the Red List of Threatened Species. This list is a comprehensive information source about the conservation status of many of the planet's animal and plant species. The IUCN is a supranational organisation that has a membership made up of national governments, conservation groups, indigenous peoples' organisations and other nongovernment organisations. It works with scientists, industries and governments to protect the environment. The Red List is often described as a 'barometer of life'. This is because it is a way of identifying the pressures that are acting on species so we can prepare conservation projects to prevent their extinction. The Red List provides information about species such as:

- ranges
- population sizes
- habitats
- threats
- potential conservation methods.

The Red List currently has a huge database of species, all of which are categorised according to factors such as range, population size, risk to habitat and risk of extinction. The list is constantly updated, and species may move category according to the risk of extinction. There are six categories for species that have been evaluated thoroughly:

- Least Concern (LC)
- Vulnerable (VU)
- Endangered (EN)
- Critically Endangered (CR)
- Extinct in the Wild (EW)
- Extinct (E)

The current aim is to have 160 000 species assessed thoroughly by 2020. By assessing species according to their risk of extinction, we can prioritise those species and habitats that require the most urgent action.

The IUCN work at local, regional and global levels to facilitate marine conservation. It has offices in more than 50 countries and has a network of more than 10 000 scientists around the globe. For example, at a regional level, it published an overview of the conservation status of corals in the Mediterranean in 2017. At a global level, it updated the Red List for sharks at a conference in 2019. At a local level, it has worked hard to assess the threat from overfishing in Lake Malawi where over one third of Malawians depend on for food.

Endangered species

The IUCN has certain criteria for classifying a species as endangered. An **endangered species** is at a high risk of extinction and will meet one of the following criteria:

- a significant reduction in population size over the last ten years or three generations
- a severely declining, fragmented or small geographical range
- a population size with fewer than 250 mature individuals.

> **KEY WORD**
>
> **endangered species:** species that are at a high risk of extinction

- a population size that is fewer than 2500 mature individuals with an ongoing sever decline in numbers
- a more than 20% risk of extinction within 20 years of five generations.

Invasive species

An invasive species is a species that has been introduced to an area outside its normal geographical range by man, either on purpose or accidentally. Invasive species pose many threats to marine environments. They may compete with native species for food or habitats, consume native species, spread diseases and alter habitats rendering them unfit for native species. Invasive species often spread quickly due to the absence of predators and decrease populations of native species.

We have accidentally and deliberately introduced many species into areas where they are not native. Organisms such as sponges and barnacles attach onto the hulls of boats and migrate around the world. It has been estimated that up to 3000 different species are transferred around the world in the ballast water of ships.

Some invasive species have escaped from aquaculture. These species may have no natural predators and so can reproduce rapidly and consume or outcompete native species, affecting ecological linkages (the ecological relationships that exist between species and their environment within an ecosystem).

Note: Ecological linkages are extension content, and are not part of your syllabus.

The Nile tilapia and European (common) carp (Figure 9.34) are invasive species now found in areas of South-East Asia. In the Murray–Darling Basin, in southeast Australia, European carp now make up to 90% of the fish. They were brought to the area in the 1850s for aquaculture but escaped into the wild. Since they have few natural predators, their population exploded, and they spread throughout the river networks of southeast Australia. The carp are herbivores and have consumed large amounts of river plants, severely affecting the food chains that depend on the plants. They have caused the river beds to be eroded and this has increased turbidity in the water. To control the populations, scientists have been researching the use of a carp herpes virus that selectively kills European carp. In the waterways of the Great Lakes of North America, Asian carp that were introduced in the 1960s and 1970s have become an invasive species. They have already replaced several native species in the Mississippi and Illinois Rivers and measures are now being taken to try to prevent the carp entering the Great Lakes themselves.

The bluestripe snapper (Figure 9.35) was introduced into Hawaii for aquaculture and has become established in the surrounding coral reefs. There are concerns that it is outcompeting native coral reef fish species.

To combat the threats posed by invasive species, the IUCNs Species Survival Commission runs the Invasive Species Specialist Group. This group of scientists and environmental experts identifies potential invasive species and areas that are at risk and develops strategies to prevent and eliminate invasive species.

Figure 9.34: European carp, an invasive species that has damaged areas of the Murray–Darling Basin in Australia.

Figure 9.35: Shoal of bluestripe snapper by a coral reef.

Viability of conservation projects

There have been many successful conservation programmes carried out to restore and protect habitats and individual species. Successful conservation is not just about releasing more individuals of a particular species into the wild and hoping that they will survive and breed. If certain conditions are not met, populations will not increase and they could even damage other species. Below is a summary of the main general methods used in conservation.

Protecting a species by banning or restricting hunting or fishing. The success of this method is illustrated by the slow recovery of some populations of whales after the International Whaling Commission placed a ban on hunting.

Increasing population sizes by increasing the amount of food present. If a species is under pressure because of food loss, efforts may be made to increase the food source. To do this in a sustainable way, the habitat has to be conserved in order to boost productivity. Grouper populations have been increased by conserving areas of mangrove where the juveniles feed.

Conservation of a habitat to protect biodiversity and the variety of species in an area. Preserving coral reefs will not only protect the reefs but also the species that depend on them as a food source and habitat. This can be done by reducing tourist damage on beaches where birds and turtles nest, controlling shipping and reducing dredging and tourist boat activities.

Enhancing and restoring habitats to increase populations. Building artificial reefs increases the populations of many fish. Replanting mangroves in areas where shrimp farming has reduced mangrove forests can help to restore mangrove populations.

Removing sources of local pollution that threaten species and habitats. Local restrictions can be placed on waste released by industrial plants and agriculture. Water treatment plants can be built to reduce the release of sewage. Recycling programmes can reduce the amount of refuse that is lost into the seas, and more environmentally sound methods of disposal can be encouraged.

Controlling global pollution. Many of the threats facing species are the result of global emissions rather than local issues. Global warming poses a threat to many habitats and species and can only be tackled by international cooperation. Legally binding treaties aim to set targets for reducing emissions such as carbon dioxide and methane in order to reduce global warming. Bans on importing the remains of endangered species, such as whale meat, reduces the demand for illegal hunting of these species.

There are many different scales of conservation projects, ranging from global involvement to local community volunteers. Global ocean treaties are set at international meetings. Charities such as the World Wide Fund for Nature (WWF) and the Marine Conservation Society increase public awareness of the need for conservation, lobby governments for action and fund projects themselves. National governments set up conservation projects for their coastal waters and employ scientists and professional conservation workers. Many charities and governments from more economically developed nations help fund conservation work in less economically developed nations. There are also many small-scale conservation projects that are run by volunteers. Many people spend their time preserving habitats, clearing litter and monitoring biodiversity. Despite the global international treaties signed by world leaders, it is often the efforts of local people who are aware of the need for a particular project that have the highest impact. Many habitats and species are still flourishing thanks to the efforts of people who give up their time.

The need to establish ecological linkages

If a population is to recover, we need to ensure that all the necessary ecological links are secure. This means that all elements of a food web must be present and that the habitat is optimal for survival. In practice, this means that there needs to be sufficient food and a variety of food types, and that the habitat has the correct shelter and other necessary features such as nursery grounds and breeding sites. Attempting to repopulate a species of coral-ingesting parrotfish will be unsuccessful if the coral reefs have been badly damaged. The reefs need protecting along with the parrotfish if the project is to be successful.

If other organisms or diseases are causing the loss of a species or habitat, those species need to be controlled. The crown-of-thorns starfish has caused the loss of large areas of the Great Barrier Reef near Australia. To help the reef recover, the starfish population needs to be reduced. Understanding the reasons for the high population of starfish will help, and recent research has pointed towards agricultural run-off of fertilisers, so conservation efforts need to focus on reducing the use of fertilisers.

Sea turtle conservation

Successful conservation programmes do not put other organisms at risk. Research in India and Florida has suggested that care must be taken when conserving populations of turtles to prevent damage to seagrasses.

Sea turtles eat seagrasses. A healthy population of sea turtles grazing on the seagrasses encourages good seagrass growth, increases the fertility of the seabed and helps disperse the seagrass. If turtle populations are too low, seagrass dies off and is replaced by algae. If turtle populations are too high, seagrass is overconsumed and dies off. Juvenile sea turtles are consumed by sharks. In many parts of the world, sharks have been overfished.

The problem with sea turtle conservation projects is that the ecological balance of many areas has been affected. Turtle populations are threatened, but shark populations are also very low because of overfishing. Strategies that successfully increase the sea turtle populations alone could lead to the loss of seagrasses and other species that feed on them (Figure 9.36). To be effective, a turtle conservation project would need to:

- increase turtle populations via habitat conservation and regulation of fishing methods
- place a ban, or restrictions, on shark fishing.

Conservation measures can have unforeseen effects on other organisms. When whaling bans were put in place for many species of large whale, species of smaller whales such as sei whales began to fall because whalers started to hunt them.

Local engagement

If conservation is to be successful, there has to be engagement with local people because the preservation of areas and species could have negative impacts on their lifestyles and wealth. If bans are placed on traditional fishing areas, it is obvious that many people

Figure 9.36: Possible effects of sea turtle conservation on seagrass. A healthy balance in the populations of sea turtles and sharks must be maintained.

could lose their livelihood or recreational areas. It is essential that local people become **stakeholders** in conservation projects and benefit from them. If a project is seen only as a cost that has been imposed from a remote government, there is little incentive to adhere to the rules and regulations. If the project offers direct benefits to local communities, there is an incentive for them to support it.

> **KEY WORD**
>
> **stakeholder:** a person who has a vested interest, for any reason, in an area or project

In parts of Indonesia where mangrove replanting projects were carried out, those areas that were replanted by non-local workers failed to become established. Where local people were paid to take part in the project, and were incentivised by financial rewards for survival of the mangroves, the success rate was far higher.

Strategies for conserving marine species

We have discussed the different threats posed by human activities to the marine environment and the factors that are essential for viable conservation projects. There are many strategies that can be employed to conserve marine species and prevent damage to the environment.

Marine protected areas and no-take zones

Marine protected areas (MPAs) are conservation areas of ocean and coasts that are tightly regulated. Their purpose is to provide areas where species can breed without human interference and increase their populations. They range in size, for example, from Echo Bay Marine Provincial Park, BC, Canada at $0.004\,\text{km}^2$ to the Pacific Remote Islands Marine National Monument at $1\,271\,500\,\text{km}^2$. Some MPAs are shown in Figure 9.37.

The activities permitted in different MPAs vary. Some areas offer general protection for all species, while others focus on a specific group of species such as sharks. Shark sanctuaries ban commercial fishing of sharks

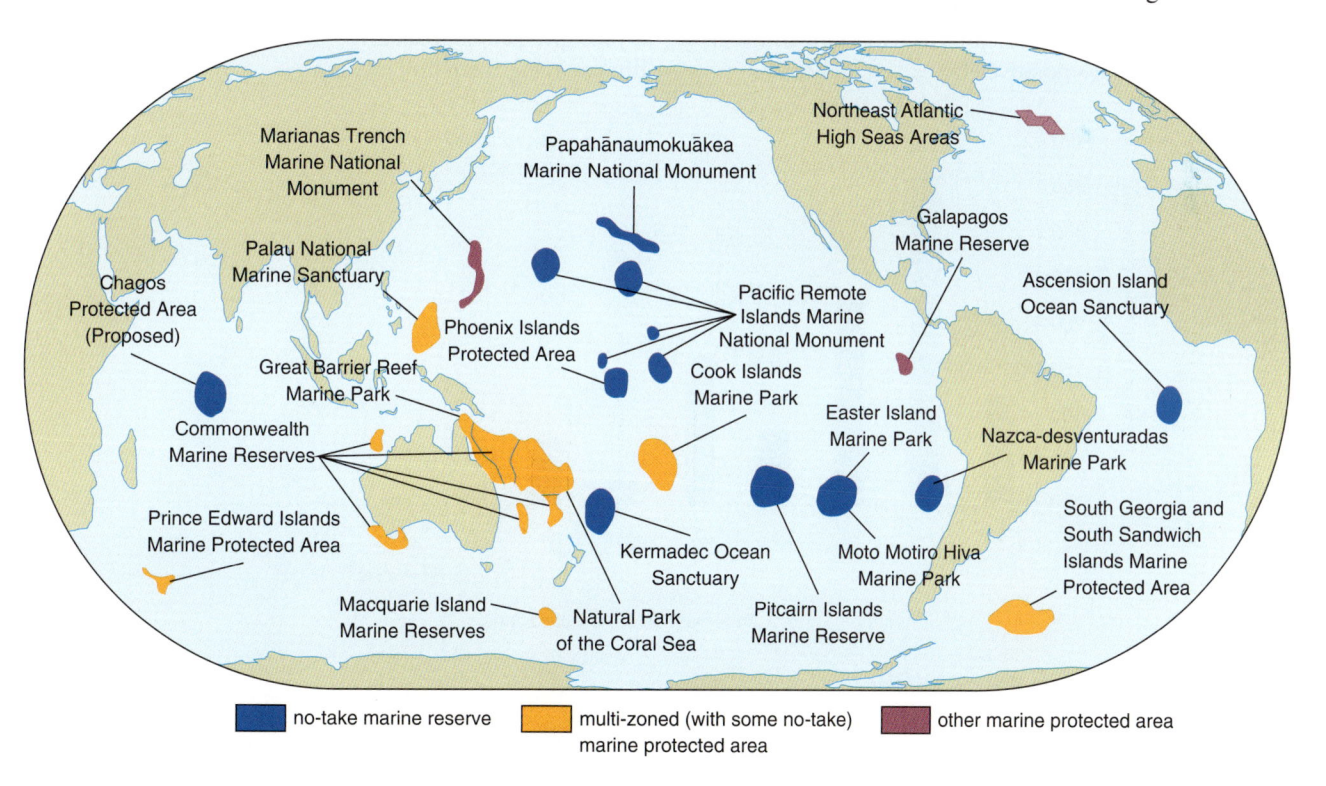

Figure 9.37: Very large marine protected areas.

and provide areas where sharks can breed without being hunted. The governments of Congo-Brazzaville, Maldives, French Polynesia, Palau, Israel and Honduras have banned all types of shark fishing within their territorial waters, including recreational fishing.

The most highly protected MPAs are 'no-take' reserves where all fishing is prohibited. In practice, only a fraction of MPAs enforce a no-take policy, with most allowing certain restricted forms of fishing in specially reserved areas. In some MPAs, no fishing, diving, agriculture or tourism is allowed, and entry is restricted to official research teams.

It is estimated that MPAs account for only between 1.8 and 2.8% of our oceans (Figure 9.38). International agreements, such as the Convention on Biological Diversity's 2011 Aichi Biodiversity Targets, have set a target for conservation at 10% coverage of the oceans by MPAs. Several scientific studies have indicated that to safeguard marine life, we actually need to have between 20 and 30% of marine areas in reserves. The concern is that it may not be until 2100 that we even reach the 10% target.

Effectiveness of MPAs

MPAs aim to create high populations of fish within the protected areas. These fish then spill over into fished areas. If healthy populations are maintained in an MPA, this can have positive effects on catches and profits for the fishing industry. New Zealand was one of the first countries to create no-take MPAs. An MPA established in 1977 at Goat Island Bay, New Zealand, successfully conserved fish stocks in the area and caused millions of eggs and larvae to drift into neighbouring areas. This increased fish catches for local fishers and helped popularise the creation of MPAs with the fishing industry. Other surveys on the effects of MPAs have found that, within the MPAs, there were twice as many large (>250 mm total length) fish species per transect, and up to fourteen times more shark biomass than in fished areas.

The ecology of MPAs needs careful monitoring as there can be unexpected impacts on food chains. In the Leigh Marine Reserve in New Zealand, predator species increased, causing a decrease in primary consumers and a subsequent increase in plants and producers. This caused the seabed to become covered with large amounts of seaweed.

Large MPAs are very costly to monitor. Preventing illegal fishing requires surveillance that can be too expensive for less economically developed nations. Local sensitivities also need to be taken into account. The UK government has set up one of the largest MPAs in the world around the Chagos Islands in the Indian Ocean. This MPA is proving to be highly controversial because it prevents people from any form of fishing or tourism, thus denying them any income.

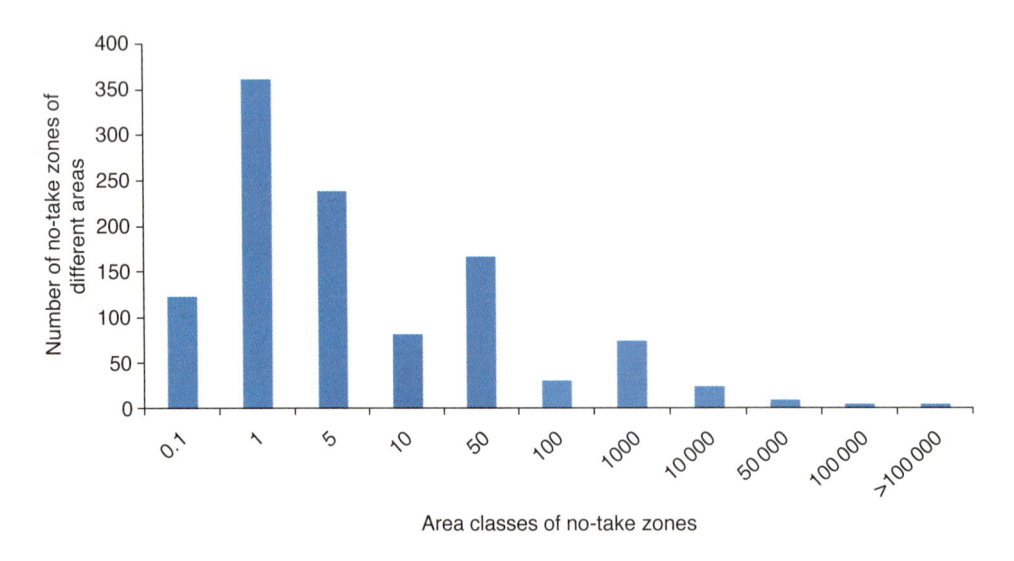

Figure 9.38: The number of marine no-take zones of different sizes in 2012.

CASE STUDY 9.2: SEA BREAM PROTECTION IN THE ADRIATIC SEA

The Torre Guaceto MPA covers 22 km^2 of the Adriatic Sea in south-eastern Italy. It was created in 2001 and in parts of it a no-take ban on fishing was enforced. By 2003, the MPA had between two to ten times as many sea breams compared with a fully fished area. Sea breams eat sea urchins, and it was found that the sea urchin population in the area was ten times lower than in fully fished areas. Because sea urchins eat seaweed, the decrease in their population led to an increase in the cover of seaweed to 47% of the seabed inside the reserve.

Surrounding fished areas had only 15% seaweed cover. Seaweed acts as an important habitat and area of shelter for many organisms (Figure 9.39).

In 2005, scientists and local fishers developed a plan to allow restricted fishing in some areas of the MPA. The aim was to maintain fishers' income while limiting negative fishing impacts. Fishing gear was designed to minimise damage to the underwater habitat and protect top-level predators and young fish. The fishers also agreed to fish only one day per week within the MPA. After regulated fishing was allowed, the fishers reported an increase in catch in the area. Within a few years, the catch was double the catch from areas outside the MPA and the income of the fishers was considerably higher than before the MPA was established.

The success of the project has made the fishers supportive of the MPA and has also increased trust between fishers and scientists. It has shown that collaboration between scientists and the fishing industry is crucial to the success of marine conservation.

Questions

1. Explain what is meant by a *no-take area*.
2. a Explain why the MPA had more seaweed than the fully fished area.
   b Suggest why the higher amounts of seaweed could help increase biodiversity.
3. Explain why the fishers are now supportive of MPAs.

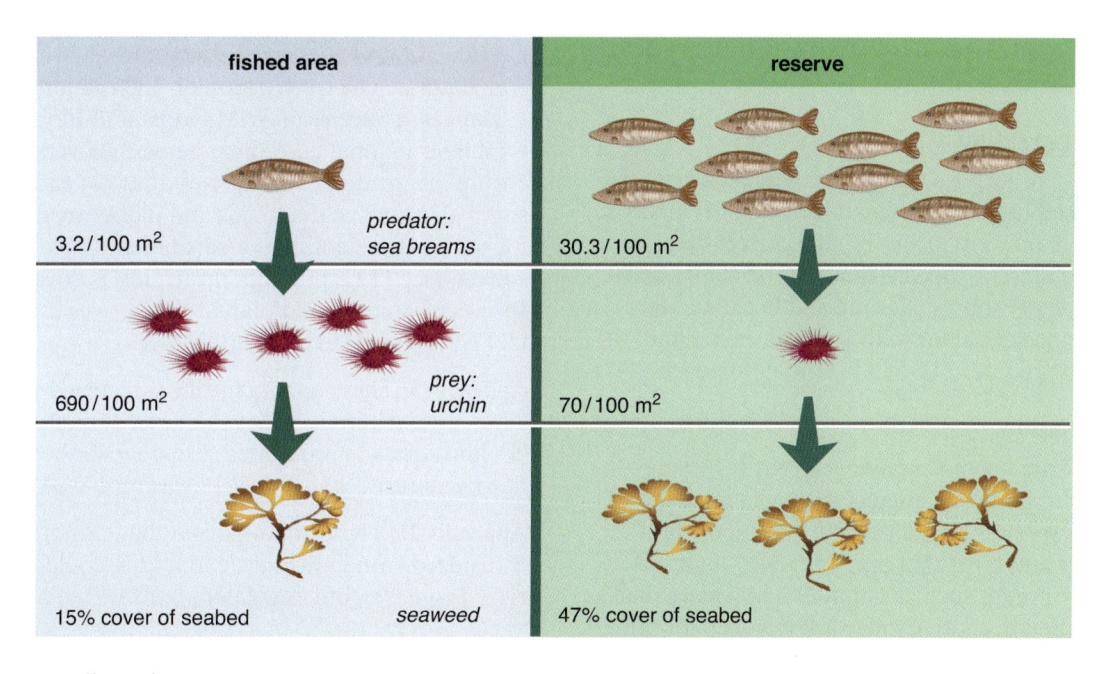

Figure 9.39: Effect of sea bream conservation on sea urchin and seaweed populations.

Captive breeding and release programmes

In Chapter 8, you studied the advantages and disadvantages of introducing cultured stock into the wild. **Captive breeding** and release programmes aim to breed species in captivity with a view to releasing them into the wild to replenish populations.

All captive breeding and reintroduction programmes require several considerations.

> ### KEY WORD
>
> **captive breeding:** the breeding of species outside of their natural area; zoos often breed organisms with a view to releasing them into the wild

Maintaining genetic diversity

Healthy populations require high genetic diversity so that they can adapt to change. If only a few individuals are used to breed, or animals that are closely related are used, the offspring will be genetically very similar. It is important to keep pedigree records, or stud books, of the animals used for breeding. Animals are sometimes moved around different zoos to ensure that they produce offspring with genetic diversity.

Habitat conservation

If animals are to be released into the wild, it is essential that the correct habitat and required ecological linkages are present. If they are to survive, the correct types of food must be present and sustainable food chains exist to ensure a steady supply. Nesting and breeding areas must also be present along with areas to shelter and escape predators.

No humanisation

Animals that are kept in captivity can easily lose the ability to hunt, forage or interact with wild animals of their own species. This is particularly important for mammals and birds that may even copy human behaviours. Animals such as dolphins and whales that have been raised in captivity may actively seek, or not avoid, human contact. It may be necessary to raise animals in areas with no human contact and efforts made to teach them how to forage for food.

In Canada and the United States, Pacific salmon populations have been supplemented by salmon spawned in hatcheries for many years. Releasing these salmon takes pressure off the wild populations that are depleted due to intense fishing. Care must be taken, however – breeding programmes need to prevent the salmon becoming inbred which could affect the genetic health of wild populations. Releasing too many salmon could also interfere with local food chains.

In the Murray–Darling Basin, Australia, pygmy perch have been successfully reintroduced after becoming extinct in the area. The fish were bred in captivity and reintroduced over a period of five years. Scientists check the DNA of the fish to ensure that genetic diversity is being maintained in the new replenished population.

Legislation

Many organisms are listed as protected species and legislation has been passed to conserve them. Legislation may prohibit hunting, capture from the wild, trading, or protect the area in which they are found. Local rules are often passed by states within countries or by national governments. National parks may be created within which habitats and species are conserved. Sometimes, however, local conservation is not enough. Many species do not remain within one area. For example, birds and whales often migrate across many national borders and some species are hunted for sale to other countries. Conservation of these species requires international cooperation. The Convention on International Trade in Endangered Species of Wild Fauna and Flora (CITES) is an international agreement between governments to ensure that trade in wild species does not endanger their survival. Many wild animals and plants are exploited for use as food, clothing, medicines and even tourist souvenirs. CITES provides protection for over 35 000 species of animals and plants. The species listed by CITES are listed in three appendices:

Appendix I: These are organisms threatened with extinction. All trade, other than exceptional circumstances, is prohibited. Figure 9.40 shows a hawksbill turtle which in 2018 was protected.

Appendix II: These are organism that, although not threatened with immediate extinction, could be at future risk. Trade is tightly regulated.

Appendix III: These are organisms that are protected in at least one country which has asked for help in control of trade. Trade is tightly controlled.

The International Whaling Commission (IWC) was established in 1946 'to provide for the proper conservation of whale stocks and thus make possible

9 Human impacts on marine ecosystems

Figure 9.40: Hawksbill turtle, a species protected by CITES.

the orderly development of the whaling industry.' It is a multinational body that had in 2019, representatives from 89 countries. The IWC carries our research on whales and dolphins to determine the health of their populations and brings in appropriate conservation measures to ensure their survival. In 1982, the IWC moratorium on whaling was introduced in response to falling populations of whales (Figure 9.41) and public opposition to whaling. The moratorium prohibits all commercial whaling. The moratorium was passed by a majority vote with some countries, such as Japan, Soviet Union and Norway lodging objections to the ban. Although commercial whaling is prohibited, Japan still catches some species of whale under IWC Special Permit Whaling, which is supposed to be for scientific research. Norway and Iceland continue to commercially catch whales, either under objection to the moratorium or under reservation to it. They set their own catch limits but must submit them to the IWC. Aboriginal subsistence whaling is practised by four nations: Denmark, Russia, the Grenadines and the United States. This is the catching of small numbers of whales by indigenous populations and is not designed to maximise profits or catches.

UNESCO biosphere reserves

Conservation projects can only succeed if local people are involved and their livelihoods considered. The United Nations Educational, Scientific and Cultural Organisation (UNESCO) has established areas around the world that try to balance the needs of humans, whilst also protecting ecosystems and species. **Biosphere reserves** are proposed and maintained by

> **KEY WORD**
>
> **biosphere reserve:** UNESCO designated area where sustainable human activity, education and research occurs alongside areas of conservation

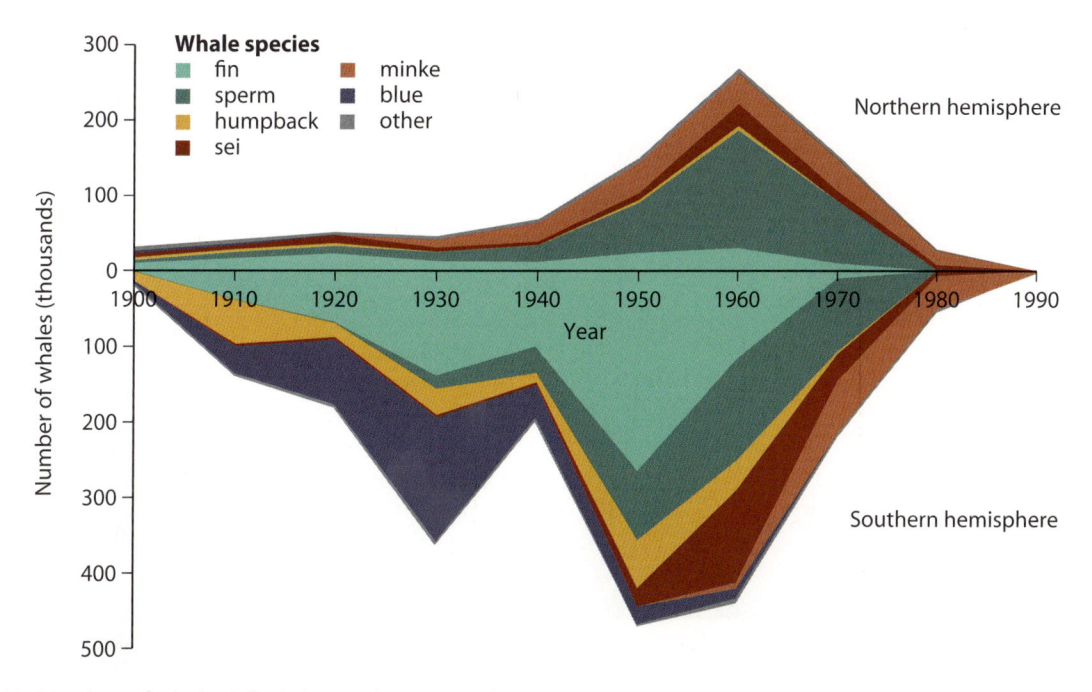

Figure 9.41: Number of whales killed during the twentieth century.

national governments but must meet strict criteria according the UNESCO rules. Each biosphere, consists of three types of area, each with a particular function. The three types are:

- **core areas**, which are protected ecosystems in which ecosystems and species are strictly protected
- **buffer, or care, areas** around the core which can be used for activities that do not damage the ecosystem; they are often used for scientific research and education
- **transition, or sustainable development, zones** where most human activity is permitted; they allow sustainable activities and promote local economic development.

By 2019, there were 686 biosphere reserves in 122 countries, many of which include marine and coastal areas. The success of biospheres is due to the engagement of local people who can benefit economically from the conservation measures that are put in place. Figure 9.42 shows part of the coastline of the Isle of Man. The Isle of Man is a self-governing British Crown dependency in the Irish Sea between Great Britain and Ireland. In 2016, it became the first entire nation to be awarded biosphere reserve status. As an island, it has an extensive coastline and areas of marine environment which are rich in biodiversity. Large populations of Atlantic cod, European eel and basking sharks are found in the surrounding waters. The seabed has reefs and areas of seagrass which are now protected under the biosphere reserve, and dolphins and minke whales are frequent visitors. Fishing is carried out sustainably and is limited to a few fishing grounds. The biosphere reserve engages the local people by bringing in tourists and school children and local people are involved in education, scientific research and conservation projects. The success of the project is primarily due to the partnership between the Isle of Man Government, the local people and nature. A map of the Isle of Man, showing the different biosphere zones is shown in Figure 9.43.

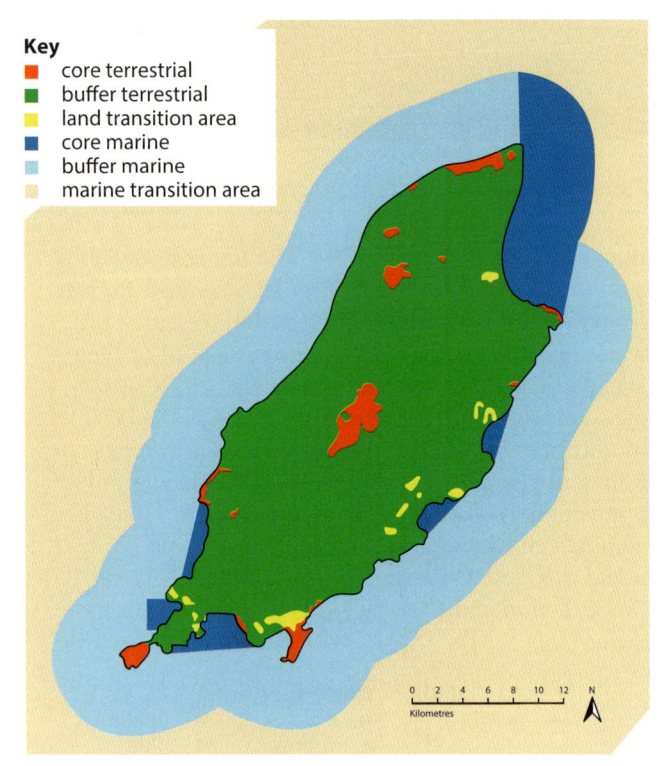

Figure 9.43: Isle of Man biosphere map. Core, buffer and transition zones are clearly marked.

Figure 9.42: Part of the coastline of the Isle of Man – a biosphere region.

Marine zoos and aquaria

Keeping marine animals in captivity, particularly mammals such as whales, is a very controversial topic. For many years, zoos and aquaria had a poor reputation and were seen as places that did not support the conservation of organisms. They frequently bought animals, sometimes endangered species, that had been trapped in the wild and them kept them in captivity for the entertainment of people. The conditions that animals were kept in were often poor, with animals given inappropriate diets, a lack of room and poor stimulation. Whales and dolphins are often trained to perform for the entertainment of humans. Large organisms such as killer whales, which may travel over 100 km a day in the open ocean, are kept in very confined conditions.

Recently, the focus of many marine zoos and aquaria has changed from being an entertainment industry to being involved in conservation projects. They are still areas where people pay to observe species that they would not be able to see in the wild, but much more care is taken to ensure animal welfare. Areas that marine zoos and aquaria are now helping with conservation include:

- safely raising animals in captivity away from hunting or habitat loss
- participating in breeding programmes to restore wild populations
- carrying out scientific research on animals
- educating visitors about the threats facing species in the wild
- using money paid by visitors to fund conservation projects in the wild.

The Florida Aquarium in Tampa, United States, embodies that approach that modern aquaria often take. It is a non-profit-making aquarium with a range of species kept with high levels of animal welfare. It carries out research on a range of species including corals and sharks and supports conservation projects such as the restoration of coral reefs. There is an extensive range of education events for all ages to help inform the public about environmental issues.

Marine zoos and aquaria will always cause a degree of controversy. Fortunately, the number of old-fashioned zoos, where animal welfare was not a high priority are decreasing. Zoos and aquaria have had to find a new, much more ethical niche that works to support and help our natural world.

Ecotourism

Since the 1970s, there has been a rise in tourism that is based on an appreciation of the natural environment. This form of tourism is called ecotourism (Figure 9.44). The aim of ecotourism is to ensure that travel is responsible, conserves the environment, sustains the well-being of local people and is also educational. The key principles of ecotourism are to:

- minimise the physical, social, behavioural and psychological impacts on the environment and local people

Figure 9.44: Comparison of (a) a sustainable ecotourist lodge in a coastal area of Tanzania and (b) a typical unsustainable mass tourist resort.

- build environmental and cultural awareness and respect
- provide positive experiences for visitors and hosts
- provide direct financial benefits for conservation
- generate financial benefits for both local people and private industry
- deliver memorable interpretative experiences to visitors that help raise sensitivity of the host countries' political, environmental and social climates
- design, construct and operate low-impact facilities
- recognise the rights and spiritual beliefs of indigenous people and work in partnership with them to create empowerment.

Ecotourism can offer local communities a means of making a profit from tourism and reducing harmful activities such as intensive aquaculture and overfishing. If the conservation of the natural environment becomes essential to the income of a local community, people will engage with it. For example, sea otters could be seen by fishers as a nuisance predator that reduce fish catches. If ecotourism depends on the survival of the sea otters and their habitats, and this ecotourism generates higher profits, there is more incentive to conserve them.

Different types of ecotourism

One problem with ecotourism is that it has been defined in many different ways. Most environmental organisations suggest that ecotourism is a nature-based, sustainably managed, conservation supporting and environmentally educating tourism. The tourist industry and governments often create the idea that ecotourism is any tourism that is linked to nature. This means that many tourist resorts that are not sustainable or environmentally sensitive are classed as ecotourist resorts. Other types of tourism are often confused with ecotourism but may be not be as environmentally sustainable.

Wildlife or nature tourism is when tourists travel to see animals and plants in their natural habitats. It can include activities such as whale watching or trips to Antarctica to see the diversity of wildlife. Although these activities are involved with nature, they are often not sustainable. Tourists may stay in large hotels, affect the behaviour of animals, interfere with breeding sites and damage local habitats.

Adventure tourism is when tourists take part in activities such as jungle trekking and whitewater rafting. It also includes reaching parts of the world that are difficult to get to. Despite being immersed in the natural world, these activities are not necessarily examples of ecotourism.

However, ecotourists can engage in many different types of activities, all of which attempt to benefit the environment and local community.

Ecolodging is when tourists stay in accommodation that has been built with environmental awareness. It may range from small hotels built using sustainable materials to remote camps where tents and small lodges are carefully sited in areas of ecological importance. The accommodation is close to the area of interest so that it can be reached easily by, for example, walking or canoeing. The tourists usually want to see species in their natural habitats, learn about local cultures and immerse themselves in the area.

Agrotourism is when tourists stay on small rural farms. They may witness sustainable farming methods, and in some cases take part in the farming to help local people. Agrotourism encourages local people to practise sustainable farming methods and helps them make additional money.

Community development can be part of ecotourism if organisations offer opportunities to tourists to join projects that protect the land of communities threatened by industry or deforestation. Tourists stay with local people and help with projects such as tree planting or building sustainable housing. They gain a better understanding of the local people and the communities benefit from the help and additional income.

Factors that must be taken into account

If ecotourism is to be truly sustainable and beneficial to nature and local people, there are several factors that have to be considered. There must be balance between the acceptable risk of these factors and helping local people gain an income. Factors to be considered include the fact that:

- Ecotourists often go to environmentally fragile areas.
- Visits may occur during sensitive periods, such as during breeding or hatching periods.
- Ecotourism could lead to mass tourism at the site if the attraction becomes better known.
- Distant locations require long flights, which cause high carbon dioxide emissions.
- There may be impacts on ecosystems such as soil erosion, disturbance of wildlife, trampling of plants, removal of vegetation (for example, collection of plants or firewood) and the introduction of invasive species on clothing or equipment.
- There is a risk that litter and refuse will be dropped unintentionally and water polluted (even though most ecotourists are interested in conservation).
- More accommodation needs to be built, which requires resources such as wood and the clearance of areas to provide more space.
- Some tourists may purchase souvenirs from threatened or endangered species, such as coral.

9 Human impacts on marine ecosystems

Responsible tourism

Unrestricted development of tourist resorts with no consideration of their impact on the marine environment is potentially very damaging and unsustainable. The goal should be responsible tourism, in which both the tourist industry and the environment benefit. When a new tourist business is being developed, certain factors should be taken into account, including **sustainable development**.

Energy conservation

Tourists fly to remote locations and then use road or boat connections to take them from the airport to the resort. This creates a large **carbon footprint** that needs to be minimised. Flights should be organised so that there are fewer of them but they operate at maximal capacity. Tourists are encouraged to use energy-efficient public transport, such as electric trams, wherever possible rather than cars. Many ecotourists travel locally by bicycle or trek. Some ecotourist companies offset their carbon footprint from the flight by planting mangroves or trees for every tour party that is flown there.

Accommodation should be energy efficient, as illustrated by the Laguna Lodge, Guatemala shown in Figure 9.45. In colder regions, buildings should be fully insulated to reduce heat loss. In warmer regions, the air conditioning should be minimised, and buildings designed to maximise natural cooling. Low-energy light bulbs and similar technology can reduce electricity consumption. Rather than using energy that is based on non-renewable fossil fuels, electricity can be generated using more environmentally friendly methods. Solar panels, wind power and wave power are used in many ecoresorts.

Recycling

Even though they may be careful, large numbers of visitors produce large amounts of refuse. Disposal of refuse, particularly plastic, is problematic but can be done responsibly. Hotels and other service industries should have recycling policies, and tourists and local people should be encouraged to place their refuse in the appropriate recycling bins. Glass, metals, paper and many forms of plastic can be recycled into other products rather than being discarded. This also creates more revenue from waste. Old plant material and food can be recycled to make fertilisers for agriculture.

Sustainable materials

Building accommodation requires raw materials such as stone, concrete and wood. Developers should be careful to harvest these in a sustainable way. It is easy to chop down forest trees to produce timber for building, but this would quickly cause deforestation and loss of biodiversity. Ideally, locally produced materials should be used. Timber should be from sites where new trees are planted, and stones and bricks from demolished buildings can be used. Figure 9.45 shows the Laguna

> **KEY WORDS**
>
> **sustainable development:** development that meets the needs of the present without compromising the ability of future generations to meet their needs
>
> **carbon footprint:** the total amount of carbon dioxide released into the atmosphere by a particular activity

Figure 9.45: (a) The Laguna Lodge in the Tzantizotz nature reserve, Guatemala, is built from local materials, including walls made from adobe and clay and lampshades from corn paper. (b) It is a zero-carbon resort, with electricity for lighting, hot water and wifi generated by 180 solar panels.

Lodge in the Tzantizotz nature reserve, Guatemala, which is built with locally sourced sustainable materials such as adobe, clay and even locally made corn paper. Similarly, structures such as new roads should be built with sustainable materials. Rather than large, concrete hotels, most ecotourist resorts tend to have small lodges that are built in the style of the local area.

Sponsorship of conservation

Tourist resorts have the potential to help conservation efforts. When visiting a nature area, even the most environmentally aware tourists can potentially affect plants and wildlife negatively. Their presence may scare animals or affect migration routes, and hiking through areas can damage habitats. However, if some of the profits generated by the tourism are used for local conservation projects and to help local people, tourism can have a very positive effect on conservation efforts. Costa Rica has a well-developed ecotourist industry and businesses use money made from tourism to sponsor conservation projects. Money is also used to sponsor the education of local people and improve resources such as sanitation and plumbing systems.

The Bosca del Cabo Rainforest Lodge

In this section, which is used as an illustration to provide some context to sustainability, we cover the Bosca del Cabo Rainforest Lodge on the Osa Peninsular, Costa Rica (Figure 9.46). It is an excellent example of a sustainable tourism project. In this section we cover the need for education, renewable energy, conservation, plus how the Rainforest Lodge reduces pollution, food miles, and how the project also helps the local people. It is a lodge from which tourists can visit areas of outstanding natural beauty around the coasts and forests of Costa Rica. It advertises itself as providing many environmentally and culturally friendly.

Educational activities include:

- providing forums for guests to learn about local conservation, wildlife programmes and general information about rainforests
- providing guidelines for workers regarding recycling at the lodge and in their own homes
- educating staff on hunting and the conservation of natural resources
- sponsoring clean-up projects and promoting beach health and raising awareness of the need to keep beaches pristine and natural
- hosting interns from around the world so that they can learn about sustainable tourism
- exposing guests to local culture, (for example through dance classes, local crafts and reading materials about the area)
- sponsoring three children of Bosque employees to attend the local bilingual school (Nueva Hoja).

Waste management policies include:

- reusing building materials from previous structures for new constructions whenever possible
- providing receptacles and transportation to recycling centres for plastic, aluminium and glass, for both staff and guests
- recycling paper, envelopes, packing materials, newspapers and any other feasible products
- reusing fresh food scraps as compost for the gardens
- donating cooked food scraps to a local farmer for feeding his pigs.

Low or zero impact practices include:

- implementing a constructed wetlands filtration system for processing of grey water
- using organic compost as fertiliser
- using mainly bamboo and plantation-grown wood for construction
- using biodegradable soaps and cleaning products whenever possible
- creating drainage around the lodge by taking erosion control measures and planting

Figure 9.46: The Bosca del Cabo Rainforest Lodge in Costa Rica.

- providing carpools for workers to decrease the number of vehicles coming and going from the town
- reducing the number of vehicles going into town by combining guest transfers whenever possible
- creating reusable bags for transporting laundry, and so on, to and from town
- providing signage in the cabins asking for cooperation in reducing water use, power use and unnecessary laundry
- using biodegradable straws and stir sticks at the bar
- participating with the Costa Rica Tourism Board in their Certificate for Sustainable Tourism (CST), a programme to protect the country's cultural and natural treasures through responsible tourism.

Alternative energy is used by:

- generating most of the lodges' power from micro-hydro and solar systems
- installing low-power consuming LED and compact florescent light bulbs for fixed lights and flashlights
- installing a non-chemical ionising system and solar-powered pool pump for pool maintenance.

There is a focus on the local community by:

- cooking with local ingredients
- preparing local dishes and typical food to encourage local Costa Rican culture and traditions
- buying the majority of food supplies locally
- buying and cooking with organically grown food when possible
- hiring local Costa Ricans as staff
- selling primarily locally or nationally crafted souvenirs in the shop
- hosting a local artisan once a week to display and sell her work directly to the guests.

Support and participation is provided by:

- hosting the annual Bosque del Cabo Jungle Golf Tournament, with all proceeds going to the women of the Osa
- hosting of the annual science meeting of the Friends of the Osa
- actively participating in Friends of the Osa and their related projects
- donating to multiple projects led by local and international organisations focused mostly on community development and conservation.

Control of invasive species

We have already discussed the threat posed by invasive species. Humans now travel further around the world than ever and so pose an increased threat. Invasive species may 'hitch a ride' on ships, in boxes of food, even on our clothes. If they are transported to an area with no natural predators and ideal conditions, their populations will rapidly increase. They can outcompete native species and over consume prey organisms. It is essential to monitor and control their spread. Controlling invasive species is often difficult and conservation groups often monitor their spread. As already stated, a range of methods have been tried to remove carp in the Murray–Darling Basin, Australia. Using electric shocks, offering a reward to people for catching carp and releasing a herpes virus that only infects carp have all been tried.

Lionfish are native to the Indo-Pacific region but were introduced around the coast of South Florida in the 1980s. It is not clear how the fish were introduced but it may have been due to accidental release from aquaria. Each fish can consume up to 460 000 prey per year and they have a very high breeding rate. They have no natural predators in the West Atlantic, Gulf of Mexico or Caribbean Sea and so their population and range has risen dramatically. By 2015, sightings had been reported among almost the entire length of the Eastern coast of north America (Figure 9.47).

Controlling the spread of lionfish is not easy. It is going to be impossible to totally remove them, so the main aim is to prevent their numbers increasing. Groupers and sharks are known to prey on lionfish in the Pacific and it may be possible to increase the population of these predatory species by protecting them from fishing. In Honduras, divers have tried to train local sharks to eat the lionfish. Lionfish are edible with well-flavoured, healthy meat and governments around the area are encouraging fishers to take as many lion fish as possible to sell to restaurants.

The New Zealand Government has reported problems with a range of invasive marine species and actively monitors marine ecosystems for the presence of new species. Pumping out ballast water from ships has been identified as a major route for invasive species. Ships may not discharge ballast water in the sea unless it is from a non-coastal source, is freshwater, is treated to destroy any species, or is released into an onshore processing plant. The hulls of ships must also be free from biofouling on arrival into New Zealand waters. If invasive species are discovered, a full survey is performed to gauge the threat that it poses, and appropriate action taken to prevent spread. Two

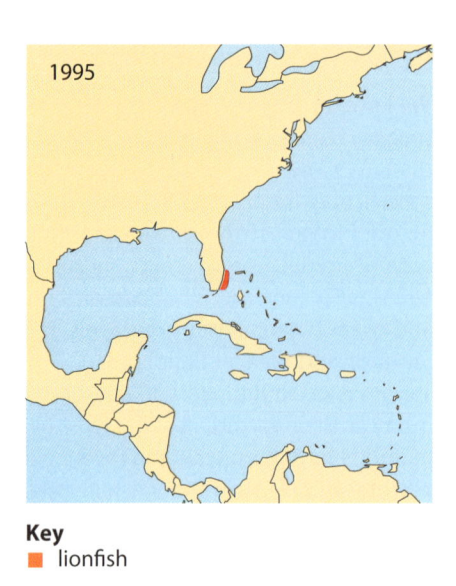

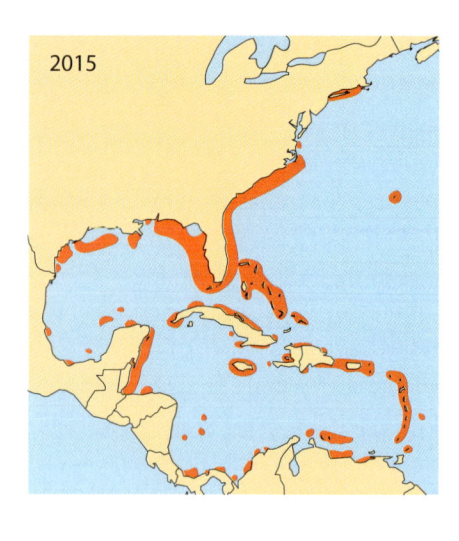

Figure 9.47: Spread of lionfish along the Eastern coast of the American continent.

invasive species that are actively controlled are the sea squirt, *Pyura doppelgangera*, and the fan worm, *Sabella spallanzanii* (Figure 9.48). Both these organisms attach to the rocks and the seabed and can compete with native species for food. They could cause economic damage by reducing the yield of mussels and other commercially import species. Boat hulls and coastal rocks are constantly monitored, and mass removal exercises performed to prevent further spread of these species.

Figure 9.48: The fan worm, *Sabella spallanzanii*, an invasive species around New Zealand.

Role of international cooperation

Most of the big issues facing the marine environment cannot be solved by the actions of one nation alone. Plastic released into the ocean by one nation will affect organisms in all parts of the ocean. Excess carbon dioxide produced by more industrial nations affects the temperature of the whole planet and causes climate change everywhere. If we are to truly conserve our marine environment, we need a coordinated approach with all nations working together. Organisations like the United Nations are intergovernmental organisations that aim to bring all nations together to help the marine environment. The problem that we have, however, is that most agreements are voluntary and require nations to work together. By 2019, CITES had been agreed by 183 nations and the IWC had 89 members. CITES, however, does not extend to those nations that have not signed. The IWC moratorium banning whaling theoretically only applies to the 89 members of the IWC. Compliance by nations that have made international agreements is also voluntary. For example, Japan still carries out whaling under the auspices of scientific whaling, while Norway and Iceland continue some whaling. To enable successful conservation, international agreements must be sought, but these will only ever be effective if most nations reach agreement.

MATHS SKILLS 9.3

STATISTICAL TESTS – STANDARD ERROR AND 95% CONFIDENCE LIMITS

In Chapter 7 you looked at standard deviation as a descriptive measure of spread of data about the mean. By calculating the standard error and 95% confidence limits of a data set we can compare the means of different sets of data with precision. It enables us to calculate the range of values within which there is 95% probability that the true mean lies.

Worked example

Table 9.15 shows the weekly number of visitors to an ecotourist resort during a 10-week period in 2017. An aquaculture project was started during 2018. The local government decided to determine whether the aquaculture project was having a negative effect on the number of visitors. The weekly number of visitors during 2019 was compared with the weekly number of visitors in 2017.

Use standard error and 95% confidence limits to determine whether there was a significant change in number of visitors after building the aquaculture project.

Week	Number of visitors per week in 2017	Number of visitors per week in 2019
1	89	65
2	78	68
3	79	56
4	124	98
5	132	101
6	116	120
7	89	102
8	82	92
9	76	75
10	78	45

Table 9.15: Weekly visitors to an ecolodge in 2017 and 2019.

Step 1 Calculate the mean number of visitors and standard deviations (see Chapter 7 for a reminder of how to calculate standard deviation.)

	2017	2019
mean	94.3	82.2
standard deviation, σ	21.3	23.9

Table 9.16: Mean and standard deviations.

Step 2 Use the formula to calculate the standard error for each year.

$$S.E. = \frac{\sigma}{\sqrt{n}}$$

Where

$S.E.$ is the standard error

σ is the standard deviation

n is the number of values

So, for 2017, the $S.E. = \frac{21.3}{\sqrt{10}} = 6.7$

and for 2019, the $S.E. = \frac{23.9}{\sqrt{10}} = 7.6$

Step 3 Calculate the 95% confidence limits. There is a probability of 95% that all values lie between a range of two standard errors above and below the mean.

In other words, 95% confidence limits = $\bar{x} \pm 2S.E.$

So, for 2017, the 95% confidence limits are 94.3 ± (2 × 6.7), which is between (94.3 + 13.4) and (94.3 − 13.4).

95% confidence limits are 80.9 to 107.7.

For 2019, the 95% confidence limits are 82.2 ± (2 × 7.6), which is between (82.2 + 15.2) and (82.2 − 15.2).

95% confidence limits are 67.0 to 97.4

Step 4 Compare the means and 95% confidence limits of the two sets of data.

From our data in Table 9.16, the mean number of visitors in 2017 is clearly higher than the mean number of visitors in 2019. We can now look at the confidence limits to see whether there is a significant difference in the number of visitors between the two years. We do this by looking to see if the confidence

CONTINUED

limits overlap. If there is no overlap, the difference between the means is statistically significant. If there is an overlap, the difference between the means is not statistically significant.

In our example, the confidence limits clearly overlap. This means that although our calculated means are different, we cannot say with 95% confidence that they are statistically significantly different. There is still a chance that the means may not be different from each other.

Figure 9.49 shows us how we can use confidence limits as error bars on graphs. This also helps us to visualise any overlaps of confidence limits. Mean values are plotted and error bars added at the upper and lower confidence limit.

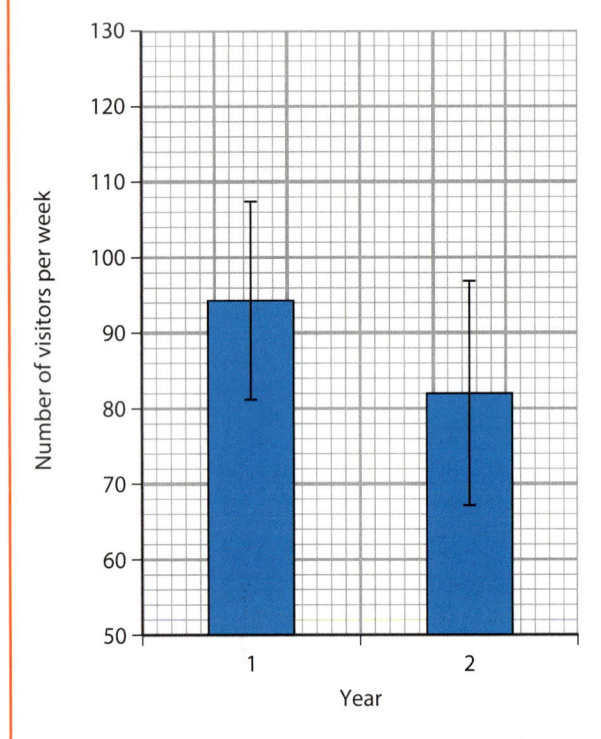

Figure 9.49: Graph of mean visitor numbers with 95% confidence limits as error bars.

Questions

1. The rates of photosynthesis for three species of marine algae that had been illuminated with the same light intensity were measured. The results are shown in Table 9.17.

Rates of photosynthesis / mm³ oxygen per hour		
Species A	Species B	Species C
15	19	21
17	22	25
12	21	28
14	25	31
18	27	27
13	21	26
12	18	27
11	17	31

Table 9.17: Rates of photosynthesis of three species of algae.

   a. Calculate the mean rate of photosynthesis for each species of alga.
   b. Calculate the standard deviation for each species of alga.
   c. Calculate the standard error for each species of alga.
   d. Comment on whether there are significantly different rates of photosynthesis between the three species of algae.

2. The number of sightings of lionfish per day were recorded in two areas of ocean. In one area, sharks that had been trained to eat lionfish had been released. The results are shown in Table 9.18. Calculate the mean number of sightings per day and use standard error and 95% confidence limits to determine whether releasing the sharks significantly affected the lionfish population.

CONTINUED

Number of lionfish sightings per day	
Area with no sharks	Area with sharks
22	18
26	11
15	25
17	4
9	11
29	23
35	12
31	14
41	11
32	6

Table 9.18: Number of lionfish sightings in two areas of ocean.

Test yourself

13 Use these words to complete the sentences below.

invasive species, conservation, bycatch, bioaccumulate, TBT, seagrass

Many human activities have damaged the environment and produced a need for _____.

There has been extensive damage to habitats such as mangrove forests, coral reefs and _____.

The fishing industry has caused fish stocks to be reduced due to overfishing and the catching of _____.

Humans have released pollutants into the oceans such as _____ and mercury which _____ along food chains.

The escape of fish from aquaculture has led to _____ affecting native populations.

14 Explain why the following are essential for a successful conservation project:
   a establishing ecological linkages
   b ensuring local engagement.

15 a List *three* reasons why conservation is important and *one* reasons why it may not be necessary.
   b Explain why the current mass extinction is different from previous mass extinctions.

16 In many areas of ocean, the number of top predators is very low because of overfishing. Explain why the conservation measures used to protect the grey seals should also include measures to protect sharks and killer whales.

17 Explain why the following activities would help ensure that ecotourism is sustainable:
   a recycling refuse
   b using solar power to generate electricity for hotels
   c using local wood and materials.

18 Summarise the roles of:
   a CITES
   b IWC moratorium
   c IUCN Red List

> **PROJECT: RAISING PUBLIC AWARENESS ABOUT THE THREAT TO OUR OCEANS**
>
> Create a series of information posters and leaflets to raise public awareness about one of the following:
>
> - the threat that plastic poses to the marine environment
> - the need for conservation of a named endangered marine species listed in the IUCN Red List
> - the threats posed to marine environments by invasive species.
>
> The posters and leaflets should be eye catching but also informative. They should be able to explain the issues to members of the general public who do not have a scientific background.
>
> **Thinking about your project**
>
> A group of learners could display their posters and leaflets in a classroom and invite people to view them. The audience could then rate each display for information quality, presentation and clarity.

> **EXAM-STYLE QUESTIONS**
>
> 1 a State what is meant by *the greenhouse effect*. [3]
>   b i Describe the possible causes of global warming. [5]
>   ii Explain the potential consequences of global warming on marine ecosystems. [7]
>   [Total: 15]
>
> 2 The concentration of mercury found in body tissues was analysed for different species of marine fish. Concentrations were compared against the mean trophic level of the fish. The mean trophic level takes account of the different types of food a fish eats.
>
> The results are shown in Table 9.19.
>
> | Species | Mean mercury concentration / ppm | Standard deviation | Mean trophic level |
> |---|---|---|---|
> | Swordfish | 0.995 | 0.870 | 4.5 |
> | bigeye tuna | 0.689 | 0.341 | 4.5 |
> | grouper | 0.448 | 0.278 | 4.2 |
> | Patagonian tooth fish | 0.354 | 0.303 | 4.3 |
> | halibut | 0.241 | 0.157 | 3.8 |
> | monkfish | 0.181 | 0.139 | 4.5 |
> | skipjack tuna | 0.144 | 0.119 | 3.8 |
> | jacksmelt | 0.081 | 0.050 | 3.1 |
> | sardine | 0.013 | 0.015 | 2.7 |
> | oyster | 0.012 | 0.035 | * |
>
> *The trophic level of oysters is difficult to assess because they filter feed on dead organic remains.
>
> **Table 9.19:** Mercury concentrations in body tissues of different fish species.

CONTINUED

a   Describe how mercury concentration changes as mean trophic level increases. [2]

b   Suggest and explain reasons why some fish species have larger standard deviations than others. [3]

c   Give an explanation for the differences in mercury concentrations of the different fish species. [4]

[Total: 9]

3   Dredging is sometimes used to clear harmful waste, such as heavy metals, from sediments at the base of estuaries. Figure 9.50 shows the effect of dredging contaminated sediment from the bottom of an estuary on the rate of cancers found in fish. The estuary once had effluent entering it from an industrial plant. The industrial plant was closed in 1983 and the river was dredged between 1989 and 1990.

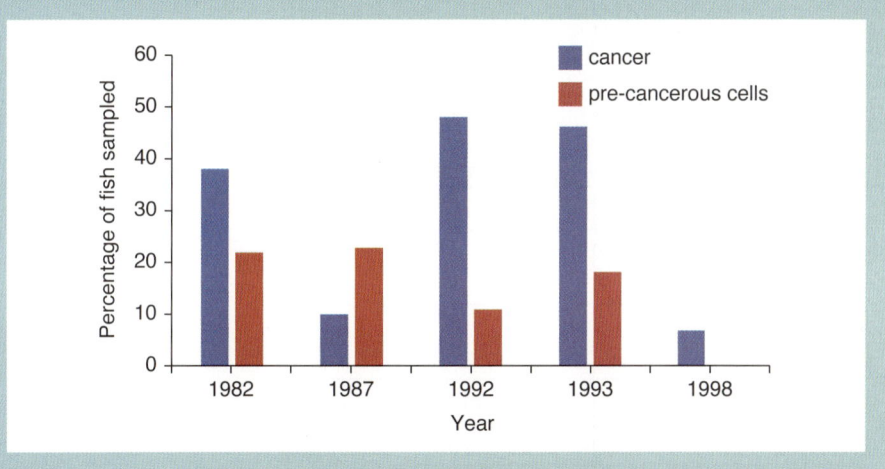

Figure 9.50: Percentage of fish sampled that had liver cancer or pre-cancerous cells.

a   i   In 1992, 84 fish were sampled. Calculate the number of fish found to have liver cancer. [2]

   ii Describe the change in number of fish with cancer and pre-cancerous cells over time. [2]

   iii Suggest an explanation for the changes in fish with cancer and pre-cancerous cells. [4]

b   Discuss other potential effects of dredging the bottom of an estuary on marine life in an estuary. [4]

[Total: 12]

4   An investigation into the effects of a desalination plant sited on the Mediterranean coast on the diversity of invertebrate animal species was carried out. Species were randomly sampled on one day in the waters near the outflow from the desalination plant and at a similar, control area further up the coast. The number of each type of species found was recorded along with several abiotic factors. The results are shown in Tables 9.20 and 9.21.

CONTINUED

Species	Number of individual animals in each location	
	Desalination plant	Control area
red sea squirt	5	27
yellow sea squirt	7	24
common brittlestar	4	5
rock crab	15	8
feather star	2	17
common sea urchin	15	7
purple sea urchin	0	16

Table 9.20: Numbers of species found in water around a desalination plant and a control area.

Abiotic factor	Desalination plant water	Control area water
pH	6.7	7.2
mean 10 m depth temperature °C	16	12
oxygen concentration / mg dm^{-3}	6	9
light penetration	low	high
salinity / %	4.0	3.4

Table 9.21: Some abiotic data for water around a desalination plant and control area.

a i Explain why the invertebrate animals were sampled at random. [1]

   ii Explain the purpose of the control site. [1]

   iii State what is meant by the term *abiotic factors*. [1]

b i Describe the general effects of the desalination plant on the invertebrate species. [3]

   ii Calculate the percentage difference in rock crabs in the water around the desalination plant compared with the control area. [2]

   iii Suggest and explain reasons for the effect of the desalination plant on the abiotic factors. [3]

   iv Suggest and explain reasons for the differences in numbers of species found in the water around the desalination plant compared to the control area. [3]

[Total: 14]

CONTINUED

5 Coho and chinook salmon populations have declined throughout the twentieth century. In 2003, a conservation programme was set up in a North American river to stop the decline in numbers of the two species of salmon. The measures taken included:

- creation of three river passages past a large dam, to allow salmon access to upstream areas of the river
- restrictions placed on the use of fertilisers on agricultural land in the upstream areas
- land near the river purchased to prevent the expansion of industries
- salmon fry cultivated in hatcheries and released into the river.

The numbers of both species of salmon found in the upstream areas each year are shown in Figure 9.51.

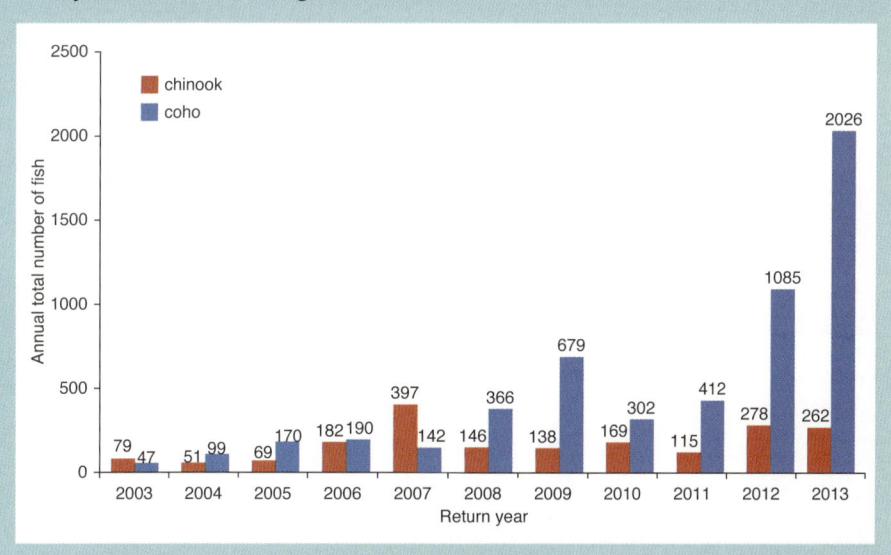

Figure 9.51: Numbers of coho and chinook salmon passing upstream of dam.

a i   Compare the effect of the conservation measures on the coho and chinook salmon. [3]
   ii Calculate the mean rate of increase in chinook salmon between 2003 and 2013. [2]
   iii Assess the success of the conservation project for both species of salmon. [3]
b i   Explain why creating the river passages could help conserve the salmon. [2]
   ii Suggest why restrictions were placed on the use of fertilisers. [3]
   iii State **one** risk of introducing cultivated salmon from hatcheries. [1]

[Total: 14]

COMMAND WORD

assess: make an informed judgement

CONTINUED

6 a Explain what is meant by:
  i conservation [2]
  ii ecotourism. [2]

 b Explain how the establishment of a conservation area around a coastal community could cause conflict with the fishing and tourist industries. [5]

 c Discuss how a tourist resort could be developed responsibly in order to minimise damage to the environment. [6]

[Total: 15]

7 Figure 9.52 shows the abundance of commercially important fish at different distances from the centre of a marine protected area (MPA). The central area of the MPA is a region with no fishing and the outer regions of the MPA have limited regulated fishing. Outside the MPA, the sea is fully fished with few restrictions.

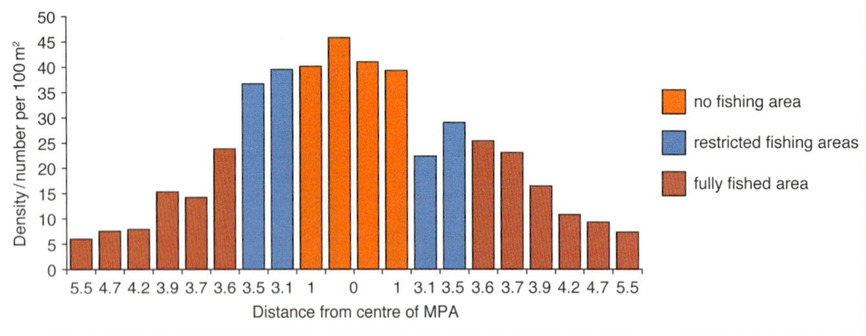

Figure 9.52: Fish density at increasing distances from the centre of a marine protected area.

 a i Describe how the density of fish changes with distance from the centre of the MPA. [2]
   ii Explain the change in density of fish as distance from the centre of the MPA increases. [3]
 b i Suggest why the local fishing industry would object to the setting up of more MPAs. [2]
   ii Suggest why the MPA could be of benefit to the local fishing industry. [3]

[Total: 10]

CONTINUED

8 Table 9.22 shows the number of ecotourists that visited some countries in 1990 and 1999.

Country	Number of visits × 1000	
	1990	1999
South Africa	1028	6026
Costa Rica	435	1027
Indonesia	2178	4700
Belize	88	157
Ecuador	362	509
Botswana	543	740

Table 9.22: Number of ecotourists visiting countries in 1990 and 1999.

a **i** Calculate the percentage increase in ecotourist visits to Costa Rica between 1990 and 1999. [2]

ii Plot a bar chart of the data in Table 9.22. [5]

b Explain how ecotourism can be beneficial for conservation and local communities. [5]

[Total: 12]

9 Figure 9.53 shows the change in area of kelp forest in a marine reserve where fishing is prohibited, and a control area that is fully fished over a period of 18 years.

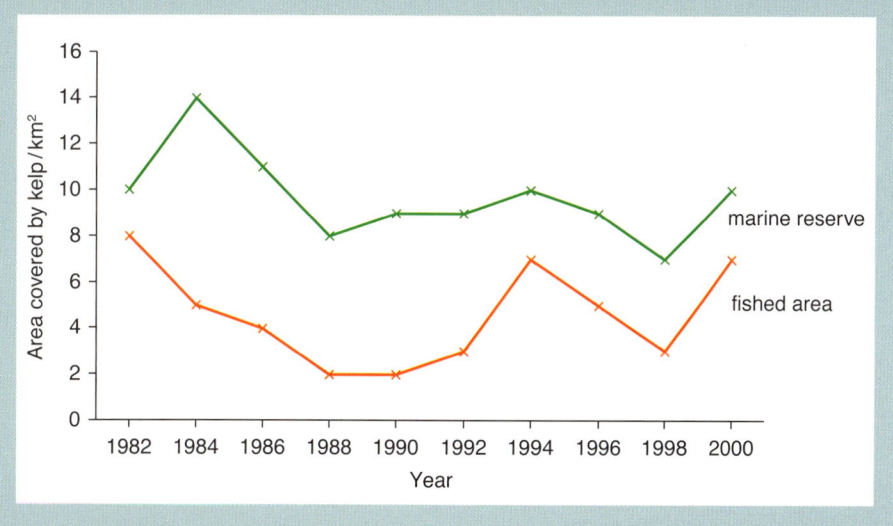

Figure 9.53: The change in area of seabed covered by kelp in a marine reserve and fully fished area.

CONTINUED

a Compare the changes in area covered by kelp in the marine reserve and the fished area. [3]

b Figure 9.54 shows part of the food web in the kelp forest. Use Figure 9.54 to explain the difference in area covered by kelp in the marine reserve and the protected area. [2]

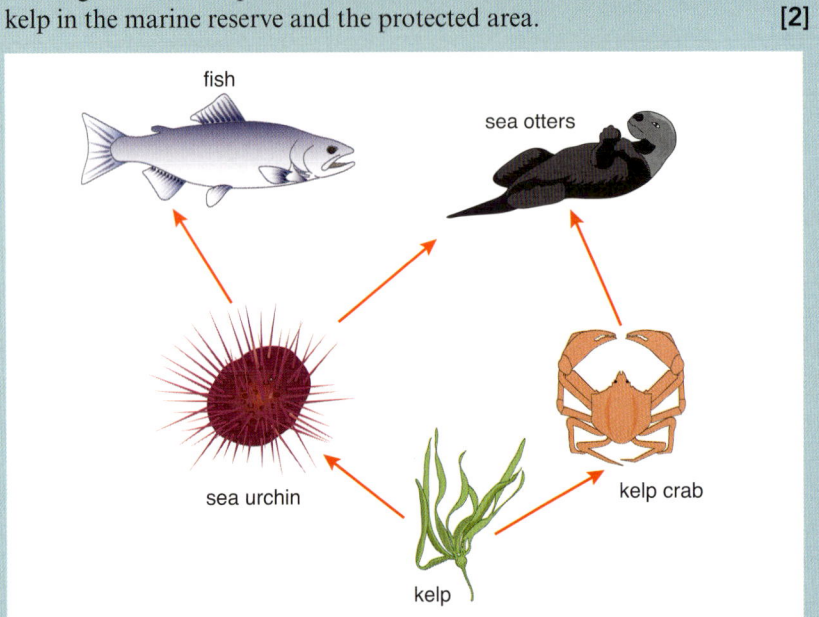

Figure 9.54: Part of kelp forest food web.

c Suggest *two* other factors that could cause the change in area covered by kelp over time. [2]

[Total: 7]

9 Human impacts on marine ecosystems

SELF-EVALUATION CHECKLIST

I can:	See section...	Needs more work	Almost there	Ready to move on
describe the effect of human activities on marine water quality, organisms and food webs	9.1			
explain the process of bioaccumulation	9.1			
describe the production of microplastics, the associated with them and ways to limit their release	9.1			
explain the natural and enhanced greenhouse effects	9.2			
describe the evidence for global warming and be able to evaluate the evidence for and against it being caused by human activity	9.2			
describe the impacts of global warming on the marine environment	9.2			
describe and explain the causes and effects of ocean acidification	9.3			
investigate the effect of pH on the loss of mass of mollusc shells	9.3			
explain the need for the conservation of marine ecosystems	9.4			
explain the roles of organisations such as the IUCN in marine conservation	9.4			
describe the threats posed by invasive species	9.4			
discuss a range of strategies for conserving marine species	9.4			

EXTENDED CASE STUDY: TROUBLE IN PARADISE – THE CHAGOS ISLANDS MARINE PROTECTED AREA

The Chagos archipelago is a collection of 55 islands in the central Indian Ocean (Figure 9.55). It is part of the British Indian Ocean Territory (BIOT). On 01 April 2010, the British government announced that Chagos would become the world's largest marine protected area (MPA). It would comprise a total surface area of 640 000 km² and would be a no-take reserve, with no fishing permitted, and there would be minimal human disturbance of the islands, beaches and ocean.

The area has one of the healthiest reef systems in the world, the largest coral atoll in the world and some of the cleanest waters, with exceptionally

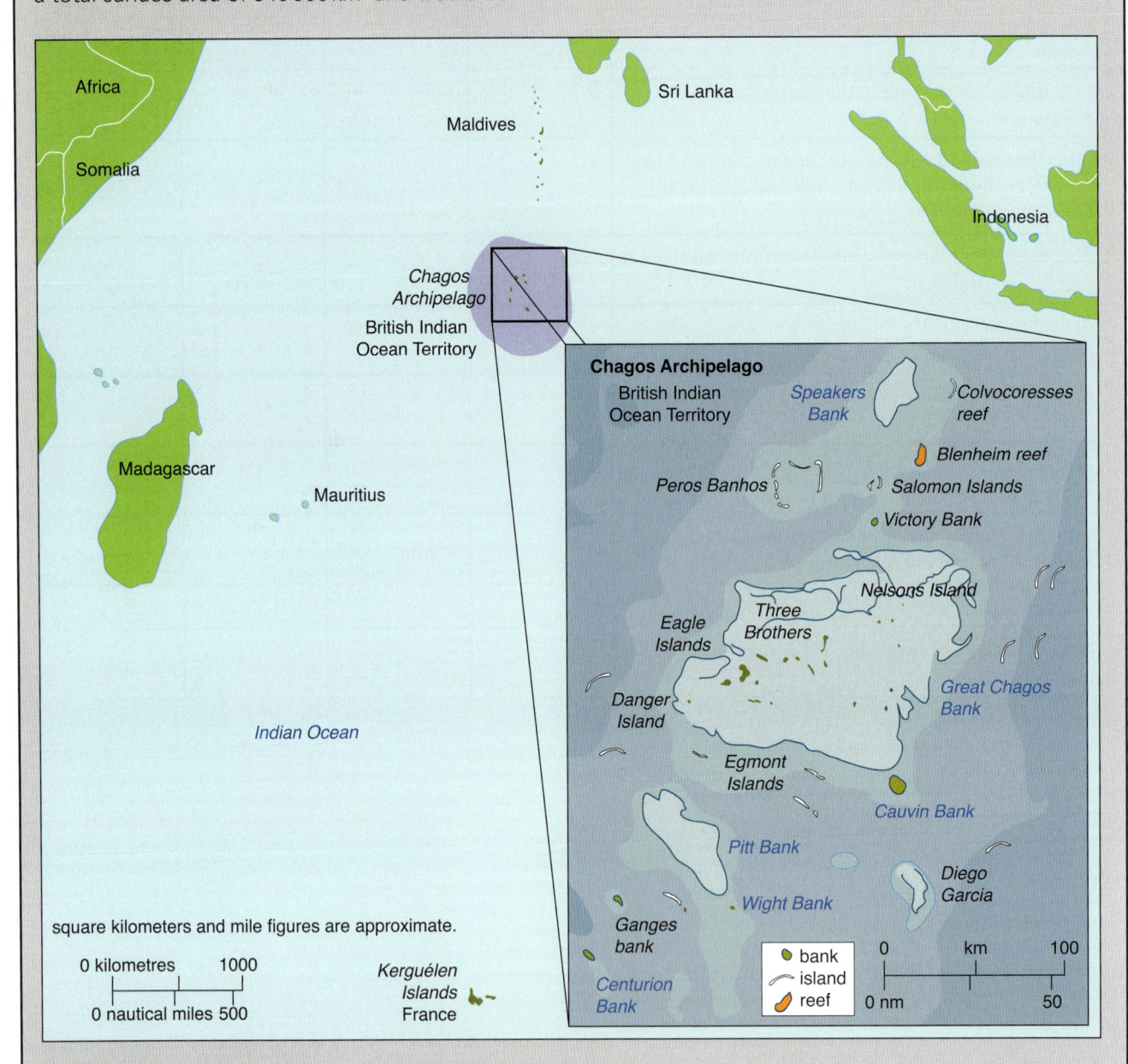

Figure 9.55: Map of the proposed Chagos marine protected area.

CONTINUED

high biodiversity. Many endangered and protected species inhabit the area.

There are more than 200 different species of coral, some of which are very rare. The reefs are very healthy and bleaching is low. Coral reefs in the Indian Ocean are under pressure from human activities, but the Chagos archipelago is an exception. The Chagos archipelago acts as a link between reefs in the east and west Indian Ocean.

There are more than 784 different species of fish found in the area. Some species, such as the Chagos clownfish, are only found in this area and it is a refuge for species of wrasse and grouper that have been hunted to extinction in other parts of the Indian Ocean. There are large populations of manta rays, sharks and tuna. Prior to the establishment of the reserve, large numbers of these fish were harvested, resulting in a collapse of their populations. The 'no-take' reserve would act as a refuge for them.

The islands are nursery sites for green and hawksbill turtles. Green turtles are classed as endangered and hawksbill turtles as critically endangered. Between 300 and 700 hawksbill and 400 to 800 green turtles are estimated to nest there annually.

The Chagos archipelago has a high diversity of sea birds. Ten of the islands are formally designated as Important Bird Areas by the conservation group Birdlife International. Protection of their habitat increases the number of nesting areas and the no-take fishing policy ensures a rich food source. In the past, rats were accidentally introduced to the islands by humans and efforts have been made to control their population because they eat eggs and chicks.

Coconut crabs are giant crustaceans that can reach more than 1 m in leg span and 3.5–5 kg in weight (Figure 9.56). The juveniles use empty coconut shells as protection, in a similar way to hermit crabs, and the adults climb trees using their claws to crack through coconuts. Coconut crabs are widely distributed but actually quite rare. They have been hunted for food, tourist souvenirs and as a fishing bait. They have also suffered from habitat loss and predation by introduced rats. The Chagos crabs are one of the most intact populations and

Figure 9.56: A coconut crab descending a tree.

act as an important source of crabs for other Indian Ocean islands.

The conservation of the area had several objectives.

- Creating one of the world's greatest conservation areas. The Chagos archipelago has a massive range of biodiversity and is as important as the Galápagos Islands or the Great Barrier Reef in ecological importance.
- Saving coral reefs. Millions of people who live in the countries bordering the Indian Ocean are dependent on coral reefs as a source for food, building materials, coastal protection and tourism revenue. The Chagos reefs are very healthy and could act as an area from which corals can be used to seed other ocean reefs that have been badly damaged.
- Saving marine wildlife and rebuilding fish stocks. The no-take zone would be a refuge area where turtles, birds and fish could breed without human impact. Animals that breed in these areas would spill over into surrounding areas, maintaining other populations.
- Food and jobs for people in the region. If the islands are protected, fishing in surrounding areas could be maintained because of the overspill of fish from the MPA. If reefs in other areas are improved, tourism would be maintained.
- Scientific research. A protected marine area with such a high biodiversity and range of habitats offers an unrivalled opportunity

CONTINUED

for scientific research, and could provide a comparison of areas with little human activity with polluted and damaged areas.

The creation of the MPA seems to be an important and highly valuable tool for global conservation. However, it has proved to be extremely controversial and there has been opposition to it. To appreciate the controversy fully, you need to understand some of the history of the islands, and know who the stakeholders in the area are.

History of the Chagos Islands

According to Maldivian tradition, fishers occasionally became stranded on some of the islands of the Chagos. They were considered to be too far from the Maldives to be colonised and remained uninhabited for many years. The first Europeans to discover them in the 1500s were Portuguese explorers who named the island group Bassas de Chagas. They were not considered to be important, and eventually the French laid claim to them in the 1700s. Coconut oil plantations were developed in the 1770s and slave labourers were brought over to work on them. In 1814, after the defeat of Napoleon, the islands passed to Great Britain and in 1840 slavery was abolished.

Many of the freed slaves remained on the island as free inhabitants, along with other people from different nationalities who moved there for work. The islands were administered from the Seychelles until 1903, when they became classed as being part of Mauritius. In 1965, the British government removed the Chagos archipelago from Mauritius to become the British Indian Ocean Territories prior to the establishment of independence in Mauritius in 1968. Mauritius retained fishing rights to the waters of the area and has disputed the sovereignty of the Chagos archipelago ever since independence.

By the late 1960s, the coconut plantations had become less profitable because of competition with larger plantations in the Far East. At this time, the Cold War was at its peak and the US was looking for a military base in the Indian Ocean. In 1966, the UK government granted a 50-year permit (until 2016), followed by an optional 20-year extension (until 2036) for the US government to use any island for defence purposes. In return for the permit, the UK government was able to purchase Polaris nuclear missiles at reduced price. Part of the agreement insisted that there was an uninhabited island on which to build a military base. Between 1967 and 1973, the entire population of native Chagossians was forcibly removed from the islands to make way for a military base on the island of Diego Garcia. More than 2000 people who had resided in the area for more than 100 years were displaced to Mauritius, the Seychelles and the UK and were officially prevented from ever returning.

The displaced Chagossian people have spent many years campaigning for the right to return. In the 1990s, conservation groups began to call for the area to be designated as an area of conservation, and restrictions were placed on fishing and visitations. By 2009, the idea of designating the whole area as a no-take MPA was formulated, leading to its formal declaration in 2010. This was welcomed by conservation groups such as Greenpeace as a major step forwards in the campaign to preserve biodiversity. In response, the government of Mauritius began a legal campaign against the MPA, stating that it breached its long-established fishing rights. Conflict occurred between the Mauritian government and Greenpeace, with Mauritius at one point refusing access to Greenpeace ships. To clarify their position, Greenpeace issued a statement declaring their support for the no-take MPA. They also stated that they did not condone the existence of the Diego Garcia military base, and supported the right of the Chagossians to return.

In 2010, the politics of the MPA took another unexpected turn. The 50-year lease was due to expire in 2016 and Diego Garcia had become increasingly important because of the increased risk of global terrorism. According to the WikiLeaks Cablegate documents, the UK government suggested that the creation of the marine reserve would safeguard the US and UK interests in these strategically important islands and make it difficult for the Chagossian people to return to their islands. If they were not permitted to fish, farm,

CONTINUED

develop tourism or any other industry, it would be all but impossible for them to make a living on the islands. This suggested that the reasons for setting up the MPA were not entirely for marine conservation.

On 18 March 2015, the Permanent Court of Arbitration in The Hague unanimously held that the MPA was illegal under the UN Convention on the Law of the Sea. It upheld the legal right of Mauritius to fish in the waters surrounding the Chagos Archipelago. In 2015, a UK government report stated that the return of the Chagossians would have minimal negative environmental impact and that they could establish good relations with any military presence on Diego Garcia.

The current situation

On 23 June 2017, in an effort to resolve the issue once and for all, the United Nations General Assembly referred the sovereignty issue between the UK and Mauritius to the International Court of Justice (ICJ). On 25 February 2019, the ICJ ruled that the Chagos Archipelago should not have been separated from Mauritius in 1952 and that the UK should return the entire archipelago to Mauritius, including Diego Garcia. The ruling is, however, only advisory and the UK has so far rejected it. Currently, the UK and Mauritius continue to negotiate on permissible levels of fishing in the area and how best to conserve the area. The Chagossian people continue to campaign for a return to the islands. It is unclear how long they will have to wait until they can eventually return to their homeland.

Questions

1 Summarise the:
   a environmental reasons for setting up the Chagos MPA
   b political reasons for setting up the Chagos MPA.

2 List the groups who could:
   a benefit from the MPA
   b be negatively affected by the MPA.

3 Explain the conflicts between:
   a conservation groups and the Mauritian government
   b the UK and US governments and the Mauritian government.

4 Suggest a strategy that could benefit all groups and the environment.

Glossary

Command words

analyse: examine in detail to show meaning, identify elements and the relationship between them

assess: make an informed judgement

calculate: work out from given facts, figure or information

compare: identify / comment on similarities and/or differences

consider: review and respond to given information

contrast: identify / comment on differences

define: give precise meaning

describe: state the points of a topic / give characteristics and main features.

discuss: write about issue(s) or topic(s) in depth in a structured way

evaluate: judge or calculate the quality, importance, amount, or value of something

explain: set out purposes or reasons / make the relationships between things evident/ provide why and/or how and support with relevant evidence.

give: produce an answer from a given source or recall / memory

identify: name / select / recognise

justify: support a case with evidence / argument

outline: set out main points

predict: suggest what may happen based on available information

sketch: make a simple freehand drawing showing the key features, taking care over proportions

state: express in clear terms

suggest: apply knowledge and understanding to situations where there are a range of valid responses in order to make proposals.

Key terms

abiotic factors: the environment's geological, physical and chemical features; the non-living part of an ecosystem

absorption spectrum: a graph of the absorbance of different wavelengths of light by a compound such as a photosynthetic pigment

abyssal plain: a flat, sandy region of the ocean floor found between trenches and the continental rise

abyssopelagic zone: the zone of the ocean between 4000 and 6000 m deep with near-freezing water temperatures and intense pressure

accessory pigment: a pigment that is not essential for photosynthesis but that absorbs light of different wavelengths and passes the energy to chlorophyll a, such as chlorophyll b, xanthophylls and phycobilins

accuracy: ensuring that measurements are close to the true value

acidic: having a pH below 7

action spectrum: a graph showing the effect of different wavelengths of light on a process, such as the rate of photosynthesis

active transport: the movement of molecules across a membrane from a region of lower concentration to a region of higher concentration; it requires the release of energy from ATP

adenosine diphosphate (ADP): an organic molecule that when combined with phosphate (P_i) during respiration produces ATP

alevin: the first larval form of salmon; they possess a yolk sac and remain within the gravel nests or redds

algal bloom: a rapid increase in a population of algae

alkaline: having a pH above 7

alternative hypothesis: there is a significant correlation between two sets of variables

amylopectin: one of the components of starch which is made from chains of glucose molecules with branches

amylose: one of the components of starch which is made from chains of glucose molecules with no branches

anaerobic respiration: the release of energy from glucose or another organic substrate in the absence of oxygen; animals produce lactate as a waste product while plants and fungi produce ethanol and carbon dioxide

Glossary

anomaly (anomalous): a result or observation that deviates from what is normal or expected; in experimental results, it normally refers to one repeated result that does not fit the pattern of the others

anthropogenic: caused by human activity

apex predator: an organism at the end of the food chain which has no natural predators

aquaculture: the rearing of aquatic animals and plants for human consumption or use

artificial reef: an underwater structure built by humans to mimic the characteristics of a natural reef

assimilation: the conversion of a nutrient into a useable form that can be incorporated into the tissues of an organism

atoll: a coral reef somewhat circular in shape with a central lagoon

atom: the smallest particle an element can be divided into and still be the same substance

atomic number: the number of protons contained in the nucleus of an atom

ATP (adenosine triphosphate): an organic molecule that provides energy to drive many processes in living cells; when broken down into ADP (adenosine diphosphate) and phosphate (P_i), it releases energy for cellular processes.

autotroph (autotrophic): an organism that can capture the energy in light or chemicals and use it to produce carbohydrates from simple molecules such as carbon dioxide

autotrophic nutrition: the ability of an organism to make its own food by taking inorganic molecules and using energy to create organic molecules

bar chart: a graph which is drawn to show the relationship between one continuous and one discontinuous variable

barrier reef: a reef separated by a lagoon from the land mass with which it is associated

basal plate: lower part of the coral calyx that separates the polyp from the substrate

bathypelagic zone: the zone of the ocean between 1000 and 4000 m deep which receives no sunlight

belt transect: sampling method involving counting of species in frame quadrats placed adjacent to the transect

benthic trawling: a fishing method that drags a net along the seabed; wooden boards at the front of the net keep the net open and stir up the seabed, causing damage

benthic zone: the lowest depth region in any body of water including the surface of the substrate

benthos: the community of organisms found in the benthic zone

binomial nomenclature: the two-part Latin name given to each species comprising the genus followed by the species

bioaccumulation: the accumulation of substances, such as pesticides, or other chemicals in an organism

biodiversity: a measure of the species, genetic and ecosystem diversity of different species

bioerosion: reef erosion caused by living organisms

biological drawing: a scientific drawing that records an image and important features of the specimen

bioluminescence: the biochemical release of light by living organisms

biomagnification: the increasing concentration of a substance, such as a toxic chemical, in the tissues of organisms at successively higher levels in a food chain

biomass: the mass of living material in an area; it can be measured as dry mass (without the water) or wet mass (with the water)

biosphere reserve: UNESCO designated area where sustainable human activity, education and research occurs alongside areas of conservation

biotic factors: the living parts of an ecosystem, which includes the organisms and their effects on each other

blades: leaf-like structures that 'hang' in the water and absorb light and minerals

blast fishing: the use of explosives to catch fish

bond: a strong force of attraction holding atoms together in a substance

bony fish: fish that have a bony skeleton and belong to the class Osteichthyes

broadcast spawning: the release of gametes freely into the water where they undergo fertilisation

buffer: a solution which can maintain a relatively stable pH

bycatch: species, caught by fishing, that are not target species

Calvin cycle: the series of reactions that occur during the light independent stage of photosynthesis; it converts carbon dioxide and other substances into glucose

calyx: the stony cup in which a coral polyp lives its life

captive breeding: the breeding of species outside of their natural area; zoos often breed organisms with a view to releasing them into the wild

carapace: the part of the exoskeleton that protects the dorsal side of the cephalothorax

carbon dioxide fixation (carbon fixation): the conversion of inorganic carbon dioxide into organic compounds such as glucose

carbon footprint: the total amount of carbon dioxide released into the atmosphere by a particular activity

carbon sequestration: long-term storage of carbon to mitigate global warming and avoid climate change

carbon sink: a natural environment that absorbs carbon dioxide from the atmosphere faster than it releases it

carnivore: an animal which feeds on other animals

carotenoid: a yellow, orange or red plant pigment used as an accessory pigment in photosynthesis

carrier proteins: membrane proteins that are involved in the transfer of substances from one side of membranes to the other; they possess a specific binding site to which substances bind and change shape as the substance is moved across the membrane

cartilaginous fish: fish that have jaws and skeletons made only of cartilage and belong to the class Chondrichthyes

catch per unit effort (CPUE): a measure of fish abundance calculated from the catch size divided by the fishing effort

cell: the smallest structural unit of an organism that is capable of independent functioning

cell sap: the fluid located inside a large permanent vacuole

cell surface membrane: a biological membrane that separates the internal contents of a cell from its external environment

cellulose: an important component of plant cell walls which is made from many straight chains of glucose molecules held together by hydrogen bonds

cell wall: a layer that surrounds some types of cells and gives strength and support; plant cell walls are made of cellulose

channel protein: membrane proteins that are involved in the transfer of substances from one side of membranes to the other; contain a pore through which substances will pass through

chemoautotroph: an organism that is able to use chemical energy to synthesise organic materials

chemosynthesis (chemosynthetic): the production of organic compounds by bacteria or other living organisms using the energy derived from reactions with inorganic chemicals

chlorophyll: a pigment found in plants and algae that is used to absorb sunlight for photosynthesis

chlorophyll (*a* and *b*): green pigments responsible for light capture in photosynthesis in algae and plants

chloroplast: the photosynthetic organelle in eukaryotes

chromatin: DNA, RNA and protein, located within the nucleus of cells

chromatography: a technique used to separate substances by their solubility

cisternae: flattened membranes of the Golgi body and endoplasmic reticulum

climate change: changes in global or regional climate patterns since the late twentieth century

cnidarians: marine animals that capture food using stinging cells

cnidocytes: stinging cells that cover the tentacles of cnidarians

commensalism: a relationship between two organisms where one organism benefits and the other is neither harmed nor benefitted

community: all the different populations interacting in one habitat at the same time

compensation point: the light intensity at which the rate of photosynthesis and the rate of respiration are equal

competition: a relationship between two organisms where both species are negatively affected as they are trying to use the same resources

compound: a substance containing two or more elements chemically bonded together

concentration gradient: the difference in concentration of molecules between two regions

Glossary

confounding variable: a variable that could affect the independent or dependent variable and therefore the results of the experiment

conservation: the protection of plants, animals and other organisms along with their habitats from extinction

consumer: an animal which feeds on other organisms to gain energy from food

continental crust: the thicker, less dense crust that makes up the foundation of the continents

continental drift: a theory supporting the possibility that continents are able to move over Earth's surface

continuous sampling: samples are taken along the whole length of the transect

continuous variable: one which can take any value (for example, temperature, time, concentration)

control experiment: a group within an investigation or study that receives exactly the same treatment as the experimental groups with the exception of the variable being tested

control variables: variables that are not being tested but that must be kept the same in case they affect the experiment

convection current: the movement of fluids or air based on density differences caused by differing temperature

convergent boundary: when two or more tectonic plates come together

coral bleaching: whitening of coral that results from the loss of a coral's symbiotic zooxanthellae

core: the dense, central region within Earth

Coriolis effect: a force that results from the Earth's rotation that causes objects or particles in motion to deflect to the right in the Northern Hemisphere and to the left in the Southern Hemisphere

counter-current (in gills): a mechanism by which gas exchange in gills is made more efficient; water and blood flow in opposite directions to maintain the diffusion gradient across the length of the gill

covalent bond: chemical bond that involves the sharing of electron pairs between atoms

cristae: folds of the inner mitochondrial membrane; they are involved in aerobic respiration

critical values of r_s: indicate when the calculated Spearman's rank is sufficient to suggest a correlation between the two sets of variables

crust: the outermost layer of rock on Earth

cructaceans: a marine invertebrate group with a hard exoskeleton, ten jointed legs and a nauplius larval stage

current: a continuous physical movement of water caused by wind or density

cyanobacteria: group of photosynthetic bacteria found in marine and fresh water

cytoplasm: all of the material, except for the nucleus, that is found within a cell

decomposers: bacteria and fungi which break down dead organic matter and release the nutrients back into the environment

delta: a low-lying triangular area at the mouth of a river formed by the deposition of sediments

denature: the loss of shape of enzymes, resulting in a loss of activity; usually the result of heating to a high temperature

density: a measure of the mass of a defined volume of water

denticles: a type of overlapping scales that provides protection and improved hydrodynamic efficiency in sharks

dependent variable: the variable being measured in an experiment

deposition: a geological process where sediments, soil and rocks are added to a landform or land mass

desalination plants: industrial facilities that remove salts from seawater to manufacture fresh water

desiccation: the removal of moisture or drying out of an organism

diatoms: group of unicellular algae found in phytoplankton characterised by silica skeletons

dichotomous key: an identification tool utilising a series of choices between alternative characters, with a direction to another stage in the key, until the species is identified

diffusion: the random movement of particles (or molecules) from a higher concentration to a lower concentration (down a concentration gradient); it is a passive process, not requiring the input of energy

dinoflagellates: group of unicellular algae found in phytoplankton characterised by the presence of two flagella

discontinuous variable: one which can only take certain values (for example, human blood type or eye colour)

disease: an illness characterised by specific signs and symptoms

dissolution: the process of being dissolved

dissolved oxygen (DO): concentration of oxygen dissolved in a solution

diurnal: occurring daily

divergent boundary: where two tectonic plates are moving away from each other

DNA (deoxyribonucleic acid): the molecule that is used as hereditary material being passed onto subsequent generations; it contains the code for all the genes of organisms.

downwelling: the downward movement of water in the sea due to density differences

dredging: the removal of material from ocean and river beds

earthquake: a sudden release of energy inside the Earth that creates seismic waves; usually caused by movement of tectonic plates or volcanic activity

echinoderms: a marine invertebrate group with pentaradial symmetry and tube feet

ecological diversity: the variation of ecosystems or habitats on a regional or global level

ecosystem: the living organisms and the environment with which they interact

ecosystem services: benefits people obtain from ecosystems, including food, flood regulation, climate control and water purification

ecotourism: sustainable tourism that is associated with an appreciation of the natural world and that minimises damage to the environment; it can benefit both environment and local populations

ectoparasite: a parasite, such as a flea or a louse, which lives on the outside of its host

electromagnetic spectrum: the range of frequencies and wavelengths of all types of electromagnetic radiation; the electromagnetic spectrum includes visible, ultra violet and infra-red light, microwaves, X rays, radio waves and gamma waves

electron: a negatively charged subatomic particle that orbits the nucleus of an atom

electron microscope: a type of microscope that uses electrons and electromagnets to magnify structures

element: a substance that cannot be chemically broken down into a simpler substance

El Niño: a warm current that develops off the coast of Ecuador around December, which can cause widespread death within local food chains

emergent properties: characteristics that are present within a compound or molecule of two or more different elements that those elements do not possess on their own

endangered species: species that are at a high risk of extinction

endoparasite: a parasite, such as a tapeworm, which lives inside the body of its host

***Endoriftia*:** symbiotic bacterial species that is found in the tube worm, *Riftia*

enhanced greenhouse effect: an elevated and imbalanced greenhouse effect caused by human activity

epipelagic zone: the zone of the ocean between 0 and 200 m deep which receives enough light for photosynthesis

erosion: a natural process where material is worn away from the Earth's surface and transported elsewhere

estuary: a partially enclosed, tidal, coastal body of water where fresh water from a river meets the saltwater of the ocean

ethical method: evaluates and chooses ways to protect the natural habitat under investigation

euryhaline: organisms that can tolerate wide changes in the salinity of water

eutrophication: the process by which a body of water becomes enriched in dissolved nutrients (such as nitrates and phosphates) that stimulate the growth of producers, usually resulting in the depletion of dissolved oxygen

evaporation: a change in state from liquid to gas below the boiling point of a substance

evenness: a measure of the relative abundance of the populations of different species in an area

excretion: the process of eliminating the waste formed from the chemical reactions within living cells

extensive aquaculture: aquaculture that uses little technology, low stocking densities and no artificial feeding

external fertilisation: when gametes such as sperm and eggs are released and fuse outside the body

Glossary

extinction: the loss of a species from the planet; some species may be extinct in the wild but still present in zoos

extremophile: an organism that is adapted to survive extreme temperature, pressure, salinity or pH

facilitated diffusion: a process by which polar substances diffuse through cell membranes via carrier or channel proteins

fatty acid: lipid molecules that are a major constituent of triglycerides and phospholipids

fecundity: the rate of reproduction of organisms; in fish the rate of egg production is often considered as a measure of fecundity

filaments: parts of gills that branch out from gill arches; they are sometimes called primary lamellae

fins: protrude from the body surface and assist in movement, stabilising position, reproduction and protection

flower: sexual reproductive organ of plants

fluid mosaic model: a model that explains the properties of cell membranes

food chain: a way to describe the feeding relationships between organisms

food web: a way to show all the different feeding relationships in an ecosystem

fossil fuels: buried organic materials from dead plants and animals which have been converted into oil, coal or natural gas by exposure to heat and pressure in the Earth's crust

frame quadrat: a plastic or metal square that sets a standard unit of area for study of the distribution of marine organisms

fringing reef: a reef close to and surrounding newer volcanic islands or that borders continental landmasses

fry: the early, small larval stage of many fish, including salmon

gas bladder: a gas-containing structure that provides buoyancy for some species of seaweed

gas (gaseous) exchange: the uptake of oxygen and release of carbon dioxide by cells or other surfaces

genetic diversity: the variety of forms of genes (alleles) within a species

geoengineering: intentionally manipulating environmental processes that affect the climate in order to reduce the impacts of climate change

ghost nets: fishing equipment that has been lost from boats but still traps and kills organisms

gills: the gaseous exchange surfaces of fish

gill slits: external openings from the gills through which water taken in at the mouth can pass back to the ocean

global ocean conveyor belt: constantly moving systems of deep-ocean water driven by thermohaline circulation

global warming: the observed and projected increases in the average temperature of Earth's atmosphere and oceans due to an enhanced greenhouse effect

glycerol: a simple molecule that is a constituent of triglycerides and phospholipids

Golgi body: cell organelle that modifies proteins

gradient: the rate of change in the y-axis value as the x-axis value increases

grana: areas in the stroma of chloroplasts where thylakoid membranes containing photosynthetic pigments are stacked on top of each other

greenhouse effect: the heating of the atmosphere due to the presence of carbon dioxide and other gases; these gases prevent infrared radiation being re-emitted into space

greenhouse gases: gases such as carbon dioxide and methane that prevent infrared radiation being released into space

growth rate: the speed of growth of a population in terms of numbers or size of individual fish

habitat: the natural environment where an organism lives

haemoglobin: protein that is found in red blood cells and transports oxygen around the body

hard corals: stony corals capable of reef-building that have a relationship with zooxanthellae

harmful algal bloom (HAB): when an excess of nutrients leads to overgrowth of marine plankton that release toxins into the water

herbivore: an animal which feeds only on producers (plants or phytoplankton)

heterotroph (heterotrophic): an organism that cannot make its own food and instead relies on consuming other organisms; all animals, fungi and protozoans are heterotrophic, as well as most bacteria

histogram: a graph which is drawn to show the frequency of one continuous variable

holdfast: strong, root-like structure that anchors the macroalgae to the seabed

Humboldt Current: a coldwater current with low salinity levels that flows north along the western coast of South America; also called the Peru current

hydrogen bond: a weak bond between two molecules due to the electrostatic attraction between a hydrogen atom in one molecule and an atom of oxygen, nitrogen or fluorine in the other molecule

hydrophilic: substances that are attracted to water molecules; will dissolve in water

hydrophobic (molecule): a molecule without a charge which repels water molecules

hydrophobic (substance): substances that will not mix with water; they will not dissolve in water

hydrothermal vent: an area where cold ocean water that has seeped into the Earth's crust is superheated by underlying magma and forced through vents in the ocean floor

hypersaline: when a body of water has a salinity level greater than 40‰

hypertonic: a solution that has a greater concentration of solutes compared to another solution

hypothesis: an explanation of an observation that can be tested through experimentation

hypotonic: a solution that has a lower concentration of solutes compared to another solution

independent variable: the variable being changed in an experiment

intensive aquaculture: aquaculture that uses intensive methods such as high stocking densities and artificial feeding to maximise production

internal fertilisation: when gametes such as sperm and eggs fuse inside the body of a parent

inter-specific competition: competition between members of different species (for example, predators-prey)

intertidal zone: area known as the seashore which is exposed at low tides and under water at high tides

intra-specific competition: competition between individuals of the same species (for example, for food or a mate)

invasive species: species that have become established in an area that is not their normal habitat due to human activity

ion: an atom or molecule that has lost or gained one or more electrons creating an electrical charge

ionic bond: chemical bond that involves the attraction between two oppositely charged ions

isotonic: a solution that has the same concentration of solutes compared to another solution

juvenile: the stage of life cycle that is not sexually mature

keystone species: an organism that plays a unique and crucial role in the way an ecosystem functions; without keystone species, the ecosystem would be dramatically different or cease to exist altogether

kinetic energy: the energy possessed by objects or particles due to movement

kinetic particle theory (particle theory): the theory of how particles (such as atoms and molecules) move in relation to each other and the amount of energy within the system

kite graph: a graph of the distribution and abundance of organisms in the littoral zone that allows zonation patterns to be easily seen

***K*-strategy:** producing few offspring but providing a large amount of parental investment

lagoon: a shallow, sheltered body of water with a soft sediment bottom

lamellae: addition branches of gill filaments that increase the surface area of the gills; they are sometimes called secondary lamellae

La Niña: a cold current that develops off the coast of Ecuador and spreads across the Pacific, reducing sea surface temperatures for extended periods of time

large permanent vacuole: a membrane bound organelle that is present in all plant and fungal cells; it contains cell sap

larvae: a planktonic stage of development which occurs between the egg and juveniles; found in nearly all species of fish and invertebrates

larval forms: the immature form of animals that undergo some metamorphosis, often having different food sources and habitats to avoid competition with the adults

lateral line: a canal on the head and the side of the fish that contains sense organs; it is externally visible in bony fish but in cartilaginous fish it is under the skin; it is externally visible in bony fish whereas in cartilaginous fish it is under the skin

leaf: photosynthetic organ of plants

Glossary

lenticel: a raised pore in the roots of a mangrove that allows gas exchange between the atmosphere and the internal tissues

life cycle: the different stages that a species passes through during its life

light dependent stage: the stage in photosynthesis whereby light energy is harvested; occurs in the thylakoid membranes of chloroplasts and produces ATP and reduced NADP

light independent stage: the stage in photosynthesis whereby carbon dioxide is converted into glucose by the Calvin cycle; occurs in the stroma of chloroplasts

light intensity: a measure of the strength or brightness of light

light microscopes: a type of microscope that uses visible light and glass lenses to magnify structures

light penetration: the depth to which light can penetrate into a material

limiting factor: the one factor, of many affecting a process, that is nearest its lowest value and hence is rate limiting; photosynthesis rate is usually limited by light intensity, temperature and/or carbon dioxide concentration

Lincoln index: a mathematical equation that can use the mark–release–recapture data to estimate the population size

line graph: a graph which is drawn to show the relationship between two continuous variables

line transect: a sampling method involving counting of species that touch the transect

lithosphere: the outermost layer of the Earth's crust

littoral zone: the benthic, or bottom, zone between the highest and lowest spring tide water marks on a shoreline, also referred to as the intertidal zone

lysosomes: membrane enclosed organelles that contain digestive enzymes

macroalgae: marine producers such as kelp and seaweeds

magnification: the process of enlarging the size of an image

mantle: a region of molten rock within the interior of the Earth, between the core and the crust

marine grasses: aquatic flowering plants that are often found in estuarine and coastal environment

marine protected area (MPA): an area of ocean or coastline where restrictions have been placed on activities; the levels of restriction may vary, some may be no-take areas where no fishing is permitted, others may allow some fishing, some may ban all access to unauthorised people, while others may allow restricted access

marine snow: particles of organic material that fall from surface waters to the deeper ocean

marine uplift: a process by which the floor of the ocean rises, possibly to the extent that it is no longer beneath the water

mark–release–recapture: a method to estimate the population size of mobile species

matrix: the fluid filled space within the inner mitochondrial membrane; it contains enzymes and sugars involved with respiration

maximum sustainable yield (MSY): the intensity of fishing that can be carried out without reducing future populations

mesopelagic zone: the zone of the ocean between 200 and 1000 m deep which receives very little light

metamorphosis: the changing of an organism from one form to another, such as the changing of a larval stage into an adult

microplastics: plastic particles that are less than 5 mm in diameter

middle lamella: a layer of pectin on the outside of plants cells; it cements neighbouring cells together

mid-ocean ridge: a mountain range with a central valley on an ocean floor at the boundary between two diverging tectonic plates, where new crust forms from upwelling magma

minimum mesh size: the smallest permitted size of the holes in fishing nets

mitochondrion: (plural: mitochondria) the organelle in eukaryotes in which aerobic respiration takes place

molecule: a group of atoms covalently bonded together

monomer: the smallest unit of a polymer; monomers are able to join chemically to form longer molecules

morphology: the study of the forms of things

mortality rate: the death rate; natural mortality is the death rate arising from natural causes, while fishing mortality is the death rate caused by fishing

mutualism (mutualistic): a relationship between two different organisms where both organisms benefit

mysis: the later larval form of crustaceans; shrimp mysis larvae drift to coastal areas

neap tide: a tide that occurs when the Moon and Sun are at right angles from each other, causing the smallest tidal range

nematocyst: the harpoon-like organelle inside of cnidocyte that contains toxin to be delivered to the prey

neutral (pH): having a pH that equals 7

neutron: neutral subatomic particles contained within the nucleus of an atom

niche: the role of a species within an ecosystem

nicotinamide adenine dinucleotide phosphate (NADP): a molecule that is reduced during the light dependent reaction; reduced NADPH is then used in the light independent reaction to convert GP into TP

nauplius: distinctive larval stage of crustaceans

nonpolar: molecules that do not have electric charge

non-sessile: when an organism is free moving (not attached to a substrate)

nucleoli (sing. nucleolus): small circular areas inside the nucleus that produce RNA for ribosomes

nucleus (atom): the positively charged central core of an atom that is made of protons and neutrons

nucleus (cell): membrane bound organelle that contains the genetic material of a cell

null hypothesis (H_0): there is no correlation between the two sets of variables

nutrient: a chemical that provides what is needed for organisms to grow, repair damaged cells or tissues, release energy or for their metabolism

nutrient cycles: the movement and exchange of elements that are essential to life, from inorganic molecules, through fixation and then into living organisms, before being decomposed back into inorganic molecules

ocean: a continuous mass of seawater on the Earth's surface, its boundaries formed by continental land masses, ridges on the ocean floor or the equator

ocean acidification: a process where the pH of the ocean is reduced over an extended period of time; generally contributed to a rise in atmospheric carbon dioxide

ocean fertilisation: the dumping of iron or other nutrients into the ocean in areas with low productivity to enhance growth of phytoplankton

oceanic crust: the dense, basaltic layer of crust that makes up the bottom of the ocean basins

oestrogen: a steroid hormone that is the primary female sex hormone

omnivore: an animal which feeds on other animals and on producers

operculum: a thin bony flap of skin covering and protecting the gills

organelle: a specialised structure within a cell that has a specific function

osmoconformer: organisms that have an internal body fluid salinity that it is the same salinity as external water

osmoregulator: organisms that regulate the internal salinity of their body fluids within a narrow range

osmosis: the movement of water from a higher water potential to a lower water potential across a selectively permeable membrane

oxidation: a chemical reaction in which an atom loses electrons

oxygen minimum layer: the layer within the ocean where the concentration of dissolved oxygen is at its lowest, typically found between the photic zone between 100 m and 1000 m deep

oxyhaemoglobin: formed when haemoglobin binds reversibly to oxygen in the gills

paleomagnetic stripes: the pattern of magnetic stripes on the ocean floor due to reversals in the Earth's magnetic field and seafloor spreading.

paper chromatography: a technique used to separate substances by their solubility

parasitism: a relationship between two organisms where the parasite obtains benefit at the expense of the host

parr: salmon stage between fry and smolt; lives in rivers and has markings along sides of body that act as camouflage

passive process: processes that occur without use of additional energy

patch reef: small, isolated reef usually located within the lagoon of a barrier reef

pelagic: zone of open ocean or sea water that is not close to the seabed or shore

pentaradial symmetry: five arms (or fans) radiating from a central body cavity

Glossary

permeability: how well water flows through a substrate

pH: a numeric value expressing the acidity or alkalinity of a solution on a logarithmic scale

pH scale: a logarithmic scale that measures the ratio of hydrogen ions to hydroxide ions

phoresis: a commensal relationship where one organism attaches itself to another in order to travel

phosphate (P_i): a compound made from phosphorus and oxygen that is combined with ADP to form ATP

photic zone: the surface layer of the ocean which receives sunlight

photoactivation: the activation of chlorophyll by light

photoautotroph: an organism that is able to use light energy to synthesise organic compounds

photolysis: the process of the breakdown of water into hydrogen and oxygen due to the effect of light during the light dependent reaction of photosynthesis

photooxidation: the loss of electrons due to the absorption of light energy

photosynthesis (photosynthetic, photosynthesise): the process of using light energy to synthesise glucose from carbon dioxide and water to produce chemical energy

photosystem: a collection of photosynthetic pigments located in the thylakoid membrane; responsible for the absorption of light energy

phycobilins: a group a light absorbing pigments that are found in red algae and cyanobacteria; it includes phycoerythrin and phycocyanin

phycocyanin: a blue-green accessory pigment that is found in some marine algae

phycoerythrin: a red accessory pigment that is frequently found in red algae

phytoplankton: microscopic photosynthetic organisms that live in the upper, sunlit layers of water

plankton: microscopic free floating marine organisms

plate tectonics: the process where large sections (plates) of the Earth's crust are in constant movement over the fluid mantle, causing earthquakes and volcanoes at the borders between the plates

polar: when opposite sides of a molecule have contrasting (partial) electrical charges

polarity: having two opposite states of being on either end (such as the North and South pole, or the positive and negative end of a magnet)

polymer: a large molecule made from many repeating sub-units

polyp: non-moving, cup-like life stage of cnidarians

population: all the individuals of the same species that live at the same place and time

porosity: how much water a substance can hold based on the empty space within it

porous: substrate with holes that allow for the passage of air and water

postlarva: the stage in the shrimp life cycle produced by metamorphosis of the mysis larva

precipitation: water that falls from the atmosphere to the Earth's surface as rain, sleet, snow or hail

precision (in experiments): this refers to the closeness of the measurements to each other; precise measurements are close to each other and there is little spread about the mean

precision (in measurements): the level of refinement in a measurement as shown by the number of significant figures given

predation: a relationship between two organisms where a predator hunts, kills and eats a prey animal

predator: an animal which hunts, kills and eats other animals

prediction: a statement of the expected results in an experiment based on the hypothesis being tested

prey: an animal which is eaten by predators

primary microplastics: microplastics, such as beads found in cosmetics, that are released directly into water

primary pigment: photosynthetic pigment that is directly involved with photosynthesis

primary producers: organisms that produce biomass from inorganic compounds; in almost all cases these are photosynthetically active organisms

primary productivity: the rate of production of new biomass through photosynthesis or chemosynthesis

principle of constant proportions: the ratio of any two major ions dissolved in seawater is constant

propagule: a reproductive structure that detaches from the parent plant and is able to grow into a new individual

protoctists: a kingdom of organisms that are characterised by the presence of a nucleus and are distinct from plants, animals and fungi; it is a diverse group that includes unicellular and multicellular organisms and organisms with and without cell walls and chloroplasts

proton: a positively charged subatomic particle contained within the nucleus of an atom

protozoea: the second-stage larva of crustaceans such as shrimp; typically, planktonic, these larvae pass through several forms as they grow

pumped ventilation: ventilation of gills by the muscle action of the mouth pumping water over the gills; it can occur when the fish is stationary

purse seine: a seine net used to capture pelagic shoals of fish; it has a series of ropes that are used to close it and trap the fish before hauling them on board

pycnocline: a layer of water between two layers of water with different densities

pyramid of biomass: a diagram that shows the biomass present in each trophic level of a food chain

pyramid of energy: a diagram that shows the amount of energy in each trophic level of a food chain

pyramid of numbers: a diagram that shows the number of organisms in each trophic level of a food chain

qualitative data: descriptive data about a variable (for example, colour or behaviour)

quantitative data: numerical data that give the quantity, amount or range of a variable (for example, concentration of oxygen or number of eggs laid)

ram ventilation: ventilation of gills by swimming with the mouth open so that a constant flow of water passes through the mouth and over the gills; it only occurs when a fish is swimming

random error: an error in measurement which is caused by factors which vary from one measurement to another

random sampling: samples are taken at random places within the sample site

recruitment: the arrival of new organisms in a population; for fish it is often considered to be the stage at which fish have reached an age when they can be caught in nets

reduction: a chemical reaction in which an atom gains electrons

reef erosion: when a coral loses more of its calcium carbonate skeleton per year than it gains

refuse: material that has been discarded

reliable: results that can be replicated by other people

renewable energy: energy that is taken from sources that are naturally replenished quickly (for example, sunlight, wind and tides)

reproductive maturity: the time when an organism is able to reproduce sexually

residence time: the average time that a particle spends in a particular system

resolution (resolving power): the smallest distance between two points that can be detected; it is a measure of the level of detail that can be seen

respiration: the process by which all living things release energy from their food by oxidising glucose

R_f value: the distance travelled by a substance on a chromatogram divided by the distance travelled by the solvent front

rhizomes: a horizontal underground structure that enable seagrasses to reproduce asexually

ribosomes: small organelles that are involved in the synthesis of proteins

ribulose biphosphate (RuBP): an organic molecule that is used in the light independent stage of photosynthesis; combined with carbon dioxide as part of the Calvin cycle

richness: the number of species in a community

Riftia: giant tube worm found around hydrothermal vents

root: structure at base of plant that anchors it to the substrate and absorbs nutrients from the sediment

rough and smooth endoplasmic reticulum: a network of flattened sacs running through the cytoplasm or eukaryotic cells; molecules, particularly proteins, can be transported through the cell inside the sacs separate from the rest of the cytoplasm; ER is continuous with the outer membrane of the nuclear envelope

r-strategy: providing large numbers of offspring while providing little parental investment

rubisco: enzyme that is involved in the first step of the Calvin cycle; it catalyses the reaction between carbon dioxide and RuBP

run-off: the flow of water from land caused by precipitation

safe method: identifies potential hazards and then reducing their risk of occurring

salinity: a measure of the quantity of dissolved solids in ocean water, represented by parts per thousand (ppt) or ‰

Glossary

scales: overlapping segments of bone covered by skin and mucus found on the outside of the fish

seas: smaller and less deep bodies of seawater that are partially enclosed by land; they are found where the ocean and land meet

scatter plot: when two sets of variables are plotted to indicate if there is a relationship between them

secondary microplastics: microplastics produced from the breakdown of larger pieces of plastic

secondary production: the rate of production of new biomass by consumers, using the energy gained by eating producers

sedimentary rock: rock formed by the deposition of particles on the ocean floor

sedimentation: the deposition of suspended particles from water

seismic: having to do with vibrations of the Earth's crust; earthquakes

semi-diurnal: occurring twice daily

sessile: when an organism is attached to a substrate and is therefore immobile

sewage: liquid and solid waste material such as waste water or urine

shells: each of a set of orbitals around the nucleus of an atom that can be occupied by electrons

Simpson's index of diversity (D): a biodiversity measure that accounts for both species richness and eveness

sink: an area where there is a net loss of material (for example, where more gas dissolves into the ocean than diffuses into the atmosphere)

smolt: form of salmon that occurs when parr lose their markings while in estuaries; they are adapted for marine life by being silver in colour and elongated in shape

soft corals: corals that do not build reefs and lack calcification

solubility: the ability of a solute to dissolve within a solvent (such as water)

solute: a solid that dissolves in a solvent

solution: a mixture of a solute dissolved in a solvent

solvent: a substance which is able to dissolve other substances

SONAR: a method that is used to detect underwater objects by the reflection of sound waves

source: an area where there is a net gain of material (for example, where more gas diffuses into the atmosphere than dissolves in the ocean)

spat: larval form of bivalve molluscs that settles and attaches to substrate

Spearman's rank correlation: a mathematical tool used to find out if there is a correlation between two sets of variables, when they are not normally distributed

species: a group of similar organisms that can interbreed naturally to produce fertile offspring

species diversity: the abundance and richness of a species in a given place

specific heat capacity: the heat required to raise the temperature of the unit mass of a given substance by one degree Celsius

spermatocyst: a pouch used to transfer sperm from male shrimp to females

splash zone: area of a rocky shore that is just above the high tide mark and receives water through the splashing of waves

spring tide: a tide that occurs when the Sun and Moon are aligned, causing the largest tidal range

stakeholder: a person who has a vested interest, for any reason, in an area or project

starch: a carbohydrate made from chains of glucose molecules joined together

stenohaline: organisms that cannot tolerate wide changes in the salinity of water

steroid hormones: steroid molecules that are used as hormones

stipe: long, tough, vertical stalk similar to the stem of plants

stroma: the liquid substance in the centre of chloroplasts, surrounding the thylakoid membranes; it is where the light independent stage occurs

subduction: the process where one lithospheric plate slides below another at a convergent plate boundary

surface area: volume ratio: an index that gives a relative measure of both surface area and volume; exchange organs generally have a very high surface area : volume ratio

sustainable development: development that meets the needs of the present without compromising the ability of future generations to meet their needs

sustainable fishing: fishing up to the maximum sustainable yield so that future fish stocks are not at risk of being depleted

swim bladder: a buoyancy organ found in bony fish

symbiosis: a relationship between two or more organisms of different species which live physically close to each other

systematic error: a consistent error which affects each measurement in the same way, normally caused by faulty measuring equipment or difficulties in reading that equipment

systematic sampling: samples are taken at fixed intervals along the transect

taxonomic hierarchy: the classification of the species within living organisms by describing the domain, kingdom, phylum, class, order, family, genus and species

testosterone: a steroid hormone that is the primary male sex hormone

theca: the walls of the calyx

theory: a well-substantiated explanation of an aspect of the natural world that has been repeatedly tested and confirmed through observation and experimentation

thermal insulator: a substance which reduces the rate of transfer of thermal energy

thermohaline circulation: large-scale ocean circulation caused by density differences due to temperature and salinity changes in the world's ocean

thylakoid membranes: membrane bound structures in the stroma of chloroplasts; stacks of thylakoids are called grana; they are where the light dependent stage of photosynthesis occurs

tidal range: the difference in height between the high-tide mark and the low-tide mark over the course of a day; also called the tidal amplitude

tidal surge: the coastal flooding of of an abnormally high seawater level associated with low pressure weather systems; also called a storm surge

tide: the periodic rise and fall of the surface of the ocean resulting from the gravitational pull of the Moon and Sun

tonoplast: the membrane found outside a large permanent vacuole in plant and fungal cells

transect: a rope or tape marked at regular intervals that sets standard distances for study of the distribution of marine organisms

transform boundary: when two plates are moving in an antiparallel direction, creating friction between them

trench: a long, narrow and deep depression on the ocean floor with relatively steep sides; caused by convergent plate boundaries

triglyceride: a type of lipid which is made from a glycerol molecule joined to three fatty acid chains

trochophore: the first larval stage of molluscs such as giant clams and oysters; they move using cilia and are planktonic

trophic level: the position an organism occupies in the food chain or food web

trophosome: organ found inside some organisms that contains symbiotic bacteria

tsunami: a seismic sea wave created by an underwater earthquake or volcanic event; not noticeable in the open ocean but building to great heights in shallow water

tube feet: tubular projections that assist in locomotion, feeding, and respiration

turbidity: the level of transparency loss water has due to the presence of suspended particles in the water; the higher the turbidity, the harder it is to see through the water

turbulence: irregular changes in the speed and direction of fluid movement

turgor pressure: the force within a plant cell that presses the cell membrane against the cell wall

upwelling: the movement of cold, nutrient-rich water from deep in the ocean to the surface

variable: a condition in an experiment that can be controlled or changed

veliger: the second-stage larva of molluscs, characterised by the presence of a vellum organ used for feeding and movement, and a shell

vesicle: small structures that consist of fluid surrounded by a membrane; they are used for transporting substances around cells

viviparous reproduction: [plants] a reproductive strategy where the seed develops into a young plant while still attached to the parent plant

volcano: a mountain or hill with a crater or vent through which lava, rock fragments, hot vapour and gas are being forced from the Earth's crust

Glossary

water bath: a container of water heated to a given temperature which can be used to either vary or control the temperature

water column: a vertical section of water from the surface to the bottom; useful concept when discussing changes in the abiotic factors within the body of water

water potential: the potential energy of water in a solution compared to pure water; water will move by osmosis from a higher water potential to a lower water potential pure water has the highest water potential at 0 kPa; dissolving solute makes the solution have a more negative kPa

water vapour: gaseous phase/state of water; produced when liquid water evaporates or boils

wavelength: the distance between two corresponding points of a wave; different colours of light have different wavelengths

weathering: the wearing down or breaking of rocks through physical, chemical or organic means

World Ocean: the combination of all major oceans into one large, interconnected body of water that encircles the world's continents

xanthophyll: a yellow or brown plant pigment used as an accessory pigment in photosynthesis

zonation: distribution of plants or animals into specific zones within an ecosystem based on a specific abiotic factor, like desiccation

zooplankton: planktonic consumers that are either floating or weakly swimming animals

zooxanthellae: symbiotic, photosynthetic dinoflagellates living within the tissues of many invertebrates

β-glucose : an isomer of the sugar, glucose; it is the monomer that cellulose is made up of

CAMBRIDGE INTERNATIONAL AS & A LEVEL MARINE SCIENCE: COURSEBOOK

> Acknowledgements

The authors and publishers acknowledge the following sources of copyright material and are grateful for the permissions granted. While every effort has been made, it has not always been possible to identify the sources of all the material used, or to trace all copyright holders. If any omissions are brought to our notice, we will be happy to include the appropriate acknowledgements on reprinting.

Cover georgnroll/Getty Images

Chapter 1: Abstract Aerial Art/GI; Stocktrek Images/GI; Science Photo Library/GI; Duncan1890/GI; Ido Meirovich/GI; Massimo Borchi/Atlantide Phototravel/GI; NASA; NASA Photo/Alamy; **Chapter 2:** Chris Frost/GI; Deagostini/GI; Henning Dalhoff/SPL; Dorling Kindersley/GI; Universal History Archive/GI; Xavier Barceló/GI; Stocktrek Images/GI; Mangiwau/GI (X2); **Chapter 3:** Wildestanimal/GI; Paulo Oliveira/Alamy; Jeff Rotman/GI; Scubaluna/GI; Jeff Rotman/GI; De Agostini Picture Library/GI; Pete Atkinson/GI; Paule858/GI; Nnehring/GI; Dr Ken Macdonald/SPL; Yva Momatiuk & John Eastcott/GI; Buck Shreck/GI; **Chapter 4:** Shur_Ca/GI; Joost Van Uffelen/GI; Dea/F. Ballanti/GI; A. Martin UW Photography/GI; Oxford Scientific/GI; Sinhyu/GI; Wim Van Egmond/SPL; Roland Birke/GI; Alexander Semenov/GI; Karen Gowlett-Holmes/GI; Deagostini/GI; Peter Johnson/Corbis/GI; Auscape/Universal Images Group/GI; Carlo Pinasco/GI; Jeff Rotman/GI; Cedric Favero/GI; Douglas Klug/GI; Farley Baricuatro/GI; Image Source/GI; Hal Beral/GI; Wildestanimal/GI; Brian Reckenbiel. Florida Fish And Wildlife Conservation Commission; NOAA's CCMA Biogeography Team; Jules Robson; Adam Glanzman/Northeastern University; photo of DSV Limiting Factor from the image gallery on the Deep Fives website https://fivedeeps.com; Biophoto Associates/SPL; **Chapter 5:** Sergiy Glushchenko/GI; Geoffrey Gilson Photography/GI; Georgette Douwma/GI; Stephen Frink/GI; Giordano Cipriani/GI; Brandi Mueller/GI; David Fleetham/GI; Federica Grassi/GI; Michael Patrick O'neill/SPL; Stephen Frink/GI; Scubazoo/SPL; Secret Sea Visions/GI; Andreas Altenburger/GI; Apomares/GI; Jeannine Nelepovitz/GI; Ricardo Lima/GI; **Practical Skills:** HASLOO/GI; Wild Horizons/Universal Images Group via Getty Image; **Chapter 6:** David Fleetham/Alamy; Science & Society Picture Library/GI; SPL; Luchschen/GI; Monty Rakusen/GI; Ed Reschke/GI; Herve Conge, Ism/SPL; Don Fawcett/SPL; Dr.Jeremy Burgess/SPL; SPL - Steve Gschmeissner/GI; Dennis Kunkel Microscopy/SPL; Dr Donald Fawcett and Robert Bolender/SPL; Biophoto Associates/SPL; SPL/GI; Dr.Jeremy Burgess/SPL; Biophoto Associates/SPL; Science Source/SPL; Herve Conge, Ism/SPL; Steve Gschmeissner/SPL/GI; Biophoto Associates/SPL; Trevor Clifford Photography/SPL; Paulo Oliveira/Alamy; Keith R. Porter/SPL; NASA/SPL; **Chapter 7:** Douglas Klug/GI; Kenneth L. Smith, Jr./GI; Ralph White/GI; Marayok/GI; **Chapter 8:** Gerard Puigmal/GI; Scott Groth, Oregon Department Of Fish And Wildlife; Benjamin Victor, Coralreeffish.Com; Barbaraaaa/GI; Dr Clive Bromhall/GI; Design Pics Inc/Alamy; Eschenfelder/GI; Undersea Vehicles Program/UNCW; Waterframe/Alamy; Romeo Gacad/GI; Frans Lanting/GI; John Gress/GI; Stockcam/GI; Boris Horvat/GI; Trieu Tuan/Shutterstock; National Geographic Image Collection/Alamy; Eye Ubiquitous/Universal Images/GI; **Chapter 9:** Paul Mccormick/GI; Matthew D White/GI; Saul Loeb/GI; Andrew Aitchison/GI; Ashley Cooper/GI; Afp/GI; Rosanne Tackaberry/Alamy; Jones/Shimlock-Secret Sea Visions/GI; Jonathan Eastland/GI; Education Images/GI; Seatops/GI; Cyril Ruoso/GI; Mooreinusa/GI; Dave Fleetham/Design Pics/GI; Antonio Camacho/GI; Annelise Pilkington/GI; Michel De Nijs/GI; Angelo Cavalli/GI; Laguna Lodge Eco-Resort And Nature Reserve; Roy Toft; Deniz Öner/GI; Gary Roberts/Alamy.

Key: GI= Getty Images, SPL= Science Photo Library, Alamy = Alamy Stock Photo

We would like to thank Paul Roobottom, as well as his A Level Marine Science students (Jake Christian, Molly Cracknell, Erin Lacy, Kristian Orchard and George Thwaites), at University College Isle of Man for their generous help with reviewing the content of the *Cambridge International AS & A Level Marine Science* coursebook. We would also like to thank Maryjane Watson for her helpful support with the practical activities in the coursebook.

Index

A

abiotic factors, in marine ecosystems, 129–131
abiotic phase, nutrient cycle, 84
absorption spectrum, 271–272
abyssal plains, 36, 40
abyssopelagic zone, 155
accessory pigments, 268–269, 273
accuracy, 193
acidic, 12
acidification, ocean, 164, 399–400
Acrophora cervicornis, 158
action spectrum, 272
active transport, 230, 232
adenosine diphosphate (ADP), 277, 288
adenosine triphosphate (ATP), 277, 288
Adriatic Sea, sea bream protection in, 415
adventure tourism, 420
aerobic respiration, 72, 288–289
age of reproductive maturity, 318–319
agriculture, effects on marine ecosystems, 374–375
agrotourism, 420
air and sea patrolling, 327
alevins, 343
algal blooms, 64, 79
    effect of agriculture on, 374
    harmful, 107, 184
    and red tides, 300–302
alkaline, 12
alternative hypothesis, 141
amino acids, 84
amylopectin, 83
amylose, 83
anaerobic respiration, 288, 289
anal fin, 114
analysis, data, 201–204, 290–292
anemones, boxer crabs and, mutualistic relationship between, 66
animacules, 212
animal cells, osmosis in, 233
anomaly (anomalous), 191
antarctic krill, 111–112
anthropogenic, 183
apex predator, 69
aquaculture, 339–356
    defined, 304
    environmental impacts, 350–353
    extensive, 340–341
    intensive, 340, 341
    mussel, 344–345
    negative effects of, minimising, 354–356
    projects, requirements for long-term success of. *See* aquaculture ventures requirements
    requirements, 339
    salmon. *See* salmon aquaculture
    shrimp, 345–347
    social and economic impacts, 353–354
    systems usage for, 339
aquaculture ventures requirements
    clean water, availability of, 347
    disease management, 348
    feed, 347–348
    labour, availability of, 348
    location, availability of, 348–349
    market demand, 349
    return on investment, 350
    stock, availability of, 347
    transport network, 349
Aral Sea, 262–264
Arctic Ocean, 155
Aristotle, 186
artificial reefs, 168–169, 337
assimilation, 82
Atlantic Ocean, 154
atmospheric gases, 85–86
atmospheric pressure, and gas solubility, 15
atolls, 160, 161
atomic number, 4
atoms
    bonding properties of. *See* bonds, atoms
    defined, 2
    kinetic particle theory, 3
    subatomic particles, 3–4
Audus apparatus, 276
Automatic Identification System (AIS), 327
Autonomous Reef Monitoring Structures (ARMS), 149
autotrophic, 66
autotrophic nutrition, 267

B

Bacon, Roger, 186
bar charts, 195
barnacle, distribution in littoral zone, 205
barrier reefs, 160, 161
basal plate, 157
basaltic rocks, 35
bathypelagic zone, 155
belt transects, 133
benthic trawling, 316–317
benthic zone, 156
benthos, 156
β-glucose, 220

binomial nomenclature, 103
bioaccumulation, 371
biodiversity
    calculation, 137–138
    defined, 125
    ecological diversity, 125
    genetic diversity, 125
    importance of, 125–127
    measurement of, 131–132
    secrets of, 149–151
    species diversity, 125
bioerosion, 164
biofouling, 387
biological drawings, 104–105
biological weathering, 41
bioluminescence, 153
biomagnification
    defined, 385
    of toxins, 385–387
biomass
    changes in, 74
    defined, 68
    pyramids of, 78–79
biosphere reserves (UNESCO), 417–418
biotic factors, in marine ecosystems, 129–131
biotic phase, nutrient cycles, 82–84
bisphenol A (BPA), 389
blades, 119
blast fishing, 384
bluestripe snapper, 410
bonds, atoms, 4–7
    covalent, 4–5
    defined, 4
    hydrogen, 4, 7
    ionic, 4, 5–6
bony fish, 112–115, 252
    defined, 106
    ecological importance of, 114–115
    economic importance of, 115
Bosca del Cabo Rainforest Lodge, 422–423
bottlenose dolphin *(Tursiops truncates)*, 306
boundaries, plate tectonics, 36–40
    abyssal plains, 40
    convergent, 37
    divergent, 36, 37
    earthquakes and, 38
    transform, 37
    trenches, 37
    tsunamis and, 38–39
    volcanoes and, 37–38
boxer crabs, and anemones, mutualistic relationship between, 66
brine, from distillation plants, 381
British Indian Ocean Territory (BIOT), 436
broadcast spawning, 307, 310–311
buffer, 189
buffer/care areas, biosphere, 418

butterfly fish, 164
bycatch, 316

C

cages, for aquaculture, 339, 340
Caligus elongatus, 65
Calvin cycle, 277–278
calyx, 157
carapace, 111
carbohydrates, 63, 83, 89
carbon cycle, 89–91, 399
carbon dioxide, 373, 398
    atmospheric concentration of, 394–396
    concentration, and rate of photosynthesis, 280
    fixation, 277
carbon footprint, 421
carbonic acid, 89
carbon sequestration, 184
carbon sink
    defined, 156
    World Ocean as, 156
carnivores, 67
carotenoids, 268
carrier proteins, 223, 231
cartilaginous fish, 116–118
    defined, 106
    ecological importance of, 116–117
    economic importance of, 117–118
catch and fishing gear, inspection of, 328
catch per unit effort (CPUE), 329
caudal fin, 113–114
Cavanaugh, Colleen, 285
cells. *See* organelles
    actual length of, 226–227
    defined, 211
    drawing, 224–225, 228–229
    history of, 211–212
    membrane. *See* cell surface membrane
    nucleus in, 216–217
    plant. *See* plant cells
    sizes of, 225
    vacuoles, 222
cell sap, 222
cell surface membrane, 212, 216
    cholesterol, 224
    phospholipids, 222–223
    proteins, 223
    structure of, 222–224
    transport of mlecules. *See* transport methods
cellulose, 83, 220
cell wall, 212, 220–221
cephalothorax, 111
Chagos archipelago, 436–439
Challenger Deep, 37
Challenger expedition, 19–20
channel proteins, 223, 231
chemical weathering, 41

Index

chemoautotrophs, 71
chemosynthesis, 285–286
chemosynthesis/chemosynthetic, 5, 66, 71
    photosynthesis *vs.*, 71
chi-squared test, 391–393
Chisso Corporation, 386
chlorophyll, 63, 75, 268
chloroplasts, 212, 220, 268
cholesterol, 224
Chondrichthyes, 116
chordates, 118–119
chromatin, 216
chromatography, 201–202
    paper, 269
    separation of photosynthetic pigments by, 269–271
circulatory systems, 246–247
cisternae, 218
climate change, 166, 177, 397, 399
climate control, 126
cnidarians, 157
cnidocytes, 157
coal, 90
command words
    analyse, 298
    assess, 431
    calculate, 23, 256
    compare, 23, 255
    consider, 260
    contrast, 96
    define, 23, 259
    describe, 23, 254
    discuss, 359
    evaluate, 98, 298
    explain, 23, 254
    give, 94, 296
    identify, 24, 296
    justify, 147, 298
    outline, 23, 359
    predict, 23, 294
    sketch, 25, 294
    state, 23, 256
    suggest, 23, 255
commensalism, 64, 65
common fisheries policy (CFP), 314
community, 64, 128–129
compensation point, 73
competition, 64, 129–130
complex life cycle, 305
    shrimp, 306–308
compounds, 2, 4
concentration gradient, 230, 231, 241
conclusions, 203–204
confounding variables, 188
conservation, 404–424
    captive breeding and release programmes, 416
    defined, 370, 404
    ecotourism. *See* ecotourism

    energy, 421
    habitat loss and, 406–408
    human activities resulted in need for, 406–409
    hunting and, 408
    International Union for the Conservation of Nature, role of, 409–410
    legislation, 416–417
    marine protected areas, 413–414
    marine zoos and aquaria, 418–419
    need for, 404–406
    overfishing and, 408
    projects, viability of, 411–413
    role of international cooperation, 424
    roles of conservationists, 404
    UNESCO biosphere reserves, 417–418
consumers
    categories, 67
    defined, 63
continental crust, 33
continental drift, 33
continuous sampling, 133
continuous variables, 195
control experiment, 187
control variables, 187
convection currents, 36
Convention on International Trade in Endangered Species of Wild Fauna and Flora (CITES), 416
convergent boundaries, 37
copepods, 108
    and marine fish, parasitic relationship between, 65
coral bleaching, 166
coral polyps, 247–248
coral reefs, 110, 126, 130, 157–169, 384
    anatomy, 157–158
    artificial reefs, 168–169
    atolls, 160, 161
    barrier reefs, 160, 161
    classification of, 157–158
    conditions required for formation, 159–160
    distribution, 159
    erosion, causes of, 164
    fringing reefs, 160–161
    hard corals, 158
    importance of, 162
    loss of, 407
    nutrition, 158–159
    patch reefs, 160, 161
    physical damage to, 166–167
    soft corals, 158
core, 33
core areas, biosphere, 418
Coriolis effect, 45, 48–49
Corliss, Jack, 285
counter-current exchanger, 249
covalent bonds, 4–5
cristae, 219
critical values of r_s, 141

crown-of-thorns starfish (COTS), 110, 164, 165–166
crust, 33
crustaceans, 110–112
    defined, 106
    ecological importance of, 111–112
    economic importance of, 112
    life cycle of, 306–308
currents
    deep, 49
    defined, 45
    surface, 48–49
curves, measuring gradients of, 400–402
cyanobacteria, 268
cytoplasm, 212, 215

D
Darwin, Charles, 160
data
    analysis, 201–204, 290–292
    comparing, 334–335
    evaluation of, 198–199
    interpretation of, 202–203
    pattern, 202
    presentation, 192–195
    qualitative, 187
    quantitative, 187
    recording, 193
    trends, 202
Dead Sea, 27–30
dead zone (Gulf of Mexico)
    defined, 99
    effects of, 100
    formation of, 99
    size, reducing, 100
decomposers, 67
decomposition, 86–87
deep currents, 49
deep-sea angler fish, life cycle of, 312–313
Deepwater Horizon disaster, 2010, 371–373
deltas, 42, 43–44
denature, 282
density, water, 17–22
    defined, 7
    formula, 17
    pressure and, 18
    temperature and, 17–18, 21–22
denticles, 116
dependent variable, 187
deposition, 42
Dermacoccus abyssi, 127
desalination plants, 381–382
desiccation, 166
diatoms, 107, 267
dichotomous key, 103
diffusion, 230–231
dinoflagellates, 107–108, 267
discontinuous variable, 195

discuss, 57
diseases, 129
disphotic zone, 74, 279
dissolution, 8
dissolved oxygen (DO), 16, 17
distance, diffusion, 231, 241
Dittmar, William, 20
diurnal tidal pattern, 44
divergent boundaries, 36, 37
DNA (deoxyribonucleic acid), 220, 268
domestic sewage, 377
Don Juan Pond, Antarctica, 9
dorsal fins, 114
dorsal neural tube, 118
downwelling, 49
dredging
    defined, 382
    mechanical, 382
    suction, 382
    water-injection, 382

E
Earth
    interior, structure of, 33
    layers, 33
    plate boundaries, 36–40
    plate tectonics theory, 33–36
earthquakes, 33, 38
echinoderms, 109–110
    defined, 106
    ecological importance of, 110
    economic importance of, 110
ecolodging, 420
ecological diversity, 125
ecosystems, marine, 127–133
    biotic and abiotic factors in, 129–131
    defined, 127
    human impacts on. *See* human impacts, on marine ecosystems
    mangrove forest. *See* mangrove forest
    open ocean, 154–157
    rocky shore, 169–171
    sandy shore, 171–172
    tropical coral reef, 157–169
ecosystem services, 156
ecotourism, 370, 419–423
    defined, 419
    energy conservation, 421
    factors to take into account, 420
    principles of, 419
    recycling, 421
    sustainable materials, 421–422
    types of, 420
ectoparasites, 65
electromagnetic spectrum, 271
electronmicrograph, 215
electron micrograph, 215–216

of chloroplast, 220
of nucleus, 217
electron microscope, 212, 213, 214
    advantages and disadvantages of, 215
electrons, 3–4
elements, 2, 4
El Niño, 51, 52
El Niño Southern Oscillation (ENSO), 51–54
Elodea, 215
emergent plants, 122
emergent properties, 4
endangered species, 408–409
endoparasites, 65
endoplasmic reticulum
    rough, 212, 217–218
    smooth, 212, 217–218
Endoriftia, 285, 286
energy, 266–302
    chemosynthesis, 285–286
    conservation, 421
    diagrams, 93–94
    kinetic, 230
    photosynthesis. *See* photosynthesis/photosynthesise
    pyramids of, 79
    renewable. *See* renewable energy
    respiration, 288–289
    transfer, through food chain, 75–77
enhanced greenhouse effect, 393
environmental impacts, aquaculture, 350–353
    competition for resources, 352
    habitat destruction, 351
    invasive species and cultured stock, 352
    native stocks, reduction in exploitation of, 353
    overexploitation of feedstocks, 351
    pollution, 351–352
    spread of disease, 352
epipelagic zone, 155
erosion
    defined, 41
    gravity, 41–42
    ice, 41
    water, 42
    wind, 42
error, sources of, 198
estuaries, 32, 43, 128
ethical method, 133
ethics, 190
euphotic zone, 279
European carp, 410
European Union (EU), 314
euryhaline fish, 252
euryhaline species, 251
eutrophication, 75, 374
evaporation, 9
evenness, 137
excretion, 85, 86–87
extensive aquaculture, 340–341

external fertilisation, 309
extinction, of species, 404, 405
extremophiles, 71
extrinsic proteins, 223

F
facilitated diffusion, 230, 231–232
fatty acids, 84, 222, 223
fecundity, 318
feed
    availability of, 347
    efficiency of use, 347–348
feeding relationships, 66–79, 129
    energy transfer through food chain, 75–77
    food chains, 68–69
    food webs, 68–69
    illustrating, 77–79
    predation, 67–68
    productivity. *See* productivity
fertilisation
    defined, 309
    external, 309
    internal, 309–310
Fick's Law, 247
filaments, 248
fins
    anal, 114
    caudal, 113–114
    defined, 113
    dorsal, 114
    pectoral, 113
    pelvic, 114
fishing, 304
    benthic trawling, 316–317
    blast, 384
    dredging, 382–383
    factory ships, 317
    policies, sociological impacts of, 335–336
    purse seine, 315–316
    rehabilitation of stocks, 336–337
    SONAR, 315
    sustainable. *See* sustainable fishing
fishing intensity, 326
fishing mortality, 319
fish lice, 112
fish stocks, rehabilitation of, 336–337
Five Deeps Expedition, 149–150
floating plants, 122
flowering plants, 122
flowers, 123
fluid-mosaic model, 222, 224
Flying fish, 113
food chains, 68–69
    defined, 67
    energy transfer through, 75–77
    influence of changes in productivity on, 75
food webs, 68–69, 406

foraminifera, 67
forked fins, 114
fossil fuels, 90
    combustion, and ocean acidification, 399–400
frame quadrat, 132, 133
frequency tables, 356–358
fresh-water fish, 252
friendly floatees, 379
fringing reefs, 160–161
fry, 343

G
Galileo, 186
gas bladders, 119
gases
    atmospheric, 85–86
    exchange. *See* gas exchange
    greenhouse, 394
    solubility in seawater, 15–16
gas exchange, 240–251
    circulatory systems, 246–247
    counter-current exchanger, 249
    defined, 240
    factors affecting rates of, 241
    in marine organisms, 241–242
    methods, examples of, 247–249
    organs, Fick's Law and, 247
    ventilation, 248–249
genetic diversity, 125
geoengineering, 183–184
Georg, Johan, 20
ghost nets, 390
gills, 112, 248–249
    counter-current mechanism, 249
gill slits, 116
Global Fishing Watch, 327
global ocean conveyor belt, 49, 50
global warming, 373, 393–399
    acidification of water, 398
    atmospheric concentration of carbon dioxide, increasing levels of, 394–396
    climate change, 397, 399
    evidence for, 394–397
    global temperatures, increasing, 394
    greenhouse effect, 394
    melting of ice, 396–398
glucose, 69, 75
glycerate phosphate (GP), 278
glycerol, 222
glycoproteins, 223
goldfish, 250
Golgi body, 212, 218–219
gradient, 17–18
grana, 220
gravity erosion, 41–42
Great Barrier Reef, 166
Great Pacific Garbage Patch, 379

greenhouse effect
    defined, 394
    enhanced, 393
greenhouse gases, 394
Grew, Nehemiah, 211
gross primary production (GPP), 72
groupers, 248
groups, marine organisms, 106–124
    bony fish, 106, 112–115
    cartilaginous fish, 106, 116–118
    crustaceans, 106, 110–112
    echinoderms, 106, 109–110
    macroalgae, 106, 119–121
    marine grasses/plants, 106, 122–124
    phytoplankton, 106, 107–108
    plankton, 106, 107
    zooplankton, 106, 108
growth rates, 319, 347
Gulf of California, 374
Gulf of Mexico dead zone, 99–100

H
habitat, 128
    loss due to range of human activities, 406–408
haemoglobin, 246
Hairy frogfish, 113, 114
halocline, 11
hard corals, 158
harmful algal bloom (HAB), 107, 184
harvesting, 89, 92
    marine species, 355
    mussels, 345
hazards, 189
Heezen, Bruce, 35
helium, atomic structure of, 4
herbivores, 67
heterocercal fins, 114
heterotrophic organisms, 67
histograms, 195, 356–358
HMS Challenger, 19–20
holdfast, 119
Homo sapiens, 370
Hooke, Robert, 211
human impacts, on marine ecosystems, 370–439
    agriculture, effects of, 374–375
    conservation of marine ecosystems. *See* conservation
    desalination plants, 381–382
    fishing practices, 382–384
    global warming. *See* global warming
    oil industry, 371–373
    refuse disposal, 378–380
    renewable energy sources, 375–377
    sewage disposal, 377–378
    toxins, bioaccumulation and biomagnification of, 385–387
Humboldt Current, 51
hunting, 408
hydrogen bonds, 4, 7

Index

hydrophilic, 223
hydrophobic, 84, 223
hydrothermal vents, 37, 39–40, 126
hypersaline, 9
hypertonic solutions, 232
hypothesis, 186
hypotonic solutions, 232

I
ice
    erosion, 41
    melting of, 396–397
igneous rocks, 35
independent variable, 187, 190
Indian Ocean, 154
indoor tanks, for aquaculture, 339, 340
industrial waste water, 378
information, for sustainable fishing
    mortality rate, 319
    recruitment, 318–319
intensive aquaculture, 340, 341
interactions, in marine ecosystems, 62–100
    feeding relationships. *See* feeding relationships
    mutualistic, 64
    nutrient cycles. *See* nutrient cycles
    parasitic relationship, 65
internal fertilisation, 309–310
International Convention on the Control of Harmful Anti-fouling Systems, 387
International Union for the Conservation of Nature (IUCN), 409–410
International Whaling Commission (IWC), 416–417
inter-specific competition, 129–130
intertidal zone, 169
intra-specific competition, 129
intrinsic proteins, 223
invasive species, 351, 352, 408, 410
    control of, 423–424
ionic bonds, 4, 5–6
ions
    defined, 5
    hydrogen, 12
    hydroxide, 12
Isle of Man, 418
isotonic solutions, 232

J
jellyfish, 108
juvenile, 308

K
kelp forests, 110, 120–121, 406
keyhole limpet hemocyanin (KLH), 127
keystone species
    defined, 106
    phytoplankton, 107–108
    plankton, 107
    zooplankton, 108

kinetic energy, 230
kinetic particle theory, 3
krill, 67, 108
    antarctic, 111–112
K-strategy, 310

L
lagoons, 160
Laguna Lodge, Guatemala, 421
lamellae, 248
La Niña, 51, 52
La Rance barrage, France, 376
larvae, 108
larval forms/stages
    advantages and disadvantages of, 305
    defined, 305
lateral line, 112–113
leaf structure, 123
lenticels, 175
Lepeophtheirus salmonis, 65
licensing, restriction by, 321–322
life, foundations on, 266
life cycles, 305–312
    complex, 305
    defined, 304
    examples of, 305–308
    external fertilisation, 309
    internal fertilisation, 309–310
    parental care. *See* parental care
    simple, 305, 306
    stages in sessile and non-sessile organisms, importance of, 309
light
    penetration in water, 272–274
    and photosynthesis, 70–71, 80–81
    ultraviolet, 388
    wavelength, 213, 274–276, 280
light dependent stage, 276–277
light independent stage, 276, 277–279
light intensity, 189, 273, 280
light microscopes
    advantages and disadvantages of, 215
    resolution and magnification, 213
light penetration, 273
limiting factors
    carbon dioxide concentration, 280
    defined, 280
    effects of changing, 280–282
    light intensity, 280
    light wavelength, 280
    temperature, 280
Lincoln index, 131–132
line graphs, 195
lines, straight, measuring gradients of, 400–402
line transects, 133
Linnaeus, Carolus, 103
lionfish, 423, 424

lipids, 84
lithosphere, 34
litmus indicator, 12
littoral zone, 32, 42–43
    barnacle distribution in, 205
    distribution and abundance of organisms in, 132–133, 134–136
liver cell, electron micrograph of, 215
location, restriction of, 322–323
long-line fishing, 324–325
lugworms *(Arenicola marina)*, 172
lunate fins, 114
lungfish, 253
lysosomes, 219

M

macroalgae, 119–121
    defined, 106
    ecological importance of, 119–120
    economic importance of, 121
Macrocystus, 119–120
magnetic polarity reversal, 35–36
magnetite, 35
magnification
    calculating, 225–226
    defined, 213
    of image, 226
    light microscopes, 213
Malpighi, Marcello, 211
mangrove forest, 174–177
    conditions for formation of, 174
    ecological importance of, 176–177
    economic importance of, 177
    loss of, 407
    red mangrove, 175–176
    replanting, 336–337
    threats to, 177
manta rays, and remora fish, commensal relationship between, 65
mantle, 33
marine aquaculture. *See* aquaculture
marine bony fish, 252
marine fish, copepods and, parasitic relationship between, 65
marine grasses/plants, 122–124
    defined, 106
    ecological importance of, 123–124
    economic importance of, 124
marine organisms
    classification of, 103–105
    distribution and abundance in littoral zone, investigation of, 132–133, 134–136
    entanglement of, 390
    gas exchange in, 241–242
    ingestion of plastics by, 390
    key groups of. *See* groups, marine organisms
    life cycles. *See* life cycles
    physiology of. *See* physiology, marine organisms

marine protected areas (MPAs), 322, 413–414
    Chagos, 436–439
    effectiveness of, 414
    Torre Guaceto, 415
marine snow, 88–89
marine uplift, 90
marine zoos and aquaria, 418–419
mark-release-recapture, 131–132
matrix, 219
maximum sustainable yield (MSY), 313
mechanical dredging, 382
mechanical weathering, 41
medicinal drugs, marine biodiversity as source of, 126–127
mercury, 385
    accumulation, 385–387
mesopelagic zone, 155
metamorphosis, 305
methylmercury, 386
micrographs, 215
    electron, 215–216
microplankton, 107
microplastics
    defined, 388
    primary, 388
    secondary, 388
    uptake and transfer of, 389
microscopes
    electron, 212, 214, 215
    light, 212, 213, 215
middle lamella, cell wall layer, 221
mid-ocean ridges, 35, 37, 39
Minamata Convention on Mercury, 386–387
minimum mesh sizes, 324
mitochondria, 219
mitochondrion, 212
molecules
    defined, 2
    transport methods. *See* transport methods
    water, 3, 4, 5
mollusc shells mass, effect of loss of pH on, 402–403
monomers, 83
morphology, of shores, 42–43
mortality rate
    defined, 319
    fishing mortality, 319
    natural mortality, 319
muddy shores, 43
mussels, 251
    aquaculture, 344–345
mutualism (mutualistic), 64, 66
myoglobin, 289
mysis, 308

N

nanoplankton, 107
National Oceanic and Atmospheric Administration (NOAA), 100

natural mortality, 319
nature tourism, 420
nauplius, 110
neap tides, 45
nematocysts, 157
net primary production (NPP), 72
neutral, 12
neutrons, 3–4
niche, 128, 129
nicotinamide adenine dinucleotide phosphate (NADP), 277
nonpolar, 223
non-sessile
    defined, 305
    life cycles stages in, importance of, 309
North Sea, sustainable fishing in, 313–315
no-take zones, 413–414
notochord, 118
nucleoli, 217
nucleus, 4, 212, 216–217
null hypothesis, 139
nurdles, 388
nutrient, 70
    cycles. *See* nutrient cycles
    defined, 82
nutrient cycles, 82–91
    abiotic phase, 84
    biotic phase, 82–84
    carbon cycle, 89–91
    reservoirs in, 85–89

O

ocean acidification, 164, 399–400
ocean fertilisation, 183–184
oceanic crust, 33
Oceanic Niño Index (ONI), 52
oceans, 153
    Atlantic Ocean, 154
    carbon cycle and, 399
    defined, 102
    and geoengineering, 183–184
    importance of, 156–157
    Indian Ocean, 154
    open, 154–157
    Pacific Ocean, 154
    surface layer, mixing of, 11–12, 19
    with war-time technology, 32
    World Ocean. *See* World Ocean
oestrogen, 218
oil industry, impact on marine ecosystems, 371–373
    food webs, effect on, 372
    indirect effects of, 373
    offshore oil platforms, drilling and setting up, 371
    physical damage to organisms, 372
    productivity, effect on, 372
    spillage. *See* oil spillage
oil spillage, 371
    cleaning-up, damage caused by, 372–373
    coastal ecosystems, damage to, 372
    effects on food webs and productivity, 372
    oxygen dead zones, 373
    physical damage to organisms, 372
    and toxicity, 371–372
omnivores, 67
open ocean, 154–157
    zones of, 155–156
operculum, 112
organelles, 211, 212. *See also* cells
    cell surface membrane. *See* cell surface membrane
    cell wall, 220–221
    Golgi body, 218–219
    mitochondria, 219
    nucleus, 216–217
    ribosomes, 218
    rough and smooth endoplasmic reticulum, 217–218
    structures and functions, 215–216
organic/biological weathering, 41
osmoconformers, 251
osmometer, 233
osmoregulation, 251–252
osmoregulators, 251
osmosis, 83, 203, 232–233
    in animal cells, 233
    defined, 230
    in plant cells, 233
overfishing, 408
over-harvesting, 177
oviparity, 312
ovoviviparity, 312
oxidation, 277
oxygen minimum layer, 16, 17
oxyhaemoglobin, 246

P

Pacific Ocean, 154
paleomagnetic stripes, 35
Pangea, 33
paper chromatography, 269
parasitism, 64, 65
parental care
    example of, 310–312
    K-strategy, 310
    r-strategy, 310
parr, 343
parrotfish, 164
particle theory, 3
passive process, 230
patch reefs, 160, 161
pattern, data, 202
pectoral fins, 113
pelagic fish, 316
pelvic fins, 114
pentaradial symmetry, 109
percent change, calculation of, 163
permeability, of substrate, 173–174

peruvian anchoveta, 115–116
pH, 189
    change in, 164
    defined, 13
    loss, impact on mollusc shell mass, 402–403
    of water, 13–14
pharyngeal slits, 118–119
phoresis, 65
phosphate, 223, 277
phospholipids, 222–223
photic zone, 70, 73
photoactivation, 277
photoautotrophs, 69
photolysis, 277
photomicrograph, 215
photooxidation, 277
photosynthesis/photosynthesise, 5, 63, 69–71, 75, 90, 126, 220, 267–283
    absorption spectrum, 271–272
    accessory pigments, 268–269
    action spectrum, 272
    chemosynthesis *vs.*, 71
    chloroplasts, 268
    electromagnetic spectrum, 271
    equation for, 267
    factors affecting, 70–71
    light dependent stage, 276–277
    light independent stage, 276, 277–279
    light intensity on rate of, 80–81
    limiting factors, 280–282
    primary pigments, 268–269
    and productivity, 279
    rate, 72–74, 274–276
photosynthometer, 276
photosystems, 276
pH scale, 13–14
phycobilins, 273
phycocyanin, 273
phycoerythrin, 273
physical weathering, 41
physiology, marine organisms, 210–264
    cells. *See* cells
    challenges, 211
    gas exchange. *See* gas exchange
    organelles. *See* organelles
    osmoregulation, 251–252
    transport of molecules, 230–233
phytoplankton, 85, 188
    defined, 16, 106
    importance of, 63–64
    species of, 107–108
picoplankton, 107
pie charts, 356–358
pigments
    accessory, 268–269, 273
    photosynthetic, separation by chromatography, 268–269
    primary, 268–269

plankton, 106, 107
planning, 187–192
    appropriate techniques, selection of, 188–190
    problem, defining, 187–188
plant cells
    chloroplasts, 220
    electron micrograph of, 216
    immersing, in solutions of different water potentials, 238–240
    large permanent vacuoles, 222
    osmosis in, 233
    walls, 221
plants, marine, 122–124
plastics, 378–379, 387–388
    impacts on marine environment, 388–390
    ingestion by marine organisms, 390
    limiting release of, 390
plate tectonics, 33–36
    boundaries, 36–40
    magnetic polarity reversal, 35–36
    seafloor spreading, 35
pneumatocysts, 119
polar, 7
polarity, 35
pollution, 107–108, 408–409
    due to waste chemicals, 381–382
    reducing, 354–355
polychlorinated biphenyls (PCBs), 389
polymers, 83
polyps, 157
polysaccharide, 220
ponds, for aquaculture, 339, 340
porosity, of substrate, 173
porous, 171
post-anal tail, 119
postlarva, 308
potatoes, in solutions of different water potentials, 235–237
practical skills, 186
    experimental planning, 187–192
    presentation of data and observations, 192–195
precipitation, 9
precision (in experiments), 193
precision (in measurements), 193
predation, 64, 67–68
predator
    apex, 69
    defined, 67
    relationship with prey, 67
prediction, 187
pressure, and density of seawater, 18
prey, 67
primary cell wall, 221
primary consumers, 67
primary microplastics, 388
primary pigments, 268–269
primary producers, 82
primary productivity, 67, 69, 72

Index

principle of constant proportions, 20, 21
productivity, 69–75
    chemosynthesis, 71
    measurement of, 72–74
    photosynthesis, 69–71, 279
    primary, 67, 69, 72
    respiration, 71–72
propagules, 174
prop roots, 176
proteins, 84
    extrinsic, 223
    intrinsic, 223
protoctists, 267
protons, 3–4
protozoea, 308
pumped ventilation, 249, 250
purse seine fishing, 315–316, 324
pycnocline, 18, 71
pyramid of numbers, 77–78, 79
pyramids of biomass, 78–79
pyramids of energy, 79
    drawing, 93–94

Q
qualitative data, 187
quantitative data, 187
quarternary consumers, 67
quotas restrictions, 321

R
ram ventilation, 249, 250
random errors, 198
random sampling, 133
recruitment, 318–320, 368
recycling, 421
Red Handfish, 113
Red List of Threatened Species, 409
red mangroves, 175–176
red muscle, in fish, 289–290
red tides, algal blooms and, 300–302
reduction, 277
reef erosion
    causes of, 164
    defined, 164
    effects of, 167–168
reef slopes, 126
refuse, 408–409
    defined, 378
    disposal, 378–380
relationships
    commensal, 65
    feeding. *See* feeding relationships
    mutualistic, 66
    parasitic, 65
    spatial, 129
    temporal, 129
reliable, 191
remora fish, manta rays and, commensal relationship between, 65

renewable energy
    defined, 375
    sources. *See* renewable energy sources
renewable energy sources
    tidal barrages, 376
    turbines, 376
    wave power devices, 376
    wind turbines, 375–376
reproductive maturity, age of, 318–319
reservoirs, in nutrient cycles, 85–89
    add nutrients to replenish, processes to, 85–88
    remove nutrients from surface layer, processes to, 88–89
residence time, 85
resolution
    defined, 213
    light microscopes, 213
respiration, 90
    aerobic, 72, 288–289
    anaerobic, 288, 289
    defined, 71
responsible tourism, 421
R_f value, 270
rhizomes, 122
ribosomes, 217, 218
ribulose biphosphate (RuBP), 278
ribulose phosphate (RuP), 278
richness, 137
Riftia
    anatomy of, 285
    defined, 285
    hydrothermal vent with, 285
Robomussels, 149
rock lobster, sustainable fishing in Western Australia, 366–368
rocky shores, 43, 126, 131, 132, 169–171
    lower shore, 171
    middle shore, 171
    splash zone, 169–170
    tide pools, 171
    upper shore, 170–171
rod and line fishing, 324
root systems, 122
rough endoplasmic reticulum (rER), 212, 217–218
rounded fins, 114
r-strategy, 310
rubisco, 278
run-off, 9, 87

S
Sabella spallanzanii, 424
safe method, 133
safety, 189
salinity, 160
    in Dead Sea water, 28–29
    defined, 9
    density of water, 18–19
    effect on freezing point of water, 10–11
    seawater, reduction in, 398

salmon, 309
    aquaculture. See salmon aquaculture
    hatcheries in North America, 338
    and trees growth, 92
salmon aquaculture, 341–344
    growing out in seawater, 343–344
    harvesting, 344
    hatching, 343
    nursery tanks, 343
    preparation of brood stock, 342
    spawning, 343
salts, 6
sandy shores, 43, 110, 132, 171–172
satellite imagery, 74
satellite tracking, 327–328
scales, 113
scatter graph, 139
scientific method, 186
sea breams, protection in Adriatic Sea, 415
sea cucumbers, 110
sea fan, 158
seafloor spreading, 35
seagrasses, 122, 123
seagrass meadows, 407–408
sea lice, 65
seals, 67
sea otters, importance in maintaining kelp forest ecosystems, 120–121
seas, 102. See also oceans
seasonal restrictions, 320–321
sea turtles, 412
seaweeds, usage of, 282–283
Secchi disc, 273–274
secondary cell wall, 221
secondary consumers, 67
secondary microplastics, 388
sedimentary rocks, 90
sedimentation, 41, 42
sediment-settling tubes, 54–55
semi-diurnal tidal pattern, 44
sessile
    defined, 305
    life cycles stages in, importance of, 309
sewage
    defined, 377
    disposal, 377–378
    domestic, 377
    New York, dumping into North-West Atlantic, 380
sharks, 67, 77, 114, 116, 310
    parental care, 311–312
shells, 4
shores, morphology of, 42–43
shrimp, 309
    aquaculture, 345–347
    biological drawing of, 111
    life cycle of, 306–308
significant figure, usage of, 287

simple life cycle, 305
    bottlenose dolphin, 306
Simpson's index of diversity, 137
sinks, 86
smolt, 343
smooth endoplasmic reticulum (sER), 212, 217–218
social and economic impacts, aquaculture
    negative outcomes, 353–354
    positive outcomes, 353
soft corals, 158
solubility, 8–17
    defined, 8
    gases, in seawater, 15–16
    impact on marine life, 16–17
    overview, 8–9
    pH scale, 13–14
    salinity, 9
    surface layer of ocean, mixing of, 11–12, 19
solute, 8
solution, 8
solvent, 7
SONAR (sound navigation), 315
sound navigation and ranging (SONAR), 32, 35
sources, 86
spatial relationships, 129
spats, 344
Spearman's rank correlation, 139–142
species
    defined, 128
    diversity, 125
    endangered, 408–409
    extinction of, 404, 405
    invasive, 351, 352, 408, 410, 423–424
specific heat capacity, 7
spermatocyst, 307
spiracle, 116
splash zone, 169–170
spring tides, 45
staghorn coral, 158
stakeholders, 413
standard error, 425–427
standard form, numbers, 284
starch, 83
starfish, 68
state of matter, 3
statistical tests, 391–393, 425–427
stenohaline species, 251
steroid hormones, 218
stipe, 119
stony coral tissue loss disease (SCTLD), 129
storm damage, mangrove forest, 177
stroma, 220, 268
subduction zone, 37
submergent plants, 122
suction dredging, 382
sulfur dioxide, 373

Index

sunlight, 160
   and photosynthesis, 70
supersaturation, 16
super subs, 149–150
surface area
   defined, 242
   and diffusion, 231
   and gaseous exchange, 241
   volume ratio of organisms, 243–246
surface currents, 48–49
surface layer of ocean, mixing of, 11–12, 19
surface run-off, 378
sustainable development, 421
sustainable development zones, biosphere, 418
sustainable fishing
   defined, 313
   information required for, 318–319
   models. *See* sustainable fishing models
   in North Sea, 313–315
   regulating, 317–319
   rock lobster, in Western Australia, 366–368
sustainable fishing models, 319–333
   air and sea patrolling, 327
   catch and fishing gear, inspection of, 328
   catch per unit effort, 329
   consumer-oriented tools, 330–331
   enforcement, 329–330
   fishing intensity, restriction of, 326
   licensing, restriction by, 321–322
   location, restriction of, 322–323
   method, restriction of, 323–325
   minimum fish sizes, restriction of, 325
   quotas, setting, restriction by, 321
   satellite tracking, 327–328
   season, restriction by, 320–321
swim bladder, 114
swordfish, 290
symbiosis, 64
systematically sampling, 133
systematic errors, 198

T

taxonomic hierarchy, 103
tectonic processes, 87–88
temperature
   and carbon dioxide, 70
   and density, 17–18, 21–22
   and diffusion of molecules, 231
   and gas exchange, 241
   and gas solubility, 15
   global, increasing, 394
   and rate of photosynthesis, 280
   water, increased, 398
temporal relationships, 129
tertiary consumers, 67
testosterone, 218
thallus, 119

Tharp, Marie, 35
theca, 158
theory, 186
thermal insulator, 18
thermocline, 11, 71
thermohaline circulation, 49, 50
Thomson, Charles Wyville, 19
thylakoid membranes, 220
tidal barrages, 376
tidal range/amplitude, 44–45
tidal surge, 45
tidal waves, 38
tides
   defined, 44
   diurnal pattern, 44
   neap, 45
   range, 44–45
   semi-diurnal pattern, 44
   spring, 45
tonoplast, 222
Torre Guaceto MPA, 415
total dissolved solids (TDS), 9
toxins, bioaccumulation and biomagnification of, 385–387
transects
   belt, 133
   defined, 132
   line, 133
transform boundaries, 37
transition zones, biosphere, 418
transport methods, 230–233
   diffusion, 230–231
trenches, 37
trends, data, 202
tributyltin oxide (TBT), 385, 387
triglycerides, 84
triose phosphate (TP), 278
trochophore larvae, 344
trophic level, 69
trophosome, 285
truncated fins, 114
tsunamiite, 61
tsunamis, 37, 38–39
   geological mark of, 59–61
   warning system, 60
tube feet, 109
tuna, 248, 250, 290
   parental care, 310–311
turbidity, 43, 272, 273–274
turbines, tidal, 377
turbulence, 15
turgor pressure, 233
   investigating using visking tubing, 234–235
turtle grass *(Thalassia testudinum)*, 123
turtles, 390, 412
twilight zone, 279

U

ultraviolet (UV) light, 388
United Nations Educational, Scientific and Cultural Organisation (UNESCO)
    biosphere reserves, 417–418
units, conversion of, 226
universal indicator, 12
upwelling, 50, 87
USCG *Duane*, 168

V

van Leeuwenhoek, Antony, 212
variables, 186
    confounding, 188
    continuous, 195
    control, 187
    dependent, 187
    discontinuous, 195
    independent, 187, 190
veliger larvae, 344
ventilation, 248–249
    pumped, 249, 250
    ram, 249, 250
ventral fins, 114
vesicle, 218
vessel detection system (VDS), 327
visking tubes, investigating turgor pressure using, 234–235
viviparity, 312
viviparous reproduction, 175–176
volcanoes, 37–38

W

water
    acidification of, 398
    density of. *See* density, water
    erosion, 42
    freezing point, effect of salinity on, 10–11
    as gaseous exchange medium, 241
    light penetration in, 272–274
    pH of, 13–14
    solubility in. *See* solubility
    temperature, and gas solubility, 15
    temperature, increased, 398
water bath, 189
water column, 17
water fleas, 112
water-injection dredging, 382
water molecules, 3, 4
    covalent bonds in, 5
water potential, 232
water vapour, 3
wavelength, light, 213, 272, 273
    effect on photosynthesis rate, 274–276
wave power devices, 376
weathering
    chemical, 41
    defined, 41
    organic/biological, 41
    physical/mechanical, 41
Wegener, Alfred, 33–34
Western Australia, sustainable rock lobster fishing in, 366–368
whales, parental care, 311
white muscle, in fish, 289–290
wildlife/nature tourism, 420
wind erosion, 42
wind turbines, 375–376
World Ocean
    as carbon sink, 156
    defined, 154
    as source of oxygen, 156
    southernmost waters of, 155
    as temperature buffer, 157

X

xanthophylls, 268

Y

Yaqui Valley, 374

Z

zonation, 169
zones, of open ocean, 155–156
zooplankton, 67, 89, 107, 379
    defined, 106
zooxanthellae, 158